the

parent soup®

Baby Name Finder

real advice from real parents who have named their babies
and lived to tell about it—with more than 15,000 names

Kate Hanley & the Parents of Parent Soup
Foreword by Nancy Evans

CB
CONTEMPORARY BOOKS

Library of Congress Cataloging-in-Publication Data

Hanley, Kate.
    The parent soup baby name finder : real advice from real parents
who have named their babies and lived to tell about it—with more
than 15,000 names / Kate Hanley and parents of Parent Soup ;
foreword by Nancy Evans.
       p.   cm.
    ISBN 0-8092-2961-7
    1. Names, Personal—Dictionaries.   I. Parent Soup.   II. Title.
CS2377.H364   1998
929.4'03—DC21   97-39946
                                            CIP

Interior production by Susan H. Hartman
Conceived by Tina Sharkey
Associate producer: Felicia Jones

Published by Contemporary Books
A division of NTC/Contemporary Publishing Group, Inc.
4255 West Touhy Avenue, Lincolnwood (Chicago), Illinois 60646-1975 U.S.A.
Copyright © 1998 by iVillage Inc.
All rights reserved. No part of this book may be reproduced, stored in a retrieval
system, or transmitted in any form or by any means, electronic, mechanical,
photocopying, recording, or otherwise, without the prior permission of
NTC/Contemporary Publishing Group, Inc.
Printed in the United States of America
International Standard Book Number: 0-8092-2961-7

18   17   16   15   14   13   12   11   10   9   8   7   6   5   4   3   2   1

many thanks to Tina Sharkey, an original member of the Parent Soup team. Tina conceived the idea for the series of Parent Soup books, and without her dedication and drive, this book would never have become a reality.

The on-line version of the Parent Soup Baby Name Finder (and therefore this book) exists because of the hard work of Macdara MacColl, who recognized that an interactive baby name finder would be useful to parents; Ed Scerbo and Vincent Press of Namease, who created the database of names; and Elaine Rubin, who brought Namease and Parent Soup together.

Thanks also to Felicia Jones, for her organizational wizardry and comforting persistence; Chaos NewMedia Limited of Charlottesville, Virginia, for their technical dexterity in transforming our database into text; Bill Moulton, for his tremendous design talents; Laurie Petersen, for her speedy proofreading; and the Parent Soupers for proving that community knows no geographical boundaries.

contents

Foreword by Nancy Evans   **vii**

Introduction   **ix**

Girls' Names A to Z   **1**

How to Deal with Flak from
Family and Friends   3, 5, 6, 9, 10, 13

Honor Thy Relatives   14, 17, 18, 21, 22, 25

When to Decide   29, 30, 32, 34, 37

"I Like the Sound of That!"   40, 43

Popularity Contest   44, 47, 51, 52, 55, 57, 58

Hollywood Kids   60, 61

"Will My Child Be Teased
Because of This Name?"   62, 65, 66, 69, 70

Names of the Weird   74, 77, 80

Real Names of Famous People   82

"What If I Never Find a Name I Like?"   86, 89

Naming for Two   93, 94, 96, 99

And Now, for a Little Levity   104

Boys' Names A to Z   **105**

Gender-Bending Names   106, 109, 110, 113, 117

How to End the Spouse Wars—Surefire
Ways to Make a Decision   118, 120, 123, 124, 127, 129

"How Do You Spell That?"   130, 134, 136, 139, 142, 145, 146

The Creative Approach   148, 151, 152, 154, 157

28 Ways to Say John   158

"Are We Normal?"   160, 162

Initially Speaking   167, 168, 171, 172, 175

What's in a Nickname?   178, 181, 183, 184, 187

How to Tell If You've Got a Keeper   190, 193, 194, 196, 199, 200, 206, 209

Unisex Names A to Z   **215**

Baby Name Finder   **229**

Flowers   230

Colors   230

Cities   230

States   231

Countries   231

Gems   232

Mountains   232

Lakes and Rivers   232

Virtues   233

Calendar   233

People—Biblical 233

People—Saints 234

Ethnic—African 235

Ethnic—Czech 236

Ethnic—Dutch 237

Ethnic—English/Welsh 238

Ethnic—French 239

Ethnic—German 240

Ethnic—Greek 242

Ethnic—Hispanic 243

Ethnic—Hungarian 246

Ethnic—Irish 246

Ethnic—Italian 247

Ethnic—Japanese 249

Ethnic—Jewish 250

Ethnic—Muslim 253

Ethnic—Norwegian 255

Ethnic—Polish 256

Ethnic—Russian 256

Ethnic—Scottish 257

Ethnic—Swedish 258

Ethnic—Swiss 258

Most Popular Girls' Names of the 1990s 259

Most Popular Boys' Names of the 1990s 260

Parent Soup's Most Popular Names 260

Parent Soup's Least Popular Names 261

The Most Popular Names of the
Past 5 Decades 261

1 Syllable 262

2 Syllables 266

3 Syllables 289

4 Syllables 301

5 Syllables 305

On-Line Baby Name
Resources 307

About the Authors 309

foreword

We started Parent Soup because there's no parent alive who can't use help with raising children. And while we all turn to parenting magazines and books for help, there's no better source of advice and comfort than other parents. At Parent Soup, an on-line gathering place found on the Web and America Online, thousands of parents meet every day to ask questions of each other and to lend a helping hand. Their collective wisdom is there to be accessed at any time of day or night—both in print in the form of messages (imagine a bulletin board covered with parenting tips) and in person in live chat rooms (imagine a moms' and dads' meeting in your living room).

Once you visit Parent Soup, you'll wonder how you got along without it, because given the time constraints that come with parenting, you need answers fast. And there's no faster way to get more information than a visit to the Soup. Not to mention, you can check in with other parents while you're in your pajamas or nursing your baby. This is a good thing.

One subject, we found, that is clearly on a lot of parents' minds is what to name their baby. When we introduced an interactive baby name finder, where you can find the meanings of thousands of names and do a customized search for the name of your dreams, it was a phenomenal hit. Parents started swapping advice on naming their babies, and pretty soon we had enough good wisdom to fill a book. So here is that book.

Lucky you that you have this book. I wound up doing all the things that good parents here say not to do. I asked my parents for advice—and took it. So the name Molly, which was my husband's first choice, bit the dust because my father said that was the name of the family cow when he was a boy. By the time I was in the delivery room, my husband and I were still negotiating vigorously over the name. We hadn't followed the advice of another wise Parent Souper that we take a list of possibilities with us to the hospital and let our daughter's personality help us make the right decision.

The truth is that naming a baby carries such freight because it's the first step toward giving your child an identity. Will the name you give your child look good on a placard if she runs for president? Or have you already nuked her chances of high office with a goofy-sounding name? Will kids find a way to make taunts from it? Will a stiff name make for a stiff kid? If your child has the same name as five other kids in his preschool class, will he have an identity crisis? On the other hand, can a unique name make your child feel like the odd kid out? And if you give a girl an androgynous name, will it help her get around gender stereotyping or cause gender confusion? No wonder naming a baby causes such consternation.

Thanks to the voices of real parents you'll hear in the pages of this book, you'll be able to cut through the fuss. You can learn what worked and what didn't. And you can come to your own decision. Most of all, you can take pleasure in the possibilities. Because as one Parent Souper says, "Remember that this naming business can be fun." So settle back and enjoy yourself. This is the beginning of a wonderful life.

~ Nancy Evans
nancy@ivillage.com

parent soup is part of
iVillage.com
THE WOMEN'S NETWORK

introduction

this book is unlike any other baby name book: what you are now holding in your hands started out on-line, within the Parent Soup Web and AOL sites. Long ago, in January 1996 (that's eons in cyberspace terms), we put our first list of 3,000 baby names and their meanings on our website. It quickly became our most highly trafficked area. (We've since increased the number of names in our database to 15,000 and added incredible search functions. The improved Baby Name Finder is still our most popular area.) Then we created a baby name message board—a place for parents to post notes to each other and engage each other in conversation about naming their babies. Thousands of posts later, that one board grew into more than 20 boards—all filled with tips on how to find the perfect baby name.

While cyberspace is great for meeting others with your interests and learning new things and swapping ideas, you can't exactly crawl into bed (the best place to dream about baby names) and snuggle up with your computer. So we decided to capture the wisdom that parents are sharing in our message boards by putting them in a book. Now you can hear the voices of our members and their advice long after it's been given and

without turning your computer on. The advice is sprinkled throughout the pages of the book, but if you're looking for a particular subject, such as unisex or trendy names, refer to the Contents.

The rest of the book is filled with names, complete with meanings, origins, and information about in what cultures each name is used (if known), from our on-line Baby Name Finder. They are broken out by gender in an easy-to-read, A-to-Z format. The book begins with a list of girls' names, then a list of boys' names, then a list of unisex names. Flip to the back of the book and you'll find 42 specialized lists of names, broken out by such criteria as nationality, popularity, and more, to help you hone your search.

We hope you like the book. More important, we hope you find a name for your baby that you love.

~ Kate Hanley
hanley@ivillage.com

girls' names

Aabidah: Arabic origin. Means: worshiper.

Aaminah: Arabic origin. Means: peace, harmony.

Aamirah: Arabic origin. Means: abundant treasure.

Aanisah: Arabic origin. Means: good-natured.

Aara: Unknown origin. Means: able, elegant.

Aarin: Unknown origin and meaning.

Aarionne: Unknown origin and meaning.

Aase: Unknown origin and meaning. Ethnic background: Norwegian.

Aasimah: Arabic origin. Means: safe, chaste.

Aasiyah: Arabic origin. Means: queen.

Aatiqah: Arabic origin. Means: free.

Aba: African origin. Means: born on Thursday, horse.

Ababno: African origin. Means: a child who returns.

Abana: Unknown origin. Means: goddess.

Abayomi: African origin. Means: come to bring joy.

Abby: Hebrew origin. Means: gives joy, father of joy, source of joy. Alternative spellings: Abbe, Abbie.

Abebi: African origin. Means: we asked and got her.

Abeo: African origin. Means: bring happiness.

Abigail: Hebrew origin. Means: a father's source of joy. 26th most popular girl's name of the '90s.

Alternative spellings and nicknames: Gael, Gayl, Ab, Abbey, Abbie, Abby, Gail, Gale, Abbigail, Abegail, Abigayle.

Abira: Hebrew origin. Means: strong.

Abra: Hebrew/Arabic origin. Means: mother, lesson.

Abrasia: Unknown origin and meaning. Ethnic background: Hispanic.

Abrianna: Unknown origin and meaning.

Acacia: Greek origin. Means: thorny, shrub, guileless.

Acantha: Greek origin. Means: pointed, thorn.

Accalia: Latin origin. Means: instigator, she wolf. Alternative spelling: Acalia.

Acima: Unknown origin. Means: judge.

Ada: Saxon origin. Means: noble, prosperous. Ethnic background: Italian. Alternative spellings and nicknames: Eadith, Addy, Addie, Aida, Ida, Edith, Eda.

Adaego: African origin. Means: daughter of wealth.

Adaeze: African origin. Means: princess.

Adah: Hebrew origin. Means: crown.

Adaha: Hebrew origin. Means: adorn. Alternative spellings: Adai, Adaiha.

Adalia: Germanic origin. Means: noble. Alternative spellings: Adaliah, Adallia, Adaia.

Adamina: Hebrew origin. Means: earth. Alternative spellings: Adaminah, Adama.

Adanma: African origin. Means: daughter of beauty.

Adara: Hebrew/Greek origin. Means: beauty, virgin, fire.

Adda: Hebrew origin. Means: happy, adorned, beautiful.

Adedewe: African origin. Means: shattered crown.

Adela: Teutonic origin. Means: noble, pleasant, humor. Ethnic background: Hispanic. Alternative spellings: Adele, Adelle.

Adelaide: Saxon origin. Means: kind, noble. Ethnic backgrounds: Italian, German. Alternative spellings and nicknames: Adelind, Adila, Adelia, Adalia, Della, Dela, Adelina, Adele, Adaline, Adela.

Adelheid: Germanic origin. Means: sweet, noble.

Adelina: Germanic origin. Means: noble, sweet, kind. Ethnic background: Italian. Alternative spellings: Adaline, Adeline.

Adeola: African origin. Means: crown brings honor.

Adiell: Hebrew origin. Means: lord, ornament. Alternative spellings: Adiel, Addielle.

Adilmira: Unknown origin and meaning. Ethnic background: Hispanic.

Adine: Hebrew origin. Means: gentle, delicate, voluptuous, noble. Alternative spellings: Adena, Adina.

Adira: Hebrew origin. Means: mighty, strong.

Adiva: Hebrew/Arabic origin. Means: gracious, pleasant, gentle.

Adiya: Hebrew origin. Means: God's treasure.

Adonia: Greek origin. Means: beautiful.

Adora: Greek/Latin origin. Means: gift.

Adorabelle: Latin origin. Means: adored, beautiful.

Adoree: Latin origin. Means: adored, glory.

Adoria: Latin/French origin. Means: worthy of divine worship.

Adorna: Latin origin. Means: adorn, beautiful.

Adret: Unknown origin. Means: a cape. Ethnic background: Jewish.

Adriana: Italian/Spanish origin. Means: dark, girl, rich, black, mysterious, dark one. 49th most popular girl's name of the '90s. Alternative spellings: Adreana, Adriane, Adrianna, Adrianne, Adria, Adrea.

Adrienne: Latin/French origin. Means: dark, woman of the sea. Alternative spelling: Adrienna.

Adwin: African origin. Means: artist.

Aenea: Greek/Latin origin. Means: praiseworthy, excellent. Alternative spellings: Aeniah, Aennela.

Afafa: African origin. Means: first child of second husband.

Afeefah: Arabic origin. Means: modest.

Affra: Hebrew origin. Means: young deer, doe. Alternative spelling: Afra.

Africa: Gaelic/Celtic origin. Means: pleasant, agreeable. Alternative spellings: Afrika, Afrikah.

Afryea: African origin. Means: born during happy times.

Agala: Hebrew origin. Means: wagon.

Agata: Latin/Celtic origin. Means: good, kind, pure. Ethnic backgrounds: Polish, Hispanic, Italian.

Agatha: Greek origin. Means: good, kind. Alternative spellings and nicknames: Ag, Agathy, Aggie, Aggy, Agathe.

Agave: Greek origin. Means: illustrious, mother.

Agnes: Greek origin. Means: pure, chaste. Ethnic background: German. Alternative spellings and nicknames: Agna, Agnese, Agneta, Agnieszka, Agnola, Nessie, Agnella, Neysa.

Aharona: Hebrew origin. Means: teaching, singing, mountain.

Ahava: Hebrew origin. Means: love.

Ahlexa: Unknown origin and meaning.

Ahola: Unknown origin. Means: girl. Alternative spellings: Aholah, Aholla.

Ahuva: Hebrew origin. Means: beloved.

How to Deal with Flak from Family and Friends

When it comes to naming babies, everyone's got an opinion. The message boards at Parent Soup are proof of that. So how do you deal with everyone else's ideas of what *your* baby should be named? The overwhelming response from Parent Soupers is: Hold your ground. Don't let looks of disbelief sway your decision on a name—if you love the name, trust your instinct. Easier said than done, maybe, but on the following pages are some voices of reason to help you face the naysayers.

Aia: Unknown origin. Means: wife.

Aida: Latin/Saxon origin. Means: happy, female.

Aideen: Irish origin. Means: little fire.

Aidel: Unknown origin and meaning. Ethnic background: Jewish.

Aileen: Greek/Irish origin. Means: light, green meadow. Alternative spellings and nicknames: Illona, Illene, Eileen, Ilene, Aline, Alene.

Aillsa: Irish origin. Means: cheer, noble. Alternative spelling: Ailsa.

Aime: French origin. Means: love, beloved. Alternative spelling: Aimee.

Aimo: Unknown origin. Means: amiable.

Ainsley: Saxon origin. Means: awe, meadow. Alternative spellings: Ainslie, Ainslee.

Airla: Greek origin. Means: tenuous. Alternative spellings: Airlee, Airlia, Airliah, Airlie.

Aisa: Unknown origin and meaning.

Aislara: Unknown origin and meaning. Ethnic background: Hispanic.

Aislinn: Irish origin. Means: vision, dream.

Aja: Unknown origin and meaning.

Akeyla: Unknown origin. Means: wisdom. Alternative spellings: Akela, Akeylah, Akeyleeah.

Akia: Unknown origin and meaning.

Akili: Arabic/Egyptian origin. Means: wisdom.

Akshara: Unknown origin and meaning.

Akuako: African origin. Means: younger of twins.

Akwate: African origin. Means: elder of twins.

Alage: Unknown origin. Means: cheerful.

Alameda: Spanish origin. Means: cottonwood, parade.

Alana: Celtic origin. Means: air, fair, bright, beautiful. Alternative spellings and nicknames: Allana, Alina, Helen, Lana, Lane, Alaina, Alanah, Alanna, Alannah, Alayna, Alaine, Alayne, Aleana.

Alani: Unknown origin and meaning.

Alara: Unknown origin and meaning.

Alarice: Saxon/Germanic origin. Means: ruler of all. Alternative spellings: Alarise, Alarica.

Alasia: Unknown origin and meaning.

Alatea: Unknown origin. Means: ivory.

Alauna: Unknown origin and meaning.

Alayla: Unknown origin and meaning.

Alba: Latin origin. Means: white, lovely.

Alberta: Saxon origin. Means: brilliant, noble. Ethnic backgrounds: German, Italian. Alternative spellings and nicknames: Berte, Bertie, Berta, Albertina, Albertine, Elberta, Bert, Albertina.

Albinia: Latin origin. Means: blond, white. Alternative spelling: Albina.

Alcina: Greek origin. Means: cared for.

Alda: Saxon origin. Means: gift, rich, old.

Aldarcy: Anglo-Saxon origin. Means: princess, chief. Alternative spellings: Aldarcie, Aldercy.

Aldora: Greek/Anglo-Saxon origin. Means: gift, noble.

Alea: Unknown origin and meaning. Alternative spelling: Aleah.

Aleda: Germanic/Saxon origin. Means: beautifully, girl, archaic, winged.

Aledis: Unknown origin. Means: friend. Alternative spelling: Aleydis.

Aleeca: Unknown origin and meaning.

Aleesa: Hebrew origin. Means: joyous.

Aleighsha: Unknown origin and meaning.

Aleldra: Unknown origin. Means: rank.

Alelina: Unknown origin and meaning. Ethnic background: Hispanic.

Alena: Greek/Slavic origin. Means: pretty, light. Ethnic background: Czech.

Alene: Celtic/Germanic origin. Means: fair, alone. Alternative spelling: Aleen.

Aleria: Latin origin. Means: city, eagle.

Alesia: Greek origin. Means: helper.

Aleta: Latin/Anglo-Saxon origin. Means: winged, little, truthful. Alternative spellings: Aletta, Alette, Alita, Alitha.

Aletheia: Greek origin. Means: truth, honesty. Alternative spellings and nicknames: Alethia, Alithea, Aletha, Alethea.

Alevtina: Unknown origin and meaning. Ethnic background: Russian.

Alexa: Greek origin. Means: defender. Ethnic backgrounds: English/Welsh, German. 43rd most popular girl's name of the '90s.

Alexandra: Greek origin. Means: defender, helper of mankind. Ethnic background: Swedish. 22nd most popular girl's name of the '90s. Alternative spellings and nicknames: Elexa, Alexa, Sandra, Sandi, Alla, Alexis, Sondra, Alix, Aleksandra, Alessandra, Allesandra, Alexondra, Alejandra, Alixandra, Alyxandra.

Alexandria: Latin origin. Means: defender of man. 41st most popular girl's name of the '90s. Alternative spellings: Alessandria, Alexandrea, Alyxandria.

Alexandrine: Latin origin. Means: defender of man.

Alexas: English origin. Means: protector of man. Alternative spellings: Alexes, Alexys, Alexee, Alix.

Alexia: Greek origin. Means: honest, defender.

Alfa: Unknown origin. Means: first. Ethnic background: Hispanic.

Alfonsine: Germanic origin. Means: noble.

Alfreda: Anglo-Saxon origin. Means: counselor, elf. Ethnic background: Polish. Nickname: Ally.

Alia: Unknown origin and meaning.

Alianna: Unknown origin and meaning.

Alice: Celtic/Teutonic origin. Means: sweet, noble. Ethnic backgrounds: Italian, German. Alternative spellings and nicknames: Elsie, Alis, Allis, Alyce, Alys, Aleece, Alicia, Alisa, Alison, Alissa, Alla, Allie, Ally, Elissa.

Aliceson: English origin. Means: son of Alice.

Alicia: Greek/Germanic origin. Means: honest, noble. 35th most popular girl's name of the '90s. Alternative spellings: Alisha, Aleysha, Alysha, Alyshia, Alyssia, Alycia, Alecia.

Alieja: Unknown origin and meaning. Ethnic background: Polish.

Alida: Germanic/Greek origin. Means: noble, archaic, winged. Alternative spelling: Alyda.

Alidis: Unknown origin. Means: friend.

Alima: Arabic origin. Means: dancing. Alternative spelling: Alimah.

Alina: Greek/Slavic origin. Means: beautiful, pretty, light. Alternative spelling: Alinna.

Aline: Germanic origin. Means: bright, noble.

Alisa: Hebrew origin. Means: joy, lovely, nature. Alternative spellings: Aliza, Alise.

Alisia: Unknown origin. Means: nature.

How to Deal with Flak

I can't stress often enough, don't bring friends and family into the name game unless you really want their input. If you tell them a name you have picked out ahead of time, they seem to take this as "What do you think of this name?" My father-in-law actually laughed at my choice for a girl's name and then said "Oh, you are serious!" From now on, they hear a name only when it is a done deal and not open to discussion, like when it's on the birth certificate!

~ Susan N., Fairhope, Alabama

Alivia: Unknown origin and meaning.

Aliyah: Hebrew origin. Means: to ascend. Alternative spellings: Aliya, Aaliyah.

Alla: Slavic origin. Unknown meaning. Ethnic background: Russian.

Allegra: Latin origin. Means: cheerful, merry. Ethnic background: Jewish.

Allena: Unknown origin. Means: noble, illustrious.

Allene: Gaelic/Irish origin. Means: fierce, beautiful.

Alleras: Unknown origin. Means: city. Alternative spellings and nicknames: Allerie, Alleris, Aleras.

Allie: Unknown origin. Means: cheerful, a cliff. Ethnic background: Irish. Alternative spellings: Alley, Ally.

Allison: Teutonic/Irish origin. Means famous, saintly, honest. 17th most popular girl's name of the '90s. Alternative spellings: Alisan, Alison, Alisyn, Allisan, Allyson, Alyson, Alysson.

Allista: Unknown origin. Means: lovely.

Allveta: Unknown origin. Means: alive.

Alma: Latin origin. Means: kind, helpful, bountiful, soul. Ethnic backgrounds: Hispanic, German.

Almaz: Unknown origin. Means: beautiful.

Almeta: Latin origin. Means: industrious, pearl. Alternative spelling: Almita.

Almira: Arabic origin. Means: clothing, exalted. Alternative spellings: Mira, Almire, Almeria.

Alocasia: Unknown origin and meaning.

Alodie: Anglo-Saxon origin. Means: prosperous. Alternative spellings: Aladee, Alodi.

Aloha: Unknown origin. Means: farewell.

Aloisa: Germanic origin. Means: famous fighter.

Aloisia: Germanic/Saxon origin. Means: famed, famous. Alternative spellings: Aloysia, Aloisus, Alyose.

Alona: Hebrew origin. Means: oak tree.

Alondra: Unknown origin and meaning.

Alora: Unknown origin and meaning.

Alpha: Greek origin. Means: first.

Alphonsa: Teutonic origin. Means: aggressive, warlike.

Alphonsine: Saxon/Germanic origin. Means: aggressive, noble.

Alrune: Unknown origin and meaning. Ethnic background: German.

Alta: Latin/Germanic origin. Means: tall, old, high.

Altagracia: Spanish origin. Means: one with high grace.

Alteh: Unknown origin and meaning. Ethnic background: Jewish. Alternative spelling: Alterkeh.

Althea: Greek origin. Means: God, wholesome, honesty, pure. Alternative spellings and nicknames: Aitheta, Althee, Thea, Althaea, Althaia.

Alufa: Hebrew origin. Means: princess, leader.

5

Alura: Anglo-Saxon origin. Means: divine counselor.

Alvina: Saxon origin. Means: blond, friend to all. Alternative spelling: Vina.

Alvita: Latin origin. Means: alive. Alternative spelling: Alveta.

Alyose: Unknown origin. Means: famed.

Alyssa: Greek/Teutonic origin. Means: sane, rational, cheerful, noble humor, nature. Alternative spellings: Alissa, Allysa, Alysa, Alysia, Alysse.

Alzena: Arabic origin. Means: woman.

Ama: African origin. Means: born on Saturday.

Amabel: Latin origin. Means: beautiful, lovable. Alternative spellings: Amabelle, Amable.

Amada: Unknown origin and meaning. Ethnic background: Hispanic.

Amadas: Unknown origin. Means: devoted. Alternative spellings: Ammadas, Ammadis.

Amadea: Latin origin. Means: loved by God.

Amaila: Unknown origin and meaning. Ethnic background: Italian.

Amal: Arabic origin. Means: bird.

Amaline: Unknown origin. Means: flattering. Alternative spelling: Amalita.

Amamda: Unknown origin and meaning.

Amana: Hebrew origin. Means: faithful.

Amanda: Latin origin. Means: love, beloved. Ethnic backgrounds: Swedish, English/Welsh, Hispanic. 9th most popular girl's name of the '90s. Nicknames: Manda, Mandy.

Amani: Unknown origin and meaning.

Amanique: Unknown origin and meaning.

Amara: Greek/Latin origin. Means: eternal, beloved.

Amarachi: Unknown origin and meaning.

Amargo: Unknown origin. Means: beauty.

Amaris: Hebrew origin. Means: given by God. Alternative spelling: Amaras.

Amary: Unknown origin. Means: God. Alternative spelling: Amari.

How to Deal with Flak

If you are absolutely in *love* with a name, then by golly, go for it! After all, you will be the one saying and hearing this name the most in years to come.

~ **Lindsay M.,
Santa Cruz, California**

Amaryllis: Greek origin. Means: sparkling. Alternative spellings: Amarillas, Amarillis.

Amata: Latin origin. Means: beloved, loved.

Amatullah: Arabic origin. Means: servant.

Amaty: Unknown origin. Means: friendly.

Amber: Arabic origin. Means: amber, immortal, jewel. 24th most popular girl's name of the '90s.

Amberlynn: Unknown origin and meaning.

Ambernesha: Unknown origin and meaning.

Ambria: Unknown origin and meaning.

Ambrosia: Greek origin. Means: food of gods, immortal.

Ambrosine: Greek origin. Means: immortal. Alternative spelling: Ambrosane.

Ameenah: Arabic origin. Means: trustworthy.

Amelia: Latin/Germanic origin. Means: flattering, industrious. Ethnic background: Italian. Alternative spellings and nicknames: Amelie, Millie, Mill, Meli, Meilie, Amalia, Amilia, Amalea, Amelija.

Amelinda: Latin origin. Means: hardworking. Alternative spelling: Amilinda.

Amena: Celtic origin. Means: honest.

America: Latin/Italian origin. Means: derived from Amerigo, Italian navigator.

Ameritia: Unknown origin and meaning.

Amethyst: Latin origin. Means: jewel, birthstone. Alternative spellings: Amethist, Amithist, Amathist.

Amice: Latin origin. Means: friendship, beloved.

Amina: Unknown origin. Means: peaceful. Ethnic background: Jewish.

Aminta: Latin origin. Means: protected, protector. Alternative spellings and nicknames: Amynta, Mindy.

Amira: Hebrew/Arabic origin. Means: speech, grain. Alternative spelling: Amirah.

Amity: Latin origin. Means: friendly, charity.

Ammaarah: Arabic origin. Means: tolerant.

Amna: Unknown origin and meaning.

Amoni: Unknown origin and meaning.

Amora: Spanish origin. Means: darling, love. Ethnic background: Hispanic.

Amorette: Latin origin. Means: darling, dearly beloved. Alternative spellings: Amarette, Amorita, Amoreta, Amoritta.

Amparo: Spanish origin. Means: to protect.

Amreen: Unknown origin and meaning.

Amrita: Unknown origin and meaning.

Amtza: Hebrew origin. Means: strength.

Amy: Latin/French origin. Means: beloved, loved. Ethnic backgrounds: English/Welsh. 46th most popular girl's name of the '90s. Alternative spellings and nicknames: Amee, Amie, Ami.

Analysia: Spanish/English origin. Unknown meaning.

Anancia: Unknown origin and meaning.

Anastasia: Greek origin. Means: resurrection. Ethnic background: Italian. Alternative spellings and nicknames: Ana, Stacey, Stacy, Anastacia, Anastasie, Anastasija, Anastazie, Annastasia.

Anatola: Greek origin. Means: from the East.

Anceline: French origin. Means: fairest maiden. Alternative spellings: Ancalin, Ancelin.

Andea: Unknown origin and meaning.

Andi: Unknown origin and meaning. Alternative spelling: Anndi.

Andorra: Unknown origin and meaning.

Andra: Scottish origin. Means: justice.

Andrea: Anglo-Saxon/Italian origin. Means: womanly. Ethnic backgrounds: Greek, German, Hungarian. 44th most popular girl's name of the '90s. Alternative spellings and nicknames: Andee, Andi, Andre, Andreana, Andria, Andriana, Andy.

Andreanna: Unknown origin. Means: fearless.

Andress: Unknown origin and meaning.

Andromeda: Greek/Latin origin. Means: justice. Alternative spelling: Andromede.

Aneesah: Arabic origin. Means: companion.

Anemone: Greek/Latin origin. Means: flower.

Angail: Unknown origin and meaning.

Angela: Greek/Latin origin. Means: angel, messenger. Ethnic backgrounds: English/Welsh, Italian. 46th most popular girl's name of the '90s. Alternative spellings and nicknames: Angie, Angy, Angelina, Angel, Angelita, Angelica, Angeline, Angele.

Angelica: Latin origin. Means: angelic, messenger. Ethnic background: Italian. Alternative spellings: Angelico, Angelika, Angeliq, Anjelic, Anjelica.

Angelou: Unknown origin and meaning.

Anibal: English origin. Unknown meaning.

Anibelis: Unknown origin and meaning.

Anika: German origin. Means: honorable ruler.

Anita: Hebrew/Spanish origin. Means: graceful. Ethnic backgrounds: Norwegian, Polish, Italian, Swedish, German. Alternative spelling: Anitra.

Anja: Unknown origin and meaning. Ethnic background: German.

Anjum: Arabic origin. Means: stars.

Anke: Germanic origin. Means: graceful.

Ann: Hebrew/Greek origin. Means: grace and mercy. Ethnic backgrounds: Swedish, English/Welsh, Scottish. Alternative spellings and nicknames: Nanete, Ninon, Nanon, Nana, Annetta, Anabella, Nanine, Ninette, Nina, Nanette, Nancy, Anora, Annie, Anabel, Annette, Anne, Anna, Nan, Annia.

Anna: Hebrew/Latin origin. Means: gracious. Ethnic backgrounds: Polish, Hungarian, Swedish, Norwegian, German, Greek, English/Welsh, Italian. 38th most popular girl's name of the '90s. Alternative spelling: Ana.

Annabell: Hebrew/Latin origin. Means: gracious, beautiful, lovable. Alternative spellings: Anabel, Annabelle, Annabella.

Annaliese: Hebrew origin. Means: grace, devoted to God. Alternative spellings: Annelies, Anneliese, Annelise, Annalee, Annalisa, Annelie, Anneloes, Analissa.

Annapurna: Hindi origin. Means: bread.

Anndrea: Greek origin. Means: valiant, strong, courageous.

Anne: Hebrew origin. Means: God has favored, prayer. Ethnic background: Norwegian.

Annegret: Unknown origin and meaning. Ethnic background: German.

Annemarie: Germanic origin. Means: grace, bitter. Ethnic background: Dutch. Alternative spellings: AnnMarie, Annamarie, Annamaria.

Annerose: Unknown origin and meaning. Ethnic background: German.

Annette: Hebrew/French origin. Means: graceful. Ethnic background: Swedish. Alternative spellings: Anett, Anette.

Annick: Saxon origin. Means: gracious. Ethnic background: French.

Annie: Hebrew origin. Means: beautiful, grace. Ethnic background: Dutch. Alternative spelling: Anni.

Annika: Germanic origin. Means: grace. Ethnic background: Swedish. Alternative spellings: Anica, Aniko, Annaka.

Annis: Greek/Anglo-Saxon origin. Means: unity, complete.

Annisia: Unknown origin and meaning. Alternative spellings: Annissa, Anissa, Anise.

Annorah: Hebrew origin. Means: grace, light. Alternative spellings: Annora, Anora.

Annunciata: Unknown origin. Means: bearer, good.

Anona: Latin origin. Means: crops.

Anquavia: Unknown origin and meaning.

Anselma: Germanic/Norse origin. Means: divine, God, protected. Alternative spellings: Ansilma, Ansela.

Anshanika: Unknown origin and meaning.

Antanae: Latin origin. Means: one of the paired, flexible, segmented, sensor.

Antanisha: Unknown origin and meaning.

Anthea: Greek origin. Means: flower. Alternative spellings and nicknames: Anthia, Biuma, Thea, Fleur, Thia, Flora, Antheia.

Antje: Germanic origin. Means: grace.

Antoinette: French origin. Means: praiseworthy, priceless. Ethnic background: German. Alternative spellings: Anntonette, Antonetta, Antonette, Antonietta, Antwanette.

Antonella: Unknown origin and meaning. Ethnic background: Italian.

Antonia: Latin origin. Means: priceless, flower. Ethnic backgrounds: German, Italian. Alternative spellings and nicknames: Nettie, Toinette, Netty, Antoinetta, Antoni, Toni, Antoinette, Netta, Antonina.

Antonina: Latin origin. Means: above praise. Ethnic background: Russian.

Antoya: Unknown origin and meaning.

Anya: Slavic origin. Means: grace. Alternative spelling: Anyah.

Anysia: Greek origin. Means: complete.

Anyssa: Unknown origin and meaning.

Aoife: Gaelic origin. Means: beauty. Ethnic background: Irish.

Aphra: Saxon/Irish origin. Means: deer, dust, dark.

Appoline: Greek/French origin. Means: sun, Apollo's gift.

April: Latin origin. Means: born, springtime. Alternative spellings: Apryl, Avrille.

How to Deal with Flak

You may not have another chance, so you may as well hold out and go with the best name you can think of.

~ Terri B.,
Bainbridge Island, Washington

Aquila: Unknown origin and meaning. Alternative spelling: Aquela.

Aquinnah: Unknown origin and meaning.

Arabella: Latin/Teutonic origin. Means: altar, beautiful, heroine, eagle. Ethnic background: Hispanic. Alternative spellings and nicknames: Arabeile, Bel, Ara, Bell, Bella, Belle, Arabela, Arabelle.

Araceli: Spanish origin. Means: sky, altar. Ethnic background: Hispanic. Alternative spelling: Aracely.

Arainne: Unknown origin and meaning.

Aral: Unknown origin and meaning.

Araminta: Hebrew origin. Means: lofty, elegant. Alternative spellings: Aramanta, Aramenta.

Arda: Anglo-Saxon origin. Means: warm, fervent, field.

Ardath: Hebrew origin. Means: flowering field. Alternative spelling: Ardeth.

Ardelle: Latin/Saxon origin. Means: enthusiasm, fervent. Alternative spellings: Ardelia, Ardella.

Ardenia: Unknown origin. Means: eagle.

Ardine: Latin/Anglo-Saxon origin. Means: enthusiasm, warm. Alternative spelling: Ardene.

Ardis: Unknown origin. Means: fervent, bold. Alternative spellings and nicknames: Ardelis, Ardra, Ardeiia, Ardeiie, Ardine, Ardene, Ardella.

Ardith: Teutonic/Anglo-Saxon origin. Means: wealthy gift, good war.

Arela: Celtic origin. Means: oath, angel, messenger. Ethnic background: Jewish. Alternative spelling: Arella.

Aretha: Greek origin. Means: beauty. Alternative spellings: Areta, Arette, Aretta.

Aretina: Unknown origin. Means: virtuous.

Argenta: Latin origin. Means: silvery.

Aria: Teutonic/Italian origin. Means: eagle, melody.

Ariadine: Greek origin. Means: holy one. Alternative spellings: Ariadne, Ariana, Ariane.

Ariana: Latin origin. Means: holy, song. Ethnic background: Jewish. Alternative spellings: Ariane, Arianna, Arriana, Aryianna.

Ariandrah: Unknown origin and meaning.

Arica: Unknown origin. Means: loving. Alternative spelling: Arika.

Arice: Unknown origin. Means: joyful.

Ariel: Hebrew origin. Means: lioness of God. Ethnic background: Hispanic. Alternative spellings: Ariela, Ariella, Arielle, Aryelle.

Arissa: Unknown origin. Means: happy. Alternative spelling: Arrissa.

Arita: Unknown origin. Means: bird, field.

Arlene: Celtic origin. Means: pledge, eagle, girl. Alternative spellings: Arlina, Arlana, Arlette, Arline, Arleen, Arlena, Arlyne.

Arleta: Celtic origin. Means: pledge.

Armelda: Teutonic origin. Means: battle, maiden. Alternative spellings: Armalda, Armilda, Armillda.

Armesha: Unknown origin and meaning.

Armida: Latin origin. Means: armed one. Ethnic background: Hispanic.

Armilla: Latin origin. Means: bracelet. Alternative spellings: Armalla, Armillas, Armillia.

Armina: Teutonic origin. Means: maid. Alternative spelling: Armine.

Armona: Unknown origin. Means: fortress. Ethnic background: Jewish.

Arnalda: Germanic/Italian origin. Means: eagle, ruler.

Arnina: Unknown origin. Means: inspired.

Arnona: Hebrew origin. Means: roaring stream.

Arola: Unknown origin. Means: sea.

Arran: Unknown origin and meaning.

Arria: Unknown origin. Means: rainmaker.

Artema: Unknown origin. Means: angels. Alternative spellings: Artima, Artamas, Arta, Artinias.

Artemisa: Greek origin. Means: vigorous.

Artemisia: Greek origin. Means: perfection, gift.

Artina: Unknown origin. Means: martial.

Arva: Latin origin. Means: from the sea, fertile.

Aselma: Gaelic origin. Means: fair, divine.

Asha: Arabic origin. Means: life, lively. Ethnic background: African. Alternative spellings: Asia, Aisha, Aishia, Ashia, Aysha.

Ashanti: Unknown origin and meaning. Alternative spelling: Ashantay.

Ashley: Old English origin. Means: ash. 3rd most popular girl's name of the '90s. Alternative spellings: Ashle, Ashlea, Ashlee, Ashlei, Ashleigh, Ashli, Ashlie, Ashly.

Ashlyn: Unknown origin and meaning. Alternative spelling: Ashlynn.

Ashti: Unknown origin. Means: fairest.

Aslaug: Norse origin. Means: devoted to God.

Aspasia: Greek origin. Means: welcome. Alternative spellings: Aspa, Aspia.

Assunta: Italian origin. Means: assumption.

Asta: Norse/Greek origin. Means: love, strength. Alternative spelling: Asstta.

Astor: Unknown origin and meaning.

Astoria: Unknown origin and meaning.

Astra: Greek/Norse origin. Means: divine, starlike. Ethnic background: Russian. Alternative spellings: Astred, Astrea, Astrid.

Astri: Unknown origin and meaning. Ethnic background: Norwegian.

Astrid: Norse origin. Means: divine strength, love. Ethnic backgrounds: German, Norwegian, Swedish.

Atalani: Unknown origin. Means: runner.

Atalie: Hebrew/Norse origin. Means: great, pure.

Athalia: Hebrew origin. Means: lord. Alternative spellings: Atalaya, Athaliah, Athalla, Athallia.

Athena: Greek origin. Means: with wisdom. Alternative spellings: Athene, Atheena.

Atiana: Unknown origin. Means: girl.

Atida: Hebrew origin. Means: future.

Atira: Hebrew origin. Means: prayer.

Atje: Unknown origin and meaning. Ethnic background: Dutch.

Atlanta: Greek origin. Means: adversary, huntress, runner, unswaying. Alternative spellings: Atalanta, Atalante.

Atronna: Unknown origin. Means: mother.

Attalie: Unknown origin. Means: maiden.

Atthia: Unknown origin. Means: gift.

Attracta: Latin origin. Means: drawn to. Ethnic background: Irish.

Auberta: Teutonic/French origin. Means: intelligent, noble. Alternative spellings: Aubarta, Auburta.

Aubine: French origin. Means: blond.

Aubree: English origin. Means: elf, supernatural being, power. Alternative spellings: Aubrie, Aubry.

Aubriana: Unknown origin and meaning.

Audrey: Old English origin. Means: noble, strength. Ethnic background: French. Alternative spellings and nicknames: Audie, Audra, Audree, Audrie, Audry, Dee.

How to Deal with Flak

Don't let your family and friends tell you, "What? You're going to name the baby that?!?!"

~ Michele C.,
Costa Mesa, California

10

Augusta: Latin origin. Means: majestic, sacred. Ethnic background: Italian. Alternative spellings and nicknames: Gussie, Austina, Augustina, Gusta, Augustine, Austine, Tina.

Aurea: Latin origin. Means: gold, breeze. Alternative spellings: Aura, Auria.

Aurelia: Latin origin. Means: golden, breeze. Ethnic backgrounds: Italian, German. Alternative spellings and nicknames: Aurie, Aurel, Aurora, Orel, Oralie, Aura, Ora, Aurelie, Aurea, Oralia.

Aurita: Unknown origin. Means: dark.

Aurora: Latin origin. Means: daybreak, dawn. Ethnic backgrounds: Hispanic, Italian. Alternative spelling: Aurore.

Austen: Latin/Saxon origin. Means: Augustus, exalted. Alternative spelling: Auston.

Austine: Latin origin. Means: majestic, little.

Autumn: Greek origin. Means: born in the fall.

Avae: Unknown origin and meaning.

Avena: Latin origin. Means: of the oatfield.

Avera: Hebrew origin. Means: born, transgressor. Alternative spelling: Avaria.

Averell: Old English origin. Means: battle, boar.

Avi: Hebrew origin. Means: father.

Aviana: Unknown origin and meaning. Alternative spelling: Avianna.

Avigail: Hebrew origin. Means: father's joy. Alternative spelling: Avigal.

Avis: Latin/Germanic origin. Means: birdlike, warlike. Alternative spellings: Avi, Ava, Avice.

Aviva: Hebrew origin. Means: spring. Alternative spelling: Avivah.

Avra: Unknown origin. Means: lord.

Ayana: Unknown origin and meaning. Alternative spelling: Ayanna.

Ayesha: Arabic origin. Means: fortunate.

Ayla: Hebrew origin. Means: an oak tree, a terebinth tree.

Aylandra: Unknown origin and meaning.

Aylworth: Teutonic origin. Means: awe-inspiring worth.

Aynet: Unknown origin and meaning.

Azalea: Hebrew/Latin origin. Means: blossom, dry earth, God. Alternative spellings: Azaleah, Azelia.

Azaria: Greek/Hebrew origin. Means: blessed by God. Alternative spellings: Azarria, Azeria.

Azbane: Unknown origin and meaning.

Azeezah: Arabic origin. Means: dear.

Aziza: Hebrew origin. Means: strong. Ethnic background: African.

Azura: Persian origin. Means: sky blue.

b

Baako: African origin. Means: firstborn.

Bab: Arabic origin. Means: from the gateway.

Babette: French origin. Means: stranger, lovely. Ethnic background: German. Alternative spellings: Babbette, Babita.

Bacall: Unknown origin and meaning.

Bahati: African origin. Means: luck.

Bailee: Unknown origin and meaning. Alternative spellings: Baylee, Bayli.

Balandria: Spanish origin. Means: of the resurrection.

Balbina: Latin origin. Means: strong, stammers. Ethnic background: Hispanic.

Baleigh: Middle English origin. Means: the outer wall of the castle.

Bambi: Italian origin. Means: child, little doll.

Banelia: Unknown origin and meaning.

Banna: Unknown origin. Means: adorn, anything.

Baptista: Latin origin. Means: baptized.

Bara: Hebrew origin. Means: to choose.

Barbara: Greek/Latin origin. Means: foreigner, exotic, mysterious. Ethnic backgrounds: Italian, Irish, Hispanic. Alternative spellings and nicknames: Barby, Babs, Babby, Barbette, Babette, Barbra, Barb, Barbi, Barbro.

Barbel: Unknown origin and meaning. Ethnic background: German.

Barbette: Unknown origin. Means: lovely.

Bardot: Unknown origin and meaning.

Basha: Hebrew/Polish origin. Means: daughter of God, stranger.

Bashir: Unknown origin and meaning.

Basia: Polish origin. Means: exotic, mysterious.

Basilia: Greek origin. Means: queenly, regal.

Bathesda: Unknown origin. Means: fountain. Alternative spelling: Bathesde.

Bathilda: Germanic origin. Means: battle, heroine. Alternative spelling: Bathelda.

Bathsheba: Hebrew origin. Means: daughter, oath. Alternative spelling: Bathsheb.

Batli: Hebrew origin. Means: I have a daughter.

Batool: Arabic origin. Means: pure, chaste.

Bayla: Hebrew origin. Means: weak, troubled. Alternative spelling: Bayle.

Baylke: Unknown origin and meaning. Ethnic background: Jewish.

Bayo: African origin. Means: there is joy.

Beata: Latin origin. Means: divinely blessed. Ethnic background: Polish. Alternative spellings and nicknames: Beate, Bea.

Beatrice: Latin/Italian origin. Means: girl, joy. Ethnic background: French. Alternative spellings and nicknames: Bea, Bee, Trix, Beatrix, Trixie, Beatriz.

Becca: Hebrew/Saxon origin. Means: to tie, beautiful.

Beda: Saxon origin. Means: warrior, maiden.

Bedelia: Unknown origin. Means: mighty.

Begga: Unknown origin. Means: bee. Alternative spelling: Bega.

Behira: Hebrew origin. Means: brilliant, clear.

Beka: Hebrew origin. Means: half. Alternative spellings: Bekah, Bekka.

Belda: French origin. Means: lovely.

Belen: Hebrew/Spanish origin. Means: house of bread. Ethnic background: Hispanic.

Belia: Slavic origin. Means: wife, pillar. Ethnic background: Hispanic.

Belicia: Unknown origin. Means: dedicated, God.

Belinda: Italian origin. Means: beautiful, serpent. Ethnic backgrounds: Hispanic, English/Welsh. Alternative spellings and nicknames: Bei, Lindie, Linda, Lindy.

Bella: Latin/Saxon origin. Means: beautiful. Ethnic background: German. Alternative spelling: Belle.

Bellaude: Unknown origin. Means: beauty.

Bellda: Unknown origin. Means: lovely. Alternative spellings: Balldame, Belldas.

Bellis: Unknown origin and meaning.

Belvia: Latin origin. Means: beautiful, view. Alternative spelling: Belva.

Bena: Hebrew origin. Means: one of wisdom. Alternative spelling: Benay.

Beneba: Unknown origin. Means: born.

Benedicta: Latin origin. Means: blessed. Alternative spellings: Benetta, Benita, Benedetta, Bendicte, Benedikta, Benedykt.

Benigna: Latin origin. Means: gentle, kind, well.

Benilda: Latin origin. Means: good. Alternative spellings: Benildas, Benilde.

Benita: Latin/Spanish origin. Means: blessed.

Bente: Latin origin. Means: blessed. Ethnic background: Norwegian.

Beora: Anglo-Saxon origin. Means: birch tree, torch. Alternative spelling: Beore.

Berdine: Greek/Germanic origin. Means: intelligent maid, glorious.

Berengaria: Anglo-Saxon origin. Means: spear maid.

Bergenia: Unknown origin and meaning.

Berit: Celtic/Germanic origin. Means: splendid, strength, intelligent. Ethnic backgrounds: Swedish, Norwegian.

How to Deal with Flak

If you fall in love with a name, use it!
~ Melissa M., Phoenix, Arizona

Berlinda: Unknown origin. Means: beauty.

Berlyn: Unknown origin. Means: beauty.

Bernadette: French/Germanic origin. Means: bear, brave, little. Ethnic backgrounds: Swiss, Hungarian. Alternative spelling: Bernadett.

Bernadine: Teutonic/Saxon origin. Means: bear, brave, intelligent. Alternative spellings and nicknames: Berna, Bernadina, Berneta, Bernetta, Bernette, Berni, Bernadette, Bernie, Bernadene, Bernardena.

Bernia: Anglo-Saxon origin. Means: battle maid.

Bernica: Unknown origin and meaning. Ethnic background: Hispanic.

Bernice: Greek origin. Means: harbinger, victorious. Alternative spellings and nicknames: Berni, Berny, Berenice.

Bernita: Greek/Germanic origin. Means: bear, brave, victory.

Bertha: Saxon/Germanic origin. Means: glorious, learning, beautiful. Ethnic backgrounds: Hispanic, Norwegian, German, Czech, Italian. Alternative spellings and nicknames: Berti, Bertie, Bertina, Berta, Berthe.

Bertilla: Teutonic origin. Means: kind, warrior maiden. Alternative spellings: Bertila, Bertilde.

Bertrade: Anglo-Saxon origin. Means: bright counselor.

Berura: Hebrew origin. Means: pure, clean.

Bess: Hebrew/Anglo-Saxon origin. Means: God's oath.

Beth: Hebrew/Saxon origin. Means: house of God.

Bethany: Hebrew origin. Means: house of figs.

Bethel: Hebrew origin. Means: house of God.

Bethesda: Greek/Hebrew origin. Means: house of mercy. Alternative spelling: Bethseda.

Bethezel: Unknown origin. Means: good. Alternative spellings: Betthel, Bettzel.

Bethia: Celtic/Hebrew origin. Means: life, God's daughter.

Bethina: Unknown origin. Means: house. Alternative spelling: Bethena.

Betsabe: Unknown origin and meaning. Ethnic background: Hispanic.

Betsy: Hebrew/Anglo-Saxon origin. Means: God's oath.

Bettina: Hebrew/Latin origin. Means: God's oath. Ethnic background: German. Alternative spelling: Betinna.

Betty: Hebrew/Anglo-Saxon origin. Means: God's oath, devoted. Alternative spellings: Bettye, Bette.

Beula: Hebrew origin. Means: married, possessed. Alternative spelling: Beulah.

Beuna: Unknown origin. Means: good.

Beverly: Anglo-Saxon origin. Means: beaver meadow, ambition. Alternative spellings and nicknames: Bevvy, Bev, Beverley.

Bianca: Italian origin. Means: air, fair, white. Alternative spelling: Bianka.

Bibi: French origin. Means: toy, bubbles.

Bibienne: Unknown origin and meaning. Ethnic background: French.

Bidelia: Irish origin. Means: protective.

Billie: Saxon origin. Means: resolution, wise. Alternative spelling: Bille.

Bina: Hebrew origin. Means: understanding, wisdom. Alternative spelling: Binah.

Binetta: Unknown origin. Means: fame. Alternative spelling: Binette.

Bira: Hebrew origin. Means: fortified city.

Birdie: Anglo-Saxon origin. Means: birdlike.

Birgit: Celtic/Gaelic origin. Means: defender. Ethnic backgrounds: German, Swedish.

Birgitta: Germanic/Swedish origin. Means: strong.

Bita: Unknown origin and meaning.

Bithia: Unknown origin. Means: girl. Alternative spelling: Bitthia.

Blaithe: Unknown origin and meaning.

Blakely: Unknown origin and meaning.

Blanche: Germanic/French origin. Means: blond, fair. Alternative spellings: Branca, Blanch, Blanca, Bianca, Blanka.

Blasia: Latin origin. Means: firebrand, stammers.

Blessing: Anglo-Saxon origin. Means: consecrated.

Blima: Unknown origin and meaning. Ethnic background: Jewish. Alternative spellings: Blimeh, Blimele.

Blinnie: Unknown origin. Means: fair.

Blossom: Old English origin. Means: fresh.

Bluma: Germanic origin. Means: flower. Ethnic background: Jewish.

Blumele: Unknown origin and meaning. Ethnic background: Jewish.

Blythe: Anglo-Saxon origin. Means: cheerful, of joy. Alternative spellings: Blisse, Bliss, Blithe.

Bobbette: Unknown origin. Means: fame.

Bobbi: Old High German origin. Means: bright fame, famous counsel. Alternative spelling: Bobbie.

Bohumila: Slavic origin. Means: God's peace. Ethnic background: Czech.

Bonita: Latin/Spanish origin. Means: pretty, good. Alternative spelling: Bonetta.

Bonnie: Latin/Scottish origin. Means: good, attractive. Alternative spellings: Boni, Bonne, Bonni, Bonny, Bonita.

Botavia: Unknown origin and meaning.

Boukje: Unknown origin and meaning. Ethnic background: Dutch.

Bozena: Slavic origin. Unknown meaning. Ethnic background: Polish.

Bracie: Unknown origin and meaning.

Honor Thy Relatives

Thinking of giving your child a family name? While this is a great way to honor a special person, there are often several other people who wish that *they* had been honored. How do you pass on a name without hurting feelings? And more important, how can you make sure that your perfect, unique child will have his or her own perfect, unique name? There are important questions to consider:

● What are your family's traditions? Do they offer any guidelines, and if so, how flexible are they?

● How can you give your child's name a sense of heritage *and* individuality?

● Will you have to differentiate between two people with the same name living under one roof?

Following are some success stories, one less-than-success story, and some suggestions to help you find that perfect combination of history and uniqueness.

Brandelyn: Unknown origin and meaning.

Brandice: Unknown origin and meaning.

Brandy: Dutch origin. Means: a fiery spirit distilled from wine. Alternative spellings: Brandee, Brandi, Brandie.

Brassica: Unknown origin and meaning.

Braulia: Unknown origin and meaning. Ethnic background: Hispanic.

Braylan: Unknown origin and meaning. Alternative spelling: Braelyn.

Brazil: Unknown origin and meaning.

Brechje: Unknown origin and meaning. Ethnic background: Dutch.

Bree: Old English origin. Means: thin broth, soup. Alternative spelling: Breah.

Breeda: Celtic/Irish origin. Means: protective, strong.

Breggin: Unknown origin and meaning.

Breina: Celtic/Irish origin. Means: strong, honor. Ethnic background: Jewish. Alternative spellings: Brainna, Brenae, Bryna, Brynna.

Brenda: Germanic/Norse origin. Means: flame, sword. Ethnic background: Irish. Nickname: Bren.

Brenna: Celtic origin. Means: raven, maiden with dark hair.

Breshan: Unknown origin and meaning.

Bretten: Unknown origin and meaning.

Bria: Unknown origin and meaning. Alternative spellings: Brhea, Brieh.

Brianna: Celtic/Gaelic/Irish origin. Means: strength. 8th most popular girl's name of the '90s. Alternative spellings: Brean, Breana, Bre-Ann, Breann, Breanna, Bre'anna, Breanne, Breeana, Breeann, Breeanna, Breyana, Breyanie, Briana, Briann, Brianne, Brieanna, Bryana, Bryanna.

Bridget: Celtic origin. Means: strong, fiery, resolute, protective. Ethnic backgrounds: Irish, German, French, Italian. Alternative spellings and nicknames: Brigette, Bridgid, Brieta, Brie, Brietta, Brita, Brigitte, Brigid, Brigida, Bridgette, Brigit, Brigitta.

Brier: Unknown origin. Means: flower.

Brietta: Celtic origin. Means: resolute, strong.

Brin: Unknown origin and meaning.

Brina: Celtic/Slavic origin. Means: defender, protector. Ethnic background: Jewish.

Brionna: Unknown origin and meaning. Alternative spellings: Breonee, Breonia, Breonna, Briona, Bryona.

Britt: Swedish origin. Means: strong. Ethnic background: Norwegian.

Britta: Celtic/Swedish origin. Means: strong, a Briton. Alternative spelling: Brita.

Brittan: Unknown origin and meaning. Alternative spelling: Brittand.

Brittany: Celtic origin. Means: of Briton. 6th most popular girl's name of the '90s. Alternative spellings: Bridney, Britanee, Britney, Britny, Brittanee, Brittani, Brittanie, Britteny, Brittnay, Brittney, Brittni, Brittny, Brytni.

Brittanylynn: Unknown origin and meaning.

Bronwen: Welsh origin. Means: dark, pure.

Brooke: Old English origin. Means: stream, to break out. 38th most popular girl's name of the '90s.

Brooklyn: Old English origin. Means: stream, to break out.

Brosine: Unknown origin. Means: immortal.

Bruna: Germanic origin. Means: brunette, brown. Ethnic background: Jewish. Alternative spelling: Brune.

Brunetta: Italian origin. Means: brunette.

Brunhilde: Germanic/Norse origin. Means: protection, fighting woman. Alternative spellings: Brunhilda, Brunhild.

Bryde: Unknown origin and meaning.

Brystol: Middle English/Anglo-Saxon origin. Means: the son of rich, rich, noble, powerful.

Bukeda: Unknown origin. Means: pretty.

Bunmi: Unknown origin. Means: my gift. Ethnic background: African.

Burgandi: Unknown origin and meaning.

Buruku: African origin. Unknown meaning.

Bushraa: Arabic origin. Means: good news.

Buttercup: Unknown origin and meaning.

C **Cabot:** Unknown origin and meaning.

Cabrina: Unknown origin and meaning.

Cacalia: Unknown origin and meaning.

Cache: French origin. Means: a hiding place.

Cadena: Anglo-Saxon origin. Means: rhythmic.

Cadence: Latin origin. Means: fall into rhythmic patterns.

Cady: Unknown origin and meaning.

Caesaria: Latin origin. Means: leader.

Cailin: Irish origin. Means: girl. Alternative spellings: Cailyn, Cailynn, Calyn.

Caitlin: Greek/Gaelic origin. Means: pure, lovely. Ethnic background: Irish. Alternative spellings: Caitlen, Caitlyn, Catlin.

Caitrianne: Unknown origin and meaning.

Caitrin: Greek/Gaelic origin. Means: pure.

Calandra: Greek origin. Means: a lark. Alternative spellings: Calendra, Calondra.

Calantha: Greek origin. Means: beautiful, blossom. Alternative spellings: Calanthe, Callantha.

Caledonia: Latin origin. Means: from Scotland.

Caleigh: Unknown origin and meaning. Alternative spelling: Calleigh.

Calia: Unknown origin. Means: instigator.

Calida: Unknown origin. Means: loving.

Calise: Unknown origin. Means: lovely.

Calla: Greek origin. Means: most beautiful.

Calliope: Greek origin. Means: one with a beautiful voice. Alternative spelling: Caliopa.

Callista: Greek origin. Means: the most beautiful. Alternative spellings and nicknames: Calysta, Kallista, Calesta, Callie, Calista.

Callula: Latin origin. Means: beautiful.

Caltha: Unknown origin. Means: flower.

Calvina: Spanish origin. Means: bright, bald. Alternative spelling: Calvinna.

Calypso: Greek/Latin origin. Means: a flower, concealer.

Camaren: Unknown origin and meaning.

Camassia: Unknown origin and meaning.

Cambre: Unknown origin and meaning.

Cambria: Anglo-Saxon origin. Unknown meaning.

Camelia: Unknown origin and meaning. Ethnic background: Hispanic. Alternative spelling: Camellia.

Camelina: Unknown origin and meaning.

Cameo: Italian origin. Means: sculptured jewel.

Camilla: Latin origin. Means: unblemished attendant. Ethnic background: Italian. Alternative spellings and nicknames: Cam, Milly, Camellia, Camille, Camelia, Camila.

Cammy: Unknown origin and meaning.

Canace: Greek origin. Means: daughter.

Candace: Latin/Greek origin. Means: glittering, glowing, pure, fire white, incandescent. Alternative spellings and nicknames: Candy, Candie, Candice, Candida, Candee, Candi.

Candenza: Latin origin. Means: rhythmic.

Candida: Latin origin. Means: bright, gleaming white. Alternative spellings: Candide, Candita.

Candra: Latin origin. Means: luminescent.

Canei: Unknown origin and meaning.

Cannon: Latin origin. Means: a mounted gun.

Caprice: Italian origin. Means: fanciful.

Carah: Celtic/Italian/Vietnamese origin. Means: friend, dear, diamond, precious, jewel. Alternative spelling: Cara.

Caren: Swedish origin. Means: pure. Ethnic background: German. Alternative spelling: Carine.

Caresse: French origin. Means: endearing.

Cari: Turkish origin. Means: flows like water.

Caridad: Latin/Spanish origin. Means: dear.

Carie: Latin/French origin. Means: strong, virile.

Honor Thy Relatives

I was named after my mother, sort of: her name is Donna; my name is LaDona. I found out when I was dating how treacherous this setup could be. One day, my boyfriend called and asked for "Dona." Mom answered and said, "This is Donna." He said, "Did you get in trouble for last night?" Mom just smiled and said, "No. Should she have?"

~ LaDona W., St. Peters, Missouri

Carina: Latin/Italian origin. Means: a keel, beloved, dear. Ethnic backgrounds: Dutch, Swedish.

Carissa: Latin origin. Means: artistic. Alternative spellings: Carisa, Caryssa.

Carita: Latin origin. Means: beloved, chary, generosity. Alternative spelling: Carrita.

Carla: Germanic origin. Means: little, strong. Ethnic background: Italian. Alternative spellings: Carlotta, Carly, Karla, Karly, Carlee, Carley, Carli, Carlie, Carlli.

Carleas: Unknown origin. Means: cheerful.

Carlene: Latin/Irish origin. Means: womanly, strong. Alternative spellings: Carleen, Carlina, Carline, Carlyn.

Carlessa: Unknown origin and meaning.

Carlianne: Unknown origin and meaning.

Carlita: Italian/Spanish origin. Means: womanly, strong.

Carlotta: French/Italian origin. Means: little, feminine. Alternative spelling: Cariota.

Carma: Sanskrit origin. Means: destiny, garden.

Carmelina: Hebrew origin. Means: garden. Alternative spellings: Carmalina, Carmelena, Carmela, Carmelita.

Carmen: Latin origin. Means: crimson, song. Ethnic backgrounds: Hispanic, German. Alternative spellings and nicknames: Carmena, Carmita, Carmina, Carmine, Carmencita.

Carmiela: Hebrew origin. Means: vineyard of the Lord. Alternative spelling: Carmiya.

Carna: Hebrew origin. Means: horn. Alternative spelling: Carni.

Carnation: Latin/French origin. Means: flesh colored, rosy.

Carol: French/Gaelic origin. Means: joyous song, strong. Alternative spellings and nicknames: Carolle, Karole, Carey, Carole, Carola, Carrie, Cary, Caryl, Karol.

Carolanne: Gaelic/French origin. Means: combination of Carol (melody, song) and Anne (God has favored, prayer).

Caroline: Latin/Saxon origin. Means: little womanly one, joy. Ethnic backgrounds: English/Welsh. 47th most popular girl's name of the '90s. Alternative spellings and nicknames: Karoline, Karolyn, Karolina, Lina, Carrie, Carolyn, Carolina, Carolin, Carola.

Carrie: Saxon origin. Means: beloved, joy.

Carsyn: Unknown origin and meaning.

Carys: Welsh origin. Means: love the ending.

Casie: Greek origin. Means: brave.

Casilda: Spanish origin. Means: solitary. Alternative spellings: Casilde, Cassilda, Cassil.

Cassandra: Greek origin. Means: one who inflames men with love, helper. Ethnic background: Hispanic. 41st most popular girl's name of the '90s. Alternative spellings and nicknames: Cassandre, Cass, Cassie, Casandra.

Cassia: Greek origin. Means: cinnamon.

Cassie: Greek origin. Means: pure.

Cassis: Unknown origin and meaning.

Casta: Greek/Spanish origin. Means: pure, modest.

Castalina: Unknown origin and meaning.

Castara: Greek origin. Means: girl. Alternative spellings: Castera, Castora.

Catalina: Greek/Spanish origin. Means: purity.

Caterina: Italian origin. Means: purity. Alternative spelling: Catrina.

Catharina: Greek origin. Means: purity. Ethnic backgrounds: Dutch, German.

Catherine: Greek origin. Means: pure. Ethnic backgrounds: English/Welsh, French, Scottish. Alternative spellings: Catharine, Cathrine, Cathryn.

Cathy: Greek origin. Means: pure.

Catima: Unknown origin. Means: reed. Alternative spelling: Cattima.

Catriona: Gaelic/Welsh origin. Means: pure. Ethnic background: Irish.

Cayla: Unknown origin and meaning.

Caylie: Greek/Old English origin. Means: to rejoice, a meadow. Alternative spellings: Cailey, Caily, Cali, Calie, Caly, Caylee, Cayley.

Ceara: Gaelic origin. Means: spear.

Cece: Unknown origin and meaning.

Cecilia: Latin origin. Means: dim-sighted, musical. Ethnic background: Swedish. Alternative spellings and nicknames: Cicily, Cis, Cissy, Cecile, Cecily, Cecelia, Celia.

Cecily: Latin origin. Means: dim-sighted. Ethnic background: Irish. Alternative spellings: Cacilie, Cecilie, Cecilla, Cicely, Cecila.

Ceirra: Latin origin. Means: a chain of hills. Alternative spellings: CeAirra, Cierra.

Celandine: Greek origin. Means: swallow.

Celeste: Latin origin. Means: heavenly. Ethnic backgrounds: Greek, Italian. Alternative spellings: Celestine, Celesta, Celestina.

Celia: Latin origin. Means: blind, heavenly. Ethnic background: Hispanic.

Celina: Latin/Greek origin. Means: heavenly, moon. Ethnic background: Italian. Alternative spellings: Celene, Celinda.

Celine: Latin origin. Means: fairest, hammer. Ethnic background: French. Alternative spelling: Celin.

Celisha: Unknown origin and meaning.

Celosia: Greek origin. Means: burning.

Ceporah: Unknown origin. Means: bird.

Cerelia: Latin/Italian origin. Means: of the spring, fruitful. Alternative spellings: Cerallua, Cerellia, Cerelly.

Cerina: Latin origin. Means: peaceful.

Cesaria: Spanish origin. Means: one with abundant hair.

Chaille: Unknown origin and meaning.

Chamaran: Unknown origin. Means: black.

Chambray: Unknown origin and meaning.

Champagne: French origin. Means: a sparkling white wine.

Chana: Hebrew origin. Means: gracious. Alternative spelling: Chani.

Chanda: Hindi origin. Means: goddess.

Chandi: Unknown origin and meaning.

Chandra: Sanskrit origin. Means: moon, brighter than stars.

Chanel: Unknown origin and meaning.

Channing: French origin. Means: canon, knowing.

Channon: Gaelic origin. Means: small, of wisdom.

Chantal: Latin/French origin. Means: song, boulder. Alternative spellings: Chantalle, Chantel, Chantell, Chantelle, Chandal, Chauntel.

Chante: Unknown origin and meaning.

Chardonnae: French origin. Means: a dry, white table wine.

Charelle: Unknown origin and meaning.

Charian: Unknown origin and meaning.

Charie: Unknown origin. Means: grace, loving. Alternative spelling: Chari.

Charis: Greek origin. Means: grace.

Charish: Unknown origin. Means: to care for, look after.

Charissa: Greek origin. Means: benevolent, loving.

Charity: Latin origin. Means: benevolent, loving. Alternative spellings and nicknames: Charry, Cherry, Charita, Chirity.

Charlene: Latin/French origin. Means: womanly, strong. Alternative spelling: Charline.

Charli: Unknown origin and meaning.

Charlotta: Italian origin. Means: strong, womanly. Ethnic background: Swedish.

Charlotte: French/Saxon origin. Means: little, noble woman. Ethnic backgrounds: English/Welsh. Alternative spellings and nicknames: Letty, Lotty, Carry, Lotte, Lottie, Lotta, Charline, Charlene, Carlotta.

Charlsie: Unknown origin and meaning.

Charmaine: Latin origin. Means: delight, singer, song. Alternative spellings: Charmain, Charmayne, Charmian.

Charra: Unknown origin and meaning.

Chasity: Unknown origin and meaning. Alternative spelling: Chassity.

Chastity: Latin origin. Means: purity.

Chateria: Unknown origin and meaning.

Chela: English origin. Unknown meaning. Alternative spellings: Chelan, Chelena.

Chelsea: Anglo-Saxon origin. Means: shipping port. 28th most popular girl's name of the '90s. Alternative spellings: Chelse, Chelsei, Chelsey, Chelsie.

Chemarin: Unknown origin. Means: black. Alternative spelling: Chemar.

Chemash: Unknown origin. Means: pacifies. Alternative spellings: Chema, Chemesh, Chemosh.

Chenelle: Unknown origin and meaning.

Cher: French origin. Means: beloved. Alternative spelling: Chere.

Cherie: French origin. Means: beloved, cherished. Alternative spellings and nicknames: Shery, Sherri, Sherry, Cheryl, Cheri, Cherye, Cheria.

Cherise: French origin. Means: beloved, cherished. Alternative spellings: Cherice, Cherish.

Cheritta: French origin. Means: treasure, beloved.

Cherokee: Native American origin. Unknown meaning.

Cherry: Latin/French origin. Means: benevolent, darling. Alternative spelling: Chery.

Cheryl: Germanic/French origin. Means: womanly, beloved, little. Alternative spellings: Cherelle, Charyl.

Chesma: Slavic origin. Means: peaceful.

Chessa: Slavic origin. Means: peaceful.

Chestnut: Greek origin. Means: edible nut.

Chevona: Unknown origin and meaning.

Chevy: Unknown origin and meaning.

Cheyann: Unknown origin and meaning. Alternative spelling: Cheyanne.

Cheye: Unknown origin and meaning.

Cheyeene: Algonquian origin. Unknown meaning.

Cheyene: Canadian French origin. Means: Native American people.

Chi: Unknown origin. Means: elder, mind.

Chiante: Unknown origin and meaning.

Chiara: Latin/Italian origin. Means: bright, clear.

Chidi: African origin. Unknown meaning.

Chika: Egyptian origin. Means: power of God. Ethnic background: African.

Chiku: African origin. Means: chatterer.

Chimene: Unknown origin. Means: heroine.

Chinasia: Unknown origin and meaning.

Chinenye: African origin. Unknown meaning.

Chipo: African origin. Means: gift.

Chiquita: Spanish origin. Means: little one.

Chita: Hebrew/Saxon origin. Means: wheat, grain, kitten.

Chiyena: Unknown origin and meaning. Ethnic background: Jewish.

Chiyoko: Japanese origin. Unknown meaning.

Chizoba: African origin. Unknown meaning.

Chloe: Greek origin. Means: verdant, blooming. 49th most popular girl's name of the '90s. Alternative spelling: Cloe.

Chlori: Greek origin. Means: flowers, blooming.

Chloris: Greek origin. Means: green, blooming. Alternative spellings: Cloris, Chloras.

Chriselda: Germanic origin. Means: strong, battle.

Chrissa: Unknown origin. Means: dearest.

Chrissie: Greek/Latin origin. Means: Christ bearer. Alternative spelling: Chrysie.

Christa: Latin/Germanic origin. Means: Christ bearer.

Christabelle: Greek/Latin origin. Means: beautiful, Christian. Alternative spelling: Cristabel.

Christiana: Latin origin. Means: Christian. Alternative spellings: Christianna, Cristiana.

Christina: Latin origin. Means: Christian. Ethnic backgrounds: English/Welsh, Greek, German, Swedish. 29th most popular girl's name of the '90s. Alternative spellings: Chrystina, Cristina.

Christine: Greek/Latin origin. Means: Christian, follower of the anointed. Ethnic backgrounds: English/Welsh, Swiss. 49th most popular girl's name of the '90s. Alternative spellings and nicknames: Teena,

Chrissy, Christabel, Chris, Tina, Chrystal, Chrissie, Christiana, Christal, Christabelle, Christina, Christa.

Christmas: Greek origin. Means: Christ's mass.

Christy: Greek/Latin origin. Means: Christ bearer. Alternative spelling: Christi.

Chyan: Irish/Gaelic origin. Means: ancient.

Chynna: Unknown origin and meaning. Alternative spelling: Chyna.

Ciandra: Unknown origin and meaning.

Ciara: Irish origin. Means: black, dark. Alternative spelling: Ciera.

Cida: Unknown origin. Means: calm.

Cilla: Latin origin. Means: learn.

Cima: Anglo-Saxon origin. Means: judge, ruler. Alternative spelling: Cimm.

Cinderella: French origin. Means: of the ashes.

Cinnamon: Greek origin. Means: spice, aroma.

Cinta: Unknown origin and meaning. Ethnic background: Hispanic.

Cinzia: Unknown origin and meaning. Ethnic background: Italian.

Cita: Unknown origin. Means: silent.

Claire: French origin. Means: clear, bright, famous. Ethnic backgrounds: English/Welsh. 43rd most popular girl's name of the '90s. Alternative spelling: Clare.

Clara: Latin origin. Means: bright, clear. Ethnic backgrounds: Polish, Hispanic, Italian. Alternative spellings: Clarine, Clareta, Clarette, Clare, Claire, Claritza.

Clarabelle: Latin/French origin. Means: beautiful, brilliant. Ethnic background: Italian. Alternative spellings: Claribel, Clarabella.

Claresta: Anglo-Saxon origin. Means: brilliant.

Clareta: Latin/Spanish origin. Means: bright, distinguished. Alternative spellings: Clarita, Clarette.

Clarimond: Germanic origin. Means: brilliant protector.

Honor Thy Relatives

In my husband's family it is a tradition to name your first son after his grandfather. My father-in-law's name is John. I wanted something with a little more character, but it was very important to my husband to follow tradition. We decided to use the Italian version of John, which is Giovanni. In the end, my father-in-law was even happier that we used Giovanni—he's very Italian, and his mother had named him John to make him sound more American. He was glad we put the Italian back!

~ Veronica S., Macedonia, Ohio

Clarinda: Latin/Spanish origin. Means: beautiful, bright, brilliant.

Clarissa: Latin origin. Means: brilliant, to be famous. Ethnic background: Italian. Alternative spellings: Clarise, Clarice, Clarisa, Clarisse.

Clasina: Unknown origin and meaning.

Claudia: Latin origin. Means: lame one. Ethnic backgrounds: German, Italian, French. Alternative spellings: Claudie, Claudina, Claudette, Claude, Claudine.

Clava: Spanish origin. Means: endearing.

Cleantha: Greek/Saxon origin. Means: in praise of flowers. Alternative spellings: Cleanthe, Cliantha.

Clematis: Greek origin. Means: brushwood, vine, flower.

Clementia: Latin origin. Means: calm, merciful. Alternative spellings: Clementas, Clementi, Clementis.

Clementine: Latin origin. Means: merciful disposition. Alternative spellings: Clementia, Clementina, Clemintina.

Cleo: Greek origin. Means: fame, glory. Alternative spelling: Clio.

Cleodal: Greek origin. Means: famous. Alternative spellings: Cleodel, Cleodell.

Cleopatra: Greek origin. Means: famous father's glory. Alternative spellings and nicknames: Cleona, Cleo, Cleopatre.

Cleva: Saxon origin. Means: cliff dweller.

Cliona: Gaelic/Irish origin. Means: princess.

Clorinda: Latin origin. Means: renowned. Alternative spelling: Clorinde.

Clotilda: Germanic/Saxon origin. Means: famous battle, heroine. Ethnic backgrounds: Italian, Hispanic. Alternative spellings: Clotilde, Clothilde.

Clover: Anglo-Saxon origin. Means: a clover, blossom. Alternative spelling: Clovah.

Clymene: Latin/Greek origin. Means: famed.

Clytie: Greek origin. Means: beautiful.

Colberdee: Unknown origin and meaning.

Colette: Latin origin. Means: army, victorious. Ethnic background: French. Alternative spelling: Collette.

Coline: Celtic/Gaelic origin. Means: dove, victory.

Colinette: Latin origin. Means: small dove. Alternative spelling: Columbine.

Colleen: Gaelic/Irish origin. Means: girl. Alternative spellings and nicknames: Coleen, Colene.

Colmbyne: Unknown origin. Means: dove.

Columbia: Latin origin. Means: dove. Alternative spellings: Colombe, Columba, Columbine.

Comfort: Latin/French origin. Means: to strengthen greatly.

Comsa: Unknown origin. Means: maidenly.

Concepcion: Spanish origin. Means: honor of the immaculate conception, understanding. Alternative spelling: Conception.

Conchita: Spanish origin. Means: honor of the immaculate conception.

Concordia: Latin origin. Means: harmony.

Connie: Latin origin. Means: consistency, faithful. Alternative spelling: Conny.

Conradine: Germanic origin. Means: bold, counsel.

Conseja: Spanish origin. Means: good counsel, holy.

Consolata: Italian origin. Means: consolation.

Constance: Latin origin. Means: unyielding, devoted. Alternative spellings and nicknames: Con, Constantia, Conni, Constantine, Constantina, Conny, Connie, Constanza.

Constantina: Latin/Italian origin. Means: constancy. Ethnic background: Greek. Alternative spelling: Constanta.

Consuela: Latin origin. Means: giver of consolation. Alternative spellings and nicknames: Connie, Consuelo.

Cora: Greek origin. Means: maiden. Alternative spellings and nicknames: Correna, Corry, Coretta, Corene, Corette, Corrie, Corinna, Coralie, Corinne, Corella.

Corabelle: Greek origin. Means: beautiful maiden.

Coral: Latin/Greek origin. Means: coral of the sea, small stone. Alternative spellings: Coralle, Corel.

Coraline: Latin/Greek origin. Means: coral of the sea, small stone.

Corazon: Latin/Spanish origin. Means: sacred heart.

Cordelia: Latin/Celtic origin. Means: heart, daughter of the sea. Alternative spelling: Cordeelia, Cordalia, Cordelie, Cordula.

Cordillera: Unknown origin and meaning.

Corette: Greek/French origin. Means: little maiden.

Coriander: Greek origin. Means: cooking plant.

Corinne: French/Greek origin. Means: French form of Cora, meaning maiden. Ethnic backgrounds: Hispanic, German, Italian. Alternative spellings: Coren, Corin,

Corina, Corinna, Corrina, Corrine, Corrinne, Correne, Corynne.

Corinthian: Greek origin. Means: ornate, luxurious.

Corisa: Greek origin. Means: maidenly.

Corlinda: Unknown origin and meaning.

Cornecia: Unknown origin and meaning.

Cornelia: Latin/Greek origin. Means: horn of the sun, queenly virtue, yellowish. Ethnic backgrounds: German, Italian. Alternative spellings and nicknames: Nellie, Nell, Cornela, Nella.

Corona: Latin/Hindi origin. Means: crown, kind. Ethnic background: Hispanic.

Corrie: Gaelic origin. Means: deep ravine or hollow.

Cosetta: French origin. Means: victorious, army. Alternative spelling: Cosette.

Cosima: Greek origin. Means: harmony, order. Ethnic background: German.

Costanza: Italian/Spanish origin. Means: constant.

Cota: Unknown origin and meaning.

Cotia: Unknown origin and meaning.

Courney: Unknown origin and meaning.

Courtney: Old French origin. Means: one who frequents the king's court. Alternative spellings: Cortney, Cortni.

Cresa: Greek origin. Means: golden.

Crescentia: Latin origin. Means: increasing, to multiply. Alternative spellings: Creseantia, Crescent, Cressentt.

22

Cressida: Greek origin. Means: golden. Alternative spelling: Cresida.

Cresusa: Unknown origin and meaning. Ethnic background: Hispanic.

Crispa: Latin origin. Means: curly, wavy. Alternative spelling: Crispas.

Cristin: Latin/Irish origin. Means: Christ's servant.

Crystal: Greek origin. Means: clear, brilliant glass. 43rd most popular girl's name of the '90s. Alternative spellings: Christal, Cristal, Chrystal.

Csilla: Hebrew origin. Means: defender. Ethnic background: Hungarian.

Cuba: Spanish origin. Means: tank, trough, born.

Cybill: Latin origin. Means: a soothsayer.

Cydney: Unknown origin and meaning.

Cyllene: Unknown origin and meaning.

Cyma: Greek origin. Means: to grow or sprout, flourish.

Cymbeline: Celtic origin. Means: child of the sun.

Cynara: Greek origin. Means: artichoke, daughter. Alternative spelling: Cynarra.

Cynthia: Greek origin. Means: moon. Alternative spellings and nicknames: Cyn, Cynth, Cindy, Cyndi, Cyndy, Cynthie.

Cypris: Greek origin. Means: from Cyprus.

Cyrena: Greek origin. Means: of Cyrena, daughter.

Cyrilla: Greek origin. Means: lordly. Alternative spelling: Cirila.

Cytherea: Greek origin. Means: of Cythera.

d

Daa'jzia: Unknown origin and meaning.

Daba: Hebrew origin. Means: kind words, bee swarm.

Dacia: Latin origin. Means: far, southerner. Alternative spellings: Dacie, Dachia, Dachi.

Daffodil: Greek origin. Means: flower. Alternative spelling: Dafodil.

Dagmar: Germanic/Danish origin. Means: joyous day, bright. Ethnic backgrounds: Czech, Swedish, Norwegian. Nickname: Dag.

Dagny: Norse origin. Means: new day, Dane's joy. Ethnic background: Norwegian.

Dahlia: Norse/Old English origin. Means: from the valley.

Daisy: Anglo-Saxon origin. Means: day's eye, flower. Alternative spelling: Daisie.

Dalia: Hebrew origin. Means: a branch, to draw water. Ethnic backgrounds: African, Hispanic. Alternative spellings: Dalya, Dalylah.

Dalila: Egyptian/Hebrew origin. Means: desired, gentle.

Damara: Greek origin. Means: gentle. Alternative spellings: Damaris, Damarra.

D'Ambra: Unknown origin and meaning.

Damita: Spanish origin. Means: lady, little nobility.

Danasia: Unknown origin and meaning.

Danette: Hebrew origin. Means: God is judge. Alternative spelling: Danete.

Dania: Hebrew origin. Means: God will judge.

Danica: Slavic origin. Means: morning star. Alternative spelling: Dannica.

Danielle: Hebrew origin. Means: my judge is the Lord. Ethnic background: French. 25th most popular girl's name of the '90s. Alternative spellings: Daniele, Danyelle, Daniella, Daniela, Denyella, Donielle, Danelle.

Danne: Unknown origin and meaning.

Danube: Unknown origin and meaning.

Danuta: Latin/Polish origin. Means: given by God.

Daphne: Greek origin. Means: laurel, bay tree, victory. Alternative spellings and nicknames: Daph, Daphie, Daphnie, Dafna.

Daquisha: Unknown origin and meaning.

Dara: Anglo-Saxon origin. Means: courageous one.

Daravia: Unknown origin and meaning.

Darbi: Unknown origin and meaning.

Darceece: Unknown origin. Means: queenly.

Darcie: Celtic origin. Means: dark, fortress. Alternative spellings: Darcia, Darcy.

Darda: Hungarian origin. Means: a dart.

Dari: Unknown origin. Means: queenly.

Daria: Persian/Spanish origin. Means: rich, preserver. Alternative spelling: Darya.

Darienne: Unknown origin and meaning.

Darina: Unknown origin and meaning.

Darla: Anglo-Saxon origin. Means: dear, loved one.

Darlene: Anglo-Saxon origin. Means: tenderly beloved. Alternative spellings: Darleen, Darline, Daryl.

Darling: Old English origin. Means: beloved one.

Darlye: English origin. Means: a grove of oak trees.

Daroma: Hebrew origin. Means: southward.

Darona: Greek/Hebrew origin. Means: gift.

Darrelle: Anglo-Saxon origin. Means: dearly beloved.

Darrien: Unknown origin and meaning.

Daruce: Unknown origin. Means: queenly.

Dasha: Unknown origin and meaning. Alternative spelling: Dashay.

Dati: Hebrew origin. Means: religiously observant.

Dativa: Unknown origin and meaning. Ethnic background: Hispanic.

Davianna: Unknown origin and meaning.

Davina: Hebrew origin. Means: beloved, loved one. Alternative spellings: Daveda, Davena, Davenia, Daveta, Davida, Davita.

Davrush: Unknown origin and meaning. Ethnic background: Jewish.

Dawn: Anglo-Saxon origin. Means: the break of day, pure. Alternative spelling: Dawnn.

Day: Sanskrit origin. Means: labor, heat, sunrise to sunset.

Dayle: Unknown origin and meaning.

Dayna: Unknown origin and meaning. Alternative spelling: Dayne.

Daysha: Unknown origin and meaning. Alternative spelling: Dayeisha.

Deanna: Latin/Anglo-Saxon origin. Means: divine, of the valley. 46th most popular girl's name of the '90s. Alternative spelling: Deana.

Deanne: Old French origin. Means: head, leader.

Dearbhail: Irish origin. Means: true desire.

Deasa: Unknown origin and meaning.

Debarath: Unknown origin. Means: cool. Alternative spellings: Deborath, Daberath.

Deborah: Hebrew origin. Means: bee, kind words. Ethnic backgrounds: English/Welsh. Alternative spellings and nicknames: Deb, Debbie, Debby, Debra, Debbra, Dabra, Dobra, Debora.

Decima: Latin origin. Means: the 10th daughter.

Dee: Old English origin. Means: dark water.

Deena: Unknown origin and meaning.

Deirdre: Celtic/Gaelic origin. Means: sorrowful one, young girl, raging compassion. Ethnic background: Irish. Alternative spellings and nicknames: Deedee, Deidre, Dee, Dyedra.

Deja: Unknown origin and meaning.

De'Jana: Unknown origin and meaning.

Deka: Greek/African origin. Means: 10, she who pleases.

Dela: Unknown origin. Means: faithful.

Delace: Latin origin. Means: delight.

Delaney: Irish origin. Means: from the river, challenger. Alternative spellings: Delanie, Delanae, Delany, Delaunay.

Delcia: Spanish origin. Means: delightful.

Delcine: Spanish origin. Means: sweet.

Deliah: Latin origin. Means: an inhabitant of Delos. Alternative spelling: Delia.

Delida: Unknown origin and meaning. Ethnic background: Hispanic.

Delight: Latin origin. Means: great pleasure.

Honor Thy Relatives

We didn't want a junior—too confusing—so we used my husband's first name as our son's middle name.

~ Lori N.,
San Francisco, California

Delilah: Hebrew origin. Means: hair, poor, temptress. Alternative spellings: Delila, Dilila.

Della: Teutonic origin. Means: one of nobility, kind. Alternative spellings and nicknames: Del, Ella.

Delma: Latin origin. Means: of the sea.

Delora: Latin origin. Means: seashore, sorrows. Alternative spellings: Dellora, Delorita.

Delphina: Greek/Latin origin. Means: of Delphi, a dolphin. Alternative spellings: Delphine, Delphinia.

Delphne: Greek origin. Means: a dolphin, calm. Alternative spelling: Delflna.

Delta: Hebrew/Greek origin. Means: born fourth, a door.

Demery: Unknown origin and meaning.

Demetria: Greek origin. Means: the harvest. Alternative spelling: Demetra.

Demi: Greek/French origin. Means: divine consideration, heraldry.

Deneane: Unknown origin and meaning.

Denedra: Unknown origin and meaning.

Denee: English origin. Unknown meaning. Alternative spelling: De'Nee.

DeNesha: Unknown origin and meaning. Alternative spelling: De'Neisha.

Denise: Greek/French origin. Means: wine, drama. Ethnic background: Irish. Alternative spellings: Denys, Denice, Deneise.

Deonsha: Unknown origin and meaning.

DeShaye: Unknown origin and meaning.

Desiah: Unknown origin and meaning.

Desiree: Latin/French origin. Means: much desired, to look to the stars, to crave. Ethnic background: Swedish. 41st most popular girl's name of the '90s. Alternative spellings: Desarea, Desirae, Desi-Rae, Dezarae, Dezaray, Dezirae, Desire.

Destiny: Latin origin. Means: fate. 37th most popular girl's name of the '90s. Alternative spellings: Destanie, Destinee, Destiney, Destini, Destinae, Destine, Destinie.

Devahuti: Sanskrit origin. Means: a God.

Devashka: Unknown origin and meaning. Ethnic background: Jewish.

Devona: Celtic/Anglo-Saxon origin. Means: divine protector, brave. Alternative spellings: Deevina, Devina, Devine, Divina, Devorna, Devirtna, Dvina.

Dexhiana: Unknown origin and meaning.

Dextra: Latin origin. Means: dexterous, right-handedness.

Deyanira: Unknown origin and meaning. Ethnic background: Hispanic.

Dhumma: Unknown origin. Means: gentle.

Diamantina: French origin. Means: diamond. Ethnic background: Hispanic. Alternative spellings: Diamanta, Diamante.

Diana: Latin origin. Means: divine. Ethnic backgrounds: Hispanic, Italian. Alternative spellings and nicknames: Deedee, Deni, Di, Deanna, Diane, Dianna, Diahann, Dianne, Dyan, Dyana, Dyane.

Diantha: Latin/Greek origin. Means: divine, flower. Alternative spellings: Dianthe, Dianthia.

Diella: Latin origin. Means: girl, worships God. Alternative spelling: Dielle.

Diethild: Germanic origin. Unknown meaning.

Dieuwertje: Unknown origin and meaning. Ethnic background: Dutch.

Dimond: Unknown origin and meaning.

Dinah: Hebrew origin. Ethnic backgrounds: Hispanic, Italian. Means: judgment, divine. Alternative spellings: Dina, Dynah.

Dioma: Unknown origin and meaning.

Dione: Greek origin. Means: daughter of heaven and earth.

Dionisia: Greek origin. Means: of wine, drama, and revelry. Ethnic background: Italian. Alternative spelling: Dionysios.

Dionna: Latin origin. Means: divine, of wine and revelry. Alternative spellings: Deonna, Dionne.

Dira: Unknown origin. Means: water.

Dirkje: Unknown origin and meaning. Ethnic background: Dutch.

Dissa: Hebrew/Norse origin. Means: praise, active. Alternative spelling: Disa.

Dixie: Anglo-Saxon/French origin. Means: dike or wall, 10th. Nickname: Dix.

Docia: Unknown origin. Means: brave.

Docie: Unknown origin. Means: good.

Docilla: Latin origin. Means: learn. Alternative spellings: Docila, Docile.

Dodie: Hebrew origin. Means: beloved friend. Alternative spelling: Dodi.

Dohnnishia: Unknown origin and meaning.

Dolly: Greek origin. Means: a vision or gift.

Dolores: Spanish origin. Means: sorrows. Alternative spellings and nicknames: Dorry, Dorrie, Dolora, Dori, Deloris, Delores.

Domel: Latin origin. Means: home lover. Alternative spellings: Domela, Domella.

Domina: Unknown origin. Means: lady. Alternative spelling: Dominae.

Dominique: Latin/French origin. Means: belonging to the Lord, born on Sunday. 49th most popular girl's name of the '90s. Alternative spellings: Domenica, Domianque, Dominga, Dominica, Domonique.

Donalda: Celtic origin. Means: dark stranger, world ruler.

Donata: Latin/Italian origin. Means: gift from God.

Donela: Celtic origin. Means: small, dark-haired girl. Alternative spelling: Donella.

Donia: Celtic/Gaelic origin. Means: dark, ruler.

Donica: Latin origin. Means: charity.

Donna: Latin/Italian origin. Means: lady, busy. Ethnic backgrounds: English/Welsh.

Dora: Greek origin. Means: a gift, gifted. Ethnic background: German.

Dorcea: Greek origin. Means: dark, gazelle, doe. Alternative spelling: Dorcia.

Dore: Greek/French origin. Means: a gift, golden.

Dorene: Gaelic/French origin. Means: golden, sullen. Alternative spellings and nicknames: Dorie, Dori, Dorine, Dory, Doreen, Dorena.

Dorin: Greek/Latin origin. Means: lady, bountiful.

Dorina: Greek origin. Means: a gift, friend.

Dorinda: Greek origin. Means: beautiful gift, bountiful.

Doris: Greek origin. Means: gift, of the ocean. Ethnic background: Swedish. Alternative spellings: Dodi, Dori, Dorisa, Dorise, Dorice, Doria.

Dorothy: Greek origin. Means: God's gift. Ethnic backgrounds: Polish, Italian, German. Alternative spellings and nicknames: Dotty, Dot, Dollie, Dolley, Dorothi, Doretta, Dore, Dora, Dolly, Dee, Dorothea, Dorthea, Dorthy, Dottie, Dorota.

Dorte: Greek origin. Means: a vision. Ethnic background: German.

Dosia: Greek/Polish origin. Means: divinely given.

Dottie: Greek origin. Means: God's gift.

Doxia: Unknown origin. Means: brave.

Doxie: Unknown origin. Means: good. Alternative spelling: Doxy.

Drahomira: Slavic origin. Means: loved ruler. Ethnic background: Czech.

Dreda: Anglo-Saxon origin. Means: friend. Alternative spelling: Drida.

Drelan: Unknown origin and meaning.

Druella: Unknown origin. Means: elfin.

Drusa: Latin origin. Means: strong. Alternative spellings: Drusie, Drucie.

Drusilla: Latin origin. Means: strong. Alternative spellings and nicknames: Drucilla, Drus, Dru, Drusie, Drusila, Drusa, Drucie.

Duana: Gaelic origin. Means: dark, song. Alternative spelling: Dwana.

Duena: Spanish origin. Means: chaperone.

Duffy: Gaelic origin. Means: dark hair, black.

Dulcie: Latin origin. Means: sweet, charming. Alternative spellings and nicknames: Dulci, Dulcine, Dulciana, Dulce, Dulcea, Dulcinea.

Duma: Unknown origin. Means: gentle. Alternative spelling: Dumah.

Duna: Unknown origin. Means: dark.

Durene: Latin origin. Means: enduring, lasting.

Durrah: Arabic origin. Means: precious pearl.

Dusha: Slavic origin. Means: spirit. Ethnic background: Jewish.

Dylana: Celtic/Welsh origin. Means: one from the sea. Alternative spelling: Dylane.

Dymphia: Gaelic origin. Means: nurse, poet. Alternative spelling: Dimphia.

Dynasty: Old English origin. Means: a succession of rulers from the same family.

Dzidzo: African origin. Means: happiness.

Eartha: Anglo-Saxon origin. Means: the earth. Alternative spellings: Erta, Ertha, Herta, Hertha, Erda.

Easter: Teutonic/Anglo-Saxon origin. Means: sunup, dawn.

Ebba: Germanic/Anglo-Saxon origin. Means: strength, return of the tide. Ethnic background: Swedish. Alternative spelling: Ebbe.

Ebere: African origin. Means: mercy.

Eberta: Teutonic origin. Means: learning, intelligent.

Ebony: Latin origin. Means: dark black wood. Alternative spellings: Ebonee, Eboni, Ebonie.

Echo: Greek origin. Means: repeated sound.

Eda: Norse/Anglo-Saxon origin. Means: poetry, blessed, fiery. Ethnic background: German. Alternative spellings and nicknames: Edie, Edda, Ede.

Edana: Celtic origin. Means: one like a flame.

Eddra: Hebrew/Anglo-Saxon origin. Means: power.

Edea: Unknown origin. Means: sorceress.

Edelgard: Teutonic origin. Means: brave guardian. Ethnic background: German.

Edeline: Germanic origin. Means: noble, gracious.

Edelmira: Unknown origin and meaning. Ethnic background: Hispanic.

Edette: Unknown origin. Means: watchtower.

Edic: Unknown origin and meaning.

Edina: Anglo-Saxon origin. Means: family, friend. Alternative spelling: Eddina.

Edissa: Unknown origin and meaning. Ethnic background: Hispanic.

Edita: Old English origin. Means: joyous, great gift. Ethnic background: Hispanic. Alternative spellings: Edyta, Edit.

Edith: Anglo-Saxon origin. Means: happy, prosperous. Alternative spellings and nicknames: Eyde, Eadith, Dita, Eadie, Edie, Editha, Eydie, Edythe, Edyth, Edy, Edna, Edithe, Ediva, Edita, Eda, Ede, Edi, Edina.

Ediva: Unknown origin. Means: gift.

Edle: Anglo-Saxon origin. Means: princess. Ethnic background: Norwegian.

Edme: Anglo-Saxon origin. Means: fortunate defender. Alternative spellings: Edmea, Edmee.

Edmonda: Old English origin. Means: prosperous protector. Alternative spellings: Edmonia, Edmunda Edmanda.

Edna: Hebrew origin. Means: rejuvenation, delight. Alternative spellings and nicknames: Eddi, Edny, Ed, Eddy, Edith, Eddie.

Edora: Unknown origin. Means: patient.

Edrea: Hebrew/Anglo-Saxon origin. Means: power, powerful. Alternative spellings and nicknames: Eddi, Eddy, Edrena, Eddie, Edra, Edris.

Eduvigis: Unknown origin and meaning. Ethnic background: Hispanic.

Edva: Unknown origin. Means: diligent. Alternative spelling: Edveh.

Edwardine: Old English origin. Means: prosperous protector.

Edwina: Old English origin. Means: fortunate friend. Alternative spellings and nicknames: Win, Winny, Wina, Edwyna, Edwine, Eadwine, Eadwina, Edina, Winnie.

Eet: Unknown origin and meaning. Ethnic background: Dutch.

Effie: Greek origin. Means: well-spoken. Alternative spellings and nicknames: Effy, Effi, Euphémie, Phemie, Eppie, Euphemia.

Efrona: Hebrew origin. Means: a fawn, a bird.

Efrosini: Hebrew origin. Means: a fawn, a bird. Ethnic background: Greek.

Efua: African origin. Means: born on Friday.

Egbertina: Anglo-Saxon origin. Means: bright, shining sword. Alternative spellings: Egberta, Egbertine.

Eglantine: Latin/French origin. Means: sweetbrier, rose, needle.

Eidel: Hebrew origin. Means: gentle, delicate.

Eileen: Greek origin. Means: bearer, light. Ethnic background: Irish. Alternative spelling: Aileen.

Eilis: Hebrew/Irish origin. Means: God's oath.

Eilysh: Unknown origin and meaning.

Eir: Norse origin. Means: peace, clemency.

Eirena: Norse origin. Means: peace.

Eithne: Gaelic/Irish origin. Means: core, kernel.

Ekaterina: Greek/Slavic origin. Means: innocent, pure. Ethnic background: Russian.

Ekechi: African origin. Means: God's creation.

Ela: Unknown origin. Means: God. Ethnic background: Hispanic.

Elah: Hebrew origin. Means: bitter, oak tree.

Elaina: Hebrew origin. Means: God has answered.

Elaine: Greek/French origin. Means: light. Ethnic background: Irish. Alternative spellings and nicknames: Laine, Lainey, Layney, Alayne, Lane, Elane, Alaine, Elana, Lani, Elayne.

Elana: Hebrew origin. Means: a tree.

Elatia: Latin origin. Means: elevated. Alternative spelling: Elata.

Elayasia: Biblical origin. Means: variation of Elijah, meaning "Yahweh is God."

Elbe: Unknown origin and meaning.

Elberta: Teutonic origin. Means: brilliant, forthright.

Elboa: Unknown origin. Means: fruitful.

Elda: Anglo-Saxon origin. Means: echo, elder, fountain.

Eldora: Spanish origin. Means: gifted, gilded, golden.

Eldreda: Anglo-Saxon origin. Means: soothsayer, friend. Alternative spelling: Eldrida.

Eldreonna: Unknown origin and meaning.

Eleanor: Greek origin. Means: light, God is my youth. Ethnic backgrounds: Irish, Scottish. Alternative spellings and nicknames: Elladine, Eleanour, Elenor, Eleonore, Elianora, El, Elnora, Ellene, Ellinor, Elna, Elnore, Elora, Leanor, Eleanora, Elyn, Elaine, Eleanore, Elena, Eleonora, Elinor, Elinore, Ella, Ellen, Elli, Ellie, Elly, Elle, Helen, Ellyn, Eileen, Elanore, Elinoar, Eleonor, Elleanor, Elenore, Elenora.

Electra: Greek origin. Means: brilliant, shining. Alternative spelling: Lectra.

Elena: Greek/Italian origin. Means: light. Ethnic backgrounds: Hispanic, Russian. 40th most popular girl's name of the '90s. Alternative spellings: Elene, Eleni, Elina, Eline, Elleen.

Elesha: Unknown origin and meaning.

Elexys: Greek origin. Means: variant of Alexis, meaning protector of men.

When to Decide

Some people were born knowing what they were going to name their children. The rest of us stress out about it until the due date is nearly upon us—or even after! When is it too late (or too early) to decide?

Elfi: Anglo-Saxon origin. Means: good elf. Ethnic background: German.

Elfrida: Old English origin. Means: counselor, peace. Ethnic background: Hispanic. Alternative spellings: Elfride, Elfreda, Elfrieda, Elfriede.

Elga: Teutonic/Slavic origin. Means: consecrated, fighter, holy. Alternative spelling: Ellga.

Eliana: Hebrew origin. Means: the Lord is God. Alternative spelling: Eliani.

Elise: French origin. Means: consecrated, God's oath. Alternative spellings: Elyse, Elysia, Eliza, Elisa, Elissa, Elisia, Alissa, Elysa.

Elisheva: Hebrew origin. Means: God's oath.

Elishka: Unknown origin and meaning.

Elisif: Unknown origin and meaning. Ethnic background: Norwegian.

Elita: Anglo-Saxon/French origin. Means: winged, chosen. Alternative spelling: Ellita.

Eliza: Hebrew origin. Means: God's oath. Alternative spellings and nicknames: Lizzie, Liza.

Elizabeth: Hebrew origin. Means: God's oath, dedicated. Ethnic backgrounds: Scottish, English/Welsh. 17th most popular girl's name of the '90s. Alternative spellings and nicknames: Elizabet,

Elsabet, Ealaside, Bessie, Besse, Belita, Bessy, Betsey, Betta, Betti, Bettine, Eilis, Elisa, Elisabet, Elisabeth, Elisabetta, Elise, Eliza, Elsa, Elsbeth, Else, Bettina, Elissa, Betty, Belle, Beth, Betsy, Bette, Babette, Bess, Elzbieta.

Elke: Hebrew/Teutonic origin. Means: oath to God, industrious. Ethnic background: German. Alternative spelling: Elka.

Ella: Germanic origin. Means: all, beautiful. Ethnic backgrounds: German, Norwegian, Italian.

Ellata: Unknown origin. Means: elevated.

Elle: French origin. Means: shortened form of Michelle, meaning who is like God?

Ellen: Greek origin. Means: light. Ethnic background: Norwegian. Alternative spellings and nicknames: Nellie, Elyn, Ellin, Eliene, Elly, Nell, Ellyn, Ellie, Elena, Elin.

Ellette: Anglo-Saxon origin. Means: light, all, small elf.

Ellice: Hebrew/Greek origin. Means: the Lord is God.

Ellie: Greek/Hebrew origin. Means: light, devoted to God, light, God of my youth. Alternative spellings: Elie, Elli, Elly, Ellee.

Ellora: Greek origin. Means: light.

Elma: Greek/Latin origin. Means: amiable, friendly, lovable.

Elmina: Teutonic origin. Means: awe, fame.

Elmira: Anglo-Saxon/Teutonic origin. Means: noble, famous. Alternative spellings: Almira, Elmina.

Elodie: Greek origin. Means: flower. Ethnic backgrounds include: French. Alternative spellings: Elodea, Elodia.

Eloise: French origin. Means: famous in battle. Alternative spellings: Louise, Louisa, Heloise, Eloisa.

Elom: Hebrew origin. Means: God loves me. Ethnic background: African.

Elondra: Unknown origin and meaning.

Elrica: Latin origin. Means: ruler, all.

Elsa: Teutonic origin. Means: noble, truth. Ethnic backgrounds: Swedish, Italian, Norwegian, German.

Alternative spellings and nicknames: Elsie, Elsy, Lisa, Lise, Else.

Elske: Unknown origin and meaning. Ethnic background: Dutch.

Elura: Unknown origin and meaning.

Elva: Anglo-Saxon origin. Means: counselor, elfin. Ethnic background: Irish. Alternative spellings and nicknames: Elfie, Elvie, Ellie, Elvia, Elvah.

Elvina: Anglo-Saxon origin. Means: friend of elves. Alternative spelling: Elvine.

Elvira: Latin/Germanic origin. Means: fair, blond, to close up. Ethnic backgrounds: Italian, Russian. Alternative spellings and nicknames: Elvie, Elire, Elwira, Elvera, Elva, Elvire.

Elwina: Anglo-Saxon origin. Means: noble friend.

Emani: Unknown origin and meaning.

Emanuela: Hebrew origin. Means: God is with us.

Emeigh: Unknown origin and meaning.

Emelda: Unknown origin. Means: flattering, industrious.

Emelia: Hebrew origin. Means: variant of Amelia, meaning work.

Emeline: Teutonic origin. Means: industrious, intellectual. Alternative spellings and nicknames: Em, Emmeline, Emmy, Emelin, Emelina, Emelyn, Emelyne, Emlynne, Emmaline.

Emer: Irish origin. Means: of myth.

Emerald: French origin. Means: green jewel. Alternative spellings and nicknames: Emeroude, Emmie, Emerant, Em, Esmeralda.

Emerencia: Latin origin. Means: earner of merit. Ethnic background: Hungarian.

Emily: Latin/Teutonic origin. Means: ambitious, flatterer, industrious. Most popular girl's name of the '90s. Alternative spellings and nicknames: Emelita, Emera, Emiline, Emlynn, Emmalyn, Emmalynne, Emmalynn, Aimil, Amala, Amalie, Amélie, Amelita, Eimile, Em, Emalia, Emaly, Ameline, Emlyn, Emeline, Emelyne, Emilia, Emelina, Emmaline, Emlynne, Emilie, Amalia, Emelin, Amelia, Amy, Emelia, Emelda, Emilee.

Emina: Latin origin. Means: lofty, noteworthy.

Emma: Teutonic origin. Means: universal, nurse, ancestress. Ethnic backgrounds: Swedish, Italian, Hispanic, French, English/Welsh. 36th most popular girl's name of the '90s. Alternative spellings and nicknames: Emmy, Emmalynne, Emmeline, Emmye, Emmie, Emmalynn, Emmi, Emie, Emi, Em, Emmalyn, Emelyne, Emeline, Emelina, Ema, Emmaline.

Emmuela: Spanish origin. Means: dedicated.

Emmylou: Unknown origin and meaning.

Emogene: Greek origin. Means: well-loved child.

Emonie: Unknown origin and meaning.

Ena: Gaelic origin. Means: ardent, fiery.

Enalda: Unknown origin. Means: omen.

Enchantra: Unknown origin and meaning.

Encratia: Unknown origin. Means: maiden. Alternative spelling: Encratis.

Endia: Unknown origin and meaning. Alternative spelling: Endya.

Endora: Greek origin. Means: light, fountain.

Engelberta: Germanic origin. Means: angel, famous, bright.

Engracia: Greek/Latin origin. Means: temperance, control, grace. Ethnic background: Hispanic.

Enice: Unknown origin. Means: happy.

Enid: Celtic origin. Means: fair, pure, purity.

Ennea: Greek origin. Means: 9th child. Alternative spelling: Enia.

Enrica: Teutonic origin. Means: head of the estate. Alternative spellings: Enrika, Enriquetta.

Enrichetta: Italian origin. Means: royal leader.

Ephemia: Unknown origin. Means: auspicious, fairest, spoken. Alternative spelling: Ephemiah.

Ephemiah: Unknown origin. Means: fairest.

Eppie: Greek origin. Means: well spoken.

Eranthe: Greek origin. Means: flower.

Erda: Teutonic origin. Means: child, earth. Alternative spellings and nicknames: Erta, Eartha, Hertha, Herta, Erdah, Erdda.

Ereaunna: Unknown origin and meaning.

Eredina: Unknown origin and meaning. Ethnic background: Hispanic.

Erela: Hebrew origin. Means: angel, messenger.

Eremita: Spanish origin. Means: eremite, desert, solitude. Ethnic background: Hispanic.

Erendira: Unknown origin and meaning.

Erica: Latin/Germanic origin. Means: the heather, powerful ruler. Ethnic backgrounds: Swiss, Hungarian, Swedish. 34th most popular girl's name of the '90s. Alternative spellings and nicknames: Ericha, Rickie, Ricky, Riki, Rikki, Rika, Ricki, Erika, Rica, Ericka, Errika.

Erida: Spanish origin. Means: loved.

Erin: Gaelic/Irish origin. Means: peace, from Ireland. 33rd most popular girl's name of the '90s. Alternative spellings: Erina, Erinna, Erine, Erinn, Erena, Eryn.

Erlia: Unknown origin. Means: fruitful.

Erlinda: Unknown origin. Means: lively.

Erline: Anglo-Saxon/Gaelic origin. Means: noble, elfin, from Ireland. Alternative spellings: Arline, Erlina, Erleena, Erlinna, Erlene.

Erma: Latin/Teutonic origin. Means: royal, powerful. Alternative spellings: Herminie, Herminia, Hermine, Hermia, Erminia, Erminie, Ermina, Hermione, Irma.

Ermelind: Teutonic origin. Means: serpent. Ethnic background: German.

Ermina: Latin origin. Means: noble. Alternative spelling: Erminna.

Erna: Teutonic/Saxon origin. Means: eagle, intent in purpose. Ethnic backgrounds: German, Norwegian.

Ernaline: Germanic origin. Means: eagle, power.

Ernestine: Teutonic origin. Means: eagle, vigor. Ethnic backgrounds: French, Italian. Alternative spellings and nicknames: Teena, Erna, Ernaline, Ernesta, Tina.

Ersha: Unknown origin. Means: earth.

Erwina: Anglo-Saxon origin. Means: friend of the sea, white river. Ethnic background: Polish.

Erzsebet: Hebrew origin. Means: devoted to God. Ethnic background: Hungarian.

Eshe: Egyptian origin. Means: life. Ethnic background: African.

Esmay: Latin/French origin. Means: esteem, to love.

Esme: French/Spanish origin. Means: beloved protector, emerald. Alternative spellings: Esma, Esmee.

Esmeralda: Greek/Spanish origin. Means: adorn, emerald, jewel. Ethnic background: Hispanic. Alternative spellings and nicknames: Esme, Esmerelda, Esmerolda.

Esperanza: Latin/Spanish origin. Means: to hope. Ethnic background: Hispanic.

Essence: Latin origin. Means: intrinsic nature.

Estee: Latin/French origin. Means: from the East. Alternative spellings: Esta, Estas.

Estelle: Persian/Latin origin. Means: the star, of the East. Alternative spellings and nicknames: Stel, Estel, Essie, Estele, Estell, Estrella, Stelle, Stella, Estrellita, Estella, Estela, Esther.

Esther: Persian origin. Means: the star, of the East. Ethnic backgrounds: Swedish, Hebrew, Italian. Alternative spellings and nicknames: Esterel, Istar, Hettie, Etty, Etti, Essy, Essie, Essa, Eister, Ettie, Stella, Hetty, Hesther, Hester, Ester, Esta, Easter.

Etana: Hebrew origin. Means: strong.

Ethel: Teutonic/Anglo-Saxon origin. Means: noble fortress. Alternative spellings: Etheline, Ethelyn, Ethyl, Ethelin, Ethelda, Ethelinda.

Ethelind: Teutonic origin. Means: intelligent, good, noble. Alternative spellings: Ethelinda, Ethelin.

Ethna: Gaelic/Irish origin. Means: kernel, graceful.

Etka: Hebrew origin. Means: household ruler.

Etta: Teutonic origin. Means: small one, home-ruler. Alternative spellings and nicknames: Etty, Eta.

Euclea: Unknown origin. Means: glorious.

Eudice: Hebrew origin. Means: praise.

Eudoca: Greek origin. Means: brave.

Eudocia: Greek origin. Means: esteemed, reputable. Alternative spellings and nicknames: Dorie, Eudoxa, Doxy, Eudosia, Doxie, Eudoxia.

Eudora: Greek origin. Means: generous gift. Alternative spellings and nicknames: Dora, Eudore.

When to Decide

I would say select three or four of your favorite names for each sex and then take your list to the hospital. You'll know which name suits your child immediately. Besides, you can't fill out the birth certificate until the child is born, and you may change your mind a million times before then.

~ **Audra H., Richmond, Texas**

Eufenia: Unknown origin and meaning. Ethnic background: Italian.

Eugenia: Greek origin. Means: well born, of nobility. Ethnic background: Italian. Alternative spellings and nicknames: Genia, Gena, Eugnie, Gene, Gina, Eugenie, Genie.

Eula: Unknown origin. Means: fair, speaking.

Eulalia: Greek origin. Means: speaks beautifully. Ethnic background: German. Alternative spellings and nicknames: Lallie, Eula, Eulalie.

Eunice: Greek origin. Means: joyfully victorious.

Euphemia: Greek origin. Means: well spoken, reputable. Alternative spellings and nicknames: Effy, Euphmie, Phemie, Effie, Eppie, Eufemia.

Euphemle: Greek origin. Means: auspicious.

Eurosia: Unknown origin and meaning.

Eurydice: Greek origin. Means: wide space, justice.

Eustacia: Greek/Latin origin. Means: fine vineyard, fruitful. Alternative spellings and nicknames: Sacy, Stacia, Sacie, Stacey, Eustacie.

Eutimia: Unknown origin and meaning. Ethnic background: Hispanic.

Eva: Hebrew/various origin. Means: life. Ethnic backgrounds: Italian, Irish, Swedish, Hungarian, Norwegian, Czech, German.

Evadne: Greek origin. Means: lucky, singer, life. Alternative spellings: Euanthe, Evadnee.

Evangeline: Greek/Latin origin. Means: brings good tidings, gospel. Alternative spellings and nicknames: Vangy, Evangelia, Vangie, Eva, Eve, Evangelina.

Evania: Greek origin. Means: tranquil. Alternative spelling: Evannia.

Evante: Greek origin. Means: blossom. Alternative spelling: Evanthe.

Eve: Hebrew origin. Means: life, mother of all things. Alternative spellings and nicknames: Evey, Evie, Evita, Evvy, Evy, Evvie, Eveline, Eveleen, Eba, Evonne, Evelina, Evaleen, Eva, Ebba, Evelyn.

Evelyn: Celtic/French origin. Means: giving, light, life. Alternative spellings and nicknames: Evaline, Evvie, Eveline, Aveline, Evaleen, Eveleen, Lena, Lina, Evalina, Evelina, Evelyne, Evlyn.

Everildis: Unknown origin and meaning.

Evetta: Celtic origin. Means: pleasant. Alternative spelling: Evette.

Evi: Unknown origin and meaning. Ethnic background: Swiss.

Evonne: Celtic origin. Means: archer. Alternative spelling: Evonee.

Eydie: Anglo-Saxon origin. Means: prosperous battle.

Ezaria: Unknown origin. Means: dear. Alternative spellings: Ezarra, Ezarras.

f

Faadilah: Arabic origin. Means: accomplished lady.

Faa'izah: Arabic origin. Means: successful.

Fabienne: Latin/French origin. Means: one who grows beans. Alternative spelling: Fabiana.

Fabiola: Latin origin. Means: bean grower, good. Alternative spellings: Fabiolas, Faviola.

Fabria: Unknown origin. Means: girl. Alternative spellings: Fabriane, Fabrianna, Fabrianne, Fabrienne.

Fadia: Unknown origin and meaning.

Faheemah: Arabic origin. Means: intelligent.

Faiga: Germanic origin. Means: a bird. Ethnic background: Jewish.

Faina: Anglo-Saxon origin. Means: joyful. Ethnic background: Russian.

Faith: Latin origin. Means: belief, faithful, trusting. Alternative spellings and nicknames: Faythe, Fae, Fayth, Fay, Faye.

Faiza: Unknown origin and meaning.

Falcon: Middle English origin. Means: bird of prey.

Fallon: Unknown origin and meaning.

Fanchet: Teutonic origin. Means: independent, free. Alternative spellings: Fanchette, Fanchon, Fanchan.

Fancy: Greek origin. Means: fantasy. Alternative spelling: Fancie.

Fanny: Teutonic origin. Means: independent, free. Alternative spellings and nicknames: Fan, Fanni, Fannie.

Fareedah: Arabic origin. Means: unique.

Farhat: Arabic origin. Means: delight.

Farica: Teutonic origin. Means: peaceable ruler. Alternative spellings: Feriga, Farika, Farrica.

Farrah: Persian origin. Means: beautiful, happy. Alternative spellings: Farra, Fayre, Farrand, Farand, Farah.

Farrow: Unknown origin and meaning.

Fatima: Arabic origin. Means: Muhammad's daughter, weaned, friend. Ethnic backgrounds: English/Welsh. Alternative spellings: Fatimah, Faatimah, Fhotima.

Fausta: Latin origin. Means: one with luck, fortunate. Alternative spellings: Faustena, Faustina, Faustine.

Favor: French origin. Means: approval.

Fawn: Latin origin. Means: deer, a young deer. Alternative spellings: Faunia, Fawnia, Fawna, Fawnessa.

Fay: Latin/French origin. Means: fairy, fidelity, raven. Alternative spellings: Fae, Fayina, Faye, Fayette.

Fayme: Old English/French origin. Means: lofty, famous.

Fayola: African origin. Means: good fortune.

Fayre: Anglo-Saxon origin. Means: beautiful.

Fealty: French origin. Means: allegiance, faithful.

Fede: Unknown origin and meaning. Ethnic background: Italian.

Fedora: Greek origin. Means: heavenly gift. Ethnic background: Italian. Alternative spelling: Theodora, Feodora.

Feechi: Unknown origin. Means: worship God. Ethnic background: African.

Feige: Hebrew origin. Means: a fig, bird.

Felda: Germanic origin. Means: field dweller.

Felicia: Latin origin. Means: happiness, happy. Ethnic background: Italian. Alternative spellings and nicknames: Falishia, Feliciana, Felicie, Felicita, Felicity, Felice, Felis, Feliza, Felita, Fee, Felicidad, Felise, Felisha, Felizitas.

Felipa: Spanish origin. Means: one who loves horses. Alternative spelling: Filippa.

Femke: Unknown origin and meaning. Ethnic background: Dutch. Alternative spelling: Fimke.

Fenella: Gaelic origin. Means: shouldered. Alternative spellings: Finelia, Finella, Finola.

Feodosia: Greek origin. Means: divine gift.

Feriga: Unknown origin. Means: loving.

Fern: Greek/Old English origin. Means: feather, delicate like a fern. Alternative spellings: Ferne, Ferna, Fernas.

Fernanda: Germanic origin. Means: peaceful journey, adventuring. Alternative spellings and nicknames: Ferdinande, Fern, Fernand, Ferdinanda, Fernandina.

Fia: Scottish origin. Means: the dark peace.

Fidelas: Latin origin. Means: faithful. Alternative spellings: Fidelia, Fidelity, Fidellia.

Fidelma: Gaelic origin. Unknown meaning. Ethnic background: Irish.

Fiep: Unknown origin and meaning. Ethnic background: Dutch.

Fifi: Hebrew/French origin. Means: she shall add, my daughter. Alternative spelling: Fifine.

Filide: Unknown origin. Means: branch.

Filma: Teutonic origin. Means: misty.

Fina: Gaelic origin. Means: vine, bright, friend.

Fiona: Gaelic origin. Means: fair complexioned. Ethnic backgrounds: Irish, English/Welsh. Alternative spellings and nicknames: Vionna, Viona, Fio, Fionna, Phiona.

Fionnula: Gaelic origin. Means: fair shouldered.

Fiora: Latin origin. Means: blooming, flower. Alternative spelling: Fiorenza.

Fitzroya: Unknown origin and meaning.

Flanna: Gaelic origin. Means: red-haired.

Flavia: Latin origin. Means: golden-haired. Ethnic background: Italian.

Fleta: Teutonic origin. Means: beautiful, swift. Alternative spellings: Fleeta, Fleda, Flita.

Fleur: French origin. Means: flower. Alternative spelling: Fleurette.

Flora: Latin origin. Means: flower. Ethnic backgrounds: Scottish, German, Italian. Alternative spellings and nicknames: Fiorry, Flossie, Florrie, Florri, Florie, Flor, Fio, Fieurette, Florella, Fiore, Floria, Floris, Flore, Fleur, Fiora.

Florence: Latin origin. Means: blooming, flourishing. Alternative spellings and nicknames: Flossi, Florie, Florrie, Floss, Flossie, Flossy, Florry, Flori, Florette, Florentia, Flor, Flo, Florinda, Floris, Florida, Florina, Flower, Florencia, Flore, Florance, Flora, Fleurette, Fleur, Fiorenza, Floria, Florine.

Florida: Latin origin. Means: blossoming, flowery.

Florina: Latin origin. Means: in bloom. Alternative spellings: Florine, Florinda, Florian.

Flos: Norse origin. Means: chieftain. Ethnic background: Dutch.

Flower: Latin origin. Means: blossom.

Foigl: Unknown origin and meaning. Ethnic background: Jewish.

Fola: African origin. Means: honor.

Fonda: Latin/Old English origin. Means: tender, foundation, profound.

Fornasa: Unknown origin and meaning. Ethnic background: Hispanic.

Forsythia: Anglo-Saxon origin. Means: flowery shrub.

Fortuna: Latin origin. Means: destiny, fortunate. Alternative spellings: Fortune, Fortunia, Fortunna.

Fotina: Teutonic origin. Means: free, friend.

Frances: Latin origin. Means: free. Alternative spellings and nicknames: Fan, Fanechka, Fania, Fanni, Fanya, Franny, Frannie, Franni, Franca, Franky, Francyne, Francie, Franci, France, Francoise, Fanchette, Fanchon, Fancy, Fannie, Fran, Fanny, Franziska, Frankie, Frank, Franciska, Francisca, Francine, Francesca.

Francesca: Latin/Italian origin. Means: free. Alternative spellings: Franchesca, Francisca, Franciska, Franziska.

Francine: Latin/French origin. Means: free.

Franzel: Unknown origin and meaning. Ethnic background: German.

Frauke: Germanic origin. Means: lady.

Freda: Teutonic origin. Means: peaceful, beautiful, joy. Alternative spellings and nicknames: Freida, Fredie, Fredeila, Frayda, Frida, Frieda.

Fredela: Teutonic origin. Means: peaceful elf. Alternative spelling: Fredella.

Frederica: Teutonic origin. Means: peaceful ruler. Alternative spellings and nicknames: Friederike, Rickie, Freddy, Freddi, Frerika, Fredericka, Rikki, Ricky, Ricki, Rica, Fritzi, Freddie, Frederique, Fred, Federica, Farica, Frederika, Friederke.

Fredneish: Unknown origin and meaning.

Freena: Unknown origin and meaning. Ethnic background: Irish.

Freidel: Germanic origin. Means: peace. Ethnic background: Jewish.

Freta: Unknown origin. Means: goddess.

Freya: Norse/Germanic origin. Means: lady, noble. Alternative spellings: Fraya, Freyah, Freia.

Freydis: Norse origin. Means: noblewoman.

Fridolf: Anglo-Saxon origin. Means: peaceful, wolf.

Frima: Unknown origin and meaning. Ethnic background: Jewish.

Frodine: Teutonic/Norse origin. Means: intelligent, wise. Alternative spelling: Frodeen.

Froma: Unknown origin. Means: girl. Ethnic background: Jewish. Alternative spelling: Fromma.

Fronde: Latin origin. Means: leafy branch.

Fronnia: Latin origin. Means: teacher, wise. Alternative spellings: Fronniah, Fronia.

Frume: Hebrew origin. Means: pious one.

Fuchsia: Latin origin. Means: crimson-flowered shrub.

Fuensanta: Spanish origin. Means: a holy fountain. Ethnic background: Hispanic.

Fuji: Japanese origin. Means: wisteria.

Fulvia: Latin origin. Means: tawny, golden. Ethnic background: Italian.

g

Gabriana: Unknown origin and meaning.

Gabriella: Hebrew/Italian origin. Means: God is my strength. Ethnic backgrounds: Swedish, Hungarian. 43rd most popular girl's name of the '90s. Alternative spellings: Gabriela, Gabrieala, Gabrielia, Gavriela, Gavriella, Gavrila.

Gabrielle: Hebrew/French origin. Means: God is my strength. 25th most popular girl's name of the '90s. Alternative spellings and nicknames: Gabie, Gaby, Gabrila, Gabey, Gavra, Gabriela, Gabi, Gabrielia, Gabriele, Gabryele, Gavrielle, Gabeiela.

Gada: Hebrew origin. Means: garden, happy, fortunate.

35

Gaea: Greek origin. Means: mother earth. Alternative spelling: Gaia.

Gail: Anglo-Saxon origin. Means: happy, vivacious. Alternative spellings: Gaylene, Gael, Gayla, Gayleen, Gale, Gayle.

Galatea: Greek origin. Means: ivory, milky white. Alternative spellings: Galatia, Galitea.

Galiana: Greek/Gaelic origin. Means: tranquil, lofty. Alternative spellings: Galiena, Galina.

Galuelle: Unknown origin and meaning. Ethnic background: French.

Ganeshia: Unknown origin and meaning.

Gardenia: Latin origin. Means: glossy, leafy flower.

Gardia: Greek origin. Means: garden.

Gari: Teutonic origin. Means: maiden, spear.

Garielle: Unknown origin and meaning.

Garlanda: Latin/French origin. Means: crowned with wreath of flowers. Alternative spelling: Garlinda.

Garnette: Latin origin. Means: a grain or seed, red jewel.

Gavra: Hebrew origin. Means: God gives me strength. Alternative spelling: Gavrah.

Gay: Teutonic origin. Means: merry, cheerful, lighthearted. Alternative spelling: Gae.

Gazella: Latin origin. Means: antelope, gazelle.

Gelasia: Greek origin. Means: love of laughter.

Gemma: Latin/Italian origin. Means: gem, precious jewel, a bud.

Genaida: Unknown origin and meaning. Ethnic background: Hispanic.

Gendel: Unknown origin and meaning. Ethnic background: Jewish.

Generosa: Spanish origin. Means: generous. Ethnic background: Hispanic.

Genesa: Unknown origin. Means: newcomer. Alternative spellings: Genesia, Genisia.

Genesis: Greek origin. Means: creation or beginning.

Geneva: French origin. Means: juniper tree. Alternative spellings and nicknames: Gena, Genevra, Janeva.

Genevieve: Celtic/Teutonic origin. Means: fair, blessed, white wave. Ethnic background: French. Alternative spellings and nicknames: Genovera, Jen, Janeva, Genny, Genevra, Gena, Guinevere, Jenny, Jennie, Gina, Gennie, Genevieve, Geneva, Genevive, Genoveva, Genovetta.

Genie: Celtic origin. Means: fair, blessed, white wave.

Genna: Hebrew/French origin. Means: newcomer, merciful.

Gennie: Unknown origin and meaning.

Georgette: Greek origin. Means: farmer, to work the earth. Ethnic background: French.

Georgia: Greek/Latin origin. Means: farmer, to work the earth. Alternative spellings and nicknames: Georginee, Georgianna, Georgetta, Geogena, Georgeanne, Georgeanna, Georgie, Georgi, Georgia, Georgina, Georgienne, Giorgia, Giorgiana, George, Georgiana, Georgianne, Georgine, Georgette.

Georgienne: Greek origin. Means: farmer, to work the earth. Alternative spelling: Georgina.

Geraldine: Teutonic origin. Means: mighty with a spear. Ethnic background: Irish. Alternative spellings and nicknames: Gerrie, Jerrie, Jere, Jeralee, Jeraldine, Gerry, Geralda, Gerri, Jeri, Giralda, Geri, Gerhardine, Geraldina, Deena, Dina, Jerry, Giralda.

Gerda: Norse origin. Means: stronghold, protection. Ethnic background: German. Alternative spellings and nicknames: Gerdi, Gerdie, Garda, Gerd.

Geri: Germanic origin. Means: proficient with the spear.

Gerita: Unknown origin. Means: bird.

Gerlind: Germanic origin. Means: delicate, with spear.

Germana: French origin. Means: from Germany. Ethnic background: Italian.

Germma: Unknown origin and meaning. Ethnic backgrounds: English/Welsh.

Gertrude: Teutonic origin. Means: well-loved warrior, spear. Ethnic backgrounds: Irish, Italian, Swedish,

German. Alternative spellings and nicknames: Gerti,
Gerty, Trudie, Trudi, Gertie, Gerta, Trudy, Trude,
Gertrudis, Gertruda, Gert, Gertrud, Gjertrud.

Ghazaalah: Arabic origin. Means: young deer.

Giacinta: Greek origin. Means: hyacinth flower.

Giacomina: Hebrew/Italian origin. Means: supplanted,
protected. Ethnic background: Italian.

Giana: Hebrew/Italian origin. Means: God is gracious.
Alternative spellings: Gianina, Gianna, Giannina.

Gilada: Hebrew origin. Means: everlasting joy.
Alternative spelling: Gila.

Gilberta: Teutonic origin. Means: a golden pledge,
brilliant. Alternative spellings and nicknames: Berty,
Gilly, Gillie, Gilli, Bertie, Berti, Berte, Gilberte,
Gilbertina, Gill, Gilbertine, Gigi, Berta.

Gilda: Celtic/Anglo-Saxon origin. Means: servant of
God, gold covered. Alternative spellings and
nicknames: Gilli, Golda.

Giletta: Unknown origin and meaning.

Gileyla: Unknown origin and meaning.

Gillian: Greek/Latin origin. Means: downy-haired
youth. Ethnic backgrounds: English/Welsh. Alternative
spellings and nicknames: Jilana, Jillie, Jilly, Jill,
Gilliana, Gilliette, Gillan.

Gina: Latin origin. Means: to rule, queen. Ethnic
background: Jewish. Alternative spellings: Geanna,
Geena.

Ginebra: Celtic origin. Means: white. Ethnic
background: Hispanic.

Ginendel: Unknown origin and meaning. Ethnic
background: Jewish.

Ginette: Hebrew/French origin. Means: gracious,
merciful.

Ginger: Latin origin. Means: flower, pure, a maiden.

Ginikanwa: African origin. Unknown meaning.

Giolia: Irish origin. Means: serves Christ. Ethnic
background: Hispanic. Alternative spelling: Giola.

Giorsal: Gaelic origin. Means: experienced battle maid.

Giovanna: Hebrew/Italian origin. Means: God's great
gift. Alternative spellings: Giavanna, GeeVana

Gisa: Hebrew/Anglo-Saxon origin. Means: hewn stone,
gift. Ethnic background: German.

Giselle: Teutonic origin. Means: oath, pledge. Ethnic
backgrounds: Hispanic, French. Alternative spellings:
Gizela, Gisella, Gisele, Gisela, Gizele.

Gitana: Spanish origin. Means: gypsy.

Gitta: Celtic/Hungarian origin. Means: strength, pearl.
Ethnic background: German.

Gittel: Hebrew origin. Means: good. Alternative
spellings: Gittle, Gita, Gitel, Gitil.

Giuditta: Hebrew/Italian origin. Means: with praise.

Giuliana: Greek/Italian origin. Means: youthful, soft-
haired. Alternative spellings: Giulia, Giulietta.

Giuseppina: Hebrew/Italian origin. Means: God shall
add.

Giustina: Latin/Italian origin. Means: just, honest.

Gladys: Latin/Welsh origin. Means: lame, flower. Ethnic
background: English. Alternative spellings and
nicknames: Glad, Gladdie, Gladi, Gladine, Gladis,
Gladyce, Gleda.

Gleda: Anglo-Saxon origin. Means: glad, gladness.

Glenda: Gaelic origin. Means: one who resides in the
valley. Alternative spellings and nicknames: Glenna,
Glynnie, Glynnis, Glennie, Glenine, Glennis, Glyn,
Glenda, Glynis, Glen, Glenn.

Glinys: Unknown origin. Means: little.

Gloria: Latin origin. Means: glorious. Ethnic backgrounds: Italian, Irish. Alternative spellings and nicknames: Glori, Glorianna, Glory, Gloriana, Gloriane.

Glucke: Unknown origin and meaning. Ethnic background: Jewish.

Godiva: Latin/Old English origin. Means: gift of God.

Golda: Old English/Hebrew origin. Means: golden. Alternative spellings and nicknames: Goldy, Goldye, Goldina, Goldia, Goldarina, Goldie.

Grace: Latin origin. Means: attractive, freely given love (of God). Ethnic background: Irish. 45th most popular girl's name of the '90s. Alternative spellings and nicknames: Gratia, Grayce, Gracye, Gracia, Grazia, Grazyna, Engracia, Gratiana, Grata, Gracie, Gray.

Graciela: Latin/Spanish origin. Means: attractive, freely given love (of God). Alternative spelling: Graciella.

Grania: Latin/Celtic origin. Means: granary, female, love. Alternative spellings: Graniah, Grannia, Granniah, Grannias, Grainne.

Gratiana: Latin origin. Means: grace. Alternative spelling: Gratianna.

Greer: Greek origin. Means: guardian.

Greet: Old English origin. Means: welcome. Ethnic background: Dutch.

Greta: Greek origin. Means: pearl. Ethnic background: Swedish. Alternative spellings: Gredel, Gretel, Gretta, Grete, Gretchen, Gretal, Gretchen.

Grimona: Unknown origin. Means: veneration. Alternative spelling: Grimonia.

Griselda: Teutonic/French origin. Means: battle, heroine. Ethnic background: Hispanic. Alternative spellings and nicknames: Selda, Grizelda, Grizel, Grissel, Griseldis, Zelda, Grishilde, Grishilda, Chriselda, Guithilda.

Gro: Norse origin. Means: to increase, gardener. Ethnic background: Norwegian.

Grunella: Unknown origin. Means: brown.

Guadalupe: Spanish origin. Means: Blessed Virgin Mary, river of the wolf.

Gudrun: Norse origin. Means: sacred story of God, wisdom. Ethnic backgrounds: German, Swedish.

Guida: French/Italian origin. Means: guide, maid.

Guillelmina: Germanic/Italian origin. Means: determined protector. Alternative spellings: Guillelmine, Guillemette.

Guinevere: Celtic origin. Means: white wave, fair complexioned. Alternative spellings and nicknames: Oona, Gwenore, Janifer, Jen, Gwenora, Jenni, Jennee, Freddy, Fredi, Gen, Guenevere, Genni, Gennifer, Freddi, Genny, Ginevra, Gena, Jenifer, Gwen, Ona, Una, Guin, Jenny, Guenna, Freddie, Gaynor, Genevieve, Jennie, Gennie.

Guiseppa: Hebrew/Italian origin. Means: he shall add. Alternative spelling: Guiseppina.

Gulai: African origin. Unknown meaning.

Gunhild: Norse origin. Means: battle maiden. Ethnic background: Norwegian. Alternative spellings: Gunhilda, Grunhild.

Gunilla: Norse/Latin origin. Means: battle maiden. Ethnic background: Swedish. Alternative spelling: Gunnel.

Gustava: Norse origin. Means: noble leader, staff of the Goths.

Gutki: Polish origin. Means: goodness.

Guva: African origin. Means: grave.

Guylaine: Teutonic origin. Means: life, warrior, guide, valley. Ethnic background: French.

Gwen: Celtic origin. Means: white browed, holy. Ethnic backgrounds: English/Welsh. Alternative spellings: Gwyn, Guenna, Gwenda.

Gwendolyn: Celtic origin. Means: white browed, holy. Alternative spellings and nicknames: Gwennie, Wendi, Wendie, Gwenny, Gwenn, Gwendolin, Gwendolen, Guendolen, Gwenni, Gwynne, Gwyneth, Gwyn, Wynn, Gwenda, Gwen, Wendy, Guenna, Gwendaline, Gwendoline, Guendalina.

Gwyneth: Celtic origin. Means: white browed, holy. Alternative spellings and nicknames: Gweneth, Winny, Gwynedd, Gwenith, Winnie, Gwynne, Gwyn.

Gwynore: Celtic origin. Means: phantom.

Gyda: Norse origin. Means: warlike. Alternative spellings: Gytha, Githa.

Gypsy: Old English origin. Means: wanderer. Alternative spellings: Gipsy, Gypsie.

Gytle: Unknown origin. Means: flatterer.

h

Haafizah: Arabic origin. Means: guardian. Alternative spelling: Hafeezah.

Haalah: Arabic origin. Means: crescent earring.

Haarisah: Arabic origin. Means: protector.

Haarithah: Arabic origin. Means: lioness.

Habbai: Egyptian origin. Means: festive.

Habeebah: Arabic origin. Means: beloved.

Habika: African origin. Means: sweetheart.

Hadasa: Hebrew origin. Means: myrtle tree. Alternative spelling: Hadaseh.

Hagai: Hebrew origin. Means: God's festival, merry festival. Alternative spellings: Haggai, Haggi, Hagi.

Haggar: Hebrew origin. Means: flees, flight.

Haidee: Greek origin. Means: honored, virtuous, considerate. Alternative spelling: Haydee.

Haily: Norse origin. Means: hero, powerful. Alternative spellings: Haile, Hailee, Halie.

Halda: Teutonic origin. Means: hero, brilliant gem.

Haldana: Teutonic origin. Means: part Dane.

Haldi: Norse origin. Means: reliable, assistant, beloved. Alternative spellings: Haldie, Haldis.

Haletta: Unknown origin. Means: queen. Alternative spelling: Halette.

Halfrida: Teutonic origin. Means: peaceful, heroine.

Hali: Greek origin. Means: the sea.

Halia: Norse origin. Means: gift, partially protected.

Halima: Egyptian origin. Means: gentle. Ethnic background: African. Alternative spelling: Haleemah.

Halimeda: Greek origin. Means: fondness for the sea. Nicknames: Hallie, Hally, Meda.

Halle: Unknown origin and meaning.

Hallela: Hebrew origin. Means: praise.

Halona: Native American origin. Means: fortunate, pleasant. Alternative spelling: Halonna.

Halsea: Unknown origin and meaning.

Hamony: Old German origin. Means: home, house.

Haneefah: Arabic origin. Means: follows truth.

Hanh: Unknown origin and meaning.

Hannah: Hebrew origin. Means: gracious and merciful, flower. Ethnic backgrounds: Irish, English/Welsh. Alternative spellings and nicknames: Hannie, Nana, Nanine, Nanon, Ninon, Hanny, Nanny, Hanni, Annice, Annetta, Nina, Nancy, Nanette, Ninetta, Anita, Hanna, Hana, Annie, Annette, Anne, Anna, Ann, Nan, Hanne, Hanneke, Hanae, Hanako.

Hannelore: Germanic origin. Unknown meaning.

Haralda: Norse origin. Means: leader in battle. Alternative spellings and nicknames: Harelda, Hallie, Hally, Harilda.

Harlie: Old English origin. Unknown meaning.

Harmony: Greek/Latin origin. Means: peace, uniting. Alternative spellings: Harmonia, Harmonie.

Harriet: Teutonic/French origin. Means: head of the estate. Ethnic backgrounds: Dutch, Swedish. Alternative spellings and nicknames: Harrott, Hatty, Hattie, Hatti, Hat, Harriot, Harriette, Harietta, Harri, Harrie.

Harshita: Unknown origin and meaning.

Haseenah: Arabic origin. Means: attractive. Alternative spelling: Hasnaa.

Hasina: Arabic origin. Means: good. Ethnic background: African. Alternative spelling: Hassaanah.

Haw-waa: Arabic origin. Means: mother of man.

Hayley: Anglo-Saxon origin. Means: from the hay meadow. Ethnic backgrounds: English/Welsh. Alternative spellings: Haylee, Hayleigh, Hayli, Haylie.

Hazel: Old English/Teutonic origin. Means: the hazel tree or nut, reddish brown.

Heather: Anglo-Saxon origin. Means: the brightly colored flower heather. Ethnic backgrounds: English/Welsh, Irish. 42nd most popular girl's name of the '90s. Alternative spelling: Heath.

Heaven: Unknown origin and meaning.

Heba: Unknown origin and meaning.

Hebe: Greek origin. Means: youth, spring.

Hedda: Teutonic origin. Means: battle maiden, strife. Ethnic backgrounds: German, Norwegian. Alternative spellings and nicknames: Hedwiga, Heddie, Heddi, Hedy, Hedwig, Heddy, Heda, Hedvige.

Hedva: Hebrew origin. Means: joy, diligent. Alternative spellings: Hedvah, Hedve, Hedveh.

Hedwig: Teutonic origin. Means: struggle, strife. Alternative spellings and nicknames: Hedwiga, Hedi, Edvig, Hedvige, Hedvig, Hedda, Heda, Avice, Hedy.

Hedy: Greek origin. Means: pleasant, agreeable, battle.

Heidi: Germanic origin. Means: of nobility, star. Ethnic background: Swiss. Alternative spellings: Heide, Heidy.

Heidrun: Norse origin. Unknown meaning. Ethnic background: German.

Heirnine: Unknown origin. Means: earth.

Heirrierte: Unknown origin. Means: estate.

Helbon: Unknown origin. Means: fruitful. Alternative spellings: Helbona, Helbonia, Helbonna, Helbonnah.

Held: Germanic origin. Means: noble, kind.

Helen: Greek/Latin origin. Means: light, ray of the sun. Ethnic backgrounds: English/Welsh, Scottish, Polish, Swedish, Czech, French, German. Alternative spellings and nicknames: Eleonore, Ellene, Eleanora, Elianora, Eleen, Elladine, Ailene, Alyne, Aila, Ellen, Elena, Eleni, Elenore, Elinor, Elinore, Ella, Elle, Elene, Eleanore, Aileen, Alaine, Aleen, Eileen, Elaine, Elana, Elane, Elayne, Eleanor, Helana, Helena, Helene.

Helga: Teutonic origin. Means: holy, happy. Ethnic backgrounds: German, Norwegian, Swedish.

Helice: Greek origin. Means: of Helicon (home of the Muses).

Hella: Germanic origin. Means: holy, happy.

"I Like the Sound of That!"

For most people, deciding on a name is not as scientific a process as you might expect. The overwhelming majority of Parent Soupers choose a name solely by the way it sounds. After all, if you're going to have to say and hear a word for the rest of your life, it may as well be easy on the ears.

Helle: Greek origin. Unknown meaning. Ethnic background: Norwegian.

Helma: Germanic origin. Means: protection, protector.

Heloise: Teutonic/French origin. Means: famous warrior.

Helsa: Hebrew origin. Means: devoted to God. Alternative spellings: Helse, Helsie.

Henda: Hebrew origin. Means: grace, gracious. Alternative spellings: Hende, Hendel, Heneh.

Henia: Germanic origin. Means: one who rules the home or estate. Ethnic background: Jewish. Alternative spellings: Henna, Henie, Henye.

Henrietta: Germanic/French origin. Means: one who rules the home or estate. Alternative spellings and nicknames: Henryetta, Hennie, Henrie, Henrieta, Henriette, Hetti, Hettie, Nettie, Henka, Netty, Etty, Eiric, Henni, Ettie, Harriette, Harriott, Hatti, Hattie, Hatty, Etti, Henrika, Hetty, Netta, Yetta, Hendrika, Enrichetta, Enriqueta, Etta, Hallie, Harriet, Henrike.

Herdis: Norse origin. Unknown meaning.

Hermelinda: Spanish origin. Means: shield of power. Ethnic background: Hispanic.

Hermina: Greek/Latin origin. Means: well born, godly. Alternative spellings: Hermine, Ione.

Hermione: Greek origin. Means: messenger, of the earth. Alternative spellings and nicknames: Hermia, Hermine, Herminia, Hermina, Ione, Erma, Herrnione.

Hermosa: Spanish origin. Means: beautiful. Alternative spelling: Herrnosa.

Hernanda: Germanic/Spanish origin. Means: bold, courageous.

Herra: Greek origin. Means: queen, lady. Alternative spelling: Herrah, Hera.

Hersilia: Latin origin. Unknown meaning. Ethnic background: Hispanic.

Hertha: Greek/Germanic origin. Means: of the earth. Alternative spellings: Erta, Ertha, Eartha, Erda, Herta.

Hertnia: Greek origin. Means: earthly, messenger. Alternative spelling: Herrntia.

Hesper: Greek origin. Means: evening star. Alternative spellings: Hespera, Hespira.

Hesta: Greek origin. Means: of the hearth. Alternative spelling: Hestia.

Hester: Persian/Latin origin. Means: star, good fortune. Alternative spellings and nicknames: Hettie, Hetty, Hett, Hesper, Esther, Hestia, Hesther.

Heti: Unknown origin. Means: beautiful.

Hetty: Persian origin. Means: evening star.

Hibernia: Latin origin. Means: one from Ireland.

Hibiscus: Latin origin. Means: with large showy flowers.

Hideko: Japanese origin. Unknown meaning.

Hidie: Germanic origin. Means: battle ready.

Hilan: Latin origin. Means: cheerful, happy.

Hilaria: Latin origin. Means: cheerful, happy.

Hilda: Teutonic origin. Means: maiden of battle, strong. Ethnic background: Czech. Alternative spellings and nicknames: Hild, Heidi, Hildie, Hildy, Hilde.

Hildar: Latin origin. Means: cheerful, happy.

Hildebrand: Germanic origin. Means: the sword of battle.

Hildegarde: Teutonic origin. Means: protective warrior maid, stronghold. Alternative spellings and nicknames: Hildagard, Hildegard, Hildagarde, Heid, Hild, Hildy, Hildie, Hilda.

Hildemar: Germanic origin. Means: glorious in battle.

Hildreth: Teutonic origin. Means: counselor of war.

Hilina: Unknown origin and meaning. Ethnic background: Polish.

Hilma: Teutonic origin. Means: helmet, protective. Alternative spelling: Helma.

Hindal: Germanic origin. Means: the deer's hind. Ethnic background: Jewish.

Hiroko: Japanese origin. Unknown meaning.

Hisaye: Japanese origin. Unknown meaning.

Hodel: Hebrew origin. Means: beautiful, honored. Alternative spelling: Hodi.

Holda: Germanic origin. Means: beloved one.

Hollah: Unknown origin. Means: girl.

Holly: Old English origin. Means: an evergreen shrub, holy. Alternative spellings: Hollie, Hollee.

Honesty: Latin origin. Means: honorable in principles and actions.

Honey: Old English origin. Means: sweet, beloved, honey.

Honora: Latin origin. Means: honorable, one with high esteem. Alternative spellings and nicknames: Norrie, Norry, Norri, Norine, Noreen, Nora, Honorine, Honoria, Honor, Honey, Norah.

Hope: Old English origin. Means: trust, optimistic faith in things to come.

Horatia: Latin origin. Means: one who marks time, to behold. Alternative spelling: Horacia.

Horiya: Hebrew origin. Means: teaching of the Lord.

Hortense: Latin origin. Means: a garden or gardener. Alternative spellings: Hortensa, Hortensia, Ortensia, Hortencia.

Hoshi: Japanese origin. Means: starlike.

Huberta: Teutonic origin. Means: one who has a bright mind.

Hudel: Hebrew origin. Means: a myrtle tree.

Hudi: Unknown origin and meaning. Ethnic background: Jewish.

Huette: Teutonic origin. Means: small intelligent girl. Alternative spellings: Hughette, Huetta, Hugette.

Hulda: Hebrew/Norse origin. Means: a weasel, much loved, sweet. Ethnic background: German. Alternative spellings and nicknames: Huldy, Huldie, Huldah.

Humairaa: Arabic origin. Means: white.

Hyacinth: Greek origin. Means: purple and white flower. Alternative spellings and nicknames: Sinty, Hyacinthie, Hyacinthia, Hyacinthe, Cinthie, Hyacintha, Jacinta, Jacynth, Cynthie, Jacky, Jackie, Jacinthe, Jacintha, Jacinda, Jacenta, Giacinta.

Hypatia: Greek origin. Means: one with superior intellect.

Ianthe: Greek origin. Means: a purple flower. Alternative spellings and nicknames: Janthina, Ianthina, Ian, Iantha, Ianthiria.

Ida: Teutonic origin. Means: industrious, prosperous. Ethnic backgrounds: German, Hispanic, Irish, Italian, Czech. Alternative spellings: Idalla, Idelle, Idette, Idalia, Idalina, Idaline.

Idalia: Greek origin. Means: one with great happiness. Alternative spellings: Idalina, Idaline, Idalis.

Idasia: Unknown origin and meaning.

Ideh: Hebrew origin. Means: praise. Alternative spelling: Idit.

Idele: Greek/Teutonic origin. Means: industrious, prosperous, happy. Ethnic background: Jewish. Alternative spellings: Idella, Idel.

Idola: Greek origin. Means: a vision of loveliness. Alternative spellings: Idolah, Idolia.

Idona: Norse/Teutonic origin. Means: industrious worker, love. Alternative spellings: Idonea, Idonia, Iduna, Idonah, Idonia, Idonna.

Iduna: Norse origin. Means: one who is actively desired. Alternative spelling: Idun.

Ierne: Latin/Irish origin. Means: one from Ireland.

Iesha: Unknown origin and meaning.

Ifigenia: Unknown origin and meaning. Ethnic background: Hispanic.

Ignacia: Latin origin. Means: one who is lively or fiery. Alternative spellings: Ignatia, Ignatzia, Ignacy.

Iheoma: African origin. Means: a welcome child.

Ijada: Unknown origin. Means: jade.

Ikeia: Unknown origin and meaning.

Ikuko: Japanese origin. Unknown meaning.

Ila: French origin. Means: from the island.

Ilana: Hebrew origin. Means: tree.

Ilaria: Latin origin. Means: one who is merry. Ethnic background: Italian.

Ilda: Teutonic origin. Means: heroine. Ethnic background: Italian.

Ildiko: Teutonic/Hungarian origin. Means: a fierce warrior.

Ileana: Greek origin. Means: bearer, light, from Troy. Ethnic background: Italian. Alternative spellings: Ilene, Illiana, Iliana.

Ilia: Hebrew origin. Means: God is Lord.

Ilka: Slavic/Teutonic origin. Means: flattering, industrious. Alternative spellings and nicknames: Ilke, Ilonka, Milka.

Illana: Unknown origin. Means: big.

Ilona: Hungarian origin. Means: beautiful, light. Alternative spelling: Ilonka.

Ilsa: Hebrew/Teutonic origin. Means: God's oath, noble maiden. Ethnic background: German. Alternative spelling: Ilse.

Ilyssa: Unknown origin and meaning.

Ima: Hebrew origin. Means: mother.

"I Like the Sound of That" Parent Poll

How did you choose your child's name?

Of 1,062 total votes:

family name	15.72%
special meaning	14.4%
we liked the sound of it	66.76%
just made it up	3.1%

1 pacifier = 100 parents

Imani: Unknown origin and meaning.

Imanuela: Hebrew origin. Means: God is with us.

Imari: Unknown origin and meaning.

Imelda: Germanic origin. Means: the whole battle. Ethnic background: Hispanic. Alternative spelling: Imalda.

Imelida: Spanish origin. Means: wistful.

Imena: Unknown origin. Means: dream.

Imogene: Latin origin. Means: image, likeness. Alternative spellings: Imojean, Imogen, Emogene.

Imperia: Latin origin. Means: imperial, commanding.

Ina: Latin origin. Means: mother, purity. Ethnic backgrounds: German, Irish. Alternative spellings and nicknames: Inesita, Ines.

Inaki: Latin origin. Means: one with intense emotion.

India: Unknown origin and meaning. Alternative spelling: Indya.

Indira: Unknown origin and meaning.

Ineke: Latin origin. Means: small. Ethnic background: Dutch.

Inez: Greek origin. Means: pure, innocent, kind. Ethnic backgrounds: Hispanic, German, Italian. Alternative spelling: Ines.

Infiniti: Unknown origin and meaning.

Ingalill: Germanic origin. Unknown meaning. Ethnic background: Swedish.

Ingalls: Germanic origin. Means: an angel.

43

Ingeborg: Norse origin. Means: fortification. Ethnic background: Swedish.

Ingegerd: Norse origin. Means: assistant. Ethnic background: Swedish. Alternative spelling: Ingjerd.

Ingrid: Norse origin. Means: the daughter of a hero. Ethnic backgrounds: Swedish, Czech, German, Norwegian. Alternative spellings: Ingunna, Ingaberg, Inge, Inga, Ingeborg, Inger.

Ingrida: Norse origin. Means: beautiful one. Ethnic background: Russian.

Iolanthe: Greek origin. Means: violet flower, a dawn cloud. Alternative spellings: Iole, Iola.

Iona: Greek origin. Means: precious violet-colored stone. Alternative spelling: Ione.

Irene: Greek origin. Means: peace, serenity. Ethnic backgrounds: Irish, Hispanic, Italian. Alternative spellings and nicknames: Rina, Rennie, Renie, Reni, Eirene, Eirena, Rene, Renny, Rena, Irina, Irena, Ira, Erena, Renata, Iren.

Ireta: Greek origin. Means: angry, wrathful. Alternative spellings: Iretta, Irette.

Iris: Greek origin. Means: the rainbow, the iris flower. Alternative spellings: Irisa, Irita.

Irma: Latin/Germanic origin. Means: powerful, noble. Ethnic background: Italian. Alternative spellings and nicknames: Irmine, Irminia, Irmina, Erme, Irmela, Irme, Irmy, Erma.

Irmgard: Germanic origin. Means: of the large settlement, war goddess.

Irra: Unknown origin. Means: castle.

Irvette: Anglo-Saxon origin. Means: lover of the sea.

Isa: Hebrew/Teutonic origin. Means: God's oath, iron willed. Ethnic background: German. Alternative spelling: Isah.

Isabel: Hebrew origin. Means: consecrated, God's oath. Ethnic backgrounds: Hispanic, Italian, Swedish, French, Polish. Alternative spellings and nicknames: Issy, Isbel, Iseabal, Ishabel, Isobel, Issie, Izabel, Izabela, Izabelle, Izabella, Nib, Tibbie, Ysabel, Issi, Isabelita, Belita, Bel, Ib, Ibbie, Ibby, Isabell, Isabelle, Isabella, Bell, Belia, Bella, Belle, Isa, Isabeau, Belicia.

Isadora: Greek origin. Means: a gift of Isis. Alternative spellings and nicknames: Isidora, Issy, Izzy, Dory, Dora, Dori.

Popularity Contest

Every decade has its popular names. Unisex names, surnames as first names, and unusually spelled names all bear the mark of the 1990s. Does this make them unworthy? Well, no, of course not, but if you're in search of an unusual name, you might want to look further. If your favorite name is enjoying a popularity streak, however, don't despair of using it—every child has a way of making a name his or her own. How can you tell how popular a name is? Check out the lists in the back of this book, read the following tips, and start perusing your local paper's birth announcements. And remember, at some point in his or her life (probably during the teen years), your child is going to hate you for your choice of names—because it's too popular, too unusual, too boring, too whatever. There's no easy way out. So find a name you love and let that cookie crumble!

Ishiko: Japanese origin. Unknown meaning.

Isis: Egyptian origin. Means: goddess of motherhood and the moon.

Isla: Scottish origin. Means: island, sweet.

Isleana: Gaelic origin. Means: a vision, sweet. Alternative spellings: Islean, Isleen, Isaeileen.

Ismenia: Irish origin. Unknown meaning. Alternative spelling: Ismey.

Isoke: African origin. Means: a satisfying gift from God.

Isolde: Celtic/Germanic origin. Means: to rule fairly. Alternative spellings: Iseult, Isolt, Isolda, Yseult, Izette.

Isotta: Unknown origin and meaning. Ethnic background: Italian.

Ita: Celtic/Gaelic origin. Means: enticing, thirst. Ethnic backgrounds: Irish, Jewish.

Iti: Hebrew origin. Means: with me.

Itka: Unknown origin and meaning. Ethnic background: Jewish.

Iveta: Unknown origin and meaning. Ethnic background: Czech.

Ivona: Hebrew/French origin. Means: God's great gift, yew tree. Ethnic background: Czech. Alternative spellings: Iva, Ivana, Ivah, Ivanna, Ivane, Ivanah, Ivonne.

Ivory: Latin origin. Means: yellowish white, a tusk.

Ivriya: Hebrew origin. Means: the Hebrew language.

Ivy: Greek/Old English origin. Means: an ivy vine, clinging. Alternative spelling: Iva.

Iwona: Polish origin. Means: an archer.

Iyana: Unknown origin and meaning.

Izebe: African origin. Means: long-expected child.

j

Jaala: Unknown origin. Means: divine.

Jacey: Unknown origin and meaning.

Jacinda: Greek origin. Means: beautiful, purple flower. Alternative spellings: Jacenta, Jacinta, Jacintha, Jacinthe, Jacynth.

Jacoba: Hebrew origin. Means: one who supplants, protects. Alternative spellings and nicknames: Jacobine, Jacki, Jakoba, Jacobina, Jacobien, Jacoby, Jakobine, Jacky, Jackie, Jacobah, Jacobba.

Jacomine: Unknown origin and meaning. Ethnic background: Dutch.

Jacoy: Unknown origin and meaning.

Jacqueline: Hebrew/French origin. Means: to protect, to hold another back. 41st most popular girl's name of the '90s. Alternative spellings and nicknames: Jacquenetta, Jacquenette, Jaquith, Jaquenette, Jaquenetta, Jacquie, Jacquette, Jaclin, Jacki, Jacklin, Jackquelin, Jackqueline, Jackelyn, Jacklynn, Jacqualyn, Jackalyn, Jackilyn, Jaqueline, Jacqui, Jacquetta, Jackie, Jacky, Jacquelyn, Jaclyn, Jacalyn, Jacalyne, Jaquelin, Jacquelyn, Jacquelynn.

Jacynth: Unknown origin. Means: beautiful.

Jade: Spanish origin. Means: jewel, precious stone. 49th most popular girl's name of the '90s. Alternative spellings: Jayda, Jayde, Jaydeen.

Jadon: Unknown origin and meaning.

Jadwiga: Polish origin. Means: peace in battle.

Jaela: Hebrew origin. Means: divine. Alternative spelling: Jala.

Jahnea: Unknown origin and meaning.

Jahnika: Unknown origin and meaning.

Jaimie: Hebrew origin. Means: one who supplants, replaces, gracious gift from God. Alternative spellings: Jaime, Jaimee, Jami, Jayme, Jaymi.

Jairia: Unknown origin. Means: enlightened.

Jakira: Unknown origin and meaning.

Jaleshia: Unknown origin and meaning. Alternative spellings: Jalicia, Ja'Leesa, Jaleesa, Ja'Leezia.

Jamece: Unknown origin and meaning.

Jamica: Unknown origin and meaning.

Jamila: Arabic origin. Means: beautiful. Ethnic background: African. Alternative spellings: Jameelah, Jameia, Jameilla, Jamiea, Jamilya, Jammal, Jimyla.

Jamisha: Unknown origin and meaning.

Janaya: Unknown origin. Means: fruit.

Jane: Hebrew origin. Means: God's gracious gift. Ethnic backgrounds: Irish, Scottish. 49th most popular girl's name of the '90s. Alternative spellings and nicknames: Janot, Janith, Janey, Jania, Jankal, Jannelle, Janyl, Jannel, Janetta, Janeczka, Janel, Janeia, Janella, Janeta, Janie, Janine, Janis, Janna, Janette, Janice, Jana, Janina, Gian, Gianina, Gianna, Jan, Gene, Janelle, Janet, Giovanna, Janae, Janay, Janee, Jayna, Jayne, Jhane.

Janelle: Hebrew/Anglo-Saxon origin. Means: God's gracious gift.

Janet: Hebrew origin. Means: God's gracious gift. Ethnic backgrounds: English/Welsh, Scottish. Alternative spellings: Jannet, Jannette, Janette.

Janice: Hebrew origin. Means: God's gracious gift. Alternative spellings: Janesa, Janessa.

Janine: Hebrew/French origin. Means: God's gracious gift. Ethnic backgrounds: English/Welsh. Alternative spellings: Janiene, Janina.

Janiqua: Unknown origin and meaning.

Janira: Unknown origin and meaning.

Janitza: Unknown origin and meaning.

Janna: Hebrew/Czech origin. Means: God's gracious gift. Alternative spelling: Jana.

Janneke: Unknown origin and meaning. Ethnic background: Dutch. Alternative spelling: Jenneke.

Jaqualia: Unknown origin and meaning.

Jaquita: Unknown origin and meaning.

Jariya: Unknown origin and meaning.

Jarmila: Czech origin. Means: grace, spring.

Jarnescia: Unknown origin and meaning.

Jaroslava: Slavic/Polish origin. Means: the glory of spring. Ethnic background: Czech.

Jasira: Unknown origin and meaning.

Jasmarie: Unknown origin and meaning.

Jasmine: Persian origin. Means: fragrantly flowered shrub. 31st most popular girl's name of the '90s. Alternative spellings and nicknames: Jasman, Jasmin, Jasmyn, Jaszmin, Jazmin, Jazmine, Jazmyne, Jazzmyne, Jessamyn, Jessamy, Jessamine, Jasmina, Jasmin, Jasmain, Yasmin, Jessie, Jess.

Jawara: Arabic origin. Means: a jewel.

Jayare: Unknown origin and meaning.

Jayla: Unknown origin and meaning. Alternative spellings: Jaylea, Jaylon, Jaylyn, Jhay-Lah.

Jeanette: Hebrew/French origin. Means: God's gracious gift. Alternative spelling: Jeannette.

Jeanne: Hebrew/French origin. Means: God's gracious gift. Alternative spellings: Jeana, Jeannae, Jeanna, Jeannie.

Jebel: Unknown origin and meaning.

Jelana: Unknown origin and meaning. Alternative spelling: Jelani.

Jemima: Hebrew/Arabic origin. Means: dove, right hand, strength. Alternative spellings and nicknames: Jemmie, Jemmy, Jemmima, Jemie, Jem, Jamima, Jemimah, Mimi, Jemina, Jemena, Jeminah, Jemine.

Jenavieve: Celtic/French origin. Means: white cheeked.

Jenaya: Unknown origin and meaning.

Jenci: Unknown origin and meaning.

Jenesia: Hebrew origin. Means: God is gracious, newcomer. Alternative spelling: Jeniece.

Jenilee: Unknown origin and meaning.

Jenna: Celtic/Old English origin. Means: one who loves peace, white cheeked. 40th most popular girl's name of the '90s. Alternative spellings: Jena, Jennah.

Jennifer: Celtic/Old English origin. Means: one who loves peace, white cheeked. Ethnic backgrounds: English/Welsh. 31st most popular girl's name of the '90s. Alternative spellings and nicknames: Genny, Jenni, Jen, Gennifer, Genni, Jennee, Jenny, Jennie, Gennie, Genna, Jenifer, Jeninfer.

Jenny: Celtic/Old English origin means: one who loves peace, white cheeked. Ethnic background: Swedish. Alternative spellings: Jennie, Jennnie.

Jeno: Greek origin. Means: heaven, well born. Ethnic background: Hungarian.

Jensen: Unknown origin and meaning.

Jerica: Unknown origin and meaning.

Jerilee: Unknown origin and meaning.

Jeritah: Unknown origin. Means: bird.

Jerri: Hebrew/Anglo-Saxon origin. Means: God will uplift, exalted. Alternative spelling: Jeri.

Jerusha: Hebrew origin. Means: married.

Jesenia: Unknown origin and meaning. Alternative spelling: Jezzenia.

Jessica: Hebrew origin. Means: one with wealth, gift. Ethnic backgrounds: English/Welsh. 5th most popular girl's name of the '90s. Alternative spellings and nicknames: Jessy, Jessalin, Jessalyn, Jess, Jessa, Jessie, Jessalynn, Jessika, Jessuca.

Jevon: Unknown origin and meaning.

Jewel: Latin/French origin. Means: precious gem, delight. Alternative spellings and nicknames: Jewell, Jewelle, Jewels, Juill.

Jezebel: Hebrew origin. Unknown meaning.

Jill: Latin origin. Means: youthful, girl. Ethnic backgrounds: English/Welsh. Alternative spellings and nicknames: Jillana, Jilli, Jillie, Jilly, Jillian.

Jinte: Unknown origin and meaning. Ethnic background: Dutch.

Jinx: Latin origin. Means: a spell or charm.

Jirina: Greek/Czech origin. Means: one who works the earth, farmer.

Jo Anne: Hebrew origin. Means: God will increase.

Jo: Hebrew origin. Means: God will increase.

Joachima: Hebrew origin. Means: the Lord judges or establishes. Alternative spellings: Joacima, Joacimah

Joan: Hebrew origin. Means: gracious gift of God. Ethnic backgrounds: English/Welsh, Irish, Polish. Alternative spellings and nicknames: Jonie, Joni, Johanna, Juanita, Jodi, Joanne, Joanna, Jody, Jodie, Joanay, Joann.

Joappa: Unknown origin. Means: lovely.

JoBeth: Unknown origin and meaning.

Jobina: Hebrew origin. Means: one who is oppressed. Alternative spellings and nicknames: Jobey, Jobie, Joby, Jobye, Jobyna.

Jocasta: Greek origin. Means: lighthearted.

Jocelyn: Hebrew/Latin origin. Means: supplanter, merry. Alternative spellings and nicknames: Josselyn, Lyn, Joycelin, Joseline, Jocelin, Lynn, Jocelyne, Jasslyn, Jazlyn, Jazzelynn, Jessalyn, Joselin, Jozlyn, Josceline, Joscelyne, Joshlyn, Joceline, Joslyn, Justine.

Jocosa: Unknown origin. Means: humorous.

Jode: Unknown origin and meaning.

Jodie: Hebrew origin. Means: praised. Ethnic backgrounds: English/Welsh. Alternative spelling: Jodi.

Joellen: Hebrew origin. Means: God is willing. Alternative spellings: Joella, Joelle, Jo Ella.

Joette: Hebrew/French origin. Means: to add, praise.

Johanna: Hebrew/Germanic origin. Means: God is gracious. Ethnic background: Dutch. Alternative spelling: Johanne.

Johneshia: Unknown origin and meaning. Alternative spellings: Johnisha, Jonisha, Johnnise, Jahneshia.

Johnette: Unknown origin and meaning.

Johnni: Unknown origin and meaning.

Johntria: Unknown origin and meaning. Alternative spelling: Johnta.

Johppa: Unknown origin. Means: lovely. Alternative spelling: Johppah.

Jola: Hebrew origin. Means: the Lord is God.

Jolande: Latin/Italian origin. Means: one who is modest or shy. Ethnic background: Dutch.

Jolanta: Latin/Polish origin. Means: pretty, violet. Alternative spellings: Jolenta, Jollanta, Jollenta.

Joletta: Latin origin. Means: violet, modest one.

Jolie: French origin. Means: pretty, with good humor.

Joline: Unknown origin. Means: increase.

Jomaralee: Unknown origin and meaning.

Jonina: Hebrew origin. Means: a dove, peaceful. Alternative spellings: Jona, Jonati.

Joplin: Unknown origin and meaning.

Jordyn: Hebrew origin. Means: flowing down, descending. Alternative spellings: Jordana, Jordann, Jordynn, Jourdan.

Jori: Unknown origin and meaning.

Jorunn: Norse origin. Means: one whom the chief loves.

Josee: Hebrew origin. Means: God will increase.

Josephine: Hebrew/French origin. Means: God will increase. Ethnic backgrounds: Dutch, German. Alternative spellings and nicknames: Pheny, Josephe, Josi, Josy, Josepha, Fifine, Josephina, Josette, Pepita, Fifi, Josie, Josefa, Joline, Joey, Joette, Jo, Giuseppina, Josefina, Fina.

Josette: Hebrew/French origin. Means: God will increase.

Joshana: Unknown origin and meaning. Alternative spelling: Joshanna.

Joshi: Hebrew origin. Means: God is my salvation.

Josie: Unknown origin and meaning. Alternative spelling: Josia.

Josnelle: Unknown origin and meaning.

Jovanah: Unknown origin and meaning. Alternative spelling: Jovanna.

Jovi: Latin origin. Means: little, jovial. Alternative spelling: Jovia.

Jovita: Latin origin. Means: joyful, little. Alternative spellings: Jovitah, Jovitta.

Joy: French/Latin origin. Means: to be merry, delight. Alternative spelling: Joya.

Juanita: Hebrew/Spanish origin. Means: God is gracious. Alternative spelling: Juana.

Juba: Unknown origin. Means: born.

Judith: Hebrew origin. Means: the praise of God. Ethnic background: Scottish. Alternative spellings and nicknames: Ju, Judye, Juditha, Judi, Judit, Judy, Jody, Jodie, Jodi, Giuditta, Judie.

Judy: Hebrew origin. Means: the praise of God. Ethnic backgrounds: English/Welsh. Alternative spellings: Judi, Judie.

Jueta: Spanish origin. Means: friend. Alternative spellings: Juetta, Juta.

Julia: Latin/French origin. Means: soft-haired one, youthful. Ethnic background: Russian. 34th most popular girl's name of the '90s. Alternative spellings and nicknames: Julita, Juliet, Julieta, Julietta, Juline, Sile, Sileas, Julienne, Julina, Julee, Gillie, Juliann, Giuletta, Juliette, Jule, Jill, Juli, Julie, Giulia, Joletta, Juliana, Juliane.

Julianna: Latin origin. Means: soft-haired one, youthful. Ethnic background: Hungarian. Alternative spellings: Juliana, Juliane, Julianne, Juliette.

Julie: Latin origin. Means: soft-haired one, youthful. Ethnic backgrounds: English/Welsh, Irish, French.

Juliza: Unknown origin and meaning.

June: Latin origin. Means: youthful, born in the sixth month. Ethnic backgrounds: English/Welsh. Alternative spellings and nicknames: Junis, Junetta, Junieta, Junine, Junina, Junie, Juniata, Junette, Junia.

Ju'nesha: Unknown origin and meaning.

Junko: Japanese origin. Unknown meaning.

Juno: Latin origin. Means: heaven, heavenly queen. Alternative spellings: Juna, Juni, Junna, Junno.

Justine: Latin origin. Means: one who is virtuous, just, upright. Alternative spellings and nicknames: Justinn, Justa, Justina, Tina, Giustina, Justise, Justyna.

Jutta: Hebrew/Germanic origin. Means: the praise of God. Ethnic background: Hispanic.

Jwahir: African origin. Means: the golden woman.

Jynx: Latin origin. Means: a spell or charm.

k

Kaatje: Unknown origin and meaning. Ethnic background: Dutch.

Kabria: Unknown origin and meaning.

Kacey: Gaelic origin. Means: vigilant, brave. Alternative spellings: Kacee, Kacie, Kacy, Kasey, Kasi, Kasie, Kaycci, Kaycee, Kaysee.

Kachine: Native American origin. Means: sacred dancer, spirit.

Kadeem: Unknown origin and meaning.

Kadence: Latin origin. Means: to fall into, rhythm.

Kadija: African origin. Means: the prophet's wife. Alternative spellings: Kadeja, Kadejiah.

Kadisha: Hebrew origin. Means: holy.

Kadiya: Hebrew origin. Means: pitcher.

Kady: Unknown origin and meaning.

Kaelyn: Greek/Old English origin. Means: to rejoice, a meadow. Alternative spellings: Kaelynn, Kailyn, Kalyn, Kaylen, Kaylin, Kaylyn.

Kahtia: Unknown origin and meaning.

Kaia: Greek origin. Means: of the earth.

Kaitlyn: Greek/Old English origin. Means: pure, a brook. 4th most popular girl's name of the '90s. Alternative spellings: Kaitlin, Kaitlynn, Kaitlinn, Kaitlan, Kaitland, Katalin, Katelin, Kateline, Katelyn, Katelynn, Katlin, Katlyn, Katlynn, Kaytlyn, Kaytlynn.

Kala: Hindi origin. Means: black.

Kalie: Sanskrit origin. Means: one with much energy. Alternative spelling: Kali.

Kalikst: Unknown origin and meaning. Ethnic background: Polish.

Kalila: Arabic origin. Means: beloved one. Alternative spelling: Kalilah.

Kalin: Unknown origin and meaning.

Kalina: Hindi origin. Means: sun. Alternative spellings: Kaleena, Kalena, Kalinda, Kalindi, Kaylena, Kaylina.

Kalli: Unknown origin and meaning. Alternative spellings: Kallie, Kaly.

Kama: Sanskrit origin. Means: loved, desired.

Kamania: African origin. Means: like the moon. Alternative spelling: Kamaria.

Kamba: African origin. Means: tortoise.

Kameko: Japanese origin. Means: child, long-lived.

Kamila: Arabic/Polish origin. Means: perfect. Alternative spellings: Kamilah, Kamillah, Kamille, Kaamilah, Kamilla.

Kamren: Unknown origin and meaning.

Kandice: Greek origin. Means: bright, light.

Kania: Hindi origin. Means: virgin. Alternative spelling: Kanya.

Kara: Greek origin. Means: one of purity, beloved. 49th most popular girl's name of the '90s. Alternative spellings: Karena, Carina, Carine.

Kareemah: Arabic origin. Means: generous.

Kareen: Unknown origin. Means: exalted.

Karen: Greek origin. Means: one of purity, beloved. Ethnic backgrounds: Irish, English/Welsh, Norwegian. Alternative spellings and nicknames: Karna, Karena, Karina, Karyna, Carin, Caren, Karyn, Karin, Kari, Kareen, Kara.

Kari: Latin/French origin. Means: one with strength, joyful song. Ethnic backgrounds: Norwegian, Russian.

Karianne: Greek origin. Means: one of purity, beloved.

Karissa: Latin origin. Means: with artistic talent. Alternative spellings: Karisten, Karisue.

Karita: Latin/Norse origin. Means: charity.

Karla: Old English/Teutonic origin. Means: womanly, strong. Ethnic background: Czech. Alternative spellings and nicknames: Karline, Karly.

Karlee: Latin origin. Means: one with strength. Alternative spellings: Karley, Karli, Karlie, Karleigh, Karly, Karlye.

Karne: Unknown origin and meaning.

Karolina: Latin/Polish origin. Means: one with strength. Ethnic background: German. Alternative spelling: Karalyn.

Karrigan: Unknown origin and meaning.

Karynza: Unknown origin and meaning.

Kashira: Unknown origin and meaning.

Kasia: Greek/Polish origin. Means: one of purity, beloved.

Kasmira: Slavic origin. Means: one who commands peace.

Kassandra: Greek origin. Means: helper, one who warns.

Kassidy: Unknown origin and meaning. Alternative spelling: Kassadi.

Kassie: Unknown origin and meaning.

Kasten: Unknown origin and meaning.

Katana: Unknown origin and meaning.

Kate: Greek origin. Means: one of purity, beloved. Nicknames: Katy, Katie.

Kathe: Greek/Germanic origin. Means: one of purity, beloved.

Katherine: Greek origin. Means: one of purity, beloved. Ethnic background: Scottish. 12th most popular girl's name of the '90s. Alternative spellings and nicknames: Katharine, Katherina, Kathrina, Kathryn, Cathee, Catherina, Cathi, Cati, Cathlene, Cathlin, Cathyleen, Cathe, Cathie, Carin, Caron, Caryn, Cassy, Catarina, Cate, Catha, Cathleen, Catherine, Cassie, Cathrine, Cathryn, Cathy, Caitlin, Catalina, Caren, Cass, Caterina, Catharina, Caitrin.

Kathleen: Greek/Irish origin. Means: pure little one, innocent. Ethnic backgrounds: English/Welsh. Alternative spellings and nicknames: Kathlene, Kittie, Kit, Kathie, Kath, Kay, Kitty, Katrina, Kate, Katie, Katrine, Kathlyn.

Katiann: Unknown origin and meaning.

Katie: Greek origin. Means: one of purity, beloved. Ethnic backgrounds: English/Welsh. 47th most popular girl's name of the '90s. Alternative spellings: Katy, Kati, Kathia, Katja, Katya, Katey.

Katina: Unknown origin and meaning.

Katrina: Greek/Norse origin. Means: one of purity, beloved. Alternative spellings: Katerina, Katarina, Katarzyna, Katrien, Katrine.

Kaye: Greek/Latin origin. Means: merry one, rejoicing. Ethnic backgrounds: English/Welsh.

Kayla: Hebrew origin. Means: a crown of laurels. 14th most popular girl's name of the '90s. Alternative spellings: Kaila, Kailah, Kaela, Kelilah, Kelila.

Kaylee: Greek/Old English origin. Means: to rejoice, a meadow. 25th most popular girl's name of the '90s. Alternative spellings: Kaylea, Kaileigh, Kailey, Kaily, Kaili, Kaleigh, Kaley, Kayley, Keleigh, Kayleigh, Kaylie.

Keaf: Arabic/Irish origin. Means: gentle, one at peace.

KeAsia: Unknown origin and meaning.

Kedma: Hebrew origin. Means: eastward.

Kefira: Hebrew origin. Means: young lioness or cub.

Keiandra: Unknown origin and meaning. Alternative spelling: Keandra.

Keiko: Japanese origin. Means: one who is adored.

Keinesha: Unknown origin and meaning.

Keisha: Unknown origin and meaning.

Kelana: Unknown origin and meaning.

Kelda: Norse origin. Means: a bubbling spring. Alternative spellings and nicknames: Kelly, Kela, Keldah, Kella, Kellda.

Kelisa: Unknown origin and meaning.

Kellie: Gaelic origin. Means: warrior of the king, brave soldier. Alternative spelling: Kelli.

Kellyn: Welsh origin. Unknown meaning.

Kelsea: Old English/Norse origin. Means: victory at
sea, island. Alternative spellings: Kelsee, Kelsi, Kelsie,
Kelsy, Kelcey, Kelcie, Kesley, Keslie.

Kelula: Hebrew origin. Means: one crowned in victory.

Kem: Old English origin. Means: one who is a
champion, warrior.

Kemara: Unknown origin and meaning.

Kenadi: Unknown origin and meaning.

Kendra: Norse/Anglo-Saxon origin. Means: one of
knowledge, understanding. Alternative spellings and
nicknames: Ken, Kendrath, Kendy, Kendrah, Kindra.

Kenesha: Unknown origin and meaning.

Kenndale: Unknown origin and meaning.

Kennedi: Unknown origin and meaning.

Kennetha: Unknown origin and meaning.

Kensey: Unknown origin and meaning. Alternative
spelling: Kenzie.

Kenta: Unknown origin and meaning.

Kenyetta: Latin origin. Means: one who is innocent,
harmless.

Kerrie: Gaelic/Anglo-Saxon origin. Means: dark one,
dark haired, ruler. Alternative spelling: Kerri.

Kerrigan: Unknown origin and meaning.

Kesey: Unknown origin and meaning.

Kesia: Unknown origin. Means: a favorite. Alternative
spelling: Kessiah.

Ketina: Aramaic origin. Means: a small child. Ethnic
background: Jewish.

Ketura: Hebrew origin. Means: incense, an offering.
Alternative spelling: Keturah.

Kevina: Unknown origin and meaning.

Keyla: Hebrew origin. Means: victorious one.

Keziah: Hebrew origin. Means: cassia plant,
cinnamonlike.

Khaalidah: Arabic origin. Means: permanent.

Khadijha: Arabic origin. Means: premature.
Alternative spelling: Khadijah.

Khalan: Unknown origin and meaning.

Khawlah: Arabic origin. Means: deer.

Kianna: Irish origin. Means: archaic one. Alternative
spellings: Keyania, Keyanna, Keyona, Keyonana,
Keyonne, Kiana, Keana, Keanna, Keeanna, Keiyyana,
Keionne.

Kiara: Irish origin. Means: black. 47th most popular
girl's name of the '90s. Alternative spellings: Kiera,
Kierra, Kierre.

Kiki: Unknown origin and meaning.

Kila: Unknown origin. Means: attractive. Alternative
spelling: Kilah.

Kileen: Unknown origin and meaning.

Kimberly: Anglo-Saxon origin. Means: of the royal
fortress, diamonds. 47th most popular girl's name of
the '90s. Alternative spellings and nicknames: Kimmy,
Kim, Kimmie, Kimberley, Kimberlee, Kymberleigh,
Kymberly, Kymberlyn.

Kineta: Greek origin. Means: one who is active, lively.

Kiona: Native American origin. Means: of the brown
hills.

Kira: Latin/Slavic origin. Means: bright light, sun.
Alternative spellings: Khira, Kiran.

Kirima: Unknown origin. Means: hill.

Kirin: Unknown origin and meaning. Ethnic
background: Swedish.

Kirstin: Latin/Scottish origin. Means: Christ bearer,
Christian. Ethnic background: Norwegian. Alternative

spellings and nicknames: Kirsti, Kirsten, Kirstie, Kirsty, Kristin, Kristina, Krysta, Kierstin, Kiersten, Kersten, Kerstin, Kerstyn, Kirsty, Kjerstin, Kyrsten, Kyrstyna, Keirston.

Kisha: Unknown origin and meaning.

Kissiah: Unknown origin. Means: favorite.

Kita: Unknown origin. Means: north.

Kitra: Hebrew origin. Means: a crown.

Kitty: Greek/Anglo-Saxon origin. Means: pure, innocent.

Klara: Latin/various origin. Means: famous one. Ethnic backgrounds: German, Hungarian. Alternative spelling: Klaartje.

Klarissa: Latin origin. Means: famous one, clear.

Klavdia: Latin/Slavic origin. Means: a lame one. Ethnic background: Russian.

Klementine: Latin/Germanic origin. Means: calm, merciful one.

Koa: Unknown origin. Means: princess. Alternative spelling: Koah.

Koleanna: Latin/Old English origin. Means: a cabbage farmer, a coal miner.

Kora: Greek origin. Means: a pure maiden. Alternative spellings and nicknames: Coriss, Corissa, Korie, Kore, Corry, Corabel, Corabella, Corena, Coretta, Corie, Corene, Koren, Corinne, Correne, Corrie, Corrina, Corrine, Corinna, Corina, Cora, Corabelle, Corella, Corette, Corey, Cori, Kori.

Korina: Greek origin. Means: a pure maiden. Alternative spellings: Koren, Korinne, Korryn, Koryn, Korie, Kore, Kori.

Kornelia: Latin origin. Means: a horn. Ethnic background: German.

Koty: Unknown origin and meaning.

Kourtney: Latin/French origin. Means: from the king's court.

Krayna: Germanic origin. Means: a crown. Ethnic background: Jewish. Alternative spellings: Kreina, Kruna, Kryna.

Kreindel: Germanic origin. Means: a crown. Ethnic background: Jewish. Alternative spelling: Krindel.

Kris: Unknown origin and meaning.

Krislyn: Unknown origin and meaning. Alternative spelling: Krislynn.

Krisol: Unknown origin and meaning.

Krista: Greek origin. Means: Christ bearer. 49th most popular girl's name of the '90s. Alternative spellings: Krysta, Kriszta.

Kristal: Greek origin. Means: Christ bearer.

Kristalen: Unknown origin and meaning. Alternative spelling: Krystalynn.

Kristaney: Unknown origin and meaning.

Kristen: Greek/Danish origin. Means: Christ bearer. Ethnic background: Norwegian. 26th most popular girl's name of the '90s. Alternative spellings: Khrystin, Kristin, Kristyn.

Kristina: Greek/Swedish origin. Means: Christ bearer. Alternative spellings: Kristena, Krisztina, Krystina, Krystyna.

Kristine: Greek/Danish origin. Means: Christ bearer. Ethnic background: Norwegian.

Kristy: Greek/Anglo-Saxon origin. Means: Christ bearer. Alternative spellings: Kristi, Kristie.

Kriten: Unknown origin and meaning.

Krystal: Greek origin. Means: brilliant, cut glass. Alternative spelling: Khrystal.

Kumiko: Japanese origin. Unknown meaning.

Kumiwa: African origin. Means: one who is brave.

Kvetoslava: Czech origin. Means: a flower. Alternative spelling: Kveta.

Kya: Unknown origin and meaning.

Kyla: Hebrew/Gaelic origin. Means: crowned in victory, attractive. Alternative spellings and nicknames: Kyl, Kilah, Kylah, Kila, Kylila.

Kyleen: Unknown origin and meaning.

Kylie: Aboriginal Australian origin. Means: a boomerang. 47th most popular girl's name of the '90s. Alternative spellings: Kylee, Kyleigh, Kyli.

Kyna: Gaelic origin. Means: one with intelligence.

Kyra: Latin origin. Means: brilliant light.

Kyrene: Greek origin. Means: God, the lord.

Kyshana: Unknown origin and meaning.

La Reina: Spanish origin. Means: queen.

La Roux: French origin. Means: red-haired.

Laa'iqah: Arabic origin. Means: worthy.

Labana: Hebrew origin. Means: white. Alternative spellings: Labanna, Labannah.

Lacey: Greek/French origin. Means: cheerful, a braid. Alternative spellings: Lacie, Lacy.

Ladda: Slavic origin. Means: lovely.

Ladonna: Unknown origin. Means: lady.

LaDrew: Unknown origin and meaning.

Lagenia: Unknown origin and meaning.

Laila: Hebrew/Norse/Egyptian origin. Means: night, born at night. Ethnic background: African. Alternative spelling: Layla.

Lais: Greek origin. Means: adored one. Alternative spellings: Laise, Laius.

Laisha: Unknown origin and meaning.

Lakayla: Unknown origin and meaning.

Lakeesha: Unknown origin and meaning. Alternative spellings: Lakeisha, Lekisha.

Laken: Unknown origin and meaning.

Lala: Greek/Slavic origin. Means: one who chatters, a tulip. Alternative spelling: Lally.

Lalage: Greek origin. Means: one who chatters. Alternative spelling: Lallage.

Lalita: Sanskrit origin. Means: one who is straightforward, pleasing. Alternative spellings: Lalitta, Lalittah.

LaMesha: Unknown origin and meaning.

Lana: Greek origin. Means: light, beautiful, fair. Alternative spellings and nicknames: Lanny, Lanna, Lanette.

Landa: Spanish origin. Means: crown of Mary.

Landrada: Unknown origin and meaning. Ethnic background: Hispanic.

Lanette: Anglo-Saxon origin. Means: a lane. Alternative spelling: Lane.

Lange: Germanic/Anglo-Saxon origin. Means: one who is tall, long.

Lania: Unknown origin and meaning. Alternative spelling: Lanea.

Lantha: Unknown origin. Means: dark.

Laquitta: Unknown origin and meaning.

Lara: Latin origin. Means: famous one, a laurel.

Lareeka: Unknown origin and meaning.

Larentia: Latin origin. Means: to foster, to nurse.

Larina: Latin origin. Means: girl, a seagull. Alternative spellings: Larine, Lareena, Lareina, Larena, Larianna, Laraine, Larine.

Larissa: Greek origin. Means: happy one, cheerful. Ethnic background: Russian. Alternative spellings and nicknames: Lacey, Lissa, Larisa, Laresa.

Lark: Old English origin. Means: skylark, sweet singing bird.

Lasca: Arabic origin. Means: a weary soldier.

LaShawnda: Unknown origin and meaning. Alternative spellings: LaShaunda, LaShawn, Lashawnteona.

LaShay: Unknown origin and meaning.

Lassie: Anglo-Saxon origin. Means: a girl.

LaTasha: Unknown origin and meaning.

Latavia: Unknown origin and meaning.

Latea: Unknown origin. Means: ivory. Alternative spelling: Lataia.

Lateefah: Arabic/Egyptian origin. Means: humor, one who is gentle. Alternative spelling: LaTeefa.

Lati: Unknown origin. Means: elevated.

Latona: Latin origin. Means: mother, of Latium. Alternative spellings: Latonia, Latoniah, Lattonia, Latonya, Latia.

Latricia: Unknown origin and meaning. Alternative spellings: Lateshia, Latishia, Latrice.

Laura: Latin origin. Means: victoriously crowned with laurels. Ethnic backgrounds: English/Welsh, Italian. 37th most popular girl's name of the '90s. Alternative spellings and nicknames: Loree, Loreen, Lorelie, Lorine, Laur, Lorie, Lorinda, Loralie, Laureen, Laure, Laurey, Laurice, Lolly, Lari, Lorette, Loren, Lorena, Lorene, Lorenza, Lori, Loretta, Laraine, Laurel, Lora, Lauren, Laurena, Laurene, Lauretta, Laurette, Lauri.

Laurel: Latin origin. Means: victoriously crowned with laurels, a little laurel. Alternative spellings and nicknames: Laurelia, Lorrie, Laurie, Lori, Lorelle, Loreal, Lorrelle.

Lauren: Latin origin. Means: victoriously crowned with laurels. 15th most popular girl's name of the '90s. Alternative spellings: Laureen, Laurene, Laurena.

Lauretta: Latin origin. Means: victoriously crowned with laurels. Alternative spellings: Laurette, Lorerta, Lorita.

Laurie: Latin/Anglo-Saxon origin. Means: victoriously crowned with laurels. Alternative spellings: Lauri, Lori.

Lavella: Latin origin. Means: cleansing. Alternative spelling: Lavelle.

Lavender: Latin origin. Means: a plant livid in color.

Laverne: Latin/French origin. Means: springlike, alder. Alternative spellings and nicknames: Laverna, La Verne, Vern, Verna, Verne, Lavergne.

Lavinia: Latin origin. Means: purified. Ethnic backgrounds: Hispanic, Italian. Alternative spellings and nicknames: Vinni, Vinnie, Vin, Lavinie, Lavena, Leah, Vinia, Vina, Lavina, Vinny.

Layne: Anglo-Saxon origin. Means: from the long meadow. Alternative spelling: Layna.

Lazine: Unknown origin and meaning.

Leah: Hebrew origin. Means: to be weary. Ethnic backgrounds: Italian, German, Hispanic. 42nd most popular girl's name of the '90s. Alternative spellings: Leeah, Lea, Leeha.

Leandra: Greek origin. Means: lioness, a woman.

Leanne: French origin. Means: to wrap around. Ethnic backgrounds: English/Welsh. Alternative spellings: Leann, Lean, LeeAnn, Leana, Leanna, Leeanna, Le'Ana.

Lebechi: African origin. Means: to watch God.

Lectra: Unknown origin. Means: brilliant.

Leda: Greek origin. Means: lady, mother of the twins. Ethnic background: Hispanic. Alternative spelling: Leta.

Leeara: Unknown origin and meaning.

Legra: Unknown origin. Means: cheerful.

Leila: Persian origin. Means: beauty, a dark complexion. Ethnic backgrounds: Irish, Hispanic. Alternative spellings and nicknames: Lela, Lelah, Leilah, Leela, Leilia, Lila, Lelia, Lee, Layla.

Leilani: Hawaiian origin. Means: child, heavenly flower.

Lelia: Greek/Teutonic origin. Means: one who is well spoken, loyal. Alternative spellings: Leala, Lealie, Leya, Laalia, Lael, Lail.

Lelith: Unknown origin. Means: wife.

Lema: Unknown origin. Means: girl. Alternative spelling: Lemiah.

Lemmuela: Hebrew origin. Means: dedicated to God. Alternative spellings: Lemuela, Lemuelah.

Lena: Greek/Hebrew origin. Means: light, allures, a dwelling place. Ethnic backgrounds: Norwegian, Swedish. Alternative spellings and nicknames: Lenette, Lina.

Leneta: Latin origin. Means: mild. Alternative spellings: Lenita, Lenis.

Lenka: Unknown origin and meaning. Ethnic background: Czech. Alternative spelling: Lenke.

Lenore: Greek origin. Means: light. Alternative spellings: Leonore, Lenora, Leonora, Lora, Leonor.

Lenqwanda: Unknown origin and meaning.

Leola: Greek/Teutonic origin. Means: dear one, lion.

Popularity Contest

When my cousin was born 10 years ago, my aunt and uncle named her Madison because they thought it was unusual. Now it's one of the most popular names, and it drives them crazy. Give your kids a name because you like it, not because it's nontrendy, trendy, or whatever. There is no telling what will be popular in the next 10 years.

~ **Michael S.,**
New York, New York

Leoma: Anglo-Saxon origin. Means: light, brightness, radiance.

Leona: Latin/Germanic origin. Means: a lion, one who is as bold as a lion. Alternative spellings and nicknames: Leonelle, Lonie, Leonia, Leoni, Leoine, Lenny, Lennie, Leonie, Leola, Lee, Leone.

Leontine: Greek/French origin. Means: a lion, one who is as bold as a lion. Alternative spellings and nicknames: Lontyne, Leontyne, Leonteen, Leontina.

Leopoldine: Teutonic origin. Means: one who is popular with the people. Alternative spellings and nicknames: Leopolda, Leopoldina, Leopoldeen, Leopola.

Leota: Teutonic origin. Means: woman of the people. Alternative spelling: Leoda.

Leotie: Native American origin. Means: a prairie flower.

Lesil: Unknown origin and meaning.

Lesly: Gaelic/Celtic origin. Means: of the holly garden, of the gray fort. Alternative spelling: Leslyane.

Letha: Greek origin. Means: forgetfulness. Alternative spellings: Leitha, Leithia, Leta, Lethia, Leda.

Letitia: Latin origin. Means: gladness, joyous. Ethnic background: Hispanic. Alternative spellings and nicknames: Leetice, Lettice, Lettie, Letty, Loutitia, Tisha, Letti, Letisha, Tish, Leticia, Laetitia, Leta, Letta, Lethia, Leda, Letizia.

Levanna: Latin origin. Means: bright moon, to raise. Alternative spellings: Levana, Levania.

Leveda: Latin origin. Means: purified. Alternative spellings: Lavetta, Lavette, Laveda.

Levina: Old English origin. Means: lightning flash, fast.

Levinicha: Unknown origin and meaning.

Levona: Hebrew origin. Means: frankincense, white.

Lewanna: Hebrew origin. Means: beaming, the moon.

Lexa: Unknown origin and meaning. Alternative spellings: Lexi, Lexy, Lexus.

Lexine: Greek origin. Means: defender of mankind.

Lia: Hebrew origin. Means: one who brings good news. Ethnic background: Italian.

Liana: Latin/French origin. Means: climbing vine, a bond. Ethnic background: Russian. Alternative spellings: Liane, Lianna, Leana, Lianne, LiAnn, LYanna.

Lianda: Unknown origin and meaning.

Liatrice: Unknown origin. Means: joyful. Alternative spellings: Liatris, Leatri, Leatrice.

Liba: Hebrew origin. Means: beloved one. Alternative spellings: Libe, Libka, Libya.

Libby: Hebrew origin. Means: dedicated to God. Alternative spellings and nicknames: Lib, Libbey, Libbie.

Libna: Unknown origin. Means: fair. Alternative spellings: Libnah, Lebna.

Lidia: Greek/Polish origin. Means: beloved of all, from Lydia. Ethnic backgrounds: Italian, Hungarian. Alternative spellings: Lida, Lidda, Liddie, Lidiya.

Lieke: Unknown origin and meaning. Ethnic background: Dutch.

Lien: Unknown origin and meaning.

Lieselotte: Hebrew/Germanic origin. Means: God's oath. Ethnic background: German.

Lilac: Persian origin. Means: lilac flower, blue color. Ethnic background: Jewish. Alternative spelling: Lilach.

Lilia: Greek/Persian origin. Means: a lily or lilac, blue-colored flower. Ethnic background: Hispanic. Alternative spellings: Lila, Lilah.

Liliane: Greek/Latin origin. Means: a lily or lilac, blue-colored flower. Ethnic background: French. Alternative spellings: Liliana, Lilianna, Lilliana.

Lilis: Greek origin. Means: lily flower. Alternative spellings: Lilias, Lillis.

Lilith: Semitic/Arabic origin. Means: wife, female demon, of the night. Alternative spellings and nicknames: Lil, Lilly, Lily, Lillith, Lilis, Lillis.

Lillemor: Unknown origin and meaning. Ethnic background: Swedish.

Lillian: Greek origin. Means: lily flower, purity. Alternative spellings and nicknames: Lilla, Lis, Lilyan, Lillie, Lillias, Lilas, Liuka, Lilles, Lillah, Lelah, Lilias, Lela, Lil, Lili, Lilian, Lily, Lilly, Lilli, Lilia, Leila, Lila, Lilah, Liliane, Lylian.

Lilly: Greek/Latin origin. Means: a lily or lilac, blue-colored flower. Ethnic background: German. Alternative spellings: Lilli, Lily.

Lilo: Hawaiian origin. Means: one who is generous. Ethnic background: Jewish.

Lilybelle: Latin origin. Means: beautiful lily. Alternative spellings and nicknames: Lilybell, Lillibel, Lilles, Lillias, Lillah, Lillie, Lilla, Lela, Lilyan, Lilias, Lelah, Lil, Lilas, Lili, Lilian, Lilli, Lilly, Lily, Lilybel, Lila, Lilah, Lilia, Liliana, Liliane, Lelia.

Lilybet: Hebrew/Greek origin. Means: God's oath, graceful.

Limbe: Unknown origin. Means: joyfulness. Ethnic background: African.

Linares: Unknown origin and meaning.

Linda: Latin/Germanic origin. Means: beautiful, gentle, soft. Ethnic backgrounds: Greek, Irish, English/Welsh. Alternative spellings and nicknames: Lindie, Lind, Lindi, Lindy, Lynda, Lynd.

Line: Norse origin. Means: distinguished one. Ethnic background: Norwegian. Alternative spelling: Lene.

Linette: Celtic/French origin. Means: one who is attractive, graceful, flax. Alternative spellings and nicknames: Lynnette, Lynnet, Linnetta, Linnet, Linn, Linet, Lynette, Netta, Lynn, Lanette, Linnette.

Linnea: Norse origin. Means: a lime-tree. Alternative spelling: Lynnea.

Linor: Unknown origin and meaning.

Linsey: Old English origin. Means: from the island of pools and linden trees. Ethnic backgrounds: English/Welsh. Alternative spellings: Lindsiann, Lindsie, Linzee, Lyndsey.

Liora: Hebrew origin. Means: the light is mine.

Lisa: Hebrew origin. Means: God's oath. Ethnic backgrounds: English/Welsh, Irish. Alternative spellings and nicknames: Lissy, Lizzie, Lisetta, Leesa, Lise, Liza, Lisette, Leeza, Lesa.

Lisbeth: Hebrew origin. Means: consecrated to God. Ethnic background: German. Alternative spellings and nicknames: Lisabette, Lisabet, Lisabetta, Lizabeth, Lyzbeth, Lisbet.

Lise-Marie: Hebrew origin. Means: God's oath, sorrow. Ethnic background: Swiss.

Lisette: Hebrew/French origin. Means: God's oath. Alternative spellings: Lissette, Lizette.

Lisha: Unknown origin. Means: of darkness. Alternative spelling: Lishe.

Lissa: Greek/Old English origin. Means: one who is sweet like honey, a bee.

Lissle: Unknown origin and meaning.

Litha: Unknown origin. Means: girl, truthful. Alternative spelling: Lithea.

Litta: Latin origin. Means: joyful one. Alternative spelling: Lita.

Liv: Norse origin. Means: defense, protection, life. Ethnic background: Norwegian.

Livei: Unknown origin and meaning.

Livia: Latin origin. Means: the olive, olive branch. Alternative spellings and nicknames: Livvie, Liv.

Liya: Unknown origin and meaning.

Liz: Unknown origin and meaning.

Lizabeth: Hebrew origin. Means: God's oath. Alternative spelling: Liesbeth.

Llisel: Hebrew/Germanic origin. Means: God's oath.

Lodah: Unknown origin. Means: lovely.

Lodema: Anglo-Saxon origin. Means: a guide.

Lodie: Unknown origin. Means: one who is prosperous.

Loes: Teutonic origin. Means: one who is holy. Ethnic background: Dutch.

Logen: Unknown origin and meaning.

Lois: Greek/Teutonic origin. Means: famed, good, one who is desired. Alternative spelling: Loise.

Lola: Latin/Spanish origin. Means: cloud, strong, womanly. Alternative spellings and nicknames: Loleta, Lolette, Lulita, Lolita.

Lolita: Latin/Spanish origin. Means: strong, womanly.

Loma: Unknown origin. Means: peaceful one.

Lomasi: Native American origin. Means: a beautiful flower.

Lona: Old English origin. Means: alone, solitary. Alternative spelling: Lonna.

Loni: Old English/Hawaiian origin. Means: alone, the sky. Alternative spelling: Lani.

Lonneke: Unknown origin and meaning. Ethnic background: Dutch.

Lopez: Unknown origin and meaning.

Lorelei: Teutonic origin. Means: a siren, alluring. Alternative spellings and nicknames: Lurleen, Lorilee, Loralei, Lurlene, Lurlina, Lura, Lurette, Lurine.

Lorena: Latin origin. Means: crowned with a laurel, victory. Alternative spellings: Lorna, Lorene, Lorenza, Laurencia, Laurentia, Laurien, Laurieann.

Loretta: Anglo-Saxon origin. Means: pure, small one. Alternative spelling: Lorette.

Loris: Latin origin. Means: victoriously crowned with laurels.

Lorna: Latin/Anglo-Saxon origin. Means: victoriously crowned with laurels, alone.

Lorola: Unknown origin. Means: family. Alternative spellings: Lorolla, Lorollas.

Lorraine: Latin/Teutonic origin. Means: a seagull, famous warrior. Ethnic background: Irish. Alternative spellings and nicknames: Lorain, Lorrayne, Laraine, Loraine, Lori.

Lotta: Germanic origin. Means: womanly. Ethnic background: Swedish. Alternative spellings: Lottie, Lotje.

Lotus: Greek origin. Means: water lily, a lotus flower, forgetfulness.

Louella: Germanic origin. Means: famous warrior.

Louise: Germanic origin. Means: famous warrior, a beautiful vision. Ethnic backgrounds: English/Welsh, French. Alternative spellings and nicknames: Lulie, Lu, Ludovika, Ludwiga, Lulita, Aloise, Loyce, Lou, Louisette, Lolita, Luise, Louisa, Lulu, Luisa, Lola, Alison, Aloisa, Aloisia, Aloysia, Eloisa, Eloise, Heloise, Lisette, Lois, Loise, Allison, Luiza.

Lourdes: Spanish origin. Means: in reference to vision of Mary. Ethnic background: Hispanic.

Love: Old English origin. Means: strong tender affection.

Lovilla: Unknown origin. Means: all.

Luana: Teutonic/Hawaiian origin. Means: a graceful maiden of battle, at leisure. Alternative spellings and nicknames: Luwana, Luwanna, Luann, Lu, Louanne, Lewanna, Luane, Lou, Louanna.

Luay: Unknown origin and meaning.

Luba: Germanic origin. Means: lover, beloved one. Ethnic background: Jewish. Alternative spellings: Lubba, Lubbi, Lubeh.

Lucerna: Latin origin. Means: a circle of light. Alternative spelling: Lucerne.

Lucette: Latin origin. Means: bringer of light. Alternative spellings: Lucida, Lucita.

Lucia: Latin origin. Means: bringer of light. Ethnic backgrounds: German, Irish, Hungarian, Hispanic, Italian. Alternative spellings: Luciana, Lucienne, Lucyna.

Lucierne: Latin origin. Means: bringer of light.

Lucille: Latin/French origin. Means: bringer of light, daybreak. Alternative spellings and nicknames: Lucilla, Lucy, Lucila, Lucile.

Lucinda: Latin origin. Means: bringer of light. Ethnic backgrounds: English/Welsh, Hispanic. Nicknames: Cindy, Lucky.

Lucretia: Latin origin. Means: bringer of light, a reward. Alternative spellings and nicknames: Lucrece, Lucrezia, Lucy, Lucrecia.

Lucy: Latin origin. Means: bringer of light, daybreak. Ethnic backgrounds: Scottish, Irish, English/Welsh. Alternative spellings and nicknames: Lucine, Lucina, Lucilla, Luce, Lu, Lulu, Luz, Lucita, Lucinda, Lucille, Lucienne, Lucie, Lucida, Luciana, Lucia, Lucette, Lucile.

Ludmila: Slavic origin. Means: lover of the people, the tribe's grace. Ethnic background: Hispanic. Alternative spellings and nicknames: Lodmilla, Ludmilla, Lyudmila, Ludie, Ludovika.

Luella: Latin/Old English origin. Means: one who makes atonement, elf. Alternative spellings and nicknames: Lula, Lu, Luelle, Ludella, Ella, Lulu, Louella, Loella, Lou.

Lulu: Germanic origin. Means: precious, famous warrior. Ethnic background: African.

Luna: Latin origin. Means: moonlight.

Lunetta: Latin/Italian origin. Means: moonlight, little moon. Alternative spellings and nicknames: Luna, Lunna.

Lupita: Latin/Spanish origin. Means: a wolf. Alternative spelling: Lupe.

Lurline: Teutonic origin. Means: an alluring temptress. Alternative spellings and nicknames: Lurlene, Lura, Lurette, Lurleen, Lurine.

Luvena: Teutonic origin. Means: little loved one.

Luz: Latin/Spanish origin. Means: reference to our lady of light. Ethnic background: Hispanic.

Lyan: Unknown origin and meaning.

Lydia: Greek origin. Means: a cultured woman from Lydia. Ethnic background: German. Alternative spellings and nicknames: Liddy, Lidia, Lydie.

Lyric: Unknown origin and meaning.

Lyris: Greek origin. Means: the lyre or harp, musical. Alternative spellings and nicknames: Lyra, Liris.

Lysandra: Greek origin. Means: liberator of mankind. Nickname: Sandra.

Lyubov: Slavic origin. Means: love, love for the people. Ethnic background: Russian.

m **Maacah:** Unknown origin and meaning.
Maaike: Unknown origin and meaning. Ethnic background: Dutch.

Maajidah: Arabic origin. Means: glorious one.

Maariyah: Arabic origin. Means: one with a light complexion.

Maartje: Unknown origin and meaning. Ethnic background: Dutch.

Mab: Celtic/Irish origin. Means: joy, filled with happiness. Alternative spellings and nicknames: Mave, Mavis, Meave.

Mabel: Latin/French origin. Means: lovable, amiable. Alternative spellings and nicknames: Mabelle, Mable, Maible, Belle, Mab, Mae, Maybelle, Amabel.

Machiko: Japanese origin. Unknown meaning.

Machute: Unknown origin. Means: a girl.

Macie: Greek/Scottish origin. Means: a pearl. Alternative spellings: Macee, Macey, Maci.

Maclain: Scottish origin. Means: from John's servant. Alternative spelling: MacLaine.

Maddie: Hebrew/Anglo-Saxon origin. Means: a high tower, one who is elevated. Alternative spellings and nicknames: Mayde, Maidy, Maidena, Magd, Maidene, Maidie, Maydena, Mayda, Magda, Maidel.

Madea: Unknown origin. Means: a sorceress.

Madelief: Unknown origin and meaning. Ethnic background: Dutch.

Madeline: Hebrew origin. Means: elevated. 26th most popular girl's name of the '90s. Alternative spellings and nicknames: Madelena, Madelina, Madid, Madlin, Mady, Dalenna, Lenna, Madel, Linn, Lynne, Mada, Maddi, Maddy, Madeleine, Madelene, Madella, Madelaine, Madelle, Madlen, Magda, Magdala, Madelon, Lynn, Madge, Lena, Madalena, Madalyn, Maddalena, Maddie, Lina, Madelline, Madelon, Madelyn, Madilyn, Madlen, Madeliene, Madelin, Madalaine, Madalena, Madalyn, Maddalena.

Madella: Hebrew origin. Means: a high tower, one who is elevated. Alternative spelling: Madelle.

Madge: Greek/Old English origin. Means: a pearl.

Madglaine: Unknown origin and meaning.

Madiah: Unknown origin. Means: adorn. Alternative spellings: Madai, Madi.

Madigan: Unknown origin and meaning.

Madisen: Teutonic/Anglo-Saxon origin. Means: of the mighty warrior, brave one. Alternative spellings: Madison, Maddison, Maddyson, Madisson, Madyson.

Madora: Greek origin. Means: a ruler.

Madra: Latin origin. Means: mother.

Madria: Unknown origin and meaning.

Mae: Hebrew/Anglo-Saxon origin. Means: one who is bitter, spring, youth.

Maelee: Unknown origin and meaning.

Magda: Hebrew/Germanic origin. Means: a high tower, one who is elevated, a maiden. Ethnic background: German.

Magdalena: Hebrew/Latin origin. Means: a high tower, one who is elevated. Ethnic backgrounds: Polish, Swedish. Alternative spellings: Magdala, Magdalen, Magdalene, Magdelyna, Magdolna.

Magena: Hebrew origin. Means: a covering, protection. Alternative spelling: Magina.

Magenta: Italian origin. Means: not available or unknown.

Maggie: Greek/Scottish origin. Means: a pearl.

Magna: Latin/Norse origin. Means: great, large, strong.

Magnificent: Unknown origin and meaning.

Magnilda: Norse/Teutonic origin. Means: fierce battle maiden.

Magnolia: French origin. Means: girl, flower of the magnolia tree. Nicknames: Mag, Nolie, Maggie, Nola.

Mahalia: Hebrew origin. Means: marrow, tenderness. Alternative spellings: Malialia, Mehala, Mahalah, Mahla, Mahala.

Mahmoodah: Arabic origin. Means: one who is praiseworthy.

Mahogany: Unknown origin. Means: a tropical tree. Alternative spelling: Maghogany.

Mai: Unknown origin and meaning.

Maia: Greek/Latin origin. Means: great, mother, nurse. Alternative spellings: Maya, Maiah, Mya.

Hollywood Kids

Celebrities set so many of our trends—what movies we see, what we wear, how we wear our hair. Why should it be any different for what we name our kids? Take a look at the names celebrities are giving their offspring and see if you think any of them are an up-and-coming naming sensation.

Kirstie Alley and Parker Stevenson	William True and Lily Price
Pamela Anderson and Tommy Lee	Brandon
Ellen Barkin and Gabriel Byrne	Jack and Romy
Kim Basinger and Alec Baldwin	Irelan Eliesse
Annette Bening and Warren Beatty	Kathlyn
Valerie Bertinelli and Eddie Van Halen	Wolfgang
Lisa Bonet and Lenny Kravitz	Zoe
Edie Brickell and Paul Simon	Adrian Edward
David Byrne	Malu Valentine
Shaun Cassidy	Caitlin and John
Phoebe Cates and Kevin Kline	Owen Joseph
Neneh Cherry	Tyson (girl)
Pam Dawber and Mark Harmon	Sean and Ty Christian
Robert DeNiro	Raphael Eugene
Danny DeVito and Rhea Perlman	Grace, Jacob, and Lucie
Neil Diamond	Marjorie, Elyn, Jesse, and Micah
Julius Erving	Jazmin
Andy Garcia	Dominick (girl), Allessandra, and Daniela
Jill Goodacre and Harry Connick, Jr.	Georgie Tatom
Whitney Houston and Bobby Brown	Bobbi Kristina
Billy Idol	Willem Wolfe
Janet Jones and Wayne Gretzky	Paulina and Ty
Wynonna Judd	Elijah and Pauline Grace
Diane Keaton	Dexter (girl)
Nicole Kidman and Tom Cruise	Isabella and Connor
Courtney Love and Kurt Cobain	Frances Bean

Bette Midler	Sophie Frederica
Demi Moore and Bruce Willis	Rumer Glenn, Scout LaRue, and Tallulah Belle
Bill Murray	Homer
Willie Nelson	Lucas Autry
Nick Nolte	Brawley King
Tatum O'Neal and John McEnroe	Kevin John and Sean Timothy
Rosie O'Donnell	Parker Jaren (P.J.)
Phylicia and Ahmad Rashad	Condola Phylea
Isabella Rosselini	Elettra-Ingrid
Susan Sarandon and Tim Robbins	Jack Henry and Miles Guthrie Tomalin
Patty Scialfa and Bruce Springsteen	Evan James and Jessica Rae
Kyra Sedgwick and Kevin Bacon	Travis Sedg and Sosie Ruth
Cybill Shepherd	Clementine, Molly Ariel, and Cyrus Zacariah
Patti Smith	Jesse Paris (girl) and Jackson Frederick
Will Smith	Trey
Darryl Strawberry	Diamond Nicole
Charlene Tilton	Cherish
John Turturro	Amadeo
Tracey Ullman	Mabel Ellen
Billy Dee Williams	Corey Dee (boy) and Hanako (girl)
Henry Winkler	Max and Zoe Emily
Stevie Wonder	Aisha (girl), Keita (boy), and Mumtaz (boy)
Robin Wright and Sean Penn	Dylan (girl) and Hopper Jack
Frank Zappa	Moon Unit, Ahmet Emuukha Rodan, Dweezil, and Diva

Maida: Anglo-Saxon origin. Means: a maiden, battle maiden. Alternative spellings: Maidel, Maidie, Mayda, Maydena.

Maika: Unknown origin and meaning.

Mailand: Anglo-Saxon origin. Means: plains, the meadowland.

Maille: Greek/Irish origin. Means: a pearl.

Mailyn: Unknown origin and meaning.

Maire: Hebrew/Gaelic origin. Means: with bitterness. Ethnic background: Irish.

Mairead: Greek/Irish origin. Means: a pearl.

Maise: Greek/Scottish origin. Means: a pearl, highest. Alternative spellings: Maice, Maisie, Mayce.

Maisha: Unknown origin and meaning.

Maite: Unknown origin and meaning.

Maitlynne: Unknown origin and meaning.

Maj: Greek/Swedish origin. Means: a pearl.

Majesta: Latin origin. Means: with dignity, power, majestic.

Makahla: Hawaiian origin. Means: myrtle. Alternative spelling: Makayla, Makaila, Macaela, Macayla.

Makena: Unknown origin and meaning. Alternative spelling: Makenna.

Makensie: Scottish origin. Means: of the handsome man.

Malaiah: Unknown origin and meaning.

Malak: Unknown origin and meaning.

Malan: Unknown origin and meaning.

Malbina: Hebrew origin. Means: to whiten, embarrass.

Malca: Hebrew/Teutonic origin. Means: active, industrious. Alternative spelling: Malcah.

Maleana: Hebrew/Germanic origin. Means: a high tower, one who is elevated. Alternative spellings: Malena, Malina, Mallina.

Malesha: Unknown origin and meaning. Alternative spelling: Malisha.

Malgorzata: Greek/Polish origin. Means: a pearl.

Mali: Hebrew/Welsh origin. Means: bitter, high.

Malia: Unknown origin and meaning.

Malinda: Greek origin. Means: gentle, sweet. Alternative spellings and nicknames: Mally, Mallie, Lindy, Melina, Malinde, Malena, Malina.

Malita: Unknown origin. Means: flower. Alternative spelling: Malleta.

Malkiya: Hebrew origin. Means: God is my king.

Mallorie: Latin/French origin. Means: one who is unlucky, ill omened. Alternative spelling: Mallory.

Malva: Greek origin. Means: soft, slender. Alternative spellings: Melba, Melva.

Malvia: Unknown origin. Means: a flower. Alternative spelling: Malvie.

Malvina: Celtic/Gaelic origin. Means: a friendly chief, polished. Ethnic background: Hispanic. Alternative spellings and nicknames: Melvie, Mal, Malva, Malvie, Mel, Melva, Melvine, Malwine.

Malynia: Unknown origin and meaning.

Mamie: Unknown origin and meaning.

Mandelyn: Unknown origin and meaning.

Mandy: Unknown origin and meaning.

Manisha: Unknown origin and meaning.

Manuela: Hebrew/Spanish origin. Means: God is with us. Ethnic background: Italian. Alternative spellings and nicknames: Manella, Mannuela, Emanuela, Ela.

"Will My Child Be Teased Because of This Name?"

Teasability is defined as the propensity of a name to invite ridicule from one's peers. It is otherwise known as *dorkiness*. And it may be the thing parents dread most as they are deciding what to name their children. Whether the name they want is old-fashioned (à la Eunice) or unusual (à la Spooky), a frequent question on the Parent Soup message boards is "Will my child be teased because of his (or her) name?" Since no one can predict the future, that question is impossible to answer. But read on for some consoling thoughts from our members.

Manya: Hebrew/Slavic origin. Means: bitter.

Mara: Hebrew origin. Means: bitter. Ethnic background: Italian. Alternative spellings: Marah, Mari, Maralina, Maraline.

Maragret: Unknown origin and meaning.

Marala: Unknown origin. Means: the sea.

Maralina: Hebrew origin. Means: bitter. Alternative spelling: Maraline.

Maranda: Unknown origin and meaning.

Maranela: Unknown origin and meaning. Ethnic background: Hispanic.

Maranne: Unknown origin and meaning.

Marcasia: Unknown origin and meaning.

Marcella: Latin origin. Means: brave, warlike, hammer. Ethnic background: Italian. Alternative spellings and nicknames: Marquita, Marcellie, Marcile, Marcy, Marcille, Marcie, Marcellina, Marcela, Marcelle, Marcellene, Marcelline.

Marcia: Latin origin. Means: of Mars, warrior. Ethnic background: Hispanic. Alternative spellings and nicknames: Marchita, Marquita, Marcelia, Marcy, Marita, Marsha, Marcile, Marcie, Marcella, Marcille.

Marciana: Latin origin. Means: warlike, hammer. Ethnic background: Hispanic.

Marelda: Teutonic origin. Means: famous maiden of battle. Alternative spellings: Marilda, Mareld, Marolda.

Marella: Teutonic origin. Means: bitter, Mary. Alternative spellings: Marela, Marelya, Maria.

Maren: Hebrew/Latin origin. Means: one who is bitter, of the sea. Ethnic background: Norwegian.

Marga: Greek/Anglo-Saxon origin. Means: the pearl. Ethnic backgrounds: German, Dutch.

Margaret: Greek origin. Means: a pearl. Ethnic backgrounds: English/Welsh, Scottish. 49th most popular girl's name of the '90s. Alternative spellings and nicknames: Maiga, Margarethe, Margarette, Marge, Maggy, Margalo, Maggi, Mag, Grethel, Grethal, Gretel, Gredel, Margarete, Marga, Margarita, Margery, Margareta, Margaretha, Margherita, Maisie, Margaretta, Madge, Gretta, Grete, Gretchen, Gretal, Greta, Daisy, Maggie, Margarete.

Margie: Greek origin. Means: a pearl. Ethnic background: Dutch.

Margila: Greek origin. Means: a pearl. Ethnic background: Hispanic.

Margot: Greek/French origin. Means: a pearl. Alternative spelling: Margo.

Margrit: Greek/Germanic origin. Means: a pearl. Alternative spellings: Margit, Margret, Margriet.

Marguerite: Greek/French origin. Means: a pearl, a daisy.

Maria: Egyptian/Hebrew origin. Means: the perfect one, bitter, with sorrow. Ethnic backgrounds: Greek, Czech, Polish, Italian, Russian, Hungarian, Hispanic, Swiss, Swedish. 48th most popular girl's name of the '90s. Alternative spelling: Mariya.

Mariam: Unknown origin and meaning. Alternative spelling: Maryam.

Marianne: Hebrew/French origin. Means: bitter, gracious. Ethnic background: Swedish. Alternative spellings: Mariaina, Marian, Mariana, Mariann, Marianna.

Mariarosa: Spanish origin. Means: lady, exalted one, bitterness, star of sea. Ethnic background: Italian.

Mariasa: Hebrew/Spanish origin. Means: bitter, gracious, rebellious.

Mariasha: Egyptian/Hebrew origin. Means: the perfect one, bitter, with sorrow.

Mariatt: Unknown origin and meaning.

Maribel: Hebrew/Latin origin. Means: one who is bitter, beautiful. Alternative spellings: Maribelle, Marybelle, Marabelle, Marabel, Marabella.

Marie: Hebrew/French origin. Means: the perfect one, bitter, with sorrow. Ethnic backgrounds: Swedish, Italian, French, Norwegian. Alternative spelling: Mari.

Marieileen: Hebrew/Greek origin. Means: bitter, light.

Mariela: Hebrew origin. Means: the perfect one, bitter, with sorrow. Alternative spellings: Mariella, Mariel, Marielle.

Mariena: Unknown origin and meaning.

Marie-Theres: Hebrew/Greek origin. Means: bitter, to reap. Ethnic background: Swiss.

Marietta: Hebrew origin. Means: bitter. Alternative spelling: Mariette.

Marigold: Old English origin. Means: the golden marigold flower. Alternative spellings: Marigolde, Marigolda, Marigolde.

Marika: Hebrew/Polish origin. Means: the perfect one, bitter, with sorrow. Ethnic background: German. Alternative spelling: Marieke.

Mariko: Japanese origin. Unknown meaning.

Marilla: Hebrew origin. Means: bitter, a flower.

Marilu: Hebrew/Germanic origin. Means: bitter, famous one.

Marilyn: Hebrew/Anglo-Saxon origin. Means: bitter, of Mary.

Marina: Latin origin. Means: of the sea. Ethnic backgrounds: Russian, Italian. Alternative spellings and nicknames: Marna, Marne, Marni, Marnie, Marinita, Marinna, Mareena, Rina, Rena.

Mariorie: Greek origin. Means: a pearl. Alternative spelling: Mariory.

Mariposa: Unknown origin and meaning.

Marisela: Unknown origin and meaning. Alternative spelling: Mariselle.

Marisol: Hebrew/Spanish origin. Means: the perfect one, bitter. Ethnic background: Hispanic.

Marissa: Hebrew/Latin origin. Means: the perfect one, bitter, sea star. Ethnic backgrounds: Hispanic, Italian. 27th most popular girl's name of the '90s. Alternative spellings: Marisa, Maresa, Myrissa, Marysia, Marrisa.

Marit: Aramaic origin. Means: a lady. Ethnic backgrounds: Norwegian, Swedish.

Marita: Hebrew/Swedish origin. Means: the perfect one, bitter. Alternative spellings: Maretta, Marette.

Marium: Hebrew/Arabic origin. Means: the perfect one, bitter.

Marjon: Greek origin. Means: a pearl. Ethnic background: Dutch.

Marjorie: Greek origin. Means: a pearl. Alternative spellings and nicknames: Mag, Marjy, Marjory, Margy, Marge, Margory, Marjie, Margo, Margie, Margery, Maggie, Marje.

Markeisa: Unknown origin and meaning.

Markel: Unknown origin and meaning.

Markie: Unknown origin and meaning. Alternative spelling: Marki.

Marla: Hebrew/Anglo-Saxon origin. Means: bitter, reference to Mary.

Marlaina: Unknown origin and meaning.

Marlee: Anglo-Saxon origin. Means: of the marshy meadow.

Marlene: Hebrew origin. Means: a high tower, one who is elevated. Ethnic background: French. Alternative spellings and nicknames: Marline, Marlyn, Marna, Marleene, Marla, Marlena, Marleen, Marleyna.

Marliese: Hebrew origin. Means: a high tower, one who is elevated. Ethnic background: German. Alternative spelling: Marlies.

Marloes: Unknown origin and meaning. Ethnic background: Dutch.

Marmara: Greek origin. Means: one who is radiant, shining.

Marney: Latin origin. Means: of the sea.

Maro: Latin origin. Means: of the sea. Alternative spelling: Marola.

Marolda: Unknown origin. Means: famous one.

Marona: Hebrew origin. Means: flock of sheep.

Marquala: Unknown origin and meaning.

Marquetta: Unknown origin and meaning.

Marra: Unknown origin. Means: the sea. Alternative spellings: Marras, Marris.

Marrigje: Unknown origin and meaning. Ethnic background: Dutch.

Marsha: Latin origin. Means: of Mars, warrior.

Marshay: Unknown origin and meaning.

Martella: Latin origin. Means: warlike.

Martha: Aramaic origin. Means: a lady, ruler of the home. Alternative spellings and nicknames: Pattie, Matty, Matti, Mart, Martie, Marti, Marth, Martelle, Martynne, Marty, Martita, Patty, Patti, Patsy, Pat, Mattie, Marta, Martina, Marthena, Marthe, Martella, Marhtha, Marthana, Marte.

Marties: Latin origin. Means: warlike. Ethnic background: Dutch.

Martina: Latin origin. Means: one who is warlike. Alternative spellings and nicknames: Teena, Martie, Marti, Marteena, Marty, Martine, Marta, Tina.

Martinique: French origin. Means: warlike.

"Will My Child Be Teased?"

When using unusual names, you have to walk a fine line. On the one hand there are unusual names that set people apart and make them sound interesting and creative (such as Willow and Raven). On the other hand there are some unusual names that just sound silly (such as Moon Unit and Dweezil).

~ Robin G.,
Chula Vista, California

Martita: Aramaic origin. Means: a lady, ruler of the home.

Marvel: Latin origin. Means: to wonder, a miracle. Alternative spellings and nicknames: Marva, Marvella, Marvelle, Marvela.

Mary: Hebrew origin. Means: the perfect one, bitter, with sorrow. Ethnic backgrounds: English/Welsh, Irish, Scottish. 30th most popular girl's name of the '90s. Alternative spellings and nicknames: Maridel, Mame, Mair, Manette, Mairi, Marea, Mall, Manon, Marianna, Marella, Maretta, Mari, Maria, Marian, Maren, Marianne, Marice, Marie, Mariam, Malia, Mae, Mamie, Manya, Mara, Marabel, Maraline, Maire.

Maryann: Hebrew/Greek origin. Means: the perfect one, bitter, with sorrow, grace. Alternative spelling: Maryanne.

Mary-Alice: Unknown origin and meaning.

Maryhelen: Unknown origin and meaning.

MaryLynn: Hebrew/Anglo-Saxon origin. Means: the perfect one, bitter, from the water.

Maryse: Unknown origin and meaning. Ethnic background: French. Alternative spelling: Marysette.

Maryvonne: Hebrew/French origin. Means: bitter, an archer.

Marzena: Latin/Polish origin. Means: warlike.

Masada: Hebrew origin. Means: foundation, support.

Masami: Japanese origin. Unknown meaning.

Matge: Greek origin. Means: a pearl.

Matilda: Germanic origin. Means: one who is fierce in battle. Ethnic background: Irish. Alternative spellings and nicknames: Matty, Tilly, Tillie, Maud, Matti, Mat, Mathilde, Tilda, Maude, Maitilde, Matilde, Mathilda, Matelda, Matylda, Mattie.

Matina: Arabic origin. Means: one who is strong. Ethnic background: Greek.

Matrona: Latin/Slavic origin. Means: a lady, noblewoman.

Matronna: Latin origin. Means: one who is brave.

Mattea: Hebrew origin. Means: a gift of God. Alternative spellings: Matthea, Matthia, Mathia, Mathea, Matta, Mattia.

Maude: Germanic origin. Means: one who is brave in battle. Alternative spellings and nicknames: Maudie, Maud.

Maura: Hebrew/Celtic origin. Means: bitter, the perfect one, dark. Ethnic background: Irish. Alternative spelling: Mora.

Mauralia: Hebrew/Celtic origin. Means: bitter, the perfect one, dark. Alternative spellings: Maurilia, Maurilla.

Maureen: Latin/Hebrew origin. Means: bitter, dark, little. Ethnic background: Irish. Alternative spellings and nicknames: Morena, Maurizia, Maurise, Maurene, Maura, Moira, Moria, Moreen, Mora, Maurita, Maurine.

Mauretta: Hebrew/Latin origin. Means: bitter, dark, little. Alternative spellings: Maurita, Moretta, Morita.

Mauri: Latin/Hebrew origin. Means: bitter, dark, little. Alternative spelling: Mori.

Maurisha: Latin/Hebrew origin. Means: bitter, dark, little.

Mauve: French origin. Means: mallow, blue-purple.

"Will My Child Be Teased?"

Ignore those who warn of grammar school teasing. If your son is confident in who he is, it is unlikely that a somewhat unconventional name will cause him much grief. If children want to pick on your child, they will no matter what his name. Unfortunately, when it comes to teasing, children can be quite creative.

~ Janice H., Brooklyn, New York

Mavis: Celtic/French origin. Means: joy, the song thrush.

Mawasi: African origin. Means: in God's hands.

Maxantia: Unknown origin and meaning. Alternative spelling: Maxentia.

Maxia: Unknown origin and meaning.

Maxima: Latin/Hebrew origin. Means: the greatest, a miracle worker. Alternative spellings: Maxama, Maxma.

Maxine: Latin origin. Means: the greatest. Alternative spellings and nicknames: Maxie, Maxime, Maxy, Max, Maxi.

May: Latin/various origin. Means: great, bitter, a pearl, kinswoman. Alternative spellings and nicknames: Maye, Mae, Maia, Maya.

Maybelle: Latin/French origin. Means: great, bitter, a pearl, kinswoman, beautiful.

Mayme: Hebrew origin. Means: bitter.

Mayra: Unknown origin and meaning.

Mayson: Unknown origin and meaning.

Mayumi: Japanese origin. Unknown meaning.

McKayla: Unknown origin and meaning.

McKenzie: Gaelic/Scottish origin. Means: of the fair man. Alternative spelling: McKenzi.

Meagan: Greek origin. Means: a pearl. 49th most popular girl's name of the '90s. Alternative spelling: Meaghan.

Meara: Gaelic/Irish origin. Means: one who is happy, mirth.

Meave: Latin/Irish origin. Means: a purple flower, joyous, intoxicating. Alternative spelling: Maeve.

Mechtild: Germanic origin. Means: one who is fierce in battle. Ethnic background: German. Alternative spelling: Mechteld.

Meda: Unknown origin. Means: justice, scholar, sea.

Medarda: Germanic origin. Means: a brave scholar. Alternative spelling: Medaras.

Medea: Greek origin. Means: to reflect, ponder. Alternative spellings: Madora, Meda, Media, Medora, Medeah, Media.

Medor: Unknown origin. Means: patient.

Medora: Greek origin. Means: to reflect, ponder, ruling.

Meg: Greek origin. Means: a pearl, great, strong. Ethnic backgrounds: English/Welsh.

Megan: Greek/Welsh origin. Means: a pearl, great, strong. 7th most popular girl's name of the '90s. Alternative spellings and nicknames: Meggie, Meggy, Meggi, Meg, Meghan, Maeghan, Maeghann, Magen.

Meghana: Unknown origin and meaning.

Megumi: Unknown origin and meaning.

Mehitabel: Hebrew origin. Means: favored by God. Alternative spellings and nicknames: Hitty, Mehitable, Metabel, Hetty, Mehetabel, Mehitabelle.

Mehla: Unknown origin. Means: melodious.

Meike: Unknown origin and meaning. Ethnic background: Dutch. Alternative spelling: Meika.

Meingolda: Unknown origin. Means: a flower. Alternative spelling: Meingoldas.

Meisha: Unknown origin and meaning.

Melanie: Greek origin. Means: black, dark. Ethnic backgrounds: French, English/Welsh. Alternative spellings and nicknames: Mellie, Melli, Milena, Melly, Melan, Melloney, Mela, Melina, Melany, Melania, Malan, Mel, Melany, Melanija, Melaine.

Melantha: Greek origin. Means: black, dark flower. Alternative spelling: Melentha.

Melba: Greek/Celtic origin. Means: soft, slender, handmaiden. Alternative spellings: Melbia, Malva, Melva.

Melda: Unknown origin. Means: wistful.

Melesha: Unknown origin and meaning. Alternative spelling: Melayshia.

Melina: Greek origin. Means: gentle, soft, yellow. Alternative spellings: Melana, Melena.

Melinda: Greek origin. Means: gentle, soft, kind. Ethnic background: Hispanic. Alternative spellings and nicknames: Melinde, Mandy, Malinde, Malinda, Lynda, Lindy, Linda, Malina, Melynda.

Melis: Unknown origin and meaning.

Melisenda: Greek/Spanish origin. Means: a bee, industrious, sweet. Alternative spelling: Melisande.

Melissa: Greek origin. Means: a bee, industrious. 40th most popular girl's name of the '90s. Alternative spellings and nicknames: Millisent, Melli, Mellie, Melly, Melosa, Millie, Milly, Misha, Missie, Missy, Melissent, Melisent, Melise, Melessa, Melesa, Malissa, Mellicent, Milicent, Melitta, Melisse, Millicent, Lisa, Melisenda, Melisande, Melisa, Melicent, Mel, Lissa, Melita, Mellisa, Mylisa, Malyssa.

Melita: Greek origin. Means: a bee, industrious, sweet. Alternative spelling: Melitta.

Mella: Unknown origin. Means: home lover, wistful.

Melody: Greek origin. Means: beautiful song, a melody. Alternative spellings and nicknames: Lodie, Mel, Melodie.

Melone: Greek origin. Means: sweet, industrious.

Melva: Celtic/Irish origin. Means: a ruler, a handmaiden.

Menjuiwe: Unknown origin. Means: trustworthy.

Meraree: Hebrew origin. Means: bitter. Alternative spellings: Merari, Mera.

Mercedes: Latin origin. Means: ransom, out of mercy. Ethnic background: Hispanic. Alternative spellings and nicknames: Merci, Mercy.

Mercia: Latin/Anglo-Saxon origin. Means: a reward, the coming kingdom. Alternative spelling: Mercie.

Mercy: Latin origin. Means: with compassion, merciful, a reward. Alternative spelling: Mercedes.

Merdyce: Unknown origin. Means: famous one.

Merete: Unknown origin and meaning. Ethnic background: Norwegian.

Merideth: Unknown origin and meaning.

Merlina: Latin/French origin. Means: a blackbird. Alternative spelling: Merline.

Merras: Latin origin. Means: of the sea. Alternative spelling: Meris.

Merry: Anglo-Saxon origin. Means: one who is mirthful, pleasant, happy. Alternative spellings and nicknames: Merrili, Marrilee, Meri, Merie, Merrie, Merrielle, Merrilee.

Mertice: Anglo-Saxon origin. Means: one who is famous.

Mertie: Unknown origin. Means: a myrtle tree.

Meryl: Latin origin. Means: a blackbird. Ethnic backgrounds: Jewish, Dutch. Alternative spellings: Merl, Merel, Maryl, Merola.

Messina: Latin origin. Means: the middle child.

Meta: Latin/Greek origin. Means: an ambitious goal, a pearl. Ethnic backgrounds: Swiss, German. Alternative spellings: Mettah, Eta, Meda.

Metis: Greek origin. Means: one with resourcefulness.

Mia: Latin/Hebrew origin. Means: belonging to me, bitter.

Miai: Unknown origin and meaning.

Miasia: Unknown origin and meaning.

Michaela: Hebrew/Anglo-Saxon origin. Means: Who is like God? 16th most popular girl's name of the '90s. Alternative spellings: Micaela, Micayla, Michaele,

Michaelsa, Michala, Mickala, Mikaela, Mikayla, Mekayla, Mekela, Mikaylah, Mikayle, Mikhayla, Michaella, Michaila.

Michaelsa: Hebrew origin. Means: Who is like God?

Micheline: Hebrew origin. Means: Who is like God? Ethnic background: French. Alternative spellings: Michaelina, Michalina.

Michelle: Hebrew/French origin. Means: Who is like God? Ethnic backgrounds: English/Welsh, Swiss, French, Italian. 38th most popular girl's name of the '90s. Alternative spellings and nicknames: Miguelita, Miguela, Midge, Micky, Mickie, Miquela, Micki, Michaeline, Michelina, Michella, Michela, Michele, Michell, Michla, Mikaela, Mickey, Micaela, Micheline, Mia, Michaela, Michaele, Michaelina, Michaella, Michel.

Michi: Japanese origin. Means: righteous.

Michiko: Unknown origin. Means: righteous.

Mieke: Hebrew/Dutch origin. Means: bitter, the perfect one.

Migdalia: Hebrew origin. Means: a fortress, a tower. Ethnic background: Hispanic.

Mignon: French origin. Means: she who is dainty, darling, delicate. Alternative spellings: Mignonne, Mignonnette, Mignonette.

Mignonette: French origin. Means: she who is dainty, darling, delicate.

MiKenna: Unknown origin and meaning.

Mikera: Unknown origin and meaning. Alternative spelling: Mikear.

Miki: Hebrew origin. Means: Who is like God?

Mikia: Unknown origin and meaning.

Mila: Slavic origin. Means: loved by all, hardworking.

Milada: Czech origin. Means: my love.

Milagros: Unknown origin and meaning.

Milda: Unknown origin. Means: battle.

Mildred: Old English origin. Means: a gentle counselor, one with mild power. Alternative spellings

and nicknames: Mil, Millie, Milly, Milli. Alternative spelling: Mildrid.

Milla: Latin origin. Means: one who is ambitious.

Millda: Old English origin. Means: mild.

Millicent: Teutonic origin. Means: strong, industrious. Alternative spellings and nicknames: Missie, Missy, Milzie, Milly, Millisent, Millie, Milli, Milissent, Melly, Mellisent, Mellie, Mil, Milicent, Lissa, Mellicent, Melicent, Melisenda, Melisande, Melicent, Mel.

Milos: Czech/Irish origin. Means: one who is pleasant, a servant. Ethnic background: Czech.

Mimba: Unknown origin. Means: born.

Mimi: Hebrew/Italian origin. Means: bitter, dove.

Mina: Germanic origin. Means: a resolute protector, love.

Mindy: Germanic origin. Means: love. Alternative spelling: Mindi.

Mine: Germanic/Japanese origin. Means: a resolute protector.

Minerva: Greek origin. Means: with wisdom, thinking. Nicknames: Minny, Min, Minette, Minnie.

Minette: Germanic/French origin. Means: a resolute protector, love. Alternative spelling: Minetta.

Minna: Teutonic origin. Means: remembrance, love, loving. Ethnic background: German. Alternative spellings and nicknames: Minny, Minnette, Minne, Mini, Min, Mindy, Minnie, Minetta, Minda, Mina, Minette.

Minta: Greek origin. Means: of the mint plant. Alternative spelling: Mintha.

Mira: Latin/Hebrew origin. Means: famous one, wonderful. Ethnic background: Russian. Alternative spellings: Mireille, Mirella, Mirelle, Mirilla, Myra, Mirra, Myrilla.

Mirabel: Latin origin. Means: very beautiful, wondrous. Alternative spellings and nicknames: Mirabelle, Mirabell, Mirabella, Bell, Mira, Belle.

Miracle: Unknown origin and meaning.

Miranda: Latin origin. Means: admirable beauty, one who is wonderful. Ethnic backgrounds: Hispanic,

Italian. 36th most popular girl's name of the '90s. Alternative spellings and nicknames: Mira, Myra, Randie, Randy, Meranda.

Miranti: Unknown origin and meaning.

Mireille: French origin. Means: to admire, a miracle. Alternative spellings: Mirella, Mirelle, Mirilla.

Mirel: Hebrew origin. Means: bitter, the perfect one. Alternative spellings: Miri, Miril.

Miriah: Unknown origin and meaning.

Miriam: Hebrew origin. Means: bitter, rebellious. Nicknames: Mimi, Minnie, Mitzi.

Mirian: Unknown origin and meaning.

Mirth: Old English origin. Means: one who rejoices with glee. Alternative spelling: Merthe.

Miru: Unknown origin. Means: harmony.

Misty: Old English origin. Means: of a thin fog, obscured.

Mita: Unknown origin. Means: industrious.

Mitzi: Hebrew/Germanic origin. Means: bitter, the perfect one. Alternative spelling: Mitzie.

Miyoshi: Japanese origin. Unknown meaning.

Mma: Unknown origin. Means: beauty. Ethnic background: African.

Modesty: Latin origin. Means: one who is moderate, restrained. Alternative spellings and nicknames: Desta, Modeste, Deste, Modesta, Modestia, Modestine.

Moina: Celtic origin. Means: one who is gentle, noble. Ethnic background: Irish. Alternative spelling: Moyna.

Moira: Hebrew/various origin. Means: bitter, of great merit, soft. Ethnic background: Irish. Alternative spellings: Moyna, Moyra, Oira, Moya, Moina, Moir.

Molly: Hebrew/Irish origin. Means: bitter one. 46th most popular girl's name of the '90s. Alternative spellings: Mollee, Mollie.

Mona: Greek/Irish origin. Means: a noble one, solitary, soft. Ethnic backgrounds: Norwegian, Swedish. Alternative spellings: Moina, Moir, Moya, Moyna, Moyra, Oira.

Monae: Unknown origin and meaning. Alternative spelling: Monaye.

Moneta: Latin origin. Means: one who admonishes. Alternative spelling: Monetta.

Monica: Greek/Latin origin. Means: admonition, a wise counselor. Ethnic backgrounds: Swedish, Italian, Swedish, Swiss, Polish, German, Norwegian, French. 45th most popular girl's name of the '90s. Alternative spellings and nicknames: Monca, Mona, Monique, Monik, Monika.

Monisha: Unknown origin and meaning.

Monserrat: Catalan origin. Means: of the jagged hill.

Monya: Unknown origin and meaning.

Morasha: Hebrew origin. Means: legacy, an inheritance.

Morette: Unknown origin. Means: darling.

Morgana: Celtic/Welsh origin. Means: a sea dweller, born by the sea. Alternative spellings: Morgan, Morganne.

Moria: Hebrew origin. Means: God is my teacher. Alternative spelling: Moriya.

Morna: Celtic/Irish origin. Means: one who is dearly beloved, gentle.

Morrin: Irish origin. Means: long-haired one.

Morrisa: Latin origin. Means: dark-skinned, Moorish.

"Will My Child Be Teased?"

Remember, Ted Bundy had a pretty normal name. What happened there could not have been much worse than if they had given him a "teasable" name!

~ Teresita I.,
Stamford, Connecticut

Morta: Latin origin. Means: of the still water, a marsh. Ethnic background: Hispanic.

Mosa: Unknown origin. Means: a fountain. Alternative spellings: Moza, Mozza.

Moselle: Hebrew origin. Means: saved from the water. Alternative spelling: Mozelle.

Mosera: Unknown origin. Means: bound. Alternative spellings: Mosira, Mosora.

Moya: Celtic origin. Means: one who is great, exceptional.

Moyra: Hebrew origin. Means: God is my teacher. Alternative spelling: Muriah.

Mudiwa: Unknown origin. Means: beloved. Ethnic background: African.

Mumtaaz: Arabic origin. Means: distinguished.

Muna: Arabic origin. Means: a wish, desire.

Muriel: Celtic/Arabic origin. Means: of the bright sea, myrrh. Ethnic background: French. Alternative spellings and nicknames: Meriel, Mur, Murielle, Merial, Murial.

Musetta: French origin. Means: a quiet tender song. Alternative spelling: Musette.

Musidora: Greek origin. Means: gift of the Muses.

Myeasha: Unknown origin and meaning.

Myliah: Unknown origin and meaning.

Myra: Greek/Latin origin. Means: abundance, beloved, wonderful. Alternative spellings: Mira, Mirilla, Myrilla.

Myrie: Unknown origin and meaning.

Myrka: Unknown origin and meaning.

Myrlene: Latin origin. Means: a blackbird.

Myrna: Celtic/Gaelic origin. Means: gentle one, beloved. Ethnic background: Irish. Alternative spellings: Moina, Morna, Mirna, Merna, Moyna, Merna.

Myrtle: Greek origin. Means: myrtle tree, victory. Alternative spellings and nicknames: Myrta, Myrtis, Myrtilla, Myrtie, Myrtia, Myrt, Mertle, Merta, Mirtle, Mertice, Myrtice, Myrtla.

n

Naadirah: Arabic origin. Means: choice, rare.

Naafi'ah: Arabic origin. Means: beneficial.

Naajidah: Arabic origin. Means: courageous.

Naamana: Hebrew origin. Means: agreeable, pleasant.

Naarah: Unknown origin. Means: a girl.

Naashom: Unknown origin. Means: enchantress.

Nabal: Unknown origin. Means: comic. Alternative spellings: Nabala, Nabalas.

Nabeha: Unknown origin and meaning.

Nabulungi: African origin. Means: beautiful one.

Nadaba: Unknown origin. Means: democratic. Alternative spelling: Nadabas.

Nadia: Slavic origin. Means: one with hope. Ethnic background: Italian. Alternative spellings: Nada, Nadda, Nadezda, Nadezhda.

Nadine: Slavic/French origin. Means: charming, one with hope.

Nadire: Unknown origin and meaning.

Nafula: African origin. Means: born during rainy season.

Naghmah: Arabic origin. Means: song.

Nahama: Hebrew origin. Means: one who comforts. Alternative spelling: Nahamas.

Nahtanha: Unknown origin. Means: corn.

Naida: Greek/Latin origin. Means: to flow, a nymph.

Naimah: Unknown origin and meaning.

Nairobi: Unknown origin and meaning.

Najia: Unknown origin and meaning.

Najmah: Arabic origin. Means: a star.

Nakedria: Unknown origin and meaning.

Nakeya: Unknown origin and meaning. Alternative spellings: Nakia, Nakiyah.

Nakisa: Unknown origin and meaning.

Nalani: Hawaiian origin. Means: the calm of the heavens.

Naliaka: African origin. Means: a wedding.

Nalyssa: Unknown origin and meaning.

Namono: African origin. Means: the younger of twins.

Nan: Hebrew origin. Means: graceful one.

Nancy: Hebrew origin. Means: graceful one.

Nanette: Hebrew origin. Means: graceful one. Ethnic background: German. Alternative spelling: Nanetta.

Nanna: Hebrew origin. Means: graceful one. Ethnic background: Norwegian.

Naomi: Hebrew origin. Means: pleasant one. Alternative spelling: Naoma.

Napea: Latin origin. Means: turnip-shaped, a nymph.

Narah: Celtic/Gaelic origin. Means: one who is happy, to be near. Alternative spelling: Narra.

Narda: Latin/Persian origin. Means: fragrantly anointed one.

Nariko: Unknown origin. Means: a loud thunder peal. Alternative spelling: Nari.

Narjis: Arabic origin. Means: flower.

Nashom: Unknown origin. Means: enchantress. Alternative spelling: Nashoma.

Nasia: Hebrew origin. Means: a miracle of God. Alternative spellings: Nasja, Nasha, Nasya.

Nasreen: Arabic origin. Means: white flower.

Nastassja: Greek/Slavic origin. Means: resurrection.

Nata: Sanskrit/Polish origin. Means: to dance, hope.

Natalie: Latin/French origin. Means: born on Christmas, to be born. Ethnic backgrounds: English/Welsh, Russian, Italian, Polish. 38th most popular girl's name of the '90s. Alternative spelling: Nathalie, Natala, Natalee, Natalia, Nataline, Natalya, Nathalia.

Natari: Unknown origin and meaning.

Natasha: Greek/Slavic origin. Means: born on Christmas, to be born. Alternative spellings: Natashja, Natasia, Natacha.

Natasiana: Unknown origin and meaning.

Nathania: Hebrew origin. Means: God has given. Alternative spelling: Nathene.

Natia: Polish origin. Means: with hope.

Natori: Unknown origin and meaning.

Navea: Unknown origin and meaning.

Nayo: African origin. Means: we have joy.

Nazeela: Unknown origin and meaning.

Neala: Celtic/Gaelic origin. Means: a champion, a noted warrior. Alternative spellings: Nealah, Neila.

Nebula: Latin origin. Means: cloudy, misty.

Necha: Hebrew origin. Means: comfort. Alternative spellings: Neche, Nechuma.

Neda: Slavic/Anglo-Saxon origin. Means: born on Sunday, a guardian. Alternative spellings: Nedda, Neddy, Nedi.

Nediva: Hebrew origin. Means: one who is noble, generous.

Nedra: Unknown origin. Means: guardian, lower. Alternative spelling: Nedrah.

Neela: Unknown origin. Means: princess. Alternative spelling: Niela.

Neeltje: Unknown origin and meaning. Ethnic background: Dutch.

Neely: Unknown origin and meaning.

Neema: Egyptian origin. Means: born during prosperous times. Ethnic background: African.

Neeoma: Unknown origin. Means: light.

Neesa: Unknown origin and meaning.

Nelda: Old English origin. Means: of the alder tree. Alternative spelling: Nellda.

Nelia: Latin/Spanish origin. Means: a horn, yellowish. Alternative spelling: Nela.

Nella: Greek origin. Means: light, a horn.

Nelleke: Latin/Dutch origin. Means: a horn. Ethnic background: Dutch.

Nelli: Greek/Celtic origin. Means: echo, light, a champion. Ethnic backgrounds: German, Russian.

Nellwyn: Anglo-Saxon origin. Means: a bright friend.

Neneh: Unknown origin and meaning.

Neom: Greek origin. Means: light, the new moon. Alternative spellings: Neoma, Neomah.

Nereida: Greek/Latin origin. Means: a sea nymph. Ethnic background: Hispanic.

Nerine: Greek origin. Means: a sea nymph. Alternative spellings and nicknames: Nerina, Nerir, Nerice, Nerissa, Nereen, Nerin, Neri, Nerita.

Nessa: Greek/Scottish origin. Means: pure, from the headland. Ethnic background: Irish. Alternative spellings: Nessi, Neisa, Neysa, Neysha.

Netra: Unknown origin and meaning.

Netta: Hebrew origin. Means: a plant or shrub. Ethnic background: Scottish. Alternative spelling: Netia.

Netzel: Unknown origin and meaning.

Neva: Old English/Spanish origin. Means: extreme, new, snowy.

Nevara: Latin origin. Means: snowy, snow. Ethnic background: Hispanic. Alternative spellings: Neveda, Navada.

Nia: Unknown origin and meaning.

Niabi: Native American origin. Means: a fawn.

Niamh: Irish origin. Means: one who is bright, beautiful.

Nichelle: Greek origin. Means: victory. Alternative spelling: Nichele.

Nicole: Greek/French origin. Means: the people's victory. Ethnic backgrounds: Irish, Italian, English/Welsh. 20th most popular girl's name of the '90s. Alternative spellings and nicknames: Nicoletta, Nikola, Nickit, Nicki, Coleitt, Nikki, Nicol, Nicolina, Niki, Nicola, Nicoline, Nicky, Nichola, Nichole, Nicholle, Nikell, Cosette, Cosetta, Nicolette, Nikole.

Nicolette: Greek/French origin. Means: the people's victory. Ethnic background: Dutch. Alternative spelling: Nicollette.

Nicoline: Greek origin. Means: the people's victory. Alternative spelling: Nicolina.

Nicoya: Unknown origin and meaning.

Niene: Unknown origin and meaning. Ethnic background: Dutch. Alternative spelling: Nienke.

Nieves: Spanish origin. Means: of the snows, in honor of Mary. Ethnic background: Hispanic.

Nike: Greek origin. Means: victory. Alternative spelling: Nika.

Niketa: Greek/Slavic origin. Means: one who is unconquerable.

Nikha: Unknown origin and meaning.

Niki: Greek/Latin origin. Means: the people's victory, of the Lord. Alternative spelling: Nikkie.

Nila: Latin origin. Means: lady, from the Nile. Alternative spelling: Nilla.

Nina: Hebrew/Spanish origin. Means: grace, a well-loved daughter. Ethnic backgrounds: English/Welsh, Norwegian, Russian. Alternative spellings: Ninon, Ninetta, Ninette, Neena.

Ninetta: Slavic/French origin. Means: grace, a well loved daughter. Alternative spelling: Ninette.

Nipha: Unknown origin. Means: snowflake.

Nisha: Unknown origin and meaning.

Nissa: Norse origin. Means: a friendly elf. Alternative spellings and nicknames: Nisse, Missy, Nissit, Nisa.

Nita: Hebrew origin. Means: one who supplants, bear. Alternative spelling: Netta.

Nix: Unknown origin. Means: hairy one.

Nixie: Germanic origin. Means: little water sprite.

Niyra: Unknown origin and meaning.

Nkeyvah: Unknown origin and meaning.

Nobuhle: Unknown origin. Means: beauty. Ethnic background: African.

Noelani: Hawaiian origin. Means: beautiful one from heaven.

Noelle: Latin/French origin. Means: birthday, born near Christmas.

Noemi: Hebrew/Italian origin. Means: beautiful one, pleasant. Ethnic background: Hispanic. Alternative spelling: Noami.

Nofiya: Hebrew origin. Means: beautiful landscape.

Noha: Unknown origin and meaning.

Nokomis: Native American origin. Means: grandmother.

Nola: Latin/Celtic origin. Means: a small bell, famous, noble lady. Alternative spelling: Nolana.

Nolita: Latin origin. Means: an unwilling lady, the olive. Alternative spellings and nicknames: Noli, Lita, Nolitta, Noleta, Noletta.

Noma: Latin/Hawaiian origin. Means: fate, the standard, peaceful.

Nona: Latin origin. Means: the ninth-born child. Alternative spellings and nicknames: Nonette, Nonie, Nonna.

Noortje: Unknown origin and meaning. Ethnic background: Dutch.

Nora: Greek/Latin origin. Means: grace, honor, light. Ethnic backgrounds: Irish, Norwegian, Italian. Alternative spellings and nicknames: Norrie, Norah.

Norberta: Teutonic origin. Means: bright hero of the North.

Nordica: Teutonic origin. Means: from the North.

Noreen: Greek/Irish origin. Means: grace, honor, light.

Norma: Latin origin. Means: the pattern, model or standard. Ethnic background: Italian. Alternative spellings and nicknames: Normie, Normi, Noreen.

Noshavyah: Unknown origin and meaning.

Notburga: Germanic origin. Means: one in want.

Novella: Latin origin. Means: new, unusual, a short novel. Ethnic background: Italian.

Novia: Latin origin. Means: new, a newcomer, a young person. Alternative spellings: Nova, Novah.

Nuala: Gaelic/Irish origin. Means: fair shouldered.

Numidia: Egyptian origin. Means: nomad from Nubia.

Nuncia: Greek origin. Means: one who announces the good news. Alternative spelling: Nunciata.

Nunu: Unknown origin and meaning. Ethnic background: Russian.

Nwaoma: African origin. Means: a beautiful child.

Nydia: Latin origin. Means: the nest, a refuge. Alternative spelling: Nidia.

Nysa: Greek origin. Means: toward the goal, the beginning point. Alternative spelling: Nyssa.

Nyshae: Unknown origin and meaning. Alternative spelling: Nyisha.

Nyx: Greek origin. Means: of night.

O

Obala: Unknown origin. Means: hills. Alternative spellings: Oballa, Obla, Obola.

Obelia: Greek origin. Means: a pointed pillar, needle. Alternative spellings: Obellia, Obel, Obiel.

Obioma: African origin. Means: one who is kindhearted.

Octavia: Latin origin. Means: the eighth born. Alternative spellings and nicknames: Tave, Tavi, Tavia, Tavie, Tavy, Octave, Octavie, Ottavia.

Oda: Germanic/Norse origin. Means: small-pointed spear.

Odeen: Unknown origin. Means: intelligent one.

Odelia: Greek/Teutonic origin. Means: little melody, wealthy, rich, one with harmony. Alternative spellings and nicknames: Othelia, Odile, Odila, Odetta, Uta,

Othilia, Otha, Odilia, Odette, Odella, Odele, Odel, Odelette, Odelet, Odell, Odelinda, Ottilie.

Odelinda: Teutonic/Anglo-Saxon origin. Means: little wealthy one.

Odera: Hebrew origin. Means: a plough.

Odessa: Greek origin. Means: a journey, voyager. Ethnic background: Hispanic.

Odette: Germanic/French origin. Means: little melody, pointed spear. Alternative spellings: Odet, Odetta.

Odine: Unknown origin. Means: intelligent one.

Ofira: Hebrew origin. Means: gold.

Ohara: Unknown origin. Means: bright.

Oira: Unknown origin. Means: great.

Okei: Japanese origin. Unknown meaning.

Olaug: Norse origin. Means: one who resembles an ancestor.

Oleia: Unknown origin and meaning.

Olenka: Slavic origin. Means: one who is holy.

Olenta: Unknown origin. Means: pretty.

Oleta: Old English origin. Means: winged one.

Oletta: Unknown origin. Means: mysterious. Alternative spelling: Olette.

Olga: Norse/Russian origin. Means: consecrated, holy. Ethnic backgrounds: Italian, German, Czech, Hungarian. Alternative spellings: Olia, Elga, Olive, Olva, Olivia, Helga, Olenka.

Oliana: Latin origin. Means: oleander, a fragrant flower.

Olida: Latin origin. Means: a fragrant flower.

Olinda: Latin origin. Means: fragrant, sweet smelling. Ethnic background: Hispanic.

Oline: Unknown origin and meaning. Ethnic background: Norwegian.

Olivia: Latin origin. Means: branch, peace, of the olive tree. Ethnic backgrounds: Italian, Irish. 25th most popular girl's name of the '90s. Alternative spellings and nicknames: Oliviah, Oliviana, Livi, Olly, Nollie,

Names of the Weird

Everyone knows of someone with a truly bizarre name, such as Pepper Roni, Royal Payne, Jack Frost. These names can make you wonder if the parents giving them were just exercising their (somewhat warped) sense of humor or if they had some sort of grudge against their newborn babies. Before you commit to the birth certificate, please make sure the name you're giving has a legacy that you yourself would be proud to carry!

Ollie, Olli, Olia, Livy, Livvy, Livvie, Liva, Livvi, Noll, Olva, Olivia, Olivette, Olga, Nolita, Nolana, Nola, Livia.

Olubayo: African origin. Means: greatest joy.

Olva: Norse origin. Means: one who is holy.

Olympia: Greek origin. Means: heavenly, from Olympus. Alternative spellings and nicknames: Olympie, Olympe, Pia, Olympias, Olimpia, Olympium.

Oma: Arabic origin. Means: commander, a ruler.

Omolara: African origin. Means: born at the right time.

Omora: Unknown origin and meaning.

Omri: Unknown origin and meaning.

Ona: Latin/Hebrew origin. Means: oneness, an only child, gracious. Alternative spelling: Oona.

Onawa: Native American origin. Means: one who is wide awake.

Ondine: Latin origin. Means: a wave. Alternative spelling: Undine.

Ondreja: Unknown origin and meaning.

Oneida: Unknown origin and meaning.

Oneshia: Unknown origin and meaning.

Onia: Unknown origin. Means: a teacher.

Onida: Native American origin. Means: desired, searching for.

Ontina: Unknown origin. Means: the brave one. Alternative spelling: Ontine.

Onyx: Greek origin. Means: a gem, a nail or claw.

Opal: Sanskrit origin. Means: a precious jewel or stone.

Opalina: Sanskrit origin. Means: a precious jewel or stone. Alternative spelling: Opaline.

Ophelia: Greek/French origin. Means: serpentlike, to help, useful. Alternative spellings and nicknames: Ophlie, Phelia, Ofelia, Ofilia, Ophelie, Ophelila, Ovelia.

Opportina: Unknown origin. Means: good. Alternative spelling: Opportuna.

Oprah: Hebrew origin. Means: a young deer, fawn, to flee or turn back. Alternative spellings: Orpah, Orpha.

Ora: Latin/Hebrew origin. Means: golden, light.

Orabel: Latin/Old English origin. Means: beautiful seacoast, beautiful one, golden. Alternative spellings: Orabelle, Oribel, Oribella, Oribelle.

Oralie: Latin/Anglo-Saxon origin. Means: beautiful seacoast, golden, light, money. Alternative spellings and nicknames: Orlene, Orlina, Ore, Oriel, Orlena, Orielda, Orali, Orelia, Oralia, Orabelle, Orabel, Ora, Oriole.

Ordella: Germanic origin. Means: elfin, pointed spear.

Orea: Greek/Latin origin. Means: from the mountain.

Oreille: Latin/French origin. Means: golden, a bird.

Orela: Unknown origin. Means: announcement.

Orella: Unknown origin. Means: a good listener. Alternative spelling: Oralla.

Orenda: Native American origin. Means: one with magic power.

Oriana: Greek/Latin origin. Means: dawning, from the mountain, golden one. Alternative spellings: Oriane, Orianna, Oria, Orian.

Oringa: Unknown origin. Means: devout one. Alternative spelling: Oringas.

Oriole: Latin/French origin. Means: beautiful one, golden, a bird. Alternative spellings: Oriel, Oreilda, Oriella, Oriola.

Orla: Gaelic/Irish origin. Means: a golden lady.

Orlanda: Germanic origin. Means: one who is famous throughout the land. Alternative spellings: Orlanta, Orlantha.

Orlena: Latin/French origin. Means: one who is golden.

Orna: Latin/Gaelic origin. Means: a tree, pale, olive colored. Ethnic background: Jewish. Alternative spellings and nicknames: Ornie, Ornas.

Ornas: Hebrew origin. Means: let there be light.

Orseline: Unknown origin and meaning. Ethnic background: Dutch.

Ortensia: Latin origin. Means: a gardener, farmer. Ethnic background: Italian.

Ortrud: Teutonic origin. Means: serpentlike. Ethnic background: German. Alternative spelling: Ortrude.

Orva: Anglo-Saxon/French origin. Means: friend in combat, gold, valuable. Alternative spellings and nicknames: Or, Orvan, Orvah.

Osana: Spanish origin. Means: health, mercy.

Osarma: Unknown origin. Means: mercy.

Oseye: Egyptian origin. Means: the happy one. Ethnic background: African.

Osithe: Old English origin. Means: of Essex. Alternative spelling: Osyth.

Otha: Anglo-Saxon origin. Means: little one who is well off. Alternative spelling: Othilia.

Otina: Unknown origin. Means: a friend.

Ottavia: Latin/Italian origin. Means: the eighth child.

Ottilie: Teutonic/Anglo-Saxon origin. Means: small battle maiden, wealthy. Ethnic background: German.

Ovida: Latin origin. Means: a poetess, industrious, a leader.

Owena: Celtic/Welsh origin. Means: youthful warrior of noble birth.

Oyama: Japanese origin. Unknown meaning.

Oza: Unknown origin. Means: a fountain.

Ozioma: African origin. Means: the good news.

Ozora: Persian origin. Means: blue as the sky.

Pacifica: Unknown origin. Means: peaceful one. Alternative spellings: Pacificia, Pacifa.

Paisley: Unknown origin and meaning.

Paiton: Unknown origin and meaning.

Palila: Unknown origin. Means: a bird.

Palla: Greek origin. Means: distinguished, knowledge. Alternative spellings: Pallua, Palua.

Palmira: Latin/Spanish origin. Means: a palm tree, born on Palm Sunday. Alternative spelling: Palmyra.

Paloma: Latin/Spanish origin. Means: a dove, one of gentleness.

Pam: Greek origin. Means: a loved one, sweet, kind.

Pamela: Greek origin. Means: a loved one, sweet, kind. Ethnic background: Italian. Alternative spellings and nicknames: Pamella, Pammi, Pammie, Pammy, Pam, Pamelina.

Pandora: Greek origin. Means: one with all gifts, talented. Alternative spelling: Dorie.

Panphila: Greek origin. Means: all-loving. Alternative spelling: Panfila.

Pansy: Greek/French origin. Means: flower, in deep thought. Alternative spellings: Pansie, Pansey.

Panthea: Greek origin. Means: of all the gods. Alternative spellings and nicknames: Panta, Panthia, Thia, Thea, Pantheas.

Panya: Egyptian/Latin origin. Means: a mouse, a twin child, victorious. Ethnic background: African.

Paradise: Indo-Iranian/Latin origin. Means: walled enclosure, heaven, perfection.

Parnella: Old English/French origin. Means: a little rock.

Parthena: Greek origin. Means: maidenly, sweet, chaste one. Alternative spellings: Parthenia, Parthinia.

Pascale: Hebrew/French origin. Means: born near Easter, Passover.

Pascasia: Hebrew/Latin origin. Means: born near Easter, Passover. Alternative spellings: Pascha, Paschasia, Pascia, Pasia.

Passion: Latin origin. Means: suffered, submitted, strong emotion.

Patience: Latin origin. Means: endurance, one who is patient. Nickname: Pate.

Patricia: Latin origin. Means: of noble birth. Ethnic background: German. Alternative spellings and nicknames: Pattie, Trish, Patty, Tricia, Patti, Patsy, Patrizia, Patrice, Patricia, Pat.

Patsy: Latin origin. Means: of noble birth. Nickname: Patti.

Paula: Latin origin. Means: little, small. Ethnic backgrounds: German, Hungarian. Alternative spellings and nicknames: Paule, Paulir, Folly, Pol, Pavia, Pauly, Faulita, Paulin, Paulie, Pauli, Pauletta, Paolina, Paulina, Paola, Paulette.

Paulette: Latin origin. Means: little, small. Ethnic background: French. Alternative spellings: Paulita, Paoletta.

Pauline: Latin/French origin. Means: little, small. Ethnic backgrounds: German, English/Welsh. Alternative spellings: Paulina, Pavlina.

Payten: Unknown origin and meaning.

Peace: Latin origin. Means: one of tranquillity.

Pearl: Latin origin. Means: a pearl, precious gem. Alternative spellings and nicknames: Perlie, Fe, Ferline, Pearia, Perle, Perl, Fearline, Pearle, Perry, Perla, Pearlina, Pearline.

Pefilia: Unknown origin and meaning. Ethnic background: Hispanic.

Names of the Weird

An early governor of Texas, Governor Hogg, named his baby girl Ima. He didn't discover what he'd done until days after it was written on her birth certificate. Luckily, she made it through life being called, "Miss Ima."

~ **Sandy D., New Jersey**

Pega: Unknown origin. Means: joined.

Peggy: Greek origin. Means: a pearl, precious gem. Alternative spellings and nicknames: Peggoty, Fe, Pegeen, Fegene.

Pegma: Unknown origin. Means: joined.

Pelagla: Greek/Hebrew origin. Means: sorrow, of the sea. Alternative spellings: Pelagie, Pelagi, Pelagia, Pelagias, Pelaga.

Penelope: Greek origin. Means: weaver, a silent worker. Alternative spellings and nicknames: Penelopa, Pennie, Pen, Penny.

Penina: Hebrew origin. Means: pearl, coral.

Penny: Greek origin. Means: weaver, a silent worker, a flower.

Penthea: Greek origin. Means: the fifth-born child. Alternative spellings: Fentheam, Fentheas, Pentha, Pentheam, Pentheas.

Peony: Greek origin. Means: the peony flower, healer. Alternative spelling: Peonie.

Peoria: Unknown origin and meaning.

Pepita: Spanish origin. Means: he shall add. Nicknames: Pepi, Peta.

Perdita: Latin origin. Means: lost one.

Perel: Unknown origin and meaning. Ethnic background: Jewish. Alternative spelling: Perele.

Perfecta: Latin/Spanish origin. Means: accomplished, perfect.

Peril: Latin origin. Means: a trial or test. Ethnic background: Jewish.

Periwinkle: Latin origin. Means: a flowering evergreen.

Pernella: French/Celtic origin. Means: a small rock, young woman. Ethnic background: Swedish. Alternative spellings: Pernelle, Parnella, Pernilla.

Pernille: Greek/Germanic origin. Means: a rock, stone. Ethnic background: Norwegian.

Peron: Unknown origin and meaning.

Perpetua: Latin origin. Means: everlasting, continuous. Ethnic background: Hispanic.

Persis: Greek origin. Means: woman from Persia. Alternative spelling: Persas.

Pesha: Greek origin. Means: born during Easter. Ethnic background: Jewish.

Peshe: Hebrew origin. Means: daughter of the oath. Alternative spelling: Pessel.

Pesye: Unknown origin and meaning. Ethnic background: Jewish.

Petra: Greek origin. Means: a rock, stone. Ethnic backgrounds: Swedish, German, Norwegian. Alternative spellings and nicknames: Petie, Petronilla, Petta, Pier, Petronille, Pet, Petrina, Peti, Peta, Perrine, Pierette, Petronia, Pete, Petronella, Petrine, Petronia.

Petula: Latin origin. Means: seeker, to ask. Alternative spellings and nicknames: Pet, Petulah, Petulia.

Petunia: Native American origin. Means: the petunia flower, reddish purple.

Pfeiffer: Unknown origin and meaning.

Phan: Unknown origin and meaning.

Pheba: Unknown origin and meaning. Alternative spelling: Phibba.

Phedra: Greek origin. Means: bright one. Alternative spellings: Phaedra, Phaidra.

Phemia: Greek origin. Means: fairest, well spoken.

Phenice: Egyptian/Hebrew origin. Means: from the palm tree. Alternative spellings and nicknames: Phenicia, Pheni, Phenica, Venice.

Phia: Unknown origin. Means: ivory, lovely, a nurse.

Philana: Greek origin. Means: lover of all God created. Alternative spellings and nicknames: Phillina, Phillane, Philine, Phila, Philina, Philida, Philene, Philana, Phil, Philona, Filomena, Mena.

Philantha: Greek origin. Means: one who loves flowers.

Philberta: Teutonic origin. Means: bright, brilliant, radiant.

Philene: Greek origin. Means: lover of all God created.

Philida: Greek origin. Means: loving one. Alternative spellings: Philina, Phillada, Phillida.

Philippa: Greek origin. Means: lover of horses. Alternative spellings and nicknames: Philipa, Philly, Phillie, Pippy, Pippa, Phil, Filippa, Felipa, Philippine, Philippe.

Philomena: Greek/Latin origin. Means: strength, lover of the moon, nightingale. Alternative spellings and nicknames: Philomel, Phil, Philomela.

Phiona: Greek origin. Means: ivory. Alternative spelling: Phionna.

Phira: Unknown origin. Means: beautiful one.

Phoebe: Greek origin. Means: shining, bright, wise. Alternative spelling: Phebe.

Phonsa: Unknown origin. Means: aggressive one.

Photina: Unknown origin. Means: friend of all.

Phylicia: Greek origin. Means: a green branch. Alternative spelling: Philicia.

Phyllis: Greek origin. Means: a green branch. Alternative spellings and nicknames: Phyllys, Phyllida, Phyl, Philis, Phylis, Phillis, Filide.

Pia: Latin/Italian origin. Means: devout, pious. Ethnic backgrounds: German, Swedish.

Piedad: Latin/Spanish origin. Means: devout, pious. Ethnic background: Hispanic.

Pierette: Greek/French origin. Means: the rock, stone. Alternative spelling: Pierrette.

Pilar: Spanish origin. Means: a pillar, foundation. Ethnic background: Hispanic.

Pink: Old English origin. Means: to pierce, of pink color.

Piper: Old English origin. Means: a pipe-player.

Pippa: Greek/Italian origin. Means: lover of horses. Alternative spelling: Pippas.

Pitana: Unknown origin and meaning. Ethnic background: Hispanic.

Placida: Latin origin. Means: calm, gentle. Alternative spellings: Placidia, Placia.

Platona: Greek origin. Means: broad one, mankind.

Pleun: Unknown origin and meaning.

Plum: Greek origin. Means: a fruit tree.

Polly: Hebrew origin. Means: little, bitter.

Pomona: Latin origin. Means: apple, fruitful.

Poonam: Unknown origin and meaning.

Poppy: Latin origin. Means: the poppy flower, fragrant.

Pora: Hebrew origin. Means: fruitful.

Porsha: Unknown origin and meaning. Alternative spelling: Porshea.

Portia: Latin origin. Means: getaway, a pig, an offering. Alternative spelling: Picia.

Precious: Latin origin. Means: with great value. Alternative spelling: Preciosa.

Presencia: Latin/Spanish origin. Means: to be present. Ethnic background: Hispanic.

Prima: Latin origin. Means: the firstborn child. Alternative spelling: Primalia.

Primavera: Latin origin. Means: born in the springtime.

Primrose: Latin origin. Means: the first rose. Alternative spellings and nicknames: Rosie, Rose, Primrosa.

Prisca: Latin origin. Means: archaic.

Priscilla: Latin origin. Means: from ancient times, of long lineage. Ethnic background: Italian. Alternative spellings and nicknames: Prissie, Prisilla, Prissy, Pris, Prisc, Sil, Priscella, Pricilla.

Pristina: Unknown origin and meaning. Ethnic background: Hispanic.

Priya: Unknown origin and meaning.

Prochora: Unknown origin. Means: a leader.

Prospera: Latin origin. Means: always fortunate.

Prudence: Latin origin. Means: having foresight, cautious. Alternative spellings and nicknames: Pru, Prud, Prudi, Prudie, Prudy, Prue, Prudencia, Prudenzia.

Prunella: Latin/French origin. Means: prune or plum colored. Alternative spelling: Prvnella.

Psyche: Greek origin. Means: the soul, breath of life.

Pulcheria: Latin origin. Means: with physical beauty. Alternative spelling: Pulchia.

Purity: Latin/Old English origin. Means: without blemish, pure, chaste.

Pyrena: Greek origin. Means: fiery, fruit, ardent.

Pythia: Greek origin. Means: diviner, a prophetess.

q **Qualisha:** Unknown origin and meaning.
Quaneria: Unknown origin and meaning.
Quanisha: Unknown origin and meaning.
Quartas: Latin origin. Means: fourth-born child. Alternative spellings: Quartis, Quartana.

Qudsiyyah: Arabic origin. Means: blessed.

Quenby: Norse origin. Means: a wife, womanly.

Quenna: Teutonic/Old English origin. Means: a woman, wife, queen. Nicknames: Queenie, Queeny, Quenie.

Querdia: Spanish origin. Means: a loved one, beloved. Alternative spellings and nicknames: Erida, Queri, Rida, Querida, Queridas.

Questa: Unknown origin. Means: a nightingale.

Quianna: Unknown origin and meaning.

Quinta: Latin origin. Means: fifth born. Alternative spellings: Quintilla, Quintina.

Quintera: Unknown origin and meaning. Ethnic background: Hispanic.

Quintessa: Unknown origin. Means: essence.

Quirita: Unknown origin. Means: citizen.

Quiteria: Unknown origin. Means: vital. Alternative spellings: Quiteris, Quita.

r **Raadhiyah:** Arabic origin. Means: pleased, happy.
Raama: Unknown origin and meaning.

Raashidah: Arabic origin. Means: righteous.

Rachaba: Unknown origin. Means: horse.

Rachel: Hebrew origin. Means: a ewe, one with purity. Ethnic backgrounds: English/Welsh, Irish. 6th most popular girl's name of the '90s. Alternative spellings and nicknames: Shellie, Shelly, Shell, Rochell, Rakel, Raquela, Ray, Shelley, Rochelle, Rey, Raquel, Rahel, Rae, Rachelle, Rachele, Rachael, Racheal, Rachell, Rachelyn, Ruchel, Ruchele.

Racine: Unknown origin and meaning.

Radcliffe: Anglo-Saxon origin. Means: from the vermilion cliffs.

Radella: Old English origin. Means: a sprite counselor. Alternative spelling: Kadilla.

Raden: Unknown origin and meaning.

Radinka: Slavic origin. Means: one who is active.

Radka: Unknown origin and meaning. Ethnic background: Czech.

Radmilla: Slavic origin. Means: one who works for the people.

Rae: Hebrew/Old English origin. Means: a ewe, with purity and grace. Alternative spellings: Raya, Ray.

Ra'eesah: Arabic origin. Means: leader.

Raelyn: Unknown origin and meaning.

Rafee'ah: Arabic origin. Means: exalted.

Rafeeqah: Arabic origin. Means: companion.

Ragnhild: Norse origin. Means: one who is wise in battle. Ethnic background: Swedish.

Rahab: Unknown origin and meaning.

Raheemah: Arabic origin. Means: affectionate.

Raihaanah: Arabic origin. Means: flowers.

Raina: Teutonic/French origin. Means: one with powerful might, a queen. Ethnic background: Jewish. Alternative spellings: Regina, Raynata, Rainah, Rayna.

Raine: Germanic origin. Means: one who advises, counsels. Ethnic background: Jewish. Alternative spelling: Rain.

Raissa: French origin. Means: believer, thinker. Ethnic background: Russian.

Ralayah: Unknown origin and meaning.

Rama: Sanskrit origin. Means: pleasing, attested.

Ramla: Egyptian origin. Means: a prophetess. Ethnic background: African.

Ramona: Teutonic/Spanish origin. Means: wise protector. Alternative spellings and nicknames: Romona, Mona, Rama, Ramonda.

Rana: Sanskrit/Norse origin. Means: to behold, of nobility, queen. Alternative spellings and nicknames: Ranice, Ranee, Rani, Rania.

Ra'naa: Arabic origin. Means: lovely.

Randi: Norse origin. Means: with great beauty.

Rannveig: Norse origin. Means: a woman from the estate. Ethnic background: Norwegian.

Raphaela: Hebrew origin. Means: God will heal. Ethnic background: German. Alternative spellings: Raffaelle, Rafaela, Raffaella.

Raquana: Unknown origin and meaning.

Rasean: Unknown origin and meaning.

RaSha: Unknown origin and meaning.

Rashida: Arabic origin. Means: righteous. Ethnic background: African. Alternative spelling: Rasheeda.

Rasia: Polish origin. Means: regal.

Names of the Weird

My husband keeps threatening that if we ever have twins he'll name them Krystal Chandeliere and Chyna Cabinyt. He came up with the names during my last pregnancy, odd spellings and all. Uggghh!

~ Rachel S.,
Freeland, Pennsylvania

Rasine: Polish origin. Means: a rose. Alternative spelling: Racine.

Rasline: Unknown origin and meaning.

Rasoliia: Unknown origin and meaning.

Rathana: Unknown origin and meaning.

Raven: Unknown origin and meaning. Alternative spelling: Rayven.

Rayanna: Unknown origin and meaning.

Raynata: Unknown origin. Means: powerful.

Rayzel: Hebrew origin. Means: a rose.

Reba: Hebrew origin. Means: to tie, bound, born fourth. Alternative spellings: Rebah, Reba, Reeba, Rebba.

Rebecca: Hebrew origin. Means: to tie, bound, enchantingly beautiful. Ethnic backgrounds: Italian, English/Welsh. 17th most popular girl's name of the '90s. Alternative spellings and nicknames: Rivi, Rivy, Ree, Riba, Rivalee, Rivkah, Becka, Becki, Beckie, Becky, Bekki, Rebekka, Reeba, Rebeca, Riva, Becca, Rebekah, Rebeka, Reba, Rebbecca, Rebeckah, Rebecka, Reebecca.

Rechaba: Unknown origin. Means: horse lover.

Reddy: Unknown origin and meaning.

Reeta: Sanskrit origin. Means: brave, honest. Alternative spelling: Rida.

Regal: Old English origin. Means: of royalty.

Regina: Latin origin. Means: a queen. Ethnic backgrounds: German, Hispanic, Italian. Alternative spellings and nicknames: Rina, Reggi, Ragina, Queenie, Gine, Regan, Reyna, Reine, Reina, Regine, Raina, Gina, Reggie.

Rehema: Egyptian origin. Means: compassion. Ethnic background: African.

Reidun: Norse origin. Means: lovely in the nest.

Reiko: Japanese origin. Means: gratitude.

Reina: Latin/Hebrew origin. Means: queen, clean. Alternative spellings: Reine, Reyna, Rayna, Raynah.

Rema: Unknown origin and meaning.

Rena: Hebrew origin. Means: with peace, joy.

Renate: Latin origin. Means: rebirth, confident. Ethnic background: German.

Renee: Latin/French origin. Means: one who is new again, reborn. Alternative spellings: Ranae, Renae.

Renita: Latin/Hebrew origin. Means: confident, self-poised, joyful song. Alternative spellings and nicknames: Riti, Rani, Reneta, Nita, Reniti, Ranita.

Reseda: Latin origin. Means: the mignonette flower, healing. Alternative spellings: Reseta, Raseta.

Reva: Latin origin. Means: to regain strength.

Rexana: Latin origin. Means: with regal grace. Alternative spellings: Rexanna, Rexanne.

Rhawann: Unknown origin and meaning.

Rhea: Greek/Latin origin. Means: stream, flowing from the earth, poppy. Alternative spellings: Rea, Rhaea.

Rhetta: Greek origin. Means: well spoken, an orator. Alternative spellings: Rheta, Reta.

Rhiamon: Unknown origin and meaning.

Rhiana: Welsh origin. Means: a maiden. Alternative spellings: Rhianne, Riana, Rianna.

Rhiannon: Celtic/Welsh origin. Means: great queen. Alternative spellings: Rhianon, Riannon, Rianon.

Rhoda: Greek origin. Means: roses, from Rhodes. Alternative spellings and nicknames: Rhody, Rodina, Rodie, Roda, Rodi, Rhodanthe, Rhodia.

Rhona: Celtic/Greek origin. Means: mighty, a rose.

Rhonda: Celtic/Welsh origin. Means: powerful river, a good lance.

Rhumani: Unknown origin and meaning.

Ria: Spanish origin. Means: from the mouth of a river.

Rica: Spanish origin. Means: famous ruler of the estate. Alternative spellings and nicknames: Rycca, Rickie, Ricca, Ricki, Rikki, Riki, Ricky.

Ricadonna: Italian origin. Means: a famous ruling lady.

Ricanora: Unknown origin and meaning. Ethnic background: Hispanic.

Ricarda: Teutonic origin. Means: a brave and powerful ruler.

Richma: Unknown origin and meaning. Alternative spellings: Richmal, Rickema.

Ricki: Teutonic/Anglo-Saxon origin. Means: strong guardian, protector of the poor. Alternative spellings: Riki, Rikki.

Ridhiyyah: Arabic origin. Means: delighted.

Riely: Unknown origin and meaning.

Rifka: Hebrew origin. Means: to bind. Alternative spelling: Rivkeh.

Riga: Unknown origin and meaning.

Rigmor: Teutonic/Norse origin. Means: a woman with great power. Ethnic background: Swedish.

Rihana: Unknown origin and meaning.

Rika: Norse origin. Means: one who is forever strong.

Rilda: Unknown origin. Means: armored, battle.

Risa: Latin origin. Means: one filled with laughter.

Rita: Greek origin. Means: a pearl. Ethnic background: Italian. Alternative spelling: Reta.

Riva: Latin/French origin. Means: to strengthen, from the shore. Alternative spellings and nicknames: Ree, Reeva, Rivalee, Rivi, Rivy.

Real Names of Famous People

A number of celebrities have attained their star status using names that aren't the ones their parents gave them. Granted, a lot of stars changed their names due to studio pressure—in the early history of Hollywood, name changing was just as common as plastic surgery is today. For instance, John Mellencamp would be awarded a record contract only if he went by Johnny Cougar. He signed the deal but gradually morphed his name back to his own as his success grew (Johnny Cougar to John Cougar Mellencamp to the original John Mellencamp, at last). Perhaps he reflects a trend among celebrities toward normal names. But then again, can you imagine a famous cowboy named Marion?

Alan Alda	Alphonse D'Abruzzo	Judy Garland	Frances Gumm
Woody Allen	Allen Konigsberg	Crystal Gayle	Brenda Gail Webb
Lauren Bacall	Betty Joan Perske	Whoopi Goldberg	Caryn Johnson
Brigitte Bardot	Camille Javal	Hulk Hogan	Terry Bollette
Tony Bennett	Antonio Benedetto	Diane Keaton	Diane Hall
Bono	Paul Hewson	Ben Kingsley	Krishna Bhanji
Michael Caine	Maurice Micklewhite	Jerry Lewis	Joseph Levitch
Dyan Cannon	Samille Diane Friesen	Toni Morrison	Chloe Wofford
Chevy Chase	Cornelius Chase	Roy Rogers	Leonard Slye
Alice Cooper	Vincent Furnier	Jane Seymour	Joyce Penelope Frankenburg
Elvis Costello	Declan McManus	Charlie Sheen	Carlos Irwin Estevez
Rodney Dangerfield	Jacob Cohen	Tina Turner	Annie Mae Bullock
John Denver	Henry John Deutschendorf, Jr.	John Wayne	Marion Morrison
Bo Derek	Mary Collins	Gene Wilder	Jerry Silbermann
Kirk Douglas	Issur Danielovitch Demsky	Stevie Wonder	Stevland Morris
Morgan Fairchild	Patsy Ann McClenny	Tammy Wynette	Virginia Wynette Pugh
Jodie Foster	Alicia Foster		

Rivera: Unknown origin and meaning.

Roanna: Latin origin. Means: one who is sweet, gracious. Alternative spellings and nicknames: Ronni, Ronny, Roana, Ranna, Roanne, Ronnie.

Roberta: Teutonic origin. Means: one with bright fame. Ethnic background: Italian. Alternative spellings and nicknames: Robenia, Ruperta, Ruberta, Robinia, Robinette, Robinett, Robine, Robina, Robi, Robena, Robby, Bertie, Bobbye, Bobina, Bobine, Bobinette, Robbi, Bobbe, Bobbi, Robin, Bobbette, Robbie, Bobbie, Bobby.

Robin: Teutonic/Anglo-Saxon origin. Means: one with bright fame, a robin. Alternative spelling: Robyn.

Rochelle: French origin. Means: a large stone. Alternative spellings and nicknames: Roch, Rochella, Rochette, Roshelle, Shell, Shelly, Shelley, Rochel, Rochele.

Roderica: Teutonic origin. Means: a noted lord, famous. Alternative spellings and nicknames: Rickie, Roddie, Rica, Roddy.

Rohana: Indic origin. Means: sandalwood, sweet incense.

Roiza: Unknown origin and meaning. Ethnic background: Jewish.

Rolanda: Teutonic origin. Means: from the land of fame. Alternative spelling: Rolande.

Roma: Latin/Italian origin. Means: wanderer, woman of Rome. Ethnic background: Jewish. Alternative spellings and nicknames: Romina, Romaine, Romelle, Romilda.

Romaine: Latin/French origin. Means: dweller of Rome.

Romilda: Teutonic origin. Means: famous woman of battle. Ethnic background: Hispanic. Alternative spellings and nicknames: Malda, Romali, Milda, Romelda, Romalda, Rumolda, Romila.

Romola: Latin origin. Means: the Roman. Alternative spellings and nicknames: Romella, Romie, Romy, Romelle.

Romy: Latin origin. Means: the sea dew, herb. Ethnic background: German.

Rona: Hebrew/Norse origin. Means: joyous, a small seal.

Ronalda: Norse origin. Means: one with powerful authority. Alternative spellings and nicknames: Ronny, Rona, Ronnie.

Roni: Hebrew origin. Means: my song of joy. Alternative spellings: Ronie, Ronee.

Ronnisia: Unknown origin and meaning.

Rosabel: Latin origin. Means: beautiful rose. Ethnic background: Hispanic. Alternative spellings: Rosabella, Rosabelle, Roselba.

Rosalba: Latin origin. Means: a lovely white rose. Ethnic background: Hispanic.

Rosalia: Latin/Italian origin. Means: a rose. Alternative spellings: Rosalie, Rosella, Roselle.

Rosalind: Latin/Germanic origin. Means: a beautiful rose, tender horse. Alternative spellings and nicknames: Rosel, Roz, Roslyn, Rosie, Rozalin, Rosalyn, Rosalini, Ros, Roselyn, Roseline, Rosaline, Rosalinda, Rosalinde, Roslin, Rosaleen, Rosalynd, Roselind, Roseline.

Rosamond: Latin/Teutonic origin. Means: a pure rose, famous protector. Alternative spellings and nicknames: Rozamund, Rozamond, Roz, Rosmunda, Rosemonde, Rosamur, Ros, Rosemund, Rosamunda, Rosamund, Rosamunde.

Rosanna: Hebrew origin. Means: the graceful rose. Ethnic background: Italian. Alternative spellings and nicknames: Roanne, Rosian, Ranna, Roseann, Rosanne, Roseanne, Roanna, Rosana, Rossana, Roseanna.

Rosary: Unknown origin and meaning.

Rose: Greek/Latin origin. Means: of Mary, a rose, love. Ethnic backgrounds: French, Irish. Alternative spellings and nicknames: Rosie, Rozalia, Rozalie, Roze, Rozele, Rozelle, Rozina, Rosene, Rhollia, Rosena, Rhody, Rosalee, Rosel, Rosetta, Rosina, Rosita, Rosy, Rosi,

Rosa, Zita, Rosaleen, Rhoda, Rois, Rosalia, Rosalie, Rosaline, Rosella, Roselle, Rozella, Roos, Rosio, Raisa, Rasia.

Rosemary: Hebrew/Latin origin. Means: Mary's rose, dew of the sea. Ethnic backgrounds: English/Welsh. Alternative spellings and nicknames: Rose Marie, Rosemay, Rosemari, Rosemarie.

Rosetta: Latin/Italian origin. Means: little rose. Alternative spellings: Rosita, Rosette.

Roshanda: Unknown origin and meaning. Alternative spelling: Roshawnda.

Rosina: Latin origin. Means: little rose. Ethnic background: Italian. Alternative spelling: Rosine.

Roswitha: Germanic origin. Means: one with famed strength. Ethnic background: German.

Rowena: Celtic/Germanic origin. Means: with flowing white hair, famous friend. Alternative spellings and nicknames: Ronny, Ranna, Ro, Row, Ronni, Ronnie, Rowe, Rena.

Roxane: Persian origin. Means: dawning, bright. Alternative spellings and nicknames: Roxanna, Roxy, Roxine, Roxie, Roxanrie, Rox, Roxi, Roxana, Rosana, Roxanne, Roxene.

Royla: Unknown origin and meaning. Alternative spelling: Roya.

Ruby: Latin origin. Means: the gem ruby, red. Alternative spellings and nicknames: Rubi, Rubetta, Rubie, Rubia, Rubina.

Rudelle: Teutonic origin. Means: famous one. Nickname: Ruda.

Rue: Greek/Teutonic origin. Means: herb of grace, with fame. Alternative spellings and nicknames: Reu, Rhu.

Ruella: Latin origin. Means: a ruler. Alternative spellings: Ruelle, Rula.

Rufano: African origin. Means: happiness.

Rufina: Greek/Latin origin. Means: red-haired. Alternative spelling: Rufena.

Rumaanah: Arabic origin. Means: a seed.

Ruskeh: Hebrew origin. Means: a ewe, one with purity.

Ruth: Hebrew origin. Means: beautiful friend. Ethnic backgrounds: German, Hispanic, Italian. Alternative spellings and nicknames: Ruthie, Ruthe, Ruthi.

Rylee: Unknown origin and meaning.

S **Saadiqah:** Arabic origin. Means: sincere.
Saahirah: Arabic origin. Means: earth, moon.
Saalihah: Arabic origin. Means: chaste.

Saarah: Arabic origin. Means: veil.

Saba: Greek/Hebrew origin. Means: woman of Sheba, aged one. Alternative spellings: Sabba, Sabah.

Sabella: Hebrew/Anglo-Saxon origin. Means: God's oath, wisdom. Alternative spelling: Sabelle.

Sabian: Unknown origin and meaning.

Sabina: Latin origin. Means: a Sabine woman. Ethnic background: German. Alternative spellings and nicknames: Savina, Bina, Sabine.

Sabra: Hebrew origin. Means: to rest, a cactus.

Sabrina: Latin/Anglo-Saxon origin. Means: from the boundary, a princess. Ethnic background: Italian. 45th most popular girl's name of the '90s. Alternative spellings and nicknames: Brina, Zabrina, Sabreena, Sabrena.

Sachiko: Japanese origin. Means: bliss. Nickname: Sachi.

Sadella: Hebrew origin. Means: a princess, noble. Nickname: Sada.

Sadey: Unknown origin and meaning. Alternative spellings: Sade, Sadie, Saide, Saydee.

Sadira: Persian origin. Means: the lotus tree, dreamy. Ethnic background: Jewish. Alternative spellings and nicknames: Sadiras, Sadirah, Dira.

Sádiyah: Arabic origin. Means: good fortune.

Sadonia: Unknown origin. Means: to ensnare.

Sadora: Unknown origin. Means: water. Alternative spelling: Sadiras.

Safiyyah: Arabic origin. Means: a close friend.

Sage: Latin origin. Means: one with great wisdom.

Sahara: Arabic/Hebrew origin. Means: desert, awakening, moon.

Saida: Arabic origin. Means: fortunate one. Ethnic background: Russian. Alternative spelling: Saidah.

Saide: Unknown origin and meaning.

Sajoir: Unknown origin and meaning.

Sakeenah: Arabic origin. Means: comfort.

Salaamah: Arabic origin. Means: salvation.

Salangi: Unknown origin and meaning. Alternative spelling: Salangia.

Salba: Unknown origin. Means: lovely.

Saleemah: Arabic origin. Means: mild.

Salina: Greek origin. Means: salty. Alternative spelling: Salena.

Sally: Hebrew origin. Means: peaceful, princess.

Salmah: Arabic origin. Means: obey.

Salome: Hebrew origin. Means: peaceful. Ethnic background: Hispanic. Alternative spellings and nicknames: Saloma, Salomi, Loma, Sally, Salom.

Salonia: Unknown origin and meaning. Ethnic background: Hispanic.

Salvia: Latin origin. Means: a wise sage. Alternative spellings: Salva, Salvina.

Sama: Unknown origin. Means: flower.

Samal: Unknown origin. Means: prayed. Alternative spelling: Samala.

Samantha: Aramaic origin. Means: the listener, attentive. Ethnic backgrounds: English/Welsh. 11th most popular girl's name of the '90s. Alternative spellings and nicknames: Sam, Sama, Sammy, Samanthia, Simantha.

Samara: Hebrew origin. Means: protected by God. Alternative spellings and nicknames: Sam, Sammy, Mara, Samaria.

Samdisha: Unknown origin and meaning.

Sameerah: Arabic origin. Means: storyteller. Alternative spelling: Samyra.

Samuela: Hebrew origin. Means: asked of God, to listen. Alternative spellings and nicknames: Samella, Samela, Samuella, Uella, Sammy, Samantha, Sam, Ela, Samuelle.

Sancia: Latin/Spanish origin. Means: companion, sanctified, sacred. Alternative spellings and nicknames: Sancha, Sanchia.

Sandip: Unknown origin and meaning.

Sandra: Greek origin. Means: defender, helper of mankind. Ethnic background: German. Alternative spellings and nicknames: Sandye, Sandi, Sandy, Sondra.

SanJuana: Hebrew/Spanish origin. Means: a gift from God.

Sanne: Unknown origin and meaning. Ethnic background: Dutch.

Sanovea: Unknown origin and meaning.

Santana: Latin origin. Means: of the saints. Ethnic background: Hispanic. Alternative spelling: Santanna.

Sanura: Egyptian origin. Means: like a kitten. Ethnic background: African.

Sapphire: Greek/Hebrew origin. Means: beautiful, blue jewel, sapphire. Alternative spellings and nicknames: Sapphi, Sephira, Saphra, Phira, Sappho, Sapir, Sapphera, Sapphira, Saphira.

Sarabeth: Hebrew origin. Means: a princess, God's oath. Alternative spelling: Sarahbeth.

Sarah: Hebrew origin. Means: a princess. Ethnic backgrounds: Scottish, English/Welsh. 2nd most popular girl's name of the '90s. Alternative spellings and nicknames: Sharo, Sherrie, Sayre, Sher, Sharona, Sheree, Sherie, Sarir, Sharai, Sadye, Saidee, Sal, Salaid, Salli, Sallie, Sarer, Saretta, Sallee, Sarita, Shara, Shari, Sara, Sheri, Sadie, Sarene, Sadella, Sari, Sally, Sarette, Sarra, Sarai, Saree.

Sarahann: Hebrew/Greek origin. Means: a gracious princess.

Sarina: Hebrew origin. Means: a princess. Alternative spellings: Sarine, Sarene.

Sarita: Hebrew/Spanish origin. Means: little princess. Alternative spellings: Saretta, Sarette.

Sasha: Unknown origin and meaning. Alternative spelling: Sascha.

Sassille: Unknown origin and meaning.

Savannah: Spanish origin. Means: from the mesa, an open plain. 45th most popular girl's name of the '90s. Alternative spelling: Savanna.

Sayah: Unknown origin and meaning.

Saychelle: Unknown origin and meaning.

Scarlet: Old English origin. Means: red. Alternative spelling: Scarlett.

Scota: Latin origin. Means: an Irish woman. Ethnic background: Irish.

Sebastiana: Greek origin. Means: from Sebasta, majestic, revered. Alternative spellings: Sebastiane, Sebastienne.

Secunda: Latin origin. Means: the second born.

Segrada: Unknown origin and meaning. Ethnic background: Hispanic.

Sela: Greek/Hebrew origin. Means: a rock. Alternative spellings: Seleta, Sella.

Selena: Greek origin. Means: heavenly, moon. 48th most popular girl's name of the '90s. Alternative spellings and nicknames: Selie, Selia, Seline, Salene, Celie, Selene, Sena, Selinda, Selina, Lena, Celine, Celinda, Celina, Celene, Sela, Selinda.

Selila: Hebrew origin. Means: path.

Selima: Arabic/Hebrew origin. Means: peaceful one. Alternative spellings: Selimah, Selema, Selemas.

Selma: Teutonic/Celtic origin. Means: protected, fair. Ethnic background: German. Alternative spellings: Zelma, Anselma, Sellma.

Semele: Greek/Latin origin. Means: to sow, one time only. Alternative spelling: Semela.

Semira: Hebrew origin. Means: from heaven.

Sena: Latin origin. Means: blessed one.

"What If I Never Find a Name I Like?"

Name-weary parents, take heart! At times it may seem like you'll never find the perfect name for your child. But thankfully, odds are in your favor that you will. When we polled parents, a whopping 82% said they'd give their kids the same name if they had it to do all over again. Phew!

Senalda: Spanish origin. Means: an omen, a sign. Nicknames: Enalda, Sena, Alda.

Senedra: Unknown origin and meaning.

Senta: Germanic origin. Means: an assistant. Ethnic background: German.

Septima: Latin origin. Means: the seventh-born child.

Sera: Unknown origin. Means: bound.

Seraphina: Hebrew/Latin origin. Means: burning ones, angels, ardent. Alternative spellings: Sera, Serafina, Serafine, Seraphine, Saraphina.

Serena: Latin origin. Means: bright, calm, serene. Ethnic background: Hispanic. Alternative spellings and nicknames: Serene, Reena, Sirene, Rena, Serenitey, Serina, Serinity.

Serica: Unknown origin. Means: silken.

Serilda: Teutonic origin. Means: armored maid of war. Alternative spellings and nicknames: Rilda, Sarilda.

Serwa: Unknown origin. Means: noble. Ethnic background: African.

Seta: Unknown origin. Means: a flower.

Sethrida: Hebrew origin. Means: appointed, chosen.

Setta: Unknown origin and meaning. Ethnic background: Hispanic.

Shafeeqah: Arabic origin. Means: affectionate.

Shahlaa: Arabic origin. Means: gray eyes.

Shaine: Hebrew origin. Means: beautiful. Alternative spelling: Shaina.

Shaiyena: Unknown origin and meaning.

Shakea: Unknown origin and meaning.

Shakeelah: Arabic origin. Means: well shaped. Alternative spellings: Shakilah, Shaklyah.

Shakira: Arabic origin. Means: to thank. Alternative spellings: Shaakirah, Shakera.

Shalia: Unknown origin and meaning.

Shalina: Unknown origin and meaning.

Shalva: Hebrew origin. Means: peace, tranquillity.

Shamaamah: Arabic origin. Means: fragrance.

Shamekia: Unknown origin and meaning. Alternative spelling: Shamika.

Shamfa: African origin. Means: sunshine.

Shamira: Hebrew origin. Means: protector, a guard.

Shamiya: Unknown origin and meaning.

Shamma: Unknown origin. Means: obedient. Alternative spelling: Shama.

Shamoodah: Arabic origin. Means: diamond.

Shanda: Unknown origin. Means: goddess.

Shandalee: Unknown origin and meaning.

Shandeigh: Old English origin. Means: boisterous, rambunctious.

Shani: Egyptian origin. Means: marvelous. Ethnic background: African. Alternative spelling: Shanee.

Shanice: Unknown origin and meaning. Alternative spellings: Shanese, Shawnese.

Shaniqua: Unknown origin and meaning.

Shannah: Hebrew/Gaelic origin. Means: a lily or rose, old, wise. Alternative spellings: Shana, Shanah, Shanna, Shania, Shauna.

Shannen: Gaelic origin. Means: small, of wisdom.

Shanta: Sanskrit origin. Means: pacified, calm, attested.

Shantrelle: Unknown origin and meaning. Alternative spellings: Shantel, Shanelle.

Shara: Unknown origin. Means: fertile.

Sharaya: Unknown origin and meaning.

Shareefah: Arabic origin. Means: noble.

Sharesa: Unknown origin and meaning.

Sharia: Unknown origin and meaning. Alternative spellings: Shari, Sharissa, Sharesa, Sharisse, Shariyah.

Sharnice: Unknown origin and meaning.

Sharon: Hebrew origin. Means: fertile, princess, plain of Sharon. Ethnic backgrounds: Irish, Hebrew, English/Welsh. Alternative spellings and nicknames: Sherri, Sherye, Sherrie, Sharry, Sharron, Sharona, Sharai, Shari, Shara, Sherry.

Shaundel: Unknown origin and meaning.

Shawna: Hebrew/Irish origin. Means: God is gracious.

Shawntae: Unknown origin and meaning.

Shay: Irish origin. Means: majestic, asked. Alternative spellings: Shaya, Shaye.

Shaylynn: Unknown origin and meaning. Alternative spellings: Shealyn, Shaelyn, Shayla.

Sheba: Hebrew origin. Means: from Sheba, daughter of our pledge. Alternative spelling: Saba.

Sheedy: Unknown origin and meaning.

Sheena: Hebrew/Gaelic origin. Means: God's gift. Ethnic background: Irish. Alternative spelling: Seanna.

Sheila: Latin/Irish origin. Means: blind, musical. Alternative spellings and nicknames: Shelagh, Shelly, Shellie, Shelli, Sheelah, Sheelagh, Sheela, Sheilah, Seila, Selia, Shelley.

Shekayl: Unknown origin and meaning.

Shelah: Hebrew/Irish origin. Means: asked, requested. Alternative spellings: Shela, Sheya, Shea, Shaya.

Shelbi: Anglo-Saxon origin. Means: from the sheltered farm.

Shelia: Hebrew origin. Means: mine is God's. Ethnic background: Irish.

Shelsie: Unknown origin and meaning.

Shenandoah: Unknown origin and meaning.

Sherika: Unknown origin and meaning.

Sherine: Unknown origin and meaning.

Sherrice: French/Old English origin. Means: beloved, from the white meadow. Alternative spelling: Sherice.

Sherry: French/Old English origin. Means: beloved, from the white meadow. Alternative spellings and nicknames: Sher, Sherye, Sherrie, Sherri, Sheree, Sheri, Shiri.

Sheryl: Germanic/French origin. Means: womanly, beloved. Alternative spelling: Sheryll.

Sheya: Unknown origin. Means: asked. Alternative spelling: Sheyanne.

Sheymonie: Unknown origin and meaning.

Shiaja: Unknown origin and meaning.

Shiana: Unknown origin and meaning. Alternative spelling: Shina.

Shira: Hebrew origin. Means: a song. Alternative spellings: Shirah, Shyra.

Shirley: Anglo-Saxon origin. Means: from the white meadow. Ethnic background: Irish. Alternative spellings and nicknames: Sherye, Sher, Shirline, Shir, Sherrie, Sherri, Sherline, Sherill, Sheree, Shirlene, Shirleen, Shirlee, Sheryl, Sheri, Sherry.

Shoshana: Hebrew/Spanish origin. Means: a rose or a lily. Alternative spelling: Shoshannah.

Shulamith: Hebrew origin. Means: peace, peaceful. Alternative spelling: Sulasmith.

Shyan: Unknown origin and meaning. Alternative spellings: Shyanne, Shyenne, Shyne.

Shydaisa: Unknown origin and meaning.

Shyla: Unknown origin and meaning.

Sibyl: Greek/Latin origin. Means: prophetess, wise. Alternative spellings and nicknames: Sybilla, Sibyll, Sybila, Sibeal, Sibella, Sibel, Sibby, Sibbie, Sib, Cybil, Sibell, Sibley, Sibylla, Sibylle, Sibilla, Sybil, Sibelle, Sybille, Cybill, Sibille.

Sida: Unknown origin. Means: a lily.

Siddra: Latin origin. Means: of the stars, shining.

Sidonia: Phoenician/Greek origin. Means: to ensnare, linen. Alternative spellings: Sadonia, Sidonie.

Sidsel: Unknown origin and meaning. Ethnic background: Norwegian.

Sieglinde: Teutonic origin. Means: a tender victory. Ethnic background: German.

Sieralyn: Unknown origin and meaning.

Sierra: Latin origin. Means: a chain of hills. 34th most popular girl's name of the '90s. Alternative spellings: Siera, Siarra.

Sigfreda: Teutonic origin. Means: triumphant peace.

Sigita: Unknown origin and meaning. Ethnic background: Russian.

Signe: Latin/Swedish origin. Means: a sign, victorious. Ethnic background: Norwegian. Alternative spelling: Signa.

Sigourney: Unknown origin and meaning.

Sigrid: Norse origin. Means: beautiful, victorious counselor, secret lore. Ethnic background: German. Alternative spelling: Sigrun.

Silda: Unknown origin. Means: solitary.

Silene: Unknown origin and meaning.

Siloam: Unknown origin and meaning. Alternative spellings: Siloum, Siloa.

Silvia: Latin origin. Means: a forest dweller. Ethnic backgrounds: Swedish, Italian. Alternative spellings: Silva, Silviane.

Sima: Aramaic/Scottish origin. Means: treasure, wealth, a listener. Alternative spelling: Simah.

Simone: Hebrew/French origin. Means: to hear or be heard. Ethnic backgrounds: Italian, English/Welsh.

"What If I Never Find a Name I Like?" Parent Poll

Would you give your child the same name if you had it to do over?

Of 1,057 total votes:

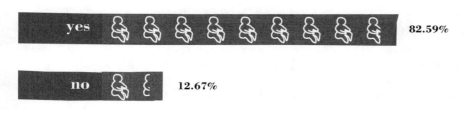

yes   82.59%

no   12.67%

maybe   4.73%

1 figure = 100 parents

Alternative spellings: Simonne, Simona, Simonetta, Simonette, Symone.

Sinead: Hebrew/Gaelic origin. Means: kindness, with God's praise. Ethnic background: Irish.

Siobhan: Hebrew/Gaelic origin. Means: kindness, with God's praise. Ethnic background: Irish.

Siorhan: Unknown origin and meaning.

Sippie: Unknown origin and meaning. Ethnic background: Dutch.

Sippora: Hebrew origin. Means: a bird. Ethnic background: Hispanic.

Sireesha: Unknown origin and meaning.

Sirel: Hebrew origin. Means: a princess. Alternative spellings: Siril, Sirke.

Sirena: Greek origin. Means: a siren, fatally beautiful temptress.

Siri: Norse origin. Means: beautiful, victorious counselor.

Sisel: Hebrew origin. Means: sweet.

Sissy: Latin/Anglo-Saxon origin. Means: blind, sister.

Sive: Irish origin. Means: goodness.

Skye: Unknown origin and meaning. Alternative spellings: Skyla, Skyler.

Sobenna: African origin. Means: follow God.

Socorro: Spanish origin. Means: ready to intercede, of Mary.

Sofonie: Unknown origin and meaning.

Sojourner: Latin origin. Means: to stay temporarily.

Solana: Greek origin. Means: one with wisdom, sunshine.

Solange: Latin/French origin. Means: good, pious.

Soledad: Latin/Spanish origin. Means: solitude, alone, of Mary.

Solerne: Unknown origin. Means: sunshine.

Solfrid: Unknown origin and meaning. Ethnic background: Norwegian.

Solita: Latin origin. Means: tranquil solitude. Alternative spellings and nicknames: Lita, Sola, Solitta.

Soloma: Hebrew origin. Means: peaceful.

Solveig: Norse origin. Means: from the powerful estate. Ethnic backgrounds: German, Norwegian, Swedish. Alternative spelling: Solvig.

Sona: Latin origin. Means: to sound, wise.

Sonesu: Unknown origin and meaning.

Sonia: Greek/Slavic origin. Means: sensible, wise. Ethnic backgrounds: English/Welsh, German. Alternative spellings and nicknames: Sonny, Sonni, Soniya, Sunny, Sonya, Sonnie, Sonja.

Sophia: Greek origin. Means: wise, sensible, discerning. Ethnic backgrounds: German, Italian, French, Dutch. 49th most popular girl's name of the '90s. Alternative spellings and nicknames: Sophey, Sophy, Sophonisba, Sophi, Soph, Sofie, Sonny, Sunny, Sophronia, Sophie, Sonni, Sonya, Sonnie, Sonja, Sonia, Sofia.

Sophronia: Greek origin. Means: wise, sensible, discerning. Alternative spellings: Sonja, Sonya.

Sorcha: Celtic/Gaelic origin. Means: intelligent, bright.

Sorele: French origin. Means: one with reddish-brown hair, sour. Ethnic background: Jewish.

Sorilda: Teutonic origin. Means: armored, battle.

Sorka: Hebrew origin. Means: a princess.

Sosthena: Unknown origin. Means: vigorous. Alternative spellings: Sosthenna, Sosthina, Sothena.

Sotoli: Unknown origin and meaning. Ethnic background: Jewish.

Speranza: Latin/Italian origin. Means: one with great hope.

Spes: Latin origin. Means: one with great hope. Ethnic background: Hispanic.

Spring: Old English origin. Means: springtime.

Staci: Greek origin. Means: one who shall rise again, resurrection.

Star: Sanskrit/Greek origin. Means: a star. Alternative spelling: Starr.

Stella: Latin origin. Means: a star. Ethnic background: Italian. Alternative spellings and nicknames: Stel, Stelle.

Stephanie: Greek origin. Means: garland, crowned in victory. Ethnic backgrounds: English/Welsh, French. 29th most popular girl's name of the '90s. Alternative spellings and nicknames: Stesha, Stephie, Stephi, Stefa, Stepliana, Stepha, Steffie, Stefana, Stephani, Stephania, Stevie, Stevena, Stevana, Stephenie, Steffi, Stefanie, Stefania, Stephney, Stepanka, Stephana, Stephanine, Stephany.

Stila: Unknown origin. Means: quiet. Alternative spellings: Stilla, Stillas.

Stina: Danish/Swedish origin. Means: Christian, pure.

Stine: Unknown origin. Means: earnest. Ethnic background: Norwegian.

Stockard: Anglo-Saxon origin. Means: a hardy tree.

Storm: Old English origin. Means: stormy, tempestuous. Nicknames: Stormi, Stormie, Stormy.

Stowe: Unknown origin and meaning.

Sughraa: Arabic origin. Means: small.

Suha: Unknown origin and meaning.

Suhailah: Arabic origin. Means: canopy.

Sula: Unknown origin. Means: bird, peace, sun.

Sultaanah: Arabic origin. Means: queen.

Suma: Egyptian/Japanese origin. Means: to ask.

Sumaali: Unknown origin and meaning.

Sumiko: Unknown origin and meaning.

Summer: Old English origin. Means: in reference to summertime. Alternative spelling: Somer.

Sunni: Unknown origin and meaning.

Sunserrea: Unknown origin and meaning.

Sura: Hebrew origin. Means: a princess.

Surele: Hebrew origin. Means: a princess. Alternative spelling: Sureli.

Suria: Unknown origin and meaning.

Susan: Hebrew/Anglo-Saxon origin. Means: a lily, a rose. Ethnic backgrounds: English/Welsh. Alternative spellings and nicknames: Suzelle, Susy, Zsa Zsa, Suzette, Suzannah, Susano, Suzy, Suzetta, Suzie, Sukey, Suzi, Siusan, Sue, Suki, Susana, Susanetta, Suzanna, Susie, Suzanne, Susi, Susette, Susanna, Susannah, Susanne, Suse, Sosanna, Susette, Susie.

Susanna: Hebrew origin. Means: a lily, a rose. Ethnic backgrounds: Swedish, Italian.

Suzu: Unknown origin. Means: a bell.

Svetlana: Greek/Slavic origin. Means: light, a star. Ethnic background: Russian. Alternative spellings: Svetlanta, Swetlana.

Swanhilda: Teutonic origin. Means: a swan battle maiden, beautiful. Alternative spellings: Swanhild, Swannhilda.

Swoosie: Unknown origin and meaning.

Sybil: Greek/Latin origin. Means: prophetess, wise. Alternative spellings: Sybilia, Sybille.

Sydelle: Hebrew origin. Means: enchantress. Alternative spelling: Sydel.

Sydni: French/Old English origin. Means: of St. Denis, of the riverside meadow. Alternative spelling: Sydnie.

Sylvan: Latin origin. Means: a forest dweller.

Sylvia: Latin origin. Means: a maiden of the forest. Ethnic background: Swedish. Alternative spellings and nicknames: Sylva, Zilvia, Sylvana, Syl, Silvie, Silvana, Silvia, Silva, Sylvie, Sylwia.

Syna: Greek origin. Means: together.

Synneove: Anglo-Saxon origin. Means: the sun's gift. Ethnic background: Norwegian.

Szeja: Unknown origin and meaning.

t **Taahirah:** Arabic origin. Means: chaste.
Taa'ibah: Arabic origin. Means: repentant.
Tabassum: Arabic origin. Means: smile.

Tabina: Unknown origin. Means: a follower.

Tabitha: Aramaic/Hebrew origin. Means: a doe, gazelle, goat. Alternative spellings and nicknames: Tabbi, Tabbie, Tabby, Tabatha, Tabita.

Tacita: Latin origin. Means: silent.

Tahanie: Unknown origin and meaning.

Tahj: Unknown origin and meaning.

Taima: Native American origin. Means: crash, thunder.

Taiwo: African origin. Means: firstborn of twins.

Taja: Unknown origin and meaning.

Takeyla: Unknown origin and meaning.

Takora: Unknown origin and meaning.

Tala: Native American origin. Means: a wolf.

Talanta: Unknown origin and meaning.

Talashah: Unknown origin and meaning.

Talia: Greek/Hebrew origin. Means: joyous, dew of heaven. Alternative spellings and nicknames: Tallie, Tally, Thalia, Talea, Talina, Talya, Taaliya.

Talis: Unknown origin and meaning.

Talitha: Aramaic origin. Means: a damsel, maiden. Ethnic background: Hispanic. Alternative spellings: Taletha, Talie.

Tallulah: Native American origin. Means: leaping water, vivacious. Alternative spellings and nicknames: Tallie, Tallou, Tallu, Tallula, Tally.

Talorian: Unknown origin and meaning.

Tama: Hebrew origin. Means: astonishment, with wonder. Alternative spellings: Tamah, Tame.

Tamara: Hebrew origin. Means: a palm tree, righteous. Ethnic backgrounds: German, Hispanic, Russian. Alternative spellings: Tamar, Temara, Tamma, Tema, Timara.

Tamatra: Unknown origin and meaning.

Tami: Japanese origin. Means: people. Alternative spelling: Tamiko.

Tamia: Unknown origin and meaning.

Tammy: Hebrew origin. Means: a palm tree, righteous, perfection. Alternative spellings: Tammi, Tammie.

Tani: Unknown origin and meaning.

Tanisha: Unknown origin and meaning. Alternative spellings: Tanaisha, Tanyasha.

Tansy: Greek/Latin origin. Means: immortal, tenacious.

Tanya: Latin/Slavic origin. Means: a fairy queen. Alternative spellings: Tania, Tanja.

Tanzenakia: Unknown origin and meaning.

Tara: Gaelic origin. Means: a hill, a rocky tower, crag. Ethnic background: Irish. Alternative spelling: Tera.

Tari: Hebrew origin. Means: fresh, ripe.

Tarkisseya: Unknown origin and meaning.

Tarrah: Aramaic origin. Means: a measurement, to carry.

Tarsila: Unknown origin and meaning. Ethnic background: Hispanic.

Taryn: Greek/Welsh origin. Means: innocent one, thunder.

Tasha: Latin/Slavic origin. Means: a birthday, Christmas.

Tashae: Unknown origin and meaning.

Tasneem: Unknown origin. Means: elevate.

Tatiana: Latin/Slavic origin. Unknown meaning. Ethnic background: Russian. Alternative spellings: Tatianas, Tatianna, Tatanisha, Tateanna, Tatia, Tatjana, Tatyana, Tayteaona.

Tatu: African origin. Means: the third born.

Tatum: Old English origin. Means: a cheerful bringer of joy.

Tauri: Unknown origin and meaning.

Tawanna: Unknown origin and meaning.

Tayana: Unknown origin and meaning.

Taybah: Arabic origin. Means: pure.

Tayla: Unknown origin and meaning.

Tayler: Unknown origin and meaning. Alternative spelling: Taelor.

Tay-yibah: Arabic origin. Means: good, sweet.

Teara: Unknown origin and meaning. Alternative spellings: Tearra, Teayrra, Teairra, Theara, Tieara, Tiera.

Tehillah: Unknown origin and meaning.

Teiko: Japanese origin. Unknown meaning.

Tempest: French origin. Means: tempestuous, stormy. Alternative spellings and nicknames: Stormy, Tempestt.

Templa: Latin origin. Means: a sanctuary. Alternative spellings: Templas, Templia, Tempa.

Tempora: Unknown origin and meaning. Ethnic background: Hispanic.

Teneah: Unknown origin and meaning.

Tenika: Unknown origin and meaning.

Terentia: Greek origin. Means: guardian.

Teri: Latin/Germanic origin. Means: polished, of the powerful tribe.

Teria: Unknown origin. Means: child, vital.

Terina: Unknown origin. Means: earthly. Alternative spellings: Terren, Terrena, Terrene, Terena.

Terrilyn: Unknown origin and meaning.

Terrishea: Unknown origin and meaning.

Tertia: Latin origin. Means: the third-born child. Alternative spellings and nicknames: Terias, Teria, Terza, Tia, Tertias, Terza, Terzas.

Teryri: Unknown origin and meaning.

Tesaura: Hebrew origin. Means: a gift. Ethnic background: Hispanic.

Tesia: Greek/Polish origin. Means: loved by God, a farmer.

Tesla: Unknown origin and meaning.

Tessa: Greek origin. Means: reaper, born fourth. Alternative spellings and nicknames: Tessy, Tessi, Tessie, Tess, Tesslyn.

Tevonna: Unknown origin and meaning.

Thaddea: Greek/Latin origin. Means: God's gift, full of praise. Alternative spellings: Thada, Thadda, Thadine.

Thaelassa: Greek origin. Means: from the sea.

Thais: Greek origin. Means: beloved girl, giving.

Thale: Unknown origin and meaning. Ethnic background: Norwegian.

Thalia: Greek origin. Means: blooming, to flourish, of comedy.

Thameenah: Arabic origin. Means: valuable.

Naming for Two

What are the considerations you need to keep in mind when naming twins, triplets, or other multiples? A lot of it is personal preference: whether you want a theme or would like to use the same first initial for each or whatever. But there *are* some things on the next few pages you might want to keep in mind.

Thea: Greek origin. Means: divine, extraordinarily beautiful. Alternative spelling: Theano.

Thecie: Greek origin. Means: divine fame. Alternative spellings: Thekla, Thecia, Thecla, Tecla, Tekia.

Thelma: Greek origin. Means: a nursling, an infant, to wish. Alternative spelling: Thelme, Thel, Telma.

Thema: Egyptian origin. Means: queen, custom. Ethnic background: African.

Themis: Greek origin. Means: custom, justice. Alternative spellings: Thema, Tema.

Thenna: Unknown origin. Means: vigorous.

Theodora: Greek origin. Means: God's divine gift. Ethnic background: German. Alternative spellings: Teodora, Tedora.

Theodosia: Greek origin. Means: God's divine gift. Alternative spellings and nicknames: Dosie, Dosia, Teodosia, Theda, Feodosia, Thede.

Theola: Greek origin. Means: God's divine gift. Alternative spellings and nicknames: Theo, Lola.

Theone: Greek origin. Means: one who is godly, divine.

Theophania: Greek origin. Means: God's appearance.

Theophila: Greek origin. Means: beloved of God. Alternative spellings: Teophila, Theophilos.

Theora: Greek origin. Means: contemplator, one who watches.

Theresa: Greek origin. Means: reaper, to reap, gleaner. Ethnic backgrounds: English/Welsh. Alternative spellings and nicknames: Tessie, Tessy, Threse, Tessi, Tresa, Trescha, Teressa, Terra, Terri, Terrie, Terrye, Tracy, Therese, Tracey, Terese, Zita, Tracie, Teresa, Tera, Tessa, Teresita, Teri, Terry, Tess.

Thesda: Unknown origin. Means: a fountain.

Thetes: Greek origin. Means: beautiful, dogmatic. Alternative spellings: Thetis, Thetisa, Thetos.

Thia: Greek origin. Means: God's divine gift.

Thila: Unknown origin and meaning. Ethnic background: Hispanic.

Thilde: Teutonic origin. Means: a battle maiden. Ethnic background: German. Alternative spelling: Thilda.

Thirze: Hebrew origin. Means: a delight, pleasantness. Alternative spellings: Thyrza, Tirza, Thirza, Thirzi, Thirzia, Thissa.

Thisbe: Greek origin. Means: from the place of the doves, loss. Alternative spelling: Thisbee.

Thomasina: Aramaic/Greek/Hebrew origin. Means: a twin. Alternative spellings and nicknames: Thomasin, Tommi, Toma, Tamzin, Tammie, Tammi, Tommy, Tommie, Tomasine, Tomasina, Thomasa, Thomasine.

Thora: Norse origin. Means: thunderous. Alternative spellings: Thordia, Thoris, Tyra, Tora, Thoraia.

Thorberta: Norse/Teutonic origin. Means: brilliance, Thor's glory.

Thorida: Norse origin. Means: the spirit of Thor. Alternative spelling: Thordis.

Thorma: Norse/Old English origin. Means: one with Thor's protection. Alternative spelling: Thormora.

Thurai-yaa: Arabic origin. Means: with luster.

Thyra: Greek origin. Means: one who carries a shield, untamed. Alternative spelling: Thera.

Tia: Anglo-Saxon origin. Unknown meaning. Alternative spellings: Tya, Teia.

Tiaja: Unknown origin and meaning.

Tiana: Unknown origin and meaning. Alternative spellings: Tianah, Tiani, Tianna, Tiona, Tyanna, Tyonna.

Tiara: Unknown origin and meaning. Alternative spellings: Tiarra, Tiaurra.

Tibelda: Germanic origin. Means: the boldest one.

Tiberia: Latin/Italian origin. Means: of the Tiber River. Nicknames: Tibbie, Tibby.

Tica: Unknown origin and meaning.

Tiffany: Greek origin. Means: God will appear, epiphany. 45th most popular girl's name of the '90s. Alternative spellings and nicknames: Tiff, Tiffa, Tiffi, Tiffie, Tiffy, Tifanie, Tiffani, Tiffanie, Tiphani.

Tikey: Unknown origin and meaning. Ethnic background: Greek.

Tilda: Teutonic origin. Means: one who is mighty in battle. Nicknames: Tildy, Tildi, Tildie.

Tima: Unknown origin and meaning.

Tina: Latin/Anglo-Saxon origin. Means: short form of names ending in *tina*.

Tinaret: Unknown origin. Means: a friend.

Tine: Anglo-Saxon origin. Means: a river. Ethnic background: Norwegian.

Tineke: Unknown origin and meaning. Ethnic background: Dutch.

Tirza: Hebrew origin. Means: delight, desirable, a cyprus tree. Alternative spelling: Tierza.

Tisbe: Unknown origin and meaning. Alternative spelling: Tisbee.

Tish: Latin origin. Means: of noble birth, gladness.

Tita: Latin origin. Means: a title of honor.

Titania: Greek origin. Means: a titan, giant. Nicknames: Tania, Tita.

Titilayo: Unknown origin and meaning.

Tivona: Hebrew origin. Means: lover of nature.

Naming for Two

I think the most important part of picking a name is that one day you'll be able to sit with the child and tell him why that name suited him as an individual.

~ **Val W., Seattle, Washington**

Toby: Hebrew/Greek origin. Means: God is good. Alternative spellings and nicknames: Tova, Tybi, Tybie, Tove, Tobi, Tobe, Tobey, Tobye.

Toiba: Hebrew origin. Means: a dove, goodly. Alternative spelling: Toibe.

Tolasa: Unknown origin and meaning. Ethnic background: Hispanic.

Tomi: Japanese origin. Unknown meaning.

Tone: Unknown origin and meaning. Ethnic background: Norwegian.

Toni: Latin origin. Means: beyond worth or praise. Alternative spellings: Tonie, Toinette, Tonia, Tonya.

Topeka: Unknown origin and meaning.

Topez: Latin origin. Means: a colorful gem. Alternative spelling: Topaza, Topaz.

Torborg: Norse/Teutonic origin. Means: a fortified place, Thorlike.

Tori: Hebrew origin. Means: my turtledove. Alternative spelling: Tory.

Torild: Norse origin. Means: Thor's cauldron.

Torkwase: African origin. Means: queen.

Tormoria: Unknown origin and meaning.

Torunn: Norse origin. Means: Thor's love.

Toshiko: Japanese origin. Unknown meaning.

Tourmaline: Singhalese origin. Means: the tourmaline gem, colorful.

Tovah: Hebrew origin. Means: good.

Traci: Greek/Latin origin. Means: brave fighter, bold, reaper. Alternative spelling: Tracie.

TraShonda: Unknown origin and meaning.

Traviata: Italian origin. Means: astray.

Trechelle: Unknown origin and meaning.

Treindel: Unknown origin and meaning. Ethnic background: Jewish.

Trela: Persian/Spanish origin. Means: evening star. Alternative spellings: Trella, Trellas.

Treva: Unknown origin. Means: home lover. Alternative spelling: Trevah.

Trevina: Unknown origin and meaning.

Triana: Unknown origin and meaning. Alternative spelling: Trana.

Tricilla: Unknown origin and meaning.

Trilby: Old English/Italian origin. Means: a fluffy hat, to sing with trills. Alternative spellings and nicknames: Trill, Trilbi, Trilly, Trilbee.

Trina: Greek origin. Means: one with purity, innocent. Ethnic background: Irish. Alternative spellings and nicknames: Trenna, Trinee, Trinia, Trena, Trine, Tryn.

Trinette: Greek/French origin. Means: one with purity, innocent. Alternative spellings and nicknames: Rinee, Trini, Trinatte, Trinetta.

Trinity: Unknown origin and meaning.

Trinotera: Unknown origin and meaning. Ethnic background: Hispanic.

Trisha: Latin origin. Means: of noble birth. Alternative spelling: Tricia.

Trista: Latin origin. Means: melancholy, full of sorrow. Alternative spellings and nicknames: Tris, Tristas, Tristan, Tristin, Tristyn, Trisus.

Trixie: Latin origin. Means: a blessing, one who brings happiness. Alternative spellings and nicknames: Trix, Trixi, Trissie, Trixy.

Trude: Norse/Germanic origin. Means: a warrior, woman with great strength. Ethnic background: German.

Trudy: Teutonic origin. Means: loved one, adored warrior. Alternative spellings and nicknames: Trudel, Trudi, Trudie, Truda.

Truth: Old English origin. Means: conformity with fact.

Tryphena: Latin origin. Means: delicate.

Tuesday: Latin/Old English origin. Means: Mars's day.

Tulip: Turkish origin. Means: a turban, bell-shaped flower.

Tullia: Latin/Gaelic origin. Means: peaceful, serene. Ethnic background: Italian.

Turid: Norse origin. Means: reference to Thor's beauty.

Turnina: Unknown origin and meaning. Ethnic background: Hispanic.

Turquoisia: French origin. Means: a sky-blue gem.

Tycell: Unknown origin and meaning.

Tyesha: Unknown origin and meaning. Alternative spelling: Ty'eshia.

Tykesha: Unknown origin and meaning.

Tylonda: Unknown origin and meaning.

Tyne: Anglo-Saxon origin. Means: a river.

Tyra: Greek/Scottish origin. Means: untamed, wild. Ethnic background: Norwegian. Alternative spelling: Tira.

Tzaitel: Hebrew origin. Means: a princess.

Tzerin: Persian/Hebrew origin. Means: a morning star.

Tzigane: Hungarian origin. Means: a gypsy.

Tzipa: Hebrew origin. Means: a bird. Alternative spelling: Tzipi.

U

Uchechi: African origin. Means: God's will.

Udele: Anglo-Saxon origin. Means: one who is wealthy, of the yew tree valley. Alternative spellings: Uda, Udelle, Udella, Udela.

Uela: Unknown origin. Means: dedicated to God. Alternative spelling: Uella.

Uganda: Unknown origin and meaning.

Ula: Celtic/Teutonic origin. Means: a jewel of the sea, estate's heir. Alternative spellings: Ylla, Ula, Ulla, Eula, Ulah.

Ulda: Unknown origin. Means: prophetess.

Ule: Unknown origin. Means: burdens.

Ulielmi: Unknown origin and meaning. Ethnic background: Hispanic.

Ulima: Unknown origin. Means: learned.

Ulla: Germanic/Norse origin. Means: one with power and riches. Ethnic background: Swedish.

Ulphi: Unknown origin. Means: lovely. Alternative spellings: Ulphia, Ulphiah.

Ulrica: Teutonic origin. Means: wolf ruler, a strong brave ruler. Ethnic backgrounds: Swedish, German. Alternative spellings and nicknames: Ulrika, Rica, Ulrika, Ulrike.

Ultima: Latin origin. Means: aloof, the final end.

Ulva: Germanic origin. Means: the wolf, courage.

Uma: Indic origin. Means: bright.

Umberlina: Unknown origin and meaning. Ethnic background: Hispanic.

Umeko: Unknown origin. Means: blossom.

Una: Latin/Gaelic origin. Means: unity, one, famine. Ethnic background: Irish. Alternative spellings: Oona, Ona.

Undine: Latin origin. Means: a wave. Alternative spelling: Ondine.

Unique: Latin origin. Means: one, the one.

Unity: Latin/Irish origin. Means: together, one.

Urania: Greek origin. Means: heavenly. Alternative spellings and nicknames: Urana, Uranie, Ranie, Rania.

Urbai: Unknown origin. Means: gentle.

Urbana: Latin origin. Means: born in the city. Alternative spellings: Urbani, Urbanna, Urbannai.

Urbi: Egyptian origin. Means: a princess. Ethnic background: African.

Naming for Two

As the mother of identical girls, I can tell you that it is much quicker to write their initials instead of writing out their full names. Every day I am thankful that we went with names that start with different letters! My suggestion— think of your absolute favorite names and use those. Not because they go together but because you want to say those names for the rest of your life.

~ Teddi B.,
Bainbridge Island, Washington

Uria: Hebrew origin. Means: God is my flame. Alternative spellings and nicknames: Urissa, Ria, Uri, Uriah, Urial.

Ursa: Latin/Germanic origin. Means: a female bear. Alternative spellings: Ursal, Ursala, Ursas.

Ursula: Latin origin. Means: a female bear. Ethnic backgrounds: German, Irish, Hispanic, Polish. Alternative spellings and nicknames: Orsa, Ursy, Ursulina, Ursulette, Ursi, Nullie, Ursie, Ursola, Ursuline, Ursule, Ursel, Ursala, Orsola, Ursa, Ursule, Ursola, Urszula.

Urta: Latin origin. Means: a spiny plant, homeland.

Uta: Teutonic origin. Means: a battle heroine, homeland.

Utas: Unknown origin and meaning.

Ute: Germanic origin. Means: one with prosperity and riches.

Utica: Native American origin. Unknown meaning. Alternative spellings: Uticas, Uttica.

Uttasta: Unknown origin and meaning.

Uzia: Hebrew origin. Means: God is my strength. Alternative spellings: Uzza, Uzial, Uzzial.

Uzoma: African origin. Means: the right way.

V **Vacla:** Unknown origin. Means: endearing.

Vaclava: Slavic/Czech origin. Means: one with greater glory.

Vadnee: Unknown origin and meaning.

Vala: Welsh origin. Means: chosen one.

Valborg: Swedish origin. Means: a powerful mountain. Ethnic background: Norwegian.

Valborga: Germanic origin. Means: a protective ruler.

Valda: Teutonic/Norse origin. Means: heroine of battle, one who rules. Alternative spellings and nicknames: Velina, Val, Valina.

Valeda: Latin origin. Means: vigorous, sound of body, brave. Alternative spellings and nicknames: Leda, Valeta, Vala, Aleda, Vale, Valeta, Valida, Vallada, Valydia.

Valentina: Latin origin. Means: one who is strong and healthy, valiant. Ethnic backgrounds: Russian, Italian. Alternative spellings and nicknames: Vally, Vallie, Valera, Valiina, Valora, Teena, Vaili, Valerie, Valeria, Valentia, Valencia, Valeda, Vale, Val, Tina, Valentine.

Valerie: Latin/French origin. Means: one who is strong and healthy, valiant. Ethnic backgrounds: Hungarian, German, Italian. Alternative spellings and nicknames: Valli, Valoree, Vallie, Valerye, Valaree, Valeree, Valrie, Vally, Valery, Valeria, Vale, Val.

Valma: Unknown origin. Means: a flower.

Vanda: Germanic/Polish origin. Means: one who wanders.

Vanessa: Greek origin. Means: a butterfly. Ethnic background: Irish. Alternative spellings and nicknames: Nessy, Vanny, Vannie, Vanni, Nessie, Vanna, Van, Nessi, Nessa, Vania, Vanessaa, Venissa.

Vani: Unknown origin. Means: child, tranquil.

Vania: Hebrew/Greek origin. Means: gift of God, a butterfly. Alternative spellings and nicknames: Van, Vanna.

Vanora: Welsh origin. Means: a white wave. Ethnic background: Hispanic.

Vanthe: Greek origin. Means: a flowering blossom.

Varda: Hebrew origin. Means: a rose.

Varina: Greek origin. Means: a stranger.

Varna: Unknown origin and meaning.

Vashti: Persian origin. Means: fairest, beautiful. Alternative spellings: Vasthia, Vastha, Vasti, Ashti, Vashtia, Vashtee.

Vasta: Unknown origin and meaning. Alternative spelling: Vastah.

Vaydell: Unknown origin and meaning.

Veda: Sanskrit/Teutonic origin. Means: knowledge, with understanding, the spirit of the forest. Alternative spellings: Vedis, Veedis.

Vedetta: Italian/French origin. Means: a guard of the watchtower. Alternative spelling: Vedette.

Vedi: Unknown origin and meaning.

Vega: Arabic/Latin origin. Means: a falling star.

Velacy: Unknown origin and meaning.

Velda: Teutonic origin. Means: wisdom of inspiration. Alternative spellings: Veleda, Valeda.

Velika: Slavic origin. Means: one who is great.

Velma: Teutonic origin. Means: firm protector, the helmet. Alternative spelling: Vilma.

Velonie: Latin origin. Means: from the vale or valley. Alternative spellings and nicknames: Val, Vallonia, Valoniah, Valonia.

Velore: Latin origin. Means: one with great valor.

Velvet: Old English origin. Means: velvety, soft.

Veneranda: Unknown origin and meaning. Ethnic background: Hispanic.

Venetia: Celtic origin. Means: blessed one.

Venice: Latin/Italian origin. Means: a palm.

Venke: Unknown origin and meaning. Ethnic background: Norwegian.

Ventura: Latin origin. Means: one with good fortune. Alternative spelling: Venture.

Venus: Latin origin. Means: possessing great beauty. Alternative spellings and nicknames: Vinnie, Vin, Venita, Vinny, Vinita.

Vera: Latin/Slavic origin. Means: faith, forthright, true. Ethnic backgrounds: Czech, Norwegian, Russian, German. Alternative spellings and nicknames: Verine, Verra, Verina, Verene, Vere, Verena, Veradis, Verla, Verada, Veradi, Veradia, Veradis.

Verbena: Latin origin. Means: a sacred bough. Alternative spellings and nicknames: Benia, Verbenia, Bena.

Verda: Latin origin. Means: springlike, fresh, new. Nickname: Verdie.

Verena: Germanic origin. Means: defender, guardian of friends. Alternative spellings: Verene, Verina.

Verla: Germanic origin. Means: defender, guardian of friends.

Verlita: Unknown origin and meaning. Ethnic background: Hispanic.

Verneta: Latin origin. Means: springlike, born in spring. Alternative spellings: Vernita, Verna, Virena, Virna.

Verona: Latin/Italian origin. Means: true, of Verona. Ethnic backgrounds: Hispanic, English/Welsh.

Veronica: Greek/Latin origin. Means: honest, true image. Ethnic background: Italian. Alternative spellings: Veroica, Veronika, Veronique.

Vespera: Latin origin. Means: an evening star.

Veste: Latin origin. Means: dweller of the hearth. Ethnic background: Hispanic. Alternative spellings: Esta, Vesta.

Vetaria: Unknown origin and meaning. Ethnic background: Hispanic.

Vevila: Celtic/Irish origin. Means: harmonious.

Vevina: Irish origin. Means: a sweet lady. Alternative spelling: Vevine.

Vianca: Unknown origin and meaning.

Vibeke: Germanic origin. Means: a small lady. Ethnic background: Norwegian.

Vicki: Latin origin. Means: victorious one. Ethnic backgrounds: English/Welsh, German. Alternative spelling: Vicky.

Victoria: Latin origin. Means: a victory, victorious. Ethnic backgrounds: English/Welsh, Irish. 18th most popular girl's name of the '90s. Alternative spellings and nicknames: Vickie, Victorie, Vikki, Vikky, Vicki, Vicky, Victoire, Victorine, Vitoria, Vittoria, Vic, Vyctoria, Viktoria.

Vida: Hebrew origin. Means: beloved one. Alternative spellings: Viddah, Vidette, Vidda, Davida.

Vidonia: Portuguese origin. Means: branch of a vine. Alternative spelling: Vidonie.

Viera: Unknown origin and meaning. Ethnic background: Czech.

Vigdis: Norse/Teutonic origin. Means: goddess of war. Ethnic background: Norwegian.

Vigilia: Latin origin. Means: one who is alert, watchful, vigilant. Alternative spelling: Vigilie.

Vignette: French origin. Means: a small vine.

Vihelmina: Germanic origin. Means: a resolute protector.

Villette: French origin. Means: from the country estate.

Vina: Spanish origin. Means: bright, sweet, a vineyard. Alternative spellings: Vinna, Veena, Vena.

Vincentia: Latin origin. Means: conqueror, to conquer. Alternative spelling: Vincenta.

Vinefrida: Unknown origin and meaning. Ethnic background: Hispanic.

Vinia: Unknown origin and meaning. Alternative spelling: Vinisa.

Vinita: Latin origin. Means: beauty, from Venice. Alternative spelling: Venita.

Vinne: Anglo-Saxon origin. Means: of the vine. Alternative spellings: Vine, Vina.

Violet: Latin origin. Means: violet, a flower. Alternative spellings and nicknames: Violetta, Yolane, Vye, Eolande, Vi, Iolande, Viole, Yolanthe, Yolande, Yolanda, Violante, Viola, Iolanthe, Violette, Violeta.

Virgilia: Latin origin. Means: bearer of the staff, thriving, strong.

Virginia: Latin/various origin. Means: she who is pure, thriving, strong. Ethnic backgrounds: English/Welsh, Italian. Alternative spellings and nicknames: Virgy, Virgini, Virgie, Jinny, Ginny, Ginnie, Ginni, Virgilia, Ginger, Virginie.

Viridas: Latin origin. Means: blooming, young. Alternative spelling: Viridis.

Vision: Latin origin. Means: one who sees.

Vita: Latin origin. Means: life, lively, intelligent. Alternative spellings: Veta, Vida, Vitia.

Viveka: Teutonic origin. Means: of the strong fortress. Ethnic background: Swedish. Alternative spellings: Viveca, Vivica.

Vivi: Latin/French origin. Means: alive, lively, full of life. Ethnic background: Norwegian. Alternative spellings: Viva, Vieva.

Vivienne: Latin/French origin. Means: alive, lively, full of life. Ethnic background: Irish. Alternative spellings: Vivyan, Viviana, Vivianna, Vivien.

Vlasta: Czech origin. Unknown meaning.

Volante: Italian origin. Means: flying.

Voleta: French origin. Means: one who is veiled, a mystery. Alternative spellings: Voletta, Vola.

Vona: Unknown origin. Means: one who is brave.

Vyera: Unknown origin and meaning. Ethnic background: Russian.

W

Waahidah: Arabic origin. Means: one, unique.

Wahkuna: Native American origin. Means: beautiful. Alternative spelling: Wakkuna.

Waka: Japanese origin. Unknown meaning. Alternative spelling: Wakako.

Walburg: Teutonic origin. Means: a mighty defender, a fortress. Ethnic background: German.

Walda: Germanic origin. Means: a ruler, leader. Alternative spellings: Waldo, Welda.

Wallis: French/Anglo-Saxon origin. Means: a foreign man, Welshman. Nicknames: Wally, Wallie.

Waltraut: Teutonic origin. Means: one with much power. Ethnic background: German.

Wanda: Teutonic origin. Means: a wanderer. Ethnic backgrounds: German, Hispanic. Alternative spellings and nicknames: Wendi, Wendye, Wendie, Wandie, Wendy, Wendeline, Wandis, Vanda, Wenda.

Wanetta: Anglo-Saxon origin. Means: she with a fair complexion. Alternative spelling: Wannett.

Warda: Teutonic/Old English origin. Means: a guardian, one who watches. Alternative spellings: Wardena, Wardah.

Waseme: African origin. Unknown meaning.

Wednesday: Latin origin. Means: day of Mercury.

Welcome: Anglo-Saxon origin. Means: to welcome, greet gladly.

Wendelin: Slavic/Teutonic origin. Means: a wanderer. Ethnic background: German. Alternative spellings and nicknames: Wendie, Wende, Wendelina, Wendolyn, Wendy, Wendeline.

Wendy: Teutonic/Celtic origin. Means: a wanderer, fair complexioned. Ethnic backgrounds: English/Welsh. Alternative spellings and nicknames: Wendi, Wendie, Wendye, Wenda, Wendeline.

Wera: Latin/Polish origin. Means: faith, forthright, true. Ethnic background: German.

Wesla: Old English origin. Means: from the western clearing. Alternative spellings and nicknames: Weslee, Wesle, Wesa, Wesley, Wes.

Wharton: Anglo-Saxon origin. Means: dweller of the estate at the hollow.

Whitlee: Anglo-Saxon origin. Means: from the white meadow.

Widnie: Unknown origin and meaning.

Wiep: Unknown origin and meaning. Ethnic background: Dutch.

Wieteke: Unknown origin and meaning. Ethnic background: Dutch.

Wilda: Anglo-Saxon origin. Means: untamed, wild one. Alternative spellings: Wilde, Wildee.

Wilesha: Unknown origin and meaning.

Wilfrede: Teutonic origin. Means: determined maker of peace. Alternative spellings and nicknames: Wildfreda, Freda.

Wilhelmina: Teutonic origin. Means: a determined protector. Ethnic backgrounds: Dutch, German. Alternative spellings and nicknames: Willeta, Billi, Willamina, Willabella, Willabel, Willabelle, Willa, Wileen, Vilhelmina, Guilema, Minny, Guglielma, Min, Minni, Billie, Willette, Willa, Wilhelmine, Wilhelma, Vilma, Velma, Valma, Billy, Willi, Guillelmina, Guillelmine, Guillemette, Helma, Mimi, Mina, Minna, Minnie, Willemien, Willemijn.

Willeke: Unknown origin and meaning. Ethnic background: Dutch.

Willette: Teutonic origin. Means: a determined protector. Alternative spelling: Wilette.

Willow: Old English origin. Means: of the willow tree, graceful.

Willtrude: Unknown origin and meaning.

Wilma: Teutonic/Anglo-Saxon origin. Means: a determined protector. Ethnic backgrounds: Hispanic, Dutch.

Wilona: Anglo-Saxon origin. Means: one who is desired. Alternative spellings: Wilonah, Wilone.

Wilva: Teutonic origin. Means: one who is determined.

Winema: Native American origin. Means: a female chief.

Winifred: Teutonic/Old English origin. Means: a peace-loving friend. Ethnic background: Irish. Alternative spellings and nicknames: Freddy, Winnifred, Winfried, Win, Winny, Freddi, Fredi, Oona, Winnie, Ona, Freddie, Una.

Winola: Germanic origin. Means: a gracious friend.

Winona: Native American origin. Means: one who is giving, firstborn girl. Alternative spellings: Winonah, Wenona, Wenonah, Wenoa, Wanonah, Wynonna.

Wira: Polish origin. Means: white.

Wiske: Unknown origin and meaning. Ethnic background: Dutch.

Wivina: Unknown origin and meaning. Alternative spellings: Wivinah, Wivinia.

Wyanda: Unknown origin and meaning.

Wynne: Welsh origin. Means: a fair one, handsome, blessed. Alternative spellings and nicknames: Wyne, Winny, Winnie.

X

Xanthe: Greek origin. Means: yellow, fair-haired, bright. Alternative spelling: Xantha.

Xantipa: Unknown origin and meaning. Ethnic background: Hispanic.

Xaviera: Arabic/Basque origin. Means: brilliant, of the new house.

Xaykevia: Unknown origin and meaning.

Xenia: Greek origin. Means: one who is hospitable to strangers. Ethnic background: German. Alternative spellings: Zena, Zenia, Xena, Xene.

Xianne: Unknown origin and meaning.

Ximena: Hebrew/Spanish origin. Means: God has heard.

Xiomara: Greek origin. Means: one who is hospitable to strangers.

Xochil: Unknown origin and meaning. Ethnic background: Hispanic.

Xylia: Greek origin. Means: of the woods. Alternative spelling: Xylina.

Xylona: Greek origin. Means: of the woods. Alternative spelling: Xylone.

Y

Yahaira: Unknown origin and meaning.

Yaira: Hebrew origin. Means: to enlighten.

Yamilet: Unknown origin and meaning.

Yamina: Unknown origin and meaning.

Yanee: Unknown origin and meaning.

Yanina: Unknown origin and meaning.

Yar: Unknown origin and meaning.

Yaritza: Unknown origin and meaning.

Yasema: Unknown origin and meaning. Alternative spelling: Yesima.

Yasmine: Persian/Arabic origin. Means: fragrantly flowered shrub. Alternative spellings: Yasmin, Yaasameen.

Yasu: Unknown origin. Means: tranquil.

Yatavia: Unknown origin and meaning.

Ydia: Unknown origin and meaning. Ethnic background: Hispanic.

Yedda: Old English origin. Means: one with a beautiful voice. Alternative spelling: Yetta.

Yelana: Greek/Slavic origin. Means: light, ray of the sun. Ethnic background: Russian.

Yesenia: Unknown origin and meaning.

Yesifin: Unknown origin and meaning.

Yette: Old English origin. Means: generous one, head of the house. Alternative spellings and nicknames: Yetida, Yetii, Yeta, Yetah, Yetta, Yetti.

Yevgenia: Greek/Slavic origin. Means: one who is well born, noble. Ethnic background: Russian. Alternative spelling: Yevgenya.

Yoko: Japanese origin. Means: positive.

Yolanda: Greek origin. Means: flower, a violet, modest. Ethnic background: Hispanic. Alternative spellings: Eolande, Iolande, Yolane, Iolanthe, Yolande, Yolanthe, Yolante.

Yomara: Unknown origin and meaning.

Yona: Hebrew origin. Means: a dove. Alternative spellings: Yonah, Yonina, Yonita.

Yoshiko: Japanese origin. Unknown meaning.

Yotti: Hebrew origin. Unknown meaning.

Yseult: Celtic/French origin. Means: the fair one. Alternative spellings: Yseulta, Yseulte.

Yudis: Unknown origin and meaning. Ethnic background: Jewish.

Yulia: Latin origin. Means: young, with youth. Ethnic background: Russian.

Yuta: Hebrew origin. Means: praise. Alternative spellings: Yute, Yutka, Yidel, Yita.

Yvette: Norse/French origin. Means: an archer, with yew-bow.

Yvonnda: Unknown origin and meaning.

Yvonne: Norse/French origin. Means: an archer, with yew-bow. Ethnic backgrounds: German, Dutch, Irish. Alternative spellings and nicknames: Von, Vonnie, Yevette, Yvette, Evonne, Ivonne.

Z

Zaahidah: Arabic origin. Means: hermit.

Zaakirah: Arabic origin. Means: glorifier.

Zabrina: Anglo-Saxon origin. Means: of noble birth. Alternative spellings and nicknames: Zabrine, Brina.

Zacarias: Hebrew origin. Means: remembrance of the Lord. Ethnic background: Hispanic.

Zaelea: Greek origin. Means: blossom, a flower. Alternative spelling: Zelea.

Zahara: Unknown origin. Means: a flower. Alternative spellings: Zaahirah, Zahira.

Zaheerah: Arabic origin. Means: ally.

Zahraa: Arabic origin. Means: beautiful.

Zahtwon: Unknown origin and meaning.

Zaida: Arabic origin. Means: lucky one. Ethnic background: Hispanic. Alternative spelling: Zada.

Zainabu: African origin. Means: beautiful.

Zaitoonah: Arabic origin. Means: olive.

Zaji: Unknown origin and meaning.

Zakiya: African origin. Means: intelligent. Alternative spellings: Zaakiyah, Zachyia.

Zakiyyah: Arabic origin. Means: pure, truthful.

Zakura: Unknown origin and meaning.

Zamara: Unknown origin and meaning.

Zandra: Greek/Latin origin. Means: defender of all mankind.

Zanna: Hebrew/Polish origin. Means: God's gracious gift.

Zapopan: Unknown origin and meaning. Ethnic background: Hispanic.

ZaQuon: Unknown origin and meaning.

Zara: Arabic/Hebrew origin. Means: brightness, a flower, princess, the coming day. Alternative spellings: Zarah, Zarrah, Zaria.

Zaragoza: Unknown origin and meaning. Ethnic background: Hispanic.

Zare: Hebrew origin. Means: morning light.

Zari: Unknown origin and meaning.

Zarna: Unknown origin and meaning.

Zarrita: Unknown origin and meaning.

Zayna: Arabic origin. Means: beauty.

Zdenka: Latin/Czech origin. Means: one from Sidon, a winding-sheet.

Zea: Latin origin. Means: one like ripe grain.

Zebada: Hebrew origin. Means: God's gift. Nickname: Zeba.

Zeenat: Arabic origin. Means: adornment.

Zeese: Unknown origin and meaning. Ethnic background: Greek.

Zela: Hebrew origin. Means: side.

Zelda: Teutonic origin. Means: a gray-haired battle heroine.

Zelia: Greek origin. Means: ardent, devoted, zealous. Alternative spelling: Zelina.

Zena: Persian/Greek origin. Means: a woman, hospitable, of Zeus. Alternative spellings: Zeena, Zenecia, Zenija, Zenia, Zina, Zinah, Zenda, Zendah.

Zenobia: Greek/Arabic origin. Means: born of Zeus, a father's pride. Alternative spellings and nicknames: Znobie, Zenna, Zenaida, Zenda, Zenia, Zena.

Zenzi: Germanic origin. Means: a good omen, to grow. Ethnic background: German.

Zera: Hebrew origin. Means: seeds. Alternative spelling: Zere.

Zerelda: Teutonic origin. Means: armored battle maiden. Alternative spellings: Zeralda, Serilda, Zarelda.

Zerlina: Teutonic origin. Means: calm, beautiful. Alternative spellings and nicknames: Zerla, Zerline, Zerlinda.

Zeta: Greek origin. Means: the one who was born last.

Zetana: Hebrew origin. Means: olive tree, an olive. Alternative spelling: Zetta.

Zeva: Greek/Hebrew origin. Means: sword, wolf.

Zevida: Hebrew origin. Means: a gift.

Zeynep: Unknown origin and meaning.

Zillah: Hebrew origin. Means: in the shade, shadow. Alternative spelling: Zilla.

Zima: Unknown origin. Means: wealth.

Zinaida: Greek/Slavic origin. Means: of Zeus, a sign. Ethnic background: Russian.

Zinnia: Latin origin. Means: the zinnia flower. Alternative spelling: Zinia.

Zipporah: Hebrew origin. Means: beauty, a bird. Alternative spellings and nicknames: Tippie, Tsiporah, Tippi, Ceporah, Zippora.

Zisel: Hebrew origin. Means: sweet.

Zita: Celtic/Spanish origin. Means: enticing, seductive, little hope. Ethnic backgrounds: German, Hispanic. Alternative spellings: Zitella, Zitah.

Zlata: Old English/Polish origin. Means: of gold, golden. Ethnic background: Jewish. Alternative spelling: Zlote.

Zoara: Unknown origin and meaning. Alternative spelling: Zoarah.

Zoba: Unknown origin. Means: a daughter. Alternative spelling: Zobe.

Zobeida: Unknown origin and meaning. Ethnic background: Hispanic.

Zoe: Greek/Latin origin. Means: daughter, life. Alternative spellings: Zoei, Zoie, Zoa.

Zoerina: Unknown origin and meaning.

Zofia: Greek/Polish origin. Means: one with wisdom.

Zoha: Hebrew origin. Means: bright light, brilliance. Alternative spellings: Zohar, Zohara.

Zoila: Unknown origin. Means: child. Alternative spellings: Zoilla, Zoi.

Zona: Hebrew origin. Means: a prostitute, girdle.

Zora: Arabic/Slavic origin. Means: Aurora, the dawn. Alternative spellings: Zorine, Zarya, Zohra, Zorah, Zorana, Zorina.

Zoraida: Unknown origin and meaning. Ethnic background: Hispanic.

Zosima: Unknown origin. Means: wealth. Alternative spellings: Zosema, Zosi.

Zsuzsanna: Hebrew/Hungarian origin. Means: a lily, a rose.

Zuhrah: Arabic origin. Means: planet Venus.

Zulay: Unknown origin and meaning.

Zuleika: Arabic origin. Means: the fair one, bright.

Zulema: Arabic/Hebrew origin. Means: peace. Ethnic background: Hispanic.

Zusa: Unknown origin and meaning.

Zwena: African origin. Means: good.

And Now, for a Little Levity

Just to make sure that you aren't taking this whole naming thing *too* seriously, we've included a joke that someone posted on our boards.

What Your Name Should Be

If:	Then your name is:
You spend a lot of time lying in the yard	Pete
You cook a lot	Stu
People owe you money	Bill
People think you're made of money	Rich
You tend to be stepped on by others	Mat
People always know where you've been	Mark
You tend to have small cuts on your body	Nick
You wake up early	Dawn/Don
You keep putting things off	Will
You're a touchy-feely type of person	Pat
People talk to you a lot	Mike
You like to steal	Rob
You can't stand emptiness	Phil
You're always looking for buried treasure	Doug
You need to shave a lot	Harry
You get beaten a lot	Tom
You end up taking a lot of crap from people	John

~ Kate P., Brooklyn, New York

104

boys' names

Aaaqil: Arabic origin. Means: wise.

Aabid: Arabic origin. Means: worshiper.

Aalam: Arabic origin. Means: universe.

Aarcus: Unknown origin and meaning.

Aaron: Hebrew origin. Means: exalted, enlightened, mountain. 39th most popular boy's name of the '90s. Alternative spellings: Haroun, Aron.

Aashiq: Arabic origin. Means: lover.

Aasif: Arabic origin. Means: intelligence.

Aasim: Arabic origin. Means: protected.

Aatiq: Arabic origin. Means: liberated.

Abaddon: Unknown origin and meaning.

Abahu: Unknown origin and meaning. Ethnic background: Jewish.

Abanobi: African origin. Unknown meaning.

Abasi: African origin. Means: stern.

Aba'ye: Hebrew origin. Means: little father.

Abbo: Unknown origin and meaning.

Abbott: Hebrew origin. Means: abbey, father. Alternative spellings: Abad, Abott, Abbot, Abbe.

Abbottson: Hebrew origin. Means: son of Abbott. Alternative spellings: Abbotsen, Abbotson.

Abdiel: Hebrew origin. Means: servant of God.

Abdon: Unknown origin and meaning.

Abdul: Arabic origin. Means: servant. Alternative spellings: Abd, Abdel.

Abdullah: Arabic origin. Means: servant of Allah.

Abe: Hebrew origin. Means: father of many.

Abednego: Aramaic origin. Means: servant.

Abeeku: African origin. Means: born on Wednesday.

Abejundio: Spanish origin. Means: relating to the *abeja* (bee).

Abel: Hebrew origin. Means: breath. Alternative spelling: Abil.

Abellard: Saxon origin. Means: ambitious, resolute. Nickname: Abbie.

Abercius: Unknown origin and meaning.

Aberlin: Unknown origin and meaning. Ethnic background: Jewish.

Abidla: Unknown origin and meaning.

Abiezer: Hebrew origin. Means: help, salvation.

Abijah: Hebrew origin. Means: Lord is father. Alternative spelling: Abisha.

Abimbola: African origin. Means: born rich.

Abimelech: Hebrew origin. Means: king, father.

Abinadab: Hebrew origin. Means: noble father.

Abioye: African origin. Unknown meaning.

Abir: Hebrew origin. Means: hero.

Abiri: Hebrew origin. Means: gallant one.

Abirio: Unknown origin and meaning. Ethnic background: Hispanic.

Abisia: Unknown origin. Means: father. Alternative spellings: Abixah, Absa.

Abner: Hebrew origin. Means: father, of light. Nicknames: Abbie, Ab.

Aboo: Arabic origin. Means: father.

Abosi: African origin. Means: life plant.

Abraar: Arabic origin. Means: pious, truthful.

Abraham: Hebrew origin. Means: father of the people. Alternative spellings and nicknames: Avram, Abie, Abram, Abe.

Abramo: Hebrew origin. Means: father of many. Ethnic background: Italian.

Abrasha: Hebrew origin. Means: father. Alternative spellings: Abrashen, Abrashke.

Absalom: Hebrew origin. Means: father of peace.

Abundio: Spanish origin. Means: full of good works.

Acacius: Unknown origin and meaning.

Ace: Latin origin. Means: unity, lucky.

Achard: Unknown origin and meaning.

Achille: Latin/Greek origin. Means: hero, lipless. Ethnic background: Italian.

Achim: Unknown origin and meaning. Ethnic background: German.

Acisclo: Unknown origin and meaning. Ethnic background: Hispanic. Alternative spelling: Acisclus.

Ackerley: Saxon origin. Means: acre, oak tree meadow, dweller. Alternative spelling: Ackley.

Adael: Hebrew origin. Means: God is witness.

Adair: Celtic origin. Means: ford.

Adal: Unknown origin. Means: courageous, noble. Alternative spellings: Adall, Adel.

Gender-Bending Names

Unisex names are incredibly popular these days. Parents are bestowing names such as Jordan, Madison, Schuyler, Devon, Bailey, Parker, and Logan on little girls *and* boys with increasing frequency. Nonsupporters say boys who share a name with girls will suffer the teasing of their classmates, à la "You've got a *girl's* name. Eww!" For a peek into the unisex debate, read on.

Adalai: Unknown origin. Means: fair.

Adalard: Germanic origin. Means: brave, noble. Alternative spellings: Adallard, Abelard.

Adalbert: Germanic origin. Means: intelligent, noble.

Adam: Hebrew/Arabic origin. Means: earth, first man. Ethnic backgrounds: Polish, Swedish, German, English/Welsh. 31st most popular boy's name of the '90s. Alternative spellings and nicknames: Addam, Addy, Adan, Addis, Ade, Bram, Adamo, Aadam, Adame, Adams, Adham, Adamek, Adamik.

Adamsen: Hebrew origin. Means: Adam (son of), earth. Alternative spellings: Adamson, Adamsun.

Adaucus: Unknown origin and meaning.

Addai: Unknown origin and meaning.

Addison: Saxon origin. Means: Adam, earth. Alternative spellings: Adis, Addis.

Ade: Saxon/African origin. Means: royal, mound or heap.

Adeeb: Arabic origin. Means: author.

Adelaido: Unknown origin and meaning. Ethnic background: Hispanic.

Adelmo: Unknown origin and meaning. Ethnic background: Italian.

Adelpho: Unknown origin. Means: brother. Alternative spelling: Adelfo.

Adeoye: Unknown origin and meaning. Ethnic backgrounds: English/Welsh.

Adewale: Unknown origin and meaning.

A'dil: Arabic origin. Means: justice. Alternative spelling: Adeel.

Adin: Hebrew origin. Means: pleasant, delicate. Alternative spelling: Adan.

Adir: Hebrew origin. Means: majestic, noble.

Adlai: Hebrew origin. Means: witness, just.

Adlar: Teutonic origin. Means: brave, eagle. Alternative spellings: Adler, Adlare.

Adlay: Hebrew origin. Means: judicious. Alternative spellings: Adlei, Adley.

Adna: Hebrew origin. Means: fortunate, adorned. Alternative spelling: Adnah.

Adney: Saxon origin. Means: island dweller.

Adolph: Germanic origin. Means: hero, noble wolf. Alternative spellings and nicknames: Dolf, Adolpho, Adolfe, Dolph, Adolphus, Adolf, Adolphe, Adulf.

Adom: Egyptian origin. Means: help from God. Ethnic background: African.

Adon: Hebrew origin. Means: Lord.

Adonaldo: Unknown origin and meaning. Ethnic background: Hispanic.

Adonijah: Unknown origin. Means: God is my Lord.

Adrian: Latin origin. Means: dark, from coast, wealthy. Ethnic backgrounds: French, English/Welsh, Hispanic, German, Italian, Dutch. Alternative spellings: Hadrian, Adrien, Adriano, Adrianus.

Adriel: Hebrew origin. Means: congregation, kingdom, majesty. Alternative spellings: Adrell, Adrial, Adriell.

Aedan: Unknown origin and meaning. Ethnic background: Irish.

Aeneas: Greek/Latin origin. Means: praiseworthy, excellent.

Afan: Unknown origin and meaning.

Afanasy: Unknown origin and meaning. Ethnic background: Russian.

Afdhaal: Arabic origin. Means: prominent.

Afililio: Unknown origin and meaning. Ethnic background: Hispanic.

Agapito: Spanish origin. Means: loved one.

Agapius: Unknown origin and meaning.

Agnar: Unknown origin and meaning. Ethnic background: Norwegian.

Agricola: Unknown origin and meaning.

Agripino: Unknown origin and meaning. Ethnic background: Hispanic.

Agueleo: Spanish origin. Means: a sumac-type plant.

Ahab: Hebrew origin. Means: uncle.

Ahad: Arabic origin. Means: unique.

Ahaziah: Unknown origin and meaning.

Ahearn: Celtic origin. Means: horses.

Aherin: Celtic/Gaelic origin. Means: owner of horses. Alternative spellings: Ahern, Aherne.

Ahimelech: Unknown origin. Means: my brother is a king.

Ahmad: Arabic origin. Means: praised one, high.

Ahmoz: Unknown origin and meaning.

Aidan: Saxon/Gaelic origin. Means: fiery, home. Alternative spellings: Aiden, Aidlan, Ayden.

Aided: Unknown origin. Means: adviser.

Aigars: Unknown origin and meaning. Ethnic background: Russian.

Aignan: Unknown origin and meaning.

Aiken: Anglo-Saxon origin. Means: oaken, Adam, large. Alternative spelling: Aikin.

Ailbhe: Unknown origin and meaning.

Ailred: Unknown origin and meaning.

Ainsworth: Saxon origin. Means: from Ann's estate.

Aiwar: Unknown origin and meaning. Ethnic background: Russian.

Aiyetoro: African origin. Means: peace on earth.

Ajax: Greek/Latin origin. Means: eagle.

Ajmal: Arabic origin. Means: handsome.

Akbar: Unknown origin and meaning.

Akeem: Nigerian origin. Unknown meaning. Alternative spellings: Akeam, Akheem.

Akevy: Unknown origin and meaning. Ethnic background: Hungarian.

Akhlaaq: Arabic origin. Means: good qualities.

Akil: Unknown origin and meaning.

Akinori: Japanese origin. Unknown meaning.

Akins: Egyptian origin. Means: a brave boy. Ethnic background: African.

Akiva: Hebrew origin. Means: to hold by the heel.

Akram: Arabic origin. Means: benevolent.

Akwasi: Unknown origin and meaning.

Akwete: African origin. Means: younger of twins.

Al: Various origin. Means: Nickname for Alan, Alistair, Albert, Alexander, Alfred, Alvin, Alphonse.

Alair: Latin origin. Means: happy, alive. Alternative spelling: Allare.

Alan: Celtic origin. Means: cheerful, harmony. Ethnic backgrounds: English/Welsh, Irish. Alternative spellings and nicknames: Alayn, All, Aland, Alano, Alain, Allan, Al, Alen.

Alanson: Celtic origin. Means: son of Alan. Alternative spellings: Alansen, Alenson, Allanson.

Alaric: Teutonic origin. Means: noble leader. Alternative spelling: Adelric.

Alastair: Greek/Scottish origin. Means: defender, helper. Alternative spellings: Alastar, Alister, Allister.

Alban: Latin origin. Means: fair. Ethnic background: Hungarian. Alternative spellings: Alben, Albin, Alva, Aubin, Albano, Albin.

Albany: Unknown origin and meaning.

Albe: Unknown origin. Means: noble.

Alberic: Teutonic origin. Means: skillful ruler. Alternative spelling: Albric.

Albert: Saxon origin. Means: brilliant, noble. Ethnic backgrounds: French, German. Alternative spellings and nicknames: Bertie, Albie, Adelbert, Bert, Alberto, Elbert, Al, Aubert, Ailbert.

Albrecht: Germanic origin. Means: noble, intelligent.

Alcot: Anglo-Saxon origin. Means: cottage.

Aldan: Saxon origin. Means: from old manor.

Aldegundo: Spanish origin. Means: battle of nobility. Ethnic background: Hispanic.

Alden: Anglo-Saxon origin. Means: old friend. Alternative spellings and nicknames: Alwin, Eldin, Elden, Aldwin, Al, Aldin, Aldwon, Aldwyn.

Alder: Anglo-Saxon origin. Means: alder tree.

Aldo: Germanic origin. Means: rich, old one. Ethnic backgrounds: French, Italian. Nickname: Al.

Aldous: Saxon origin. Means: of the old house. Alternative spellings: Aldis, Aldus, Aldas.

Aldred: Anglo-Saxon origin. Means: wise adviser.

Aldrich: Anglo-Saxon/Teutonic origin. Means: king, old sage. Alternative spellings: Aldridge, Alredge, Aldric.

Alec: Greek origin. Means: defender.

Alemet: Unknown origin. Means: hidden. Ethnic background: Hebrew.

Aleron: Latin/French origin. Means: eagle, knight.

Alessio: Unknown origin and meaning. Ethnic background: Italian.

Alexander: Greek origin. Means: defender, helps. Ethnic backgrounds: English/Welsh, German, Swedish, Scottish, Hispanic, Russian. 13th most popular boy's name of the '90s. Alternative spellings and nicknames: Allister, Al, Sandy, Saunders, Sanders, Alex, Alessandro, Alexis, Alastair, Alec, Alexio, Alexzander, Alejandro, Aleksandr, Alessandro, Alexandro, Alexandros.

Alexei: Greek/Slavic origin. Means: defender of man. Ethnic background: Russian. Alternative spellings: Aleksei, Alexey, Alexja.

Gender-Bending Names

Why can't boys use names once they've been used by girls? Do they have cooties?

~ **Rain W., Simi Valley, California**

Alf: Norse/Germanic origin. Means: underworld, wise. Ethnic background: Swedish.

Alfalfa: Unknown origin and meaning.

Alfeus: Unknown origin. Means: God.

Alford: Anglo-Saxon origin. Means: ancient.

Alfred: Anglo-Saxon origin. Means: counselor, elf. Ethnic backgrounds: German, Polish, Swiss. Alternative spellings and nicknames: Alfie, Alfredo, Fred, Alf, Al.

Alger: Anglo-Saxon origin. Means: noble one. Alternative spelling: Algar.

Algernon: French origin. Means: beard. Nicknames: Algie, Algy, Al.

Ali: Arabic origin. Means: eminent, the greatest.

Alicio: Unknown origin and meaning. Ethnic background: Hispanic.

Alipi: Unknown origin and meaning. Ethnic background: Czech.

Alireza: Unknown origin and meaning.

Alisen: Unknown origin. Means: fame.

Allajawaan: Unknown origin and meaning.

Allard: Anglo-Saxon/Teutonic origin. Means: brave, noble. Alternative spelling: Alard.

Allen: Celtic origin. Means: cheerful, small cliff, harmony. Ethnic backgrounds: Irish, English/Welsh. Alternative spelling: Allan.

Allward: Unknown origin. Means: guardian.

Almagor: Unknown origin. Means: fearless.

Almo: Anglo-Saxon origin. Means: famous, noble.

Almund: Anglo-Saxon origin. Means: temple defender, German.

Alois: Germanic origin. Means: famous warrior. Ethnic backgrounds: German, Polish, Hispanic. Alternative spellings: Aloysius, Aloisio.

Alonso: Spanish origin. Means: battle.

Alonza: Spanish origin. Means: noble.

Alonzo: Italian origin. Means: nobleman's estate.

Alpar: Unknown origin and meaning. Ethnic background: Hungarian.

Alpheus: Greek origin. Means: river god. Alternative spelling: Alphaeus.

Alphonse: Saxon/Teutonic origin. Means: noble, battle ready. Alternative spellings and nicknames: Lonny, Alfonso, Alonzo, Lon, Alphonzo, Alfons, Alphonso.

Alpin: Scottish origin. Means: blond.

Alric: Teutonic origin. Means: universal ruler. Alternative spelling: Alrick.

Alroy: Latin/Gaelic origin. Means: red-haired, royal.

Alston: Anglo-Saxon origin. Means: from an old estate. Alternative spellings and nicknames: Al, Alton.

Alsworth: Unknown origin. Means: great.

Alter: Hebrew origin. Means: old one.

Altman: Germanic origin. Means: wise man.

Alula: Arabic origin. Means: firstborn.

Alvado: Unknown origin and meaning.

Alvah: Unknown origin. Means: exalted.

Alvar: Latin/Norse origin. Means: elf, warrior, fair. Alternative spellings: Alvaro, Alver.

Alvin: Saxon/Teutonic origin. Means: friend, loved. Alternative spellings: Alvin, Alwin, Elvin, Elwin, Alvan, Alvin, Alwyn.

Alvis: Norse origin. Means: wise.

Alvord: Anglo-Saxon origin. Means: ancient, old ford.

Alzado: Unknown origin and meaning.

Amaan: Arabic origin. Means: safety. Alternative spellings: Aman, Amman.

Amadeo: Latin origin. Means: beloved. Ethnic background: Hispanic. Alternative spellings: Amado, Amando.

Amadeus: Latin origin. Means: loves God. Ethnic background: German.

Amadour: Latin origin. Means: lover.

Amadus: Unknown origin. Means: God. Alternative spelling: Amandus.

Amalio: Unknown origin and meaning. Ethnic background: Hispanic.

Amancio: Latin origin. Means: to love. Ethnic background: Hispanic.

Amaramto: Unknown origin and meaning. Ethnic background: Hispanic.

Amasa: Hebrew origin. Means: bearer, heavy.

Amazu: African origin. Unknown meaning.

Ambert: Teutonic/Saxon origin. Means: intelligent.

Ambrose: Greek/Latin origin. Means: divine, immortal. Ethnic backgrounds: Italian, Irish, Hispanic, German, Hungarian. Alternative spellings and nicknames: Nam, Ambrogio, Ambros, Ambrosi, Ambrosio, Ambrosius, Ambrus.

Ameer: Arabic origin. Means: commander.

Amerigo: Latin/Teutonic origin. Means: industrious. Alternative spelling: Americo.

Amery: Latin/Germanic origin. Means: divine, lover, hardworking. Alternative spelling: Amory.

Amias: Latin origin. Means: devoted to God. Alternative spelling: Amyas.

Amichai: Hebrew origin. Means: my nation lives.

Amiel: Hebrew origin. Means: God of my people.

Amin: Arabic origin. Means: honest.

Amit: Unknown origin and meaning.

Amitan: Hebrew origin. Means: faithful.

Ammon: Hebrew/Egyptian origin. Means: faithful.

Amnon: Hebrew origin. Means: hidden.

Amor: Unknown origin and meaning.

Amos: Hebrew origin. Means: burden, carried.

Gender-Bending Names

Whether we like it or not, boys get teased for having girls' names, whereas girls can get away with it. A girl can wear pants or a suit, but a boy can't wear a dress without being stereotyped. Yes, it's unfair, and yes, we can all rail about inequality in our society. But I certainly wouldn't give my son a girl's name, knowing that he'd be teased, just to prove a point about equality.

~ **Trudi R., Brooklyn, New York**

Ampah: Unknown origin. Means: trust. Ethnic background: African.

Amund: Norse origin. Means: protector, divine.

Ananias: Unknown origin and meaning.

Anarolio: Unknown origin. Means: east.

Anas: Arabic origin. Means: friend. Alternative spelling: Annas.

Anastacio: Spanish origin. Means: of the resurrection. Ethnic background: Hispanic.

Anastatius: Greek origin. Means: reborn.

Anatol: Greek origin. Means: east, dawn, of the East. Ethnic background: German. Alternative spellings: Anatole, Anatolio, Anatoly.

Andre: Greek origin. Means: manly. Ethnic backgrounds: French, Swiss. Alternative spellings: Andreas, Andrei, Andres, Andrej, Andrey, Andrzej, Andrzey.

Andrere: Unknown origin and meaning.

Andrew: Greek origin. Means: manly, with strength. Ethnic backgrounds: English/Welsh, Scottish. 15th most popular boy's name of the '90s. Alternative spellings and nicknames: Andrien, Anders, Drew, Andy, Andreas, Andre.

Andronicus: Latin origin. Unknown meaning.

Andy: Greek origin. Means: manly.

Anfanio: Unknown origin and meaning. Ethnic background: Hispanic.

Angelo: Greek/Italian origin. Means: angel, messenger. Alternative spellings and nicknames: Angie, Angell, Angelos, Angelus, Anjel.

Angits: Celtic origin. Means: one of strength, exceptional.

Angus: Celtic origin. Means: choice. Ethnic backgrounds: Scottish, Irish. Nicknames: Gus, Gussie.

Anh: Unknown origin and meaning.

Ankoma: African origin. Means: last born of parents.

Annan: Celtic origin. Means: from the stream.

Annibale: Phoenician origin. Means: grace, favor. Ethnic background: Italian.

Anniel: Unknown origin and meaning.

Anscom: Anglo-Saxon origin. Means: from the valley. Alternative spelling: Anscomb.

Ansell: French origin. Means: adherent, nobleman.

Anselm: Germanic origin. Means: divine, helmet. Alternative spellings and nicknames: Anse, Ansel, Anselme, Anselmo.

Anshel: Hebrew origin. Means: blessed, fortunate. Alternative spellings: Anshel, Anshl.

Anskar: Unknown origin and meaning.

Anson: Anglo-Saxon origin. Means: awe, son of Ann.

Antal: Latin origin. Means: beyond praise. Ethnic background: Hungarian.

Antero: Unknown origin and meaning. Ethnic background: Hispanic.

Anthony: Latin origin. Means: inestimable, above worth. Ethnic backgrounds: English/Welsh. 21st most popular boy's name of the '90s. Alternative spellings and nicknames: Antoni, Tony, Anton, Antonio, Antony.

Antipas: Greek origin. Means: father.

Anton: Germanic/Slavic origin. Means: inestimable. Ethnic backgrounds: Swiss, Russian, Dutch, Czech. Alternative spellings: Antonin, Antoine, Antwainn, Antwon.

Anwaar: Arabic origin. Means: light.

Anwar: Saxon origin. Means: wild.

Anwyl: Saxon origin. Means: beloved. Alternative spellings: Anwyll, Anwell.

Anyon: Celtic/Saxon origin. Means: anvil.

Apollo: Greek origin. Means: handsome.

Apolonio: Unknown origin and meaning. Ethnic background: Hispanic.

Aquan: Unknown origin and meaning.

Aracin: Unknown origin and meaning.

Araldo: Unknown origin. Means: army.

Aralt: Irish origin. Means: army, leader.

Arber: Latin origin. Means: gardener.

Arbogast: Unknown origin and meaning. Ethnic background: German.

Archard: Germanic/Anglo-Saxon origin. Means: powerful, sacred. Alternative spelling: Archerd.

Archer: Latin origin. Means: bowman.

Archibald: Saxon/Germanic origin. Means: bold, distinguished. Alternative spellings and nicknames: Arch, Archie, Archer, Archibaldo, Arcibaldo.

Archie: Unknown origin and meaning.

Ardan: Unknown origin. Means: height. Ethnic background: Irish.

Ardell: Anglo-Saxon origin. Means: dell. Alternative spelling: Ardel.

Arden: Latin origin. Means: ardent, eagle. Alternative spelling: Ardin.

Ardley: Saxon origin. Means: home lover.

Ardolph: Anglo-Saxon origin. Means: home, wolf.

Areeb: Arabic origin. Means: wise.

Arelus: Unknown origin. Means: friend.

Aren: Old Irish origin. Means: peace.

Arend: Germanic origin. Means: eagle, powerful. Alternative spellings: Ahren, Ahrens.

Argus: Greek origin. Means: guardian, vigilant. Nickname: Gus.

Argyle: Celtic/Irish origin. Means: belonging. Alternative spelling: Argile.

Aribert: Unknown origin and meaning. Ethnic background: German.

Aribold: Unknown origin. Means: addition.

Aries: Latin origin. Means: ram.

Arik: German origin. Means: powerful, rich ruler. Alternative spellings: Aric, Arek.

Arild: Norse origin. Means: battle commander.

Ario: Hebrew origin. Means: lion, warlike. Alternative spellings: Ari, Arrio.

Aris: Unknown origin and meaning.

Aristides: Greek/French origin. Means: best, excellence.

Arjan: Unknown origin and meaning. Ethnic background: Dutch. Alternative spelling: Arjun.

Arkady: Unknown origin and meaning. Ethnic background: Russian.

Arki: Unknown origin and meaning. Ethnic background: Jewish. Alternative spelling: Arko.

Arkin: Norse origin. Means: king's son.

Arledge: Anglo-Saxon origin. Means: dweller.

Arlen: Celtic origin. Means: pledge.

Arley: Anglo-Saxon origin. Means: hare, rabbit.

Arlo: Saxon origin. Means: protected, fortified hill.

Armand: Germanic/French origin. Means: armed, army. Alternative spellings: Armond, Arman, Armando, Armin.

Armoni: Hebrew origin. Means: castle, palace.

Armro: Unknown origin. Means: noble. Alternative spelling: Arms.

Armstrong: Scottish/Saxon origin. Means: strong arms.

Arnold: Germanic/Saxon origin. Means: eagle, power. Alternative spellings and nicknames: Arnie, Arne, Arno, Arnaldo, Arnall, Arnaud, Arnell, Arnoldo, Arnoux.

Arnon: Hebrew origin. Means: roaring stream, swift.

Arnot: Germanic origin. Means: eagle. Alternative spellings: Arnott, Arnart, Arnett.

Arnulf: Unknown origin and meaning. Ethnic backgrounds: German, Norwegian.

Aroldo: Teutonic origin. Means: eagle, strong. Ethnic background: Italian.

Arpad: Hungarian/Hebrew origin. Means: seed, wanderer. Alternative spelling: Arvad.

Arrigo: Germanic/Italian origin. Means: rules the estate. Ethnic background: Italian.

Arsenio: Greek origin. Means: strong.

Arshad: Arabic origin. Means: honest.

Arshaq: Arabic origin. Means: handsome.

Art: Celtic/Gaelic origin. Means: strong as a bear. Ethnic background: Irish.

Artemio: Unknown origin and meaning. Ethnic background: Hispanic.

Arthur: Latin/Celtic origin. Means: noble, strength, bear. Ethnic backgrounds: English/Welsh, Scottish, German, Polish, Russian, Hispanic, Italian. Alternative spellings and nicknames: Arv, Arvy, Arvin, Artus, Artie, Arvie, Arturo, Art, Artur, Artair.

Arundel: Anglo-Saxon origin. Means: eagle's dell. Alternative spellings: Arundell, Arondel, Arondell.

Arvai: Unknown origin and meaning.

Arvel: Saxon origin. Means: wept. Alternative spellings: Arvell, Arval.

Arvid: Norse origin. Means: eagle tree. Alternative spelling: Arve.

Arvidas: Unknown origin and meaning. Ethnic background: Russian.

Aryell: Hebrew origin. Means: lion of God.

Asa: Hebrew/Arabic origin. Means: physician, heal.

Asad: Arabic origin. Means: lion.

Asbjorn: Norse origin. Means: divine bear. Ethnic background: Norwegian.

Ascot: Anglo-Saxon origin. Means: cottage. Alternative spelling: Ascott.

Asgar: Arabic origin. Means: smallest.

Asharious: Unknown origin and meaning.

Ashby: Anglo-Saxon origin. Means: ash tree.

Asher: Hebrew origin. Means: fortunate, happy.

Ashfaaq: Arabic origin. Means: kindness.

Ashford: Anglo-Saxon origin. Means: ash (tree). Alternative spellings: Ashley, Ashton.

Ashlin: Anglo-Saxon origin. Means: ash tree, pool.

Ashraf: Arabic origin. Means: of noble birth.

Ashton: Anglo-Saxon origin. Means: ash tree.

Ashur: Semitic origin. Means: warlike.

Asifa: Unknown origin. Means: storm.

Aslam: Arabic origin. Means: very safe.

Asmus: Unknown origin and meaning. Ethnic background: German.

Asner: Unknown origin and meaning.

Aspah: Unknown origin. Means: collector.

Asriel: Hebrew origin. Means: prince of God.

Astin: Unknown origin and meaning.

Aswin: Unknown origin. Means: friend.

Ataa': Arabic origin. Means: gift.

Ateeq: Arabic origin. Means: ancient.

Athanasius: Greek/Latin origin. Means: immortal. Alternative spellings: Atanasio, Atanas.

Athar: Arabic origin. Means: most pious.

Atherton: Anglo-Saxon origin. Means: dweller of spring farm.

Atilano: Unknown origin and meaning. Ethnic background: Hispanic.

Gender-Bending Names

My husband, daughter, and I were at the park last week when we heard a dad calling out, "Logan! Logan!" You will never believe what happened next: three children came running, two boys and one girl!

~ Jackie T.,
Ft. Bragg, North Carolina

Atinuwa: Unknown origin and meaning.

Atley: Unknown origin. Means: dweller.

Atsu: Egyptian origin. Means: younger of twins. Ethnic background: African.

Attila: Hungarian origin. Unknown meaning. Ethnic background: German. Alternative spellings: Attilio, Attalas.

Atwater: Anglo-Saxon origin. Means: waterside dweller.

Atwell: Anglo-Saxon origin. Means: spring dweller.

Atwood: Anglo-Saxon origin. Means: forest dweller.

Atworth: Anglo-Saxon origin. Means: farmstead dweller.

Atyab: Arabic origin. Means: refined.

Aubin: Latin/French origin. Means: blond, fair. Alternative spellings: Auben, Aubyn.

Aubrey: Germanic/French origin. Means: blond, elf, king. Alternative spellings and nicknames: Alberik, Brey, Bree.

Audley: Anglo-Saxon origin. Means: prospering, of the meadow. Alternative spelling: Audly.

Audras: Unknown origin. Means: fortunate. Alternative spelling: Audres.

Audric: Germanic/French origin. Means: noble, old. Alternative spelling: Audrie.

Audwin: Germanic origin. Means: rich, friend.

August: Latin origin. Means: dignitary, venerable, majestic. Ethnic background: German. Alternative spellings and nicknames: Gus, Augus, Augie, Gussie, Austin, Augustus, Auguste, Augustine, Augustin, Augusto, Agostina, Agusto.

Aurelius: Latin origin. Means: golden, friend. Alternative spelling: Aurelio.

Aust: Unknown origin and meaning.

Austin: Latin origin. Means: Augustus, exalted, majestic. 12th most popular boy's name of the '90s. Alternative spelling: Austyn.

Autry: Unknown origin and meaning.

Avan: Unknown origin. Means: proud.

Avenall: Latin/French origin. Means: dweller of oat field. Alternative spellings: Avenel, Avenell.

Averill: Anglo-Saxon origin. Means: April, boar hunter.

Avery: French/Anglo-Saxon origin. Means: ruler of elves, favor. Nickname: Av.

Aviaz: Hebrew origin. Means: father of strength.

Avinoam: Unknown origin and meaning.

Aviv: Hebrew origin. Means: springtime.

Avniel: Hebrew origin. Means: God is my rock.

Avrom: Hebrew origin. Means: father of multitudes. Alternative spellings: Avrum, Avrumel, Avrumke.

Avrumtchick: Unknown origin and meaning. Ethnic background: Jewish.

Awet: Unknown origin and meaning.

Axel: Hebrew/Germanic origin. Means: father of peace, divine source of life. Ethnic background: Swedish. Alternative spelling: Axl.

Axton: Anglo-Saxon origin. Means: swordsman's stone.

Aylmer: Teutonic/Old English origin. Means: famous, noble.

Aylward: Teutonic/Saxon origin. Means: awe inspiring, protector. Alternative spelling: Aylsworth.

Aylwin: Teutonic/Saxon origin. Means: awe-inspiring friend.

Azariah: Hebrew origin. Means: helped by God.

Azeez: Arabic origin. Means: beloved.

Azhar: Arabic origin. Means: glittering.

Aziz: Hebrew origin. Means: strength.

Azrae: Unknown origin. Means: angel.

Azriel: Hebrew origin. Means: God helps, angel.

Azubuike: African origin. Means: support is strength.

b

Baaqee: Arabic origin. Means: perpetual.

Baaqir: Arabic origin. Means: wealthy.

Baaree: Arabic origin. Means: deity, creator.

Bacilio: Unknown origin and meaning. Ethnic background: Hispanic.

Badee: Arabic origin. Means: rare.

Badru: Egyptian origin. Means: born at full moon. Ethnic background: African.

Bahaa: Arabic origin. Means: beauty.

Bailby: Unknown origin. Means: indirect.

Bailey: Old English origin. Means: able, bailiff. Alternative spellings: Bailie, Baily.

Bainbridge: Anglo-Saxon/Gaelic origin. Means: bridge, sea.

Baird: Celtic origin. Means: ballad, fiery, poet. Alternative spellings: Bard, Barde, Beard, Baard.

Baker: Anglo-Saxon origin. Means: one who bakes.

Balbo: Latin origin. Means: speaker, indirect.

Baldassarre: Italian origin. Means: wise man, protector.

Baldemar: Germanic origin. Means: princely.

Balder: Norse/Saxon origin. Means: ruler, brave, army. Alternative spelling: Baldur.

Baldomero: Germanic origin. Means: famous, bold, brave. Ethnic background: Hispanic.

Baldovino: Unknown origin and meaning. Ethnic background: Italian.

Baldric: Germanic origin. Means: bold.

Baldwin: Germanic/Saxon origin. Means: bold, friend. Alternative spellings: Baldain, Baudoin, Balduin.

Baleegh: Arabic origin. Means: eloquent.

Balfour: Saxon/Gaelic origin. Means: hill, meadow. Alternative spelling: Balfore.

Balint: Latin origin. Means: healthy, strong. Ethnic background: Hungarian.

Ballard: Germanic origin. Means: bold, strong.

Balogun: African origin. Means: the chief of war.

Balthasar: Persian origin. Means: battle, king, protected by God. Ethnic background: German. Alternative spellings: Balthazar, Baltasar.

Bancroft: Anglo-Saxon origin. Means: from the bean field.

Banning: Celtic origin. Means: blond, little one.

Baptist: Latin origin. Means: to dip. Ethnic background: German.

Barabas: Hebrew origin. Means: loyal, exhortation. Alternative spelling: Barabbas.

Baram: Hebrew origin. Means: son of the nation.

Barclay: Anglo-Saxon origin. Means: birch tree, wood.

Barden: Anglo-Saxon origin. Means: near boar's den.

Bardo: Aramaic/Germanic origin. Means: farmer, plowman.

Bardrick: Anglo-Saxon origin. Means: ax, ruler.

Bardulf: Anglo-Saxon origin. Means: ax, wolf. Ethnic background: German. Alternative spelling: Bardolf.

Barend: Germanic origin. Means: bear. Ethnic background: Dutch.

Barker: Old English origin. Means: logger.

Barkley: Unknown origin and meaning.

Barlow: Anglo-Saxon origin. Means: of the bare hill.

Barn: Unknown origin. Means: pointed.

Barnaby: Hebrew origin. Means: consolation, from prophecy. Alternative spellings and nicknames: Barna, Barny, Barnabas, Barney, Barnaba.

Barnett: Anglo-Saxon origin. Means: leader.

Barney: Hebrew/Germanic origin. Means: bear, consolation.

Barnum: Anglo-Saxon origin. Means: of a noble home.

Baron: Anglo-Saxon/Teutonic origin. Means: warrior, nobleman. Alternative spelling: Barron.

Barr: Anglo-Saxon origin. Means: gateway.

Barret: Saxon origin. Means: bear, great strength. Alternative spelling: Barrett.

Barrington: Unknown origin and meaning.

Barris: Saxon origin. Means: son of Harry.

Barry: Celtic/Gaelic origin. Means: marksman, of the barrier. Ethnic backgrounds: English/Welsh, Irish.

Bart: Hebrew/Anglo-Saxon origin. Means: ploughman, barley farmer. Ethnic background: Dutch.

Bartholomew: Hebrew origin. Means: farmer. Alternative spellings and nicknames: Barth, Bat, Bart, Barthelemy, Bartholomaus, Bartolme, Bartolomeo.

Bartkus: Unknown origin. Means: farmer.

Bartley: Hebrew/Anglo-Saxon origin. Means: farmer, Bart's meadow. Alternative spellings: Barthel, Bartel.

Barton: Anglo-Saxon origin. Means: barley, farmer. Nicknames: Barth, Bart.

Baruch: Hebrew origin. Means: blessed.

Baruett: Hebrew origin. Means: one who is blessed. Nicknames: Barrey, Barrie, Barry.

Bas: Unknown origin and meaning. Ethnic background: Dutch.

Baseer: Arabic origin. Means: wise. Alternative spellings: Basheer, Basir.

Bashaarat: Arabic origin. Means: good news.

Basie: Unknown origin and meaning.

Basil: Latin/Greek origin. Means: kingly, royal. Alternative spellings: Basile, Basilio, Basilius, Basillio.

Bastian: Unknown origin and meaning. Ethnic background: German.

Bates: Unknown origin and meaning.

Baudier: Unknown origin. Means: army.

Baudoin: French/Germanic origin. Means: bold.

Baudric: Unknown origin. Means: bold.

Baum: Unknown origin and meaning.

Baxter: Saxon origin. Means: a baker. Nickname: Bac.

Bayard: French/Teutonic origin. Means: fiery, brown.

Baylet: Unknown origin. Means: bailiff.

Baylor: Anglo-Saxon origin. Means: one who trains horses.

Bazak: Hebrew origin. Means: flash of light.

Bela: Unknown origin. Means: city.

Bear: Anglo-Saxon/Germanic origin. Means: a bear.

Beathan: Gaelic origin. Means: of the right hand, life.

Beatty: Gaelic origin. Means: blesses.

Beau: Latin/French origin. Means: beautiful, handsome.

Beaufort: French origin. Means: beautiful fortress. Alternative spelling: Beaufert.

Beaumont: French origin. Means: beautiful mountain.

Beauregard: French origin. Means: handsome, well regarded.

Beauvais: French origin. Means: fair.

Beck: Norse/Saxon origin. Means: brook.

Beckett: Unknown origin and meaning.

Bedad: Unknown origin. Means: lonely.

Bedford: Unknown origin and meaning.

Belden: Anglo-Saxon origin. Means: beautiful land. Alternative spelling: Beldon.

Belino: Unknown origin and meaning. Ethnic background: Hispanic.

Belisario: Spanish origin. Means: arrow or bowman. Ethnic background: Hispanic.

Bellamy: Latin/French origin. Means: beautiful, friend.

Belshazzar: Hebrew origin. Means: king's guardian.

Beluchi: African origin. Means: provided God approves.

Ben: Hebrew origin. Means: son, righteous. Alternative spelling: Benn.

Benedict: Latin origin. Means: blessed. Alternative spellings and nicknames: Dixon, Ben, Bennett, Benny, Bendix, Benedetto, Benedicto, Benedikt.

Benesh: Latin/Hebrew origin. Means: blessed. Alternative spelling: Benish.

Bengt: Latin/Slavic origin. Means: blesses. Ethnic background: Swedish.

Benigno: Latin origin. Means: gentle, kind, well. Ethnic background: Hispanic.

Benjamin: Hebrew origin. Means: of the right hand. Ethnic backgrounds: English/Welsh, German, Hispanic. 25th most popular boy's name of the '90s. Alternative spellings and nicknames: Bennie, Benjy, Benny, Benson, Ben, Bejamin, Beniamino.

Bennett: Latin origin. Means: blessed. Alternative spellings: Bennet, Benoit, Benito.

Benno: Germanic origin. Means: bear.

Benny: Hebrew origin. Means: of the right hand.

Benoni: Hebrew origin. Means: son of my sorrows.

Benson: Hebrew origin. Means: son of Benjamin.

Bentley: Old English origin. Means: bent-grass meadow, clearing. Alternative spelling: Bently.

Benton: Anglo-Saxon origin. Means: bent, from the moors. Nickname: Ben.

Beppe: Unknown origin and meaning. Ethnic background: Italian.

Ber: Germanic origin. Means: bear. Ethnic background: Jewish.

Berel: Unknown origin and meaning. Ethnic background: Jewish.

Beresford: Anglo-Saxon origin. Means: from the barley ford.

Berg: Germanic origin. Means: mountain.

Gender-Bending Names

Can you imagine your daughter coming home and announcing she has met her perfect match? And then saying, "Oh, and by the way, Mom, his name is the same as mine!"

~ Samantha S.,
Summit, New Jersey

Berger: Saxon/French origin. Means: shopkeeper, shepherd.

Berget: Unknown origin. Means: resolute. Alternative spelling: Beret.

Bergren: Germanic origin. Means: from the mountain stream.

Berkeley: Anglo-Saxon origin. Means: from the birch meadow. Alternative spellings: Berkley, Barclay.

Bermudo: Unknown origin and meaning. Ethnic background: Hispanic.

Bernal: Unknown origin and meaning. Ethnic background: Hispanic.

Bernard: Germanic/Anglo-Saxon origin. Means: bear, hardy, bold. Ethnic background: French. Alternative spellings and nicknames: Barnet, Barnard, Barney, Bernhard, Bernie, Bern, Barn, Bernado, Bernardo, Burnard.

Berndt: Germanic origin. Means: brave as a bear. Ethnic background: Swedish. Alternative spellings: Bernd, Berend, Bernt.

Berne: Germanic origin. Means: bear, brave. Alternative spelling: Bern, Berno.

Bernie: Germanic origin. Means: bold as a bear. Alternative spelling: Berneen.

Bert: Various origins. Means: bright, brilliant, glorious, radiant. Ethnic background: Dutch.

Berthold: Germanic origin. Means: brilliant, famous ruler. Alternative spellings: Bertold, Bertoldi, Bertoldo, Bertoud.

Bertil: Germanic origin. Means: intelligent, brilliant. Ethnic background: Swedish. Alternative spelling: Bertell.

Berton: Teutonic/Saxon origin. Means: brilliant, fortified town.

Bertram: Latin/Germanic origin. Means: brilliant raven, illustrious. Alternative spellings and nicknames: Bertie, Bertrand, Bartram, Bert, Barthram.

Bertrand: Teutonic/French origin. Means: brilliant raven, illustrious. Alternative spelling: Bertrando.

Berwick: Anglo-Saxon origin. Means: barley grange.

Bevan: Celtic origin. Means: young soldier, well born. Alternative spellings: Beven, Beaven, Beavan, Bevin.

Bevis: Teutonic/French origin. Means: archer, fair. Alternative spelling: Bevus.

Biagio: Greek/Italian origin. Means: stammerer, royal.

Bichri: Hebrew origin. Means: my eldest.

Bilaal: Arabic origin. Means: water. Alternative spelling: Bilal.

Billy: Germanic/French origin. Means: resolution, wise.

Bing: Germanic origin. Means: hollow.

Bink: Anglo-Saxon origin. Means: from the bank.

Birch: Anglo-Saxon origin. Means: birch tree. Alternative spellings: Birk, Burch.

Birchard: Unknown origin and meaning.

Birkett: Old English origin. Means: dweller of the birch land. Alternative spellings and nicknames: Berkett, Berk, Birk.

Birkey: Old English origin. Means: birch tree island.

Birley: Old English origin. Means: cattle, a byre. Alternative spelling: Berley.

Bishop: Old English origin. Means: overseer, bishop.

Bjorn: Norse origin. Means: bear. Ethnic backgrounds: Swedish, German. Alternative spellings: Bjarne, Bjorg.

Black: Anglo-Saxon origin. Means: dark.

Blade: Old English origin. Means: glory, prosperous.

Blagden: Anglo-Saxon origin. Means: from the dark valley.

Blaine: Gaelic origin. Means: lean, thin. Alternative spellings: Blayn, Blayne, Blane, Blain.

Blaise: Greek/Latin origin. Means: stammerer. Alternative spelling: Blas.

Blakeley: Old English origin. Means: black.

Blakeslee: Unknown origin and meaning.

Blakey: Anglo-Saxon origin. Means: fair.

Blanco: Germanic/Spanish origin. Means: blond.

Blanford: Anglo-Saxon origin. Means: gray-haired, crossing.

Blaze: Latin/Germanic origin. Means: fiery, stutters. Alternative spellings: Blase, Blayze, Blaise.

Bligh: Anglo-Saxon origin. Means: happiness.

Boas: Hebrew origin. Means: swiftness. Alternative spellings: Boase, Boaz.

Bob: Germanic/Saxon origin. Means: famous. Ethnic backgrounds: English/Welsh. Alternative spelling: Bobby.

Bobar: Unknown origin. Means: beaver.

Boden: French origin. Means: herald, messenger. Alternative spellings: Bodin, Bodan, Bodo.

Bogart: Germanic/Gaelic origin. Means: bow, a soft marsh, bog.

Bogdan: Slavic origin. Means: God's gift. Ethnic backgrounds: Russian, Polish.

Boguslaw: Slavic/Polish origin. Means: God's glory. Alternative spelling: Bohuslav.

Bolger: Unknown origin and meaning.

Bolivar: Spanish origin. Means: strong, warlike.

Bolton: Anglo-Saxon origin. Means: farm. Alternative spelling: Bolten.

Bonar: Unknown origin. Means: courteous, gentle.

Bonavento: Unknown origin and meaning. Ethnic background: Hispanic.

Bonesh: Hebrew origin. Means: good.

How to End the Spouse Wars—Surefire Ways to Make a Decision

If you and your spouse can't agree, or if you just can't commit to one name, there's still hope. Other parents were finally able to pick the name that would appear on the birth certificate using some pretty creative compromises. Hopefully, the ideas that follow will help you reach a decision that leaves everyone happy.

Bonifatius: Latin/Germanic origin. Means: good fate. Alternative spellings: Boniface, Bonifacio.

Bono: Unknown origin and meaning.

Boone: Latin/French origin. Means: good.

Booth: Norse/Teutonic origin. Means: dweller, herald. Alternative spellings: Boote, Both, Boot, Boothe.

Boquet: Unknown origin and meaning.

Borden: French/Anglo-Saxon origin. Means: den of boars, cottage. Alternative spelling: Bordon.

Borg: Norse origin. Means: castle.

Boris: Slavic/Russian origin. Means: battler, fighter, small. Ethnic background: German.

Borlow: Unknown origin. Means: bare.

Bosworth: Anglo-Saxon origin. Means: surrounded by trees, cattle.

Botolf: Anglo-Saxon origin. Means: herald.

Boume: Unknown origin. Means: brook.

Bourke: Old English origin. Means: fortification, hill.

Boutros: Unknown origin and meaning.

Bowen: Celtic origin. Means: little, son of Owen, warrior.

Bowie: Celtic/Gaelic origin. Means: blond-haired.

Boyce: Teutonic/Welsh origin. Means: dweller, forest.

Boyd: Celtic origin. Means: blond-haired.

Boyden: Celtic/Saxon origin. Means: blond, messenger.

Boyne: Gaelic origin. Means: white cow.

Brad: Anglo-Saxon origin. Means: broad valley, sun. Alternative spellings: Bradan, Braden.

Bradburn: Anglo-Saxon origin. Means: broad, brook.

Bradbury: Unknown origin and meaning.

Bradford: Anglo-Saxon origin. Means: broad ford.

Bradley: Anglo-Saxon origin. Means: broad meadow. 43rd most popular boy's name of the '90s. Alternative spelling: Bradly.

Bradwell: Anglo-Saxon origin. Means: broad spring.

Brady: Gaelic/Irish origin. Means: broad, spirited. Alternative spelling: Bradyan.

Brainard: Anglo-Saxon/Teutonic origin. Means: bold, raven. Alternative spelling: Braynard.

Bram: Old English/Celtic origin. Means: bramblebush, raven. Alternative spellings: Bramwell, Brahm.

Bran: Celtic origin. Means: raven, youth. Ethnic background: Irish. Alternative spelling: Brandt.

Branch: Latin origin. Means: an extension, appendage.

Brand: Norse/Anglo-Saxon origin. Means: a firebrand, sword. Alternative spellings: Brant, Brander.

Brando: Italian origin. Means: brilliant raven. Alternative spelling: Brandio.

Brandon: Teutonic/Old English origin. Means: from the beacon hill. 17th most popular boy's name of the '90s. Alternative spellings: Branden, Brandin, Brandyn.

Branford: Unknown origin and meaning.

Branson: Unknown origin and meaning. Alternative spelling: Branston.

Brawley: Anglo-Saxon origin. Means: hillside meadow.

Braxton: Anglo-Saxon origin. Means: badger, town. Alternative spelling: Braxten.

Brayan: Unknown origin and meaning.

Brayden: Old English origin. Means: to broaden, make spacious, widen. Alternative spellings: Braydon, Brayton.

Bredo: Unknown origin and meaning. Ethnic background: Norwegian.

Brelain: Unknown origin and meaning.

Bremel: Unknown origin and meaning. Ethnic background: Jewish. Alternative spelling: Breml.

Brendan: Celtic/Latin origin. Means: aflame, prince, bright light. Ethnic backgrounds: Irish, English/Welsh. 46th most popular boy's name of the '90s. Alternative spellings: Brandan, Branden, Brandon, Brendon, Brennan, Brenden, Brendn, Brendon, Brynden.

Brennan: Celtic origin. Means: brave, raven, little.

Brent: Old English origin. Means: high, hill. Alternative spelling: Brenton.

Breshawn: Unknown origin and meaning.

Brett: Celtic/Old English origin. Means: Briton, from Brittany. 46th most popular boy's name of the '90s. Alternative spelling: Bret.

Brewster: Old English origin. Means: a brewer of beer. Alternative spelling: Brewer.

Breyer: Unknown origin and meaning.

Brian: Celtic origin. Means: honor, high, strong leader. Ethnic background: Irish. 33rd most popular boy's name of the '90s. Alternative spellings: Brion, Brient, Bryon, Bryan, Brien, Briant, Bryant, Brieon.

Brice: Celtic/Anglo-Saxon origin. Means: ambitious, quick. Alternative spelling: Bryce.

Bridger: Anglo-Saxon origin. Means: near the bridge.

Brig: Old English origin. Means: a bridge.

Brigham: Old English origin. Means: bridge, homestead.

Brigido: Unknown origin and meaning. Ethnic background: Hispanic.

How to End the Spouse Wars

My husband and I both agreed that we could each choose one name and whichever first name–middle name combination sounded the best would be the name we chose. So if your husband wants Patrick and you want Austin, tell him that you'll use his choice and you can use yours. Austin Patrick (even Patrick Austin) sounds great, and you will both be happy.

~ **Jamie C., Chesapeake, Virginia**

Brinkley: Unknown origin and meaning.

Brock: Gaelic/Anglo-Saxon origin. Means: badger.

Brockley: Anglo-Saxon origin. Means: of the badger meadow.

Broderick: Teutonic/Saxon origin. Means: broad, flat land or ridge. Alternative spellings and nicknames: Derick, Derrick, Roderick.

Brodie: Irish origin. Means: of the muddy place. Alternative spelling: Brody.

Brogan: Unknown origin and meaning.

Bromleigh: Anglo-Saxon origin. Means: broom-covered meadow. Alternative spelling: Bromley.

Bronislaw: Slavic origin. Means: protection, glory. Ethnic background: Polish.

Bronson: Old English origin. Means: brown, darker.

Bronte: Greek origin. Means: thunder.

Brooks: Old English origin. Means: stream, to break out.

Brougher: Anglo-Saxon origin. Means: fortress.

Broughton: Anglo-Saxon origin. Means: fortress town.

Bruce: French origin. Means: brewer, dweller of the brush.

Bruno: Teutonic origin. Means: brown. Ethnic backgrounds: German, Italian, Swiss.

Bryce: Anglo-Saxon/Celtic origin. Means: noble, rich, speckled, swift.

Bryshane: Unknown origin and meaning.

Bryson: Unknown origin and meaning.

Buck: Old English origin. Means: buck, deer, graceful. Nicknames: Buckey, Bucky.

Buckley: Old English/Irish origin. Means: of the buck meadow, boy.

Budd: Old English origin. Means: herald of kings, winner. Alternative spellings and nicknames: Budde, Buddie, Buddy, Bud.

Buffalo: Latin origin. Means: large wild oxen.

Bundy: Anglo-Saxon origin. Means: free.

Buni: Hebrew origin. Means: constructed.

Bunim: Hebrew origin. Means: good.

Bunji: Japanese origin. Unknown meaning.

Burbank: Anglo-Saxon origin. Means: of the castle's hill.

Burdett: Anglo-Saxon origin. Means: little bird.

Burdon: Anglo-Saxon origin. Means: castle dweller.

Burford: Anglo-Saxon origin. Means: of the castle ford.

Burgard: Unknown origin. Means: castle. Alternative spelling: Burgaud.

Burgess: Teutonic origin. Means: citizen of town. Alternative spellings and nicknames: Burg, Bergess, Berg, Berger.

Burhaan: Unknown origin. Means: evidence.

Burke: Teutonic origin. Means: castle, dweller of the castle. Alternative spellings: Bourk, Berk, Berke, Burk, Burkett.

Burkhard: Germanic origin. Means: protection, brave, a castle's strength. Alternative spellings: Burchard, Burkhart.

Burl: Anglo-Saxon origin. Means: wine cup bearer. Alternative spellings: Burle, Byrle, Berle.

Burleigh: Old English origin. Means: castle, of the hilly meadow. Alternative spelling: Burley.

Burnaby: Norse origin. Means: warrior's estate.

Burne: Anglo-Saxon origin. Means: from the brook. Alternative spelling: Byrne.

Burnell: French/Anglo-Saxon origin. Means: reddish brown, a brook. Alternative spelling: Burrell.

Burney: Anglo-Saxon origin. Means: brook island dweller. Alternative spelling: Birney.

Burns: Anglo-Saxon origin. Means: son of Byrne.

Burr: Norse/Saxon origin. Means: youth, prickly covering.

Burt: Anglo-Saxon origin. Means: hill town, glorious.

Burton: Anglo-Saxon origin. Means: dweller, famous one. Alternative spellings and nicknames: Bert, Berton, Burt.

Busby: Norse origin. Means: village dweller.

Buster: Anglo-Saxon origin. Means: to burst or break.

Butler: Unknown origin and meaning.

Bwerani: African origin. Means: welcome.

Byford: Anglo-Saxon origin. Means: from a river crossing.

Byram: Anglo-Saxon origin. Means: cattle yard, ancient.

Byrd: Anglo-Saxon origin. Means: birdlike.

Byron: French origin. Means: cottage.

C **Cab:** French origin. Means: a driver's cabin.
Cabell: Unknown origin and meaning.
Cadby: Norse/Saxon origin. Means: warrior's settlement.

Caddock: Welsh origin. Means: battle.

Cade: Anglo-Saxon origin. Means: round, lumpish.

Cadel: Anglo-Saxon origin. Means: military. Alternative spellings: Cadal, Cadell.

Caden: Unknown origin and meaning.

Cadman: Celtic origin. Means: battle, warrior. Alternative spelling: Cadmann.

Cadmar: Greek/Welsh origin. Means: warrior, great battle. Alternative spelling: Cadmarr.

Cadmus: Greek origin. Means: of the East, adorn.

Cain: Hebrew origin. Means: bright, possessed. Alternative spellings: Caine, Cainen.

Calder: Celtic/Anglo-Saxon origin. Means: from the brook, river.

Caldwell: Anglo-Saxon origin. Means: from the cold spring.

Caleb: Hebrew origin. Means: bold, faithful, dog. Alternative spellings and nicknames: Cal, Cale.

Calen: Unknown origin and meaning. Alternative spelling: Cailun. Kalen

Caley: Gaelic origin. Means: slender.

Calhoun: Celtic/Gaelic origin. Means: forest dweller, warrior.

Calixto: Latin origin. Means: a chalice. Ethnic background: Hispanic.

Calum: Latin/Celtic origin. Means: dove.

Calvert: Anglo-Saxon origin. Means: herdsman. Nickname: Calbert.

Calvin: Latin/French origin. Means: bald. Alternative spelling: Calvino. Nickname: Cal.

Camden: Gaelic/Saxon origin. Means: of the crooked valley. Alternative spelling: Camdyn.

Camerero: Unknown origin. Means: chamberlain.

Camillo: Latin origin. Means: servant. Ethnic background: German. Alternative spelling: Camilo.

Campbell: Latin/Gaelic origin. Means: field, crooked mouth. Alternative spelling: Campball.

Camrin: Celtic origin. Means: bent nose, crooked nose.

Camron: Unknown origin and meaning.

Canaan: Unknown origin and meaning.

Candido: Latin origin. Means: white. Ethnic background: Hispanic.

Canute: Latin/Norse origin. Means: white-haired, knot. Alternative spelling: Canuto.

Canyon: Latin origin. Means: steep-sided valley.

Caractacus: Unknown origin and meaning.

Cardew: Celtic origin. Means: of the black fort.

Carel: French origin. Means: strong. Ethnic background: Dutch.

Carew: Latin/Celtic origin. Means: to run, fortress dweller.

Carino: Unknown origin and meaning. Ethnic background: Hispanic.

Carl: Germanic origin. Means: city, manly. Ethnic backgrounds: Norwegian, English/Welsh.

Carleton: Germanic/Saxon origin. Means: Carl's, farmer's, free. Alternative spelling: Carlton.

Carlisle: Old English origin. Means: castle, walled city. Alternative spelling: Carlyle.

Carlos: Italian/Spanish origin. Means: manly, strong. Alternative spelling: Carlo.

Carmelo: Hebrew origin. Means: vineyard, garden.

Carmichael: Gaelic origin. Means: friend.

Carmiel: Hebrew origin. Means: the Lord is my vineyard.

Carney: Celtic origin. Means: soldier: victorious. Alternative spellings: Carny, Carnay.

Carollan: Unknown origin. Means: champion.

Carr: Norse/Celtic origin. Means: marshland, fighter.

Carrew: Unknown origin. Means: fortress.

Carrick: Gaelic/Irish origin. Means: rocky headland.

Carson: Welsh origin. Means: marsh dweller, son of Carr.

Carsten: Latin/Old English origin. Means: Christian, stony marsh. Ethnic backgrounds: German, Norwegian.

Carswell: Anglo-Saxon origin. Means: of the water-filled spring.

Carter: Anglo-Saxon origin. Means: cart driver/maker. Alternative spellings: Cart, Cartier.

Cartland: Anglo-Saxon origin. Means: of the land between the streams.

Carvel: Old English origin. Means: from the villa by the marsh. Alternative spelling: Carvell.

Carver: Old English origin. Means: wood-carver.

Carvey: Unknown origin. Means: athlete.

Case: French origin. Means: a chest or box.

Casiano: Unknown origin and meaning. Ethnic background: Hispanic.

Casimir: Slavic origin. Means: proclaimer of peace. Ethnic background: Polish. Alternative spelling: Casimiro.

Caspar: Persian/Germanic origin. Means: a treasurer, wise man. Alternative spellings and nicknames: Cassy, Jasper, Kasper, Cass, Casper.

Caspian: Unknown origin and meaning.

Cass: Latin origin. Means: one who is proud of his appearance. Alternative spellings: Cash, Caz.

Cassell: Unknown origin and meaning.

Cassidy: Celtic/Gaelic origin. Means: clever, inventor.

Cassius: Latin origin. Means: vain, protective cover.

Castellan: Unknown origin. Means: castle.

Casto: Unknown origin and meaning. Ethnic background: Hispanic.

Castor: Latin origin. Means: beaver.

Cata: Unknown origin. Means: carve, catfish, grasp, lizard.

Cathal: Celtic origin. Means: battle, rule. Ethnic background: Irish.

Cathmor: Gaelic origin. Means: great warrior.

Cato: Latin origin. Means: wise, cautious. Ethnic background: Norwegian. Alternative spellings: Caton, Catto, Catton.

Cavan: Gaelic origin. Means: handsome.

Cavell: Teutonic origin. Means: bold, active. Alternative spellings: Cavil, Cavill.

How to End the Spouse Wars

We have a system that gives respect to all suggestions—we both put names on the list. You can only totally veto a name if you absolutely couldn't live with it. But all the names have to be put on the list before they can be taken off. No one's ideas are stupid or shouldn't be considered. Especially when choosing a baby's name, you have to give it a chance to take hold.

~ Cathie P.,
Virginia Beach, Virginia

Cawley: Norse origin. Means: ancestral.

Cayetano: Latin/Spanish origin. Means: from Caieta. Ethnic background: Hispanic.

Cecil: Latin origin. Means: one who is blind, sixth. Alternative spellings and nicknames: Cicile, Cece, Cecile, Cecilio.

Cedric: Celtic origin. Means: battle, war chief. Ethnic background: French. Alternative spelling: Cedrick.

Ceferino: Unknown origin and meaning. Ethnic background: Hispanic.

Celedonio: Unknown origin and meaning. Ethnic background: Hispanic.

Celestino: Latin origin. Means: heavenly. Ethnic background: Hispanic.

Celso: Latin origin. Means: lofty, high. Ethnic background: Hispanic.

Cerf: French origin. Means: deer.

Cesar: Latin origin. Means: born, cut, hair. Ethnic background: Hispanic. Alternative spellings: Caesar, Cesare.

Chad: Celtic/Anglo-Saxon origin. Means: protector, warlike. Alternative spelling: Chadd.

Chadburn: Anglo-Saxon origin. Means: from the brook.

Chadwick: Anglo-Saxon origin. Means: from the warrior's town, protector.

Chaffee: Unknown origin and meaning.

Chaika: Hebrew origin. Means: life. Alternative spellings: Chaikeh, Chaikel, Chaiki, Chai.

Chaim: Hebrew origin. Means: life.

Chalmers: Old English/Teutonic origin. Means: king of household.

Chan: Unknown origin. Means: old.

Chanan: Aramaic origin. Means: gracious. Ethnic background: Jewish. Alternative spelling: Chanina.

Chancellor: Old English origin. Means: chief minister of state.

Chandler: Latin/French origin. Means: candle maker/seller. Alternative spelling: Chandlor.

Chang: Unknown origin. Means: bow, constantly, mountain, open.

Chanoch: Hebrew origin. Means: dedicated, educated.

Chapell: French origin. Means: from the chapel.

Chapen: French origin. Means: chaplain. Alternative spellings: Chapin, Chapland, Chaplin.

Chapman: Anglo-Saxon origin. Means: citizen, merchant.

Charilaos: Unknown origin and meaning. Ethnic background: Greek.

Charles: Germanic origin. Means: manly, strong, free. Ethnic backgrounds: Greek, French, English/Welsh. 39th most popular boy's name of the '90s. Alternative spellings and nicknames: Charley, Karl, Charlie, Carlos, Carlo, Carl, Chuck.

Charlton: Old English origin. Means: farmstead, free.

Chase: French origin. Means: hunter, the chase.

Chaskel: Unknown origin and meaning. Ethnic background: Jewish.

Chatham: Anglo-Saxon origin. Means: soldier's land.

Chatwin: Anglo-Saxon origin. Means: warring friend.

Chaucer: Latin origin. Means: chancellor.

Chauncey: Latin origin. Means: chancellor, record keeper. Alternative spellings: Chauncy, Chancey, Chance, Chaunce.

Chavakuk: Assyrian origin. Means: garden plant. Ethnic background: Jewish.

Chavivi: Hebrew origin. Means: my beloved.

Chaz: Unknown origin and meaning.

Che: Unknown origin and meaning.

Chen: Unknown origin. Means: great.

Cheney: French origin. Means: dweller, forest. Alternative spellings: Chenay, Cheyney.

Chermon: Hebrew origin. Means: sacred.

Chester: Latin/Anglo-Saxon origin. Means: camp, of a walled town. Nicknames: Clies, Chet.

Chet: Latin origin. Means: camp, fortress. Alternative spelling: Chett.

Chetwin: Anglo-Saxon origin. Means: of the cottage on the path.

Chevalier: French origin. Means: knight, with high honor.

Chew: Unknown origin. Means: hill.

Chiamaka: African origin. Means: God is splendid.

Chibale: Egyptian origin. Means: kinship. Ethnic background: African.

Chiel: Hebrew origin. Means: God lives.

Chijioke: African origin. Means: God owns gifts.

Chikosi: African origin. Means: the wreck.

Chilton: Anglo-Saxon origin. Means: of the farm by a river.

Chimanga: African origin. Means: maize.

Chin: Unknown origin. Means: grasp, increase, tree.

Chiram: Hebrew origin. Means: lofty, exalted.

Chiura: Japanese origin. Unknown meaning.

Chiztam: Unknown origin and meaning.

Chovev: Hebrew origin. Means: friend, lover.

Chow: Unknown origin. Means: everywhere. Alternative spelling: Chou.

Christian: Latin origin. Means: anointed, follows Christ. Ethnic backgrounds: German, Scottish, Norwegian, Swiss. 32nd most popular boy's name of the '90s. Alternative spellings and nicknames: Christ, Christie, Chris, Christain, Christiano, Chrystien, Cristiano, Cristian.

Christodoulous: Greek origin. Means: Christ bearer.

Christopher: Greek origin. Means: Christ bearer. Ethnic backgrounds: English/Welsh. 6th most popular boy's name of the '90s. Alternative spellings and nicknames: Kit, Chrissy, Kris, Kester, Chris, Christoph, Christophe, Cristofer, Cristoforo, Cristopher.

Christos: Greek origin. Means: Christlike.

Chuck: Germanic/French origin. Means: manly, strong.

Chuhei: Japanese origin. Unknown meaning.

Chuna: Hebrew origin. Means: comfort. Alternative spelling: Chuneh.

Churchill: Anglo-Saxon origin. Means: from the church hill.

Cian: Gaelic origin. Means: ancient.

Cicero: Latin origin. Means: chickpea.

Ciprian: Greek origin. Means: from Cyprus. Alternative spelling: Cipriano.

How to End the Spouse Wars

I suggest flipping a coin. When I am choosing between two things that I like equally, I flip a coin, and if I'm disappointed in the outcome, then I know that in my heart of hearts I like the other choice better.

~ Julie J., Darien, Connecticut

Ciriaco: Latin/Greek origin. Means: devotion, Lord. Ethnic background: Italian.

Cirill: Latin/Greek origin. Means: devotion, Lord.

Cirillo: Greek/Spanish origin. Means: lordly, noble. Ethnic background: Italian. Alternative spelling: Cirilo.

Ciro: Greek origin. Means: lordly, sun. Ethnic backgrounds: Hispanic, Italian.

Claiborn: Germanic/French origin. Means: boundary of clovers. Alternative spelling: Claiborne.

Clair: French origin. Means: clear, bright, famous.

Clancy: Gaelic origin. Means: red warrior, offspring.

Clarence: Latin origin. Means: famous, clear one.

Clark: Latin/Anglo-Saxon origin. Means: scholar, clergyman. Alternative spelling: Clarke.

Claude: Latin origin. Means: lame. Ethnic background: French. Alternative spellings: Claud, Claudius, Claudio.

Claus: Greek/Germanic origin. Means: victory. Ethnic background: Dutch.

Clavero: Spanish origin. Means: keeper.

Clay: Old English origin. Means: brook, clay, earth.

Clayborne: Anglo-Saxon origin. Means: born of the clay brook, mortal. Alternative spellings: Claybourne, Clayborn.

Clayton: Anglo-Saxon origin. Means: mortal, of clay. Nickname: Clay.

Cleary: Gaelic origin. Means: scholar.

Cleavon: Old English origin. Means: steep bank.

Clement: Latin origin. Means: gentle, merciful. Alternative spellings and nicknames: Clem, Klemens, Clim, Clemence, Clemente, Clemens, Clementius.

Cleofas: Unknown origin and meaning. Ethnic background: Hispanic.

Cleon: Latin/Saxon origin. Means: from the cliffs, famous.

Cleveland: Saxon origin. Means: cliff dweller.

Clifford: Old English origin. Means: cliff crossing. Nickname: Cliff.

Clifton: Anglo-Saxon origin. Means: from a cliff town.

Cline: Unknown origin. Means: little.

Clinton: Anglo-Saxon origin. Means: estate, from a hill town. Nickname: Clint.

Clive: Anglo-Saxon origin. Means: cliff dweller. Alternative spelling: Cleve.

Clovis: Germanic origin. Means: famous warrior, a clover.

Clske: Unknown origin and meaning. Ethnic background: Dutch.

Cluny: Gaelic origin. Means: from the meadow.

Clwe: Unknown origin. Means: cliff.

Clyde: Celtic/Welsh origin. Means: river, warm, heard from a distance.

Cocinero: Unknown origin. Means: cook.

Colby: Anglo-Saxon origin. Means: black, dark, farm, a coal town. Alternative spelling: Colbey.

Cole: Old English origin. Means: of the dark town, victory.

Coleman: Latin/Irish origin. Means: dove, dark town, chief. Alternative spelling: Colman.

Colier: Anglo-Saxon origin. Means: charcoal, coal miner.

Colin: Celtic/Gaelic origin. Means: victorious, cub or pup. Ethnic backgrounds: English/Welsh. Alternative spellings: Colan, Cole.

Colis: Anglo-Saxon origin. Means: son of a dark man. Alternative spelling: Collis.

Collier: Anglo-Saxon origin. Means: charcoal merchant. Alternative spellings: Collyer, Colyer.

Collin: Gaelic/Irish origin. Means: virile. 46th most popular boy's name of the '90s.

Colm: Gaelic/Irish origin. Means: dove, servant.

Colson: Unknown origin and meaning.

Colten: Old English origin. Means: a coal town. Alternative spellings: Colton, Coltson, Coltun, Coltin.

Colter: Anglo-Saxon origin. Means: herds horses.

Colum: Greek/Gaelic origin. Means: victory, dove. Ethnic background: Irish.

Columbus: Latin origin. Means: dove. Alternative spelling: Columban.

Colwen: Anglo-Saxon origin. Means: coal miner. Alternative spellings: Colwin, Colvin.

Commodore: Dutch/French origin. Means: a commissioned rank in the navy.

Como: Italian origin. Means: of the lake.

Conall: Celtic origin. Means: strong wolf. Ethnic background: Irish.

Conan: Celtic origin. Means: with wisdom. Alternative spelling: Conant.

Conde: Unknown origin. Means: count.

Coniah: Unknown origin. Means: gift. Alternative spellings: Conias, Conah.

Conlan: Gaelic/Irish origin. Means: hero, wise. Alternative spellings: Conlin, Conlon, Conleth.

Connor: Gaelic/Irish origin. Means: desire, wise, hound keeper. 26th most popular boy's name of the '90s. Alternative spellings: Conor, Conner, Connnor.

Conrad: Germanic/Anglo-Saxon origin. Means: bold, counsel. Alternative spellings and nicknames: Con, Curt, Cort, Connie, Konrad, Conrade.

Conrado: Germanic/Spanish origin. Means: counselor, adviser. Ethnic background: Hispanic.

Conroy: Celtic origin. Means: persistent, wise.

Constant: Latin origin. Means: regular, constant.

Constantine: Latin origin. Means: loyal, steadfast. Ethnic background: Greek. Alternative spellings and nicknames: Conn, Connie, Constant, Konstantin, Constantin, Constantino, Costantin, Costantino, Costanzo, Constancio.

Conway: Greek/Celtic origin. Means: great, hound of the plain.

Cooney: Irish origin. Means: handsome.

Cooper: Latin/Saxon origin. Means: barrel, cask maker.

Corbet: French/Old English origin. Means: raven. Alternative spellings: Corbett, Corbin, Corby.

Corcoran: Gaelic/Irish origin. Means: reddish.

Cord: Old French/Latin origin. Means: a rope.

Cordaro: Unknown origin and meaning.

Cordell: Latin/French origin. Means: a rope. Alternative spelling: Cordilio.

Corey: Celtic/Gaelic origin. Means: chosen one; of the hill, hollow, or pool. Alternative spelling: Cory.

Cormick: Gaelic/Irish origin. Means: brave, charioteer. Alternative spellings: Cormac, Cormack.

Cornall: Unknown origin. Means: colored. Alternative spelling: Cornel.

Cornelio: Latin origin. Means: horn of the sun. Ethnic background: Italian.

Cornelius: Latin origin. Means: horn of battle, wise. Ethnic background: German. Alternative spellings and nicknames: Cornel, Neil, Cornell, Neal.

Corodon: Greek origin. Means: helmet, lark. Alternative spelling: Corydon.

Corrado: Italian origin. Means: bold. Alternative spelling: Contrado.

Cort: Greek/Norse origin. Means: honest adviser of court, short.

Cortez: Spanish origin. Means: legal body.

Corvin: Anglo-Saxon origin. Means: friend. Alternative spelling: Convin.

Coryell: Unknown origin. Means: battle.

Cosell: Greek origin. Means: order.

Cosmo: Greek origin. Means: harmony, order. Alternative spellings: Cosme, Cosimo.

Cotton: Anglo-Saxon origin. Means: of the cotton plant.

Coty: Unknown origin and meaning.

Country: Middle English/Old French origin. Means: a nation or a state.

Court: French origin. Means: from the court.

Courtland: Anglo-Saxon origin. Means: from the court or farm.

Covell: Anglo-Saxon origin. Means: from the cave slope.

Cowan: Gaelic/Irish origin. Means: from the hillside, twin.

How to End the Spouse Wars

I know a woman whose husband persisted through her entire pregnancy that the baby should be named Cyrus. When the baby was born, he suggested Kirk, and she was so relieved that she agreed instantly. Turns out he wanted to name it Kirk all along.

~ **Jill B., Chico, California**

Coyle: Gaelic origin. Means: battle monger.

Craddock: Welsh origin. Means: beloved, abounding.

Craig: Celtic/Gaelic origin. Means: of the mountain crag or stony hill. Ethnic backgrounds: English/Welsh.

Crandale: Old English origin. Means: from the crane valley. Alternative spellings: Crandall, Crandell.

Cranley: Old English origin. Means: from the crane meadow.

Cranston: Old English origin. Means: of the crane town.

Crawford: Old English origin. Means: from the crow's lake or ford.

Creighton: Gaelic/Old English origin. Means: border settlement, creek.

Crenshaw: Unknown origin and meaning.

Crescin: Latin origin. Means: growing. Alternative spellings: Crescint, Crescen, Crescencio.

Cris: Latin origin. Means: growing.

Crisanto: Unknown origin and meaning. Ethnic background: Hispanic.

Crisoforo: Unknown origin and meaning. Ethnic background: Hispanic.

Crispin: Latin origin. Means: curly, wavy. Alternative spellings: Crispino, Crespin.

Crist: Welsh origin. Means: Christian. Alternative spelling: Cristo.

Cristobal: Spanish origin. Means: Christ bearer. Ethnic background: Hispanic.

Crofton: Anglo-Saxon origin. Means: from the enclosed field.

Crompton: Old English origin. Means: from the winding farm.

Cromwell: Anglo-Saxon origin. Means: from the winding brook.

Crosby: Anglo-Saxon origin. Means: from the town's crossroad. Alternative spellings: Crosbie, Crosbey, Crosley.

Csaba: Hungarian origin. Means: from mythology.

Ctirad: Unknown origin and meaning. Ethnic background: Czech.

Cubbenah: Unknown origin. Means: born.

Cudjo: Unknown origin. Means: born.

Cuffy: Unknown origin. Means: born.

Culbert: Teutonic/Saxon origin. Means: brilliant, seaman. Alternative spellings: Colvert, Colbert.

Cullen: Celtic origin. Means: handsome, young pet. Alternative spellings: Cullan, Cullin.

Culley: Gaelic origin. Means: woodland dweller. Alternative spelling: Cully.

Culver: Latin origin. Means: dove. Alternative spelling: Colver.

Currey: Gaelic origin. Means: champion. Alternative spellings: Curry, Curran.

Curtis: Latin/French origin. Means: tent enclosure, courteous one. Alternative spellings and nicknames: Kurt, Court, Curt.

Cuthbert: Anglo-Saxon origin. Means: brilliant, famous. Alternative spellings and nicknames: Cuddy, Cuthburt.

Cutler: Anglo-Saxon origin. Means: knife maker. Alternative spellings: Cutlor, Cuttler.

Cutter: Unknown origin and meaning.

Cyler: Irish origin. Means: chapel, devoted. Alternative spellings: Cuyler, Cyle.

Cynric: Anglo-Saxon origin. Means: powerful, royal.

Cyprian: Greek/Polish origin. Means: from Cyprus. Alternative spelling: Cyprio.

Cyrano: Greek origin. Means: of Cyrene.

Cyril: Greek origin. Means: lordly. Alternative spellings: Cyrille, Cyrillus.

Cyrus: Persian/Greek origin. Means: throne, sun. Alternative spellings and nicknames: Cy, Rus, Ciro.

Czeslaw: Polish origin. Means: fortress, glory.

d

Daan: Unknown origin and meaning. Ethnic background: Dutch.

Dabney: Hebrew origin. Means: beloved.

Dadyeh: Hebrew origin. Means: beloved.

Daegal: Saxon origin. Means: dawn, from the dark brook.

Dag: Norse/Germanic origin. Means: day. Ethnic background: Norwegian.

Dagan: Semitic origin. Means: earth, little fish. Alternative spelling: Dagon.

Dagfinn: Norse origin. Means: bright Finn.

Dagobert: Germanic origin. Means: glorious day.

Dagwood: Old English origin. Means: forest of the bright one.

Dahn: Hebrew origin. Means: judge.

Daigoro: Japanese origin. Unknown meaning.

Dainis: Unknown origin and meaning. Ethnic background: Russian.

Daiyaan: Arabic origin. Means: mighty ruler.

Dajon: Unknown origin and meaning.

Dakarai: Unknown origin and meaning.

Dakotah: Native American origin. Means: the Santee branch of the Sioux.

Dalbert: Germanic/Anglo-Saxon origin. Means: bright valley, proud. Alternative spelling: Delbert.

Daley: Gaelic/Anglo-Saxon origin. Means: assembly, from the valley. Ethnic backgrounds: English/Welsh. Alternative spellings: Daly, Dali.

Dalson: Anglo-Saxon origin. Means: Daegal's.

Dalton: Anglo-Saxon origin. Means: from the valley town. Alternative spellings: Daulton, Delton.

Dalziel: Gaelic origin. Means: from the small field.

Damal: Unknown origin. Means: conqueror. Alternative spellings: Damalas, Damali, Damalis.

Damario: Unknown origin and meaning. Ethnic background: Hispanic. Alternative spelling: D'Mario.

Damaso: Greek origin. Means: to subdue. Ethnic background: Hispanic. Alternative spelling: Damasus.

Damick: Unknown origin. Means: earth. Alternative spellings: Damicke, Damek.

Damien: Greek origin. Means: divine power, fate. Ethnic background: Irish.

Damon: Greek/Latin origin. Means: tame one, spirit. Alternative spellings: Damian, Damion, Damien, Damiano, Damaun, Daymiane, Daymond, Deman.

Dane: Hebrew/Norse origin. Means: God will judge, from Denmark. Alternative spelling: Dain.

Daniel: Hebrew origin. Means: my judge is the Lord. Ethnic backgrounds: French, Swedish, Swiss, Hispanic, English/Welsh, Scottish, German. 11th most popular boy's name of the '90s. Nicknames: Dan, Dannie, Danny, Danilo.

Dano: Unknown origin and meaning. Ethnic background: Swiss.

Danson: Unknown origin and meaning.

Dante: Latin origin. Means: to endure. Ethnic background: Hispanic.

Daquill: Unknown origin and meaning.

Darby: Norse origin. Means: deer settlement, free.

Darius: Egyptian/Latin origin. Means: kingly, wealthy. Alternative spellings: Dariusz, Darriuss, Dario.

How to End the Spouse Wars

When I first found out I was pregnant, I immediately started drawing up lists of names, but my husband couldn't have cared less. I could not get him involved in a discussion about it at all, and I was totally exasperated. Then we went for the sonogram and found out we're having a boy. On the ride home, my husband suddenly started saying, "What do you think of this name? What do you think of that name?"

I think that early in the pregnancy men have trouble grasping the tremendous realization that, yes, there actually *is* going to be a baby! It seems like a theoretical concept, whereas women know the baby is inside us, and we're much more connected to the idea from the start. So if you're fairly early in your pregnancy, don't be upset if your husband's not paying that much attention. He'll figure it out.

~ Trudi R., Brooklyn, New York

Darnell: French origin. Means: hidden, of the rye grass.

Darom: Hebrew origin. Means: south.

Darr: Unknown origin and meaning.

Darrell: Anglo-Saxon origin. Means: dearly beloved. Alternative spellings: Darryl, Daryl.

Darrin: Gaelic/Saxon origin. Means: great, rocky hill, kingly. Alternative spellings: Darrian, Darrion, Daren, Darien, Darin, Darren, Daron, Dehryen.

Darris: Unknown origin. Means: the son of Harry.

Darsey: Celtic/French origin. Means: dark, fortress.

Darshaun: Hindi origin. Unknown meaning. Alternative spelling: Darshan.

Dartagnon: Unknown origin and meaning.

Darton: Anglo-Saxon origin. Means: from the deer park, water.

Darwen: Unknown origin. Means: brave. Alternative spelling: Darivin.

Darwin: Anglo-Saxon origin. Means: lover of the sea.

Daryel: English origin. Means: a grove of oak trees.

Daulah: Unknown origin. Means: happiness.

David: Hebrew origin. Means: beloved one. Ethnic backgrounds: Swedish, Scottish, German, English/Welsh. 19th most popular boy's name of the '90s. Alternative spellings and nicknames: Davy, Davie, Dave, Davis, Davide.

Davin: Norse origin. Means: bright, alert, a Finn. Alternative spellings: Daven, Davon.

Davis: Hebrew/Saxon origin. Means: beloved, son of David. Ethnic background: Scottish. Alternative spelling: Deivis.

Dawan: Old English origin. Means: deer, doe.

Dawson: Hebrew origin. Means: son of David.

Daxeur: Unknown origin and meaning.

Daylen: Unknown origin and meaning.

DeAjah: Unknown origin and meaning.

Dean: Latin/Anglo-Saxon origin. Means: supervisor, of the valley. Ethnic backgrounds: English/Welsh. Alternative spellings: Dene, Deane.

DéAndre: Unknown origin and meaning.

DeAngelo: Unknown origin and meaning. Alternative spelling: DeAngelio.

Dearborn: Anglo-Saxon origin. Means: deer brook dweller.

Declan: Irish origin. Unknown meaning.

Decus: Unknown origin and meaning.

Dedric: Teutonic origin. Means: ruler of the people. Alternative spellings: Deddrick, Dedrick, Detrick, Didrik, Dietrich.

Deems: Anglo-Saxon origin. Means: to judge.

Deen: Arabic/Hebrew origin. Means: faith, God's judgment.

Defoe: Unknown origin and meaning.

DeForest: Anglo-Saxon origin. Means: to clear the land.

Degas: French origin. Unknown meaning.

Degenhard: Unknown origin and meaning. Ethnic background: German.

Deion: Unknown origin and meaning. Alternative spellings: Deionte, Deon, Deondre, Deonte.

Dejuan: Unknown origin and meaning. Alternative spelling: Dejean.

Dekari: Unknown origin and meaning.

Del: Latin origin. Means: of the sea.

Delano: French/Gaelic origin. Means: healthy, of the dark.

Delanos: Unknown origin. Means: alder.

Delante: Unknown origin and meaning.

Delbert: Anglo-Saxon origin. Means: bright day, brilliant. Alternative spellings and nicknames: Dal, Bert, Dalbert, Del.

Delf: Greek origin. Means: from Delphi. Ethnic background: German. Alternative spelling: Delfino.

Delling: Norse origin. Means: shining.

Delmar: Latin origin. Means: of the sea. Alternative spelling: Delmer, Delmore.

Delon: Unknown origin and meaning.

Delvin: Greek origin. Means: a dolphin.

Demarcus: Unknown origin and meaning. Alternative spellings: DeMarc, Damarcus.

Demas: Greek origin. Means: the dignified one.

"How Do You Spell That?"

Are you thinking of giving your baby's name a twist by spelling it untraditionally? There are usually at least five different ways to spell any name (Kate, Cait, Kayte, Cait, K8 . . .). So why not set your child apart with a different take on an old favorite? The issue has sparked much debate among Parent Soupers. Read on to hear some arguments pro and con.

Demeko: Unknown origin and meaning.

Demetrio: Greek/Spanish origin. Means: gift, earth. Ethnic backgrounds: Hispanic, Italian. Alternative spellings: Demetrios, Demetrig.

Demetrius: Greek origin. Means: lover of the earth. Alternative spellings and nicknames: Demmy, Dimitri, Dmitri, Demitri, Demitrios, Demetress, Dimitrje, Dymtrias, Da'Metrius.

Demier: Unknown origin and meaning.

Deminko: Unknown origin and meaning.

Demonde: Latin/French origin. Means: society, mankind.

Denby: Norse origin. Means: of a Danish settlement. Alternative spelling: Danby.

Deney: Unknown origin and meaning.

Deniko: Unknown origin and meaning.

Dennis: Greek origin. Means: of wine, drama, and revelry. Alternative spellings: Denes, Denis, Deniz.

Denoriel: Unknown origin and meaning.

Denzel: Anglo-Saxon origin. Unknown meaning. Alternative spelling: Danzel.

Derek: Teutonic origin. Means: famous ruler of the people. Ethnic background: Irish. 41st most popular boy's name of the '90s. Alternative spellings: Dereck, Derreck, Derrek, Derik, Darick, Darrick, Derrick, Derrik, Derrico.

Dermell: Unknown origin and meaning.

Dermot: Celtic/Old English origin. Means: one who is free, moat. Ethnic background: Irish. Alternative spelling: Dermott.

Derry: Celtic/Anglo-Saxon origin. Means: one of red color, oak tree.

Derwin: Teutonic/Saxon origin. Means: friend of the beasts and water. Alternative spellings: Darwin, Erwin, Durwin.

Desean: Unknown origin and meaning. Alternative spellings: DeShawn, Deshon, Dashawn, DShaun.

Desi: Latin origin. Means: desire.

Desiderio: Latin/Spanish origin. Means: desired.

Desmond: Latin/Celtic origin. Means: protector of mankind, from the South. Ethnic background: Irish. Alternative spellings and nicknames: Desi, Desman, Demond.

Detlef: Germanic origin. Means: inheritance.

Detmar: Unknown origin and meaning. Ethnic background: German. Alternative spelling: Detmer.

Devan: Celtic origin. Means: variation of Devin, meaning poet. Alternative spelling: Deven.

DeVanta: Unknown origin and meaning. Alternative spellings: DeVante, Devauntae, Devonté, Devonte, Devonzia, Davonte, Dyvonta.

Devir: Hebrew/Arabic origin. Means: innermost room.

Devlin: Hebrew/Gaelic origin. Means: beloved, fierce.

Dewar: Unknown origin. Means: pilgrim.

Dewey: Welsh origin. Means: beloved.

DeWitt: Flemish origin. Means: blond, white.

Dexter: Latin origin. Means: dexterous, right-handedness. Nicknames: Deck, Dex.

Dhaamin: Arabic origin. Means: helper.

Dhariel: Unknown origin and meaning.

Diamon: Anglo-Saxon origin. Means: bridge protector.

DiAndre: Unknown origin and meaning.

Diante: Greek origin. Means: variation of Diantha, meaning heavenly flower.

Diarmaid: Gaelic origin. Means: free man. Ethnic background: Irish.

Diarmit: Unknown origin. Means: envious.

Diaya: Unknown origin and meaning.

Dibia: African origin. Means: healer.

Dibn: Unknown origin. Means: eloquent. Alternative spellings: Dibrin, Dibru, Dibbrun.

Dick: Teutonic origin. Means: strong ruler.

Dickens: Teutonic origin. Means: strong ruler.

Didier: Latin/French origin. Means: longing, desired.

Diego: Spanish origin. Means: one who supplants, replaces.

Dieter: Germanic origin. Means: people's ruler. Alternative spellings: Detier, Dietbert.

Diethelm: Germanic origin. Unknown meaning.

Dillard: Unknown origin and meaning.

Dillon: Celtic/Welsh origin. Means: faithful, near the sea. Alternative spellings: Dillan, Dillion, Dylan.

Dimant: Unknown origin and meaning. Ethnic background: Russian.

Dimas: Slavic origin. Means: strong fighter. Ethnic background: Hispanic.

Dino: Greek/Germanic origin. Means: small, old sword. Ethnic background: Italian.

Dion: Greek origin. Means: of wine, drama, and revelry.

Dionysus: Greek origin. Means: divine, of wine and revelry. Alternative spellings: Dionigi, Dionsio, Dionisio.

Dirk: Germanic origin. Means: famous ruler of the people. Alternative spelling: Dierk.

Dixon: Teutonic/Anglo-Saxon origin. Means: strong leader, son of Richard. Alternative spelling: Dickson.

Dlyon: Unknown origin and meaning.

Doane: Celtic origin. Means: from the sand dune.

Dolan: Celtic/Old English origin. Means: black-haired, bend in stream or valley.

Dom: Latin origin. Means: belonging to the Lord.

Dominic: Latin origin. Means: belonging to the Lord. Ethnic backgrounds: Irish, Italian, Hispanic, German, Polish, Czech. Alternative spellings and nicknames: Dommie, Nick, Dom, Dominick, Domenico, Domingo, Dominico, Dominik.

Domitilo: Latin origin. Means: tamed. Ethnic background: Hispanic.

Donaciano: Unknown origin and meaning. Ethnic background: Hispanic.

Donahue: Gaelic origin. Means: dark warrior.

Donald: Celtic origin. Means: dark stranger, world ruler. Ethnic background: Scottish. Alternative spellings and nicknames: Donny, Donnie, Donnell, Don, Donall, Donal, Donaldo.

Donat: Celtic/Polish origin. Means: stranger, gift from God. Ethnic background: Irish. Alternative spelling: Donato.

Donavon: Irish/Celtic/Scottish origin. Means: brown stranger, proud ruler.

Dong: Unknown origin. Means: copper.

Donkor: Egyptian origin. Means: a humble person. Ethnic background: African.

Donnan: Irish origin. Means: dark, brown. Alternative spelling: Donan.

Donnell: Celtic origin. Means: a hill.

Donogh: Celtic origin. Means: mighty warrior. Ethnic background: Irish.

Donovan: Gaelic origin. Means: dark, warrior. Ethnic backgrounds: English/Welsh.

Dontavis: Unknown origin and meaning.

Donte: Unknown origin and meaning.

Dontrell: Unknown origin and meaning.

Donzeal: Unknown origin and meaning.

Dooley: Gaelic origin. Means: dark hero.

Doran: Greek/Celtic origin. Means: a gift, wanderer, stranger.

Dorcus: Greek origin. Means: forest, gazelle.

Dorian: Greek origin. Means: of the ocean or sea. Alternative spellings and nicknames: Dim, Dorey, Dorien, Dore, Dory.

Doroteo: Greek origin. Means: God's gift. Ethnic background: Hispanic.

Dorr: Hebrew origin. Means: a generation.

Dorsett: Old English origin. Means: of the water tribe.

Dorwin: Unknown origin. Means: animal.

Douglas: Celtic/Gaelic origin. Means: dark stranger or stream. Ethnic backgrounds: English/Welsh. Alternative spellings and nicknames: Doug, Douglass, Dougal.

Douwe: Unknown origin and meaning. Ethnic background: Dutch.

Dov-Ber: Hebrew origin. Means: bear.

Dow: Irish origin. Means: dark-haired.

Doyle: Celtic origin. Means: dark stranger.

Drake: Latin/Germanic origin. Means: dragon, duck.

Draven: Unknown origin and meaning.

Drayton: Unknown origin and meaning.

Drea: Unknown origin and meaning.

Drew: Greek/Norse origin. Means: manly, wise, with foresight. Alternative spellings and nicknames: Drue, Druce, Dru.

Druce: Celtic/Saxon origin. Means: son of Drew, wise.

Drummond: Scottish origin. Means: from the hilltop.

Drury: Unknown origin. Means: darling.

Dryden: Anglo-Saxon origin. Means: dry valley dweller.

Duane: English origin. Means: a meadow.

Dub: Gaelic origin. Means: dark.

Duco: Unknown origin and meaning. Ethnic background: Dutch.

Dudas: Irish origin. Means: small pipe or piper.

Dudel: Unknown origin and meaning. Ethnic background: Jewish.

Dudley: Anglo-Saxon origin. Means: from the meadow or clearing. Ethnic backgrounds: English/Welsh. Nicknames: Dud, Lee.

Dudu: Hebrew origin. Means: beloved. Alternative spellings: Dudya, Dudyeh.

Duer: Celtic origin. Means: battle's hero.

Duff: Gaelic origin. Means: dark hair, black.

Dugald: Gaelic origin. Means: dark stranger.

Dugan: Gaelic origin. Means: dark-skinned.

Duke: Latin origin. Means: leader of the people. Alternative spelling: Duque.

Dumisani: African origin. Means: herald.

Duncan: Celtic origin. Means: a dark one, chief. Ethnic backgrounds: English/Welsh, Scottish. Nickname: Dunc.

Dunley: Anglo-Saxon origin. Means: of the hill's meadow.

Dunmore: Scottish origin. Means: from the hill fortress.

Dunn: Old English origin. Means: dark, brown.

Dunstan: Anglo-Saxon origin. Means: of the brown stone hill. Alternative spelling: Dunston.

Dunton: Anglo-Saxon origin. Means: hill farm dweller. Alternative spelling: Duntson.

Durand: Latin origin. Means: one who endures. Alternative spellings: Durante, Dante.

Durstin: Unknown origin. Means: heart. Alternative spellings: Durst, Durston.

Durward: Persian/Anglo-Saxon origin. Means: gatekeeper, guard. Alternative spellings: Derwood, Durware, Durwood.

Dusan: Czech origin. Means: soul, spirit.

Dustin: Teutonic origin. Means: valiant. Alternative spellings: Dusten, Dusty.

Duvall: Unknown origin and meaning.

Duvid: Unknown origin and meaning. Ethnic background: Jewish.

Duy: Unknown origin and meaning.

Dwayne: Celtic origin. Means: of song, dark. Alternative spellings: Dwane, Duane, Dawayne, DeWayne.

Dwight: Anglo-Saxon origin. Means: blond, white, fair.

Dygal: Unknown origin. Means: born. Alternative spellings: Dygall, Dagall.

Dylan: Celtic/Welsh origin. Means: one from the sea. 23rd most popular boy's name of the '90s. Alternative spelling: Dylen.

Dzintars: Unknown origin and meaning. Ethnic background: Russian.

Eamon: Old English/Irish origin. Means: fortunate warrior. Alternative spelling: Eamonn.

Earl: Anglo-Saxon origin. Means: warrior, nobleman. Alternative spellings: Earle, Erl, Erle, Errol.

Eaton: Anglo-Saxon origin. Means: from the town near the river.

Eben: Hebrew origin. Means: foundation, rock. Alternative spelling: Even.

Ebenezer: Hebrew origin. Means: help, foundation stone. Ethnic background: Scottish. Nicknames: Eb, Eben.

Ebsen: Unknown origin and meaning.

Eckart: Germanic origin. Means: sacred. Alternative spellings: Eckbert, Eckhard, Ekkehard.

Econah: Unknown origin. Means: gift.

Edan: Celtic origin. Means: one like a flame.

Edelbert: Teutonic origin. Unknown meaning. Ethnic background: German.

Edelmar: Anglo-Saxon origin. Means: noble, famous.

Edesio: Unknown origin and meaning. Ethnic background: Hispanic.

Edgar: Old English origin. Means: prosperous warrior, spear. Ethnic background: German. Alternative spellings and nicknames: Eddy, Ned, Ed, Eddie, Edgardo.

Edison: Old English origin. Means: son of Edward. Alternative spelling: Edson.

Edlun: Germanic origin. Means: nobility, prosperous.

Edmar: Anglo-Saxon origin. Means: rich sea.

Edmund: Old English/Italian origin. Means: prosperous protector. Ethnic background: German. Alternative spellings and nicknames: Ed, Eddy, Ned, Eddie, Edmond, Edmondo, Edmundo.

Edolf: Unknown origin. Means: prosperous.

Edrees: Unknown origin and meaning.

Edrei: Hebrew origin. Means: leader, my flock. Alternative spelling: Edroi.

Edric: Anglo-Saxon origin. Means: prosperous, rich rule.

Edrick: Anglo-Saxon origin. Means: rich sea.

Edsard: Unknown origin and meaning. Ethnic background: Dutch.

Edsel: Anglo-Saxon origin. Means: of Edward's estate/hall, prosperous.

Edward: Old English origin. Means: prosperous protector. Ethnic backgrounds: English/Welsh. 45th most popular boy's name of the '90s. Alternative spellings and nicknames: Teddy, Ed, Ned, Eddie, Ted, Edoardo, Edouard, Eduard, Eduardo, Edwardo, Edwald, Edi, Edvard, Edvards.

Edwin: Old English origin. Means: fortunate friend. Ethnic background: German. Alternative spellings and nicknames: Ed, Eddie, Edvin.

Edy: Old English origin. Means: a whirlpool. Ethnic background: Swiss.

Eelco: Unknown origin and meaning. Ethnic background: Dutch.

Efrain: Unknown origin and meaning. Ethnic background: Hispanic.

Efrat: Hebrew origin. Means: honored.

Efron: Hebrew origin. Means: a fawn or a bird.

Egan: Gaelic/Anglo-Saxon origin. Means: ardent, formidable.

Egarton: Anglo-Saxon origin. Means: from the edge of town. Alternative spelling: Egerton.

Egbert: Anglo-Saxon origin. Means: bright, shining sword. Ethnic background: German. Nicknames: Bertie, Bert.

Egidio: Greek/Italian origin. Means: squire, shield keeper.

Egil: Norse/French origin. Means: the edge or point, a sting.

Egmont: Anglo-Saxon origin. Means: corner of the mountain. Ethnic background: German.

Egon: Germanic/Gaelic origin. Means: point of a sword, fighter.

Egwin: Unknown origin. Means: brilliant. Alternative spelling: Egin.

Ehren: Germanic origin. Means: honorable.

Ehrenfried: Germanic origin. Means: honor, peace. Ethnic background: German.

Ehrnd: Unknown origin. Means: lonesome. Alternative spelling: Ehud.

Eibe: Unknown origin and meaning.

Eigil: Norse origin. Means: frightening.

Eike: Unknown origin and meaning. Ethnic background: German.

Einar: Norse origin. Means: leader, warrior.

Eisig: Hebrew origin. Means: he who laughs. Alternative spellings: Eisik, Eizik.

Eitan: Hebrew origin. Means: strong, permanent.

Eivind: Unknown origin and meaning. Ethnic background: Norwegian.

Ejonte: Unknown origin and meaning.

Ekechukwu: African origin. Means: God's creation.

Elad: Hebrew origin. Means: forever, eternal.

Elbert: Teutonic origin. Means: brilliant, forthright. Alternative spellings and nicknames: Bertie, Albert, Bert, Elburt, Elbart, Edbert.

Eldar: Hebrew origin. Means: habitation of God.

Elden: Teutonic/Saxon origin. Means: elf, old friend. Alternative spelling: Eldin.

Elder: Old English origin. Means: of shrubs/trees, old.

Eldon: Teutonic/Anglo-Saxon origin. Means: hill's edge, antiquity.

Eldra: Unknown origin and meaning.

Eldred: Old English origin. Means: wise counsel.

Eldric: Unknown origin. Means: old.

Eldrid: Norse/Saxon origin. Means: spirit, adviser.

Eldridge: Anglo-Saxon origin. Means: king's counsel, old hills.

Eldwen: Old English origin. Means: adviser. Alternative spelling: Eldwin.

Eleph: Unknown origin. Means: ox.

Eleuterio: Greek origin. Means: free. Ethnic background: Hispanic. Alternative spelling: Eleutherios.

Eli: Hebrew origin. Means: highest, uplift, Lord. Ethnic background: Norwegian. Alternative spelling: Ely.

Eliab: Unknown origin and meaning.

Elias: Hebrew/Greek origin. Means: the Lord is God. Ethnic background: Hispanic. Alternative spellings: Elihu, Ellis, Elliott, Elliot, Elijah, Eliot, Eliath, Eliathan, Eliathas, Elia, Elio, Elya, Elyeh.

Elidad: Hebrew origin. Means: God is a friend.

Eliezer: Hebrew origin. Means: God has helped. Alternative spellings: Eleizer, Eleazar, Eleazaro, Eleszer, Elazar.

Elijah: Hebrew origin. Means: the Lord is God. Alternative spellings: Elijha, Elighjah, Eligio, Elihu, Elijahuan.

Elimelech: Hebrew origin. Means: father is the king.

Eliphaz: Unknown origin and meaning.

Eliseo: Hebrew/Spanish origin. Means: the Lord is God. Ethnic backgrounds: Italian, Hispanic.

Elkan: Hebrew origin. Means: possessed by God. Alternative spelling: Elkin.

Ellard: Old English/Germanic origin. Means: alder tree, brave, strong. Alternative spellings: Ellerd, Ellord.

Ellerey: Teutonic origin. Means: alder tree, elder. Alternative spelling: Ellery.

Elliot: Hebrew/French origin. Means: the Lord is God. Alternative spellings: Elliott, Eliot.

Ellison: Hebrew/Anglo-Saxon origin. Means: son of Ellis. Alternative spelling: Elison.

Elmar: Old English/Teutonic origin. Means: of noble fame, awe inspiring. Ethnic background: German. Alternative spellings: Elmer, Aylmer.

Elmo: Germanic origin. Means: friendly, helmet.

Elmore: Anglo-Saxon origin. Means: from the moor of elm trees.

Elon: Latin origin. Means: invincible, spirited. Alternative spelling: Ellon.

Elrad: Hebrew origin. Means: God is the ruler.

Elroy: Latin origin. Means: king, royal. Alternative spellings and nicknames: Eroy, Roy.

Elryck: Unknown origin and meaning.

Elsdon: Anglo-Saxon origin. Means: from the noble hill.

Elstan: Old English origin. Means: of the noble town. Alternative spelling: Elston.

Elsworth: Anglo-Saxon origin. Means: from the noble estate.

Elton: Old English origin. Means: dweller of the old estate.

Eltren: Unknown origin. Means: honorable.

Elviro: Unknown origin and meaning.

Elvis: Norse origin. Means: all, a sage.

Elvy: Old English origin. Means: elfin, warrior.

Elway: Unknown origin and meaning.

Elwell: Anglo-Saxon origin. Means: from the old spring.

Elwyn: Anglo-Saxon origin. Means: one who is friend to elves, noble friend. Alternative spellings and nicknames: Winn, Wynn, Elvin, Elwin.

Elwood: Old English origin. Means: one of the old forest. Alternative spelling: Ellwood.

Elysian: Unknown origin and meaning.

Emanuel: Hebrew origin. Means: God is with us. Ethnic background: German. Alternative spellings and nicknames: Manny, Emmanuel, Immanuel, Manuel, Emanuele.

Emee: Unknown origin. Means: fortunate.

Emerson: Germanic origin. Means: industrious, son of Emory. Alternative spelling: Emersen.

"How Do You Spell That?"

I worry about some of these children when I see what they are named! Some of these creative spellings look like the parents just can't spell.

~ **Leigh N., Macon, Georgia**

Emeterio: Greek origin. Unknown meaning. Ethnic background: Hispanic.

Emil: Teutonic origin. Means: flattering, industrious. Ethnic backgrounds: Swedish, German. Alternative spellings: Emile, Emlyn, Emilio.

Emmerich: Unknown origin and meaning. Ethnic background: German.

Emmett: Hebrew/Anglo-Saxon origin. Means: truth, industrious. Alternative spellings and nicknames: Emmy, Em, Emmet, Emmott.

Emory: Germanic origin. Means: industrious, ruler. Alternative spellings: Emery, Merrick, Emeri, Emereo.

Enda: Gaelic origin. Means: bird. Ethnic background: Irish.

Ender: Unknown origin. Means: fountain. Alternative spellings: Endor, Endoro.

Endre: Greek/Hungarian origin. Means: manly.

Eneas: Greek origin. Means: praise.

Eng: Unknown origin. Means: place.

Engedi: Unknown origin. Means: fame.

Engelbert: Germanic origin. Means: angel, famous, bright. Alternative spelling: Englebert.

Enn: Unknown origin and meaning. Ethnic background: Russian.

Ennis: Greek origin. Means: child, wine, revelry.

Enoch: Hebrew origin. Means: one who is devoted, consecrated.

Enrique: Germanic/French origin. Means: head of the estate. Ethnic background: Hispanic. Alternative spelling: Enrico.

Eoin: Hebrew/Gaelic origin. Means: God is gracious and merciful. Ethnic background: Irish.

Ephraim: Hebrew origin. Means: abounding, one who is fruitful. Alternative spellings and nicknames: Ef, Efraim, Ephrem, Efrem, Ephram, Ephriam, Efram, Effram.

Epifanio: Unknown origin and meaning. Ethnic background: Hispanic.

Epitacio: Unknown origin and meaning. Ethnic background: Hispanic.

Eradis: Unknown origin. Means: forthright.

Eraldo: Unknown origin and meaning.

Erasmus: Greek origin. Means: kindly, lovable. Ethnic background: German. Alternative spellings: Erasme, Erasmo.

Erastus: Greek origin. Means: beloved, honored. Alternative spellings: Erastes, Erasatus.

Erhard: Germanic origin. Means: respected warrior.

Eric: Germanic/Norse origin. Means: ever kingly, powerful ruler, honor. Ethnic backgrounds: English/Welsh. 27th most popular boy's name of the '90s. Alternative spellings and nicknames: Erich, Erik, Ric, Rick, Ricky, Eirick, Eryk, Erick, Erics.

Erland: Norse/Germanic origin. Means: from a strange land, honor. Ethnic background: Swedish. Alternative spelling: Erlond.

Erling: Norse/Saxon origin. Means: nobleman's son.

Ermanno: Teutonic/Italian origin. Means: mighty warrior.

Ernald: Germanic origin. Means: eagle, power. Alternative spelling: Ernaldus.

Ernest: Teutonic origin. Means: eagle, vigor. Ethnic background: Irish. Alternative spellings and nicknames: Ern, Ernie, Ernesto, Ernestus.

Ernst: Teutonic origin. Means: seriousness, earnest. Ethnic backgrounds: German, Swedish, Swiss. Alternative spelling: Erno.

Errol: Latin origin. Means: wandering.

Erskine: Old English/Scottish origin. Means: Irish, from the high cliff.

Erving: Gaelic/Hungarian origin. Means: handsome, seaman. Alternative spelling: Ervin.

Erwin: Anglo-Saxon origin. Means: friend of the sea, white river. Ethnic background: German.

Esau: Hebrew origin. Means: hairy.

Escriba: Spanish origin. Means: scribe.

Eshel: Hebrew origin. Means: tamarisk tree.

Eskil: Norse origin. Means: divine sacrifice. Ethnic background: Swedish. Alternative spelling: Eskill.

Esmero: Unknown origin and meaning. Ethnic background: Hispanic.

Esmond: Old English origin. Means: gracious protector.

Espen: Germanic origin. Means: bear of God. Ethnic background: Norwegian.

Esquilo: Spanish origin. Means: with great modesty. Ethnic background: Hispanic.

Estacada: Unknown origin and meaning.

Estanislao: Unknown origin and meaning. Ethnic background: Hispanic.

Este: Latin origin. Means: from the East.

Esteban: Spanish origin. Means: victorious. Alternative spellings: Estaban, Estelan, Estevan.

Estes: Latin origin. Means: an inlet, tide. Alternative spelling: Estis.

Estlin: Unknown origin and meaning.

Estus: Unknown origin. Means: honored.

Ethan: Hebrew origin. Means: firm, permanent. 44th most popular boy's name of the '90s. Alternative spelling: Etam.

Ethaniel: Unknown origin and meaning.

Ethban: Unknown origin. Means: gracious. Alternative spellings: Ethben, Ethbin.

Etienne: Greek/French origin. Means: crowned. Ethnic background: Swiss.

Ettore: Greek origin. Means: steadfast, loyalty. Ethnic background: Italian.

Etzal: Germanic origin. Means: noble father.

Eudo: Greek origin. Means: well regarded, gift.

Eugene: Greek origin. Means: well born, of nobility. Ethnic background: French. Alternative spellings and nicknames: Gene, Eugen, Eugenio.

Eulalio: Unknown origin and meaning. Ethnic background: Hispanic.

Eunan: Gaelic origin. Means: great fear. Ethnic background: Irish.

Eusebio: Greek origin. Means: pious, respectful. Ethnic backgrounds: Italian, Hispanic. Alternative spelling: Eusebius.

Eustachio: Greek/Italian origin. Means: fine vineyard, fruitful. Alternative spellings: Eustasius, Eustazio.

Eustrate: Unknown origin and meaning.

Evan: Hebrew/Celtic origin. Means: gracious, youthful warrior. 38th most popular boy's name of the '90s.

Evander: Latin/Greek origin. Means: well respected.

Evangelos: Greek origin. Means: brings good tidings. Alternative spelling: Evangelista.

Everard: Old English/Teutonic origin. Means: strength of a boar. Alternative spellings: Evered, Everardo, Eberhard, Eberardo, Evert.

Everett: Anglo-Saxon/Germanic origin. Means: strong warrior. Alternative spelling: Everhart.

Evers: Anglo-Saxon origin. Means: with strength and bravery.

Evreml: Hebrew origin. Means: mighty father. Alternative spellings: Evromel, Evromele.

Evren: Unknown origin and meaning.

Ewald: Germanic origin. Means: just ruler, bearer, lab. Alternative spelling: Ewold.

Ewan: Celtic origin. Means: young, born. Alternative spelling: Ewen.

Eward: Germanic origin. Means: with great strength. Ethnic background: Dutch.

Ewert: Anglo-Saxon origin. Means: ewe, shepherd.

Ewing: Anglo-Saxon origin. Means: one who knows the law, friend.

Eynar: Unknown origin and meaning. Ethnic background: Russian.

Ezeamaka: African origin. Means: king is splendid.

Ezekiel: Hebrew origin. Means: God will strengthen. Alternative spellings and nicknames: Zeke, Ezechiel, Ezechiele, Ezequiel.

Ezenachi: African origin. Means: the king rules.

Ezeoha: African origin. Means: the people's king.

Ezio: Greek/Latin origin. Means: eagle.

Ezra: Hebrew origin. Means: the helpful one, salvation. Alternative spellings and nicknames: Ez, Esra, Esdras, Ezar.

f

Faakhir: Arabic origin. Means: excellent.

Fabian: Latin origin. Means: one who grows beans. Ethnic backgrounds: German, Hispanic. Alternative spellings and nicknames: Fabe, Fabien, Fabiano.

Fabrin: Latin origin. Means: craftsman, smith. Alternative spellings: Fabrioni, Fabrice, Fabrizio.

Fabron: Latin origin. Means: blacksmith, mechanic.

Fachan: Irish origin. Means: enterprising. Alternative spelling: Fachanan.

Facundo: Unknown origin and meaning. Ethnic background: Hispanic.

Fagan: Anglo-Saxon origin. Means: joyful, fiery. Alternative spelling: Fagin.

Faheem: Arabic origin. Means: learned.

Fairfax: Anglo-Saxon origin. Means: yellow- or fair-haired one.

Faizon: Unknown origin and meaning.

Fakhr: Arabic origin. Means: glory.

Faldo: Unknown origin and meaning.

Faline: Unknown origin. Means: catlike.

Falk: Hebrew origin. Means: circling, falcon. Ethnic background: German.

Falkner: French/Anglo-Saxon origin. Means: one who trains or hunts falcons. Alternative spellings: Fowler, Faulkner.

Fane: Anglo-Saxon origin. Means: glad.

Faraji: African origin. Means: consolation.

Fareed: Arabic origin. Means: unique.

"How Do You Spell That?"

I have trouble picturing a Hilaree Rodham Clinton or Hilari Rodham Clinton. There has to be a balance between creativity and functionality.

~ Robyn G.,
Chula Vista, California

Farkas: Hebrew/Hungarian origin. Means: wolf.

Farley: Anglo-Saxon origin. Means: of the wayside, bull's meadow.

Farnall: Anglo-Saxon origin. Means: of the fern slope. Alternative spellings: Farnell, Fernald.

Farnham: Anglo-Saxon origin. Means: from the fern field.

Farnley: Anglo-Saxon origin. Means: of the bull's meadow.

Farold: Anglo-Saxon origin. Means: mighty traveler.

Farr: Anglo-Saxon origin. Means: sojourner.

Farrell: Celtic origin. Means: valorous one. Alternative spellings: Farell, Farrel, Ferrell, Fergal.

Farris: Greek origin. Means: solid, rocklike. Alternative spelling: Ferris.

Farro: Unknown origin. Means: well. Alternative spellings: Farron, Faro.

Fasta: Spanish origin. Means: sacrifices. Alternative spelling: Fasto.

Fattah: Arabic origin. Means: victory.

Faust: Latin origin. Means: one with luck, fortunate. Alternative spellings: Faustino, Fausto, Faustus.

Favian: Unknown origin. Means: man. Alternative spellings: Favient, Favin, Favianus.

Faxan: Teutonic/Anglo-Saxon origin. Means: with thick hair. Alternative spellings: Faxen, Faxon.

Febronio: Unknown origin and meaning. Ethnic background: Hispanic.

Fedde: Unknown origin and meaning. Ethnic background: Dutch.

Feibush: Latin/Greek origin. Means: bright one. Ethnic background: Jewish.

Feivel: Latin/Greek origin. Means: bright one. Ethnic background: Jewish.

Felimy: Unknown origin and meaning. Ethnic background: Irish.

Felipe: Spanish origin. Means: one who loves horses. Alternative spellings: Felipo, Filippo.

Felix: Latin origin. Means: the lucky, happy one. Ethnic backgrounds: Irish, Hispanic, German, Czech, Swiss.

Felton: Old English origin. Means: of the garden estate.

Fenimore: Unknown origin and meaning.

Fenton: Old English origin. Means: of the settlement near the marsh.

Feodor: Greek origin. Means: divine gift. Ethnic background: Russian. Alternative spelling: Fedor.

Ferdinand: Germanic origin. Means: peaceful journey, adventuring. Ethnic background: French. Alternative spellings and nicknames: Ferd, Ferde, Ferdie, Fernando, Fernand, Hernando, Ferdinando, Ferdnando.

Ferenc: Latin/Hungarian origin. Means: independent, free.

Fergus: Gaelic origin. Means: manly, strong. Ethnic background: Irish.

Ferrand: Unknown origin. Means: gray. Alternative spellings: Ferrant, Farrand, Farrant.

Festatus: Latin origin. Means: festive, steadfast. Alternative spelling: Festus.

Fhoki: Japanese origin. Unknown meaning.

Fiachra: Gaelic origin. Means: raven. Ethnic background: Irish.

Fidel: Latin origin. Means: faithful. Ethnic background: Hispanic. Alternative spellings: Fidelis, Fidele, Fidelio.

Fielding: Anglo-Saxon origin. Means: field dweller.

Filbert: Anglo-Saxon origin. Means: brilliant, radiant. Alternative spellings: Filberte, Filiberto, Fulbert.

Fillander: Unknown origin and meaning. Alternative spelling: Fillender.

Fillmore: Anglo-Saxon origin. Means: famous. Alternative spellings: Filmer, Filmore.

Filomeno: Greek/Latin origin. Means: lover of songs or man. Ethnic background: Hispanic.

Finbar: Gaelic/Irish origin. Means: fair-haired, handsome. Ethnic background: Irish. Alternative spellings: Finbur, Finnbar.

Finch: Unknown origin and meaning.

Fineas: Unknown origin and meaning. Ethnic background: Hispanic.

Finian: Celtic/Irish origin. Means: handsome.

Finlay: Gaelic origin. Means: fair warrior. Alternative spellings: Finley, Findlay, Findley.

Finn: Gaelic origin. Means: fair, white. Ethnic background: Norwegian.

Fintan: Unknown origin and meaning. Ethnic background: Irish.

Firman: Anglo-Saxon origin. Means: distant traveler, strong, firm. Alternative spellings: Firmin, Farman, Farmann, Fermin.

Fishel: Hebrew origin. Means: fish, multiply. Alternative spelling: Fishke.

Fisk: Old English/Swedish origin. Means: fisherman. Alternative spelling: Fiske.

Fitch: Anglo-Saxon origin. Means: ermine, a white-tailed weasel.

Fitz: Teutonic/Anglo-Saxon origin. Means: son of.

Fitzgerald: Teutonic/Anglo-Saxon origin. Means: son of Gerald, mighty. Alternative spelling: Fitzger.

Fitzhugh: Anglo-Saxon origin. Means: intelligent, son of Hugh.

Fitzpatrick: Teutonic/Anglo-Saxon origin. Means: son of Patrick, regal.

Flannan: Gaelic origin. Means: red, ruddy. Ethnic background: Irish. Alternative spelling: Flann.

Flavian: Latin origin. Means: golden-haired. Alternative spellings: Flavio, Flavius.

Fletcher: Germanic origin. Means: an arrowsmith. Nickname: Fletch.

Flint: Old English origin. Means: the brook, stream.

Flip: Anglo-Saxon origin. Means: nimble, talkative.

Florentin: Latin origin. Means: blooming, flourishing. Ethnic background: German. Alternative spelling: Florencio.

Floyd: Celtic origin. Means: one with gray hair.

Flynn: Gaelic origin. Means: one with red hair. Alternative spelling: Flinn.

Folke: Teutonic/Norse origin. Means: guardian of the people. Ethnic background: Swedish.

Forbes: Greek/Gaelic origin. Means: flowering plant, fields.

Forrester: French/Anglo-Saxon origin. Means: forest dweller, guardian. Alternative spellings and nicknames: Foss, Forrie, Forster, Forester, Foster, Forest, Forrest.

Fortuno: Latin origin. Means: destiny, chance. Ethnic background: Hispanic. Alternative spelling: Fortunio.

Foster: Latin/Anglo-Saxon origin. Means: forest keeper, shearer.

Fraime: Unknown origin and meaning. Ethnic background: Jewish.

Fraine: Anglo-Saxon origin. Means: foreigner. Alternative spellings: Frayne, Freyne.

Franchot: Latin/Teutonic origin. Means: free.

Francisco: Latin/Spanish origin. Means: free. Ethnic background: Hispanic. Alternative spellings: Francesco, Fransisco.

François: French origin. Means: free, of France.

Frank: Latin/Germanic origin. Means: spear, Frenchman, free. Alternative spellings: Franck, Franco, Frankie.

Franklin: Latin/Teutonic origin. Means: a free man who owns land. Alternative spellings and nicknames: Francklyn, Francklin, Franklyn, Frank, Frankie.

Frantisek: Teutonic origin. Means: free. Ethnic background: Czech.

Franz: Germanic origin. Means: free. Ethnic background: Swiss. Alternative spelling: Frans.

Fraser: French/Scottish origin. Means: strawberry flowers. Alternative spellings: Frasier, Frazer, Frazier.

Fred: Teutonic origin. Means: peaceful ruler.

Frederick: Teutonic origin. Means: peaceful ruler. Ethnic background: Scottish. Alternative spellings and nicknames: Freddy, Fred, Freddie, Frederic, Fredric, Fritz, Frederico, Frederik, Fredrich, Fredrik, Friedrich, Federico.

Freeman: Anglo-Saxon origin. Means: a free man.

Fremont: Teutonic origin. Means: free, noble protector.

Frewen: Anglo-Saxon origin. Means: free, noble friend. Alternative spelling: Frewin.

Frey: Anglo-Saxon origin. Means: Lord.

Frick: Anglo-Saxon origin. Means: bold.

Fridmann: Germanic origin. Means: man of peace.

Fridolin: Unknown origin and meaning. Ethnic background: German.

Fridtjof: Unknown origin and meaning. Ethnic background: Norwegian.

Friso: Anglo-Saxon origin. Means: curly haired. Ethnic background: Dutch.

Fritz: Germanic origin. Means: peaceful ruler, free. Ethnic background: Swiss. Alternative spelling: Fritzi.

Frode: Norse origin. Means: wise, well informed.

Fromel: Unknown origin and meaning. Ethnic background: Jewish.

Frost: Germanic origin. Means: extreme coldness.

Froyim: Unknown origin and meaning. Ethnic background: Jewish. Alternative spelling: Froyimke.

Fu: Unknown origin. Means: teacher.

Fukuda: Japanese origin. Means: field. Alternative spelling: Furuta.

Fuller: Old English origin. Means: cloth, to thicken.

Fulton: Anglo-Saxon origin. Means: one who is from the farm.

Fysal: Unknown origin and meaning.

g

Gaal: Unknown origin. Means: angry.

Gabai: Hebrew origin. Means: communal official.

Gabel: French origin. Means: little Gabriel. Alternative spelling: Gable.

Gabino: Hebrew/Spanish origin. Means: God is my strength. Ethnic background: Hispanic.

Gabor: Hebrew/Hungarian origin. Means: God is my strength. Alternative spelling: Gibor.

Gabriel: Hebrew origin. Means: man of God, who is my strength. Ethnic backgrounds: Hispanic, German, Swedish. 44th most popular boy's name of the '90s. Nicknames: Gabby, Gabe, Gabie.

Gad: Hebrew origin. Means: happy, fortunate warrior.

Gadil: Arabic origin. Means: God is my wealth. Ethnic background: Jewish. Alternative spellings: Gidil, Gedil.

Gadmann: Unknown origin. Means: fortunate. Alternative spelling: Gadmon.

Gaerity: Unknown origin and meaning.

Gage: Old English/French origin. Means: pledge, pawn.

Gaile: Anglo-Saxon origin. Means: happy, vivacious.

Gainer: Unknown origin. Means: fair. Alternative spelling: Gainor.

Gaius: Latin origin. Means: merry.

Galen: Greek/Gaelic origin. Means: calm, wise, bright. Alternative spelling: Galan.

Gall: Celtic/Gaelic origin. Means: foreigner, stranger.

Gallagher: Celtic/Gaelic origin. Means: eager assistant. Ethnic background: Irish.

Galton: Anglo-Saxon origin. Means: of the hill estate.

Galvan: Celtic/Gaelic origin. Means: shiny or bright white, sparrow. Alternative spellings and nicknames: Galven, Galvin, Vin, Vinny.

Gamal: Hebrew/Arabic origin. Means: a camel. Alternative spelling: Gamali.

Gamaliel: Hebrew origin. Means: the Lord, God is my reward.

Gamba: African origin. Means: warrior.

Gamel: Norse origin. Means: elderly, old.

Gannon: Gaelic origin. Means: blond one, fair complexion.

Garbick: Unknown origin and meaning.

Garcia: Teutonic/Spanish origin. Means: brave in battle, strength, spear.

Gardal: Teutonic origin. Means: careful protector. Alternative spellings: Gardel, Gardell.

Gardiner: Teutonic origin. Means: one who loves plants, gardener. Alternative spellings: Gardener, Gardner, Gairdner.

Gareth: Celtic origin. Means: a garden, gentle, strong.

Garett: Old English/French origin. Means: mighty spear, to guard. Alternative spellings and nicknames: Gerry, Jaret, Jary, Garet, Gerard, Gary, Garth, Garrett, Garreth, Gareth, Garry, Garret, Garritt.

Garfield: Old English origin. Means: of the triangular field.

Garibald: Unknown origin. Means: addition. Alternative spellings: Garibold, Garibaldo.

Garlan: Latin/French origin. Means: crowned with a wreath of flowers.

Garmond: Anglo-Saxon origin. Means: protector, spearman. Alternative spellings: Garmund, Garman.

Garner: Teutonic origin. Means: noble guardian of the army.

Garnett: Latin origin. Means: a grain or seed, red jewel.

Garnock: Welsh origin. Means: of the alder-tree meadow.

Garonne: Unknown origin and meaning.

"How Do You Spell That?"

On behalf of the creative spellers out there: This is the United States of America, and much blood has been shed to ensure your right to spell *Tom* with a *Q* if you so desire. Every baby is unique, and I can certainly understand the desire of many parents to express that uniqueness in the baby's name. Personally, I'm trying very hard to make sure that the child I'm expecting won't share a name with 10 other kids in his preschool class. But we have to be careful when we change a classic name and give it a creative spelling. Remember that our spelling will be giving others a first impression of our children, often before they have had a chance to do so in person (as on a résumé, for instance).

~ **Maura S., Alexandria, Virginia**

Garretson: French/Anglo-Saxon origin. Means: son of Garret, to guard.

Garrick: Teutonic origin. Means: mighty warrior, one who wields a spear. Alternative spellings and nicknames: Garick, Rick, Ricky.

Garrison: French origin. Means: the troop's fort.

Garroway: Anglo-Saxon origin. Means: spear, warrior.

Garson: Anglo-Saxon origin. Means: son of Gar, spear.

Garth: Norse origin. Means: of the garden, yardkeeper.

Garton: Anglo-Saxon origin. Means: dweller of the field near the town.

Garvey: Gaelic origin. Means: spear bearer, difficult peace.

Garvin: Gaelic origin. Means: friend, military ally. Alternative spelling: Garwin.

Garwood: Anglo-Saxon origin. Means: dweller of the fir forest.

Gary: Germanic/Anglo-Saxon origin. Means: spear bearer, warrior. Ethnic backgrounds: English/Welsh. Alternative spellings: Gari, Garey, Garry, Garii, Garry.

Gaspar: Persian origin. Means: holder of treasure. Ethnic backgrounds: Hispanic, Italian. Alternative spellings: Gasper, Gaspare.

Gaston: Germanic/French origin. Means: guest, stranger, of Gascony. Ethnic backgrounds: French, German, Hispanic, Italian. Alternative spelling: Gastone.

Gati: Unknown origin. Means: family. Alternative spellings: Gatian, Gatias.

Gaudenz: Unknown origin and meaning. Ethnic background: Swiss.

Gauthier: Teutonic origin. Means: powerful leader.

Gavin: Scottish/Welsh origin. Means: young hawk. Ethnic backgrounds: English/Welsh. Alternative spellings: Gavan, Gaven, Gavino.

Gavril: Hebrew/Slavic origin. Means: God is my strength. Alternative spellings: Gavrel, Gavrilke.

Gaylord: French origin. Means: lively, dandy, brave. Alternative spellings: Gayler, Gallard.

Gayner: Gaelic/Irish origin. Means: fair-haired one's son.

Gazo: Unknown origin. Means: leader. Alternative spelling: Gazzo.

Geary: Anglo-Saxon origin. Means: changeable. Alternative spelling: Gery.

Gebhard: Germanic origin. Means: one with a gift of strength. Ethnic background: German.

Geddy: Unknown origin and meaning.

Gedraitis: Unknown origin. Means: calm.

Geert: Germanic origin. Means: brave strength. Ethnic background: Dutch.

Gefen: Hebrew origin. Means: vine.

Gehrig: Unknown origin and meaning.

Geier: Norse origin. Means: spear, vulture. Alternative spellings: Geir, Garr, Geyer.

Gelasias: Greek origin. Means: love of laughter. Alternative spelling: Gelasius.

Geminian: Unknown origin. Means: born. Alternative spelling: Geminius.

Gemino: Unknown origin and meaning. Ethnic background: Hispanic.

Genaro: Spanish origin. Means: consecrated to God.

Gene: Greek origin. Means: well born, fortunate.

Gennady: Unknown origin and meaning. Ethnic background: Russian.

Gentilis: Latin origin. Means: of the same clan or kind.

Gentry: French origin. Means: well bred.

Geoffrey: Germanic origin. Means: God's peace. Ethnic backgrounds: English/Welsh, Irish. Alternative spellings and nicknames: Jeffers, Geof, Geoff, Jeffry, Jeff, Jeffery, Godfrey.

George: Greek origin. Means: farmer, to work the earth. Ethnic background: Scottish. 43rd most popular boy's name of the '90s. Alternative spellings and nicknames: Georgie, Jorin, Georges, Jorge, Joris, Jurgen, Georgios, Georg, Georgy, Giorgio.

Geraint: Greek/Welsh origin. Means: old, elderly.

Gerald: Teutonic origin. Means: mighty ruler and spearman. Ethnic background: French. Alternative spellings and nicknames: Jer, Jerold, Gerrald, Gereld, Garold, Jerrold, Gerry, Jerry, Gery, Geraldo, Gerold, Giraldo.

Gerard: Germanic origin. Means: brave warrior, spear. Ethnic background: French. Alternative spellings: Garrard, Gerardo, Geraud, Gerault, Gerrard, Gerhard, Gerrit, Gerrid, Gherardo, Giraud.

Gerben: Unknown origin and meaning. Ethnic background: Dutch.

Gerbold: Germanic origin. Means: bold spear.

Gere: Greek origin. Means: holy fame.

Geremia: Greek/Italian origin. Means: sacred name. Alternative spelling: Giroiamo.

Gereron: Greek origin. Means: battle, old.

Gerius: Unknown origin. Means: steadfast.

Gerlac: Germanic origin. Means: spear-wielding soldier.

Germain: Latin origin. Means: brother, brotherhood. Ethnic background: French. Alternative spelling: Germayn.

German: Teutonic origin. Means: warrior. Ethnic background: Hispanic. Alternative spellings: Germaun, Germin.

Gernot: Germanic origin. Means: spear buyer.

Gerolamo: Unknown origin and meaning. Ethnic background: Italian.

Gersham: Hebrew origin. Means: exiled stranger. Alternative spellings: Gershom, Gershon.

Gert: Teutonic origin. Means: warrior. Ethnic background: Dutch.

Gertjan: Unknown origin and meaning. Ethnic background: Dutch.

Gervas: Teutonic origin. Means: honorable, spear holder. Alternative spellings and nicknames: Jarv, Jarvey, Jervis, Gervase, Gervais, Jarvis, Gervaso.

Getzel: Hebrew/Germanic origin. Means: peace of God. Alternative spellings: Getz, Gotz.

Gevante: Unknown origin and meaning.

Geza: Hungarian origin. Unknown meaning.

Ghanee: Arabic origin. Means: wealthy.

Ghulaam: Arabic origin. Means: servant.

Giachem: Unknown origin and meaning. Ethnic background: Swiss.

Giacomo: Hebrew/Italian origin. Means: supplanted, protected.

Gian: Hebrew/Italian origin. Means: God is gracious. Alternative spelling: Gianni.

Gianpaolo: Unknown origin and meaning.

Gibbon: Unknown origin. Means: born. Alternative spelling: Gibeon.

Gibe: French origin. Means: famous pledge.

Gibrian: Unknown origin. Means: aristocrat.

Gibson: Anglo-Saxon origin. Means: son of Gilbert, trusted.

Gideon: Hebrew origin. Means: cuts down, great, indomitable warrior. Alternative spelling: Gadeone.

Gifford: Germanic origin. Means: great gift, bravery. Alternative spellings and nicknames: Giff, Gifferd.

Gil: Greek origin. Means: bearded, kid, protector. Ethnic background: Jewish.

Gilane: Unknown origin. Means: downy.

Gilbert: Teutonic origin. Means: a golden pledge, brilliant. Ethnic backgrounds: French, Irish. Alternative spellings and nicknames: Gib, Gibb, Gil, Gill, Bert, Giberto, Guilbert, Guibert.

Gilboa: Unknown origin. Means: bubbly.

Gilby: Unknown origin. Means: estate.

Gilchrist: Gaelic/Irish origin. Means: servant of Christ.

Gildas: Celtic/Anglo-Saxon origin. Means: servant of God, gold-covered.

Gildor: Anglo-Saxon origin. Means: a goldsmith. Ethnic background: Jewish.

Giles: Greek origin. Means: bearded companion, kid, protector. Ethnic background: Irish.

Gilford: Anglo-Saxon origin. Means: of Gill's ford.

Gillead: Arabic origin. Means: camel's hump, mountainous. Alternative spellings: Gilleod, Gilead.

Gilles: Greek/French origin. Means: protective shield.

Gilmer: Teutonic origin. Means: famous captive.

Gilmore: Gaelic origin. Means: devoted to St. Mary. Alternative spellings: Gilmour, Gillmore.

Gilroy: Gaelic origin. Means: son of the red-haired one.

Gilson: Hebrew/Anglo-Saxon origin. Means: son of Gil, joy.

Gilus: Unknown origin. Means: heritage. Alternative spelling: Gildus.

Gimpel: Germanic origin. Means: bright. Ethnic background: Jewish.

Gino: Germanic/Italian origin. Means: famous in battle.

Gioacchino: Hebrew/Italian origin. Means: the Lord will establish.

Gionata: Unknown origin and meaning. Ethnic background: Italian.

Giordano: Unknown origin. Means: descending.

Giosue: Hebrew/Italian origin. Means: the Lord is my salvation.

Giovanni: Hebrew/Italian origin. Means: God's great gift. Alternative spelling: Giovanny.

Girvan: Gaelic origin. Means: rough. Alternative spellings: Girven, Girvin.

Gisbert: Unknown origin and meaning. Ethnic backgrounds: Dutch, German.

Gisleno: Unknown origin and meaning.

Giulio: Greek/Italian origin. Means: youthful, soft-haired.

Giuseppe: Hebrew/Italian origin. Means: God shall add.

Giustino: Latin/Italian origin. Means: just, honest. Alternative spelling: Giusto.

Givon: Hebrew origin. Means: heights.

Gjest: Norse origin. Means: stranger.

Gladwin: Anglo-Saxon origin. Means: cheerful friend.

Glen: Gaelic origin. Means: one who resides in the valley. Alternative spellings: Glenn, Glynn, Glynas.

Glenden: Gaelic origin. Means: of the dark glen. Alternative spelling: Glendon.

Goar: Unknown origin. Means: fighter. Alternative spelling: Goer.

Goddard: Old English/Teutonic origin. Means: firm, divinely steadfast. Alternative spellings: Godard, Godderd, Godred.

Godfrey: Germanic origin. Means: God's peace. Alternative spellings: Goffredo, Gottfried.

Godric: Anglo-Saxon origin. Means: with God's rule. Alternative spelling: Godrich.

Godwin: Old English origin. Means: faithful friend of God. Alternative spellings: Goodwyn, Goodwin.

Goeffrey: Unknown origin. Means: divinely.

Golding: Anglo-Saxon origin. Means: golden, son of God.

Goldwin: Anglo-Saxon origin. Means: precious friend, loves gold.

Goliath: Hebrew origin. Means: exiled stranger.

Golin: Unknown origin and meaning.

Gomar: Hebrew origin. Means: thorough, complete. Alternative spelling: Gomer.

Gonzago: Unknown origin and meaning. Ethnic background: Hispanic.

Gonzales: Spanish origin. Means: wolf. Alternative spellings: Gonsalve, Gonzalo.

Goodman: Anglo-Saxon origin. Means: good servant.

Goodrich: Unknown origin. Means: good.

Goos: Unknown origin and meaning. Ethnic background: Dutch.

Goral: Hebrew origin. Means: fate, lot.

Gordon: Gaelic/Anglo-Saxon origin. Means: hero, of the triangular field. Ethnic backgrounds: English/Welsh. Alternative spellings and nicknames: Gordy, Gordie, Gordan, Gorden.

Gore: Anglo-Saxon origin. Means: hero, a cathedral.

Gorje: Unknown origin and meaning.

Gorman: Gaelic/Irish origin. Means: blue, blue-eyed.

Goro: Japanese origin. Unknown meaning.

Gothar: Unknown origin. Means: flocks.

Gotthard: Teutonic origin. Means: with God's rule. Ethnic background: German. Alternative spelling: Gothard.

Gottlieb: Germanic origin. Means: loves God. Alternative spelling: Gottlob.

Gould: Unknown origin and meaning.

Gower: Welsh origin. Means: pure.

Gowon: African origin. Means: rainmaker.

Grady: Gaelic origin. Means: illustrious, noble.

Graham: Old English origin. Means: of the gray place or home. Ethnic backgrounds: English/Welsh. Alternative spellings and nicknames: Graeme, Ham.

Granger: Anglo-Saxon/French origin. Means: farmer.

Grant: Old English origin. Means: one who is great.

Grantland: Old English origin. Means: from the grand meadow, deeded. Alternative spellings: Grantham, Grantley.

Granville: French origin. Means: from the big town.

Graves: Unknown origin and meaning.

Gray: Old English origin. Means: to shine.

Grayson: Old English origin. Means: the reeve's son. Ethnic backgrounds: English/Welsh.

"How Do You Spell That?"

Who cares if your name comes preprinted on brushes and pencils?

~ Kristina M., Sunderland, Massachusetts

Greeley: Anglo-Saxon origin. Means: of the gray meadow.

Greene: Germanic origin. Means: to grow.

Greg: Greek origin. Means: vigilant, watchful. Alternative spelling: Gregg.

Gregory: Greek origin. Means: vigilant, watchful. Ethnic background: Irish. 47th most popular boy's name of the '90s. Alternative spellings and nicknames: Gregorie, Greg, Gregg, Gregor, Gregorio, Greger, Gergely, Gergory, Grigory, Grigor, Grigorij, Grzegorz.

Greyson: Unknown origin. Means: judge's. Alternative spelling: Grey.

Grier: Unknown origin and meaning.

Griffith: Celtic/Welsh origin. Means: with great faith, chief. Alternative spellings and nicknames: Griff, Griffin, Griffey.

Grimbal: Old English origin. Means: bold, fierce. Alternative spelling: Grimbald.

Griswold: Teutonic origin. Means: of the gray, wild forest.

Grover: Anglo-Saxon origin. Means: tends to the grove or trees.

Gualtiero: French/Spanish origin. Means: a general, strong warrior. Ethnic background: Italian.

Gudmund: Norse origin. Means: leader.

Guglielmo: Germanic/Italian origin. Means: determined protector.

Guido: French/Italian origin. Means: rope guide, valley. Ethnic background: German.

Guillaume: Germanic/French origin. Means: determined protector. Alternative spelling: Guillermo.

Guin: Gaelic origin. Means: blond.

Gumersindo: Germanic origin. Means: one who follows the path. Ethnic background: Hispanic.

Gunde: Unknown origin and meaning. Ethnic background: Swedish.

Gunnar: Germanic origin. Means: fierce warrior. Ethnic backgrounds: Norwegian, Swedish.

Gunter: Teutonic origin. Means: army, brave fighter. Ethnic background: German. Alternative spelling: Gunther.

Gurias: Unknown origin. Means: family.

Guryon: Hebrew origin. Means: lion.

Gus: Teutonic origin. Means: staff of God. Ethnic background: Dutch.

Gustaf: Norse/Germanic origin. Means: noble leader, staff of the Goths. Ethnic background: Swedish. Alternative spellings: Gustaff, Gustav, Gustave, Gustavo.

Guthrie: Gaelic origin. Means: windy, free.

Guy: Various origin. Means: life, warrior, guide, valley. Ethnic background: French, Jewish. Alternative spelling: Gai.

Gwynn: Celtic origin. Means: white browed, holy.

Gyorgy: Greek origin. Means: watchful, vigilant. Ethnic background: Hungarian.

Gyozo: Unknown origin and meaning. Ethnic background: Hungarian.

Gyula: Greek/Hungarian origin. Means: lightly bearded.

h

Haadee: Arabic origin. Means: guide, leader.

Haafiz: Arabic origin. Means: guardian.

Haakon: Arabic origin. Unknown meaning. Ethnic background: Norwegian.

Haaris: Arabic origin. Means: planter.

Haas: Unknown origin. Means: hare.

Habakkuk: Hebrew origin. Means: to embrace.

Habeeb: Arabic origin. Means: beloved.

Habimama: African origin. Means: God exists.

Hachiro: Japanese origin. Unknown meaning.

Hachman: Unknown origin. Means: learned. Alternative spellings: Hachmann, Hachmin.

Hackett: Germanic origin. Means: little hacker.

Hadad: Unknown origin and meaning.

Hadden: Anglo-Saxon origin. Means: of the heath valley. Alternative spellings: Haddan, Haddon, Haden.

Hadley: Anglo-Saxon origin. Means: of the heath meadow.

Hadrian: Greek origin. Means: of rich, dark soil.

Hadriel: Hebrew origin. Means: splendor of the Lord.

Hadwin: Teutonic origin. Means: ally in battle. Alternative spelling: Hadwyn.

Hagar: Hebrew origin. Means: flees, flight.

Hagen: Teutonic/Gaelic origin. Means: young warrior. Ethnic background: German. Alternative spellings: Haggen, Hagan.

Hagley: Anglo-Saxon origin. Means: of the hedged enclosure. Alternative spelling: Hawley.

Haig: Anglo-Saxon origin. Means: of the hedged enclosure.

Haike: Unknown origin and meaning. Ethnic background: Dutch.

Haines: Anglo-Saxon origin. Means: vine-covered cottage. Alternative spellings: Hanus, Haynes.

Hakan: Norse origin. Means: noble, fiery. Ethnic background: Swedish.

Hakeem: Arabic origin. Means: wise sage. Alternative spellings: Hakim, Hakeen.

Hako: Unknown origin. Means: exalted.

Hal: Teutonic origin. Means: army leader.

Haland: Anglo-Saxon origin. Means: Henry's. Alternative spelling: Halland.

Halbert: Teutonic origin. Means: hero, brilliant gem. Nicknames: Hal, Bert.

Haldas: Unknown origin. Means: reliable.

Halden: Teutonic origin. Means: part Dane. Alternative spellings: Haldin, Haldane, Haldan, Halfdan.

Haldor: Norse origin. Means: thunder, rock.

Hale: Teutonic origin. Means: a robust. Alternative spelling: Hal.

Halford: Anglo-Saxon origin. Means: from the ford's hall.

Hall: Anglo-Saxon origin. Means: of the manor.

Hallam: Anglo-Saxon origin. Means: hall dweller.

Halliwell: Anglo-Saxon origin. Means: dweller of the holy spring.

Halsey: Anglo-Saxon origin. Means: from Hal's island. Alternative spelling: Halsy.

Halstead: Anglo-Saxon origin. Means: of the manor house. Alternative spelling: Halsted.

Halston: Swedish origin. Means: rock or stone.

Halton: Anglo-Saxon origin. Means: estate on the hill.

Halvard: Norse origin. Means: castle, defender. Alternative spellings: Halvor, Hallvard.

Ham: Hebrew origin. Means: warm.

Hamal: Arabic origin. Means: lamb.

Hamar: Norse origin. Means: ingenuity, hammer.

Hamid: Arabic origin. Means: God, praised.

Hamill: Unknown origin and meaning.

Hamilton: Anglo-Saxon origin. Means: of the flat-topped hill, home lover.

Hamish: Hebrew/Gaelic origin. Means: may God protect, one who supplants.

Hamlet: Germanic origin. Means: home, enclosed area.

Hamlin: Germanic origin. Means: one who loves a small home. Alternative spelling: Hamlyn.

Hamon: Germanic origin. Means: a home, faithful. Nickname: Hamo.

Hamor: Unknown origin and meaning.

Han: Germanic origin. Means: God's gift.

The Creative Approach

If you've tried the rational approach to finding a name (poring over books, talking to friends and family, scouring your family tree) with no luck, maybe it's time to mix it up a little. Start looking around and expect the unexpected. Sit still and listen to your inner voice. After all, inspiration works in mysterious ways.

Hanani: Hebrew origin. Means: gracious. Alternative spelling: Hananiah.

Haneef: Arabic origin. Means: professes truth.

Hanford: Anglo-Saxon origin. Means: dweller of the high ford. Alternative spelling: Hamford.

Hanisi: African origin. Means: born on Thursday.

Hank: Teutonic origin. Means: ruler of the estate.

Hanley: Anglo-Saxon origin. Means: one who is from the high pasture. Alternative spellings: Henley, Hanleigh.

Hannibal: Phoenician origin. Means: grace of God. Alternative spellings and nicknames: Hanno, Hanni.

Hans: Hebrew/Germanic origin. Means: gracious gift of God. Ethnic backgrounds: Swiss, Dutch, Norwegian, Swedish.

Hansel: Hebrew/Germanic origin. Means: one who is a gift from God. Alternative spelling: Hansuli.

Haqq: Arabic origin. Means: truth.

Harbin: French origin. Means: glorious warrior.

Harcourt: Teutonic/Anglo-Saxon origin. Means: the courtyard of the soldiers.

Harden: Anglo-Saxon/French origin. Means: of the hare's meadow, lively. Alternative spellings: Hardin, Hardunn, Hardan.

Hardwin: Anglo-Saxon origin. Means: brave friend.

Hardy: Old English/Germanic origin. Means: bold, hardy, robust. Alternative spellings: Hardie, Hardey, Harday, Harding.

Harel: Hebrew origin. Means: mountain of God.

Hargrave: Anglo-Saxon origin. Means: of the grove. Alternative spelling: Hargrove.

Harim: Germanic origin. Means: protective.

Harlan: Teutonic/Old English origin. Means: battleground, land with many rabbits. Alternative spelling: Harland.

Harlow: Norse/Anglo-Saxon origin. Means: army leader, protected hill.

Harmon: Greek/Latin origin. Means: peace, uniting.

Harod: Hebrew origin. Means: heroic, loud. Alternative spelling: Harrod.

Harold: Old English origin. Means: powerful ruler or warrior, army. Alternative spellings and nicknames: Areldo, Herold, Hal, Harald, Harry, Haroldo.

Harper: Anglo-Saxon origin. Means: one who plays the harp.

Harrison: Teutonic/Anglo-Saxon origin. Means: son of Harry, estate head. Alternative spellings and nicknames: Harri, Harrus, Harris, Harro.

Harry: Teutonic/Old English origin. Means: head of the house, warrior.

Harsho: Unknown origin. Means: tricky.

Hart: Anglo-Saxon/Teutonic origin. Means: deer, stag.

Hartmann: Germanic origin. Means: austere, heart, strong man. Alternative spelling: Hartman.

Hartmut: Unknown origin and meaning. Ethnic background: German.

Hartwell: Teutonic origin. Means: from the deer's spring.

Haruki: Japanese origin. Unknown meaning.

Harvey: Old English/Germanic origin. Means: battle worthy, protector. Alternative spellings and nicknames: Harv, Harve, Hervey.

Hasheem: Arabic origin. Means: destroyer. Alternative spelling: Hashim.

Hashum: Arabic origin. Means: rich. Alternative spelling: Heshum.

Hasin: Arabic origin. Means: laughing. Alternative spellings: Hassin, Hasen.

Haskel: Hebrew origin. Means: understanding, wisdom. Alternative spellings: Haskell, Heskel.

Hassan: Arabic origin. Means: wise, handsome. Alternative spellings: Hasim, Hassim.

Hasso: Unknown origin and meaning. Ethnic background: German. Alternative spelling: Hasson.

Hastings: Latin/Anglo-Saxon origin. Means: spear, severe, violent.

Havelock: Norse origin. Means: a contest at sea.

Hawthorne: Old English origin. Means: of the thorny hedge.

Haydon: Anglo-Saxon/Teutonic origin. Means: from the hedged valley, hay. Alternative spellings: Hayden, Hayton.

Haye: Scottish origin. Means: from the stockade. Ethnic background: Dutch.

Haymo: Unknown origin. Means: amiable.

Hayward: Anglo-Saxon origin. Means: guardian of the hedged enclosure. Alternative spelling: Heyward.

Hazael: Old English/Teutonic origin. Means: the hazel tree or nut, reddish brown. Ethnic background: Hispanic.

Hearn: Anglo-Saxon origin. Means: a hunter. Alternative spelling: Hearne.

Heath: Anglo-Saxon origin. Means: one who is from a wasteland.

Heathcliff: Anglo-Saxon origin. Means: from the cliff of the wasteland.

Hector: Greek origin. Means: a steadfast defender, restraining. Ethnic background: Hispanic. Alternative spellings and nicknames: Heck, Hekter.

Hein: Germanic origin. Means: home. Ethnic background: Dutch. Alternative spellings: Heiiri, Heiner, Heini, Heinlich.

Heinz: Germanic origin. Means: ruler of the home. Ethnic background: Swiss.

Helge: Teutonic origin. Means: holy, happy. Ethnic backgrounds: German, Swedish, Norwegian.

Heliodoro: Spanish origin. Means: gift of sun.

Hellfried: Germanic origin. Unknown meaning.

Helmand: Germanic origin. Unknown meaning.

Helmar: Germanic origin. Means: fierce battle.

Helmut: Germanic origin. Means: helmet, protector, courage.

Heman: Hebrew origin. Means: steady, a faithful man.

Hendrick: Germanic origin. Means: one who rules the home or estate. Alternative spellings: Hendrik, Heinrich.

Henech: Hebrew origin. Means: educated, dedicated. Ethnic background: Jewish. Alternative spelling: Henach.

Henry: Germanic origin. Means: one who rules the home or estate. Ethnic background: Scottish. Alternative spellings and nicknames: Hal, Hank, Harry, Hendrick, Hendrik, Henri, Henryk, Henrik, Henny.

Henson: Germanic origin. Means: son of Henry, head of the house.

Heraldo: Unknown origin and meaning.

Herb: Teutonic origin. Means: a bright warrior or army.

Herbert: Teutonic origin. Means: a bright warrior or army. Ethnic background: Swedish. Alternative spellings and nicknames: Herbie, Herb, Bert, Herberto.

Herman: Teutonic origin. Means: high-ranking soldier. Ethnic background: Dutch. Alternative spellings: Hermon, Hermann, Hermino, Heremon, Harmen.

Hermenegildo: Teutonic/Spanish origin. Means: great sacrifice.

Hermon: Hebrew origin. Means: sacred, consecrated. Ethnic background: Irish.

Hernando: Germanic/Spanish origin. Means: adventuring, bold, courageous. Alternative spelling: Hernan.

Herrick: Germanic/Norse origin. Means: military leader.

Herrod: Greek origin. Means: conqueror, to watch over. Alternative spelling: Herod.

Herschel: Hebrew origin. Means: deer. Alternative spellings and nicknames: Hershel, Hershele, Hersch, Hertz, Hertzel, Hertzl, Hesh, Hirsch, Hirsh, Hirshl.

Herve: Teutonic/French origin. Means: a warrior ready for battle.

Hessel: Unknown origin and meaning. Ethnic background: Dutch.

Heston: Unknown origin and meaning.

Hevel: Hebrew origin. Means: breath, vapor.

Heywood: Old English origin. Means: one who is from a hedged forest. Alternative spellings and nicknames: Woody, Haywood.

Hezekiah: Hebrew origin. Means: God is my strength. Alternative spellings and nicknames: Hesiquio, Hezeklah, Zeke.

Hidalgo: Unknown origin and meaning.

Hidde: Germanic origin. Means: battle ready. Ethnic background: Dutch.

Hideaki: Japanese origin. Unknown meaning.

Hideyo: Japanese origin. Unknown meaning.

Hifz: Arabic origin. Means: preserve.

Higinio: Unknown origin and meaning. Ethnic background: Hispanic.

Hilario: Norse/Spanish origin. Means: cheerful, happy. Ethnic background: Hispanic. Alternative spelling: Hillario.

Hilel: Hebrew origin. Means: one who is praised greatly. Alternative spellings: Hillel, Hillell.

Hilliard: Teutonic origin. Means: a war guardian.

The Creative Approach

Try spelling a common name backward. For example, Evelyn = Nyleve. I personally think that's beautiful. Just try it, and maybe you'll come up with something good and unique.

~ **Rita C., Bronx, New York**

Hilton: Anglo-Saxon origin. Means: hill dweller. Alternative spellings: Hylton, Hillten, Hiltan.

Hiram: Hebrew origin. Means: one who is exalted and noble. Nicknames: Hi, Hy.

Hiramatsu: Unknown origin. Means: flat.

Hiroshi: Japanese origin. Means: one who is generous.

Hirza: Unknown origin. Means: delight.

Ho: Unknown origin. Means: congratulate.

Hoashis: Unknown origin. Means: God.

Hobert: Germanic origin. Means: Bert's hill.

Hoffman: Germanic origin. Means: influential man.

Hogan: Gaelic origin. Means: youth.

Holbert: Unknown origin. Means: brook. Alternative spelling: Hilbert.

Holcomb: Anglo-Saxon origin. Means: dweller of the deep valley.

Holden: Germanic/Anglo-Saxon origin. Means: of the hollow, gentle.

Holger: Norse origin. Means: island, spear. Ethnic background: German.

Hollis: Anglo-Saxon origin. Means: one who dwells in the holly tree grove. Nicknames: Holl, Holly.

Holmain: Teutonic origin. Means: one who dwells on the river's island. Alternative spellings: Holman, Holmen.

Holmes: Teutonic/Norse origin. Means: one who dwells on the river's island.

Holmfrid: Unknown origin and meaning. Ethnic background: Swedish.

Holt: Anglo-Saxon origin. Means: one who dwells in the forest.

Homer: Greek origin. Means: a pledge or security, a hostage. Alternative spellings: Homere, Omero.

Honda: Unknown origin. Means: base.

Hong: Unknown origin. Means: flank.

Horace: Latin origin. Means: one who marks time, to behold. Alternative spellings and nicknames: Horry, Race, Horacio, Horatio.

Horst: Germanic origin. Means: a wooded hill.

Horton: Latin/Anglo-Saxon origin. Means: a gardener, one from the gray estate.

Hosaam: Arabic origin. Means: sword.

Hosea: Hebrew origin. Means: one of salvation.

Hosni: Unknown origin and meaning.

Houghton: Anglo-Saxon origin. Means: dweller of the estate on the bluff.

Houston: Anglo-Saxon origin. Means: of the house in the town.

Howard: Teutonic/Anglo-Saxon origin. Means: chief guardian or protector.

Howe: Germanic/Anglo-Saxon origin. Means: of the high hill.

Howell: Welsh origin. Means: one who is alert, eminent.

Howland: Anglo-Saxon origin. Means: one from the chief's land. Alternative spellings: Howlend, Howlond, Howlyn.

Hubbard: Germanic origin. Means: one with grace.

Hubert: Teutonic origin. Means: one who has a bright mind. Alternative spellings and nicknames: Hube, Hugh, Bert, Huberto, Hobart, Hubie, Hobey, Hobbie, Hobie, Bart, Hebert.

Hudson: Anglo-Saxon origin. Means: son of Hudd, hooded.

The Creative Approach

My husband woke up one morning and said, "I've got it. I dreamt it last night—we have to name him Keenan Isaiah." So here he is, four months later, and everyone asks us, "Where in the world did you get the name Keenan?" You should see the looks on their faces when we tell them my husband dreamt it!

~ **Kim T., Upperco, Maryland**

Hudya: Hebrew origin. Means: praise.

Huey: Teutonic origin. Means: bright mind and spirit.

Hugh: Teutonic origin. Means: bright mind and spirit. Ethnic backgrounds: Scottish, English/Welsh, Irish. Alternative spelling: Hughes.

Hugo: Teutonic/Latin origin. Means: bright mind and spirit.

Hulbard: Germanic origin. Means: brilliant, graceful. Alternative spellings: Hulbert, Hulburt.

Humbert: Teutonic origin. Means: a bright home, shining warrior. Alternative spelling: Humberto.

Hume: Norse/Scottish origin. Means: of the hill by the water.

Humphrey: Teutonic origin. Means: guardian or protector of peace. Alternative spellings: Humfry, Humphry.

Hunter: Old English origin. Means: one who searches or hunts. 47th most popular boy's name of the '90s.

Huntington: Old English origin. Means: from the hunting estate.

Huntley: Old English origin. Means: of the hunter's farm.

Hurd: Unknown origin. Means: hard.

Hurley: Gaelic origin. Means: the tide of the sea.

Hurst: Anglo-Saxon origin. Means: forest dweller.

Husain: Arabic origin. Means: pious.

Hutton: Anglo-Saxon origin. Means: of the ridge estate.

Huxford: Anglo-Saxon origin. Means: from the ash-tree field.

Huxley: Anglo-Saxon origin. Means: from the ash-tree field.

Hwang: Japanese origin. Means: yellow.

Hyman: Hebrew origin. Means: life, from the high place. Alternative spellings and nicknames: Hy, Hymen, Hymie.

Iaap: Unknown origin and meaning. Ethnic background: Dutch.

Iacopo: Unknown origin and meaning. Ethnic background: Italian.

Ian: Hebrew/Gaelic origin. Means: God is gracious. Ethnic backgrounds: English/Welsh. 33rd most popular boy's name of the '90s. Alternative spelling: Iain.

Ibeamaka: African origin. Means: the agnates are splendid.

Ibratum: Arabic origin. Means: father. Alternative spelling: Ibraaheem.

Icario: Greek origin. Unknown meaning. Ethnic background: Hispanic.

Ichabod: Hebrew origin. Means: without glory.

Ichal: Unknown origin and meaning. Ethnic background: Jewish. Alternative spelling: Ichel.

Iden: Gaelic/Anglo-Saxon origin. Means: a wealthy man. Alternative spelling: Idden.

Idil: Hebrew origin. Means: praise.

Idress: Arabic origin. Means: teaches a lesson.

Ieronimo: Unknown origin and meaning. Ethnic background: Italian.

Ifeanacho: African origin. Means: the desired child.

Iftikhaar: Arabic origin. Means: honor.

Iggy: Greek/Latin origin. Means: one who is lively or fiery.

Ignace: Greek/French/Latin origin. Means: one who is lively or fiery. Ethnic backgrounds: Hispanic, Polish, German. Alternative spellings: Ignacio, Ignazio, Ignatius, Ignatus, Ignaze, Ignaz.

Igor: Norse origin. Means: the hero. Ethnic backgrounds: Czech, Russian.

Ihsaan: Arabic origin. Means: kindness.

Ihtishaam: Arabic origin. Means: magnificence.

I'jaaz: Arabic origin. Means: miracle.

Ike: Hebrew origin. Means: one who laughs.

Ikenna: African origin. Means: father's power.

Ikhlaas: Arabic origin. Means: sincerity.

Ikraam: Arabic origin. Means: honoring.

Ilario: Latin origin. Means: one who is merry. Ethnic background: Italian.

Ildebrando: Unknown origin and meaning. Ethnic background: Italian.

Ildefonso: Unknown origin and meaning. Ethnic background: Hispanic.

Ilya: Hebrew/Slavic origin. Means: the Lord is my God. Alternative spelling: Ilyash.

Imaad: Arabic origin. Means: pillar.

Imaam: Arabic origin. Means: leader.

Immanuel: Hebrew origin. Means: God is with us. Ethnic background: German. Alternative spelling: Imanuel.

Imre: Germanic/Hungarian origin. Means: supervisor, innocent.

Imrich: Unknown origin and meaning. Ethnic background: Czech.

Inaayat: Arabic origin. Means: bounty.

Inazo: Japanese origin. Unknown meaning.

Indalecio: Latin origin. Unknown meaning. Ethnic background: Hispanic.

Ingar: Norse origin. Means: son's army.

Inglebert: Germanic origin. Means: bright angel.

Ingmar: Norse origin. Means: the hero's son. Alternative spelling: Ingemar.

Ingo: Germanic/Old English origin. Means: the meadow.

Ingolf: Norse origin. Means: wolf. Ethnic background: German.

Ingraham: Norse origin. Means: raven. Alternative spelling: Ingram.

Ingvar: Norse origin. Means: army, warrior. Ethnic background: Swedish.

Inigo: Basque/Teutonic origin. Means: one strong with emotion.

Innes: Gaelic/Anglo-Saxon origin. Means: one from the island. Alternative spellings: Inness, Innis.

Inocencio: Latin/Spanish origin. Means: innocence. Ethnic background: Hispanic. Alternative spelling: Innocenzo.

Ioannis: Unknown origin and meaning. Ethnic background: Greek.

Ippolito: Greek/Italian origin. Means: of the horse plain.

Iqbaal: Arabic origin. Means: prosperity. Alternative spelling: Iqbal.

Ireneusz: Greek/Polish origin. Means: peace, serenity.

Irfaan: Arabic origin. Means: wisdom.

Irshaad: Arabic origin. Means: to guide, instruct.

Irving: Gaelic/Anglo-Saxon origin. Means: handsome, lover of the sea. Ethnic background: Jewish. Alternative spellings: Erwin, Irvin, Irvine, Irwin, Irvine.

Isaac: Hebrew origin. Means: he who laughs. Ethnic background: Hispanic. Alternative spellings and nicknames: Izaak, Isaak, Iz, Izzy, Ike, Isacco, Issac, Itz, Itzig, Itzik, Izak.

Isaiah: Hebrew origin. Means: the Lord is my salvation. Alternative spellings: Isiah, Issaiah, Issiah.

Isami: Japanese origin. Unknown meaning. Alternative spelling: Isamu.

Isao: Japanese origin. Unknown meaning.

Isauro: Greek origin. Means: the soft breeze. Ethnic background: Hispanic.

Isham: Anglo-Saxon origin. Means: of the iron estate.

Ishmael: Hebrew origin. Means: God will hear. Alternative spellings: Isamel, Ishmiel, Ismaa'eel, Ismael, Ismail, Ismiel.

Ishmul: Unknown origin. Means: wanderer.

Ishrnael: Unknown origin. Means: wanderer.

Ishtiyaaq: Arabic origin. Means: desire, eagerness.

Isidore: Greek/Latin origin. Means: gift of Isis, strong gift. Ethnic backgrounds: Italian, German, Hispanic. Alternative spellings and nicknames: Iz, Issy, Isador, Dore, Izzy, Isidor, Dory, Dorian, Isidoro.

Islam: Unknown origin and meaning.

Isman: Unknown origin. Means: husband. Alternative spelling: Isma.

Israel: Hebrew origin. Means: prince of God, wrestled with God.

Isser: Egyptian origin. Means: God saves. Ethnic background: Jewish. Alternative spelling: Isserel.

The Creative Approach

We argued for six years before we found a girl's name. I wanted to name our daughter one of the many (I thought) fabulous names from my family. Unfortunately these names made my husband gag. Luckily, our first child was a boy. When I got pregnant again, we'd be up until midnight with our 10 baby books and a genealogy book that goes back to Adam and Eve (literally), arguing the whole time. So one night we were doing this (and please remember I am a fairly rational person, because this is going to sound really, really weird), and I got up to go to the bathroom (ahhhh the joys of being pregnant). And as I was sitting there preparing to heave my pregnant belly back to bed, I heard this strange whisper. It wasn't my husband . . . it wasn't my mother . . . it wasn't my son. And all it said was "Rebecca James." So I freaked out and went dashing back to our room. I told my husband, and he said that he had never thought of it but somehow it seemed right. I told my mother, and she said the same thing. And I *certainly* had never thought of it—not my sort of name for a child either. But we remained up in the air about a name. Then, in the delivery room after the baby was born, my mother asked, "What are you going to name her so we can call your father?" But we *still* hadn't settled on a name. So we were suggesting them, Carlyn Rose, Rebecca James, and a couple of others. And every time someone said "Rebecca James," the baby stopped crying and smiled. *Really*—we have it on video! So she chose her name, and she *IS* Rebecca James. By the way, my father's name was James. He was so excited that "we" named the baby for him.

~ Tarrant F., Eugene, Oregon

Istifaa: Arabic origin. Means: to prefer.

Istvan: Greek/Hungarian origin. Means: crowned in victory.

Ithaman: Unknown origin. Means: man.

Ithnan: Unknown origin. Means: sailor.

Itmar: Hebrew origin. Means: island of palms.

Itsche: Unknown origin and meaning. Ethnic background: Jewish.

Ivan: Hebrew/Slavic origin. Means: God's gracious gift. Ethnic backgrounds: Hungarian, Russian.

Ivar: Norse origin. Means: army bowman, archer. Ethnic background: Russian. Alternative spellings and nicknames: Ivon, Yves, Ives, Ivo, Ivor, Iver, Iven.

Iwata: Unknown origin. Means: field.

Izzie: Greek origin. Means: great gift, gift of Isis. Ethnic background: Jewish. Alternative spelling: Izzy.

j

Jaabir: Arabic origin. Means: comforter.

Jaak: Finnish origin. Unknown meaning. Ethnic background: Russian.

Jaaziniah: Hebrew origin. Means: God hears. Alternative spelling: Jaazaniah.

Jabari: Egyptian origin. Means: brave. Ethnic background: African.

Jabbaar: Arabic origin. Means: mighty.

Jabez: Hebrew origin. Means: full of sorrow.

Jabin: Unknown origin. Means: born. Alternative spellings: Jabon, Jaban.

Jabrial: Unknown origin and meaning.

Jabulani: African origin. Means: be happy.

Jacari: Unknown origin and meaning. Alternative spellings: Ja'Carree, Jakory.

Jace: Unknown origin and meaning.

Jacek: Polish origin. Means: handsome.

Jacinto: Greek/Spanish origin. Means: handsome, purple flower.

Jack: Hebrew/Anglo-Saxon origin. Means: God's gracious gift. 45th most popular boy's name of the '90s. Nicknames: Jocko, Jock, Jake.

Jackson: Hebrew/Anglo-Saxon origin. Means: son of Jack, God's gift. Alternative spelling: Jaxon.

Jacob: Hebrew origin. Means: he who supplants, replaces. Ethnic backgrounds: German, Hispanic, Norwegian, Swedish. 4th most popular boy's name of the '90s. Alternative spellings and nicknames: Jakie, Jacques, Jake, Jakeb, Jacobo, Jacoby, Jakob.

Jaddan: Unknown origin. Means: man. Alternative spellings: Jadda, Jaddo.

Jaden: Unknown origin and meaning. Alternative spelling: Jayden.

Ja'far: Arabic origin. Means: small river.

Jagger: Anglo-Saxon origin. Means: carter.

Jahdal: Unknown origin. Means: directs. Alternative spellings: Jahdiel, Jahdol, Jahdai.

Jahod: Unknown origin and meaning.

Jai: Unknown origin and meaning.

Jaime: Unknown origin and meaning.

Jairus: Hebrew origin. Means: the Lord enlightens. Alternative spellings: Jairis, Jayrus, Jair, Jarius.

Jakeem: Unknown origin and meaning. Alternative spelling: Jahkim.

Jalaal: Arabic origin. Means: grandeur. Alternative spelling: Jalil.

Jalen: Unknown origin and meaning. Alternative spellings: JaLon, Jalyn, Jaylen.

Jamarcus: Unknown origin and meaning.

Jamarius: Unknown origin and meaning. Alternative spellings: Jamarrius, Jamario.

James: Hebrew origin. Means: one who supplants, replaces. Ethnic backgrounds: English/Welsh, Irish, Scottish. 20th most popular boy's name of the '90s. Alternative spellings and nicknames: Shamus, Jemmie, Jem, Jamesy, Jemmy, Jim, Hamish, Seamus, Jimmy, Jimmie, Jamie, Jacob.

Jametrius: Unknown origin and meaning.

Jamil: Arabic origin. Means: handsome one. Alternative spellings: Jamill, Jamel, Jamal.

Jamin: Unknown origin. Means: right-handed. Alternative spelling: Jammin.

Jamir: Unknown origin and meaning.

Jamison: Hebrew/Anglo-Saxon origin. Means: son of James, supplanter.

Jamnes: Unknown origin. Means: magician. Alternative spelling: Jamnis.

Jamonte: Unknown origin and meaning.

Janal: Unknown origin and meaning. Alternative spellings: Janult, Ja'Neal.

JanMeer: Unknown origin and meaning.

Jano: Hebrew origin. Means: God's gracious gift. Ethnic background: Hispanic. Alternative spelling: Janos.

Janusz: Hebrew/Polish origin. Means: God is gracious. Alternative spelling: Januse.

Japhet: Hebrew origin. Means: handsome. Alternative spelling: Japheth.

Jaquaad: Unknown origin and meaning. Alternative spelling: Jaquaid.

Jaquale: Unknown origin and meaning.

Jaquan: Unknown origin and meaning. Alternative spellings: JayQuan, JahQuan, Jul'Quawn.

Jared: Hebrew origin. Means: the descendant. 41st most popular boy's name of the '90s. Alternative spellings: Jarid, Jarred, Jarrod.

Jarlath: Irish origin. Means: a tributary, Lord.

Jarle: Unknown origin and meaning. Ethnic background: Norwegian.

Jaromir: Unknown origin and meaning. Ethnic background: Czech.

Jaron: Unknown origin and meaning.

Jaroslav: Slavic/Polish origin. Means: the glory of spring. Ethnic background: Czech. Alternative spelling: Jaroslaw.

Jarqueese: Unknown origin and meaning.

Jarreau: Unknown origin and meaning.

Jarren: Unknown origin and meaning.

Jarrett: French origin. Means: to watch.

Jarvis: Unknown origin and meaning.

Jason: Greek origin. Means: one with healing powers. Ethnic backgrounds: English/Welsh, Irish. 36th most popular boy's name of the '90s. Alternative spellings: Jashawn, Jayson.

Jasper: Persian/Greek origin. Means: a treasurer, colorful stone. Ethnic background: German. Alternative spellings and nicknames: Kass, Gasper, Kasper, Cass, Casper, Jesper.

Jauhar: Unknown origin. Means: diamond.

Javaris: Unknown origin and meaning.

Javier: Arabic/Spanish origin. Means: bright, intelligent. Ethnic background: Hispanic.

Javon: Unknown origin and meaning. Alternative spellings: Javone, Jayvon, Javaun, Jevaun, Jovon.

Javont: Unknown origin and meaning. Alternative spellings: Javontae, Jevontae, JeVonte.

Jawaad: Arabic origin. Means: generous.

Jawon: Unknown origin and meaning. Alternative spellings: Juwan, Jawuan.

Jedediah: Hebrew origin. Means: friend of the Lord, beloved of God. Alternative spellings: Jediah, Jed.

Jefferson: Anglo-Saxon origin. Means: son of Geoffrey/Jeffrey, peace.

Jeffrey: Anglo-Saxon/Teutonic origin. Means: gift of peace. 43rd most popular boy's name of the '90s. Alternative spellings and nicknames: Jeffy, Jeff, Jeffery, Jeffray.

Jehu: Unknown origin. Means: Lord.

Jelinek: Unknown origin. Means: deer.

Jelmer: Unknown origin and meaning. Ethnic background: Dutch.

Jenario: Unknown origin and meaning.

Jennings: Hebrew/Anglo-Saxon origin. Means: son of John/Jean, God's gift.

The Creative Approach

If you want a true melting pot of cultural names, have a California telephone book mailed out to you.

~ Samantha S.,
Summit, New Jersey

Jens: Hebrew/Norse origin. Means: God's great gift. Ethnic background: Swedish.

Jephum: Unknown origin. Means: prepared. Alternative spelling: Jepum.

Jerald: Teutonic origin. Means: with the strength of a spear.

Jeremy: Hebrew origin. Means: God will uplift, exalted. Ethnic backgrounds: English/Welsh. 41st most popular boy's name of the '90s. Alternative spellings and nicknames: Jeremiah, Jeremias, Jerry, Jeramiah, Jeramy, Jereme, Jeremia, Jeramey, Jeremias, Jeremie, Jerime, Jeromy.

Jericho: Unknown origin and meaning.

Jermaine: Latin origin. Means: brother. Alternative spellings: Jerman, Jahmaine.

Jerome: Greek/Latin origin. Means: a holy name. Ethnic background: French. Alternative spellings and nicknames: Gerome, Gerry, Jerry, Jeroen, Jeron, Jeronimo.

Jerrell: Unknown origin and meaning.

Jerry: Hebrew/Anglo-Saxon origin. Means: God will uplift, exalted.

Jervis: Teutonic/Old English origin. Means: keen, sharp as a spear. Alternative spelling: Jarveis.

Jesh: Unknown origin. Means: man. Alternative spellings: Jesher, Jeuz.

Jesus: Aramaic/Hebrew origin. Means: savior, God will help. Ethnic background: Hispanic.

Jethro: Hebrew origin. Means: abundance, riches, excellence. Alternative spellings and nicknames: Jeth, Jetro, Jett.

Jeu: Unknown origin. Means Lord.

Jezreel: Unknown origin. Means: God's.

Jianni: Unknown origin and meaning.

Jibril: Unknown origin and meaning.

Jiichiro: Japanese origin. Unknown meaning.

Jiles: Unknown origin and meaning.

Jim: Hebrew origin. Means: one who supplants, replaces. Alternative spellings: Jimi, Jimmie, Jimmy.

Jindrich: Germanic/Czech origin. Means: head of the house.

Jiri: Greek/Czech origin. Means: one who works the earth, farmer.

Jiro: Japanese origin. Unknown meaning.

Jivon: Hindi origin. Means: one who values life.

Joab: Hebrew origin. Means: God is the father.

Joachim: Hebrew origin. Means: the Lord judges or establishes. Ethnic background: German. Alternative spelling: Joakim.

Joah: Hebrew origin. Means: fatherhood.

Joakirna: Unknown origin. Means: judge.

Joaquin: Spanish origin. Means: one who is prepared.

Joash: Unknown origin. Means: God. Alternative spelling: Joashus.

Job: Hebrew origin. Means: one who is oppressed.

Jobin: Unknown origin and meaning.

Jochbed: Hebrew origin. Means: God's glory. Alternative spelling: Jochebed.

Jochen: Hebrew/Germanic origin. Means: established by God.

Joe: Hebrew origin. Means: God will increase. Alternative spelling: Joey.

Joed: Unknown origin. Means: goodness.

Joel: Hebrew origin. Means: God is willing.

Joep: Unknown origin and meaning. Ethnic background: Dutch.

Joewand: Unknown origin and meaning.

Johan: Hebrew/Germanic origin. Means: God is gracious. Ethnic backgrounds: Dutch, Norwegian, Swedish. Alternative spellings: Johanan, Johann, Johannes.

Johiah: Hebrew origin. Means: Jehovah.

John: Hebrew origin. Means: the Lord is gracious, gift of God. Ethnic backgrounds: Greek, English/Welsh, Scottish. 10th most popular boy's name of the '90s. Alternative spellings and nicknames: Jonpie, Jonny, Shaughn, Jock, Shaun, Jon, Juan, Sean, Shawn, Zane, Ivan, Johnny, Shane, Gian, Johann, Johan, Jevon, Evan, Jack, Jan, Ian, Hans, Giovanni, Johnnie.

Johnico: Unknown origin and meaning.

Johnson: Hebrew/Scottish origin. Means: son of John, God's gift.

Johnston: Hebrew/Scottish origin. Means: from John's farm, God's gift.

Jojo: African origin. Means: born on Monday.

Jokichi: Japanese origin. Unknown meaning.

Joktan: Unknown origin. Means: tiny.

Jollie: French origin. Means: one with good humor.

Jomo: Unknown origin. Means: burning.

Jonah: Hebrew origin. Means: a dove, peaceful. Alternative spellings and nicknames: Jone, Jonas.

Jonathan: Hebrew origin. Means: the Lord is gracious, gift of God. Ethnic backgrounds: Irish, English/Welsh. 20th most popular boy's name of the '90s. Alternative spellings and nicknames: Jon, Jonathon, Jonnathan, Johnathan, Johnathan.

Jones: Hebrew/Anglo-Saxon origin. Means: John, God's gift.

Jonovan: Unknown origin and meaning.

Joop: Hebrew/Dutch origin. Means: God shall increase.

Joos: Unknown origin and meaning. Ethnic background: Swiss.

Joost: Latin/Dutch origin. Means: one who is just.

28 Ways to Say John

Say your spouse is dead-set on naming your son John. You were hoping for something a little more, well, exotic. There is hope! Practically any classic name has numerous incarnations in other languages. Who knew that there were 28 ways (and probably more) to say John?

Gian, Gianni, Giovanni	Italian
Jean	French
Johann, Johannus, Hans, Hansel	German
Ivan, Vanya	Russian
Shane, Sean	Irish
Shawn	Scottish
Juan, Juanito	Spanish
Sian, Ian	Welsh
Jan, Jansen, Janus	Norse
Joao	Portugese
Yanni	Greek
Jancsi	Hungarian
Janek, Zane	Polish
Jens	Norwegian
Jonam	Swedish
Jack	American

Jord: Hebrew/Norse origin. Means: to flow down, night. Ethnic background: Dutch.

Jorgen: Greek/Norse origin. Means: one who farms the earth. Ethnic background: Swedish. Alternative spellings: Jorg, Jorge.

Joris: Greek/Norse origin. Means: one who farms the earth. Ethnic background: Dutch.

Jorren: Unknown origin and meaning. Ethnic background: Dutch.

Jorrit: Unknown origin and meaning. Ethnic background: Dutch.

Jory: Hebrew/Norse origin. Means: God will uplift, a farmer.

Jos: Unknown origin and meaning. Ethnic background: Dutch.

Joseph: Hebrew origin. Means: God will increase. Ethnic backgrounds: French, German, Swiss, Hispanic. 14th most popular boy's name of the '90s. Alternative spellings and nicknames: Joe, Joey, Josef, Josefat, Josephus, Joses, Jozef, Jozsef.

Joshua: Hebrew origin. Means: God is my salvation. 9th most popular boy's name of the '90s. Alternative spellings and nicknames: Josh, Joshuah, Je'hoshua, Jeshua, Joshuanayri, Joshwuan.

Josiah: Hebrew/Arabic origin. Means: the Lord supports, fire of God. Alternative spelling: Josias.

Jost: Unknown origin and meaning. Ethnic background: German.

Jostein: Norse origin. Unknown meaning. Ethnic background: Norwegian.

Josue: Hebrew/Spanish origin. Means: God is my salvation.

Jotham: Hebrew origin. Means: the Lord is perfect. Alternative spelling: Jothan.

Joub: Unknown origin. Means: praise the Lord.

Jourdan: Unknown origin and meaning. Alternative spelling: Jordanny, Jordin.

Jovani: Unknown origin and meaning.

Juan: Hebrew/Spanish origin. Means: God is gracious. Ethnic background: Hispanic.

Jucundo: Unknown origin and meaning. Ethnic background: Hispanic.

Judah: Hebrew origin. Means: the praise of God. Alternative spellings and nicknames: Judas, Judd, Jude, Jud, Judus.

Judsen: Unknown origin. Means: son of Judd. Alternative spelling: Judson.

Jules: Latin/French origin. Means: one lightly bearded. Alternative spelling: Jule.

Julio: Latin/Spanish origin. Means: lightly bearded, youthful.

Julius: Latin origin. Means: soft bearded, youthful. Ethnic backgrounds: German, Polish. Alternative spellings and nicknames: Juley, Jules, Jule, Julian.

Junaid: Arabic origin. Means: small army.

Junius: Latin origin. Means: forever youthful.

Juraj: Unknown origin and meaning. Ethnic background: Czech.

Jurgen: Greek/Germanic origin. Means: one who farms the earth. Ethnic background: Swiss. Alternative spelling: Jurg.

Justin: Latin origin. Means: one who is virtuous, just, upright. Ethnic backgrounds: Czech, Irish. Alternative spellings: Justan, Justen, Justis, Jestin, Justyn.

Juvencio: Latin origin. Means: forever youthful. Ethnic background: Hispanic.

k

Kaare: Unknown origin and meaning. Ethnic background: Norwegian.

Kadar: Arabic origin. Means: powerful one. Alternative spelling: Kedar.

Kade: Unknown origin and meaning.

Kaden: Arabic origin. Means: a companion.

Kai: Norse/Scottish origin. Means: fowl, fire.

Kailer: Unknown origin and meaning.

Kale: Germanic origin. Means: bald one.

Kaleb: Hebrew/Arabic origin. Means: heart, messenger, brave.

Kaleem: Arabic origin. Means: speaker.

Kalen: Unknown origin and meaning.

Kalil: Arabic origin. Means: a good friend. Alternative spellings: Kahaleel, Kahlille, Khalil, Khaleel, Khalil.

Kalvin: Latin origin. Means: bald one.

Kamau: African origin. Means: quiet warrior.

Kamil: Arabic/Polish origin. Means: perfection. Ethnic background: Czech. Alternative spellings: Kamal, Kaamil.

Kampihe: African origin. Means: go and see.

Kamron: Unknown origin and meaning.

Kamulira: African origin. Means: lamentable.

Kamuzu: African origin. Means: medicinal.

Kanaye: Hebrew/Japanese origin. Means: zealous one.

Kane: Gaelic/Celtic origin. Means: battle, tribute, intelligent. Alternative spellings: Kaine, Kain, Kainoah, Kanean, Kayne.

Kang: Unknown origin. Means: bay.

Kani: Hebrew/Arabic origin. Means: a reed, a spear. Alternative spelling: Kaniel.

Kanichi: Japanese origin. Unknown meaning.

Kanko: Unknown origin and meaning.

Kanton: Unknown origin and meaning.

Kaoru: Japanese origin. Unknown meaning.

Kapel: Unknown origin and meaning. Ethnic background: Jewish.

Kapil: Hindi origin. Unknown meaning.

Kareem: Arabic origin. Means: bountiful. Alternative spellings: Karaamat, Karam.

Karl: Old English/Teutonic origin. Means: manly, strong, farmer. Ethnic backgrounds: German, Swedish, Norwegian, Swiss. Alternative spelling: Karoly.

Karmel: Hebrew origin. Means: a vineyard.

Karson: Anglo-Saxon origin. Means: son of Carr.

Karsten: Greek/Germanic origin. Means: blessed, anointed one. Ethnic backgrounds: Dutch, Norwegian.

Kashaun: Unknown origin and meaning. Alternative spellings: Kershawn, Keyshawn.

Kasheif: Unknown origin and meaning.

Kasimir: Slavic origin. Means: one who commands peace. Ethnic background: German.

"Are We Normal?"

Still squabbling with your spouse? You are not alone. While nearly 40 percent of parents polled named their kids with no problem, for the majority of us there's a certain degree of haggling that goes hand in hand with naming babies. What category do you fall into?

Kasiya: Egyptian origin. Means: departure. Ethnic background: African.

Kaski: Hebrew origin. Means: God is my strength.

Kaspar: Germanic/Polish origin. Means: treasurer, treasure, imperial. Alternative spelling: Kasper.

Kasril: Hebrew origin. Means: God is my crown. Alternative spelling: Kasrileke.

Kassidy: Unknown origin and meaning.

Katsu: Japanese origin. Unknown meaning.

Kauffman: Germanic origin. Means: a merchant.

Kayode: African origin. Means: he brought joy.

Kazimierz: Slavic/Polish origin. Means: famous warrior.

Kazuhiro: Japanese origin. Unknown meaning. Alternative spelling: Kazuo.

Kea: Unknown origin. Means: small.

Keaira: Unknown origin and meaning.

Kealy: Irish origin. Means: handsome.

Kean: Gaelic/Irish origin. Means: bold, handsome, ancient. Alternative spellings: Keane, Keanu, Keene.

Keanjaho: African origin. Means: heap of beans.

Keats: Unknown origin and meaning.

Keefe: Arabic/Irish origin. Means: gentle, one at peace.

Keegan: Gaelic origin. Means: one who is fiery. Alternative spellings: Keagan, Kegan, Keigan.

Keenen: Gaelic origin. Means: ancient, fiery one. Alternative spellings: Keenan, Kienan.

Kees: Latin/Dutch origin. Means: a horn.

Keifer: Unknown origin and meaning.

Keiichi: Japanese origin. Unknown meaning.

Keir: Celtic/Norse origin. Means: the dark-skinned one, marshland. Alternative spellings: Keiron, Kieran.

Keirrick: Unknown origin. Means: royal.

Keith: Gaelic/Welsh origin. Means: one who is of the wooded battlefield. Ethnic backgrounds: English/Welsh, Irish.

Kelechi: African origin. Means: thank God.

Kell: Norse origin. Means: of the bubbling spring.

Kellan: Unknown origin and meaning. Alternative spelling: Kellen.

Keller: Gaelic origin. Means: a companion, champion.

Kelvan: Celtic/Gaelic origin. Means: from the narrow river. Alternative spellings: Kelven, Kelvin, Kelwen, Kelwin.

Kemp: Old English origin. Means: one who is a champion, warrior.

Kenay: Unknown origin. Means: brave one.

Kenaz: Unknown origin. Means: a hunter.

Kendal: Celtic origin. Means: ruler of the bright river valley. Alternative spellings: Kendale, Kendel, Kyndall.

Kenden: Unknown origin and meaning.

Kendrick: Anglo-Saxon/Gaelic origin. Means: son of Henry, a fearless leader. Alternative spelling: Kendric.

Kenelm: Anglo-Saxon origin. Means: a brave family defender.

Kenlay: Anglo-Saxon origin. Means: dweller of the king's headland. Alternative spellings: Kenleigh, Kenley.

Kenn: Welsh origin. Means: bright, clear water.

Kennan: Unknown origin and meaning.

Kenneth: Gaelic origin. Means: one who is handsome, of fire. Ethnic backgrounds: English/Welsh. Alternative spellings and nicknames: Ken, Kenney, Kenny, Kent, Kenith.

Kensell: Unknown origin. Means: brave.

Kenshiro: Unknown origin and meaning.

Kent: Celtic/Anglo-Saxon origin. Means: a border, white.

Kentac: Unknown origin and meaning.

Kentaro: Japanese origin. Unknown meaning.

Kenton: Old English origin. Means: of the river estate, royal, keen.

Kenward: Old English origin. Means: a brave, royal guardian. Alternative spellings: Kenard, Kennard.

Kenway: Old English origin. Means: a brave, royal warrior. Alternative spelling: Kenweigh.

Kenyon: Celtic/Gaelic origin. Means: one who has fair hair. Alternative spellings and nicknames: Ken, Kenny, Kenyan.

Keon: Unknown origin and meaning. Alternative spelling: Keonta.

Kerill: Greek origin. Means: of royalty, lordly. Ethnic background: Irish.

Kermit: Celtic/Gaelic origin. Means: a free man, son of Diarmaid, no envy. Alternative spellings and nicknames: Dermot, Kerry.

Kerr: Norse origin. Means: from the marshy land.

Kerrith: Unknown origin and meaning. Ethnic backgrounds: English/Welsh.

Kerwin: Gaelic origin. Means: black, dark-haired one. Alternative spellings and nicknames: Kirwin, Kerwen, Kerwon, Kern.

Keskel: Hebrew origin. Means: God will strengthen. Alternative spelling: Keskil.

Kester: Greek/Latin origin. Means: Christ bearer, of the Roman camp.

Keto: Unknown origin and meaning. Ethnic background: Russian.

Kevin: Celtic/Gaelic origin. Means: one who is gentle, handsome. Ethnic backgrounds: English/Welsh, Irish. 31st most popular boy's name of the '90s. Alternative spellings and nicknames: Kev, Kevan, Keven, Kevellin, Kavan, Kayvaun.

Khabeer: Arabic origin. Means: informer.

Khalid: Arabic/Egyptian origin. Means: eternal, immortal. Alternative spelling: Khaalid.

Khari: Arabic origin. Means: one who is charitable.

Khateeb: Arabic origin. Means: orator.

Kheino: Unknown origin and meaning. Ethnic background: Russian.

Kian: Welsh/Irish origin. Unknown meaning.

Kiari: Unknown origin and meaning.

Kiefer: Arabic/Irish origin. Means: peaceful one.

Kilby: Teutonic origin. Means: dweller of the spring farm.

Killian: Latin/Gaelic origin. Means: blind, innocent, a retreat. Ethnic background: Irish. Alternative spellings: Kilian, Kilan.

Kilmer: Unknown origin and meaning.

Kiln: Gaelic/Irish origin. Means: black.

Kimani: Unknown origin and meaning.

Kimbal: Anglo-Saxon/Welsh origin. Means: glorious ruler, noble warrior. Alternative spellings and nicknames: Kemble, Kim, Kimble, Kimball.

Kimon: Unknown origin and meaning. Ethnic background: Greek.

"Are We Normal?" Parent Poll

How difficult was it for you and your spouse to agree on a name?

Of 924 total votes:

not difficult at all	39.17%
somewhat difficult	25.43%
very difficult	10.28%
still haven't agreed	25.1%

1 figure = 100 parents

Kincaid: Unknown origin. Means: battle.

Kingdon: Anglo-Saxon origin. Means: of the king's hall.

Kingsley: Anglo-Saxon origin. Means: of the king's meadow.

Kingston: Anglo-Saxon origin. Means: of the king's town.

Kingswell: Anglo-Saxon origin. Means: of the king's spring.

Kinji: Japanese origin. Unknown meaning.

Kinnard: Gaelic origin. Means: dweller of the high hill.

Kinnell: Gaelic origin. Means: one from the cliffs. Alternative spelling: Kenil.

Kino: Unknown origin and meaning.

Kinofe: Unknown origin and meaning.

Kinsley: Anglo-Saxon origin. Means: of the king's forest.

Kip: Unknown origin and meaning.

Kipling: Old English origin. Means: a cured fish.

Kirby: Old English/Teutonic origin. Means: from the church town. Alternative spellings: Kerby, Kerr.

Kirk: Norse/Old English origin. Means: one who dwells near the church.

Kirkley: Norse/Old English origin. Means: of the church meadow.

Kirkpatrick: Latin/Norse origin. Means: noble one who dwells near the church.

Kirkwood: Norse/Old English origin. Means: one who dwells near the church forest.

Kiss: Old English origin. Unknown meaning.

Kitei: Japanese origin. Unknown meaning.

Kitron: Hebrew origin. Means: a crown.

Kitson: Unknown origin and meaning.

Kiva: Hebrew origin. Means: protected, supplanted. Alternative spelling: Kiveh.

Kiyomi: Japanese origin. Unknown meaning.

Kiyoshi: Japanese origin. Unknown meaning.

Kjell: Germanic/Swedish origin. Means: manly, strong, sacrificial cauldron. Ethnic background: Norwegian.

Klaus: Greek/Germanic origin. Means: popular victory. Alternative spellings: Klaas, Klas.

Klein: Germanic origin. Means: little, small one. Alternative spelling: Kline.

Klemen: Latin/Germanic origin. Means: merciful one. Ethnic background: Hungarian.

Kleon: Latin origin. Means: famous one.

Klox: Unknown origin. Means: hills.

Knight: Anglo-Saxon origin. Means: a noble soldier.

Knox: Anglo-Saxon origin. Means: a hill dweller.

Knut: Norse origin. Means: a knot, a short man. Ethnic background: Norwegian. Alternative spelling: Knute.

Ko: Unknown origin. Means: yellow.

Koen: Germanic origin. Means: a trustworthy adviser. Ethnic background: Dutch.

Koi: Unknown origin and meaning.

Koji: Japanese origin. Unknown meaning.

Kolby: Unknown origin and meaning.

Kole: Latin/Old English origin. Means: a cabbage farmer, a coal miner.

Kolin: Unknown origin and meaning.

Kolton: Unknown origin and meaning. Alternative spelling: Koltyn.

Konad: Unknown origin. Means: one who is bold.

Konane: Unknown origin. Means: bright one.

Kong: Unknown origin. Means: hole.

Konrad: Germanic origin. Means: a bold, wise adviser. Ethnic background: Swiss.

Konstantin: Latin origin. Means: one who is steady, firm. Alternative spelling: Konstanty.

Kontar: Egyptian origin. Means: an only son. Ethnic background: African.

Koos: Unknown origin and meaning. Ethnic background: Dutch.

Koppel: Hebrew origin. Means: supplanted, protected.

Korey: Latin/Gaelic origin. Means: a helmet, of the ravine. Alternative spelling: Kori.

Kornel: Latin/Polish origin. Means: a horn. Ethnic backgrounds: Dutch, Hungarian.

Korwin: Unknown origin. Means: a friend.

Kosey: Egyptian origin. Means: lion. Alternative spelling: Kosse.

Kostas: Latin origin. Means: one who is steady, firm. Ethnic background: Greek.

Kota: Unknown origin and meaning.

Kotaro: Japanese origin. Unknown meaning.

Kramer: Old English origin. Means: a traveling shopkeeper, peddler.

Krijn: Unknown origin and meaning. Ethnic background: Dutch.

Krishna: Sanskrit/Hindi origin. Means: black, dark, delightful. Alternative spellings: Krishnah, Krisha.

Kriss: Unknown origin and meaning. Ethnic backgrounds: English/Welsh.

Krister: Greek/Swedish origin. Means: Christ bearer.

Kristian: Greek/Swedish origin. Means: Christ bearer.

Kristopher: Greek origin. Means: Christ bearer. Alternative spellings: Krystopher, Kristofer, Kristoffer, Kryzstof, Krzysztof, Kristolf.

Krolik: Unknown origin. Means: a hare.

Ksawery: Arabic/Polish origin. Means: one with great intelligence.

Kub: Unknown origin and meaning. Ethnic background: Polish.

Kune: Unknown origin. Means: a hare.

Kunibert: Germanic origin. Means: brave one.

Kunle: African origin. Means: home is full with honors.

Kuroda: Unknown origin. Means: black.

Kurt: Germanic origin. Means: bold, brave one; an adviser. Ethnic background: Swiss. Alternative spelling: Kirt.

Kurtis: Latin/French origin. Means: an enclosure, courtesy.

Kusuo: Japanese origin. Unknown meaning.

Kwabena: African origin. Means: born on Tuesday.

Kwacha: African origin. Means: morning.

Kwaco: Unknown origin. Means: born.

Kwame: Unknown origin. Means: born.

Kwan: Unknown origin. Means: shut.

Kwasi: Unknown origin. Means: born.

Kye: Unknown origin and meaning.

Kyle: Gaelic origin. Means: he who is handsome, fair. 19th most popular boy's name of the '90s. Alternative spellings: Kile, Kyler.

Kyne: Anglo-Saxon origin. Means: bold, royal.

Kynos: Unknown origin and meaning. Ethnic background: Czech.

Kyo: Japanese origin. Unknown meaning.

Kyras: Unknown origin and meaning. Ethnic background: Irish. Alternative spellings: Kyree, Kyron.

Kyutaro: Japanese origin. Unknown meaning.

Kyuzo: Japanese origin. Unknown meaning.

Label: Hebrew origin. Means: lion.

Labib: Unknown origin and meaning.

Lach: Anglo-Saxon origin. Means: lives near the water.

Lachlan: Gaelic/Old English origin. Means: warlike, an enclosure.

Lachus: Unknown origin. Means: invincible. Alternative spelling: Lachish.

Ladarius: Unknown origin and meaning.

Ladd: Anglo-Saxon origin. Means: an attendant.

Ladislaus: Latin origin. Means: famous ruler. Ethnic background: German. Alternative spellings: Ladislao, Ladislav, Lazlo.

La'eeq: Arabic origin. Means: clever.

Lagee: Swedish origin. Means: of the sea.

Laird: Scottish origin. Means: the Lord, a wealthy landowner.

Lajos: Teutonic/Hungarian origin. Means: famous one, holy.

Lakelyn: Unknown origin and meaning.

Lamar: Latin/Teutonic origin. Means: of the sea, famous, renowned.

Lambert: Teutonic origin. Means: wealthy in land, brilliant. Ethnic background: German. Alternative spellings and nicknames: Bertie, Lanbert, Bert, Lamberto, Landbert, Landberto.

Lamont: Norse origin. Means: one who knows the law. Alternative spellings: Lammond, Lamond.

Lancaster: Old English origin. Unknown meaning.

Lancelot: Latin/French origin. Means: a small spear, serves. Alternative spellings and nicknames: Launce, Launcelot, Lancey, Lance, Lancinet.

Lander: Latin/Anglo-Saxon origin. Means: a lion, from the grassy plain. Alternative spellings: Landers, Landor, Landis.

Landre: Anglo-Saxon origin. Means: local leader, rough land. Alternative spellings: Landri, Landry.

Lane: Old English origin. Means: from the narrow passage.

Lanfranco: Unknown origin and meaning. Ethnic background: Italian.

Lang: Germanic origin. Means: long.

Langford: Old English origin. Means: dweller of the long river crossing.

Langston: Anglo-Saxon origin. Means: one who is esteemed, of the long estate. Alternative spellings: Langdon, Langley, Landon.

Langworth: Unknown origin. Means: enclosure.

Laoghaire: Irish origin. Means: calf herder, a shepherd.

Largent: Unknown origin and meaning.

Larimer: Unknown origin. Means: lover of horses. Alternative spelling: Larimor.

Laron: French origin. Means: a thief.

Larry: Latin/Teutonic origin. Means: victoriously crowned with laurels.

Lars: Latin/Norse origin. Means: victoriously crowned with laurels. Ethnic backgrounds: Swedish, Norwegian.

Larson: Latin/Norse origin. Means: son of Lars, crowned.

Lasse: Greek origin. Means: the people's victory. Ethnic background: Norwegian.

Lathan: Unknown origin. Means: nearby.

Lathrop: Anglo-Saxon origin. Means: from the village barn.

Latimer: Anglo-Saxon origin. Means: one who translates or interprets.

Latton: Unknown origin. Means: man. Alternative spelling: Laughton.

Lavonte: Unknown origin and meaning.

Lawford: Anglo-Saxon origin. Means: of the hill ford.

Lawler: Gaelic origin. Means: one who mumbles.

Lawley: Anglo-Saxon origin. Means: of the hill meadow.

Lawrence: Latin/Anglo-Saxon origin. Means: victoriously crowned with laurels. Alternative spellings and nicknames: Lonin, Larrance, Laurents, Lorenz, Lorenzo, Loren, Lon, Lauren, Laurance, Lars, Larry, Laurence, Lawrence, Laurenz, Laurent, Lauro, Lawry, Lorant, Lorne.

Lawton: Anglo-Saxon origin. Means: from the town on the hill.

Lazarus: Hebrew origin. Means: God has helped. Alternative spellings: Lazario, Lazaro, Leeser.

Lazauskas: Unknown origin. Means: willow.

Lazer: Hebrew origin. Means: God will help.

Le Var: Unknown origin and meaning.

Leal: French origin. Means: one who is faithful.

Leander: Greek origin. Means: lion, a man. Alternative spellings: Leandre, Leandro.

Lear: Anglo-Saxon origin. Means: one who is joyful.

Lech: Polish origin. Means: founder of the Polish race.

Leger: Unknown origin and meaning.

Leggitt: French origin. Means: a delegate. Alternative spellings: Liggett, Laggett.

Leif: Norse origin. Means: one who is well loved, the heir. Ethnic backgrounds: Swedish, Norwegian.

Leith: Celtic/Scottish origin. Means: dweller of the river's meadow.

Leland: Anglo-Saxon origin. Means: of the meadowland. Alternative spellings: Leighland, Leighton.

Lemuel: Hebrew origin. Means: dedicated to God. Nicknames: Lem, Lemmie, Lemmy.

Lendl: Old English origin. Means: of the river near the alders.

Lennon: Gaelic/Old English origin. Means: a small cloak, a river near the house.

Leno: Native American origin. Means: man. Alternative spelling: Lenno.

Lenox: Gaelic/Old English origin. Means: from the elm forest, chief.

Leo: Latin origin. Means: a lion, one who is as bold as a lion. Ethnic background: Irish. Alternative spellings: Lyonel, Leon, Lionel.

Leon: Latin/Spanish origin. Means: a lion, one who is as bold as a lion. Ethnic backgrounds: Russian, Hispanic, French.

Leonard: Teutonic origin. Means: a lion, one who is as bold as a lion. Alternative spellings and nicknames: Lennie, Lenny, Len, Lenard, Lennart, Leny, Leonarda, Leonardo, Leone, Leonce, Leonid, Leonidas.

Leopold: Teutonic origin. Means: one who is popular with the people. Ethnic backgrounds: German, Polish. Alternative spellings and nicknames: Lepp, Leo, Leopoldo.

LeRon: Unknown origin and meaning.

Lerone: Hebrew origin. Means: the song is mine.

Leroy: French origin. Means: the king. Alternative spellings and nicknames: Leroi, Lee, Roy, Elroy, Rex, Laroy.

Leshem: Hebrew origin. Means: precious stone.

Lester: Latin origin. Means: one who is from the army camp. Nickname: Les.

Leszek: Polish origin. Means: Polish father.

Lev: Hebrew/Slavic origin. Means: a heart, a lion.

Levan: Latin origin. Means: to raise. Ethnic background: Russian. Alternative spelling: Levon.

Leverett: French origin. Means: a young rabbit.

Leverton: Anglo-Saxon origin. Means: farm dweller.

Levi: Hebrew origin. Means: joined to, associated. Alternative spelling: Levy.

Levin: Unknown origin. Means: a friend.

Lewis: Teutonic/French origin. Means: celebrated warrior, renowned fighter. Alternative spellings and nicknames: Lewes, Ludorick, Lew, Louie, Louis, Lou, Clovis, Lewy.

Liam: Teutonic/Gaelic origin. Means: helmet, determined protector.

Lian: French origin. Means: to bind or tie.

Liban: Unknown origin and meaning.

Liberato: Latin origin. Means: with freedom, liberty. Ethnic background: Hispanic.

Lidio: Greek origin. Unknown meaning. Ethnic background: Hispanic.

Lieber: Hebrew/Germanic origin. Means: one who is beloved.

Liman: Unknown origin. Means: man. Alternative spelling: Limann.

Linc: Unknown origin and meaning.

Lincoln: Latin/Anglo-Saxon origin. Means: of the lake colony.

Lindberg: Germanic origin. Means: of the linden-tree mountain.

Lindell: Anglo-Saxon origin. Means: of the linden-tree meadow.

Linden: Old English origin. Means: flexible, like a lime tree. Alternative spelling: Lindo.

Initially Speaking

So you've finally decided on a name for your little girl. It meets all your requirements, your spouse likes it—heck, even your in-laws like it. Let's just say, for argument's sake, that the name you've found is Priscilla Isadora Gump. What's wrong with this picture? *The initials spell* PIG. Is it time to march straight back to that drawing board?

Lindley: Anglo-Saxon origin. Means: of the linden-tree valley. Alternative spelling: Lindly.

Liney: Unknown origin. Means: field.

Linford: Old English origin. Means: of the linden-tree ford.

Link: Old English origin. Means: of the river's bank, an enclosure.

Lino: Latin/French origin. Means: praise, a flaxen-type weave. Ethnic background: Hispanic. Alternative spelling: Lins.

Linton: Old English origin. Means: of the flaxen enclosure, linden lined.

Linus: Greek/Latin origin. Means: a boy with flaxen hair. Alternative spelling: Lynus.

Lionel: Latin/French origin. Means: youthful lion. Alternative spelling: Leonel.

Lipman: Germanic origin. Means: lover of mankind. Ethnic background: Jewish.

Lisandro: Spanish origin. Means: a liberator.

Lisimba: Egyptian origin. Means: torn, a lion. Ethnic background: African.

Liska: Unknown origin. Means: fox.

Litton: Old English origin. Means: dweller of the hill estate, a small town.

Livingston: Anglo-Saxon origin. Means: from lief's town.

Llewellyn: Celtic origin. Means: one who is lionlike.

Lloyd: Welsh origin. Means: one with gray hair. Alternative spelling: Floyd.

Locke: Anglo-Saxon origin. Means: from the fortified enclosure.

Lockwood: Anglo-Saxon origin. Means: of the deep forest.

Loeb: Germanic origin. Means: a lion. Ethnic background: Jewish.

Lombard: Latin/Teutonic origin. Means: he with a long beard. Alternative spellings: Lombardo, Lombardy.

London: Latin/Old English origin. Means: a fortress of the moon.

Lorcan: Gaelic/Irish origin. Means: little fierce one.

Loredo: Latin origin. Means: crowned with laurels. Ethnic background: Greek.

Lorimer: Latin origin. Means: maker of horse harnesses.

Loring: Germanic origin. Means: famous in battle, crowned.

Lot: Hebrew origin. Means: to envelop, protect, to veil.

Lotachukwu: African origin. Means: remember God.

Louis: Germanic origin. Means: famous warrior. Ethnic backgrounds: French, Irish. Alternative spellings: Lou, Luis.

Lowell: Anglo-Saxon origin. Means: one who is loved, beloved. Alternative spelling: Lovell.

Lubbock: Unknown origin and meaning.

Lubomir: Slavic/Czech origin. Means: a great love, famous.

Initially Speaking

You have to think about what the initials will spell. You may or may not want them to make a word. My sister's initials are SAM, and she goes by the nickname Sam. But you wouldn't want your child's initials to spell something such as COW, BAT, or DUD.

~ Elizabeth C.,
Raleigh, North Carolina

Lucas: Latin origin. Means: light. Ethnic background: Hispanic. 41st most popular boy's name of the '90s. Alternative spellings: Loukas, Lukas, Luca, Lucano, Luykas.

Lucius: Latin origin. Means: bringer of light, daybreak. Alternative spellings: Lucian, Lucien, Luciano, Lucio.

Lucky: Greek origin. Means: one who is fortunate.

Ludlow: Germanic/Anglo-Saxon origin. Means: a famous battle, the prince's hill. Alternative spellings: Ludek, Ludlew.

Ludly: Anglo-Saxon origin. Means: dweller of the valley.

Ludolf: Unknown origin and meaning. Ethnic background: German.

Ludwig: Germanic origin. Means: famous warrior. Alternative spellings: Ludvig, Ludvik, Ludwik.

Luigi: Germanic/Italian origin. Means: famous warrior.

Luke: Latin origin. Means: bringer of light. Ethnic background: Irish. 43rd most popular boy's name of the '90s. Alternative spellings: Lucais, Lucas.

Lundy: Scottish origin. Means: from the island grove.

Lunn: Irish origin. Means: one who is fierce, strong.

Lunt: Norse origin. Means: of the grove.

Lutero: Unknown origin. Means: a flute player. Ethnic background: Hispanic.

Lutf: Arabic origin. Means: courtesy.

Luther: Teutonic origin. Means: celebrated warrior. Alternative spellings: Lothair, Lothario, Lothar, Luthais.

Lutz: Germanic origin. Means: famous warrior. Ethnic background: German.

Luzero: Unknown origin and meaning.

Lydell: Anglo-Saxon origin. Means: a dell, hill, or slope.

Lyle: French origin. Means: one who comes from the isle. Alternative spelling: Lisle.

Lyman: Anglo-Saxon origin. Means: one who lays bricks, of the valley. Alternative spelling: Lymann.

Lynd: Anglo-Saxon origin. Means: from the linden-tree woods.

Lyndon: Old English origin. Means: one who lives at the hill of linden trees. Alternative spelling: Lindon.

---

m **Mablevi:** African origin. Means: do not deceive.

Mac: Celtic/Scottish origin. Means: the son of. Alternative spelling: Mack.

MacAdam: Gaelic/Scottish origin. Means: son of Adam, earth.

Macario: Spanish origin. Means: one who is happy. Ethnic background: Hispanic. Alternative spelling: Macarius.

MacDonald: Scottish origin. Means: son of Donald, mighty ruler.

MacDougal: Scottish origin. Means: son of Dougal, dark stranger.

Macedonio: Slavic origin. Means: of Macedonia. Ethnic background: Hispanic.

MacEgan: Scottish origin. Means: son of Egan, powerful.

MacKinley: Scottish origin. Means: son of Kinley, leader.

168

Macklin: Unknown origin and meaning.

MacMurray: Celtic/Scottish origin. Means: son of Murray, mariner, of the sea.

MacNair: Gaelic origin. Means: the heir's son.

Maddock: Celtic/Welsh origin. Means: one who is kind and bountiful, beneficent. Alternative spellings: Maddoc, Madocock, Maddox, Madox.

Madu: Egyptian origin. Means: of the people. Ethnic background: African.

Madzimoyo: African origin. Means: water of life.

Magaidi: Unknown origin. Means: a fighter.

Magdaleno: Hebrew/Spanish origin. Means: a high tower, one who is elevated.

Magne: Norse origin. Means: fierce warrior.

Magnus: Latin origin. Means: one who is great. Ethnic backgrounds: Norwegian, Swedish.

Mahatma: Sanskrit origin. Means: high souled, one who is magnanimous.

Maher: Irish origin. Means: generous one. Ethnic background: Jewish.

Mahluli: African origin. Means: the victor.

Maimon: Arabic origin. Means: luck, good fortune. Ethnic backgrounds: Jewish.

Maisel: Persian origin. Means: warrior, warlike. Ethnic background: Jewish. Alternative spelling: Meisel.

Maitland: Old English origin. Means: plains, from the meadowland.

Major: Latin origin. Means: great, a champion.

Makio: Japanese origin. Unknown meaning.

Makoto: Japanese origin. Unknown meaning.

Malachi: Hebrew origin. Means: an angel, God's messenger. Alternative spellings: Malakhi, Malachy, Malchus.

Malawa: African origin. Means: flowers.

Malcolm: Latin/Celtic origin. Means: a disciple of St. Columbia, a dove. Ethnic backgrounds: English/Welsh, Scottish. Alternative spellings: Malcoln, Malcom.

Malik: Arabic origin. Means: master. Alternative spelling: Malek.

Malise: Celtic/Gaelic origin. Means: a disciple of Jesus.

Maloney: Gaelic/Irish origin. Means: a servant of St. John, devoted. Alternative spelling: Malone.

Manasseh: Hebrew origin. Means: one who is forgetful. Alternative spelling: Manases.

Manchester: Old English origin. Means: a camp of soldiers.

Manchu: Chinese origin. Means: one who is pure.

Mandel: Latin/French origin. Means: almond, garment designer. Alternative spellings: Mandell, Mandella.

Manfred: Teutonic origin. Means: hero, a peaceful man. Ethnic background: German. Nickname: Fred.

Manley: Old English origin. Means: one who is virile, of the hero's common. Alternative spelling: Manly.

Mann: Old English/Germanic origin means: a hero, man. Ethnic background: Jewish. Alternative spelling: Mannes, Manning.

Mannis: Gaelic origin. Means: with greatness. Ethnic background: Jewish. Alternative spellings: Manish, Manus.

Mansfield: Anglo-Saxon origin. Means: of the river's field.

Manshel: Hebrew origin. Means: one who comforts.

Manton: Anglo-Saxon origin. Means: from Mann's estate, a hero.

Manuel: Hebrew/Spanish origin. Means: God is with us. Ethnic background: Hispanic. Nicknames: Manny, Mani.

Manville: Latin origin. Means: of the grand estate. Alternative spellings and nicknames: Melville, Mel, Manvil, Manvel, Manvell.

Mao: Unknown origin and meaning.

Marcellus: Latin origin. Means: warlike, hammer. Alternative spellings: Marcial, Marcel, Marcelino, Marcellas, Marcello, Marcelo, Marsilio.

Marcin: Latin/Polish origin. Means: warlike.

Marcus: Latin origin. Means: of Mars, warlike. Alternative spellings: Marcos, Marco, Markus.

Margarito: Greek origin. Means: a pearl. Ethnic background: Hispanic.

Marino: Latin origin. Means: of the sea.

Mario: Latin origin. Means: one who is bitter or rebellious, virile. Ethnic backgrounds: Italian, Hispanic. Alternative spellings: Marion, Marius, Marios, Mariano.

Mark: Latin origin. Means: warlike, a warrior. Ethnic backgrounds: English/Welsh. 47th most popular boy's name of the '90s. Alternative spellings: Marc, Marco, Marcus, Marek.

Marlin: Anglo-Saxon/French origin. Means: one who is as cunning, a falcon. Alternative spellings: Merlin, Marlon.

Marlow: Teutonic origin. Means: from a hill by a lake. Alternative spelling: Marlowe.

Marmaduke: Celtic origin. Means: a sea leader or steward. Ethnic background: Irish. Nickname: Duke.

Marmion: French/Gaelic origin. Means: small one, a sparkling flame.

Marnin: Hebrew origin. Means: one who creates joy.

Mároof: Arabic origin. Means: famous.

Marquel: Unknown origin and meaning.

Marques: French origin. Means: a sign or mark.

Marquise: French origin. Means: a nobleman.

Marsden: Anglo-Saxon origin. Means: marsh valley dweller. Alternative spellings and nicknames: Denny, Mardon, Marston, Marsdon, Marden, Marland, Marsh.

Marshall: Germanic/French origin. Means: one who is in charge of the horses. Alternative spelling: Marshal.

Marshawn: Unknown origin and meaning.

Marston: Anglo-Saxon origin. Means: from the farm by the spring.

Martial: Latin origin. Means: warlike.

Martin: Latin origin. Means: warlike. Ethnic backgrounds: Swiss, Hispanic, Swedish, Norwegian, English/Welsh, Irish. Alternative spellings and nicknames: Martie, Mart, Marty, Martino, Marten, Mark, Marton, Maarten, Martijn.

Marv: Latin origin. Means: to wonder, a miracle.

Marvin: Teutonic origin. Means: famous friend of the sea. Alternative spellings and nicknames: Marwin, Marv, Mervin, Merwin, Merwyn, Merv.

Marwood: Anglo-Saxon origin. Means: of the forest lake.

Masaaki: Japanese origin. Unknown meaning.

Masajiro: Japanese origin. Unknown meaning. Alternative spelling: Masaji.

Masamba: African origin. Means: leaves.

Masamitsu: Japanese origin. Unknown meaning.

Masanao: Japanese origin. Unknown meaning.

Masayuki: Japanese origin. Unknown meaning.

Mashael: Unknown origin and meaning.

Maslin: French origin. Means: a little one.

Mason: Germanic/French origin. Means: one who builds with stone, to make.

Ma'soom: Arabic origin. Means: innocent.

Massimiliano: Latin origin. Means: the best. Ethnic background: Italian. Alternative spelling: Massimo.

Masura: Japanese origin. Unknown meaning.

Mather: Anglo-Saxon origin. Means: from the great army.

Matin: Arabic origin. Means: one who is strong. Ethnic backgrounds: English/Welsh.

Matisse: Unknown origin and meaning.

Matland: Unknown origin. Means: of the plains.

Mato: Native American origin. Means: one who is brave.

Matteson: Unknown origin and meaning.

Matthew: Hebrew origin. Means: a gift of God. Ethnic backgrounds: English/Welsh. 3rd most popular boy's name of the '90s. Alternative spellings and nicknames: Mat, Matty, Mattias, May, Mateo, Mathias, Matt, Mathew, Mata, Matan, Mathi, Matthia, Mathieu, Mats,

Matteo, Matthaeus, Matthee, Matthias, Matthijs, Mayhew.

Matunde: African origin. Means: fruits.

Maurice: Greek/Latin origin. Means: one who is dark, dark-haired. Ethnic background: French. Alternative spellings and nicknames: Morrie, Maury, Morris, Marurice, Mauricio, Maurizio, Morio, Morrice.

Mawali: African origin. Means: there is a God.

Mawulolo: African origin. Means: God is great.

Max: Latin origin. Means: the greatest. Ethnic backgrounds: French, Swiss.

Maxfield: Unknown origin and meaning.

Maximilian: Latin origin. Means: the greatest. Ethnic background: Polish. Alternative spellings and nicknames: Maxie, Max, Maxim, Maximillian, Maximillion, Maxmilian, Maxamillion, Maximiano.

Maxwell: Anglo-Saxon origin. Means: from the large spring. Nicknames: Maxie, Max.

Mayer: Latin origin. Means: great.

Mayfield: Anglo-Saxon origin. Means: of the soldier's field.

Maynard: Teutonic origin. Means: a powerful, mighty man, brave, steady. Alternative spelling: Menard.

Mayor: Latin origin. Means: great, one who is first.

Mays: Unknown origin and meaning.

Mayuko: Unknown origin and meaning.

Mazal: Hebrew origin. Means: a star, luck.

McGill: Latin origin. Means: son of Gill, youth.

McKay: Latin origin. Means: son of Kay, with glory.

McLean: Scottish origin. Means: of John's servant.

Meade: Anglo-Saxon origin. Means: meadow dweller. Alternative spelling: Mead.

Medwin: Teutonic/Anglo-Saxon origin. Means: a true friend.

Mehmet: Unknown origin and meaning.

Meindert: Germanic origin. Means: one who is firm, strong. Ethnic background: Dutch. Alternative spellings: Meinhard, Meinrad.

Melanio: Greek origin. Means: black, dark. Ethnic background: Hispanic.

Melar: Unknown origin. Means: a prince.

Melbourne: Anglo-Saxon origin. Means: from the brook near the mill. Alternative spellings: Melburn, Milburn, Milburt, Millburn.

Melchizedek: Hebrew origin. Means: my king is righteousness.

Melchor: Hebrew origin. Means: the king. Ethnic background: Hispanic.

Meldon: Latin/Anglo-Saxon origin. Means: of the hillside mill.

Meletius: Latin/Greek origin. Unknown meaning. Alternative spelling: Meletios.

Melito: Greek origin. Means: a bee, industrious. Ethnic background: Hispanic.

Melquiades: Unknown origin and meaning. Ethnic background: Hispanic.

Melville: Old English origin. Means: of the mill estate.

Melvin: Celtic/Old English origin. Means: a chief, a famous friend. Alternative spellings: Melvina, Melvyn, Malvin, Malwin.

Menas: Unknown origin and meaning. Ethnic background: Hispanic.

Mendel: Old English origin. Means: one who repairs, knowledge. Ethnic background: Jewish. Alternative spellings: Mendl, Menka, Menke, Menla, Menlin.

Mensa: Egyptian origin. Means: third son. Ethnic background: African.

Menshel: Hebrew origin. Means: one who comforts. Alternative spelling: Menshl.

Merced: Unknown origin and meaning.

Mercer: French origin. Means: a merchant. Alternative spellings: Merce, Merceer.

Mercurio: Unknown origin and meaning. Ethnic background: Hispanic. Alternative spelling: Mercury.

Merial: Hebrew/Celtic origin. Means: bitter, bright sea.

Meridith: Celtic/Welsh origin. Means: guardian of the sea.

Merrick: Teutonic/Old English origin. Means: a powerful ruler, sea ruler.

Merrill: Teutonic/Old English origin. Means: one who is famous, a body of water.

Merton: Anglo-Saxon origin. Means: of the sea estate.

Meshach: Unknown origin and meaning.

Messiah: Unknown origin and meaning.

Metzger: Unknown origin. Means: from the butchery.

Meyer: Teutonic/various origin. Means: to brighten, an attendant, a farmer. Alternative spelling: Myer.

Micah: Hebrew origin. Means: who is like God?

Michael: Hebrew origin. Means: who is like God? Ethnic backgrounds: Greek, English/Welsh, Irish, Hebrew, Swedish. Alternative spellings: Michail, Michal, Micheal, Mickael, Miguel, Mihaly, Mikael, Mikal, Mikeal, Mikel, Mikhail, Mikkel, Miquel, Mykal.

Michener: Unknown origin and meaning.

Mickey: Hebrew/Anglo-Saxon origin. Means: who is like God? Nickname: Mick.

Mieczyslaw: Polish origin. Means: a glorious man.

Miklos: Greek/Hungarian origin. Means: a victory for the people. Alternative spellings: Mikis, Mikoali, Mikos.

Initially Speaking

Even if you carefully choose a name, your daughter may end up with funny initials. After I married, my initials became PMS. My husband had it monogrammed on my bowling ball.

~ Paula S.,
Canton Center, Connecticut

Milan: Latin origin. Means: a warrior, one with grace. Ethnic background: Czech.

Miles: Latin origin. Means: a soldier, warrior. Ethnic background: Irish. Alternative spelling: Myles.

Milford: Anglo-Saxon origin. Means: of the mill's crossing.

Milhous: Unknown origin and meaning.

Millard: Latin/French origin. Means: one who flatters, a miller, strong. Alternative spelling: Miller.

Miller: Latin origin. Means: a miller, one who mills grain.

Millford: Anglo-Saxon origin. Means: of the mill's crossing.

Millman: Anglo-Saxon origin. Means: man, a miller. Alternative spelling: Milman.

Milo: Latin origin. Means: a soldier, warrior.

Milore: Unknown origin. Means: a prince. Alternative spelling: Mylor.

Miltiades: Unknown origin and meaning. Ethnic background: Greek.

Milton: Anglo-Saxon origin. Means: from the mill town. Nickname: Milt.

Minoru: Japanese origin. Unknown meaning.

Miroslav: Slavic/Czech origin. Means: one who is gloriously famous.

Mirsab: Arabic origin. Means: prudent one.

Misael: Hebrew origin. Means: borrowed.

Mischa: Hebrew/Slavic origin. Means: who is like God?

Mitchell: Hebrew/Anglo-Saxon origin. Means: who is like God? 48th most popular boy's name of the '90s. Alternative spellings and nicknames: Mike, Mitch, Mitchel, Michel.

Mitsuo: Japanese origin. Unknown meaning.

Mitsuyoshi: Japanese origin. Unknown meaning.

Modesto: Latin/Italian origin. Means: one who is moderate, restrained. Ethnic background: Hispanic.

Moises: Hebrew/Spanish origin. Means: from the water. Alternative spelling: Moishe.

Molton: Unknown origin. Means: a mule.

Monet: Latin/French origin. Means: one who admonishes.

Monroe: Latin/Celtic origin. Means: from the red swamp or marsh. Alternative spellings: Munro, Monro.

Montague: Latin origin. Means: of the peaked hill or mountain. Alternative spelling: Montagu.

Montana: Latin origin. Means: of the mountain.

Montero: Unknown origin. Means: a huntsman.

Montgomery: Latin/French origin. Means: of the mountain, castle. Nicknames: Monte, Monty.

Monty: Anglo-Saxon origin. Means: of the rich man's mountain. Alternative spelling: Monte.

Moore: French origin. Means: one with dark skin, a wasteland.

Mordecai: Hebrew origin. Means: warlike. Alternative spelling: Mordcheh.

Morel: Latin origin. Means: dark colored. Alternative spellings: Moreno, Morey, Morrell, Morril, Mauro, Maury.

Moreland: Anglo-Saxon origin. Means: of the moors.

Morgen: Celtic/Welsh origin. Means: a sea dweller, born by the sea.

Morley: Anglo-Saxon origin. Means: from the pasture marsh.

Morris: Latin/Anglo-Saxon origin. Means: dark skinned, Moorish. Ethnic background: Jewish. Alternative spellings: Morice, Morrise, Morse, Moritz.

Morrison: Latin/Scottish origin. Means: son of Maurice, dark skinned. Alternative spelling: Morison.

Mort: Latin origin. Means: of the still water, a marsh.

Mortimer: Latin/Old English origin. Means: one who is like still water, of the sea. Ethnic background: Irish. Alternative spellings and nicknames: Mortie, Mort, Morton.

Morton: Old English origin. Means: of the estate near the moor or sea. Alternative spellings and nicknames: Morty, Mort, Morten.

Morven: Celtic/Gaelic origin. Means: the sea, of the big gap or peak, pale. Alternative spelling: Morvin.

Moses: Hebrew origin. Means: saved from the water. Alternative spellings and nicknames: Moss, Moe, Mose, Mosie, Moshke.

Motel: Persian/Hebrew origin. Means: warlike. Alternative spellings: Moti, Motta.

Mouldon: Anglo-Saxon origin. Means: of the mule farm. Alternative spellings: Moulton, Muldon.

Mubaarak: Arabic origin. Means: blessed.

Muel: Hebrew origin. Means: God has dedicated.

Muhammad: Arabic origin. Means: praised one, to praise. Alternative spelling: Mohamed.

Muir: Scottish origin. Means: of the moor.

Mukhtaar: Arabic origin. Means: selected, chosen one.

Muki: Hebrew origin. Means: one who brightens. Ethnic background: Jewish.

Mulogo: African origin. Means: wizard.

Muncie: Unknown origin and meaning.

Muneer: Arabic origin. Means: splendid.

Mungo: Celtic origin. Means: lovable, a dear friend.

Muntean: Unknown origin and meaning. Ethnic background: Hungarian.

Muraad: Arabic origin. Means: desire.

Murdoch: Celtic/Scottish origin. Means: a protector of the sea, a seaman. Alternative spelling: Murdock.

Murray: Celtic origin. Means: a mariner, one who dwells by the sea. Alternative spelling: Murry.

Murtough: Gaelic/Irish origin. Means: a sea warrior. Alternative spellings: Murtagh, Murrough.

Muslim: Egyptian/Arabic origin. Means: a believer, professes.

Mustafa: Unknown origin. Means: chosen.

Mutka: Persian/Hebrew origin. Means: warlike.

Myron: Greek origin. Means: myrrh, fragrant or sweet oil. Alternative spelling: Myreon.

n Naam: Hebrew origin. Means: agreeable, pleasant.

Naaman: Hebrew origin. Means: agreeable, pleasant. Alternative spellings: Naamann, Naam.

Naasir: Arabic origin. Means: defender.

Nabor: Unknown origin and meaning. Ethnic background: Hispanic.

Nachmanke: Hebrew origin. Means: compassionate one, one who comforts.

Nadab: Unknown origin. Means: one with ideas. Alternative spellings: Nadabb, Nadabus.

Nadav: Hebrew origin. Means: noble, a generous one.

Nadeem: Unknown origin and meaning.

Naftali: Hebrew origin. Means: to wrestle.

Nagy: Unknown origin. Means: husky.

Nahash: Unknown origin and meaning.

Nahshu: Unknown origin. Means: enchanter. Alternative spellings: Nahshun, Nahshunn, Nahson, Nahshon.

Nahum: Hebrew origin. Means: one who comforts.

Naim: Hebrew origin. Means: pleasant one.

Nakisisa: African origin. Means: child of the shadows.

Naldo: Teutonic origin. Means: one with wise power.

Nalon: Unknown origin and meaning.

Nalor: Old English origin. Means: a sailor.

Naman: Hebrew origin. Means: agreeable.

Namir: Hebrew origin. Means: leopard. Alternative spelling: Namer.

Nando: Unknown origin and meaning. Ethnic background: Italian.

Nandor: Germanic/Hungarian origin. Means: one who is prepared for a journey.

Naoichi: Japanese origin. Unknown meaning.

Naoto: Japanese origin. Unknown meaning.

Napoleon: Greek origin. Means: from the new city. Alternative spelling: Napolean.

Narcissus: Latin origin. Means: a lily, daffodil. Alternative spelling: Narciso.

Nash: Unknown origin and meaning.

Nassor: Arabic origin. Means: the victorious one. Ethnic background: African. Alternative spellings: Naseer, Nasir.

Nassos: Unknown origin and meaning. Ethnic background: Greek.

Natal: Latin/Spanish origin. Means: born on Christmas, to be born. Alternative spellings: Natale, Natalio.

Nathan: Hebrew origin. Means: God has given. 48th most popular boy's name of the '90s. Alternative spellings and nicknames: Nat, Nate, Natan.

Nathaniel: Hebrew origin. Means: God has given. 34th most popular boy's name of the '90s. Alternative spellings and nicknames: Nat, Natanael, Nataniel, Nate, Nathanael, Nathanial, Nathaneal.

Naum: Slavic origin. Means: one who is clever. Ethnic background: Russian.

Naveed: Unknown origin and meaning.

Naylor: Old English origin. Means: a sailor.

Nayton: Unknown origin and meaning.

Nazar: Arabic origin. Means: charity.

Nazario: Hebrew/Spanish origin. Means: of Nazareth, a branch. Ethnic background: Hispanic.

Initially Speaking

My best friend's husband has a three-year-old son by a previous marriage. The little boy's name is James Taryn, and my friend calls him JT. She asked him the other day what everyone else called him. He answered, "My mommy calls me Taryn, my daddy calls me Bubba and Junior, and my grandpa calls me trouble."

~ Debi F., Russianville, Indiana

Nazarius: Unknown origin. Means: aloof.

Nazheer: Arabic origin. Means: precedent. Alternative spelling: Nazir.

Nduka: African origin. Means: life is supreme.

Neal: Celtic/Gaelic origin. Means: a champion, a noted warrior. Ethnic backgrounds: English/Welsh, Irish. Alternative spellings: Niles, Niels, Nials, Nels, Neill, Neall, Nils, Niall, Neil, Neale, Neils, Nial.

Nebedaeus: Unknown origin and meaning.

Nebuchadnezzar: Babylonian origin. Unknown meaning.

Neco: Unknown origin and meaning.

Nehemiah: Hebrew origin. Means: one who is comforted by God.

Nelson: Celtic/Gaelic origin. Means: son of Neal, champion. Alternative spellings: Nilson, Nealson.

Neman: Unknown origin and meaning.

Nemesio: Latin origin. Means: one who is just. Ethnic background: Hispanic.

Nemo: Greek origin. Means: of the glen.

Nepomuceno: Unknown origin and meaning. Ethnic background: Hispanic.

Ness: Hebrew origin. Means: a miracle. Alternative spellings: Nes, Nisim.

Nessan: Irish origin. Unknown meaning.

Nestor: Greek origin. Means: homecoming, with wisdom. Ethnic background: Hispanic.

Netanel: Hebrew origin. Means: God's gift.

Nevil: Latin/French origin. Means: of the new settlement. Alternative spellings: Nevile, Neville.

Nevlin: Unknown origin. Means: a sailor.

Newbold: Old English origin. Means: of the town by the tree.

Newcomb: Unknown origin. Means: a stranger.

Newland: Anglo-Saxon origin. Means: from the new settlement.

Newlin: Celtic/Welsh origin. Means: one from near the new spring. Alternative spelling: Newlyn.

Newman: Anglo-Saxon origin. Means: a newcomer, stranger.

Newt: Anglo-Saxon origin. Means: one from the new settlement. Alternative spelling: Newton.

Ngoli: African origin. Means: happiness.

Niamke: African origin. Means: God's gift.

Nicanor: Greek origin. Means: man's victory. Ethnic background: Hispanic.

Nicholas: Greek origin. Means: the people's victory. Ethnic backgrounds: Irish, English/Welsh, Greek. 2nd most popular boy's name of the '90s. Alternative spellings and nicknames: Niles, Nicholl, Nichol, Nicolas, Nicky, Klaus, Colin, Claus, Nick, Nicholaus, Nicholes, Nickolas, Nickolaus, Nicolus, Nikolas, Nichloas, Nicholai, Nicklaus, Nicol, Nicolaas, Nicolai, Nicos, Nikos, Nikolai, Niklas, Nikko, Niko, Niklaus, Nykolahs, Nicco.

Nicodemus: Greek origin. Means: the people's conqueror, victory.

Nicomedes: Greek origin. Means: one who ponders the victory. Ethnic background: Hispanic.

Nidri: Hebrew origin. Means: my oath.

Nigel: Latin origin. Means: one who is dark, swarthy. Ethnic backgrounds: English/Welsh. Alternative spellings: Niger, Nygel.

Nikhil: Unknown origin and meaning.

Nikita: Greek/Slavic origin. Means: one who is unconquerable.

Nikon: Unknown origin and meaning. Ethnic background: Greek.

Nile: Egyptian origin. Means: of the Nile.

Nils: Greek/Swedish origin. Means: the people's victory. Ethnic backgrounds: German, Norwegian.

Nino: Hebrew/Italian origin. Means: God is gracious. Ethnic background: Hispanic.

Nipsey: Unknown origin and meaning.

Niven: Gaelic/Scottish origin. Means: nephew, a saint servant. Alternative spelling: Nevin.

Nixon: Greek/Anglo-Saxon origin. Means: son of Nicholas, people's victory.

Nizaam: Arabic origin. Means: order.

Nli: Unknown origin and meaning.

Noah: Hebrew origin. Means: comfort from work, rest. 46th most popular boy's name of the '90s.

Noam: Unknown origin and meaning.

Noaz: Hebrew origin. Means: bold, one who is daring.

Noble: Latin origin. Means: one who is well born.

Noboru: Japanese origin. Unknown meaning.

Nobutaka: Japanese origin. Unknown meaning.

Nodab: Unknown origin and meaning.

Noe: Hebrew/Spanish origin. Means: comfort, peace. Ethnic background: Hispanic.

Noel: Latin/French origin. Means: birthday, born near Christmas. Alternative spelling: Nowell.

Noga: Hebrew origin. Means: bright, sparkling.

Nolan: Celtic/Gaelic origin. Means: famous champion, noble.

Nolizwe: African origin. Means: country.

Nomikos: Greek origin. Unknown meaning.

Noor: Arabic origin. Means: light.

Norbert: Teutonic origin. Means: bright hero of the North. Ethnic backgrounds: Italian, Hispanic. Alternative spelling: Norberto.

Norman: Teutonic/French origin. Means: from the North, a Norseman. Ethnic backgrounds: English/Welsh. Alternative spellings and nicknames: Norm, Normie, Norris.

Norsalus: Unknown origin and meaning.

Northrop: Anglo-Saxon origin. Means: from the north farm.

Norton: Anglo-Saxon origin. Means: from the north farm.

Norval: Scottish origin. Means: of the north valley. Alternative spellings: Norvall, Norvel, Norvil, Norville.

Norward: Teutonic/Anglo-Saxon origin. Means: guardian of the north gate.

Norwell: Anglo-Saxon origin. Means: from the north spring.

Norwin: Teutonic/Anglo-Saxon origin. Means: a friend from the north. Ethnic background: Swiss. Alternative spellings: Norvin, Norwyn.

Norwood: Anglo-Saxon origin. Means: from the north forest.

Norword: Anglo-Saxon origin. Means: from the north.

Nosson: Hebrew/Norse origin. Means: a gift.

Nuncio: Latin origin. Means: one who announces the good news.

Nuri: Hebrew origin. Means: my fire, my light. Alternative spellings: Nuriel, Nuris.

Nuteh: Unknown origin and meaning. Ethnic background: Jewish.

Nwabudike: African origin. Means: child is power.

Nyagwa: Unknown origin. Means: a ruler.

Nye: Latin/Welsh origin. Means: with honor.

Nyrell: Unknown origin and meaning.

Oakes: Anglo-Saxon origin. Means: from the oak, an oak trader.

Oakley: Anglo-Saxon origin. Means: of the oak-tree meadow.

Obed: Hebrew origin. Means: servant of God. Alternative spellings: Obeded, Obadiah.

Obert: Germanic origin. Means: brilliant one, wealthy.

Obiajulu: African origin. Means: the heart is consoled.

Obinna: African origin. Means: dear to the father.

Obispo: Spanish origin. Means: bishop. Ethnic background: Hispanic.

Octavius: Latin origin. Means: the eighth born. Alternative spellings and nicknames: Octavian, Octavus, Tavey, Octave, Octavio, Ottavito.

Odab: Unknown origin and meaning.

Oddvar: Norse origin. Means: the spear's point.

Ode: Egyptian/Teutonic origin. Means: born on the road, wealthy. Ethnic background: African.

Odericus: Unknown origin. Means: good.

Odilo: Teutonic origin. Means: refined, one who is well off. Alternative spellings: Odlo, Odo.

Odin: Norse origin. Means: of the sky.

Odoardo: Old English origin. Means: prosperous protector. Ethnic background: Italian.

Odolf: Teutonic origin. Means: wealthy.

Odoric: Unknown origin. Means: good. Alternative spelling: Odrick.

Ofar: Hebrew origin. Means: a young deer, fawn.

Ofelio: Unknown origin and meaning. Ethnic background: Hispanic.

Ogden: Anglo-Saxon origin. Means: from the valley of oaks.

Ogilvie: Scottish origin. Means: from the mountain's peak.

Oglesby: Anglo-Saxon origin. Means: inspires awe.

Oisin: Celtic origin. Unknown meaning. Ethnic background: Irish.

Okpara: Egyptian origin. Means: firstborn. Ethnic background: African.

Olaf: Norse origin. Means: one who resembles an ancestor. Ethnic backgrounds: Hebrew, German. Alternative spellings and nicknames: Olini, Ola, Olin, Olav, Olof.

Olcott: Unknown origin. Means: cottage.

Oldrich: Germanic/Czech origin. Means: one with riches and power.

Oleg: Slavic/Norse origin. Means: one who is holy. Ethnic background: Russian.

Olegario: Slavic/Norse origin. Means: one who is holy. Ethnic background: Hispanic.

Olen: Norse origin. Means: one who resembles an ancestor. Alternative spellings: Olin, Ole.

Oliver: Latin origin. Means: branch, peace, of the olive tree. Ethnic backgrounds: Irish, English/Welsh. Alternative spellings and nicknames: Olivier, Noll, Nollie, Nolly, Ollie, Oliverio, Oliviero.

Olnay: Anglo-Saxon origin. Means: from Olney. Alternative spellings: Olney, Olnton.

Olpe: Unknown origin and meaning.

Omar: Arabic origin. Means: the highest, firstborn son, long life. Alternative spellings: Omarr, Omer, Omor.

Omari: Arabic origin. Means: one who is well born.

Omen: Latin origin. Means: faithful, a sign. Ethnic background: Jewish.

Ondrej: Greek/Czech origin. Means: manly, with strength.

Onesimo: Unknown origin and meaning. Ethnic background: Hispanic.

Onofre: Unknown origin and meaning. Ethnic background: Hispanic.

Oram: Anglo-Saxon origin. Means: of the riverside settlement.

Oran: Gaelic/Irish origin. Means: pale, a pale green, a willow.

Orazio: Latin/Italian origin. Means: to see or behold.

Orbelin: Unknown origin and meaning.

Ordway: Anglo-Saxon origin. Means: a spear-wielding fighter.

Orel: Unknown origin and meaning.

Oren: Hebrew/Gaelic origin. Means: pale, a pine tree. Alternative spellings: Orren, Orrin, Orin.

Orenthal: Hebrew/Old English origin. Means: a tall pine tree, pale.

Orestes: Greek origin. Means: from the mountain. Ethnic background: Hispanic. Alternative spelling: Oreste.

Orford: Anglo-Saxon origin. Means: from the cattle farm.

Ori: Hebrew origin. Means: my light.

Orion: Greek origin. Means: son of fire, of the East. Alternative spellings: Orien, Oryon, Orian.

Orlan: Old English origin. Means: of the steep hill.

Orlando: Germanic origin. Means: one who is famous throughout the land. Ethnic background: Italian. Alternative spelling: Orland.

Orman: Teutonic/Anglo-Saxon origin. Means: a mariner, spearman. Alternative spelling: Ormond.

Oro: Latin/Spanish origin. Means: golden, gold.

Oron: Latin origin. Means: light, of the East. Ethnic background: Hebrew.

Oroville: Latin/Anglo-Saxon origin. Means: light, of the East.

Orrick: Anglo-Saxon origin. Means: of the valley of the ancient oaks.

Orsola: Latin origin. Means: one who is like a bear. Ethnic background: Italian.

Orson: Latin/French origin. Means: one who is like a bear. Alternative spellings: Orsine, Orsini, Orsin, Orsino.

Orten: Unknown origin. Means: great. Alternative spellings: Ortin, Ortwin.

Orterd: Unknown origin. Means: cattle.

Ortfried: Unknown origin and meaning. Ethnic background: German.

Orton: Teutonic/Anglo-Saxon origin. Means: wealthy one, from the seaside.

What's in a Nickname?

Nearly every name can be shortened into a nickname. At their best nicknames are used to show affection. At their worst they are belittling. Used well, the nickname can allow a child's name to grow along with him or her. Some names, such as Peg (from Margaret) or Sasha (from Alexander), are strict derivatives of other names. So, if you are planning to call your daughter Peg, should you go through the formality of putting Margaret on her birth certificate?

Orval: Anglo-Saxon origin. Means: one who wields the spear mightily. Alternative spellings: Orvas, Orvil.

Orville: Anglo-Saxon/French origin. Means: of the golden estate, a lord.

Orvin: Anglo-Saxon origin. Means: a spear-wielding companion.

Orwell: Unknown origin and meaning.

Orwin: Unknown origin. Means: divine.

Osakwe: African origin. Means: if God agrees.

Osamu: Japanese origin. Unknown meaning.

Osbert: Old English origin. Means: brilliant, famous one. Nicknames: Bertie, Berty, Oz, Bert, Ozzie.

Osborn: Norse/Old English origin. Means: bear, fierce warrior, divine.

Oscar: Norse/Celtic origin. Means: divine, perfect spear. Ethnic backgrounds: Irish, Hispanic. Alternative spellings and nicknames: Ossie, Oskar, Ozzie, Oszkar.

Osceola: Unknown origin and meaning.

Osediame: Unknown origin and meaning.

Osgood: Norse/Teutonic origin. Means: divine creator.

Oshri: Unknown origin. Means: my good fortune. Ethnic background: Jewish.

Osman: Teutonic/Anglo-Saxon origin. Means: God's divine protection. Alternative spellings: Osmar, Osmen, Osmo, Osmond, Osmund.

Osred: Anglo-Saxon origin. Means: a divine counselor.

Osric: Teutonic/Anglo-Saxon origin. Means: divine ruler. Alternative spellings: Osrick, Osrock.

Oswald: Old English origin. Means: God's rule, divine power. Ethnic background: German. Alternative spellings and nicknames: Ossie, Oz, Ozzie, Osvaldo, Oswell.

Oswin: Old English origin. Means: friend of God.

Otakar: Unknown origin and meaning. Ethnic background: Czech.

Othieno: African origin. Means: born in the night.

Othineil: Hebrew origin. Means: my strength is in God. Alternative spelling: Otniel.

Othman: Germanic origin. Means: he who is well off.

Otis: Greek/Germanic origin. Means: one with keen hearing, wealthy. Alternative spelling: Ottis.

Otmar: Germanic origin. Means: one who is famously wealthy.

Otto: Teutonic origin. Means: one who is prosperous, wealthy. Ethnic backgrounds: Polish, German. Alternative spelling: Ottone.

Ovid: Latin origin. Means: poet, industrious, a leader. Alternative spelling: Ovidio.

Owen: Celtic/Welsh origin. Means: youthful warrior of noble birth. Ethnic background: Irish. Alternative spellings: Owan, Evan, Ewen, Own.

Oxford: Anglo-Saxon origin. Means: of the oxen farm or crossing.

Oyvind: Unknown origin and meaning. Ethnic background: Norwegian.

Ozan: Unknown origin. Means: man.

Ozias: Greek origin. Means: the Lord is strong.

Ozire: Unknown origin and meaning.

Ozmo: Unknown origin and meaning.

Ozzie: Hebrew/Old English origin. Means: one with strength, divine power. Alternative spelling: Ozzy.

Pablo: Latin/Spanish origin. Means: little, small.

Pacian: Unknown origin and meaning. Alternative spellings: Pacien, Pace.

Paco: Latin/Spanish origin. Means: a free man.

Padget: French origin. Means: an attendant. Alternative spellings: Padgett, Pagas.

Pageman: Greek/Anglo-Saxon origin. Means: the knight's young attendant.

Paine: Latin origin. Means: one from the country, rustic, earthy. Alternative spelling: Payne.

Paki: Egyptian origin. Means: a witness. Ethnic background: African.

Pallas: Greek origin. Means: distinguished, knowledge. Alternative spelling: Palnas.

Pallaton: Native American origin. Means: a brave warrior. Alternative spelling: Palladin.

Palma: Latin origin. Means: a palm tree, born on Palm Sunday.

Palmer: Latin/Anglo-Saxon origin. Means: a pilgrim who bears palms, crusader.

Palti: Hebrew origin. Means: my escape.

Panagiotis: Greek origin. Means: consecrated, holy one.

Panama: Spanish origin. Means: a hat made from palms.

Pancrazio: Greek/Italian origin. Means: supreme ruler, all powerful. Alternative spelling: Pankraz.

Panfilo: Unknown origin and meaning. Ethnic background: Hispanic.

Panos: Greek origin. Means: the rock.

Pantaleon: Unknown origin and meaning. Ethnic background: Hispanic.

Pantias: Unknown origin and meaning. Ethnic background: Greek.

Paolo: Latin/Italian origin. Means: little one, small.

Paris: Greek origin. Means: an abductor.

Parke: Old English origin. Means: dweller of the enclosed land, forest. Alternative spelling: Park.

Parker: Old English origin. Means: guardian of the forest.

Parnell: Old English/French origin. Means: a little rock. Alternative spellings: Pernel, Parle.

Parrish: Greek/Old English origin. Means: neighborhood, lives near the church.

Parry: Welsh origin. Means: son of Harry. Alternative spelling: Parrie.

Parthik: Unknown origin and meaning.

Partholon: Aramaic/Gaelic origin. Means: a hill or furrow, a ploughman. Ethnic background: Irish. Alternative spelling: Parlan.

Pascal: Hebrew/Latin origin. Means: born near Easter, Passover. Ethnic backgrounds: French, Italian. Alternative spellings: Pasco, Pascual.

Paterson: Unknown origin and meaning.

Patrick: Latin origin. Means: of noble birth. Ethnic backgrounds: Scottish, French, Irish. 34th most popular boy's name of the '90s. Alternative spellings and nicknames: Partric, Paddy, Patrik, Patty, Pat, Patricio, Patrizio, Patroncinio, Patryck.

Patton: Anglo-Saxon origin. Means: from the combatant's town.

Paul: Latin origin. Means: little, small. Ethnic backgrounds: Irish, French, English/Welsh. 48th most popular boy's name of the '90s. Alternative spellings and nicknames: Paulie, Pablo, Paulo, Pawel.

Pavlof: Latin/Slavic origin. Means: little, small. Alternative spelling: Pavel.

Paxon: Teutonic origin. Means: a trader from afar. Alternative spellings: Packston, Packton.

Payton: Latin/Anglo-Saxon origin. Means: of royal birth, the warrior's camp. Alternative spellings: Paton, Payten.

Peabo: Unknown origin and meaning.

Pecos: Unknown origin and meaning.

Pedaias: Unknown origin and meaning. Alternative spelling: Pedaiah.

Pedro: Greek/Spanish origin. Means: a rock, stone.

Peer: Unknown origin and meaning. Ethnic background: German.

Pegasus: Greek origin. Means: attendant, winged.

Pelle: Greek/Norse origin. Means: the rock, stone. Ethnic background: Swedish. Alternative spellings: Pele, Pelee.

Pelton: Unknown origin and meaning.

Pembroke: Anglo-Saxon/Welsh origin. Means: from the headland.

Penley: Anglo-Saxon origin. Means: from the enclosed farm.

Penn: Latin/Germanic origin. Means: a pen or quill, a commander.

Penrod: Germanic origin. Means: famous commander.

Penrose: Unknown origin and meaning.

Pentige: Unknown origin and meaning.

Pentz: Unknown origin and meaning.

Penuel: Hebrew origin. Means: face of God.

Pepin: Unknown origin. Means: a petitioner.

Peppino: Hebrew/Italian origin. Means: he shall add.

Percival: French origin. Means: valley piercer. Alternative spellings and nicknames: Perc, Perce, Perceval, Percy.

Peregrino: Latin origin. Means: one who wanders. Ethnic background: Hispanic.

Perfecto: Latin origin. Means: accomplished, perfect. Ethnic background: Hispanic.

Perikles: Greek origin. Unknown meaning.

180

What's in a Nickname?

I think children should be given formal names, at least on the birth certificate. It gives them a choice later in life. It may not be right, but people judge us by our names before they even meet us. And a formal name gives our kids the chance to present themselves in a more respected and professional manner than a nickname does.

~ Eva D.,
Lighthouse Point, Florida

Perkin: Anglo-Saxon origin. Means: little rock. Alternative spelling: Parkin.

Perrin: Greek/French origin. Means: little rock. Alternative spellings: Perrine, Pero, Per.

Perry: Anglo-Saxon origin. Means: from the pear tree. Nickname: Perr.

Peter: Greek origin. Means: a rock, stone. Ethnic backgrounds: English/Welsh, Scottish, Swiss, Hungarian, German, Irish. 45th most popular boy's name of the '90s. Alternative spellings and nicknames: Pearce, Pernell, Petey, Petie, Petrie, Pedro, Perrin, Pete, Pierce, Pierre, Pietro, Parnell, Petr, Petro, Petronilo, Petros, Petrus, Petter, Piet, Pieter, Pietro, Piotr, Pyotr.

Pethuel: Unknown origin and meaning.

Peverel: Latin/French origin. Means: of the piper, seeds of climbing shrub. Alternative spellings: Peverell, Peveril.

Phelan: Celtic/Gaelic origin. Means: little wolf.

Phelgen: Unknown origin and meaning. Alternative spelling: Phelgon.

Philander: Greek origin. Means: lover of all God created. Alternative spelling: Philender.

Philbert: Teutonic origin. Means: bright, brilliant, radiant.

Philemon: Greek origin. Means: affectionate, a great thinker. Alternative spelling: Philo.

Philetus: Unknown origin and meaning.

Phillip: Greek origin. Means: lover of horses. Ethnic backgrounds: Scottish, English/Welsh, German, Irish. 44th most popular boy's name of the '90s. Alternative spellings: Philipp, Philip, Phelps, Phillipi, Phil, Philippe, Philan.

Phineas: Egyptian/Hebrew origin. Means: the Nubian, oracle. Alternative spelling: Phinehas.

Photius: Unknown origin and meaning. Ethnic background: Greek.

Picardus: Unknown origin and meaning. Ethnic background: Hispanic.

Pickford: Anglo-Saxon origin. Means: of the ford's peak.

Pico: Unknown origin and meaning.

Pierce: Greek/Anglo-Saxon origin. Means: a stone, rock. Ethnic background: Irish.

Pierre: Greek/French origin. Means: rock, a stone. Ethnic backgrounds: English/Welsh.

Pierrepont: Latin/French origin. Means: from the stone bridge. Alternative spelling: Pierpont.

Pierson: Greek/Anglo-Saxon origin. Means: son of Peter/Pierce, the rock. Alternative spellings: Peirsen, Pearson.

Pim: Unknown origin and meaning. Ethnic background: Dutch.

Pincas: Egyptian/Hebrew origin. Means: dark complexioned, oracle. Alternative spellings: Pineleh, Pinkeh.

Pinya: Hebrew origin. Unknown meaning. Alternative spelling: Pina.

Pioquinto: Unknown origin and meaning. Ethnic background: Hispanic.

Pippin: French origin. Means: royal. Ethnic background: Dutch.

Pirney: Unknown origin. Means: from the island.

Pius: Latin origin. Means: one who is dutiful, religious. Ethnic background: German.

Placido: Latin origin. Means: calm, gentle. Ethnic background: Hispanic.

Plan: Latin origin. Means: flat, level.

Platinum: Latin/Spanish origin. Means: silver metal.

Plato: Greek origin. Means: broad one, mankind.

Policarpo: Greek origin. Means: with much fruit. Ethnic background: Hispanic.

Polk: Unknown origin and meaning.

Pollard: Teutonic origin. Means: a man with short hair. Alternative spellings: Pollerd, Polard.

Pollock: Anglo-Saxon origin. Means: little rock.

Pollux: Greek/Latin origin. Means: a crown.

Polo: Unknown origin and meaning.

Polonice: Unknown origin and meaning. Ethnic background: Hispanic.

Polygnotos: Greek origin. Unknown meaning.

Pomeroy: French origin. Means: from near the apple orchard.

Pomposo: Unknown origin and meaning. Ethnic background: Hispanic.

Ponce: Spanish origin. Means: fifth born. Alternative spelling: Ponciano.

Pontias: Greek origin. Means: lover of the sea. Alternative spellings: Pontius, Pontus.

Pope: Greek origin. Means: a bishop, father.

Porfirio: Greek/Spanish origin. Means: a purple stone. Ethnic background: Hispanic.

Porter: Latin/French origin. Means: gatekeeper, porter, to carry. Alternative spelling: Portero.

Powell: Celtic/Welsh origin. Means: son of Howell, eminent.

Pratt: Unknown origin and meaning.

Praxedes: Unknown origin and meaning. Ethnic background: Hispanic.

Prentice: Latin origin. Means: an apprentice, scholar.

Prescott: Anglo-Saxon origin. Means: from the priest's dwelling. Alternative spelling: Preston.

Presley: Anglo-Saxon origin. Means: dweller of the priest's meadow.

Preto: Unknown origin and meaning. Ethnic background: Hispanic.

Price: Welsh origin. Means: son of Rhys, ardent.

Primitivo: Unknown origin and meaning. Ethnic background: Hispanic.

Primo: Latin/Italian origin. Means: the firstborn child.

Prine: Unknown origin and meaning.

Prisciliano: Latin origin. Means: from ancient times, of long lineage. Ethnic background: Hispanic.

Procopio: Latin origin. Means: the declared leader. Ethnic background: Hispanic.

Procter: Latin origin. Means: administrator, leader. Alternative spelling: Proctor.

Prosper: Latin origin. Means: always fortunate. Alternative spellings: Prospero, Prosperus.

Publias: Latin origin. Means: a hero. Alternative spelling: Publius.

Purvis: Anglo-Saxon/French origin. Means: food, to provide.

Q

Qaadir: Arabic origin. Means: powerful. Alternative spelling: Qawee.

Quaco: Unknown origin and meaning.

Quadai: Unknown origin and meaning.

Quadrey: Unknown origin and meaning.

Quamere: Unknown origin and meaning.

Quami: Unknown origin and meaning.

Quanah: Unknown origin and meaning.

What's in a Nickname?

I am in favor of having a nickname and a formal name. My name is Kristina, and I often go by Kris or Krissy with my friends. But at work I am Kristina. I love having an elegant name but also a fun nickname to use informally.

~ **Kristina M.,**
Sunderland, Massachusetts

Quao: Unknown origin and meaning.

Quartus: Latin origin. Means: fourth-born child.

Quashee: Egyptian origin. Means: one who is born on Sunday.

Quasimodo: Unknown origin and meaning. Ethnic background: Hispanic.

Quddos: Arabic origin. Means: holy one, pure.

Quentin: Latin origin. Means: the fifth-born child. Alternative spellings and nicknames: Quent, Quenton, Quint, Quinten, Quintin, Quinton, Quintino, Quinto.

Quertnel: Unknown origin and meaning.

Quesstin: Unknown origin and meaning.

Quigley: Gaelic/Irish origin. Means: distaff, unruly.

Quillan: Greek origin. Means: youth, youngster, a cub.

Quilmes: Unknown origin and meaning. Ethnic background: Hispanic.

Quinby: Norse origin. Means: dweller of the woman's estate, womanly. Alternative spelling: Quimby.

Quincy: Latin/French origin. Means: of the fifth son's estate.

Quinlan: Gaelic/Irish origin. Means: well shaped, graceful. Alternative spelling: Quinlin.

Quintez: Unknown origin and meaning.

Quirino: Unknown origin and meaning. Ethnic background: Hispanic.

Qunicy: Unknown origin and meaning.

Quontavius: Unknown origin and meaning.

r **Raaghib:** Arabic origin. Means: willing, desirous.

Raashid: Arabic origin. Means: pious.

Rab: Teutonic origin. Means: with bright fame. Ethnic background: Scottish.

Rabbaanee: Arabic origin. Means: devotee.

Rabbi: Hebrew origin. Means: my master.

Rabul: Unknown origin and meaning. Ethnic background: Hispanic.

Rachins: Unknown origin and meaning.

Racqueab: Unknown origin and meaning.

Radbert: Anglo-Saxon origin. Means: one who advises the ambassador, red. Nickname: Rad.

Radborne: Anglo-Saxon origin. Means: one who dwells near the red brook. Alternative spellings: Radbourne, Radburn.

Radcliff: Anglo-Saxon origin. Means: from the vermilion cliffs.

Radley: Anglo-Saxon origin. Means: dweller of the red field. Alternative spellings: Redley, Ridley.

Radnor: Anglo-Saxon origin. Means: dweller of the red shore.

Radolf: Anglo-Saxon origin. Means: one who counsels the wolves, warriors.

Radomir: Unknown origin and meaning. Ethnic background: Czech.

Raeshon: Unknown origin and meaning. Alternative spellings: Rayshawn, Rashone, Reshawn.

Rafeé: Arabic origin. Means: of nobility.

Rafeeq: Arabic origin. Means: friend.

Rafferty: Gaelic origin. Means: one who is prosperous.

Raffin: Hebrew origin. Means: God has healed, exalting. Alternative spelling: Rafi.

Raghib: Unknown origin and meaning.

Ragnar: Germanic/Norse origin. Means: a wise leader. Ethnic background: Norwegian.

Rahmaan: Arabic origin. Means: most kind. Alternative spellings: Raheem, Rahmat.

Rainer: Germanic origin. Means: army, prudent leader.

Raleigh: Anglo-Saxon/French origin. Means: dweller of the deer (or bird's) meadow. Alternative spellings: Ralaigh, Ralleigh.

Ralik: Unknown origin and meaning.

Ralis: Unknown origin and meaning.

Ralph: Teutonic/Norse origin. Means: fearless adviser, an agile wolf. Ethnic background: Swiss. Alternative spellings and nicknames: Rafe, Raff, Ralf, Rolf, Rolph.

Ralston: Old English origin. Means: a dweller of Ralph's estate. Alternative spellings: Ralfston, Rolfston

Ramah: Sanskrit origin. Means: pleasing, attested.

Rambert: Germanic origin. Means: brilliant one with power. Alternative spelling: Ramburt.

Ramel: Unknown origin and meaning. Alternative spelling: Raymel.

Rami: Hebrew origin. Means: high, exalted. Alternative spelling: Ramiah.

Ramiro: Germanic/Spanish origin. Means: one who is famous through decisions. Ethnic background: Hispanic.

Ramsden: Anglo-Saxon origin. Means: of the ram's lair.

Ramsey: Old English/Scottish origin. Means: mighty strong island, garlic island. Alternative spelling: Ramsay.

Rance: French origin. Means: exquisite marble.

Ranceford: Unknown origin and meaning.

Randall: Teutonic origin. Means: the shield's edge, a wolf. Alternative spellings: Randal, Randell.

What's in a Nickname?

My son's full name is Giovanni Antonio, and we call him Gino, which isn't the official nickname for Giovanni (Gian, Gianni, Vanni are), but it was a combo between his first and middle names. We liked being able to be creative and to add our own twist to his name.

~ **Veronica S., Macedonia, Ohio**

Randolph: Teutonic origin. Means: the shield's edge, a wolf. Ethnic background: Irish. Alternative spelling: Randolf.

Ranen: Hebrew origin. Means: to be joyous.

Ranger: French origin. Means: keeper of the forest. Alternative spelling: Rainger.

Rankin: Anglo-Saxon origin. Means: little shield, a row or range.

Ransell: Unknown origin and meaning. Alternative spelling: Rancell.

Ransford: Anglo-Saxon origin. Means: from the raven's ford.

Ransley: Anglo-Saxon origin. Means: from the raven's meadow.

Ransom: Anglo-Saxon origin. Means: son of Rand, raven, shield. Alternative spelling: Ransome.

Rante: Unknown origin and meaning.

Raoul: Teutonic/French origin. Means: fearless adviser, an agile wolf. Alternative spellings: Rahul, Rule.

Raphael: Hebrew origin. Means: God will heal. Alternative spellings: Rafael, Rafaelle, Rafaello, Rafal, Refael.

Rashad: Arabic origin. Means: one with good sense. Alternative spellings: RaShaad, Rashard.

Rashard: Unknown origin and meaning.

Rasheed: Arabic origin. Means: righteous.

Rashidi: Egyptian origin. Means: good council. Ethnic background: African.

Rasmus: Greek origin. Means: lovable, one who is well liked.

Rasool: Arabic origin. Means: messenger.

Raul: Teutonic/Spanish origin. Means: one with wisdom and strength. Ethnic background: Hispanic. Alternative spelling: Raunel.

Ravid: Hebrew origin. Means: ornament.

Rawdan: Teutonic origin. Means: from the deer hill. Alternative spellings: Rawden, Rawdin, Rawdon.

Rawlins: Anglo-Saxon origin. Means: son of Ralph/Raleigh, counsel. Alternative spelling: Rawson.

Ray: Teutonic origin. Means: a wise protector.

Raybourne: Anglo-Saxon origin. Means: from the deer brook. Alternative spellings: Rayburn, Raybin.

Raymond: Teutonic origin. Means: a wise protector. Ethnic backgrounds: French, Irish. Alternative spellings and nicknames: Ramond, Ramone, Ray, Raymund, Ramon, Raimondo, Raimund, Raimundo, Raymon, Raymeen.

Raynard: Teutonic origin. Means: brave and wise warrior. Alternative spelling: Raynor.

Razi: Hebrew origin. Means: my secret.

Redford: Anglo-Saxon origin. Means: dweller of the red ford. Alternative spellings: Radford, Ruford, Rufford.

Redman: Anglo-Saxon origin. Means: red-haired adviser.

Redmond: Old English origin. Means: protective counsel. Alternative spellings: Redmund, Radrnund, Redwald.

Reed: Anglo-Saxon origin. Means: red-haired. Alternative spellings: Read, Redd, Reid.

Reese: Welsh origin. Means: ardent, a stream. Alternative spelling: Reece.

Reeve: Old English origin. Means: a bailiff, steward. Alternative spelling: Reave.

Regan: Celtic/Gaelic origin. Means: a king, regal. Alternative spellings: Raegen, Reagan, Reagen, Regen.

Reginald: Teutonic origin. Means: a powerful ruler. Alternative spellings and nicknames: Reggy, Raynold, Reg, Reinhold, Reynold, Reggie, Reginaldo.

Regis: French origin. Means: a ruler.

Regulo: Latin origin. Means: a rule. Ethnic background: Hispanic.

Rehoboam: Unknown origin and meaning.

Reidar: Norse origin. Means: protector of the home. Ethnic background: Norwegian.

Reilly: Unknown origin. Means: valiant. Alternative spellings: Reilley, Ryley.

Reinhard: Germanic origin. Means: one who gives brave advice.

Remigio: Unknown origin and meaning. Ethnic background: Hispanic.

Remington: Anglo-Saxon origin. Means: from the raven farm.

Remus: Latin origin. Means: Rome's founder. Alternative spelling: Remo.

Renato: Latin origin. Means: rebirth, mighty.

Renaud: Teutonic/French origin. Means: with brave and wise power. Alternative spelling: Renault.

Renferd: Teutonic origin. Means: a peacemaker. Alternative spelling: Renfred.

Reno: Unknown origin and meaning.

Renshaw: Anglo-Saxon origin. Means: a dweller of the raven's forest.

Renton: Anglo-Saxon origin. Means: of the raven farm.

Renwick: Teutonic origin. Means: from where the ravens nest.

Renzo: Latin/Italian origin. Means: a laurel.

Reshard: Unknown origin and meaning.

Reuben: Hebrew origin. Means: behold, a son. Alternative spellings and nicknames: Rube, Ruben, Ruby, Rubin, Rubel, Ruva.

Rex: Latin origin. Means: a king.

Rexford: Latin/Anglo-Saxon origin. Means: dweller of the king's castle. Alternative spellings and nicknames: Rexfourd, Rex, Rexferd.

Rey: Latin origin. Means: a king. Alternative spelling: Reyes.

Reynard: Teutonic/French origin. Means: powerful, decisive, a fox. Alternative spellings and nicknames: Rennard, Reinhardt, Renaud, Renard, Reinhard, Raynard, Ray, Rey.

Reynold: Teutonic origin. Means: lasting, decisive ruler. Alternative spellings: Reinald, Reinaldo, Reinhold, Reinold, Renaldo, Rennold, Rinaldo.

Rhett: Old English/Welsh origin. Means: a small stream, with enthusiasm.

Rhodes: Anglo-Saxon origin. Means: one who lives near the crucifix.

Rian: Irish origin. Means: a little king.

Riao: Unknown origin and meaning.

Ribal: Unknown origin. Means: an addition.

Ricardo: Teutonic/Spanish origin. Means: a brave and powerful ruler. Ethnic background: Hispanic. Alternative spellings: Ricard, Riccardo, Rico.

Rice: Anglo-Saxon/Welsh origin. Means: one who is ardent, intense.

Richard: Teutonic origin. Means: a brave and powerful ruler. Ethnic backgrounds: Irish, Scottish, English/Welsh. 38th most popular boy's name of the '90s. Alternative spellings and nicknames: Ritch, Riocard, Ritchie, Richy, Richie, Dicky, Rickie, Rich, Dickie, Rick, Ricki, Ricky, Rico, Rickert, Riki, Ric, Ricard, Ricardo, Riccardo, Dick, Richart, Richerd, Ryszard.

Richman: Anglo-Saxon origin. Means: a powerful man.

Richmond: Teutonic origin. Means: strong guardian, protector of the poor.

Richshae: Unknown origin and meaning.

Rickard: Teutonic/Norse origin. Means: strong guardian, protector of the poor. Ethnic background: Irish. Alternative spellings: Rick, Ricker, Rickert, Rickey, Rickward, Rickwood, Ricky, Rik, Rikkert.

Riddock: Irish origin. Means: from the flatland.

Rider: Old English origin. Means: a horseman, knight. Alternative spelling: Ryder.

Ridge: Anglo-Saxon origin. Means: one who is from the ridge. Alternative spellings: Ridgeway, Rigg.

Ridglee: Old English origin. Means: from the meadow's edge. Alternative spellings: Ridgley, Ridglea.

Ridhaa: Arabic origin. Means: pleasure.

Riemer: Unknown origin and meaning. Ethnic background: Dutch.

Rif'at: Arabic origin. Means: dignity.

Rigby: Anglo-Saxon origin. Means: dweller of the ruler's valley.

Rimon: Hebrew origin. Means: a pomegranate.

Ring: Greek/Old English origin. Means: a ring. Alternative spelling: Ringo.

Riordan: Gaelic origin. Means: the king's poet. Nicknames: Dannie, Dan, Danny.

Rip: Latin/Dutch origin. Means: riverbank, mature, ripe.

Ripley: Anglo-Saxon origin. Means: from the field of the shouter. Alternative spellings and nicknames: Leigh, Rip, Lee, Riply.

Rishab: Unknown origin and meaning.

Rishon: Hebrew origin. Means: first.

Rito: Unknown origin and meaning. Ethnic background: Hispanic.

Rivan: Unknown origin and meaning.

River: Latin origin. Means: flowing water.

Riyaadh: Arabic origin. Means: gardens.

Roald: Teutonic/Norse origin. Means: notable sovereign, mighty ruler. Ethnic background: Norwegian.

Roan: Unknown origin and meaning.

What's in a Nickname?

If people want to be lawyers or other professionals, their names, no matter how unusual or cutesy, won't keep them from it.

~ Angie F., Frisco, Texas

Roar: Teutonic/Norse origin. Means: a famous spearman.

Roarke: Gaelic origin. Means: famed sovereign. Alternative spellings: Rorke, Rourke, Ruark.

Robert: Teutonic origin. Means: one with bright fame. Ethnic backgrounds: English/Welsh, Swiss, Scottish, Irish, French, Polish. 25th most popular boy's name of the '90s. Alternative spellings and nicknames: Robby, Riobard, Robers, Nob, Rob, Rupert, Ruprecht, Roberto, Robinson, Ruperto, Robbie, Robin, Rip, Rab, Bobby, Bobbie, Bob, Bert, Robb.

Robinson: Teutonic/Anglo-Saxon origin. Means: son of Robin, bright fame.

Rocco: Unknown origin and meaning.

Rochester: Old English origin. Means: a rocky citadel. Nicknames: Rockie, Rock, Chet, Chester, Rocky.

Rock: Old English/French origin. Means: a rock, stone.

Rockwell: Old English origin. Means: from the rocky well.

Rocky: Germanic/Anglo-Saxon origin. Means: to rest.

Roderick: Teutonic origin. Means: a noted lord, famous. Ethnic background: Irish. Alternative spellings and nicknames: Rodrique, Rodrigue, Roderigo, Roddie, Rodd, Ruy, Roderic, Rory, Roderich, Rurik, Rodrigo, Rodrick, Roddy, Rod, Ricky, Rick, Broderick, Roderik, Rodriego, Rodrecus.

Rodman: Teutonic/Old English origin. Means: courageous knight's aide, a land clearer. Alternative spellings and nicknames: Roddie, R[...] Roddy, Rod.

Rodney: Teutonic origin. Means: a noted ruler. Nicknames: Rodd, Roddie, Roddy, Rod.

Rodwell: Anglo-Saxon origin. Means: from the spring near the path.

Roemello: Unknown origin and meaning.

Rogan: Irish origin. Means: red-haired one.

Roger: Teutonic origin. Means: a famous spearman. Ethnic background: French. Alternative spellings and nicknames: Rogers, Ruttger, Ruggiero, Rog, Rodgie, Rodge, Rodger, Rutger, Rudiger, Rogerio, Rogelio, Rutgerus, Ruggero.

Roland: Teutonic origin. Means: from the land of fame. Ethnic backgrounds: German, Swiss. Alternative spellings and nicknames: Rolly, Rollo, Roley, Lanny, Lannie, Rollie, Rowland, Rollins, Rolland, Roldan, Rolando, Orlando, Rollin.

Rolf: Germanic origin. Means: famous wolf. Ethnic backgrounds: Swedish, Swiss, Norwegian. Alternative spelling: Rolph.

Rollin: Teutonic origin. Means: famous wolf. Alternative spellings: Rollins, Rollie.

Rolshawn: Unknown origin and meaning.

Rolt: Unknown origin. Means: curving.

Roman: Latin origin. Means: from Rome. Ethnic backgrounds: German, Hispanic. Alternative spellings: Romain, Romanus, Rome.

Rombert: Unknown origin. Means: one who prayed.

Romeo: Latin/Italian origin. Means: pilgrim to Rome, fame. Alternative spellings: Romeon, Romero.

Romney: Latin/Welsh origin. Means: a Roman, from the curving river.

Romulus: Latin origin. Means: citizen/founder of Rome. Alternative spelling: Romulo.

Ronald: Norse origin. Means: one with powerful authority. Ethnic backgrounds: English/Welsh, Irish. Alternative spellings and nicknames: Raghnall, Ranald, Ronny, Renaldo, Ron, Ronnie, Ronaldus.

Ronan: Celtic/Irish origin. Means: an oath, a small seal.

Rondell: Unknown origin and meaning.

Ronson: Norse/Anglo-Saxon origin. Means: son of Ronald, mighty.

Rooney: Gaelic/Irish origin. Means: red-haired hero. Alternative spellings: Rowney, Rowen, Rowan.

Roosevelt: Germanic origin. Means: from the rose field.

Roper: Anglo-Saxon origin. Means: a rope maker.

Roque: Unknown origin. Means: a soldier. Ethnic background: Hispanic.

Rosalio: Unknown origin and meaning. Ethnic background: Hispanic.

Roscoe: Norse origin. Means: from the deer forest. Alternative spellings and nicknames: Ros, Rossie, Rossy, Roz, Ross.

Ross: Teutonic/Gaelic origin. Means: of the peninsula, headland. Ethnic background: Irish. Nicknames: Rossie, Rossy.

Roswell: Teutonic origin. Means: a mighty horse.

Roth: Germanic origin. Means: red-haired one.

Rothwell: Norse origin. Means: from the red spring.

Rotislav: Slavic origin. Means: one who seizes glory. Ethnic background: Russian.

Rover: Anglo-Saxon origin. Means: rambler, one who wanders.

Rovonte: Unknown origin and meaning.

Rowan: Gaelic/Norse origin. Means: little red one, a rowan tree. Alternative spellings: Rowe, Rowen, Rohan.

Rowell: Anglo-Saxon origin. Means: from the deer spring.

Rowley: Old English origin. Means: dweller of the wooded land.

Roy: French/Celtic origin. Means: king, red-haired. Alternative spellings: Ruy, Rey, Roi.

Royal: Latin/French origin. Means: kingly, regal.

Royce: Latin/Old English origin means: king, royal one. Alternative spellings: Roy, Roice.

Royd: Norse origin. Means: dweller of the forest clearing.

Royden: Old English/French origin. Means: from the royal hill.

Rudo: Unknown origin. Means: love. Ethnic background: African.

Rudolph: Teutonic origin. Means: famous wolf. Alternative spellings and nicknames: Dolf, Rudolfo, Rudie, Rollo, Rolfe, Rodolphe, Rodolf, Dolph, Rudolf, Rolph, Rollin, Rodolph, Rodolfo, Raoul, Rudy, Rolf.

Rudyard: Teutonic/Old English origin. Means: eminence, of the red enclosure. Nicknames: Ruddie, Ruddy, Rudd, Rudy.

Rufus: Latin origin. Means: red-haired. Alternative spellings and nicknames: Rufe, Ruff, Ruffe, Rufino.

Rugby: Anglo-Saxon origin. Means: dweller of the raven's estate.

Ruiz: Unknown origin and meaning.

Rumford: Anglo-Saxon origin. Means: dweller of the wide ford.

Rune: Norse origin. Means: secret lore. Ethnic background: Swedish.

Rupert: Germanic origin. Means: one with bright fame. Ethnic background: Irish. Alternative spellings: Ruperto, Ruprecht.

Rurik: Norse/Slavic origin. Means: a famous king.

Rush: French/Old English origin. Means: red-haired one, a grassy plant.

Rushford: Anglo-Saxon origin. Means: dweller of the rush ford.

Ruskin: French origin. Means: red-haired one.

Ruslan: Unknown origin and meaning. Ethnic background: Russian.

Russell: Latin/French origin. Means: little red-haired one. Ethnic backgrounds: English/Welsh. Alternative spellings and nicknames: Rustie, Rus, Russ, Russel, Rusty.

Rustice: Unknown origin. Means: country. Alternative spelling: Rusticus.

Rusty: Old English/French origin. Means: ruddy. Alternative spellings: Rust, Rustem.

Rutherford: Anglo-Saxon origin. Means: from the cattle ford. Alternative spellings and nicknames: Ford, Rutherfurd.

Rutledge: Anglo-Saxon origin. Means: from the red pool.

Rutley: Anglo-Saxon origin. Means: dweller of the root meadow. Alternative spelling: Rutland.

Ruvim: Unknown origin and meaning.

Ryan: Celtic/Gaelic origin. Means: the king's descendant, laughing. Ethnic backgrounds: Irish, English/Welsh. 8th most popular boy's name of the '90s.

Rye: Old English origin. Means: a cereal grass.

Ryker: Unknown origin and meaning.

Rylan: Old English origin. Means: dweller of the rye meadow. Alternative spellings: Ryland, Rycroft.

Ryle: Unknown origin and meaning.

Ryman: Old English origin. Means: a rye merchant.

Ryne: Welsh origin. Means: a ruler.

Ryoichiro: Japanese origin. Unknown meaning.

Ryton: Old English origin. Means: from the rye enclosure.

S

Sa'aadat: Arabic origin. Means: prosperity.

Saadiq: Arabic origin. Means: true.

Saber: French origin. Means: a sword.

Sabino: Latin origin. Means: a Sabine man. Ethnic background: Hispanic.

Sabiryhan: Arabic origin. Means: one who is patient. Ethnic background: Russian. Alternative spellings: Sabir, Saboor.

Sabola: Egyptian origin. Means: pepper. Ethnic background: African.

Sabu: Unknown origin. Means: boy.

Saburo: Japanese origin. Unknown meaning.

Sacco: Unknown origin and meaning. Ethnic background: Dutch.

Sa'd: Arabic origin. Means: felicity.

Sadakichi: Japanese origin. Unknown meaning.

Sadao: Japanese origin. Unknown meaning.

Sadir: Unknown origin and meaning. Ethnic background: Jewish.

Sadoc: Unknown origin. Means: sacred.

Saeed: Arabic origin. Means: one who is happy, lucky. Alternative spelling: Sa'eed.

Safdar: Arabic origin. Means: warrior.

Safford: Anglo-Saxon origin. Means: from the willow ford.

Sageon: Unknown origin and meaning.

Sagiv: Hebrew/Arabic origin. Means: mighty, with strength.

Sagrario: Unknown origin and meaning. Ethnic background: Hispanic.

Sahl: Arabic origin. Means: easy, smooth.

Saif: Arabic origin. Means: sword.

Sainvilus: Unknown origin and meaning.

Sair: Unknown origin. Means: a hermit. Alternative spelling: Saire.

Salaam: Arabic origin. Means: salvation. Alternative spelling: Saalim.

Saleem: Arabic origin. Means: mild, healthy, peace. Alternative spellings: Salaah, Salim.

Salinger: Unknown origin and meaning.

Salisbury: Anglo-Saxon origin. Means: of the fortified guard.

Salvador: Latin origin. Means: of the savior. Ethnic background: Hispanic. Alternative spellings and nicknames: Savior, Sauveur, Sallie, Sal, Xavier, Salvatore, Sally, Salvator.

189

Sam: Hebrew origin. Means: asked of God, to listen. Alternative spellings and nicknames: Shem, Sammie, Sammy.

Sameer: Arabic origin. Means: storyteller. Alternative spelling: Samir.

Samson: Hebrew origin. Means: the brilliant sun. Alternative spellings and nicknames: Sammie, Shem, Sim, Simson, Simpson, Sansone, Sammy, Sam, Sampson, Sanson, Sansen.

Samuel: Hebrew origin. Means: asked of God, to listen. Ethnic backgrounds: Irish, Scottish. 26th most popular boy's name of the '90s. Alternative spellings and nicknames: Sammie, Shem, Sam, Sammy, Samuele, Samual.

Sanborn: Old English origin. Means: from the sandy stream. Alternative spellings and nicknames: Sanburn, Sandy, Sanborne.

Sancho: Latin/Spanish origin. Means: companion, sanctified, sacred. Ethnic background: Hispanic.

Sanders: Greek origin. Means: defender, helper of all men. Alternative spellings and nicknames: Sanderson, Sandor, Sandy, Saunders, Saunderson, Sander, Sandro.

Sanderson: Greek origin. Means: son of Alexander, defender. Alternative spellings: Saunders, Saunderson.

Sandon: Anglo-Saxon origin. Means: from the sandy hill. Alternative spelling: Santon.

Sanford: Anglo-Saxon origin. Means: from the sandy river crossing. Alternative spellings and nicknames: Sandford, Sandy, Sanferd, Sanfourd, Sanfo.

Sanfred: Unknown origin. Means: counsel.

Sanger: Unknown origin and meaning.

Santiago: Spanish origin. Means: in honor of Saint James, his protection. Ethnic background: Hispanic.

Santino: Unknown origin and meaning.

Santo: Spanish origin. Means: holy, protected by the saints.

Sargent: Latin origin. Means: a military attendant, officer. Alternative spellings and nicknames: Sarge, Sargie, Sergeant, Sergent.

Sarna: Unknown origin and meaning.

How to Tell If You've Got a Keeper

When will this name search ever end? It's not as if bells and whistles will go off when you stumble on the name your child was meant to have. But there are tests to see if you've found *the one*. Some are tangible; some rely on more of a gut instinct. But don't be afraid to trust your feelings—after all, your child's name will represent him or her to the world. If the name sounds good but something inside of you doesn't like it, it may be best to find another one.

Satoru: Japanese origin. Unknown meaning.

Saturnino: Latin/Italian origin. Means: agriculture, vegetation, full. Ethnic background: Hispanic.

Saud: Unknown origin and meaning.

Saul: Hebrew origin. Means: prayed for, longed for. Nicknames: Solly, Zollie, Sollie, Zolly, Sol.

Saulat: Arabic origin. Means: dignity.

Saval: Unknown origin and meaning.

Savando: Unknown origin and meaning.

Saverio: Basque/Italian origin. Means: the new house, bright.

Savil: Latin origin. Means: from the willow farm. Alternative spellings: Savill, Saville.

Sawandi: Unknown origin. Means: founder.

Sawao: Japanese origin. Unknown meaning.

Sawyer: Celtic origin. Means: a woodcutter, woodsman. Alternative spellings and nicknames: Saw, Sawyere.

Saxon: Teutonic origin. Means: man of the sword. Nicknames: Sax, Saxe.

Schulz: Unknown origin and meaning.

Schuyler: Dutch origin. Means: scholar, a wise man, shelter. Ethnic background: Dutch. Nickname: Sky.

Scott: Latin origin. Means: one from Scotland. Ethnic backgrounds: English/Welsh. 47th most popular boy's name of the '90s. Alternative spellings and nicknames: Scot, Scotti, Scottie, Scotty.

Seamus: Hebrew/Gaelic origin. Means: supplanted. Ethnic background: Irish.

Sebald: Anglo-Saxon origin. Means: a bold victory. Ethnic background: German.

Sebastian: Greek origin. Means: from Sebasta, majestic, revered. Ethnic backgrounds: English/Welsh, Hispanic. Alternative spellings and nicknames: Sib, Bastien, Basty, Sebastiano, Sebastien, Bastian.

Sedgwick: Old English origin. Means: from near the trees with sharp leaves. Alternative spellings: Sedgewick, Sedgewinn.

Seff: Hebrew origin. Means: a wolf.

Segel: Hebrew origin. Means: treasure.

Seito: Japanese origin. Unknown meaning.

Sekani: Egyptian origin. Means: one rich with laughter. Ethnic background: African.

Sekel: Unknown origin and meaning. Ethnic background: Jewish.

Selby: Teutonic origin. Means: from the farm by the estate. Alternative spelling: Shelby.

Seldon: Old English origin. Means: from the vale of willows. Alternative spellings and nicknames: Donny, Selden, Donnie, Don.

Seled: Hebrew origin. Means: praise, leap for joy.

Selfridge: Unknown origin and meaning.

Selig: Germanic/Old English origin. Means: blessed, holy. Ethnic background: Jewish.

Selwyn: Anglo-Saxon origin. Means: a good friend. Alternative spellings and nicknames: Winny, Wyn, Winnie, Wynn, Selwin.

Sennett: French origin. Means: with wisdom.

Seon: Unknown origin and meaning. Ethnic background: Irish.

Sepp: Hebrew/Germanic origin. Means: God shall add. Ethnic background: German.

Septimus: Latin origin. Means: the seventh.

Serafiel: Unknown origin and meaning. Ethnic background: Hispanic.

Seraphim: Hebrew/Latin origin. Means: burning ones, angels, ardent. Ethnic background: Greek. Alternative spellings: Serafin, Seraphin.

Serapio: Unknown origin and meaning. Ethnic background: Hispanic.

Sereno: Latin origin. Means: bright, calm, serene. Ethnic background: Italian.

Serge: Latin/French origin. Means: attendant, a server. Alternative spellings: Sergio, Sergius, Sergei, Sergeant, Sergei, Sergent, Sergias, Sergius, Sergu, Sergio, Sergeio.

Serle: Teutonic origin. Means: armor, well armed.

Servacio: Unknown origin and meaning. Ethnic background: Hispanic. Alternative spelling: Servando.

Sessue: Japanese origin. Unknown meaning.

Seth: Hebrew origin. Means: appointed, chosen.

Seton: Anglo-Saxon origin. Means: from the coast.

Severen: Latin/Anglo-Saxon origin. Means: severe, from the river boundary. Alternative spellings: Severn, Seve, Severin, Severo.

Sewall: Anglo-Saxon origin. Means: the powerful sea. Alternative spelling: Sewald.

Seward: Anglo-Saxon origin. Means: victorious guardian of the sea. Alternative spelling: Siward.

Sewell: Anglo-Saxon/Teutonic origin. Means: triumphant at sea. Alternative spellings: Sewel, Sewald, Sewall, Sewole, Sewoll.

Sexton: Old English origin. Means: an officer of the church.

Sextus: Latin origin. Means: the sixth-born child.

Seymour: Latin/Old English origin. Means: from the moor by the sea, famous. Nicknames: Morry, Morie, Morrie, Morey.

Shaafee: Arabic origin. Means: healer.

Shadoe: Unknown origin and meaning.

Shadrach: Babylonian origin. Unknown meaning. Alternative spelling: Sadrach.

Shahaab: Arabic origin. Means: flame, brightness.

Shakeel: Arabic origin. Means: handsome.

Shakur: Arabic origin. Means: to thank.

Shalah: Unknown origin and meaning.

Shalem: Hebrew origin. Means: peace, whole. Alternative spellings: Shaleem, Shalom, Sholem, Sholom.

Shalin: Unknown origin and meaning.

Shamel: Unknown origin and meaning.

Shamir: Hebrew origin. Means: a diamond.

Shamrose: Unknown origin and meaning.

Shams: Arabic origin. Means: sun.

Shanahan: Irish origin. Means: sagacious, wise.

Shane: Hebrew/Gaelic origin. Means: God is gracious. Ethnic background: Irish. Alternative spellings: Shayne, Sheign.

Shanley: Irish origin. Means: an ancient hero.

Shareef: Arabic origin. Means: noble.

Sharif: Arabic origin. Means: honest.

Sharvay: Unknown origin and meaning.

Shateek: Unknown origin and meaning.

Shatner: Unknown origin and meaning.

Shatz: Hebrew origin. Unknown meaning.

Shaun: Hebrew/Irish origin. Means: God is gracious. Ethnic backgrounds: English/Welsh, Irish.

Shaw: Old English/Scottish origin. Means: dweller of the grove, terse.

Sheehan: Gaelic/Irish origin. Means: small, peaceable.

Shefer: Hebrew origin. Means: beautiful, pleasant.

Sheffield: Old English origin. Means: from the uneven field. Nicknames: Sheffie, Sheff, Field, Sheffy, Fields.

Sheikh: Unknown origin and meaning.

Sheldon: Anglo-Saxon origin. Means: from the ledge of the hill. Alternative spellings and nicknames: Shelly, Shell, Shelton, Shelley.

Shelton: Anglo-Saxon origin. Means: of the farm near the ledge.

Shep: Old English origin. Means: from the sheep's meadow.

Shepherd: Old English origin. Means: a tender of sheep. Alternative spellings and nicknames: Shepard, Shepp, Sheppard, Shepperd, Sheppy, Shep.

Shepley: Old English origin. Means: from the sheep's meadow. Alternative spellings: Sheply, Shipley.

Shepsil: Hebrew origin. Means: a sheep. Alternative spellings: Shabsi, Shebsil.

Sherard: Anglo-Saxon origin. Means: valorous, courageous. Alternative spelling: Sherrard.

Sherborne: Anglo-Saxon origin. Means: from the clear brook. Alternative spelling: Sherbourn.

Sherlock: Anglo-Saxon origin. Means: light-haired one. Alternative spelling: Sherlocke.

Sherman: Anglo-Saxon origin. Means: a shearer of sheep. Nicknames: Mannie, Manny, Sherm, Shermie, Shermy, Man.

Shermarke: African origin. Means: bringer of good fortune.

Sherrod: Unknown origin and meaning.

Sherwin: Anglo-Saxon origin. Means: one who is quick as the wind, loyal. Alternative spellings and nicknames: Sherwynd, Win, Winny, Winnie.

Sherwood: Anglo-Saxon origin. Means: from the bright forest. Nicknames: Woodie, Woody, Wood.

Shet: Hebrew origin. Means: appointed, garment.

Shianhan: Unknown origin and meaning.

You've Got a Keeper

Can you see the name on a résumé?

~ Elizabeth S.,
New Philadelphia, Ohio

Shigeo: Japanese origin. Unknown meaning.

Shiloh: Unknown origin and meaning.

Shinsei: Japanese origin. Unknown meaning.

Shipton: Anglo-Saxon origin. Means: dweller of the sheep town. Alternative spelling: Skipton.

Shivon: Unknown origin and meaning.

Shloimeh: Hebrew origin. Means: with peace.

Shmiel: Hebrew origin. Means: God has dedicated. Alternative spelling: Shmelke.

Shohaci: Japanese origin. Unknown meaning.

Shoji: Japanese origin. Unknown meaning.

Shota: Unknown origin and meaning. Ethnic background: Russian.

Shotaro: Japanese origin. Unknown meaning.

Shoze: Japanese origin. Unknown meaning.

Shraga: Aramaic origin. Means: light. Ethnic background: Jewish.

Shujaa: Arabic origin. Means: bold.

Siblee: Greek/Anglo-Saxon origin. Means: an oracle, friendly.

Sid: French/Old English origin. Means: of St. Denis, of the riverside meadow.

Siddell: Anglo-Saxon origin. Means: from the wide valley.

Siddeq: Arabic origin. Means: just, true.

Siddon: Unknown origin. Means: a fisherman.

Sidon: Phoenician/Greek origin. Means: to ensnare, linen. Alternative spelling: Sidonius.

Sidras: Latin origin. Means: of the stars, shining.

Sidwel: Celtic/Anglo-Saxon origin. Means: from the broad well, sea. Alternative spellings: Sidwell, Sidwohl.

Siegbert: Germanic origin. Means: famous in victory.

Siegfried: Teutonic origin. Means: triumphant peace. Alternative spellings and nicknames: Siffre, Sig, Siggy, Sigfrid, Sigvard, Siegfrid, Sigfrido.

Siff: Norse origin. Unknown meaning. Ethnic background: Jewish.

Sigleif: Unknown origin and meaning. Ethnic background: Norwegian.

Sigmund: Teutonic origin. Means: protective victory. Alternative spellings and nicknames: Siggie, Sigismundo, Sigsmond, Sig, Sigismondo, Sigismund, Sigismond, Siegmund.

Sigurd: Norse origin. Means: a winning defender. Ethnic background: German. Alternative spelling: Sigvard.

Sigwald: Germanic origin. Means: a victorious ruler.

Sihon: Unknown origin and meaning. Alternative spellings: Sihonn, Sihun, Sihunn.

Silaah: Arabic origin. Means: arms, weapons.

Silas: Greek/Hebrew origin. Means: wood, to ask or borrow.

Silsby: Anglo-Saxon origin. Means: from Sill's farm.

Silvanus: Latin origin. Means: from the forest. Alternative spellings and nicknames: Silvan, Silvain, Sil, Silvano, Sylvanus, Sylvan, Silvio, Silas.

Silverio: Unknown origin and meaning. Ethnic background: Hispanic.

Silvester: Latin origin. Means: person of the woods, woodcutter. Alternative spellings and nicknames: Vest, Silvestre, Silvestro, Sylvester.

Silvio: Latin/Italian origin. Means: silver. Ethnic backgrounds: Hispanic, Swiss.

Simon: Hebrew origin. Means: to hear or be heard. Ethnic backgrounds: Hispanic, English/Welsh. Alternative spellings and nicknames: Siomonn, Sim, Simeon, Simon, Simone, Simeone, Shimon.

Simpson: Hebrew origin. Means: son of Simon, hears. Alternative spelling: Simson.

Sinclair: Latin/French origin. Means: illustrious light, of St. Claire. Nicknames: Sinc, Clair, Clare.

Sion: Hebrew/Welsh origin. Means: God is gracious, exalted.

Siraaj: Arabic origin. Means: sun, a candle.

Sishe: Hebrew origin. Means: sweet. Alternative spelling: Syshe.

Sivan: Assyrian origin. Means: the ninth Jewish month. Ethnic background: Jewish.

Sixto: Latin origin. Means: the sixth-born child. Ethnic background: Hispanic.

Sjoerd: Norse origin. Means: a victorious guardian. Ethnic background: Dutch.

Skelly: Gaelic origin. Means: historian, one who tells stories.

Skelton: Anglo-Saxon origin. Means: dweller of the ledge estate.

Skerrit: Unknown origin and meaning.

Skerry: Norse origin. Means: from the rocky island.

Skip: Norse origin. Means: a ship captain. Alternative spellings and nicknames: Skippie, Skippy, Skipper, Skipp.

Sky: Unknown origin and meaning. Alternative spelling: Skye.

Skyler: Unknown origin and meaning.

Slade: Anglo-Saxon origin. Means: child, valley dweller. Alternative spelling: Slader.

Slate: French origin. Unknown meaning.

Slavario: Unknown origin and meaning.

Slaven: Gaelic origin. Means: mountaineer. Alternative spellings: Slavin, Sleven, Slevin.

Slawomir: Slavic/Polish origin. Means: one with glory and fame.

Slerd: Unknown origin and meaning. Ethnic background: Dutch.

You've Got a Keeper

Try to imagine yelling the name out the back door as loud as you can.

~ Blair F.,
Charlotte, North Carolina

Sly: Latin origin. Means: person of the woods, woodcutter.

Smedley: Anglo-Saxon origin. Means: from the flat meadow.

Smith: Old English origin. Means: blacksmith. Nicknames: Smitty.

Snake: Old English origin. Means: a snake.

Snowden: Anglo-Saxon origin. Means: of the snowy hill.

Snyder: Unknown origin. Means: a tailor.

Socrates: Greek origin. Means: teacher.

Sofio: Greek origin. Means: wisdom. Ethnic background: Hispanic.

Sohil: Unknown origin and meaning.

Sol: Latin/Spanish origin. Means: the beautiful sun. Ethnic background: Jewish.

Solomon: Hebrew origin. Means: a wise man of peace. Alternative spellings and nicknames: Zollie, Solly, Zolly, Sollie, Salomone, Salomo, Salmon, Salomon, Sol, Shalom, Saloman.

Solon: Greek origin. Means: a sage.

Soma: Hungarian origin. Means: a horn.

Somerset: Old English origin. Means: from the summer place. Alternative spellings: Somerton, Somerville.

Sonio: Greek/Slavic origin. Means: sensible, wise. Ethnic background: Hispanic.

Sonnie: Unknown origin and meaning.

Soo: Unknown origin and meaning.

Sorrell: French origin. Means: one with reddish brown hair, sour.

Soslan: Unknown origin and meaning. Ethnic background: Russian.

Sotero: Unknown origin and meaning. Ethnic background: Hispanic.

Southwell: Anglo-Saxon origin. Means: from the southern spring.

Sowa: Unknown origin. Means: an owl.

Spalding: Anglo-Saxon origin. Means: dweller of the split meadow. Alternative spelling: Spaulding.

Speed: Anglo-Saxon origin. Means: prosperity, success.

Spencer: Old English origin. Means: dispenser of supplies, provisioner. 48th most popular boy's name of the '90s. Alternative spellings and nicknames: Spence, Spense, Spenser.

Spengler: Germanic origin. Means: a tinsmith.

Spiridon: Greek/Latin origin. Means: the spirit or soul.

Spiro: Latin origin. Means: breath, to breathe. Ethnic background: Greek.

Sprage: Teutonic origin. Means: one who is quick, alert. Alternative spelling: Sprague.

Sproule: Old English origin. Means: active one. Alternative spelling: Sprowle.

Spyros: Greek origin. Unknown meaning.

Squire: Anglo-Saxon/French origin. Means: attendant, a shield bearer.

Sroli: Unknown origin and meaning. Ethnic background: Jewish.

Stacie: Greek origin. Means: one who shall rise again, resurrection.

Stafford: Old English origin. Means: from the river crossing, the ford. Alternative spellings: Staffard, Staford.

Stan: Old English origin. Means: from the rocky clearing.

Stanbury: Old English origin. Means: from the stone fortress.

Stancliff: Old English origin. Means: dweller of the rocky cliff.

Standfield: Old English origin. Means: dweller of the rocky meadow. Alternative spelling: Stanfield.

Standice: Old English origin. Means: from the rocky grove. Alternative spelling: Standish.

Stanford: Old English origin. Means: from the stone river crossing. Alternative spellings and nicknames: Stan, Ford, Stamford.

Stanhope: Old English origin. Means: from the rocky hollow.

Stanislaus: Slavic/Latin origin. Means: a glorious governor. Ethnic background: Polish. Alternative spellings and nicknames: Stan, Stanislas, Stanislav, Stanislaw.

Stanley: Old English origin. Means: from the rocky clearing. Ethnic background: Irish. Alternative spellings and nicknames: Stannie, Stanly, Lee, Stan, Stanleigh.

Stanmore: Unknown origin and meaning.

Stanton: Old English origin. Means: from the stony place. Alternative spellings and nicknames: Stan, Staunton.

Stanway: Old English origin. Means: from near the stony road.

Stanwick: Old English origin. Means: from the stony town.

Stanwin: Unknown origin and meaning.

Stanwood: Old English origin. Means: from the rocky wood.

Stashu: Unknown origin and meaning.

Stathis: Unknown origin and meaning. Ethnic background: Greek.

Stavros: Unknown origin and meaning. Ethnic background: Greek.

Stedman: Old English origin. Means: farmer, farmstead owner. Alternative spelling: Stedmann.

Steele: Unknown origin and meaning.

Stein: Germanic/Norse origin. Means: hard as a stone, rock. Alternative spellings: Sten, Stijn, Stone.

Steinar: Norse origin. Means: a rock-hard warrior.

Stephen: Greek origin. Means: garland, crowned in victory. Ethnic backgrounds: English/Welsh. 28th most popular boy's name of the '90s. Alternative spellings and nicknames: Stephanus, Stevy, Stefon, Estevan, Stevie, Steven, Steve, Stephan, Stefan, Etienne, Esteban, Steffen, Stephone, Staffan, Stefano, Stepan, Stephane, Stephanio, Stephanos.

Stephenson: Greek origin. Means: son of Stephen, crowned.

Sterne: Old English origin. Means: austere. Alternative spellings: Stern, Stearn, Stearne.

Steve: Greek origin. Means: garland, crowned in victory. Ethnic backgrounds: English/Welsh.

Stevenson: Greek origin. Means: son of Steven, crowned.

Stewart: Old English origin. Means: a bailiff, estate manager. Alternative spellings and nicknames: Stu, Stew, Stuart, Steward.

Stillman: Anglo-Saxon origin. Means: tranquil, peaceful.

Stilwell: Anglo-Saxon origin. Means: a quiet, calm stream.

Stinson: Unknown origin and meaning.

Stockley: Old English origin. Means: from the tree-lined meadow.

Stockwell: Old English origin. Means: from the tree-lined spring.

Stoddard: Old English origin. Means: a person who tends horses.

Stoke: Old English origin. Means: a village dweller.

Stonwin: Unknown origin and meaning.

Strahan: Irish origin. Means: a poet.

Stratford: Old English origin. Means: from the river's street crossing.

Strom: Greek origin. Means: a bed or mattress.

Stroud: Old English origin. Means: from the thicket.

Struthers: Old English origin. Means: from the stream.

Styles: Old English origin. Means: of the stiles.

Suffield: Old English origin. Means: from the southern field.

Sujith: Unknown origin and meaning.

Sullivan: Irish origin. Means: black-eyed one.

Sully: Old English origin. Means: from the southern meadow.

Sultan: Arabic origin. Means: king, power. Ethnic background: Russian. Alternative spelling: Sultaan.

Sumner: Latin/French origin. Means: a caller, one who summons.

Sun: Greek origin. Means: reference to the sun.

Sunny: Unknown origin and meaning.

Surem: Unknown origin and meaning. Ethnic background: Russian.

Susi: Unknown origin. Means: horseman. Alternative spelling: Sussi.

Suskov: Unknown origin. Means: a gopher.

Sutcliff: Old English origin. Means: from the south cliff.

Sutemi: Japanese origin. Unknown meaning.

Sutherland: Norse origin. Means: one from the southern lands.

Sutton: Old English origin. Means: from the southern estate.

Sven: Norse/Swedish origin. Means: one with youth. Alternative spelling: Svein.

You've Got a Keeper

Think about how the name will look in print, on graduation day, on wedding announcements.

~ **Audra H., Richmond, Texas**

Sverre: Norse origin. Means: to swirl about, restless.

Swain: Teutonic origin. Means: a young helper. Alternative spellings and nicknames: Swane, Swaine, Swayne, Sweyn.

Sweeney: Irish origin. Means: a little hero.

Swithbart: Old English origin. Means: a landowner. Alternative spelling: Swithbert.

Sybren: Unknown origin and meaning. Ethnic background: Dutch.

Symington: Anglo-Saxon origin. Means: from Simon's dwelling.

Synjin: Unknown origin and meaning.

Taaj: Arabic origin. Means: crown.

Taalib: Arabic origin. Means: inquirer.

Tab: Germanic/Anglo-Saxon origin. Means: brilliant, a drummer. Alternative spelling: Tabb.

Tabansi: African origin. Means: one who endures patiently.

Tabber: Persian origin. Means: drummer, a drum. Alternative spellings: Taber, Tabor.

Tacio: Unknown origin and meaning. Ethnic background: Hispanic.

Tadaatsu: Japanese origin. Unknown meaning.

Tadashi: Japanese origin. Unknown meaning.

Tadd: Welsh origin. Means: father.

Tadeo: Aramaic/Spanish origin. Means: courageous, one who praises. Alternative spellings: Taddeo, Tadeusz.

Taggert: Gaelic origin. Means: a prelate, religious dignitary.

Tahaw-wur: Arabic origin. Means: bravery.

Tailor: Latin/French origin. Means: to cut, a tailor.

Takahiro: Unknown origin and meaning.

Takashi: Japanese origin. Unknown meaning. Alternative spelling: Takeshi.

Takehide: Japanese origin. Unknown meaning.

Takeo: Japanese origin. Unknown meaning.

Takuji: Japanese origin. Unknown meaning.

Tal'at: Arabic origin. Means: appearance.

Talbot: French origin. Means: a bloodhound, pillager. Alternative spellings and nicknames: Tallie, Tally, Talbert, Tallbot, Talbott, Tallbott.

Talmadge: Anglo-Saxon origin. Means: the lake between the towns.

Talyn: Unknown origin and meaning.

Tamarcus: Unknown origin and meaning.

Tamayo: Unknown origin and meaning.

Tameez: Arabic origin. Means: judgment.

Tamio: Japanese origin. Unknown meaning.

Tamir: Arabic/Hebrew origin. Means: pure, tall, stately.

Tamkeen: Arabic origin. Means: power.

Tancredo: Germanic/Italian origin. Means: of thoughtful counsel. Ethnic background: Hispanic.

Tanel: Hebrew origin. Means: God is my judge.

Tanton: Old English origin. Means: from the river estate.

Taqee: Arabic origin. Means: devout.

Taran: Celtic/Welsh origin. Unknown meaning.

Taray: Unknown origin and meaning.

Tariq: Arabic origin. Means: to come at night, morning star. Alternative spelling: Taariq.

Tarleton: Old English origin. Means: from the thunderous estate.

Taro: Unknown origin and meaning.

Tarp: Unknown origin and meaning.

Tarrant: Welsh origin. Means: thunder.

Tarrsus: Unknown origin and meaning. Alternative spelling: Tarsus.

Tartan: Unknown origin. Means: chief. Alternative spellings: Tarton, Tarttan.

Tarus: Unknown origin and meaning.

Tasadduq: Arabic origin. Means: to give alms.

Tasheem: Unknown origin and meaning. Alternative spelling: Tashiem.

Tate: Teutonic/Anglo-Saxon origin. Means: one who is cheerful. Alternative spellings: Tait, Taite.

Tau: Egyptian origin. Means: a lion. Ethnic background: African.

Taurino: Unknown origin. Means: bull-like. Ethnic background: Hispanic. Alternative spelling: Taurean.

Tavanna: Unknown origin and meaning.

Tavaris: Unknown origin and meaning. Alternative spelling: Tavoris.

Tavis: Celtic/Gaelic origin. Means: a twin. Alternative spellings and nicknames: Tav, Tavish, Tevis.

Tavon: Unknown origin and meaning.

Tawqeer: Arabic origin. Means: honor.

Tayib: Indic origin. Means: delicate, good. Alternative spelling: Tay-yib.

Tayon: Unknown origin and meaning.

Tayor: Unknown origin and meaning.

Taysean: Unknown origin and meaning.

Teague: Gaelic/Irish origin. Means: a poet. Alternative spelling: Teage.

Tearle: Old English origin. Means: serious, austere, harsh. Alternative spelling: Terle.

Teclo: Greek origin. Means: divine, renowned fame. Ethnic background: Hispanic.

Ted: Greek origin. Means: God's divine gift.

Teddman: Teutonic/Anglo-Saxon origin. Means: protector of the nation. Alternative spellings: Tedman, Tedmann, Tedmond, Tedmund.

Teillo: Unknown origin. Means: bright. Alternative spelling: Teilo.

Teivel: Hebrew origin. Means: beloved one.

Telesforo: Greek origin. Means: to bring to an end. Ethnic background: Hispanic.

Telford: Latin/French origin. Means: a shallow stream, an iron cutter. Alternative spellings: Tellford, Telfor, Telfore, Telfour.

Telly: Greek origin. Means: God's divine gift.

Teman: Hebrew origin. Means: the right side.

Templeton: Old English origin. Means: from the city of the temple. Nicknames: Temp, Temple.

Teng: Unknown origin. Means: mound.

Teniya: Unknown origin and meaning.

Tennessee: Native American origin. Unknown meaning.

Tennyson: Greek origin. Means: son of Dennis, of wine, drama, and revelry.

Teo: Greek origin. Means: God's divine gift. Ethnic background: Hispanic.

Teofilo: Greek/various origin. Means: God's beloved. Ethnic background: Hispanic.

Teogenes: Greek origin. Unknown meaning. Ethnic background: Hispanic.

Tereso: Unknown origin and meaning. Ethnic background: Hispanic.

Terje: Norse origin. Means: of Thor's spear.

Terrance: Latin origin. Means: polished, tender. Alternative spellings: Terencio, Terrence, Terrerce.

Terrell: Teutonic/Old English origin. Means: warlike, thunderous ruler. Alternative spellings: Tirrell, Terrill, Tarrell, Tyrell, Tyrelle.

Terris: Latin/Teutonic origin. Means: son of Terry, polished. Alternative spelling: Terrezz.

Territus: Unknown origin and meaning. Alternative spelling: Teritus.

Tesei: Unknown origin and meaning.

Tesfay: Unknown origin. Means: hope.

Tetsuo: Japanese origin. Unknown meaning.

Tevin: Unknown origin and meaning. Alternative spelling: Tevyn.

Thaabit: Arabic origin. Means: brave.

Thackeray: Old English origin. Means: one who works on roofs.

Thad: Unknown origin and meaning.

My husband's method is to put it on his business card to see if it looks strange—or if he gets any visions of exotic dancers.

~ **Tarrant F., Eugene, Oregon**

Thaddeus: Greek/Latin origin. Means: God's gift, full of praise. Alternative spellings and nicknames: Taddeusz, Taddy, Tad, Thaddaus, Thad, Taddeo, Tadd, Tadeo, Thaddaeus, Thaddous, Thadeus.

Thambo: African origin. Means: ground.

Thane: Anglo-Saxon origin. Means: attendant, one who follows. Alternative spellings: Thaine, Thayne.

Tharwat: Arabic origin. Means: influence.

Thatcher: Anglo-Saxon origin. Means: one who thatches roofs. Alternative spellings and nicknames: Thaxter, Thacher, Thatch, Thackeray.

Thayer: Teutonic origin. Means: of the national army. Nickname: Thay.

Thelonious: Teutonic/Latin origin. Means: famous ruler of the people.

Themetri: Unknown origin and meaning.

Themistoklis: Greek origin. Unknown meaning.

Theobald: Teutonic origin. Means: bravest prince of the people. Alternative spellings and nicknames: Toiboid, Tiebout, Tibold, Thibaut, Thibaud, Thebault, Teddy, Teddie, Tedd, Dietbold, Theo, Teobaldo, Tybalt, Ted.

Theodore: Greek origin. Means: God's divine gift. Alternative spellings and nicknames: Tedd, Theodorous, Thodore, Theo, Tad, Feodore, Dode, Teddy, Teddie, Tudor, Theodor, Teodoro, Teodor, Ted, Feodor, Dore, Teodardo, Teodosio, Teodulo, Theodoris, Theodoros, Theodorus.

Theodoric: Teutonic origin. Means: ruler of the people. Alternative spellings and nicknames: Teodorico, Tedric, Teddy, Teddie, Derk, Theo, Tedd, Rick, Ted, Dietrich, Dieter, Dirk, Derrick, Derek.

Theon: Greek origin. Means: one who is godly, divine.

Theophrastos: Greek origin. Unknown meaning.

Theron: Greek origin. Means: a hunter. Alternative spelling: Therron.

Thierry: Teutonic/French origin. Means: of the people's rule.

Thomas: Aramaic/Greek/Hebrew origin. Means: a twin. Ethnic backgrounds: Scottish, English/Welsh, Irish. 22nd most popular boy's name of the '90s. Alternative spellings and nicknames: Tome, Thoma, Thom, Tammie, Massey, Tam, Tommy, Tommie, Tomas, Tomlin, Tomkin, Tomaso, Tammy, Tamas, Tom, Thommy.

Thor: Norse origin. Means: thunderous. Alternative spellings and nicknames: Tyrus, Torre, Torin, Thorin, Tor, Tore, Thorr, Torr.

Thorald: Teutonic origin. Means: ruler of thunder. Alternative spellings: Torald, Thorold.

Thorbert: Norse/Teutonic origin. Means: brilliance, Thor's glory. Alternative spellings: Torbart, Torbert.

Thoreau: Unknown origin and meaning.

Thorley: Norse/Teutonic origin. Means: from Thor's meadow. Alternative spelling: Torley.

Thorndike: Old English origin. Means: from the bank of thorns. Alternative spellings and nicknames: Thorn, Thornie, Thorny, Thorndyke.

Thorne: Old English origin. Means: one who dwells near the thorn tree.

Thornley: Old English origin. Means: from the thorny meadow.

Thornton: Old English origin. Means: from the thorny village. Nicknames: Thorn, Thornie, Thorny.

Thorpe: Teutonic/Anglo-Saxon origin. Means: from the small town.

Thurber: Unknown origin and meaning.

Thurgood: Norse/Old English origin. Means: Thor is good.

Thurlow: Norse/Old English origin. Means: from Thor's mountain. Alternative spelling: Thorlow.

Thurman: Norse/Old English origin. Means: protected by Thor, his servant. Alternative spellings: Thurmond, Thorman, Thurmann, Thorman, Thormond, Thormund.

Thurston: Norse/Old English origin. Means: Thor's precious stone. Alternative spellings: Thorstein, Thorsten, Thurstan.

Tiberio: Latin/Italian origin. Means: of the Tiber River. Ethnic background: Hispanic. Alternative spellings: Tibor, Tiburcio.

Tierell: Unknown origin. Means: serious.

Tiernan: Gaelic/Anglo-Saxon origin. Means: in reference to the Lord, regal. Ethnic background: Irish. Alternative spelling: Tierney.

Ties: Unknown origin and meaning. Ethnic background: Dutch.

Tilden: Anglo-Saxon origin. Means: from the rich valley.

Tilford: Anglo-Saxon origin. Means: one from the productive ford. Alternative spellings: Tillford, Tillfourd.

Tillio: Unknown origin. Means: captive. Alternative spelling: Tillo.

Tilton: Anglo-Saxon origin. Means: from the good estate.

Tim: Greek origin. Means: one who honors and fears God. Ethnic backgrounds: English/Welsh.

Timon: Greek origin. Means: one who honors and fears God. Ethnic background: Hispanic.

Timothy: Greek origin. Means: one who honors and fears God. Ethnic backgrounds: Irish, English/Welsh. 33rd most popular boy's name of the '90s. Alternative spellings and nicknames: Tymon, Timothee, Timofei, Timmie, Timotheus, Timoteo, Timmy, Tim, Timeth.

Tirso: Greek origin. Means: a vine-decked staff. Ethnic background: Hispanic.

Titus: Greek origin. Means: a titan, giant. Nicknames: Tite, Tito.

Tobias: Hebrew/Greek origin. Means: God is good. Ethnic background: Hispanic. Alternative spellings and nicknames: Tobit, Tobie, Tobiah, Tobe, Tobia, Toby, Tobin, Tobias.

Toda: Hebrew origin. Means: thanks, thankful.

Todd: Latin/Old English origin. Means: a fox. Ethnic backgrounds: English/Welsh. Alternative spellings and nicknames: Toddie, Toddy, Tod.

Toft: Old English origin. Means: from the small farm.

Tokunosuke: Japanese origin. Unknown meaning.

Toland: Anglo-Saxon origin. Means: from land that is taxed. Alternative spelling: Tolland.

Tollman: Anglo-Saxon origin. Means: a collector of taxes. Alternative spellings: Tollmann, Tolman, Tolmann.

Tom: Aramaic/Greek/Hebrew origin. Means: a twin.

Tomer: Hebrew origin. Means: a palm tree, righteous.

Tomiek: Unknown origin and meaning.

Tomkin: Anglo-Saxon origin. Means: little Tom.

Tomlin: Anglo-Saxon origin. Means: the little twin.

Tomo: Aramaic/Japanese origin. Means: a twin.

Tonino: Unknown origin and meaning. Ethnic background: Italian.

Tony: Latin origin. Means: inestimable, above worth.

Tooru: Japanese origin. Unknown meaning.

Torbjorn: Norse/Teutonic origin. Means: a bear, (Thorlike).

Torfinn: Unknown origin and meaning. Ethnic background: Norwegian.

Torgrim: Unknown origin and meaning. Ethnic background: Norwegian.

Toribio: Latin origin. Unknown meaning. Ethnic background: Hispanic.

Torkild: Norse origin. Means: Thor's cauldron.

Tormey: Irish origin. Means: spirit of the thunder.

Torolf: Norse origin. Means: a wolf, Thorlike.

Torpin: Unknown origin and meaning.

Torrance: Gaelic/Irish origin. Means: from the knolls. Alternative spellings and nicknames: Torrence, Torr, Torry, Tore, Torrey, Torey.

Torray: Celtic origin. Means: from the tower. Alternative spellings: Totty, Torey.

Torrlow: Unknown origin and meaning.

Torsten: Norse origin. Means: the stone of Thor. Ethnic backgrounds: German, Swedish. Alternative spelling: Torstein.

Torvald: Norse origin. Means: Thor's rule.

Towland: Unknown origin and meaning.

Townley: Anglo-Saxon origin. Means: from the town's meadow.

Townsend: Anglo-Saxon origin. Means: from the end of town. Alternative spellings and nicknames: Town, Townie, Towny, Towson.

Towrey: Unknown origin and meaning. Alternative spelling: Towroy.

Toyd: Unknown origin and meaning.

Toyokazu: Japanese origin. Unknown meaning.

Tracay: Greek/Latin origin. Means: brave fighter, bold, reaper.

Trahern: Celtic/Welsh origin. Means: one with strength of iron. Alternative spellings and nicknames: Tray, Trahurn.

Tranquilino: Unknown origin and meaning. Ethnic background: Hispanic.

Traugott: Teutonic origin. Means: God's truth. Ethnic background: German.

Travis: Latin/French origin. Means: from the road crossing. 44th most popular boy's name of the '90s. Alternative spellings: Traver, Travers.

Trayvarous: Unknown origin and meaning.

Tre: Unknown origin and meaning.

Treat: Unknown origin and meaning.

Tredway: Anglo-Saxon origin. Means: mighty warrior.

Tremayne: Celtic/Welsh origin. Means: ruins, from near the circle of stones. Alternative spelling: Tremain.

Trenton: Latin/Welsh origin. Means: from the stream with swift current. Alternative spellings: Trenten, Trent, Trynton.

Trevon: Unknown origin and meaning. Alternative spellings: TreVaughn, Trevino.

Trevor: Celtic/Welsh origin. Means: man of wisdom, discreet. Alternative spellings and nicknames: Trev, Treavor, Trevar.

Trey: Unknown origin and meaning.

Trigg: Norse origin. Means: true.

Trinidad: Latin/Spanish origin. Means: three, the trinity. Ethnic background: Hispanic.

Tripp: Anglo-Saxon origin. Means: a traveler.

Tristram: Latin/Celtic origin. Means: full of sorrow, intrepid. Alternative spellings: Tristen, Tristian, Tristin, Trysten.

Trivini: Unknown origin and meaning. Ethnic background: Italian.

Troy: French origin. Means: one who has curly hair.

Troyal: Unknown origin and meaning.

Truesdale: Anglo-Saxon origin. Means: from the beloved's farm.

Truls: Unknown origin and meaning. Ethnic background: Norwegian.

Truman: Anglo-Saxon origin. Means: a faithful man, loyal.

Trumble: Anglo-Saxon origin. Means: one with boldness and strength.

Trygve: Norse origin. Means: trustworthy, trust.

Tsalani: African origin. Means: good-bye.

Tsutomu: Japanese origin. Unknown meaning.

Tucker: Old English origin. Means: a thickener or tucker of cloth. Nicknames: Tucky, Tuck, Tuckie.

Tudor: Greek/Welsh origin. Means: God's gracious gift.

Tullio: Latin/Spanish origin. Means: lively. Ethnic background: Italian. Alternative spelling: Tulio.

Tullius: Latin/Italian origin. Means: a king, a rank. Alternative spellings: Tuli, Tullus, Tullusus.

Tully: Latin/Gaelic origin. Means: religious, serene, with God's peace. Alternative spellings and nicknames: Tull, Tulley.

Tupper: Anglo-Saxon origin. Means: one who raises rams.

Turlough: Gaelic origin. Means: an instigator. Ethnic background: Irish.

Turner: Latin/French origin. Means: a lathe worker, tournament champion.

Tutto: Unknown origin and meaning.

Tuxford: Norse origin. Means: from the spearman's ford.

Twain: Old English origin. Means: to cut in two.

Twimell: Unknown origin and meaning.

Twyford: Anglo-Saxon origin. Means: of the crossing at the double river.

Ty: Latin/Anglo-Saxon origin. Means: of Tyre, an enclosure. Alternative spelling: Tye.

Tybalt: Teutonic origin. Means: one who can lead the people. Alternative spellings and nicknames: Thibaut, Tybald, Theobald, Ty.

Tyberrius: Unknown origin and meaning.

Tychon: Unknown origin. Means: a winegrower. Alternative spellings: Tychonn, Tichon, Tichonn, Ticon.

Tyece: Unknown origin and meaning. Alternative spelling: Tiyeze.

Tykearon: Unknown origin and meaning.

Tylar: Anglo-Saxon origin. Means: a maker of tiles or bricks. Alternative spelling: Tylor.

Tylow: Unknown origin and meaning.

Tynan: Gaelic origin. Means: dark, sovereign. Nickname: Ty.

Tyran: Unknown origin and meaning.

Tyre: Latin origin. Means: one from Tyre. Alternative spellings: Tyree, Tyreie.

Tyriek: Unknown origin and meaning.

Tyrone: Greek origin. Means: a ruler with absolute power. Nickname: Ty.

Tyshawn: Unknown origin and meaning.

Tyson: Teutonic/French origin. Means: son of the German. Alternative spellings and nicknames: Sonny, Ty, Tysson.

Tyus: Unknown origin and meaning.

U

Uba: African origin. Means: wealthy.

Ubald: Unknown origin. Means: brave one. Alternative spellings: Ubaldo, Ube.

Ubanwa: African origin. Means: wealth in children.

Uberio: Unknown origin and meaning. Ethnic background: Italian.

Udeh: Hebrew origin. Means: praise.

Udel: Anglo-Saxon origin. Means: one who is wealthy.

Udell: Anglo-Saxon origin. Means: from the valley of the yew tree. Alternative spellings and nicknames: Dell, Del, Udale, Udall.

Udenwa: African origin. Means: child's fame.

Udo: Teutonic origin. Means: one with great fortune, prosperous. Ethnic background: German.

Udolf: Teutonic/Anglo-Saxon origin. Means: prosperous one, wolf.

Ugo: African/Italian origin. Means: eagle, of bright mind and spirit. Ethnic background: Swiss.

Ulas: Unknown origin and meaning.

Ulbrich: Unknown origin and meaning. Ethnic background: German.

Ulf: Norse origin. Means: wolf. Ethnic backgrounds: Norwegian, Swedish.

Ulfat: Arabic origin. Means: friendship.

Ulfred: Anglo-Saxon origin. Means: a wolf of peace. Alternative spelling: Ulfrido.

Ulgar: Anglo-Saxon origin. Means: a wolf spear.

Ulick: Norse/Teutonic origin. Means: the spirit of play, a noble ruler. Ethnic background: Irish.

Ulland: Teutonic origin. Means: of the noble land. Alternative spellings: Ullund, Uland.

Ullock: Anglo-Saxon origin. Means: wolf's sport.

Ulmer: Norse/Anglo-Saxon origin. Means: famous wolf. Alternative spelling: Ulmar.

Ulric: Teutonic origin. Means: wolf ruler, a strong brave ruler. Alternative spellings and nicknames: Rickie, Ulrick, Ricky, Rick, Ric, Ulrich, Ulrico.

Ultan: Gaelic/Irish origin. Means: a man from Ulster. Alternative spelling: Ultann.

Ulysses: Greek/Latin origin. Means: wrathful, to hate. Alternative spellings: Ulises, Ulick, Ulisse, Ulysee, Ulyses.

Umar: Arabic origin. Unknown meaning. Ethnic background: Russian.

Umberto: Germanic/Italian origin. Means: a famous warrior.

Unitas: Unknown origin and meaning.

Unwin: Anglo-Saxon origin. Means: one who is unfriendly.

Updike: Unknown origin and meaning.

Upton: Anglo-Saxon origin. Means: from the town on the hill.

Upwood: Anglo-Saxon origin. Means: from the upper forest.

Urban: Latin origin. Means: city dweller, worldly wise. Alternative spellings: Urbanus, Urbain, Urbano, Urbaine.

Uri: Hebrew origin. Means: God is my flame. Alternative spelling: Ury.

Urian: Greek origin. Means: from heaven, greatest. Alternative spelling: Urion.

Urias: Unknown origin and meaning. Ethnic background: Hispanic. Alternative spelling: Uraeus.

Urien: Celtic/Welsh origin. Means: one of privileged birth.

Urs: Latin/Germanic origin. Means: a bear. Ethnic background: Swiss. Alternative spelling: Urso.

Usaid: Arabic origin. Means: small lion.

Usaku: Japanese origin. Unknown meaning.

Utz: Teutonic/Germanic origin. Means: wolf ruler, a strong brave ruler. Ethnic background: German.

Uwe: Teutonic origin. Means: a universal ruler. Ethnic backgrounds: German, Swiss.

Uziel: Hebrew origin. Means: God is my strength.

Uzondu: African origin. Means: the way of life.

V

Vachel: French origin. Means: one who tends the cattle. Alternative spellings: Vachil, Vachell, Vachill.

Vail: Anglo-Saxon origin. Means: residing in the valley. Alternative spellings: Valle, Vale.

Vakhtang: Unknown origin and meaning. Ethnic background: Russian.

Valdes: Teutonic/Norse origin. Means: battle hero, one who rules. Alternative spellings: Valdis, Valdas, Vladas, Vlad.

Valentin: Latin/French origin. Means: one who is strong and healthy, valiant. Ethnic backgrounds: Russian, German. Alternative spellings: Valente, Valentino.

Valerian: Latin origin. Means: one who is strong and healthy, valiant. Alternative spellings and nicknames: Valerius, Val, Valeria, Valerio.

Valery: Germanic/French origin. Means: one with foreign powers. Ethnic background: Russian.

Vallis: French origin. Means: a Welshman.

Van Ness: Dutch origin. Means: dwells near the headland.

Van Wyck: Dutch origin. Unknown meaning.

Van: Dutch origin. Means: signifies of or from.

Vance: Dutch origin. Means: son of Van, thresher. Alternative spelling: Van.

Vancouver: Unknown origin and meaning.

Vander: Dutch origin. Means: signifies of or from.

Vandyke: Dutch origin. Means: dwells near the dike. Alternative spelling: Van Dyke.

Varden: Celtic/French origin. Means: from the green hill. Alternative spellings: Verdon, Vardon.

Vareck: Anglo-Saxon origin. Means: from the stronghold. Alternative spelling: Varick.

Varian: Latin origin. Means: capricious, variable. Alternative spellings: Varien, Varion.

Vasallo: Unknown origin. Means: a vassal.

Vasco: Basque/Spanish origin. Means: a crow.

Vasilek: Unknown origin. Means: a protector.

Vasilios: Greek origin. Means: with royal blood, regal. Alternative spellings: Vasilis, Vassilis, Vassily, Vasso.

Vasyuta: Unknown origin and meaning.

Vaughn: Celtic/Welsh origin. Means: little one. Alternative spelling: Vaughan.

Vegard: Norse origin. Means: protection.

Velvel: Hebrew origin. Means: a wolf.

Venancio: Unknown origin and meaning. Ethnic background: Hispanic.

Venceslao: Slavic/Czech origin. Means: one with great glory. Ethnic background: Hispanic.

Venerio: Unknown origin and meaning. Ethnic background: Hispanic.

Verald: Unknown origin and meaning.

Verek: Unknown origin and meaning.

Veremundo: Unknown origin and meaning. Ethnic background: Hispanic.

Verge: Anglo-Saxon origin. Means: one who owns four acres.

Vern: Latin origin. Means: one who is youthful.

Verney: French origin. Means: from the alder grove. Alternative spelling: Varney.

Vernon: Latin/French origin. Means: springlike, youthful, of the alders. Alternative spellings and nicknames: Lavern, Laverne, Vern, Verne, Verney.

Vero: Unknown origin and meaning. Ethnic background: Hispanic.

Verrall: French origin. Means: true. Alternative spellings: Verrell, Veryl, Verrill, Vere.

Vic: Latin/French origin. Means: the victor, one from the town. Alternative spelling: Vick.

Victor: Latin origin. Means: victorious, a conqueror. Ethnic backgrounds: French, Russian, Hispanic, Swiss. Alternative spellings and nicknames: Vitorio, Vic, Vick, Vittorio, Viktor, Vittore.

Vidal: Spanish origin. Means: vital, life. Ethnic background: Hispanic.

Viggo: Danish/Latin origin. Means: pertaining to war. Ethnic background: Norwegian.

Vigor: Latin origin. Means: with force, energy.

Vince: Latin origin. Means: conqueror, to conquer.

Vincent: Latin origin. Means: conqueror, to conquer. Ethnic backgrounds: Czech, French, Irish. 47th most popular boy's name of the '90s. Alternative spellings and nicknames: Vin, Vincentius, Vincenty, Vinnie, Vicente, Vince, Vincente, Vincenz, Vinny, Vincenzo, Vinzenz.

Vinson: Latin/Anglo-Saxon origin. Means: son of Vincent, conqueror's son.

Virgil: Latin origin. Means: bearer of the staff, thriving, strong. Alternative spellings and nicknames: Virgie, Vergil, Virgy, Virg, Virgilio, Verge, Virge.

Virtudes: Latin/Spanish origin. Means: with manly qualities, virtuous. Ethnic background: Hispanic.

Vitaly: Latin origin. Means: life, lively. Ethnic background: Russian.

Viterbo: Unknown origin and meaning. Ethnic background: Hispanic.

Vitezslav: Unknown origin and meaning. Ethnic background: Czech.

Vitold: Unknown origin and meaning. Ethnic background: Russian.

Vitus: Latin origin. Means: of life, lively. Ethnic background: German. Alternative spellings: Vito, Vite.

Viviano: Latin origin. Means: alive, lively, full of life. Ethnic background: Hispanic.

Vladimir: Slavic origin. Means: prince of all, of royal fame. Ethnic backgrounds: Czech, Russian. Alternative spellings and nicknames: Vladamir, Wladimir, Waldemar, Vladimar, Vladi, Vladamar, Valdemar.

Vladislav: Slavic origin. Means: one of great glory. Alternative spelling: Vyacheslav.

Vlastibor: Unknown origin and meaning. Ethnic background: Czech.

Vlastimil: Slavic origin. Unknown meaning. Ethnic background: Czech.

Volf: Anglo-Saxon/Hebrew origin. Means: a wolf, strength.

Volker: Teutonic origin. Means: of the people's army. Ethnic background: German.

Volkhard: Unknown origin and meaning. Ethnic background: German.

Volkov: Unknown origin. Means: a wolf. Alternative spelling: Volkow.

Volney: Teutonic origin. Means: the spirit of the people. Alternative spelling: Volny.

Voss: Unknown origin. Means: a fox.

Vovcenko: Unknown origin. Means: a wolf.

Vyatt: Unknown origin and meaning.

W **Wade:** Anglo-Saxon origin. Means: a rover, living at the river crossing. Alternative spelling: Wayde.

Wadley: Anglo-Saxon origin. Means: from the advancer's meadow. Alternative spelling: Weddell.

Wadsworth: Anglo-Saxon origin. Means: from the advancer's estate. Alternative spellings and nicknames: Waddie, Waddy, Wadesworth.

Wagner: Germanic origin. Means: one who makes wagons.

Wahab: Arabic origin. Means: a gift.

Waheed: Arabic origin. Means: unique.

Wainwright: Old English origin. Means: one who makes wagons. Alternative spellings and nicknames: Wain, Wayne, Wright.

Waite: Old English origin. Means: a watchman, protector.

Wake: Anglo-Saxon origin. Means: alert.

Wakefield: Old English origin. Means: dweller of Wake's field, wetland. Nicknames: Field, Wake.

Wakeley: Old English origin. Means: dweller of Wake's meadow.

Wakeman: Old English origin. Means: a watchman, protector.

Walcott: Anglo-Saxon origin. Means: from the Welsh cottage, full cloth. Alternative spelling: Walcot.

Waldemar: Teutonic origin. Means: famous sovereign, strong, powerful. Ethnic background: German. Alternative spellings and nicknames: Waldimar, Wallie, Wally, Valdemar, Wald, Waldo.

Walden: Teutonic origin. Means: mighty ruler, from the forest.

Waldo: Teutonic origin. Means: a powerful ruler. Alternative spellings and nicknames: Wally, Wallie, Wald, Waldron, Waldos.

Waldon: Anglo-Saxon origin. Means: from the Welshman's hill.

Waldron: Teutonic origin. Means: a powerful raven, authoritative.

Walford: Anglo-Saxon origin. Means: from the ford of the Welshman.

Walker: Anglo-Saxon origin. Means: a cloth thickener. Nicknames: Wallie, Wally.

Wallace: French/Anglo-Saxon origin. Means: a foreign man, Welshman. Alternative spellings and nicknames: Welch, Wally, Wallie, Wallas, Welsh, Walsh, Wallis, Wallache.

Waller: Germanic/Anglo-Saxon origin. Means: an army leader, a mason.

Wallmond: Teutonic origin. Means: a strong protective ruler. Alternative spellings: Walmund, Walmond, Warmond.

Walston: Unknown origin and meaning.

Walt: Teutonic origin. Means: powerful warrior, ruler.

Walter: Teutonic origin. Means: powerful warrior, ruler. Ethnic backgrounds: Scottish, Swiss. Alternative spellings and nicknames: Wally, Wat, Walther, Walters, Wallie, Gautier, Gualterio, Wal, Gualtiero, Walt, Gauthier.

Walton: Old English origin. Means: from the walled town, the Welsh town. Nicknames: Wallie, Wally, Walt.

Walworth: Anglo-Saxon origin. Means: from the Welshman's farm.

Walwyn: Anglo-Saxon origin. Means: a Welsh friend.

Wandell: Unknown origin and meaning.

Wang: Unknown origin. Means: a prince, yellow.

Warburton: Unknown origin. Means: of the castle.

Ward: Old English/Teutonic origin. Means: a guardian, watchman. Alternative spellings: Worden, Warde, Warden.

Wardell: Anglo-Saxon origin. Means: from the watchman's hill.

Wardley: Anglo-Saxon origin. Means: of the guardian's meadow.

Ware: Anglo-Saxon origin. Means: one who is wary, wise, shrewd.

Warfeld: Old English origin. Means: from the field by the dam. Alternative spellings: Warfield, Warfold.

Warford: Old English origin. Means: from the ford by the dam. Alternative spelling: Warfourd.

Warren: Teutonic/Anglo-Saxon origin. Means: a game warden, a loyal protector. Alternative spellings: Ware, Waring, Warrin.

Warrick: Teutonic/Anglo-Saxon origin. Means: a protective ruler, a fortress.

Warring: Latin/Teutonic origin. Means: true, cautious, protection. Alternative spelling: Waring.

Warton: Anglo-Saxon origin. Means: from the town by the dam.

Warwick: Teutonic/Anglo-Saxon origin. Means: strong protecting ruler, fortress. Alternative spellings: Aurick, Vareck, Varick, Warrick.

Washburn: Old English origin. Means: from the flooded stream. Nicknames: Burn, Wash, Burnie, Burny.

Washington: Anglo-Saxon origin. Means: from the wise one's estate, wet, damp. Nickname: Wash.

Watende: African origin. Means: no revenge.

Wather: Unknown origin and meaning.

Watkins: Teutonic/Anglo-Saxon origin. Means: son of Walter/Watt, powerful.

Watson: Teutonic/Anglo-Saxon origin. Means: son of Walter/Watt, powerful.

Wayland: Old English origin. Means: from the land by the road. Alternative spellings and nicknames: Waylen, Land, Way, Waylon.

Wayne: Old English origin. Means: a maker of wagons, craftsman. Ethnic backgrounds: English/Welsh.

Wazeer: Arabic origin. Means: adviser.

Webb: Old English origin. Means: one who weaves, a weaver. Alternative spellings: Weber, Webster.

Webley: Old English origin. Means: from the weaver's meadow.

Webster: Old English origin. Means: one who weaves, a weaver. Nicknames: Web, Webb.

Welborne: Anglo-Saxon origin. Means: dweller of the spring stream.

Welby: Norse origin. Means: from the farm by the well.

Weldon: Teutonic origin. Means: from the hill spring.

Welford: Anglo-Saxon origin. Means: from the well by the ford.

Welk: Unknown origin. Means: a wolf.

Wellington: Anglo-Saxon origin. Means: from the rich man's estate.

Wells: Old English origin. Means: from the springs.

Welton: Anglo-Saxon origin. Means: dweller of the spring farm.

Wenceslaus: Slavic/Germanic origin. Means: one with the greatest glory.

Wenston: Unknown origin and meaning.

Wentworth: Anglo-Saxon origin. Means: from the white estate.

Wenzel: Slavic/Germanic origin. Means: one with the greatest glory.

Werdah: Unknown origin and meaning.

Werner: Teutonic origin. Means: of the protective army. Ethnic backgrounds: German, Czech, Swiss. Alternative spellings: Wernher, Warner.

Wes: Old English origin. Means: from the western clearing.

Wescott: Old English origin. Means: from the western cottage. Alternative spelling: Westcott.

Wesley: Old English origin. Means: from the western clearing. Alternative spellings and nicknames: Westleigh, Westley, Lee, Leigh, Wes, Wesly, Westley.

Westbrook: Old English origin. Means: from the western brook.

Weston: Old English origin. Means: from the western town. Nicknames: West, Wes.

Wetherby: Old English origin. Means: from the farm.

Wetherell: Unknown origin and meaning.

Wetherly: Old English origin. Means: from the meadow.

Weylin: Celtic origin. Means: son of the wolf.

Wheatley: Anglo-Saxon origin. Means: dweller of the wheat meadow.

Wheaton: Unknown origin and meaning.

Wheeler: Old English origin. Means: one who makes wheels.

Whistler: Old English origin. Means: a piper.

Whitby: Norse/Old English origin. Means: from the white farmstead.

White: Germanic origin. Means: white in color.

Whitelaw: Anglo-Saxon origin. Means: from the white hill.

Whitfield: Anglo-Saxon origin. Means: from the white field.

Whitford: Old English origin. Means: from the white ford.

Whitley: Anglo-Saxon origin. Means: from the white meadow.

Whitlock: Anglo-Saxon origin. Means: stronghold, one with fair hair.

Whitman: Anglo-Saxon origin. Means: one with fair hair.

Whitmore: Anglo-Saxon origin. Means: from the white moor.

Whittaker: Old English origin. Means: dweller of the white meadow. Nickname: Whit.

Wickham: Anglo-Saxon origin. Means: from the enclosed meadow.

Wickley: Anglo-Saxon origin. Means: from the enclosed meadow.

Wier: Latin/Polish origin. Means: faith, forthright, true.

Wieslav: Slavic origin. Means: one with great glory. Ethnic background: Polish. Alternative spelling: Wieslaw.

Wilbur: Old English/Teutonic origin. Means: one who loves his fortress, brilliant. Alternative spellings: Wilbert, Wilburt, Wilber.

Wilde: Teutonic origin. Means: untamed, wild one.

Wildon: Anglo-Saxon origin. Means: from the wooded hillside.

Wiley: Unknown origin. Means: wet meadow of willows. Alternative spelling: Wylie.

Wilford: Old English origin. Means: from the ford by the willows.

Wilfred: Teutonic origin. Means: determined maker of peace. Alternative spellings and nicknames: Willy, Fred, Freddie, Wilfrid, Will, Willie, Wilfrid, Wilfrido, Wilfried, Walfred.

Wilkes: Unknown origin and meaning.

Will: Teutonic/Anglo-Saxon origin. Means: a determined protector.

Willamson: Teutonic/Anglo-Saxon origin. Means: son of William, a protector.

Willard: Teutonic/Anglo-Saxon origin. Means: one who is firm, courageous. Nicknames: Willy, Willie, Will.

Willebald: Teutonic origin. Means: one with desire and courage. Ethnic background: Dutch.

William: Teutonic origin. Means: a determined protector, a helmet. Ethnic backgrounds: Scottish, English/Welsh, Irish. 16th most popular boy's name of the '90s. Alternative spellings and nicknames: Wilkie, Willy, Willet, Williamson, Bill, Lyam, Vilhelm, Uilleam, Uilliam, Wilek, Wilkes, Wilson, Wilmer, Wilmar, Willis, Willie, Willi, Willem, Guillermo, Billie, Billy, Wilhelm, Guillaume, Wiley, Will, Guglielmo.

Willie: Teutonic/Anglo-Saxon origin. Means: a determined protector.

Willis: Teutonic origin. Means: son of William, a protector.

Willoughby: Old English/Norse origin. Means: from the farm by the willows.

Wilmer: Teutonic origin. Means: a determined protector, with fame.

Wilmot: Teutonic origin. Means: one who is determined, dearly loved.

Wilson: Teutonic origin. Means: son of William, a protector.

Wilt: Old English origin. Means: from the well of the town.

Wilton: Old English origin. Means: from the well of the town. Nicknames: Willy, Willie, Will, Wilt.

Winchell: Anglo-Saxon origin. Means: one who draws the well's water.

Windsor: Teutonic/Anglo-Saxon origin. Means: from the river's bend, from Windsor.

Winfield: Anglo-Saxon origin. Means: from the field of a friend. Nicknames: Field, Win, Winny, Winnie.

Wingate: Old English origin. Means: of the victorious gate, winding.

Wink: Germanic origin. Means: to signal.

Winslow: Teutonic/Old English origin. Means: from the hill of a friend, victory. Nicknames: Win, Winny, Winnie.

Winston: Anglo-Saxon origin. Means: a friendly town, of the Winston estate. Alternative spellings and nicknames: Winny, Win, Winton, Winnie, Wynston.

Winthrop: Teutonic/Old English origin. Means: from the village of a friend. Nicknames: Winny, Win, Winnie.

Winton: Old English origin. Means: from the enclosed (or willow) pasture. Alternative spelling: Wynton.

You've Got a Keeper

My 13-month-old is Lydia, a name I love because it is lyrical, historical, and untrendy. Her older sister's name is Leah, another name I love for the same reasons. But even though I handpicked both my girls' names, I mix them up quite easily. I would advise anyone naming siblings to say the names together *a lot* before deciding—some days I can never get it right!

~ Denise H.,
Asheville, North Carolina

Winward: Old English origin. Means: from the forest of a friend.

Wirt: Teutonic/Anglo-Saxon origin. Means: the master, one who is worthy.

Witold: Teutonic/Polish origin. Means: ruler of the wide forest.

Witt: Anglo-Saxon origin. Means: a wise man.

Witter: Anglo-Saxon origin. Means: a wise warrior.

Witton: Anglo-Saxon origin. Means: from the estate of the wise one.

Wojciech: Slavic/Polish origin. Means: a consoling soldier.

Wolcott: Old English origin. Means: dweller of the wolf's cottage.

Wolf: Teutonic/Anglo-Saxon origin. Means: a wolf. Ethnic background: German. Alternative spellings and nicknames: Wolfie, Wolfy, Wolfe, Wulff.

Wolfgang: Teutonic origin. Means: an advancing wolf. Ethnic background: German. Nicknames: Wolfie, Wolfy, Wolf.

Wolfram: Teutonic origin. Means: with wolf- and ravenlike characteristics.

Wong: Unknown origin. Means: a body.

Woodley: Anglo-Saxon origin. Means: from the meadow with many trees.

Woodman: Anglo-Saxon origin. Means: a woodcutter or hunter.

Woodrow: Anglo-Saxon origin. Means: dweller of a place near the woods. Nicknames: Wood, Woodie, Woody.

Woodruff: Anglo-Saxon origin. Means: a bailiff.

Woodward: Anglo-Saxon origin. Means: a warden of the forest.

Woolcott: Old English origin. Means: dweller of the wolf's cottage.

Woolsey: Old English origin. Means: victorious wolf.

Worcester: Anglo-Saxon origin. Means: one who dwells in the alder forest.

Wordsworth: Old English origin. Means: a guardian of all, from the farmstead.

Worth: Old English origin. Means: from the farmstead. Alternative spelling: Worthy.

Worthington: Old English origin. Means: a riverside dweller.

Worton: Old English origin. Means: from the vegetable farm.

Wouter: Teutonic/Dutch origin. Means: powerful warrior, ruler.

Wright: Anglo-Saxon origin. Means: an artisan with wood, a carpenter.

Wyatt: French origin. Means: small warrior, a guide. Alternative spellings and nicknames: Wiatt, Wye.

Wyborn: Norse origin. Means: a war bear.

Wycliff: Anglo-Saxon origin. Means: from the white cliff.

Wylie: Anglo-Saxon origin. Means: one who charms, enchanting. Alternative spellings and nicknames: Wye, Leigh, Wiley, Lee.

Wyman: Anglo-Saxon origin. Means: warrior.

Wymer: Anglo-Saxon origin. Means: one who is famous in battle.

Wyndham: Anglo-Saxon origin. Means: from the windy village, via a winding path.

Wynn: Welsh origin. Means: a fair one, handsome, blessed. Nicknames: Winny, Winn, Winnie, Wynee.

Wystan: Old English origin. Means: war stone, stone of battle. Alternative spelling: Wystand.

Wythe: Anglo-Saxon origin. Means: from near the willow tree.

X

Xanthus: Greek/Latin origin. Means: yellow, fair-haired, bright.

Xavier: Arabic/Basque origin. Means: brilliant, of the new house. Alternative spellings: Xever, Javier, Xaver.

Xenophon: Greek origin. Means: an unfamiliar voice. Nicknames: Xeno, Zennie.

Xenos: Greek origin. Means: a guest, a stranger.

Xerxes: Persian origin. Means: a prince or king. Nickname: Zerk.

Ximenes: Hebrew/Spanish origin. Means: God has heard.

Xipto: Unknown origin and meaning. Ethnic background: Hispanic.

Xylon: Greek origin. Means: of the woods.

Y

Yaameen: Arabic origin. Means: blessed.

Yachna: Hebrew origin. Means: God is gracious, kindness.

Yadon: Hebrew origin. Means: he will judge.

Yadua: Hebrew origin. Means: celebrity, that which is known.

Yagil: Hebrew origin. Means: to rejoice.

Yakar: Hebrew origin. Means: precious, beloved one.

Yale: Old English origin. Means: one who provides, sloping land.

Yamato: Japanese origin. Unknown meaning.

Yancy: Native American origin. Means: an Englishman. Alternative spellings and nicknames: Yance, Yankee, Yank, Yancey.

Yanis: Hebrew origin. Means: God's gift. Ethnic background: Greek. Alternative spellings: Yannis, Yantsha.

Yankel: Hebrew origin. Means: he who supplants, replaces. Alternative spellings: Yaki, Yakov, Yekel.

Yardley: Anglo-Saxon origin. Means: from the enclosed meadow.

Yarkon: Hebrew origin. Means: green.

Yarom: Hebrew origin. Means: he will raise up.

Yasir: Arabic origin. Means: one who is well off, rich.

Yasmuji: Japanese origin. Unknown meaning.

Yasuo: Japanese origin. Unknown meaning.

Yasutaro: Japanese origin. Unknown meaning.

Yave: Unknown origin and meaning. Ethnic background: French.

Yazeed: Arabic origin. Means: increasing.

Yeats: Anglo-Saxon origin. Means: one who dwells near the gate. Alternative spelling: Yates.

Yediel: Hebrew origin. Means: knowledge of the Lord.

Yehoshua: Hebrew origin. Means: God is salvation.

Yehuda: Hebrew origin. Means: praise of the Lord. Alternative spelling: Yehudi.

Yemin: Hebrew origin. Means: right-handed.

Yemyo: Japanese origin. Unknown meaning.

Yens: Unknown origin and meaning.

Yeoman: Anglo-Saxon origin. Means: retainer, a young man.

Yero: Unknown origin and meaning.

Yesel: Unknown origin and meaning.

Yesher: Hebrew origin. Means: honest one.

Yevgeny: Greek/Slavic origin. Means: one who is well born, noble. Ethnic background: Russian.

Yianni: Unknown origin and meaning.

Yigal: Hebrew origin. Means: he will redeem.

Yisrael: Hebrew origin. Means: prince of God, to contend.

Yitzhak: Hebrew origin. Means: he will laugh. Alternative spellings and nicknames: Yitz, Yitzchak.

Yngvar: Norse origin. Means: of Ing's army.

Yobachi: African origin. Means: pray to God.

Yogi: Sanskrit origin. Means: one who practices yoga.

Yojiro: Japanese origin. Unknown meaning.

Yoosef: Hebrew/Arabic origin. Means: God shall add, a prophet. Alternative spelling: Yosef.

Yoran: Hebrew origin. Means: to sing.

York: Old English/Norse origin. Means: of the boar estate, the sacred yew tree. Alternative spelling: Yorke.

Yosemite: Native American origin. Unknown meaning.

Yoshe: Hebrew origin. Means: the Lord is my salvation.

Yoshiaki: Japanese origin. Unknown meaning.

Yoshikatsu: Japanese origin. Unknown meaning.

Yoshinobu: Japanese origin. Unknown meaning.

Yoshio: Japanese origin. Unknown meaning.

Yossel: Hebrew origin. Means: God will add. Alternative spellings: Yoska, Yossi.

Yosuke: Japanese origin. Unknown meaning.

Yudel: Hebrew origin. Means: praise. Alternative spelling: Yudi.

Yui: Unknown origin and meaning.

Yuji: Japanese origin. Unknown meaning.

Yukichi: Japanese origin. Unknown meaning.

Yukio: Hebrew/Japanese origin. Means: God will nourish.

Yukon: Unknown origin and meaning.

Yule: Anglo-Saxon/Norse origin. Means: born during Christmas. Alternative spelling: Yul.

Yuma: Native American origin. Means: the chief's son.

Yurik: Greek/Slavic origin. Means: farmer, to work the earth. Ethnic background: Russian. Alternative spellings and nicknames: Yuri, Yuris.

Yursa: Unknown origin. Means: bear.

Yves: Norse/French origin. Means: an archer, with yew bow. Alternative spellings: Yvon, Ivar, Ives, Yvan.

Z

Zaahid: Arabic origin. Means: devotee.

Zaahir: Arabic origin. Means: blooming flower.

Zabulon: Hebrew origin. Means: to exalt or honor. Ethnic background: Hispanic.

Zacchaeus: Hebrew origin. Means: remembrance of the Lord.

Zacharias: Hebrew origin. Means: remembrance of the Lord. Ethnic background: German. Alternative spellings: Zaccaria, Zacharia, Zackariah, Zakariya, Zacaria, Zechariah.

Zachary: Hebrew origin. Means: remembrance of the Lord. 7th most popular boy's name of the '90s. Alternative spellings and nicknames: Zacnry, Zakarias, Zachy, Zacharie, Zacanas, Zeke, Zechariah, Zak, Zacharias, Zachariah, Zach, Zacaria, Zacarias, Zack, Zachery, Zackary, Zackery, Zackory, Zakary, Zakory, Zacary.

Zadok: Hebrew origin. Means: one who is just, righteous.

Zafar: Arabic origin. Means: victory.

Zafeer: Arabic origin. Means: firm intention.

Zaheer: Arabic origin. Means: protector.

Zahur: Egyptian origin. Means: a flower. Ethnic background: African.

Zaid: Arabic origin. Means: abundance. Alternative spelling: Zade.

Zaimel: Unknown origin and meaning.

Zaire: Unknown origin and meaning.

Zajac: Unknown origin. Means: a hare. Alternative spelling: Zajicka.

Zak: Hebrew origin. Means: remembrance of the Lord. Alternative spelling: Zach.

Zakaa: Arabic origin. Means: keen perception. Alternative spelling: Zakee.

Zakai: Aramaic/Hebrew origin. Means: innocent, one who is pure.

Zakoc: Unknown origin. Means: just.

Zale: Greek origin. Means: power of the sea.

Zalkin: Hebrew origin. Means: peace. Alternative spelling: Zalki.

Zalman: Hebrew origin. Means: peace.

Zamir: Hebrew origin. Means: singing, a songbird. Alternative spelling: Zemir.

Zander: Greek/Latin origin. Means: defender of all mankind.

Zane: Hebrew origin. Means: God will nourish.

Zanique: Unknown origin and meaning.

Zanvil: Hebrew origin. Means: God will nourish.

Zaphnozy: Unknown origin and meaning.

Zared: Hebrew origin. Means: ambush.

Zarek: Unknown origin and meaning.

Zavad: Hebrew origin. Means: gift, a dowry.

Zavier: Basque origin. Means: brilliant, of the new house.

Zbigniew: Slavic/Polish origin. Means: one who leaves anger behind.

Zbik: Unknown origin. Means: a wildcat.

Zdenek: Latin/Czech origin. Means: one from Sidon, a winding-sheet.

Zebadiah: Hebrew origin. Means: God's gift. Alternative spellings and nicknames: Zeb, Zebe, Zebedee.

Zebe: Hebrew origin. Means: to exalt, to dwell.

Zebulon: Hebrew origin. Means: to exalt, to dwell. Nicknames: Lonny, Zeb.

Zedekiah: Hebrew origin. Means: God is mighty and just. Nickname: Zed.

Zeeman: Dutch origin. Means: a seaman.

Zeff: Hebrew origin. Means: a wolf. Alternative spellings: Zev, Ziff.

Zeidel: Hebrew origin. Means: grandfather. Alternative spelling: Zaydel.

Zek: Hebrew origin. Means: he who laughs.

Zeke: Hebrew origin. Means: God will strengthen.

Zelig: Teutonic/Hebrew origin. Means: happy, blessed, holy.

Zelotes: Greek origin. Means: zealous.

Zemel: Hebrew origin. Means: bread.

Zenaido: Greek origin. Unknown meaning. Ethnic background: Hispanic.

Zenas: Greek origin. Means: living, gift of God.

Zeno: Greek origin. Means: of Zeus. Ethnic background: Italian.

Zenobio: Greek/Arabic origin. Means: born of Zeus, a father's pride. Ethnic background: Hispanic.

Zenon: Greek origin. Means: friendly. Ethnic backgrounds: Polish, Hispanic.

Zephaniah: Hebrew origin. Means: God has treasured. Alternative spellings and nicknames: Zeph, Zephan.

Zerah: Hebrew origin. Means: shining, dawning.

Zerem: Hebrew origin. Means: a stream.

Zero: Arabic origin. Means: empty.

Zetan: Hebrew origin. Means: olive tree, an olive.

Zeus: Greek origin. Means: father, king.

Zevon: Unknown origin and meaning.

Zhorzh: Unknown origin and meaning. Ethnic background: Russian.

Ziegier: Unknown origin. Means: brick.

Ziggy: Unknown origin and meaning.

Zimmerman: Unknown origin. Means: a carpenter. Alternative spelling: Zimmermann.

Zintars: Unknown origin and meaning. Ethnic background: Russian.

Zintis: Unknown origin and meaning. Ethnic background: Russian.

Zion: Unknown origin and meaning.

Zissa: Hebrew origin. Means: sweet. Alternative spellings: Zisseh, Zushe, Zussel.

Ziv: Hebrew origin. Means: with brilliance, bright.

Ziyaad: Arabic origin. Means: surplus.

Zjateek: Unknown origin and meaning.

Zoilo: Germanic origin. Means: one's duty, the cost. Ethnic background: Hispanic.

Zokaa: Arabic origin. Means: sun.

Zoltan: Arabic/Hungarian origin. Means: a ruler, prince.

Zoser: Unknown origin and meaning.

Zosimo: Unknown origin and meaning. Ethnic background: Hispanic.

Zotico: Greek origin. Unknown meaning. Ethnic background: Hispanic.

Zsolt: Unknown origin and meaning. Ethnic background: Hungarian.

Zuberi: Egyptian origin. Means: strong. Ethnic background: African.

Zufar: Arabic origin. Means: brave man.

Zundel: Unknown origin and meaning. Ethnic background: Jewish.

Zuriel: Hebrew origin. Means: the stone of God.

Zussman: Germanic/Hebrew origin. Means: a sweet man.

213

unisex names

Abba: Arabic/Aramaic origin. Means: father, born. Ethnic background: Jewish.

Abbey: Latin/French origin. Means: father.

Abelino: Spanish origin. Means: from Avellino, from near the hazelnut trees.

Aberdeen: Unknown origin and meaning.

Aconcagua: Unknown origin and meaning.

Adar: Hebrew origin. Means: fire, fiery, noble.

Adi: Hebrew origin. Means: ornament, my adornment.

Adonis: Greek origin. Means: handsome, lord.

Agape: Greek origin. Means: brotherly love.

Agate: Greek/Celtic origin. Means: good.

Akaka: Unknown origin and meaning.

Akira: Scottish/Japanese origin. Means: anchor.

Akron: Unknown origin and meaning.

Alain: Gaelic/French origin. Means: cheerful, bright.

Alaska: Unknown origin and meaning.

Alcott: Anglo-Saxon origin. Means: cottage.

Aleutian: Unknown origin and meaning.

Alexandre: Latin/French origin. Means: defender of man.

Alexis: Greek origin. Means: helper. 13th most popular girl's name of the '90s.

Alexus: Latin/Greek origin. Means: defender of man. Alternative spelling: Alex.

Allyn: Celtic origin. Means: handsome, beautiful.

Alpine: Unknown origin and meaning. Alternative spellings: Alp, Alpena.

Altai: Unknown origin and meaning.

Altinure: Unknown origin and meaning. Ethnic background: Irish.

Alva: Latin origin. Means: fair, blond.

Amadis: Latin origin. Means: devoted, beloved, God.

Amarillo: Unknown origin and meaning.

Amazon: Unknown origin and meaning.

Amedee: French origin. Means: loves God.

Amir: Hebrew/Arabic origin. Means: prince, princess, mighty.

Amur: Unknown origin and meaning.

Anders: Greek/Germanic origin. Means: manly, strong. Ethnic backgrounds: Norwegian, Swedish.

Anderson: Greek/Norse origin. Means: son of Ander.

Andes: Latin origin. Means: from the Andes.

Andras: Norse origin. Means: breath. Ethnic background: Hungarian.

Angel: Greek/Latin origin. Means: messenger. Ethnic background: Hispanic.

Angola: Unknown origin and meaning.

Annacotty: Unknown origin. Means: little boat. Ethnic background: Irish.

Annapolis: Unknown origin and meaning.

Ansley: Unknown origin. Means: awe, meadow.

Anstice: Greek origin. Means: resurrected, reassure.

Ara: Greek/Hebrew origin. Means: able, altar, to gather.

Ararat: Unknown origin and meaning.

Arbor: Latin origin. Means: herb gardener.

Ardara: Unknown origin and meaning. Ethnic background: Irish.

Ardeen: Latin origin. Means: ardent, warm. Ethnic background: Irish.

Arizona: Unknown origin and meaning.

Armani: Unknown origin and meaning.

Artemas: Greek origin. Means: angels, Artemis.

Aruba: Arabic origin. Means: love of spouse.

Ashland: Unknown origin and meaning.

Aspen: Unknown origin and meaning.

Aster: Unknown origin and meaning.

Astilbe: Unknown origin and meaning.

Asuncion: Spanish origin. Means: assumption.

Atlas: Greek origin. Means: a titan.

Audris: Teutonic origin. Means: fortunate.

Auguste: Latin/French origin. Means: majestic, dignitary.

Austria: Unknown origin and meaning.

Averil: Latin/Old English origin. Means: born in April, boar, open.

Avril: Old English origin. Means: boar, battle, April. Ethnic background: Jewish.

b

Ba: Unknown origin and meaning.

Baikal: Unknown origin and meaning.

Baines: Unknown origin and meaning.

Balkan: Unknown origin and meaning.

Bay: Anglo-Saxon origin. Means: reddish-brown hair.

Beecher: Anglo-Saxon origin. Means: by the beech tree.

Bela: Hebrew/Slavic origin. Means: destruction, bright. Ethnic background: Hungarian.

Bell: Slavic/French origin. Means: white, beautiful.

Bergen: Germanic origin. Means: dweller of hill/mountain.

Berry: Anglo-Saxon origin. Means: manor.

Beryl: Greek/Hebrew origin. Means: green, precious stone. Ethnic backgrounds: English/Welsh. Alternative spellings and nicknames: Berryle, Berri, Berrie, Berry.

Bevin: Celtic origin. Means: soldier, youthful, singer.

Bhutan: Unknown origin and meaning.

Blair: Gaelic origin. Means: of the field.

Blake: Old English origin. Means: both black (dark) and white (pale). 48th most popular boy's name of the '90s.

Blanc: Unknown origin and meaning.

Bo: Norse origin. Means: to live, dwell, commander. Ethnic background: Swedish.

Boise: Unknown origin and meaning.

Bolivia: Unknown origin and meaning.

Boston: Old English origin. Means: town near a thicket.

Brasenia: Unknown origin and meaning.

Brea: Old English origin. Means: thin broth.

Bristol: Anglo-Saxon origin. Means: rich, noble.

Brit: Celtic/Slavic origin. Means: strong, a Briton. Ethnic backgrounds: Jewish, Norwegian.

Brook: Old English origin. Means: stream.

Bryn: Welsh origin. Means: hill. Alternative spelling: Brynn.

Burgundy: Unknown origin and meaning.

Burnett: Anglo-Saxon origin. Means: brown.

Butte: French origin. Means: isolated hill/mountain.

Cairo: Unknown origin and meaning.

Calcite: Unknown origin and meaning.

Calgary: Unknown origin and meaning.

California: French origin. Means: successor.

Cameron: Celtic/Gaelic origin. Means: crooked, individuality. Ethnic backgrounds: English/Welsh. Alternative spellings and nicknames: Cam, Camm, Camryn.

Candelario: Spanish origin. Means: candle, feast.

Canice: Gaelic origin. Means: handsome, fair one.

Canton: Unknown origin and meaning.

Cardamine: Unknown origin and meaning.

Carey: Welsh origin. Means: castle dweller, dark one. Alternative spelling: Cary.

Carlin: Gaelic origin. Means: champion. Alternative spelling: Carling.

Carly: Teutonic/Gaelic origin. Means: champion, strong. Ethnic backgrounds: English/Welsh.

Carmel: Hebrew origin. Means: garden, vineyard. Alternative spellings and nicknames: Carmella, Carmela, Carmelita.

Carroll: Celtic origin. Means: valiant champion. Ethnic background: Irish. Alternative spellings: Carel, Carol, Carole, Caryl.

Cascade: Latin origin. Means: steep, rocky waterfall.

Casey: Celtic/Gaelic origin. Means: brave, vigilant.

Cerulean: Latin origin. Means: deep blue.

Chadron: Unknown origin and meaning.

Champaign: Latin/French origin. Means: level, open field.

Charcoal: Old English origin. Unknown meaning.

Charleston: Germanic/Saxon origin. Means: Charles's farm.

Charlock: Unknown origin and meaning.

Charlot: French origin. Means: son of Charlemagne. Ethnic background: Irish.

Chervil: Unknown origin and meaning.

Cheyenne: Algonquian origin. Unknown meaning.

Chicago: Unknown origin and meaning.

China: Unknown origin and meaning.

Chris: Greek/Latin origin. Means: Christian, Christ bearer.

Chuma: Egyptian origin. Means: wealth. Ethnic backgrounds: African, Jewish.

Citrine: Unknown origin. Means: resembling topaz.

Cleve: Saxon origin. Means: cliff dweller.

Cobalt: Greek origin. Means: silver-white metal.

Cody: Anglo-Saxon origin. Means: cushion. Alternative spellings: Codie, Codey.

Coffee: Arabic origin. Means: seeds/berries of coffee plants.

Colima: Unknown origin and meaning.

Collins: Gaelic/Irish origin. Means: virile.

Colorado: Latin origin. Means: color and strength.

Compassion: Unknown origin and meaning.

Concord: Latin origin. Means: agreement, accord.

Congo: Unknown origin and meaning.

Consistency: Latin origin. Means: steadfast to principles.

Consuelo: Latin origin. Means: giver of consolation. Ethnic background: Hispanic.

Cook: Latin origin. Means: to cook.

Copper: Latin origin. Means: metal, for brass/bronze.

Corcovado: Unknown origin and meaning.

Cori: Gaelic/Irish origin. Means: ravine, rounded hill.

Corliss: Anglo-Saxon origin. Means: kindly, strong.

Cornelian: Latin origin. Means: horn of the sun.

Cosmos: Greek origin. Means: harmony, order.

Courtesy: Old English origin. Means: social conduct.

Courtney: French origin. Means: from court or farmstead. Alternative spellings: Courtenay, Courtland,Courtnie, Courteney.

Crimson: Spanish origin. Means: a deep purple.

Cruz: Spanish origin. Means: agony at the cross. Ethnic background: Hispanic.

Cyd: Latin origin. Means: public hill.

Cyperus: Greek origin. Means: from Cyprus. Alternative spellings: Cypress, Cyprus.

d

Dacey: Celtic origin. Means: southerner. Alternative spellings: Dacy.

Dakota: Native American origin. Unknown meaning.

Dale: Germanic/Anglo-Saxon origin. Means: valley or dale dweller. Alternative spellings: Dail, Daile, Dalton.

Dallas: Celtic/Old English origin. Means: a valley house by a waterfall, wise. Nickname: Dal.

Dama: Hebrew/Latin origin. Means: a lady, to resemble.

Dana: Hebrew/Latin origin. Means: to judge, pure, bright. Ethnic backgrounds: Czech, Irish, Jewish. Alternative spellings: Dain, Dane.

Darcy: Celtic/French origin. Means: dark, fortress. Ethnic background: Irish. Alternative spellings: Darcey, Darsy, Darsey.

Darian: Persian origin. Means: king, royalty.

Daryl: Anglo-Saxon origin. Means: beloved.

Dashen: Unknown origin and meaning.

Dayton: Anglo-Saxon origin. Means: cheerful town.

Deandre: Unknown origin and meaning.

Deane: Latin/Anglo-Saxon origin. Means: supervisor, of the valley.

December: Latin origin. Means: 10th month in Roman calendar.

Dempsey: Gaelic/Anglo-Saxon origin. Means: proud, judge, blame. Alternative spellings: Denys, Denzil, Denny, Dennison, Dennie, Denis, Dion.

Denver: Anglo-Saxon origin. Means: from the valley edge.

Deverell: Welsh origin. Means: from the river's bank.

Devin: Celtic origin. Means: one who writes verse, poet. Alternative spelling: Devyn.

Devon: Anglo-Saxon origin. Means: of Devon, near river.

Diamond: Greek/Latin origin. Means: precious stone, bright.

Didi: Hebrew origin. Means: beloved.

Dnieper: Unknown origin and meaning.

Dody: Hebrew origin. Means: beloved friend.

Donell: Norse origin. Means: ruler.

Dorcas: Greek origin. Means: dark, gazelle, doe.

Dory: French origin. Means: golden, blond.

Dothan: Hebrew origin. Means: the law.

Duluth: Unknown origin and meaning.

Durango: Spanish origin. Unknown meaning.

Durham: Anglo-Saxon origin. Means: stock breeding.

e

Eavan: Gaelic origin. Means: fair. Ethnic background: Irish.

Ebro: Unknown origin and meaning.

Edel: Hebrew/Germanic origin. Means: gentle, brave, noble.

Eden: Hebrew origin. Means: delight, adornment. Alternative spelling: Edin.

Edlyn: Anglo-Saxon origin. Means: adviser, noble one. Nickname: Lyn.

Edmonton: Anglo-Saxon origin. Unknown meaning.

Egypt: Unknown origin and meaning.

Eiger: Unknown origin and meaning. Ethnic background: Dutch.

Elbruz: Unknown origin and meaning.

Elisha: Hebrew origin. Means: the Lord is my salvation.

Ellis: Hebrew/Greek origin. Means: the Lord is God.

Ellsworth: Anglo-Saxon origin. Means: of the noble estate.

Emelin: Teutonic origin. Means: busy, industrious.

Emlen: Teutonic/Welsh origin. Means: busy, waterfall. Alternative spelling: Emlyn.

England: Latin origin. Unknown meaning.

Erebus: Greek origin. Unknown meaning.

Erie: Celtic origin. Means: from Ireland.

Etna: Greek origin. Unknown meaning.

Eustace: Greek/French origin. Means: fine vineyard, fruitful. Ethnic background: Polish.

Everest: Unknown origin and meaning.

Ewa: Hebrew/Polish origin. Means: life.

Eyre: Unknown origin and meaning.

f

Fabia: Latin origin. Means: grower of beans.

Fall: Greek origin. Means: autumn.

Farand: Teutonic origin. Means: one who is attractive, pleasant. Alternative spellings and nicknames: Farant, Ran, Rand, Farrand, Randy.

Fargo: Unknown origin and meaning.

February: Latin origin. Means: expiation period.

Fiji: Unknown origin and meaning.

Fisher: Old English origin. Means: one who fishes.

Foluke: African origin. Means: in God's hands.

Ford: Old English origin. Means: cattle, river crossing.

Fortune: Latin/French origin. Means: destiny, chance.

Francis: Latin/Teutonic origin. Means: free, liberated. Ethnic backgrounds: English/Welsh, French. Alternative spellings and nicknames: Fran, François, Frank, Franz.

Freedom: Old English origin. Means: being at liberty.

Friday: Old English origin. Means: Freya's day.

Fujita: Japanese origin. Means: field.

g

Gabi: Hebrew origin. Means: God is my strength.

Gale: Celtic/Anglo-Saxon origin. Means: energetic, merry, sing. Alternative spellings: Gayl, Gayle, Gail, Gaile.

Ganges: Unknown origin and meaning.

Garland: Latin/French origin. Means: crowned with wreath of flowers. Alternative spelling: Garlan.

Garnet: Latin origin. Means: a grain or seed, red jewel. Alternative spellings: Garnett, Garnette.

Gaynor: Gaelic/Irish origin. Means: fair-haired one's son. Ethnic backgrounds: English/Welsh.

Gentle: Latin origin. Means: of the same clan.

Geode: Greek origin. Means: earthlike, hollow stone.

Germaine: Latin origin. Means: brother, brotherhood. Alternative spellings: Germana, Jermaine, Germain.

Gertrudis: Teutonic origin. Means: well-loved warrior, spear. Ethnic background: Hispanic.

Gigi: Unknown origin and meaning. Ethnic background: Italian.

Gijs: Anglo-Saxon origin. Means: wise, well learned. Ethnic background: Dutch.

Gill: Latin/French origin. Means: youthful.

Gleason: Unknown origin and meaning.

Glomma: Norse origin. Unknown meaning.

Glyn: Welsh origin. Means: valley dweller.

Glynis: Gaelic origin. Means: valley dweller. Alternative spelling: Glynnis.

Godavari: Unknown origin and meaning.

Gold: Latin/Anglo-Saxon origin. Means: superiority, blond.

Goodness: Germanic origin. Means: morally virtuous.

Guam: Unknown origin and meaning.

Guri: Hebrew/Norse origin. Means: a young lion, beautiful.

Gwynne: Celtic origin. Means: white-browed, holy.

h

Haley: Greek/Irish origin. Means: clever, hero, ingenious. Alternative spellings: Haleigh, Hailey.

Hampton: Old English origin. Means: town or village.

Happy: Old English origin. Means: joyful.

Harley: Anglo-Saxon origin. Means: of the hare's meadow. Alternative spellings and nicknames: Arlie, Harl, Hartley, Arley, Harleigh, Hart.

Hartford: Anglo-Saxon origin. Means: of the stag's forest.

Hashi: Unknown origin. Means: bridge.

Haven: Old English origin. Means: safety, harbor, port.

Hawaii: Polynesian origin. Unknown meaning.

Hayes: Anglo-Saxon origin. Means: hunter, hay farmer. Alternative spelling: Hays.

Helicon: Greek origin. Means: of Helicon (home of the Muses).

Herval: Unknown origin and meaning.

Hibbing: Unknown origin and meaning.

Hillary: Latin origin. Means: cheerful, happy. Ethnic backgrounds: English/Welsh. Alternative spellings: Hilaire, Hillery, Hilari, Hillarey, Hilary.

Himalaya: Unknown origin and meaning.

Hirata: Unknown origin. Means: field.

Holiness: Old English origin. Means: sanctity, one who is devout.

Holland: Norse origin. Unknown meaning.

Honor: Latin origin. Means: honorable, one with high esteem.

Hood: Germanic origin. Means: a head covering.

Hospitality: Latin origin. Means: friendly reception of friends and strangers.

Huila: Teutonic origin. Means: bright mind and spirit.

Humble: Latin origin. Means: a feeling of insignificance, lowly.

Humility: Latin origin. Means: one who is humble, a modest sense.

Huron: Native American origin. Unknown meaning.

Hyatt: Anglo-Saxon origin. Means: from the high gate.

i

Idowu: African origin. Means: born after twins.

Indiana: Latin origin. Unknown meaning.

Indigo: Indian/Greek origin. Means: blue plant dye.

Indus: Unknown origin and meaning.

Ingemar: Norse origin. Means: the famous one. Ethnic background: Swedish.

Inger: Norse origin. Means: son's army. Ethnic background: Swedish.

Ira: Hebrew origin. Means: watcher, one with vision. Ethnic background: German.

j

Jacinth: Greek origin. Means: attractive, purple flower.

Jackie: Hebrew origin. Means: God is gracious, supplanter.

Jada: Old English/French origin. Means: an old horse, a precious stone.

Jadeite: Spanish origin. Means: form of jade.

Jael: Hebrew origin. Means: to ascend, a mountain goat.

Jamaal: Arabic origin. Means: beauty, handsome.

Jamaica: Unknown origin and meaning.

Jamie: Hebrew origin. Means: one who supplants, replaces. Ethnic backgrounds: English/Welsh.

Jan: Hebrew/Norse origin. Means: God is gracious. Ethnic backgrounds: Dutch, Swedish, Polish, German, Norwegian. Alternative spelling: Janne.

Janis: Hebrew origin. Means: God's gracious gift. Ethnic background: Russian.

January: Latin origin. Unknown meaning.

Jari: Unknown origin and meaning.

Jay: Latin origin. Means: a lively bird.

Jaya: Hindi origin. Means: victory.

Jean: Hebrew/French origin. Means: God's gracious gift. Ethnic backgrounds: Scottish, Swiss, English/Welsh. Alternative spellings and nicknames: Jeanie, Jeannine, Gene, Jeanette, Jeanne, Jeannette.

Jehan: French origin. Means: God's gift.

Jerzy: Greek/Polish origin. Means: one who works the earth, farmer.

Jesse: Hebrew origin. Means: one with wealth, gift. Alternative spellings and nicknames: Jess, Jessie.

Jet: Hebrew origin. Means: abundance, riches, excellence. Ethnic background: Dutch.

Jody: Hebrew origin. Means: praised.

Jordan: Hebrew origin. Means: flowing down, descending. Alternative spellings: Jorden, Jordon, Jordaan.

Jorie: Hebrew origin. Means: God will uplift.

Jose: Hebrew/Spanish origin. Means: God will increase. Ethnic background: Hispanic.

Joyce: Latin origin. Means: to be merry, delight. Alternative spellings and nicknames: Joyous, Joice, Joy.

Julian: Latin/French origin. Means: soft-haired one, youthful. Ethnic backgrounds: English/Welsh. Alternative spelling: Julien.

July: Latin origin. Means: Julius Caesar.

Justice: Latin origin. Means: the act of rightfulness.

Justus: Latin/Norse origin. Means: one who is virtuous, just, upright.

K

Kameron: Celtic/Gaelic origin. Means: one with the crooked nose.

Karel: Latin/French origin. Means: one with strength, joyful song. Ethnic backgrounds: Czech, Dutch. Alternative spellings: Karole, Karyl, Karol.

Kay: Greek/Latin origin. Means: merry one, rejoicing. Alternative spellings: Caye, Kaye.

Keaton: Unknown origin and meaning.

Keelan: Celtic origin. Means: slender one. Ethnic background: Irish.

Keely: Gaelic origin. Means: handsome, beautiful. Alternative spellings: Keelia, Keeley.

Kelby: Unknown origin. Means: from the farm.

Kelly: Gaelic origin. Means: warrior of the king, brave soldier. Ethnic backgrounds: Irish, English/Welsh. Alternative spellings: Keli, Kellie, Kelli, Kelley.

Kelsey: Old English/Norse origin. Means: victory at sea, island. Alternative spelling: Kelcey.

Kemi: Unknown origin and meaning.

Kendall: Celtic origin. Means: ruler of the bright river valley. Alternative spelling: Kendell.

Kennedy: Gaelic/Old English origin. Means: an unattractive head, royal.

Kennison: Gaelic/Anglo-Saxon origin. Means: son of Kenneth, handsome.

Kenya: Latin/Slavic origin. Means: one who is innocent, harmless.

Kerinci: Unknown origin and meaning.

Kerry: Celtic/Gaelic origin. Means: dark one, dark-haired, ruler. Ethnic backgrounds: English/Welsh.

Khaki: Persian origin. Means: dusty, yellowish brown.

Khiem: Unknown origin. Means: humble.

Khingan: Unknown origin and meaning.

Kiah: Unknown origin. Means: beginning.

Kiley: Unknown origin and meaning.

Kim: Old English origin. Means: glorious ruler, noble. Ethnic backgrounds: English/Welsh.

King: Anglo-Saxon origin. Means: one of royalty, a ruler.

Kinsey: Anglo-Saxon origin. Means: royal, victorious.

Knowledge: Old English origin. Means: retention of truth or principles.

Kody: Norse/Anglo-Saxon origin. Means: a cushion.

Kolyma: Slavic origin. Unknown meaning.

Koryak: Unknown origin and meaning.

Kurile: Unknown origin and meaning.

Ky: Unknown origin. Means: to abstain.

Labor: Latin origin. Means: work, for economic gain.

Lawson: Latin/Anglo-Saxon origin. Means: son of Lawrence, crowned.

Le: Hebrew origin. Means: weary, pear, plums.

Lee: Anglo-Saxon/Gaelic origin. Means: of the meadow, poetic one. Ethnic backgrounds: English/Welsh. Alternative spellings: Leigh, Lea, Leann, Leeanna.

Lesley: Gaelic/Celtic origin. Means: of the holly garden, of the gray fort. Ethnic backgrounds: English/Welsh. Alternative spellings and nicknames: Lezlie, Lesli, Les, Lesly, Leslie.

Li: Unknown origin. Means: black, plums.

Lin: Anglo-Saxon origin. Means: from the waterfall, a brook. Ethnic backgrounds: English/Welsh.

Lindsay: Old English origin. Means: from the island of pools and linden trees. Ethnic backgrounds: English/Welsh. Alternative spellings: Lindsy, Lindsey.

Lindy: Old English origin. Means: linden tree, attractive.

Ling: Unknown origin. Means: forest.

Loden: Unknown origin and meaning.

Logan: Gaelic origin. Means: from the hollow.

Loire: French origin. Unknown meaning.

Lon: Latin/Norse origin. Means: fierce, lionlike.

Lonnie: Old English/Germanic origin. Means: solitary, of nobility.

Loren: Latin origin. Means: crown, laurels.

Lykaon: Unknown origin and meaning.

Lynn: Anglo-Saxon origin. Means: a cascade, waterfall. Alternative spellings: Lynne, Lynelle, Lynna, Lyn, Linn, Lynette.

Mackenzie: Scottish origin. Means: of the handsome man. Alternative spellings: Mackensie, Makenzie.

Macon: Unknown origin and meaning.

Macy: Unknown origin. Means: the bearer.

Madison: Teutonic/Anglo-Saxon origin. Means: God's, mighty.

Magic: Greek origin. Means: of sorcery, witchcraft.

Maize: Native American origin. Means: yellowish, corn.

Malaysia: Unknown origin and meaning.

Malin: Teutonic/Anglo-Saxon origin. Means: a high tower, little warrior. Ethnic background: Swedish.

Mallory: Latin/French origin. Means: one who is unlucky, ill omened.

March: Latin/Germanic origin. Means: month of Mars, a boundary.

Mariah: Egyptian/Hebrew origin. Means: the perfect one, bitter, God has taught.

Marice: Hebrew/Latin origin. Means: bitter, the sea, dark.

Marion: Latin origin. Means: warlike, bitter.

Maris: Latin origin. Means: a sea star. Ethnic background: Russian. Alternative spellings: Marys, Marris, Meris, Marissa, Marisa, Mari, Marras.

Marley: Anglo-Saxon origin. Means: from the marsh or lake.

Maroon: Italian origin. Means: chestnut, dark reddish brown.

Marquis: French origin. Means: a nobleman.

Marsalis: Greek/Gaelic origin. Means: a pearl.

Massif: French origin. Means: massive, a compacted mountain range.

Massillion: Unknown origin and meaning.

Matana: Hebrew origin. Means: a gift of God.

Mathia: Hebrew origin. Means: a gift of God.

Matsuda: Unknown origin. Means: field.

Matsuhira: Japanese origin. Means: flat.

Matsukawa: Japanese origin. Means: pine. Nickname: Matsu.

Matsumoto: Japanese origin. Means: origin.

Matsunaka: Japanese origin. Means: middle.

Matsuo: Unknown origin. Means: little.

Matsuoka: Japanese origin. Means: hill.

Matsushima: Japanese origin. Means: island.

Matsushita: Japanese origin. Means: below.

Matsuyama: Japanese origin. Means: mountain.

Mattie: Hebrew/French origin. Means: a gift of God, fierce in battle.

Matza: Persian origin. Means: a warrior, warlike. Ethnic background: Jewish.

Mayon: Unknown origin and meaning.

Mayotte: Unknown origin and meaning.

McKenna: Anglo-Saxon origin. Means: son of Kenneth, royal.

McKinley: Scottish origin. Means: son of Kinley, of the fair herd.

Medina: Unknown origin and meaning.

Meir: Hebrew origin. Means: giving light.

Mel: French/Greek origin. Means: of the infertile land, industrious.

Memphis: Egyptian origin. Unknown meaning.

Meredith: Celtic/Welsh origin. Means: guardian of the sea. Alternative spellings and nicknames: Meridth, Merridie, Meridith, Merry.

Merle: Latin/French origin. Means: a blackbird. Alternative spellings and nicknames: Merla, Meria, Merl, Merola, Myrie, Merl, Meryl, Myrlene, Merlina, Merline.

Merritt: Latin origin. Means: valuable, of merit. Alternative spellings and nicknames: Merit, Merri, Merry.

Mesen: Unknown origin and meaning.

Mette: Greek origin. Means: an ambitious goal, a pearl. Ethnic background: Norwegian.

Miami: Native American origin. Unknown meaning.

Michael: Hebrew origin. Means: who is like God? Ethnic backgrounds: Greek, English/Welsh, Irish, Swedish, German. Most popular boy's name of the '90s. Alternative spellings and nicknames: Mickie, Micky, Mike, Mikael, Michel.

Mikenzie: Scottish origin. Means: son of the fair man.

Ming: Unknown origin. Means: bright.

Mink: Unknown origin and meaning.

Minnesota: Unknown origin and meaning.

Missoula: Unknown origin and meaning.

Missouri: Unknown origin and meaning.

Mitchella: Hebrew/Anglo-Saxon origin. Means: who is like God?

Moline: Unknown origin and meaning.

Monaco: Unknown origin and meaning.

Monday: Latin origin. Means: moon's day.

Moonstone: Greek origin. Means: adularia.

Morgan: Celtic/Welsh origin. Means: a sea dweller, born by the sea. Ethnic background: Irish. Alternative spelling: Morgen.

Moriah: Hebrew origin. Means: God is my teacher.

Mosi: Egyptian origin. Means: firstborn. Ethnic background: African.

Mura: Hebrew/Slavic origin. Means: bitter, a village.

Murphy: Irish origin. Means: a sea warrior.

Musa: Egyptian/Arabic origin. Means: of the water.

Muta: Latin/Persian origin. Means: of silence, warlike. Ethnic background: Jewish.

Naka: Unknown origin. Means: middle.

Nara: Celtic/Gaelic origin. Means: one who is happy, to be near.

Natividad: Latin/Spanish origin. Means: to be born (of the Virgin Mary).

Nebraska: Native American origin. Means: the flat water.

Nell: Greek/Celtic origin. Means: echo, light, a champion.

Nepal: Unknown origin and meaning.

Nesta: Greek/Welsh origin. Means: innocent, pure, chaste. Ethnic backgrounds: English/Welsh.

Nevada: Latin origin. Means: snow, snowy. Alternative spellings and nicknames: Nava, Vada, Navada, Neva.

Ngozi: Egyptian origin. Means: a blessed one, blessing. Ethnic background: African.

Niagara: Unknown origin and meaning.

Nico: Greek/Italian origin. Means: the people's victory.

Nikki: Greek/Latin origin. Means: the people's victory, of the Lord.

November: Latin origin. Means: the 9th Roman month.

Nuru: Egyptian origin. Means: born during daylight. Ethnic background: African.

Nyasa: Greek origin. Means: toward the goal, the beginning point.

Obsidian: Latin origin. Means: to besiege.

October: Latin origin. Means: 8th month of the Roman calendar.

Odd: Norse origin. Means: the spear's point. Ethnic background: Norwegian.

Odell: Teutonic origin. Means: a melody, prosperous, wealthy.

Oka: Unknown origin. Means: hill.

Ola: Norse origin. Means: one who resembles an ancestor. Ethnic backgrounds: Jewish, Norwegian.

Olean: Unknown origin and meaning.

Oleander: Latin origin. Means: a plant with fragrant flowers.

Olenek: Slavic origin. Means: one who is holy.

Ollie: Latin/Anglo-Saxon origin. Means: branch, peace, of the olive tree.

Olympus: Greek origin. Means: heavenly, from Olympus.

Onega: Slavic origin. Unknown meaning.

Ontario: Unknown origin and meaning.

Orange: Sanskrit origin. Means: citrus.

Orchid: Latin origin. Means: tropical flower.

Oregon: Unknown origin and meaning.

Orinoco: Unknown origin and meaning.

Orola: Unknown origin. Means: family.

Oslo: Unknown origin and meaning.

Ossa: Unknown origin and meaning.

Ove: Norse origin. Means: the spear's point, awe. Ethnic background: Swedish.

Page: Greek/Anglo-Saxon origin. Means: the knight's young attendant. Alternative spelling: Paige.

Pat: Latin origin. Means: of noble birth.

Patty: Latin origin. Means: of noble birth.

Paxton: Latin/Teutonic origin. Means: town of peace, a trader from afar.

Paz: Hebrew/Spanish origin. Means: gold, peace, our lady of peace reference.

Pechora: Unknown origin and meaning.

Pelion: Greek origin. Unknown meaning.

Pepper: Latin origin. Means: of the piper, seeds of climbing shrub.

Peridot: Unknown origin and meaning.

Peyton: Latin/Anglo-Saxon origin. Means: of regal birth, royal.

Pham: Unknown origin. Means: to commit.

Phoenix: Greek/Latin origin. Means: eagle, mythological bird, rebirth.

Pity: Latin origin. Means: with sympathetic grief.

Potter: Old English origin. Means: to swell.

Pyrenees: Greek origin. Means: stone of the fruit.

Qamar: Arabic origin. Means: moon.

Quartz: Slavic/Greek origin. Means: crystallike mineral.

Quinn: Celtic/Gaelic origin. Means: one who is intelligent and wise. Ethnic background: Irish.

Rabi: Arabic origin. Means: a breeze, harvest, the spring.

Rainier: Germanic/French origin. Means: a decisive warrior.

Randy: Teutonic origin. Means: admired, the shield's edge, a wolf. Alternative spelling: Randie.

Red: Anglo-Saxon origin. Means: red-haired, ruddy complexion.

Refugio: Spanish origin. Means: in honor of Mary.

Remy: Latin origin. Means: oarsman, to work.

Renata: Latin/Italian origin. Means: rebirth, confident. Ethnic backgrounds: Russian, Hispanic. Alternative spellings and nicknames: Rennie, Renie, Renae, Renate, Renee, Rene.

Rene: Latin/French origin. Means: one who is new again, reborn. Ethnic backgrounds: Swiss, Hispanic, French. Nickname: Renie.

Renny: Irish origin. Means: wealthy, charming, mighty.

Rhine: Unknown origin and meaning.

Rhone: Unknown origin and meaning.

Riley: Old English/Gaelic origin. Means: of the rye meadow, courageous. Alternative spellings: Reilly, Ryley, Rileigh, Ryleigh.

Rio: Spanish origin. Means: river.

Robin: Teutonic/Anglo-Saxon origin. Means: one with bright fame, a robin. Ethnic backgrounds: English/Welsh. Alternative spellings and nicknames: Robina, Robby, Robinia, Robinette, Robinett, Robine, Robena, Robbin, Robbi, Robi, Robenia, Robyn, Robbie.

Rodas: Greek/Italian origin. Means: a rose garden, roses. Ethnic background: Hispanic.

Rory: Teutonic/Gaelic origin. Means: a famous king, red hair/complexion. Ethnic background: Irish. Alternative spellings: Rorry, Rorie, Rurik.

Rosario: Latin/Spanish origin. Means: a beautiful rose, reference to Mary. Ethnic background: Hispanic.

Russet: Latin origin. Means: ruddy.

Rwanda: Unknown origin and meaning.

Sacha: Greek/Slavic origin. Means: defender of mankind.

Saka: Unknown origin. Means: slope.

Saki: Unknown origin. Means: cape.

Salem: Arabic origin. Means: peace.

Salud: Latin/Spanish origin. Means: salvation, reference to Mary.

Salween: Unknown origin and meaning.

Sana: Unknown origin and meaning.

Sandy: Greek/Anglo-Saxon origin. Means: defender, helper of all men.

Sangay: Unknown origin and meaning.

Sardonyx: Greek origin. Unknown meaning.

Saturday: Latin origin. Means: Saturn's day, the 7th day.

Sean: Hebrew/Irish origin. Means: God is gracious. Ethnic backgrounds: English/Welsh.

Seine: Greek origin. Means: a fishing net.

Sepia: Greek origin. Means: a cuttlefish, brownish.

September: Latin origin. Means: the 7th Roman month.

Shamil: Unknown origin and meaning. Ethnic background: Russian.

Shandy: Old English origin. Means: boisterous, rambunctious.

Shannon: Gaelic origin. Means: small, of wisdom.

Shasta: Unknown origin and meaning.

Shawn: Hebrew/Irish origin. Means: God is gracious.

Shea: Irish origin. Means: majestic, asked.

Shelby: Anglo-Saxon origin. Means: from the sheltered farm.

Shelley: Anglo-Saxon origin. Means: from the ledge or shelly meadow. Ethnic background: Irish. Alternative spellings and nicknames: Shell, Shelly, Shelli, Shellie, Shelly, Shell.

Sheridan: Celtic/Irish origin. Means: savage, wild, untamed. Nicknames: Dannie, Dan, Danny, Sherry.

Shima: Native American origin. Means: mother, island.

Sibley: Greek/Anglo-Saxon origin. Means: an oracle, friendly.

Sidney: French/Old English origin. Means: of St. Denis, of the riverside meadow. Alternative spellings and nicknames: Syd, Sid, Sydney.

Sidra: Latin origin. Means: of the stars, shining. Alternative spellings: Siddra, Sidras.

Sienna: Italian origin. Means: a brownish pigment.

Silvano: Latin origin. Means: from the forest. Ethnic background: Hispanic.

Silver: Anglo-Saxon origin. Means: white.

Skylar: Dutch origin. Means: sheltering.

Sloan: Celtic/Gaelic origin. Means: a warrior. Alternative spelling: Sloane.

Sobriety: Latin origin. Means: temperance, moderation.

Sola: Unknown origin. Means: alone, hermit.

Song: Old English origin. Means: a melody.

Spokane: Unknown origin and meaning.

Stacy: Greek origin. Means: one who shall rise again, resurrection. Alternative spellings and nicknames: Stace, Stacey, Stacie.

Sterling: Old English origin. Means: little star, truly valuable. Alternative spelling: Stirling.

Stevie: Greek/Anglo-Saxon origin. Means: garland, crowned in victory.

Stockton: Old English origin. Means: from the tree-lined estate.

Sunday: Greek origin. Means: day of the sun.

Sydney: French/Old English origin. Means: of St. Denis, of the riverside meadow. Alternative spellings and nicknames: Syd, Sidney, Sid, Sidonie, Sidonia.

Sympathy: Greek origin. Means: with great compassion.

Syria: Unknown origin and meaning.

t

Tacoma: Unknown origin and meaning.

Taft: Anglo-Saxon origin. Means: a river.

Tagawa: Unknown origin. Means: a field.

Tahoe: Unknown origin and meaning.

Tal: Hebrew origin. Means: dew of heaven.

Tambora: Unknown origin and meaning.

Tanabe: Unknown origin and meaning.

Tanaka: Unknown origin and meaning.

Tanana: Unknown origin and meaning.

Tanner: Old English origin. Means: a preparer of leather. Nicknames: Tann, Tannie, Tanny, Tan.

Tansey: Greek/Latin origin. Means: immortal, tenacious.

Tarim: Unknown origin and meaning.

Taupe: Latin origin. Means: mole, dark brown-gray.

Taylor: Latin/French origin. Means: to cut, a tailor. Alternative spelling: Tailor.

Teal: Germanic origin. Means: a small duck.

Tegan: Celtic origin. Means: a doe.

Temperance: Latin origin. Means: mixed in proper proportions.

Tengger: Unknown origin and meaning.

Terence: Latin origin. Means: polished, tender. Ethnic background: Irish. Alternative spellings and nicknames: Terencio, Terrence, Terry, Torrance.

Terry: Latin/Germanic origin. Means: polished, of the powerful tribe.

Tethyan: Unknown origin and meaning.

Teton: Native American origin. Unknown meaning.

Thabana: Unknown origin and meaning.

Thanksgiving: Anglo-Saxon origin. Means: to give thanks.

Thien: Unknown origin. Means: an expert.

Thieu: Unknown origin and meaning.

Thistle: Old English origin. Means: a prickly plant.

Tho: Unknown origin and meaning.

Thursday: Norse/Latin origin. Means: Thor's day, thunderous.

Timothea: Greek origin. Means: one who honors and fears God. Alternative spellings and nicknames: Timi, Timmi, Timmie, Timotea, Thea, Tim, Timmy.

Tobago: Unknown origin and meaning.

Tomila: Unknown origin and meaning.

Torrens: Gaelic/Irish origin. Means: from the knolls.

Torrey: Celtic/Gaelic origin. Means: from the tower or knolls.

Toy: Unknown origin and meaning.

Toyo: Japanese origin. Means: plentiful.

Tracy: Greek/Latin origin. Means: brave fighter, bold, reaper. Ethnic backgrounds: English/Welsh. Alternative spellings and nicknames: Trace, Tracie, Tracey, Tracey, Tracie.

Tran: Unknown origin. Means: forehead.

Tristan: Latin/Welsh origin. Means: full of sorrow, noisy. Ethnic backgrounds: German, Hispanic. Nicknames: Tris.

True: Anglo-Saxon origin. Means: faithful, loyal.

Turquois: French origin. Means: a sky-blue gem. Alternative spelling: Turquoise.

Tyler: Anglo-Saxon origin. Means: a maker of tiles or bricks. 5th most popular boy's name of the '90s. Alternative spellings and nicknames: Tiler, Ty.

U

Uda: Teutonic origin. Means: one with great fortune, prosperous. Ethnic background: Jewish.

Ulexite: Unknown origin and meaning.

Unni: Norse origin. Means: modest.

Ural: Unknown origin and meaning.

Uriah: Hebrew origin. Means: God is my flame. Alternative spellings: Urias, Uriel.

Utah: Spanish origin. Means: mountain dwellers.

V

Vaclav: Slavic/Czech origin. Means: one with greater glory.

Val: Latin origin. Means: one with strength and bravery.

Valentine: Latin origin. Means: one who is strong and healthy, valiant. Ethnic background: Irish. Alternative spellings and nicknames: Valentijn, Valiant, Valentino, Valente, Val, Valentin.

Valeska: Slavic origin. Means: glorious leader. Ethnic background: German.

Vasya: Greek/Slavic origin. Means: with royal blood, regal.

Verne: Latin origin. Means: springlike, born in spring. Alternative spelling: Verda.

Vesuvius: Latin origin. Unknown meaning.

Vistula: Unknown origin and meaning.

Vivian: Latin/French origin. Means: alive, lively, full of life. Alternative spellings and nicknames: Viv, Vyvyan, Vivianne, Vivie, Vevay, Vivia, Viviane, Viv, Vi, Vivien, Vivi, Vivyan, Vivienne, Vivien, Viviana.

Volga: Slavic origin. Unknown meaning.

W **Waverly:** Old English origin. Means: from the field of wavering aspens. Nicknames: Leigh, Lee.

Weaver: Old English origin. Means: from the path by the water, weaves.

Wendell: Slavic/Teutonic origin. Means: a wanderer. Alternative spelling: Wendel.

Wentforth: Unknown origin and meaning.

Whitney: Anglo-Saxon origin. Means: from the white island. Nickname: Whit.

Wichita: Unknown origin and meaning.

Wilmar: Teutonic origin. Means: a determined protector, with fame.

Winfred: Teutonic/Old English origin. Means: a peace-loving friend. Ethnic background: Irish. Alternative spellings and nicknames: Win, Winfrid, Winifred.

Wing: Old English origin. Means: warm, of flight.

Winter: Anglo-Saxon origin. Means: born in the winter.

Wisconsin: Unknown origin and meaning.

Wisdom: Old English origin. Means: wise with knowledge.

Wray: Norse origin. Means: one who dwells in the corner.

Wyoming: Unknown origin and meaning.

Y **Yama:** Hebrew origin. Means: toward the sea, westward.

Yangtze: Chinese origin. Unknown meaning.

Z **Zagros:** Unknown origin and meaning.

Zambesi: Unknown origin and meaning.

Zimra: Hebrew/Arabic origin. Means: song of praise, choice fruit. Ethnic background: Hebrew.

Zoisite: Unknown origin and meaning.

baby name finder

What follows is 42 separate lists of names divided into every category we could think of. If your baby's name has to fit certain specifications, here is your easy reference guide. If you know you want a three-syllable first name to go with your one-syllable last name, the names are divided out for you by syllable. If you really want a Czechoslovakian name, they're also listed by nationality. Or for a name with a biblical namesake, you've come to the right place.

Here's how it works: Each list contains first names only. Scan each list for names that catch your eye, then flip to the front of the book to look up that name's definition and origin. Repeat until you've found a name you like. Easy, right?

Happy hunting!

Flowers

Alfalfa	Daffodil
Alocasia	Dahlia
Althaea	Daisy
Amaryllis	Daphne
Andromeda	Erica
Angelica	Forsythia
Anise	Fuchsia
Artemisia	Ginger
Aster	Heather
Astilbe	Iris
Azalea	Ivy
Basil	Jasmine
Bellis	Lavender
Bergenia	Lilac
Blephilia	Lily
Brasenia	Maize
Brassica	Marigold
Burnet	Mariposa
Buttercup	Melissa
Cacalia	Mitchella
Calanthe	Oleander
Caltha	Orchid
Camassia	Peony
Camelina	Petunia
Camellia	Rose
Cardamine	Rosemary
Carnation	Sage
Charlock	Silene
Chervil	Tulip
Cicely	Veronica
Cinnamon	Violet
Clover	Willow
Coriander	
Cosmos	
Cyperus	
Cypress	

Colors

Amber	Red
Bay	Royal
Black	Ruby
Burgundy	Russet
Cassis	Rust
Cerulean	Scarlet
Charcoal	Sepia
Chestnut	Sienna
Cobalt	Silver
Coffee	Slate
Copper	Taupe
Crimson	Teal
Fuchsia	Thistle
Garnet	Turquoise
Gold	Violet
Hazel	Willow
Heather	
Hunter	
Indigo	
Ivory	
Jade	
Khaki	
Lavender	
Loden	
Magenta	
Mahogany	
Maize	
Maroon	
Mink	
Olive	
Periwinkle	
Pink	
Plum	

Cities

Aberdeen
Ada
Addison
Akron
Albany
Alexandria
Alpena
Amarillo
Anderson
Annapolis
Ashland
Aspen
Astoria
Atlanta
Augusta
Austin
Beatrice
Blythe
Boise
Boston
Branson
Bristol
Buffalo
Butte
Cairo
Calgary
Camden
Canton
Casper
Chadron
Champaign
Charlotte
Cheyenne
Chicago
Clinton
Clovis
Cody
Columbia
Columbus
Concord
Cortez
Craig

			States	**Countries**
Dallas	Macon	Salem	Alaska	Andorra
Dayton	Madison	Salina	Arizona	Angola
Denver	Manchester	Savannah	California	Antigua
Dillion	Marion	Sidney	Carolina	Aruba
Dothan	Marshall	Spokane	Colorado	Austria
Duluth	Massillion	Stockton	Dakota	Bhutan
Durango	Medina	Sydney	Florida	Bolivia
Durham	Memphis	Tacoma	Georgia	Burma
Edmonton	Merced	Topeka	Hawaii	Chad
Elmira	Miami	Towson	Indiana	China
Eugene	Milan	Trenton	Kansas	Cyprus
Everett	Milford	Troy	Kentucky	Egypt
Fargo	Missoula	Tyler	Minnesota	England
Flint	Moline	Vernon	Missouri	Fiji
Florence	Monroe	Victoria	Montana	Georgia
Fulton	Montgomery	Warren	Nebraska	Guam
Gary	Muncie	Webster	Nevada	Holland
Hamilton	Nairobi	Wichita	Oregon	Jamaica
Hampton	Norman	Willow	Tennessee	Jordan
Hartford	Oakley	Wilmar	Texas	Libya
Hays	Odessa	Winslow	Utah	Malaysia
Helena	Olean	Yuma	Virginia	Mali
Hibbing	Olympia		Wisconsin	Martinique
Houston	Orlando		Wyoming	Mayotte
Hugo	Oroville			Monaco
Jackson	Oslo			Nepal
Jasper	Paris			Niger
Joplin	Paterson			Panama
Lamar	Peoria			Rwanda
Lawrence	Phoenix			Syria
Lawton	Pierre			Tobago
Lincoln	Pratt			Trinidad
London	Prescott			
Lowell	Quincy			
Lubbock	Racine			
	Raleigh			
	Regina			
	Reno			
	Richmond			
	Riga			
	Rio			
	Roswell			

Gems

Agate
Amethyst
Aquamarine
Calcite
Citrine
Copper
Cornelian
Crystal
Diamond
Emerald
Garnet
Geode
Gold
Ivory
Jacinth
Jade
Jadeite
Jasper
Jet
Moonstone
Obsidian
Onyx
Opal
Pearl
Peridot
Platinum
Quartz
Ruby
Sapphire
Sardonyx
Silver
Topaz
Turquois
Ulexite
Zoisite

Mountains

Aconcagua	Kerinci
Aleutian	Khingan
Alp	King
Alpine	Kirkpatrick
Altai	Kolyma
Andes	Koryak
Annapurna	Logan
Ararat	Lykaon
Atlas	Massif
Balkan	Mayon
Blanc	McKinley
Brooks	Nevada
Carstenz	Olympus
Cascade	Ossa
Colima	Pavlof
Columbia	Pelee
Cook	Pelion
Corcovado	Pico
Cordillera	Pyrenees
Cristobal	Rainier
Cyllene	Rocky
Dashen	Ruiz
Eiger	Sangay
Elbert	Shasta
Elbruz	Sierra
Elias	Storm
Ellsworth	Tambora
Erebus	Tengger
Etna	Tethyan
Everest	Teton
Fuji	Thabana
Helens	Tomila
Helicon	Ural
Himalaya	Vesuvius
Hood	Vinson
Hubbard	Washington
Hudson	Whitney
Huila	Wilhelm
Ida	Zagros
Jan	
Jaya	
Jebel	

Lakes and Rivers

Akaka	Helmand
Albert	Henry
Amazon	Herval
Amur	Hudson
Aral	Huron
Arthur	Indus
Baikal	James
Barkley	Kemi
Bowen	Kolyma
Case	Kurile
Caspian	Lawrence
Chad	Lena
Chari	Livingston
Chelan	Loire
Churchill	Mackenzie
Colorado	Madison
Como	Magdalena
Congo	Marion
Constance	Matana
Cooper	Meade
Danube	Meredith
Darling	Mesen
Darya	Mississippi
Della	Murray
Dnieper	Nelson
Don	Neman
Dvina	Ness
Ebro	Neva
Elbe	Niagara
Erie	Nigel
Eyre	Niger
Francis	Nile
Fraser	Nyasa
Gairdner	Olenek
Ganges	Onega
Garonne	Ontario
Geneva	Orange
Georgia	Oreille
Gila	Orinoco
Glomma	Pearl
Godavari	Pechora
Helena	Pecos
	Powell

232

	Virtues	Calendar	People—Biblical	
Rayburn	Charity	April	Aaron	Daniel
Rhine	Chastity	Arbor	Abaddon	Darius
Rhone	Compassion	August	Abdon	David
Rio	Consistency	Autumn	Abednego	Deborah
Salween	Constance	Christmas	Abel	Demetrius
Seine	Courtesy	December	Abimelech	Diana
Sidney	Faith	Easter	Abinadab	Dorcas
Sinclair	Gentle	Fall	Abraham	Drusilla
Snake	Goodness	February	Absalom	Eleazar
Stirling	Harmony	Friday	Adam	Eli
Stockton	Holiness	January	Adonijah	Eliab
Summer	Honesty	July	Aeneas	Elijah
Tahoe	Honor	June	Ahab	Elimelech
Tallulah	Hope	Labor	Ahaziah	Eliphaz
Tanana	Hospitality	March	Ahimelech	Elisha
Tarim	Humbleness	May	Alphaeus	Elizabeth
Torrens	Humility	Monday	Amman	Enoch
Tully	Joy	November	Amnon	Ephriam
Ural	Justice	October	Amos	Esau
Victoria	Kindness	Saturday	Ananias	Esther
Vistula	Knowledge	September	Andrew	Ethan
Volga	Love	Summer	Andronicus	Eunice
Walker	Patience	Sunday	Anna	Eve
Wentforth	Peace	Thanksgiving	Annas	Ezekiel
Wilson	Pity	Thursday	Aquila	Ezra
Yangtze	Purity	Tuesday	Ariel	Festus
Yosemite	Sobriety	Wednesday	Asher	Gabriel
Yukon	Sympathy	Winter	Athaliah	Gad
Zambesi	Temperance		Azariah	Gaius
	Truth		Barabbas	Gideon
	Wisdom		Barnabas	Goliath
			Bartholomew	Gomer
			Bathsheba	Habakkuk
			Belshazzar	Hadad
			Benjamin	Hagar
			Boaz	Haggai
			Cain	Hamor
			Caleb	Hanani
			Cornelius	Hananiah
				Hannah

			People— Saints	
Ichabod	Nahash	Tabitha	Aaron	Anysia
Isaac	Naomi	Tamar	Abbo	Apollo
Isaiah	Nathan	Thaddaeus	Abercius	Athanasius
Ishmael	Nathanael	Thomas	Abraham	Attalas
Jaazaniah	Nebedaeus	Timothy	Acacius	Augustine
Jacob	Nebuchadnezzar	Titus	Achard	Aurea
James	Nehemiah	Uriah	Acisclus	Balbina
Jason	Nicodemus	Uriel	Adam	Barbara
Jeremiah	Noah	Vashti	Adaucus	Bardo
Jesse	Obadiah	Zacchaeus	Addai	Barnard
Jesus	Paul	Zadok	Adela	Basil
Jezebel	Peter	Zebedee	Adrian	Beatrice
Joab	Pethuel	Zechariah	Adulf	Benedict
Joanna	Philemon	Zedekiah	Afan	Bernard
Job	Philetus	Zephaniah	Afra	Berno
Joel	Philip	Zerah	Agape	Bertha
John	Phinehas		Agapius	Birgitta
Jonah	Phoebe		Agatha	Blaise
Jonathan	Priscilla		Agnes	Boniface
Joseph	Rachel		Agricola	Bruno
Josephus	Rahab		Aidan	Caesaria
Joshua	Rebekah		Aignan	Casimir
Josiah	Rehoboam		Ailbhe	Caspar
Judas	Reuben		Ailred	Catherine
Lazarus	Rhoda		Alban	Cecilia
Leah	Rufus		Albert	Charles
Levi	Ruth		Alexander	Christina
Lot	Samson		Alexis	Christmas
Luke	Samuel		Alice	Christopher
Lydia	Sarah		Amadeus	Clare
Maacah	Saul		Amadour	Claudia
Manasseh	Shadrach		Ambrose	Cleopatra
Mark	Shemaiah		Ammon	Constantine
Martha	Shiloh		Anastasia	Cornelius
Mary	Silas		Andrew	Cyril
Matthew	Simeon		Angela	Damasus
Melchizedek	Simon		Angelico	Daniel
Micah	Solomon		Angelo	David
Michael	Stephen		Anskar	Dominic
Mordecai			Anthony	Donald
Moses			Antonia	Edbert
			Antony	Edith
				Edmund

Ethnic—African

Edward	Judith	Peter	Aba	Beluchi
Edwin	Julian	Philip	Ababno	Bunmi
Elizabeth	Julius	Phoebe	Abanobi	Buruku
Emily	Justin	Prisca	Abasi	Bwerani
Eric	Katherine	Priscilla	Abayomi	Chiamaka
Eugene	Kenneth	Ralph	Abebi	Chibale
Eugenia	Kevin	Raphael	Abeeku	Chidi
Eurosia	Kieran	Raymund	Abeo	Chijioke
Eustace	Laurence	Reinold	Abimbola	Chika
Everildis	Lelia	Richard	Abioye	Chikosi
Fabian	Leo	Rita	Abosi	Chiku
Faith	Leonard	Robert	Adaego	Chimanga
Felix	Louis	Romanus	Adaeze	Chinenye
Florian	Lucy	Rose	Adanma	Chipo
Francis	Luke	Rufus	Ade	Chizoba
Frederick	Macarius	Rupert	Adedewe	Chuma
Gabriel	Magnus	Sabina	Adeola	Dalia
George	Marcellus	Sanchia	Adom	Deka
Gerard	Margaret	Sebastian	Adwin	Dibia
Gertrude	Maria	Silvester	Afafa	Donkor
Gilbert	Marian	Simeon	Afryea	Dumisani
Godfrey	Martin	Simon	Aisha	Dzidzo
Gregory	Mary	Stephen	Aiyetoro	Ebere
Guy	Matthias	Teresa	Akins	Efua
Hedda	Maura	Thea	Akuako	Ekechi
Henry	Maurice	Theodore	Akwate	Ekechukwu
Herbert	Maximillian	Thomas	Akwete	Elom
Hilary	Melaine	Timothy	Ama	Eshe
Hilda	Michael	Valentine	Amazu	Ezeamaka
Hope	Mildred	Veronica	Ampah	Ezenachi
Hubert	Monica	Victor	Ankoma	Ezeoha
Hugh	Natalia	Victoria	Asha	Faraji
Ida	Nicholas	Vincent	Atsu	Fayola
Isaac	Nino	Virgil	Aziza	Feechi
Isabel	Olaf	Walter	Azubuike	Fola
James	Oliver	Wilfrid	Baako	Foluke
Jason	Oswald	William	Badru	Gamba
Jeremy	Otto	Wolfgang	Bahati	Ginikanwa
Jerome	Patrick	Zachary	Balogun	Gowon
Joachim	Paul	Zoe	Bayo	Gulai
Joan	Pelagia			Guva
John				Habika
Joseph				Habimama

Halima	Matunde	Rehema		**Ethnic—** **Czech**
Hanisi	Mawali	Rudo	Alena	Kveta
Hasina	Mawasi	Rufano	Alipi	Kvetoslava
Ibeamaka	Mawulolo	Sabola	Anastazie	Kynos
Idowu	Mensa	Sanura	Anton	Ladislav
Ifeanacho	Mma	Sekani	Antonin	Lenka
Iheoma	Mosi	Serwa	Berta	Lubomir
Ikenna	Mudiwa	Shamfa	Blanka	Ludek
Isoke	Mulogo	Shani	Bohumila	Ludvik
Izebe	Nabulungi	Shermarke	Bohuslav	Maria
Jabari	Nafula	Sobenna	Ctirad	Matylda
Jabulani	Nakisisa	Tabansi	Dagmar	Michal
Jamila	Naliaka	Taiwo	Dana	Milada
Jojo	Namono	Tatu	Drahomira	Milan
Jwahir	Nassor	Tau	Dusan	Milos
Kadija	Nayo	Thambo	Eva	Miroslav
Kamania	Nduka	Thema	Felix	Oldrich
Kamau	Neema	Torkwase	Frantisek	Olga
Kamba	Ngoli	Tsalani	Gabriela	Ondrej
Kampihe	Ngozi	Uba	Gustav	Otakar
Kamulira	Niamke	Ubanwa	Hana	Pavel
Kamuzu	Nobuhle	Uchechi	Helena	Pavlina
Kasiya	Nolizwe	Udenwa	Hilda	Petr
Kayode	Nuru	Ugo	Ida	Radka
Keanjaho	Nwabudike	Urbi	Igor	Radomir
Kelechi	Nwaoma	Uzoma	Imrich	Rudolf
Kontar	Obiajulu	Uzondu	Ingrid	Stanislav
Kumiwa	Obinna	Waseme	Iveta	Stepanka
Kunle	Obioma	Watende	Ivona	Teodor
Kwabena	Ode	Yobachi	Jana	Vaclav
Kwacha	Okpara	Zahur	Jarmila	Vera
Layla	Olubayo	Zainabu	Jaromir	Viera
Lebechi	Omolara	Zakiya	Jaroslav	Vincent
Limbe	Osakwe	Zuberi	Jaroslava	Vitezslav
Lisimba	Oseye	Zwena	Jindrich	Vladimir
Lotachukwu	Othieno		Jiri	Vlasta
Lulu	Ozioma		Jirina	Vlastibor
Mablevi	Paki		Josef	Vlastimil
Madu	Panya		Juraj	Werner
Madzimoyo	Ramla		Justin	Zdenek
Mahluli	Rashida		Kamil	Zdenka
Malawa	Rashidi		Karel	
Masamba			Karla	
			Karol	

Ethnic—
Dutch

Adrianus	Fedde	Johan	Marloes	Ties
Aleen	Femke	Johanna	Marrigje	Tineke
Alette	Fiep	Jolande	Marties	Tryn
Annelies	Fimke	Joop	Martijn	Van
Anneloes	Flos	Joost	Matthijs	Vander
Annemarie	Francisca	Jord	Mechteld	Vandyke
Annie	Friso	Joris	Meike	Wiep
Anton	Geert	Jorren	Meindert	Wieteke
Arjan	Gerben	Jorrit	Merel	Wilhelmina
Atje	Gerrit	Jos	Mieke	Willebald
Barend	Gert	Josephine	Neeltje	Willeke
Bart	Gertjan	Kaatje	Nelleke	Willem
Bas	Gijs	Karel	Nick	Willemien
Berend	Gisbert	Karsten	Nicolaas	Willemijn
Bert	Goos	Katrien	Nicolette	Wilma
Boukje	Greet	Kees	Niene	Wiske
Brechje	Guus	Klaartje	Nienke	Wouter
Carel	Haike	Klaas	Noortje	Yvonne
Carina	Hanne	Koen	Orseline	
Catharina	Hanneke	Koos	Petrus	
Claus	Hans	Kornel	Piet	
Clske	Harmen	Krijn	Pieter	
Conny	Harriet	Laurien	Pim	
Daan	Haye	Lennart	Pippin	
Deman	Hein	Lieke	Riemer	
Detmer	Herman	Liesbeth	Rikkert	
Dieuwertje	Hessel	Loes	Roderik	
Dirkje	Hidde	Lonneke	Ronaldus	
Douwe	Hilbert	Lotje	Roos	
Duco	Iaap	Lynda	Rutgerus	
Edsard	Ineke	Maaike	Sacco	
Eelco	Jacobien	Maarten	Sander	
Eet	Jacomine	Maartje	Sanne	
Eibe	Jan	Madelief	Schuyler	
Eiger	Janne	Marga	Sippie	
Elisabeth	Janneke	Margie	Sjoerd	
Elsbeth	Jelmer	Margriet	Slerd	
Elske	Jenneke	Marhtha	Sophie	
Eward	Jeroen	Marieke	Stijn	
	Jet	Marjon	Sybren	
	Jinte			
	Joep			

Ethnic—
English/Welsh

Adam	Darren	Janine	Louise	Samantha
Adeoye	Darryl	Jannette	Lucinda	Sarah
Adrian	David	Jason	Lucy	Scott
Alan	Dean	Jayne	Malcolm	Sean
Alexa	Deborah	Jean	Margaret	Sebastian
Alexander	Debra	Jennifer	Mark	Sharron
Alison	Divina	Jeremy	Martin	Shaun
Allan	Donna	Jessica	Mary	Simon
Amanda	Donovan	Jill	Matin	Simone
Amy	Douglas	Joanna	Matthew	Sonia
Andrew	Dudley	Joanne	Meg	Stacey
Angela	Duncan	Jodie	Melanie	Stephanie
Ann	Edward	John	Michael	Stephen
Anna	Elizabeth	Jonathan	Michelle	Steve
Annabelle	Emma	Jonathon	Natalie	Steven
Anthony	Eric	Joslyn	Neal	Stuart
Arthur	Fatima	Judy	Neil	Susan
Barry	Fiona	Julian	Nesta	Susannah
Belinda	Francis	Julie	Nicholas	Theresa
Benjamin	Garry	June	Nicky	Thomas
Beryl	Gary	Karen	Nicola	Tim
Beverley	Gavin	Kathleen	Nigel	Timothy
Bob	Gaynor	Kathryn	Nina	Todd
Brendan	Geoffrey	Katie	Norman	Tracy
Cameron	Germma	Kaye	Oliver	Venissa
Carl	Gillian	Keith	Paul	Verona
Carly	Gladys	Kelly	Pauline	Vicki
Caroline	Gordon	Kenneth	Peter	Victoria
Catherine	Graham	Kerrith	Philip	Virginia
Charles	Grayson	Kerry	Pierre	Wayne
Charlotte	Gwen	Kevin	Rachel	Wendy
Christina	Hannah	Kim	Rebecca	William
Christine	Hayley	Kirsty	Richard	
Christopher	Hayton	Kriss	Robert	
Claire	Heather	Laura	Robin	
Clare	Helen	Leanne	Ronald	
Colin	Hilary	Lee	Rosemary	
Craig	Hugh	Lesley	Russell	
Daley	Ian	Lin	Ryan	
Damian	Irina	Linda		
Daniel	James	Lindsay		
	Jamie	Linsey		
	Janet	Lisa		

Ethnic—
French

Adrian	Edmond	Ignace	Maurice	Sebastien
Adrien	Edouard	Isabelle	Max	Seraphin
Alain	Elodie	Jacqueline	Melanie	Serge
Albert	Emile	Jacques	Michel	Silviane
Aldo	Emilie	Jean	Michele	Simone
Alexandre	Emma	Jeanne	Micheline	Sophie
Amedee	Ernestine	Jeannie	Mickael	Stephan
Andre	Etienne	Jehan	Mireille	Stephane
Annick	Eugene	Jerome	Monique	Stephanie
Antoine	Evelyne	Joseph	Muriel	Suzanne
Armand	Fabienne	Josette	Nicolas	Sylvie
Arnaud	Fabrice	Jules	Nicole	Therese
Audrey	Ferdinand	Julie	Noelle	Thierry
Aurelie	Fernand	Julien	Octave	Veronique
Barthelemy	Francis	Laetitia	Pascal	Victor
Beatrice	Franck	Laurence	Pascale	Vincent
Bendicte	François	Laurent	Patrick	Virginie
Benoit	Frederic	Leon	Paul	Yave
Bernadette	Gabrielle	Leonce	Paulette	Yvan
Bernard	Galuelle	Liliane	Perrine	Yves
Bibienne	Gaston	Louis	Philippe	Yvette
Brigitte	Genevieve	Louise	Pierre	Yvonne
Catherine	Georges	Lucien	Raymond	
Cedric	Georgette	Lucienne	Regine	
Celine	Gerald	Lylian	Rene	
Chantal	Gerard	Madeleine	Renee	
Charles	Germain	Marc	Robert	
Christophe	Gilbert	Marcel	Roger	
Claire	Gilles	Marguerite	Romain	
Claude	Ginette	Marie	Rose	
Claudie	Gisele	Marielle	Rosy	
Colette	Guillaume	Marius		
Daniel	Gustave	Marlene		
Daniele	Guy	Marthe		
Danielle	Guylaine	Martine		
Denis	Helene	Maryse		
Denise	Henri	Marysette		
Didier	Hermann	Maryvonne		
Dominique	Herve	Mathieu		
	Honorine			
	Hughes			

Ethnic—
German

Achim	Annegret	Bertram	Detier	Emmerich
Adalbert	Anneliese	Bettina	Detlef	Engelbert
Adam	Annerose	Bianka	Detmar	Erasmus
Adelaide	Anselm	Birgit	Dierk	Erhard
Adelheid	Anselma	Bjorn	Dietbert	Erich
Adolf	Antje	Blanka	Dieter	Ermelind
Adrian	Antoinette	Bodo	Diethelm	Erna
Adriane	Anton	Bonifatius	Diethild	Ernst
Agathe	Antonia	Boris	Dietrich	Erwin
Agnes	Arbogast	Brigitta	Dominik	Etzal
Albert	Archibald	Brigitte	Dora	Eugen
Alberta	Arend	Brunhild	Dorothea	Eugenie
Albertine	Aribert	Bruno	Dorte	Eulalia
Albin	Armin	Burkhard	Eberhard	Eva
Albrecht	Arno	Cacilie	Eckart	Ewald
Alexa	Arnulf	Camillo	Eckbert	Fabian
Alexander	Aron	Candita	Eckhard	Falk
Alfons	Artur	Caren	Edda	Fedor
Alfred	Asmus	Carmen	Edelbert	Felix
Alice	Astrid	Carola	Edelgard	Felizitas
Aline	Attila	Carsten	Edgar	Feodora
Alma	August	Catharina	Edmund	Ferdinand
Alois	Aurelia	Christa	Eduard	Fidelio
Aloisia	Axel	Christian	Edwin	Flora
Alrune	Babette	Christina	Effi	Florentin
Alwin	Balduin	Christoph	Egbert	Frank
Amadeus	Balthasar	Claudia	Egmont	Franz
Amalia	Baptist	Claudius	Egon	Franzel
Amandus	Barbel	Clemens	Ehrenfried	Franziska
Ambrosius	Bardulf	Constantin	Eike	Frauke
Anatol	Barnabas	Cordula	Elfi	Freia
Andrea	Barthel	Corinna	Elfriede	Frida
Andreas	Bastian	Cornelia	Elisa	Fridmann
Anett	Beate	Cornelius	Elisabeth	Fridolin
Angelika	Beatrix	Cosima	Elke	Friederke
Angelus	Bella	Dagmar	Ella	Friedrich
Anita	Benedikt	Dagobert	Elli	Fritz
Anja	Benjamin	Daniel	Elmar	Gabriel
Anke	Benno	David	Elsa	Gabriele
Anna	Bernd	Degenhard	Elsbeth	Gaston
	Bernhard	Delf	Emanuel	Gebhard
	Berta	Delila	Emil	Genoveva
	Berthold		Emile	Georgine

Gerda	Helmar	Jutta	Margit	Raimund
Gerhard	Helmut	Karin	Margrit	Rainer
Gerlind	Hendrik	Karl	Marianna	Raphaela
Gernot	Henrike	Karolina	Marika	Rebekka
Gertrud	Herta	Kasimir	Marius	Regina
Gisa	Hilde	Kaspar	Marliese	Reinhold
Gisbert	Holger	Katarina	Mathilde	Renate
Gitta	Horst	Kathe	Matthias	Roderich
Gottfried	Hulda	Katja	Maxi	Roland
Gotthard	Ida	Kerstin	Mechtild	Rolf
Gottlieb	Ignaz	Kilian	Meinhard	Roman
Gottlob	Ilse	Klara	Meta	Romy
Gotz	Immanuel	Klaus	Michael	Rosalinde
Gregor	Ina	Konrad	Michel	Rosi
Grete	Ines	Kornelia	Minna	Rosine
Grunhild	Ingo	Kunibert	Mirabell	Roswitha
Gudrun	Ingolf	Ladislaus	Monika	Rudiger
Guido	Ingrid	Lambert	Nanette	Rudolf
Gunter	Ira	Lea	Nelli	Ruprecht
Gunther	Irma	Leonie	Nils	Ruth
Gustav	Irmela	Leopola	Notburga	Sabine
Hagen	Irmgard	Leopold	Oda	Salvator
Hanna	Isa	Liane	Odo	Sandra
Hannelore	Isidor	Lieselotte	Olaf	Sebald
Hans	Jacob	Lilli	Olga	Selma
Harald	Jakob	Lisbeth	Ortfried	Senta
Harro	Jakobine	Lorenz	Ortrud	Sepp
Hartmann	Jan	Lothar	Ortwin	Severin
Hartmut	Jasper	Lucia	Oswald	Sibylle
Hasso	Jeannette	Ludolf	Otmar	Siegbert
Hedda	Joachim	Ludwig	Ottilie	Sieglinde
Heide	Jochen	Luise	Otto	Siegmund
Heidrun	Johann	Lukas	Pankraz	Sigrid
Hein	Johanna	Lutz	Patricia	Sigrun
Heiner	Jonas	Lydia	Paula	Sigurd
Heinrich	Jorg	Magda	Pauline	Solveig
Heinz	Josef	Malwin	Peer	Sonja
Hekter	Josefa	Malwine	Peter	Sophia
Helene	Josephine	Manfred	Petra	Stefan
Helga	Jost	Marcel	Philip	Steffen
Helge	Juliane	Marga	Pia	Steffi
Hella	Julius	Margaretha	Pius	Suse
Hellfried	Jurgen			

Tamara
Tanja
Tatjana
Thaddaus
Thekla
Theodor
Theodora
Thilde
Torsten
Traugott
Tristan
Trude
Udo
Ulbrich
Ulla
Ulrich
Ulrike
Ursula
Ute
Utz
Uwe
Valentin
Valeria
Valeska
Vera
Veronika
Vicki
Viktoria
Vinzenz
Viola
Vitus
Volker
Volkhard
Walburg
Waldemar
Waltraut
Wanda
Wendelin

Wenzel
Wera
Werner
Wernher
Wilfried
Wilhelm
Wilhelmine
Wolf
Wolfgang
Xaver
Xenia
Yvonne
Zacharias
Zenzi
Zita

Ethnic— Greek

Alex
Alexandros
Andrea
Andreas
Angelos
Anna
Ariadne
Aristides
Athena
Celeste
Charilaos
Charles
Christina
Christodoulous
Christos
Chrysie
Constantina
Constantine
Daphne
Demetra
Demetrios
Demitrios
Dimitri
Dino
Dionysios
Efrosini
Elaine
Eleni
Eleutherios
Elia
Elias
Elie
Eusebius
Eustrate
Evangelos
George
Georgios
Helen
Ioannis
John

Katrina
Kimon
Kostas
Leonidas
Linda
Loredo
Maria
Marios
Matina
Meletios
Michael
Mikis
Mikos
Miltiades
Nassos
Nicholas
Nicos
Nikon
Nikos
Nomikos
Olympia
Panos
Pantias
Perikles
Petro
Petros
Photius
Polygnotos
Seraphim
Silas
Solon
Spiridon
Spiro
Spyros
Stathis
Stavros
Stephanos

Telly
Thalia
Theano
Themistoklis
Theodoris
Theodoros
Theophrastos
Thomas
Tikey
Vasilios
Vassilis
Vasso
Yanis
Yannis
Zeese

Ethnic—
Hispanic

Abegail	Ambrosio	Benilde	Cipriano	Dimas
Abejundio	Americo	Benito	Ciro	Dina
Abelino	Amora	Benjamin	Clara	Dionisio
Abil	Amparo	Bermudo	Claudio	Dolores
Abirio	Ana	Bernal	Clemente	Domingo
Abrasia	Anabel	Bernica	Cleofas	Domitilo
Abundio	Analissa	Berta	Clotilde	Donaciano
Acisclo	Anastacio	Betsabe	Columba	Donaldo
Adalberto	Anatolio	Blanca	Concepcion	Doroteo
Adame	Andres	Blas	Conrado	Drusila
Adela	Anfanio	Bolivar	Conseja	Dulce
Adelaido	Angel	Bonavento	Constancio	Eberardo
Adelfo	Anselmo	Bonifacio	Consuelo	Edelmira
Adilmira	Antero	Brandio	Corazon	Edesio
Adolfo	Antonio	Braulia	Cordilio	Edissa
Adonaldo	Apolonio	Brigido	Corina	Edita
Adrian	Arabela	Caliopa	Corona	Edmundo
Afililio	Araceli	Calixto	Cosme	Eduardo
Agapito	Ariela	Camelia	Crescencio	Eduvigis
Agata	Armando	Camilo	Crespin	Efrain
Agripino	Armida	Candido	Cresusa	Ela
Agueleo	Arnoldo	Canuto	Crisanto	Eleazar
Agusto	Artemio	Caridad	Crisoforo	Elena
Aislara	Arturo	Carino	Cristian	Eleonor
Albano	Asuncion	Carisa	Cristo	Eleuterio
Alberto	Atanasio	Carlos	Cristobal	Elfrida
Aldegundo	Atilano	Carmen	Cruz	Elias
Alejandro	Aurelio	Carolina	Dalia	Eligio
Alelina	Aurora	Casiano	Damario	Elisabeth
Alfa	Bacilio	Casimiro	Damaso	Eliseo
Alfonso	Balbina	Cassandra	Damian	Elviro
Alfredo	Baldomero	Casto	Daniel	Emereo
Alicio	Baltasar	Catalina	Dante	Emeterio
Alma	Barbara	Caton	Dario	Emilio
Aloisio	Bartolme	Cayetano	Dativa	Emma
Altagracia	Beatriz	Cecilio	Debora	Endoro
Amable	Belen	Ceferino	Delfino	Engracia
Amada	Belia	Celedonio	Delida	Enrique
Amadeo	Belinda	Celestino	Demetrio	Epifanio
Amalio	Belino	Celia	Desiderio	Epitacio
Amancio	Belisario	Celso	Deyanira	Erasmo
Amanda	Benedicto	Cesar	Diamantina	Eredina
Amaramto	Benigno	Cinta	Diana	Eremita

Ernesto	Genaro	Imelda	Lorenzo	Melquiades
Esdras	Generosa	Indalecio	Lotario	Menas
Esmeralda	Genoveva	Ines	Lourdes	Mercedes
Esmero	Geraldo	Inocencio	Lucano	Mercurio
Esperanza	Gerardo	Irene	Lucas	Migdalia
Esquilo	German	Isaac	Lucia	Miguel
Estanislao	Gertrudis	Isabel	Lucinda	Miranda
Esteban	Gilberto	Isamel	Ludmila	Modesto
Estela	Ginebra	Isauro	Luis	Moises
Eufemia	Giolia	Isidoro	Lutero	Morio
Eugenio	Gisela	Jacinto	Luz	Morta
Eulalio	Gonzago	Jacobo	Macario	Nabor
Eusebio	Graciela	Jano	Macedonio	Narciso
Eutimia	Grata	Javier	Magdaleno	Natalio
Evangelina	Gregorio	Jeronimo	Malvina	Natividad
Everardo	Griselda	Jesus	Manuel	Nazario
Fabian	Guadalupe	Joaquin	Maranela	Nemesio
Facundo	Guillermo	Jorge	Marcelino	Nepomuceno
Faustino	Gumersindo	Jose	Marcia	Nereida
Febronio	Gustavo	Josefat	Marcial	Nestor
Federico	Haroldo	Juan	Marciana	Nevara
Felipo	Hazael	Jucundo	Marcos	Nicanor
Felix	Hector	Judit	Margarita	Nicolas
Fermin	Heliodoro	Julio	Margarito	Nicomedes
Fernando	Herberto	Jutta	Margila	Nieves
Fidel	Hermelinda	Juvencio	Maria	Nino
Filiberto	Hermenegildo	Ladislao	Mariana	Noe
Filomeno	Hermino	Landrada	Mario	Noemi
Fineas	Hernanda	Lauro	Marisa	Norberto
Flavio	Hersilia	Lavinia	Marisol	Obispo
Florencio	Hesiquio	Lazaro	Marsilio	Octavio
Fornasa	Higinio	Lea	Marta	Odessa
Fortuno	Hilario	Leda	Martin	Odilia
Francisco	Honoria	Leila	Mateo	Ofelio
Fuensanta	Horacio	Leon	Matilde	Olegario
Gabino	Hortencia	Leonardo	Mauricio	Olinda
Gabrieala	Humberto	Leonor	Maximiano	Onesimo
Gabriel	Icario	Leticia	Maya	Onofre
Garcia	Ida	Liberato	Melanio	Orestes
Gaspar	Ifigenia	Lidio	Melchor	Oscar
Gaston	Ignacio	Lilia	Melinda	Ovelia
Gemino	Ildefonso	Lino	Melisa	Ovidio
Genaida		Lisandro	Melito	Paco

Panfilo	Ramiro	Santiago	Teodulo	Vero
Pantaleon	Ramon	Sara	Teofilo	Verona
Pascual	Raquel	Saturnino	Teogenes	Vesta
Patricio	Raul	Sebastian	Tereso	Vetaria
Patroncinio	Rebeca	Segrada	Tesaura	Vicente
Paulo	Refugio	Serafiel	Thila	Victor
Paz	Regina	Serafin	Tiberio	Vidal
Pedro	Regulo	Serapio	Tiburcio	Vinefrida
Pefilia	Reinaldo	Serena	Timon	Viola
Peregrino	Remigio	Sergio	Timoteo	Violeta
Perfecto	Renata	Servacio	Tirso	Virgilio
Perla	Rene	Servando	Tito	Virtudes
Perpetua	Reyes	Setta	Tobias	Viterbo
Petronilo	Ricanora	Severo	Tolasa	Viviano
Picardus	Ricardo	Sigfrido	Tomas	Wanda
Piedad	Rito	Silvano	Toribio	Wilfrido
Pilar	Roberto	Silverio	Tranquilino	Wilma
Pioquinto	Rodas	Silvestre	Trena	Xantipa
Pitana	Rodolfo	Silvio	Trinidad	Xipto
Placido	Rodrigo	Simon	Trinotera	Xochil
Policarpo	Rogelio	Sippora	Tristan	Ydia
Polonice	Roldan	Sixto	Tulio	Yolanda
Pomposo	Roman	Socorro	Turnina	Zabulon
Ponciano	Romilda	Sofio	Ubaldo	Zacarias
Porfirio	Roque	Soledad	Ulfrido	Zaida
Praxedes	Rosa	Sonio	Ulielmi	Zapopan
Preciosa	Rosabel	Sotero	Ulises	Zaragoza
Presencia	Rosalba	Spes	Ulrico	Zenaido
Preto	Rosalio	Susano	Umberlina	Zenobio
Primitivo	Rosana	Tabita	Urbano	Zenon
Prisciliano	Rosario	Tacio	Urias	Zita
Pristina	Rufino	Talitha	Uriel	Zobeida
Procopio	Rumolda	Tamara	Ursula	Zoilo
Prudencia	Ruperto	Tancredo	Valente	Zoraida
Quasimodo	Ruth	Tarsila	Valerio	Zosimo
Quilmes	Sabino	Taurino	Valydia	Zotico
Quintera	Sagrario	Teclo	Vanora	Zulema
Quinto	Salome	Telesforo	Venancio	
Quirino	Salonia	Telma	Venceslao	
Rabul	Salud	Tempora	Veneranda	
Rafael	Salvador	Teo	Venerio	
Raimundo	Sancho	Teodardo	Veremundo	
	Santana	Teodoro	Verlita	

Ethnic— Hungarian

Akevy	Jozsef
Alban	Judit
Alpar	Julianna
Ambrus	Karoly
Andras	Katalin
Andrea	Klara
Aniko	Klemen
Anna	Kornel
Antal	Kriszta
Arpad	Krisztina
Attila	Lajos
Balint	Laszlo
Barnabas	Lenke
Bela	Lidia
Bernadett	Lucia
Csaba	Magdolna
Csilla	Margit
Denes	Maria
Emerencia	Mariann
Endre	Marta
Erika	Mihaly
Erno	Miklos
Ervin	Muntean
Erzsebet	Olga
Eva	Oszkar
Ferenc	Paula
Gabor	Peter
Gabriella	Sandor
Gergely	Tamas
Geza	Tibor
Gyorgy	Valeria
Gyozo	Zoltan
Gyula	Zsolt
Henrik	Zsuzsanna
Ildiko	
Ilona	
Imre	
Iren	
Istvan	
Ivan	
Janos	
Jeno	

Ethnic— Irish

Aedan	Conor	Felimy
Aileen	Cormac	Felix
Alan	Damien	Fergal
Allen	Dana	Fergus
Allie	Darcy	Fiachra
Altinure	Dearbhail	Fidelma
Angus	Declan	Finbar
Annabella	Deirdre	Finian
Annacotty	Denise	Finnbar
Aoife	Derek	Finola
Ardan	Dermot	Fintan
Ardara	Desmond	Fiona
Ardeen	Diarmaid	Flann
Art	Dominick	Flannan
Attracta	Donal	Freena
Barbara	Donall	Gallagher
Barry	Donat	Garret
Berneen	Donogh	Geoffrey
Bidelia	Eamon	Geraldine
Bran	Eamonn	Gertrude
Breeda	Eavan	Gilbert
Brenda	Eileen	Giles
Brendan	Eilis	Gloria
Brian	Eithne	Gorden
Bridget	Elaine	Grace
Brigit	Eleanor	Grainne
Bryan	Elva	Gregory
Caitlin	Emer	Hannah
Carleen	Emmet	Heather
Carroll	Enda	Heremon
Cathal	Eoin	Hermon
Catriona	Ernest	Hugh
Cecily	Ethna	Ida
Charlot	Eunan	Ina
Ciara	Eva	Irene
Cliona		Ismenia
Colm		Ismey
Colman		Ita
Colum		Ivor
Columban		Izett
Conall		
Conleth		
Connor		

James	Matilda	Quinn	Ulick	Abramo
Jana	Maura	Quintin	Ultan	Achille
Jane	Maureen	Rachel	Una	Ada
Jarlath	Michael	Randolph	Unity	Adamo
Jason	Miles	Raymond	Ursula	Adelaide
Jeninfer	Moina	Richard	Valentine	Adele
Joanne	Moira	Rickard	Vanessa	Adelina
Jonathan	Molly	Robert	Victoria	Adelmo
Julie	Mona	Roderick	Vincent	Adolfo
Justin	Morgan	Ronald	Vivienne	Adriano
Karen	Morrin	Ronan	William	Agata
Kathleen	Mortimer	Rory	Winfred	Agnese
Keelan	Murphy	Rose	Winifred	Agostino
Keith	Murrough	Ross	Yvonne	Alberta
Kelly	Murtough	Rupert	Zephan	Alberto
Kerill	Myles	Ryan		Aldo
Kevin	Myrna	Samuel		Alessandra
Kian	Neal	Scota		Alessandro
Kieran	Neil	Seamus		Alessio
Killian	Nessa	Sean		Alfonso
Kyras	Nessan	Seon		Alfredo
Laoghaire	Niall	Shane		Alice
Laurence	Niamh	Sharon		Amaila
Leila	Nicholas	Shaun		Ambrogio
Leo	Nicola	Shawn		Amelia
Linda	Nora	Sheena		Anastasia
Lisa	Noreen	Sheila		Andrea
Lorcan	Nuala	Shelia		Angela
Lorraine	Oisin	Shelley		Angelica
Louis	Oliver	Shirley		Angelo
Lucia	Olivia	Sinead		Anita
Lucy	Orla	Siobhan		Anna
Luke	Oscar	Sive		Annabella
Maeve	Owen	Stanley		Annamaria
Maille	Parlan	Suzanne		Annibale
Maire	Partholon	Tara		Anselmo
Mairead	Patrick	Terence		Antonella
Malachy	Paul	Teresa		Antonia
Malone	Peter	Thomas		Antonio
Manus	Philip	Tiernan		Arcibaldo
Marmaduke	Pierce	Timothy		Armando
Martin		Trina		Arnaldo
Mary		Turlough		Aroldo

Arrigo	Chiara	Egidio	Flavio	Giulietta
Arturo	Cinzia	Elena	Flora	Giulio
Assunta	Ciriaco	Eleonora	Franca	Giuseppe
Attilio	Cirillo	Elio	Franco	Giuseppina
Augusta	Ciro	Elisa	Frederico	Giustina
Augusto	Clara	Elisabetta	Fulvia	Giustino
Aurelia	Clarabella	Eliseo	Gabriele	Giusto
Aurelio	Clarice	Ella	Gabriella	Gloria
Aurora	Clarissa	Elsa	Gadeone	Goffredo
Baldassarre	Claudia	Elvira	Garibaldo	Grazia
Baldovino	Claudio	Emanuele	Gaspare	Gregorio
Barbara	Clemintina	Emilia	Gastone	Gualtiero
Barnaba	Cloe	Emilio	Genovetta	Guendalina
Bartolomeo	Clotilde	Emma	Geraldina	Guglielmo
Basillio	Corinna	Enrichetta	Gerardo	Guido
Beatrice	Cornelia	Enrico	Geremia	Guiseppa
Belinda	Cornelio	Eraldo	Germana	Guiseppina
Benedetto	Corrado	Ermanno	Gerolamo	Gustav
Beniamino	Cosimo	Ernesta	Gertrude	Iacopo
Beppe	Costantino	Ernesto	Gervaso	Ida
Berenice	Costanza	Ester	Gherardo	Ieronimo
Bernado	Costanzo	Ettore	Giacomina	Ignazio
Berta	Cristiana	Eufenia	Giacomo	Ilaria
Bertoldo	Cristiano	Eugenia	Gian	Ilario
Bertrando	Cristina	Eugenio	Gianna	Ilda
Biagio	Cristoforo	Eusebio	Gianni	Ildebrando
Bianca	Damiano	Eustachio	Giannina	Ileana
Bonifacio	Daniela	Eva	Gigi	Ines
Brigida	Dario	Evangelina	Gilberto	Innocenzo
Bruno	Davide	Evelina	Gino	Ippolito
Camilla	Debora	Fabiano	Gioacchino	Irene
Carla	Delia	Fabrizio	Giola	Irma
Carlo	Demetrio	Fausto	Gionata	Isabella
Carlotta	Diana	Fede	Giorgia	Isacco
Carmine	Dina	Federica	Giorgiana	Isidore
Carolina	Dino	Federico	Giorgio	Isotta
Casimiro	Dionigi	Fedora	Giosue	Ivo
Caterina	Dionisia	Felice	Giovanna	Lamberto
Cecilla	Domenico	Felicita	Giovanni	Lanfranco
Celeste	Dorotea	Ferdinando	Giroiamo	Laura
Celestina	Edgardo	Filippo	Giuditta	Lavinia
Celina	Edmondo	Fiorenza	Giulia	Lea
Cesare	Edoardo	Flavia	Giuliana	Leonardo

				Ethnic— Japanese
Leone	Natale	Remo	Teobaldo	Akinori
Leonora	Natalia	Renata	Teodora	Akira
Leopoldo	Nicola	Renzo	Teodoro	Bunji
Letizia	Nino	Riccardo	Teodosio	Chiura
Lia	Noemi	Rinaldo	Teresa	Chiyoko
Lidia	Nora	Rita	Timoteo	Chuhei
Liliana	Norberto	Roberta	Tito	Daigoro
Lorenzo	Norma	Roberto	Tobia	Fhoki
Luca	Novella	Rodolfo	Tomaso	Fujita
Lucia	Odoardo	Rodrigo	Tonino	Goro
Luciano	Olga	Rolando	Trivini	Hachiro
Lucio	Olimpia	Romeo	Tullia	Haruki
Lucrezia	Olivia	Rosa	Tullio	Hideaki
Luigi	Oliviero	Rosalinda	Uberio	Hideko
Luisa	Orazio	Rosanna	Ugo	Hideyo
Maddalena	Oreste	Rosella	Ulisse	Hiroko
Manuela	Orlando	Rosina	Ulrico	Hiroshi
Mara	Orsola	Rossana	Umberto	Hisaye
Marcella	Ortensia	Ruggero	Valentina	Ikuko
Marcello	Osvaldo	Ruth	Valentino	Inazo
Marco	Ottavia	Sabrina	Valeria	Isami
Margherita	Ottavito	Salvatore	Valerio	Isamu
Maria	Ottone	Samuele	Veronica	Isao
Mariano	Pamela	Sandro	Vincenzo	Ishiko
Mariarosa	Pancrazio	Sara	Virginia	Iva
Marie	Paola	Saverio	Vittore	Jiichiro
Marina	Paoletta	Sebastiano	Vittoria	Jiro
Mario	Paolo	Sereno	Vittorio	Jokichi
Marisa	Pascal	Sergio	Viviana	Junko
Marta	Patrizia	Sibilla	Zaccaria	Kanaye
Martino	Patrizio	Silvestro	Zeno	Kanichi
Massimiliano	Peppino	Silvia		Kaoru
Massimo	Pietro	Silvio		Katsu
Matilde	Priscella	Simeone		Kazuhiro
Matteo	Prudenzia	Simone		Kazuo
Mattia	Quintino	Sofia		Keiichi
Maurizio	Quinto	Speranza		Keiko
Mauro	Rachele	Stefania		Kentaro
Melania	Raffaella	Stefano		Kinji
Michele	Raimondo	Stella		Kitei
Miranda	Rebecca	Susanna		Kiyomi
Monica	Regina	Taddeo		Kiyoshi
Nadia	Reginaldo	Tecla		Koji
Nando				Kotaro

Ethnic—
Jewish

Kumiko	Shoji	Aaron	Amichai	Berura
Kusuo	Shotaro	Aba'ye	Amina	Bichri
Kyo	Shoze	Abahu	Amira	Bira
Kyutaro	Suma	Abba	Amitan	Blima
Kyuzo	Sutemi	Abel	Amtza	Blimeh
Machiko	Tadaatsu	Abir	Anshel	Blimele
Makio	Tadashi	Abira	Anshil	Bluma
Makoto	Takashi	Abiri	Anshl	Blumele
Mariko	Takehide	Aberlin	Arela	Bonesh
Masaaki	Takeo	Abrasha	Ariana	Breina
Masaji	Takeshi	Abrashen	Ariela	Bremel
Masajiro	Takuji	Abrashke	Arki	Breml
Masami	Tamio	Adael	Armona	Brina
Masamitsu	Teiko	Adam	Armoni	Brit
Masanao	Tetsuo	Adar	Arnona	Bruna
Masayuki	Tokunosuke	Adena	Asriel	Brune
Masura	Tomi	Adi	Atida	Buni
Mayumi	Tomo	Adiel	Atira	Bunim
Michi	Tooru	Adir	Avi	Carmel
Mine	Toshiko	Adira	Aviaz	Carmiel
Minoru	Toyo	Adiva	Avigal	Carmiela
Mitsuo	Toyokazu	Adiya	Avniel	Carmiya
Mitsuyoshi	Tsutomu	Adret	Avril	Carna
Miyoshi	Usaku	Agala	Avrom	Carni
Naoichi	Waka	Aharona	Avrum	Chai
Naoto	Wakako	Ahava	Avrumel	Chaika
Noboru	Yamato	Ahuva	Avrumke	Chaikeh
Nobutaka	Yasmuji	Aidel	Avrumtchick	Chaikel
Okei	Yasuo	Akiva	Basha	Chaiki
Osamu	Yasutaro	Alemet	Bara	Chana
Oyama	Yemyo	Alisa	Baram	Chanan
Reiko	Yojiro	Alissa	Baruch	Chani
Ryoichiro	Yoko	Alita	Batli	Chanina
Saburo	Yoshiaki	Aliza	Bayla	Chanoch
Sachiko	Yoshikatsu	Allegra	Bayle	Chaskel
Sadakichi	Yoshiko	Almagor	Baylke	Chavakuk
Sadao	Yoshinobu	Alona	Bazak	Chavivi
Satoru	Yoshio	Alteh	Behira	Chermon
Sawao	Yosuke	Alter	Ben	Chiyena
Seito	Yuji	Alterkeh	Benesh	Chiel
Sessue	Yukichi	Alufa	Benish	Chiram
Shigeo	Yukio	Alysa	Ber	
Shinsei	.	Amana	Berel	
Shohaci				

Chita	Eizik	Gabai	Henia	Ita
Chovev	Elad	Gabi	Henna	Iti
Chuma	Elazar	Gabriel	Henye	Itka
Chuna	Eldar	Gabriella	Hersh	Itmar
Chuneh	Eli	Gadil	Hershel	Itsche
Daba	Elinoar	Gai	Hershele	Itz
Dabra	Elisheva	Gavrel	Hertz	Itzig
Dadyeh	Elka	Gavriela	Hertzel	Itzik
Dalya	Elkan	Gavril	Hertzl	Ivriya
Dana	Elkin	Gavrilke	Hesh	Izzie
Daniel	Elrad	Gedil	Heskel	Izzy
Darom	Elya	Gefen	Hevel	Jeremiah
Daroma	Elyeh	Gendel	Hillel	Joel
Darona	Emmet	Gershom	Hindal	Joella
Dati	Erela	Getz	Hirsh	Joshua
David	Eshel	Getzel	Hirshl	Kadisha
Davida	Ester	Gibor	Hodel	Kadiya
Davrush	Etka	Gidil	Hodi	Kaniel
Deborah	Evreml	Gil	Horiya	Kapel
Delila	Evromel	Gilada	Hudel	Karmel
Devashka	Evromele	Gildor	Hudi	Kaski
Devir	Faiga	Gimpel	Hudya	Kasril
Dina	Feibush	Gina	Ichal	Kasrileke
Dissa	Feige	Ginendel	Ichel	Kayla
Dobra	Feivel	Gita	Ideh	Kedma
Dodi	Fishel	Gitel	Idele	Kefira
Dov-Ber	Fishke	Gitil	Idil	Kelila
Dudel	Foigl	Givon	Idit	Keskel
Dudu	Fraime	Glucke	Ilya	Keskil
Dudya	Frayda	Goral	Ilyash	Ketina
Dudyeh	Freidel	Guryon	Imanuel	Kitra
Dusha	Frima	Hadasa	Imanuela	Kitron
Duvid	Froma	Hadaseh	Irvin	Kiva
Eden	Fromel	Hadriel	Irvine	Kiveh
Efrat	Froyim	Hallela	Irving	Koppel
Efron	Froyimke	Harel	Isaac	Krayna
Efrona	Frume	Haskel	Isaiah	Kreina
Eidel		Henach	Ishmael	Kreindel
Eisig		Henda	Isser	Krindel
Eisik		Hende	Isserel	Kruna
Eitan		Hendel		Kryna
		Henech		
		Heneh		

Label	Mendl	Nofiya	Razi	Shimon
Lazer	Menka	Noga	Rebecca	Shloimeh
Leeser	Menke	Nosson	Refael	Shmelke
Leshem	Menla	Nuri	Reina	Shmiel
Lev	Menlin	Nuteh	Rifka	Shraga
Levi	Menshel	Odera	Rimon	Siff
Levona	Menshl	Ofar	Rishon	Sirel
Liba	Merel	Ofira	Rivkeh	Siril
Libe	Michael	Ola	Rochel	Sirke
Libka	Michla	Olaf	Rochele	Sisel
Lieber	Minda	Omen	Roiza	Sishe
Lilach	Mirel	Orali	Roma	Sivan
Lilo	Miri	Oren	Rubel	Sol
Liora	Miril	Ori	Ruchel	Sorele
Lipman	Moishe	Orna	Ruchele	Sorka
Loeb	Morasha	Oron	Ruskeh	Sotoli
Luba	Mordcheh	Oshri	Ruva	Sroli
Lubeh	Moriya	Otniel	Sadir	Sura
Magena	Morris	Palti	Sadira	Surele
Magina	Moshke	Penina	Sagiv	Sureli
Maher	Motel	Penuel	Sahara	Syshe
Maimon	Moti	Perel	Sapir	Tamir
Maisel	Motta	Perele	Sara	Tanel
Malachi	Muel	Peril	Seff	Tari
Malbina	Muki	Perl	Segel	Teivel
Malkiya	Muta	Pesha	Sekel	Tema
Mani	Mutka	Peshe	Seled	Teman
Manish	Nachmanke	Pessel	Selig	Tivona
Mann	Nadav	Pesye	Selila	Tobias
Mannes	Naftali	Pina	Seth	Toda
Mannis	Namer	Pineleh	Shabsi	Toiba
Manshel	Namir	Pinkeh	Shaine	Toibe
Mara	Natan	Pinya	Shalem	Tomer
Mariasha	Necha	Pora	Shalom	Tori
Marnin	Neche	Rachel	Shalva	Trana
Marona	Nechuma	Raina	Shamir	Treindel
Masada	Nediva	Raine	Shamira	Tuli
Mata	Nes	Raisa	Sharon	Tzaitel
Matan	Netanel	Rami	Shatz	Tzerin
Matza	Netta	Ranen	Shebsil	Tzipa
Mazal	Nidri	Ravid	Shefer	Tzipi
Meisel	Nisim	Rayna	Shepsil	
Mendel	Noaz	Rayzel	Shet	

Ethnic—Muslim

Uda	Yudel	Aaaqil	Ashfaaq	Haadee
Udeh	Yudi	Aabid	Ashraf	Haafiz
Udel	Yudis	Aabidah	Aslam	Haafizah
Uriah	Yuta	Aadam	Ataa'	Haalah
Uriel	Yute	Aalam	Ateeq	Haaris
Varda	Yutka	Aaminah	Athar	Haarisah
Velvel	Zak	Aamirah	Atyab	Haarithah
Volf	Zakai	Aanisah	Ayesha	Habeeb
Yachna	Zalki	Aashiq	Azeez	Habeebah
Yadon	Zalkin	Aasif	Azeezah	Hafeezah
Yadua	Zalman	Aasim	Azhar	Hakeem
Yagil	Zamir	Aasimah	Baaqee	Haleemah
Yaira	Zanvil	Aasiyah	Baaqir	Haneef
Yakar	Zavad	Aatiq	Baaree	Haneefah
Yaki	Zaydel	Aatiqah	Badee	Haqq
Yankel	Zeff	Abd	Bahaa	Haseenah
Yantsha	Zeidel	Aboo	Baleegh	Hasnaa
Yarkon	Zek	Abraar	Baseer	Hassaanah
Yarom	Zelig	Adeeb	Bashaarat	Hassan
Yediel	Zemel	Adeel	Batool	Haw-waa
Yehoshua	Zemer	A'dil	Bilaal	Hifz
Yehuda	Zera	Afdhaal	Burhaan	Hosaam
Yekel	Zerem	Afeefah	Bushraa	Humairaa
Yemin	Zetan	Ahad	Daiyaan	Husain
Yesher	Zev	Ahmad	Daulah	Ibraaheem
Yidel	Zevida	Ajmal	Deen	Idress
Yigal	Ziff	Akhlaaq	Dhaamin	Iftikhaar
Yisrael	Zimra	Akram	Durrah	Ihsaan
Yita	Zisel	Ali	Faadilah	Ihtishaam
Yitz	Zissa	Amaan	Faa'izah	I'jaaz
Yitzchak	Zisseh	Amatullah	Faakhir	Ikhlaas
Yona	Zlata	Ameenah	Faatimah	Ikraam
Yonita	Zlote	Ameer	Faheem	Imaad
Yoran	Zohar	Ammaarah	Faheemah	Imaam
Yosef	Zundel	Anas	Fakhr	Inaayat
Yoshe	Zusa	Aneesah	Fareed	Iqbaal
Yoska	Zushe	Anjum	Fareedah	Irfaan
Yossel	Zussel	Anwaar	Farhat	Irshaad
Yossi	Zussman	Areeb	Fattah	Ishtiyaaq
Yotti		Arshad	Ghanee	Ismaa'eel
		Arshaq	Ghazaalah	Istifaa
		Asad	Ghulaam	
		Asgar		

253

Jaabir	Naadirah	Sa'aadat	Siddeq	Zaahid
Jabbaar	Naafi'ah	Saadiq	Silaah	Zaahidah
Ja'far	Naajidah	Saadiqah	Siraaj	Zaahir
Jalaal	Naasir	Saahirah	Sughraa	Zaahirah
Jamaal	Naghmah	Saalihah	Suhailah	Zaakirah
Jameelah	Najmah	Saalim	Sultaan	Zaakiyah
Jauhar	Narjis	Saarah	Sultaanah	Zafar
Jawaad	Nasreen	Saboor	Taahirah	Zafeer
Junaid	Nazar	Sa'd	Taa'ibah	Zaheer
Kaamil	Nazheer	Sa'diyah	Taaj	Zaheerah
Kaamilah	Nizaam	Sa'eed	Taalib	Zahraa
Kaleem	Noor	Safdar	Taariq	Zaid
Karaamat	Qaadir	Sahl	Tabassum	Zaitoonah
Karam	Qamar	Saif	Tahaw-wur	Zakaa
Kareem	Qawee	Sakeenah	Tal'at	Zakee
Kareemah	Quddos	Salaah	Tameez	Zakiyyah
Khaalid	Qudsiyyah	Salaam	Tamkeen	Zeenat
Khaalidah	Raadhiyah	Salaamah	Taqee	Ziyaad
Khabeer	Raaghib	Saleem	Tasadduq	Zokaa
Khaleel	Raashid	Saleemah	Tasneem	Zufar
Khateeb	Raashidah	Salmah	Tawqeer	Zuhrah
Khawlah	Rabbaanee	Sameer	Tay-yib	
Laa'iqah	Ra'eesah	Sameerah	Tay-yibah	
La'eeq	Rafee'	Saulat	Taybah	
Lateefah	Rafee'ah	Shaafee	Thaabit	
Lutf	Rafeeq	Shaakirah	Thameenah	
Maajidah	Rafeeqah	Shafeeqah	Tharwat	
Maariyah	Raheem	Shahaab	Thurai-yaa	
Mahmoodah	Raheemah	Shahlaa	Ulfat	
Ma'roof	Rahmaan	Shakeel	Usaid	
Ma'soom	Rahmat	Shakeelah	Waahidah	
Mirsab	Raihaanah	Shamaamah	Wahab	
Mubaarak	Ra'naa	Shamoodah	Waheed	
Muhammad	Rasheed	Shams	Wardah	
Mukhtaar	Rasheedah	Shareef	Wazeer	
Mumtaaz	Rasool	Shareefah	Yaameen	
Muneer	Ridhaa	Shujaa	Yaasameen	
Muraad	Ridhiyyah		Yazeed	
Muslim	Rif'at		Yoosef	
	Riyaadh			
	Rumaanah			

Ethnic— Norwegian

Aase	Edle	Haakon	Kaare	Nanna
Agnar	Egil	Haldis	Karen	Nils
Alf	Eigil	Haldor	Kari	Nina
Anders	Einar	Halfdan	Karin	Nora
Andreas	Eirik	Halvard	Karl	Odd
Anette	Eivind	Halvor	Karsten	Oddvar
Anita	Eli	Hans	Katrine	Ola
Anna	Elin	Harald	Kirsten	Olaf
Anne	Eline	Hedda	Kirstin	Olaug
Arild	Elisif	Hedvig	Kjell	Olav
Arne	Ella	Helga	Knut	Ole
Arnulf	Ellen	Helge	Kristen	Oline
Arve	Elsa	Helle	Kristin	Ove
Arvid	Else	Herdis	Kristine	Oyvind
Asbjorn	Erik	Hilde	Kristoffer	Per
Aslaug	Erling	Idun	Laila	Pernille
Asta	Erna	Inga	Lars	Petra
Astri	Espen	Ingar	Lasse	Petrine
Astrid	Eva	Ingeborg	Leif	Petter
Baard	Even	Inger	Lena	Ragnar
Beate	Finn	Ingjerd	Lene	Ragnhild
Benedikte	Fredrik	Ingrid	Line	Randi
Bente	Freya	Ingvar	Lise	Rannveig
Beret	Freydis	Ivar	Liv	Reidar
Berit	Frida	Iver	Magne	Reidun
Berta	Fridtjof	Jakob	Magnus	Roald
Bjarne	Frode	Jan	Maren	Roar
Bjorg	Geir	Janne	Margit	Rolf
Bjorn	Gerd	Jarle	Marie	Sidsel
Blrger	Gjertrud	Jens	Marit	Sigleif
Bredo	Gjest	Johan	Marius	Signe
Brit	Grete	Johanne	Markus	Sigrid
Britt	Gro	Johannes	Marta	Sigrun
Carl	Gudmund	Jon	Marte	Sigurd
Carsten	Gudrun	Jonas	Martin	Siri
Cato	Gunhild	Jorunn	Merete	Solfrid
Cecilie	Gunnar	Jostein	Mette	Solveig
Christian	Guri		Mikkel	Stein
Dag	Gyda		Mona	Steinar
Dagfinn			Monika	Sten
Dagmar			Morten	Stine
Dagny				Svein
Didrik				

	Ethnic— Polish			Ethnic— Russian
Sven	Adam	Ignacy	Magdalena	Afanasy
Sverre	Agata	Ignatius	Malgorzata	Aigars
Synneove	Agnieszka	Irena	Marcin	Aiwar
Terje	Alfred	Ireneusz	Marek	Aleksandr
Thale	Alfreda	Iwona	Maria	Aleksandra
Tine	Alicja	Izabela	Marian	Aleksei
Tone	Aloysius	Izabella	Marta	Alevtina
Tor	Andrzej	Izak	Marysia	Alexei
Tora	Andrzey	Jacek	Marzena	Alla
Torbjorn	Anita	Jadwiga	Maximilian	Amelija
Torborg	Anna	Jan	Michal	Anastasija
Tore	Artur	Janina	Michalina	Anatoly
Torfinn	Beata	Januse	Mieczyslaw	Andrei
Torgrim	Benedykt	Janusz	Mikoali	Andrey
Torild	Bogdan	Jaroslaw	Monika	Anton
Torkild	Boguslaw	Jerzy	Natalia	Antonina
Torolf	Bozena	Joanna	Otto	Arkady
Torstein	Bronislaw	Jolanta	Paulina	Artur
Torunn	Casimir	Jozef	Pawel	Arvidas
Torvald	Clara	Julius	Piotr	Astra
Trine	Czeslaw	Justyn	Rafal	Bogdan
Truls	Danuta	Justyna	Rasia	Boris
Trygve	Dariusz	Kalikst	Rasine	Dainis
Turid	Dominik	Kamilla	Robert	Dimant
Tyra	Dorota	Karol	Ryszard	Dmitri
Ulf	Edyta	Kasia	Slawomir	Dzintars
Unni	Elzbieta	Katarzyna	Stanislaus	Eduard
Valborg	Erwina	Kazimierz	Stanislaw	Ekaterina
Vegard	Eustace	Konstanty	Stefan	Elena
Venke	Ewa	Krystyna	Sylwia	Elvira
Vera	Florian	Kryzstof	Tadeusz	Enn
Veronika	Grazyna	Krzysztof	Teresa	Eynar
Vibeke	Grzegorz	Ksawery	Urszula	Faina
Vigdis	Gutki	Kub	Wieslav	Fedor
Viggo	Hanna	Kyrstyna	Wieslaw	Feodor
Vivi	Helena	Lech	Witold	Galina
Yngvar	Henryk	Leopold	Wojciech	Garii
	Hilina	Leszek	Zbigniew	Gennady
		Lidia	Zenon	Georgy
		Lucyna	Zofia	Grigorij
		Ludwik		Grigory

			Ethnic— Scottish	
Igor	Pavel	Yakov	Alastair	Rab
Ingrida	Pyotr	Yelana	Alexander	Richard
Irina	Raisa	Yevgenia	Andrew	Robert
Ivan	Raissa	Yevgeny	Angus	Samuel
Ivanna	Renata	Yevgenya	Ann	Sarah
Ivar	Rotislav	Yulia	Arthur	Thomas
Jaak	Ruslan	Yuri	Benjamen	Walter
Janis	Rustem	Yurik	Catherine	William
Julia	Sabiryhan	Yuris	Christian	
Kari	Saida	Zhorzh	Daniel	
Katerina	Sergei	Zinaida	David	
Keto	Shamil	Zintars	Davis	
Kheino	Shota	Zintis	Donald	
Klavdia	Sigita		Duncan	
Larissa	Soslan		Ebenezer	
Leon	Stanislav		Eleanor	
Leonid	Stepan		Elizabeth	
Levan	Sultan		Flora	
Liana	Surem		Frederick	
Lidiya	Svetlana		George	
Lina	Svetlanta		Helen	
Luiza	Tamara		Henry	
Lyubov	Tatiana		Hugh	
Lyudmila	Tatyana		James	
Maria	Umar		Jane	
Marina	Vakhtang		Janet	
Maris	Valentin		Jannet	
Mariya	Valentina		Jean	
Melanija	Valery		John	
Mikhail	Vassily		Judith	
Mira	Vera		Katherine	
Nadezda	Victor		Lucy	
Nadezhda	Viktor		Malcolm	
Natalia	Vitaly		Margaret	
Natalya	Vitold		Mary	
Naum	Vladas		Netta	
Nelli	Vladimir		Patrick	
Nikolai	Vyacheslav		Peter	
Nina	Vyera		Philip	
Nunu				
Oleg				
Olga				

Ethnic— Swedish

Adam	Ebba	Inga	Martin
Agneta	Edit	Ingalill	Mats
Alexander	Edvard	Ingeborg	Michael
Alexandra	Edvin	Ingegerd	Mikael
Alf	Eleonora	Ingemar	Mona
Amanda	Elin	Inger	Monica
Anders	Elisabet	Ingrid	Monika
Anita	Elisabeth	Ingvar	Niklas
Ann	Elsa	Isabella	Nils
Anna	Emil	Jakob	Olof
Annette	Emma	Jan	Oskar
Annika	Erik	Jenny	Ove
Arne	Erika	Jens	Patrik
Astrid	Erland	Jesper	Pelle
Axel	Ernst	Joakim	Per
Barbro	Eskil	Johan	Pernilla
Bengt	Ester	Jonas	Petra
Berit	Eva	Jorgen	Pia
Berndt	Evert	Karin	Ragnhild
Bernt	Folke	Karl	Rebecka
Bertell	Fredrik	Katarina	Rigmor
Bertil	Gabriel	Kerstin	Rolf
Birgit	Gabriella	Kirin	Rune
Birgitta	Gertrud	Klas	Silvia
Bjorn	Greger	Krister	Solveig
Bo	Greta	Kristina	Staffan
Britt	Gudrun	Lars	Stefan
Britta	Gunde	Leif	Stina
Carina	Gunilla	Lena	Susanna
Cecilia	Gunnar	Lennart	Sven
Charlotta	Gunnel	Lillemor	Sylvia
Christina	Gustaf	Lisbet	Tomas
Dagmar	Gustav	Lotta	Torsten
Daniel	Hakan	Magdalena	Ulf
David	Hans	Magnus	Ulla
Desiree	Harriet	Maj	Ulrika
Doris	Hedvig	Malin	Viktoria
	Helena	Margareta	Viveka
	Helga	Maria	
	Helge	Marianne	
	Henrik	Marie	
	Herbert	Marit	
	Holmfrid	Markus	

Ethnic— Swiss

Alfred
Andre
Andreas
Anton
Ariane
Armin
Bernadette
Bernhard
Bruno
Christian
Christine
Daniel
Dano
Edi
Edy
Ekkehard
Erich
Erika
Ernst
Etienne
Evi
Felix
Franz
Fritz
Gaudenz
Giachem
Gottfried
Hans
Hansuli
Heidi
Heini
Heinrich
Heinz
Jacques
Jean
Joos
Josef
Jothan
Jurg
Jurgen
Karin
Karl
Konrad

Kurt
Lise-Marie
Marcel
Maria
Marie-Theres
Markus
Marlies
Martin
Max
Meinrad
Meta
Michel
Michela
Monika
Niklaus
Norwin
Peter
Ralph
Rene
Rico
Robert
Roland
Rolf
Rudolf
Silvio
Stefan
Stephan
Ugo
Ulrich
Urs
Uwe
Victor
Walter
Werner
Willi

Most Popular Girls' Names of the 1990s (1990–1996)

1. Emily
2. Sarah
3. Ashley
4. Kaitlyn
5. Jessica
6. Brittany
   Rachel
7. Megan
8. Brianna
9. Amanda
   Hannah
10. Taylor
11. Samantha
12. Katherine
13. Alexis
14. Courtney
    Haley
    Kayla
15. Lauren
16. Michaela
17. Allison
    Elizabeth
    Rebecca
18. Victoria
19. Madison
20. Nicole
21. Alyssa
22. Alexandra
23. Morgan
24. Amber
    Shelby
25. Danielle
    Gabrielle
    Kaylee
    Olivia

26. Abigail
    Kristen
    Madeline
27. Lindsey
    Marissa
28. Chelsea
29. Christina
    Jordan
    Mackenzie
    Stephanie
30. Mary
31. Jasmine
    Jennifer
32. Sydney
33. Erin
34. Erica
    Julia
    Sierra
35. Alicia
    Carly
    Kelly
36. Emma
    Miranda
37. Bailey
    Destiny
    Kelsey
    Laura
38. Anna
    Brooke
    Casey
    Michelle
    Natalie
    Paige
39. Cassidy
40. Elena
    Jenna
    Melissa

41. Alexandria
    Cassandra
    Cheyenne
    Desiree
    Holly
    Jacqueline
42. Heather
    Leah
43. Alexa
    Claire
    Crystal
    Gabriella
    Shannon
    Ariana
    Deja
    Jamie
44. Andrea
45. Grace
    Mariah
    Monica
    Sabrina
    Savannah
    Tiffany
46. Amy
    Angela
    Deanna
    Molly
47. Caroline
    Katie
    Kiara
    Kimberly
    Kylie
48. Maria
    Selena

49. Adriana
    Chloe
    Christine
    Dominique
    Jade
    Jane
    Kara
    Krista
    Margaret
    Meagan
    Sophia
    Tatiana
50. Brandi
    Isabella
    Janae
    Kiana
    Zoe

Most Popular Boys' Names of the 1990s (1990–1996)

1. Michael
2. Nicholas
3. Matthew
4. Jacob
5. Tyler
6. Christopher
7. Zachary
8. Ryan
9. Joshua
10. John
11. Daniel
12. Austin
13. Alexander
14. Joseph
15. Andrew
16. William
17. Brandon
18. Justin
19. David
    Kyle
20. James
    Jonathan
21. Anthony
22. Thomas
23. Dylan
24. Cody
25. Benjamin
    Robert
26. Connor
    Samuel
27. Eric
28. Stephen
29. Jordan
30. Sean

31. Adam
    Kevin
32. Christian
33. Brian
    Ian
    Timothy
34. Nathaniel
    Patrick
35. Jesse
36. Jason
37. Logan
38. Evan
    Richard
39. Aaron
    Charles
    Devin
40. Taylor
    Tristan
41. Cameron
    Corey
    Derek
    Garrett
    Jared
    Jeremy
    Lucas
42. Dustin
43. Bradley
    Dakota
    George
    Jeffrey
    Luke
44. Elijah
    Ethan
    Gabriel
    Phillip
    Travis

45. Caleb
    Chad
    Chase
    Edward
    Jack
    Peter
46. Brendan
    Brett
    Collin
    Noah
    Trevor
47. Alex
    Gregory
    Hunter
    Jose
    Mark
    Scott
    Vincent
48. Blake
    Mitchell
    Nathan
    Paul
    Spencer
49. Quentin
50. Alan
    Colton
    Jake
    Liam
    Mason

Parent Soup's Most Popular Names

And now, in no particular rank, and gathered by no particularly scientific means, are the baby names that Parent Soupers are talking about the most. They reflect a decided trend toward unisex (U) names, but that's another subject (see page 215). We wouldn't be surprised if these names became the Jessicas, Jennifers, and Michaels of tomorrow:

Aislinn (F)	Logan (U)
Alexa (F)	Madison (U)
Austin (M)	Mason (M)
Bailey (U)	Max (M)
Brianna (F)	Mackenzie (U)
Bryce (U)	Megan (F)
Caitlin (F)	Nicole (F)
Cheyenne (F)	Noah (M)
Cole (M)	Owen (M)
Connor (M)	Parker (U)
Dakota (U)	Preston (M)
Devon (U)	Quinn (M)
Dylan (M)	Riley (U)
Emily (F)	Ryan (U)
Emma (F)	Savannah (F)
Ethan (M)	Sierra (F)
Evan (M)	Spencer (M)
Grayson (M)	Sydney (F)
Hannah (F)	Taylor (U)
Hunter (U)	Tyler (U)
Isabella (F)	Zachary (M)
Jackson (M)	
Jacob (M)	
Jared (M)	
Jordan (U)	
Kayleigh (F)	
Kendall (F)	
Kyle (U)	
Kyra (F)	

Parent Soup's Least Popular Names

Again, there is no particular order to or any particular vendetta against any of these names. But when we asked what everybody's least favorite name was, this is what we got. If you disagree, or think we've left out a particularly heinous name, come to either AOL Keyword: parentsoup or www.parentsoup.com on the Web, and post a message on the Baby Name message boards with your most and least favorite names. That way we can institute "best" and "worst" lists that will reflect up-to-the-minute trends.

Amber	Fern	Melissa
Amy	Fred	Mike
Annette	Gertrude	Muffy
Ashley	Greg	Myron
Bambi	Gus	Oscar
Beatrice	Harry	Ralph
Bertha	Heather	Randy
Blaine	Irving	Reginald
Brenda	Irwin	Roger
Bruce	Janelle	Stacy
Bud	Janet	Tammy
Buffy	Jennifer	Tiffany
Caitlin	Jud	Tina
Connie	Kay	Ursula
Courtney	Kenny	Vicky
Darlene	Kitty	
Debbie	Krystal	
Denny	Laura	
Dick	Louise	
Doug	Lydia	
Elmer		
Emily		

The Most Popular Names of the Past 5 Decades

1940s

GIRLS	BOYS
Mary	James
Maria	John
Linda	Robert
Barbara	William
Patricia	Charles
Betty	David
Sandra	Jerry
Carolyn	Thomas
Gloria	Richard
Martha	Jose

1950s

GIRLS	BOYS
Linda	Robert
Mary	Michael
Patricia	James
Susan	John
Deborah	David
Kathleen	William
Barbara	Thomas
Nancy	Richard
Sharon	Gary
Karen	Charles

1960s

GIRLS	BOYS
Mary	Michael
Susan	David
Lisa	James
Karen	John
Linda	Robert
Deborah	William
Kimberly	Mark
Donna	Richard
Patricia	Jeffrey
Cynthia	Charles

1 Syllable

GIRLS	BOYS
Michelle	Michael
Jennifer	Robert
Kimberly	David
Lisa	James
Tracy	John
Kelly	Jeffrey
Nicole	Steven
Angela	Christopher
Pamela	Brian
Christine	Mark

1980s

GIRLS	BOYS
Jennifer	Michael
Sarah	Christopher
Nicole	Matthew
Jessica	David
Katherine	Jason
Stephanie	Daniel
Elizabeth	Robert
Amanda	Eric
Melissa	Brian
Lindsay	Joseph

Abe	Bink	Bryn
Ace	Birch	Buck
Ade	Black	Budd
Al	Blade	Burke
Alf	Blaine	Burl
Alp	Blair	Burne
Ánh	Blaithe	Burns
Ann	Blake	Burr
Anne	Blanc	Burt
Arms	Blanch	Butte
Art	Blas	Byrd
Aust	Blaze	Cab
Ba	Bligh	Cache
Bab	Bliss	Cade
Baines	Blythe	Cain
Baird	Bo	Cal
Barb	Boase	Cale
Barn	Bob	Carl
Barr	Boone	Carr
Bart	Booth	Cart
Bas	Borg	Case
Bates	Boume	Cass
Baum	Bourke	Cerf
Bay	Boyce	Chad
Bayle	Boyd	Chaim
Bear	Boyne	Chan
Beate	Brad	Chang
Beau	Bram	Chase
Beck	Bran	Chaz
Bell	Branch	Che
Belle	Brand	Chen
Ben	Breann	Cher
Bengt	Bree	Chet
Ber	Brent	Chew
Berg	Brett	Cheye
Berk	Brice	Chi
Berndt	Brier	Chiel
Berne	Brig	Chin
Bert	Brin	Chow
Beryl	Brit	Chris
Bess	Brock	Chuck
Beth	Brook	Chyan
Bette	Bruce	Cimm
Bing	Brune	Claire

Clark	Don	Flint	Goar	Heinz
Claude	Dong	Flip	Gold	Held
Claus	Dorr	Flos	Goos	Herb
Clay	Dow	Floyd	Gore	Hersch
Cliff	Doyle	Flynn	Gotz	Hifz
Cline	Drake	Forbes	Gould	Ho
Clint	Drew	Ford	Grace	Holmes
Clive	Duane	Fraime	Grant	Holt
Clwe	Dub	Fraine	Graves	Hong
Clyde	Duff	Fran	Gray	Hood
Cole	Duke	Frank	Greene	Hope
Colm	Dunn	Franz	Greer	Horst
Cook	Durst	Fred	Greet	Howe
Cord	Duy	Frey	Greg	Hugh
Cort	Dwayne	Frick	Grete	Hume
Court	Dwight	Fritz	Grey	Hurd
Coyle	Earl	Frode	Grier	Hurst
Craig	Eet	Fronde	Gro	Hwang
Cris	Eir	Frost	Guam	Ike
Crist	Elle	Frume	Guin	Itz
Cruz	Eng	Fu	Guus	Ives
Curt	Enn	Gaal	Guy	Jaak
Cyd	Ernst	Gad	Gwen	Jace
Cyle	Eve	Gage	Gwynn	Jack
Daan	Eyre	Gai	Haas	Jade
Dag	Faith	Gail	Haig	Jai
Dahn	Falk	Gall	Haines	Jair
Dale	Fall	Garr	Hal	Jake
Dane	Fane	Garth	Hale	James
Darr	Farr	Gay	Hall	Jan
Dave	Faust	Geert	Ham	Jane
Dawn	Fawn	Geir	Han	Jarle
Day	Fay	Gene	Hanh	Jay
Dayle	Fayme	George	Hank	Jean
Dean	Fayre	Gere	Hans	Jeanne
Dee	Fern	Gert	Haqq	Jed
Deems	Fiep	Gian	Hart	Jeff
Deen	Finch	Gijs	Haye	Jens
Del	Finn	Gil	Hayes	Jesh
Delf	Fisk	Giles	Hays	Jess
Dick	Fitch	Gill	Hearn	Jet
Dirk	Fitz	Gilles	Heath	Jeu
Doane	Flann	Gjest	Hebe	Jill
Dom	Fleur	Glen	Hein	Jim

Jinx	Keith	Lang	Mab	Nell
Jo	Kell	Lange	Mac	Ness
Joan	Kem	Lark	Madge	Newt
Job	Kemp	Lars	Mae	Nick
Jode	Kenn	Leal	Mai	Nile
Joe	Kent	Lean	Maille	Nils
Joel	Kern	Lear	Maire	Nix
John	Kerr	Lech	Maize	Nli
Jones	Khiem	Lee	Maj	Noam
Joop	Kiln	Leif	Mann	Noor
Joos	Kim	Leith	Mao	Nye
Joost	King	Len	March	Oakes
Jord	Kip	Lev	Mark	Odd
Jorg	Kirk	Libe	Marsh	Ode
Jos	Kiss	Lien	Marv	Olpe
Josh	Kjell	Lin	Matt	Own
Jost	Klaus	Linc	Maude	Pace
Joub	Klein	Ling	Mauve	Page
Joy	Klox	Link	Max	Paine
Joyce	Knight	Lins	May	Pam
Juan	Knox	Lise	Mayme	Parke
Judd	Knut	Lisle	Mays	Parle
Jude	Ko	Liv	Meade	Pat
Juill	Koi	Liz	Meg	Paul
Jules	Kole	Lloyd	Mel	Paz
June	Kong	Locke	Merle	Peace
Jurg	Koos	Loeb	Mick	Pearl
Jynx	Kris	Loes	Miles	Peer
Kade	Kub	Loise	Ming	Penn
Kai	Kune	Lon	Mink	Pentz
Kale	Kurt	Lorne	Mirth	Per
Kane	Kwan	Lot	Mitch	Pete
Kang	Kye	Lou	Moir	Pham
Karl	Kyle	Love	Moore	Phan
Kate	Kyne	Luke	Morse	Pierce
Kay	Lach	Lunn	Mort	Pim
Kayne	Ladd	Lunt	Myles	Pink
Keaf	Lail	Lutf	Naam	Plan
Kean	Laird	Lutz	Nan	Pleun
Keats	Lais	Luz	Nash	Plum
Keefe	Laise	Lyle	Nate	Polk
Kees	Lance	Lynd	Naum	Ponce
Keir	Lane	Lynn	Neal	Pope

Pratt	Roth	Shyne	Tahj	Twain
Price	Rourke	Sid	Tal	Ty
Prine	Rowe	Siff	Tame	Tyece
Quao	Roy	Skip	Tarp	Tyne
Quartz	Royce	Sky	Tate	Tyre
Quinn	Royd	Slade	Tau	Ulf
Rab	Rube	Slate	Taupe	Urs
Rad	Rue	Slerd	Teague	Utz
Rae	Rufe	Sloan	Teal	Vail
Raine	Rule	Sly	Tearle	Val
Ralph	Rune	Smith	Ted	Van
Rance	Rush	Snake	Teng	Vance
Ray	Ruth	Sol	Tess	Vaughn
Reave	Rye	Song	Thad	Vere
Red	Ryle	Soo	Thale	Verge
Reed	Ryne	Speed	Thane	Vern
Reese	Sage	Spes	Thieu	Verne
Reeve	Sahl	Sprage	Tho	Veryl
Rex	Saif	Spring	Thor	Vic
Rey	Sair	Sproule	Thorne	Vince
Rhaea	Sam	Squire	Thorpe	Virge
Rhett	Saud	Stan	Tim	Vlad
Rhine	Saul	Star	Tine	Volf
Rhodes	Schulz	Steele	Tish	Voss
Rhone	Scott	Stein	Todd	Wade
Rice	Sean	Stelle	Toft	Waite
Rick	Seff	Sterne	Tom	Wake
Ridge	Seine	Steve	Tone	Wald
Ring	Sepp	Stine	Toy	Walsh
Rip	Serge	Stoke	Toyd	Walt
Roan	Serle	Storm	Tran	Wang
Roar	Seth	Stowe	Tre	Ward
Roarke	Shaine	Strom	Treat	Ware
Robb	Shams	Stroud	Trent	Wayne
Rock	Shane	Styles	Trey	Webb
Rod	Shatz	Sun	Trigg	Welk
Roi	Shaw	Suse	Trine	Wells
Rolf	Shawn	Sven	Tripp	Wes
Rolt	Shay	Swain	Troy	White
Rome	Shea	Taaj	Trude	Wier
Ron	Sheikh	Tab	True	Wilde
Rose	Shep	Tadd	Truls	Wilkes
Ross	Shet	Taft	Truth	Will

2 Syllables

Wilt	Aaaqil	Adi	Aimo	Alfa
Wing	Aabid	Adiell	Ainsley	Alford
Wink	Aalam	A'dil	Ainsworth	Alfred
Wirt	Aara	Adin	Airla	Alger
Witt	Aarcus	Adine	Aisa	Ali
Wolf	Aarin	Adir	Aislinn	Alice
Wong	Aaron	Adlai	Aiwar	Aline
Worth	Aase	Adlar	Aja	Alise
Wray	Aashiq	Adlay	Ajax	Alla
Wright	Aasif	Adna	Ajmal	Allard
Wynn	Aasim	Adney	Akbar	Allen
Wythe	Aatiq	Adolph	Akeem	Allene
Xene	Aba	Adom	Akhlaaq	Allie
Yale	Abba	Adon	Akil	Allward
Yar	Abbey	Adrell	Akins	Allyn
Yave	Abbo	Adret	Akram	Alma
Yeats	Abbott	Adwin	Akron	Almaz
Yens	Abdiel	Aedan	Akwete	Almire
Yette	Abdon	Afan	Alain	Almo
Yitz	Abdul	Afdhaal	Alaine	Almund
York	Abel	Affra	Alair	Alois
Yule	Abir	Agnar	Alan	Alpar
Yute	Abner	Agnes	Alard	Alpha
Yves	Aboo	Ahab	Alba	Alphonse
Zach	Abra	Ahad	Alban	Alpin
Zaid	Abraar	Ahearn	Albe	Alpine
Zale	Abram	Aherin	Albert	Alric
Zane	Absa	Ahmad	Albrecht	Alroy
Zare	Achard	Ahmoz	Albric	Alrune
Zebe	Achim	Aia	Alcot	Alston
Zeese	Ackley	Aida	Alcott	Alsworth
Zeff	Ada	Aidan	Alda	Alta
Zeus	Adael	Aided	Aldan	Altai
Zev	Adaeze	Aideen	Alden	Alteh
Zhorzh	Adai	Aidel	Alder	Alter
Ziv	Adair	Aigars	Aldo	Altman
Zobe	Adal	Aignan	Aldous	Alva
Zoi	Adam	Aiken	Aldred	Alvah
Zsolt	Adar	Ailbhe	Aldrich	Alvar
	Adda	Aileen	Alec	Alvin
	Addai	Ailred	Alene	Alvis
	Addis	Ailsa	Alette	Alvord
	Adeeb	Aime	Alex	Alyose

Ama	Annick	Aren	Asha	Audrey
Amaan	Annie	Arend	Ashby	Audric
Amal	Anniel	Arette	Asher	Audris
Amber	Annis	Argus	Ashfaaq	Audwin
Ambert	Anscom	Argyle	Ashford	Auguste
Ambrose	Ansell	Arice	Ashland	Austin
Ameer	Anselm	Aries	Ashley	Austine
Amice	Anshel	Arik	Ashlin	Autry
Amiel	Anskar	Arild	Ashlyn	Autumn
Amin	Ansley	Aris	Ashraf	Avae
Amir	Anson	Arjan	Ashti	Avan
Amit	Anstice	Arki	Ashton	Avi
Ammon	Antal	Arkin	Ashur	Avis
Amna	Antje	Arko	Aslam	Aviv
Amnon	Anton	Arledge	Aslaug	Avniel
Amor	Anwaar	Arlen	Asmus	Avra
Amos	Anwar	Arlene	Asner	Avril
Ampah	Anwyl	Arley	Aspah	Avrom
Amreen	Anya	Arlo	Aspen	Awet
Amtza	Anyon	Armand	Asta	Axel
Amund	Aoife	Armine	Aster	Axton
Amur	Aphra	Armro	Astin	Ayla
Amy	April	Armstrong	Astor	Aylmer
Anas	Aquan	Arnold	Astra	Aylward
Anders	Ara	Arnon	Astri	Aylwin
Andes	Aral	Arnot	Astrid	Aylworth
Andi	Aralt	Arnulf	Aswin	Aynet
Andra	Arbor	Arpad	Ataa'	A'yonne
Andras	Archard	Arran	Ateeq	Azbane
Andre	Archer	Arshad	Athar	Azeez
Andress	Archie	Arshaq	Atje	Azhar
Andrew	Arda	Arta	Atlas	Aziz
Andy	Ardan	Arthur	Atley	Azrae
Angail	Ardath	Arva	Atsu	Baako
Angel	Ardell	Arvai	Atwell	Baaqee
Angits	Ardeen	Arvel	Atwood	Baaqir
Angus	Ardelle	Arvid	Atworth	Baaree
Anja	Arden	Aryell	Atyab	Babette
Anjum	Ardis	Asa	Aubin	Bacall
Anke	Ardith	Asad	Aubine	Badee
Anna	Ardley	Asbjorn	Aubree	Badru
Annan	Ardolph	Ascot	Aubrey	Bahaa
Annette	Areeb	Asgar	Audley	Baikal

Bailby	Bartkus	Beldon	Betty	Boden
Bailee	Bartley	Belen	Beula	Bodo
Bailey	Barton	Bella	Beuna	Bogart
Bainbridge	Baruch	Bellaude	Bevan	Bogdan
Baker	Baruett	Bellda	Bevis	Bohuslav
Balbo	Baseer	Bellis	Bhutan	Boise
Balder	Basha	Belva	Bibi	Bolger
Baldric	Bashir	Bena	Bichri	Bolton
Baldwin	Basia	Bendix	Bilaal	Bonar
Baleegh	Basie	Benesh	Billie	Bonesh
Baleigh	Basil	Bennett	Billy	Bonnie
Balfour	Bastian	Benno	Bina	Bono
Balint	Bathsheb	Benny	Binette	Boquet
Balkan	Batli	Benson	Bira	Borden
Ballard	Batool	Bente	Birchard	Boris
Bambi	Baudier	Bentley	Birdie	Borlow
Bancroft	Baudoin	Benton	Birgit	Boston
Banna	Baudric	Beppe	Birkett	Bosworth
Banning	Baxter	Berdine	Birkey	Botolf
Baptist	Bayard	Berel	Birley	Boukje
Bara	Bayla	Berend	Bishop	Boutros
Baram	Baylet	Berenice	Bita	Bowen
Barbel	Baylke	Bergen	Bjorn	Bowie
Barbette	Baylor	Berger	Blagden	Boyden
Barbra	Bayo	Berget	Blakeley	Bracie
Barclay	Bazak	Bergren	Blakely	Bradan
Barden	Bcla	Berit	Blakeslee	Bradburn
Bardo	Beathan	Berlyn	Blakey	Bradford
Bardot	Beatty	Bernal	Blanca	Bradley
Bardrick	Beaufort	Bernard	Blanco	Bradwell
Bardulf	Beaumont	Bernice	Blanford	Brady
Barend	Beauvais	Bernie	Blasia	Brainard
Barker	Becca	Berry	Blessing	Brainna
Barkley	Beckett	Bertha	Blima	Brander
Barlow	Beda	Bertil	Blinnie	Brandice
Barnett	Bedad	Bertold	Blossom	Brando
Barney	Bedford	Berton	Blrger	Brandon
Barnum	Beecher	Bertrade	Bluma	Brandy
Baron	Begga	Bertram	Boas	Branford
Barret	Beka	Bertrand	Bobar	Branson
Barris	Bela	Berwick	Bobbette	Brawley
Barry	Belda	Bethel	Bobbi	Braxton
Barthram	Belden	Betsy	Bobby	Brayan

Brayden	Broughton	Cadence	Cardew	Cassis
Braylan	Bruna	Cadman	Carel	Casta
Brazil	Brunhild	Cadmar	Caren	Casto
Brea	Bruno	Cadmus	Caresse	Castor
Bre-Ann	Bryde	Cady	Carew	Cata
Breanne	Bryshane	Cailin	Carey	Cathal
Brechje	Bryson	Cailun	Cari	Cathmor
Bredo	Buckley	Cainen	Carie	Cathy
Breeda	Bucky	Cairo	Carla	Cato
Breggin	Buddy	Caitlin	Carlene	Cavan
Brelain	Bundy	Caitrin	Carlin	Cavell
Bremel	Buni	Calcite	Carling	Cawley
Brenda	Bunim	Calder	Carlisle	Cayla
Brendan	Bunji	Caldwell	Carlos	Caylie
Brenna	Bunmi	Caleb	Carly	Cece
Brennan	Burbank	Caleigh	Carma	Cecil
Brenton	Burchard	Calen	Carmel	Cedric
Breshan	Burdett	Caley	Carmen	Celeste
Breshawn	Burdon	Calhoun	Carna	Celine
Bretten	Burford	Calise	Carney	Celso
Brewster	Burgard	Calla	Carol	Cesar
Breyer	Burgess	Caltha	Carrew	Chadburn
Bria	Burhaan	Calum	Carrick	Chadron
Brian	Burkett	Calvert	Carrie	Chadwick
Bridger	Burkhard	Calvin	Carroll	Chaffee
Bridget	Burleigh	Cambre	Carson	Chaikeh
Brigham	Burnell	Camden	Carsten	Chaille
Brina	Burnett	Camille	Carswell	Chalmers
Brinkley	Burney	Cammy	Carsyn	Chambray
Bristol	Burton	Campbell	Carter	Champagne
Britney	Busby	Camrin	Cartland	Champaign
Britta	Bushraa	Canaan	Carvel	Chana
Brittan	Buster	Canace	Carver	Chanan
Brockley	Butler	Candace	Carvey	Chanda
Brodie	Byford	Candide	Cary	Chandi
Brogan	Byram	Candra	Carys	Chandler
Bromleigh	Byron	Canei	Cascade	Chandra
Bronson	Cabell	Canice	Casey	Chanel
Bronte	Cabot	Cannon	Casie	Channing
Bronwen	Cadby	Canton	Caspar	Channon
Brooklyn	Caddock	Canyon	Cassell	Chanoch
Brosine	Cadel	Caprice	Cassie	Chantal
Brougher	Caden	Carah	Cassil	Chante

Chapell	Cheyney	Clarette	Colum	Country
Chapen	Chidi	Clarimond	Colwen	Courney
Chapman	Chika	Clarisse	Comfort	Courteney
Charcoal	Chiku	Claudette	Como	Courtland
Charelle	Chilton	Clava	Comsa	Covell
Charie	Chimene	Clayborne	Conah	Cowan
Charis	China	Clayton	Conall	Craddock
Charish	Chipo	Cleanthe	Conan	Crandale
Charlene	Chiram	Cleary	Concord	Cranley
Charles	Chita	Cleavon	Conde	Cranston
Charli	Chiztam	Clement	Congo	Crawford
Charlock	Chloe	Cleo	Conlan	Creighton
Charlot	Chlori	Cleon	Connie	Crenshaw
Charlotte	Chloris	Cleva	Connor	Cresa
Charlsie	Chovev	Cleveland	Conrad	Crescin
Charmaine	Chrissie	Clifford	Conroy	Crimson
Charra	Christa	Clifton	Constance	Crispa
Chaskel	Christian	Clinton	Constant	Crispin
Chatham	Christine	Clorinde	Conway	Cristin
Chatwin	Christmas	Clothilde	Cooney	Crofton
Chaucer	Christoph	Clover	Cooper	Crompton
Chauncey	Christos	Clovis	Copper	Cromwell
Chela	Christy	Clske	Cora	Crosby
Chelsea	Chuhei	Cluny	Coral	Crystal
Chemar	Chuma	Clymene	Corbet	Csaba
Chemash	Chuna	Clytie	Cordell	Csilla
Chenay	Churchill	Cobalt	Corette	Ctirad
Chenelle	Chynna	Cody	Corey	Cuba
Cheney	Cian	Coffee	Cori	Cudjo
Cherie	Cida	Colbert	Corinne	Cuffy
Cherise	Cilla	Colby	Corliss	Culbert
Chermon	Cima	Coleman	Cormick	Cullen
Cherry	Cindy	Colette	Cornall	Culley
Chervil	Cinta	Colin	Corrie	Culver
Cheryl	Cirill	Coline	Cortez	Currey
Chesma	Ciro	Colis	Corvin	Curtis
Chessa	Cita	Colleen	Coryell	Cuthbert
Chester	Citrine	Collin	Cosell	Cutler
Chestnut	CJ	Collins	Cosette	Cutter
Chetwin	Claiborn	Colmbyne	Cosmos	Cybill
Chevy	Clancy	Colson	Cota	Cydney
Cheyann	Clara	Colten	Cotton	Cyler
Cheyenne	Clarence	Colter	Coty	Cyllene

Cyma	Danube	Daysha	Derek	Dione
Cynric	Danzel	Dayton	Dermell	Dira
Cypress	Daphne	Deanne	Dermot	Dirkje
Cyril	Daquill	Dearbhail	Derry	Dissa
Cyrus	Dara	Dearborn	Derwin	Dixie
Czeslaw	Darbi	Debra	Desean	Dixon
Daa'jzia	Darby	Declan	DeShaya	Dlyon
Daba	Darceece	Decus	Desi	Dnieper
Dabney	Darcey	Dedric	Desmond	Docia
Dacey	Darcy	Deena	Destine	Docie
Dacia	Darda	Defoe	Detlef	Docile
Dadyeh	Dari	Degas	Detmar	Dody
Daegal	Darla	Deion	Devin	Dolan
Dagan	Darlene	Deirdre	Devine	Dolly
Dagfinn	Darling	Dej'a	Devir	Domel
Dagmar	Darlye	Deja	Devlin	Donald
Dagny	Darnell	Dejuan	Devon	Donat
Dagwood	Darom	Deka	Dewar	D'ondre
Dainis	Darrin	Dela	Dewey	Donkor
Daisy	Darris	Delcine	DeWitt	Donna
Daiyaan	Darshaun	Delight	Dexter	Donnan
Dajon	Darton	Della	Dextra	Donnell
Dalbert	Daruce	Delling	Dhaamin	Donnie
Daley	Darwen	Delma	Dhumma	Donogh
Dallas	Darwin	Delmar	Diamon	Donte
Dalson	Darya	Delon	Diamond	Dontrell
Dalton	Daryel	Delphine	Dianne	Donzeal
Dalya	Daryl	Delphne	Diarmaid	Dooley
Dalziel	Dasha	Delta	Diarmit	Dora
Dama	Dashawn	Delvin	Dibn	Doran
Damal	Dashen	Demas	Dibru	Dorcas
D'Ambra	Dati	Demi	Dickens	Dore
Damick	Daulah	Demier	Didi	Dorene
Damon	Daven	Demonde	Dieter	Dorin
Dana	David	Dempsey	Diethelm	Doris
Danette	Davin	Denby	Diethild	Dorsett
Daniel	Davis	Deneane	Dillard	Dorte
Danielle	Davrush	De'Nee	Dillon	Dorwin
DAnne	Dawan	Deney	Dimant	Dory
Danny	Dawson	Denise	Dimas	Dothan
Dano	Daxeur	Dennis	Dinah	Dottie
Danson	Daylen	Denver	Dino	Douglas
Dante	Dayna	Denzel	Dion	Douwe

Dov-Ber	Dylan	Edva	Elden	Elvire
Doxia	Dylane	Edward	Elder	Elvis
Doxie	Dzidzo	Edwin	Eldon	Elvy
Draven	Dzintars	Edy	Eldra	Elway
Drayton	Eamon	Eelco	Eldred	Elwell
Drea	Eartha	Effie	Eldric	Elwln
Dreda	Easter	Efrain	Eldrid	Elwood
Drelan	Eaton	Efrat	Eldridge	Emee
Drummond	Eavan	Efron	Eldwen	Emeigh
Drury	Ebba	Egan	Eleph	Emer
Drusa	Eben	Egbert	Elfi	Emil
Dryden	Ebere	Egil	Elfriede	Emlen
Duco	Ebro	Egmont	Elga	Emma
Dudas	Ebsen	Egon	Eli	Emmett
Dudel	Echo	Egwin	Eliab	Ena
Dudley	Eckart	Egypt	Elise	Enda
Dudu	Eda	Ehren	Elkan	Ender
Duer	Edan	Ehrnd	Elke	Endre
Duffy	Eddra	Ehud	Ella	Endya
Dugald	Edea	Eibe	Ellard	England
Dugan	Edel	Eidel	Ellen	Enice
Dulcie	Edelgard	Eiger	Ellette	Enid
Duluth	Eden	Eigil	Ellice	Ennis
Duma	Edette	Eike	Ellie	Enoch
Duna	Edgar	Eileen	Ellis	Eoin
Duncan	Edic	Eilis	Ellsworth	Ephraim
Dunley	Edith	Eilysh	Elma	Eppie
Dunmore	Edle	Einar	Elmar	Erda
Dunstan	Edlun	Eisig	Elmo	Erhard
Dunton	Edlyn	Eisik	Elmore	Eric
Durand	Edmar	Eitan	Elom	Erie
Durene	Edme	Eithne	Elon	Erin
Durham	Edmund	Eivind	Elrad	Erland
Durrah	Edna	Ejonte	Elroy	Erline
Durstin	Edolf	Ela	Elryck	Erling
Durward	Edrees	Elad	Elsa	Erma
Dusan	Edrei	Elah	Elsbeth	Erna
Dusha	Edric	Elaine	Elsdon	Ernald
Dustin	Edrick	Elbe	Elske	Ernest
Duvall	Edroi	Elbert	Elstan	Ernie
Duvid	Edsard	Elbruz	Elton	Erno
Dwana	Edsel	Elda	Eltren	Errol
Dygal	Edson	Eldar	Elva	Ersha

Erskine	Ewa	Farro	Fintan	Friday
Erving	Ewald	Farrow	Firman	Fridmann
Erwin	Ewan	Fasta	Fishel	Fridolf
Esau	Eward	Fattah	Fisher	Fridtjof
Esdras	Ewert	Fausta	Fitzger	Friederke
Eshe	Ewing	Faustus	Fitzhugh	Frima
Eshel	Eydie	Favin	Flanna	Friso
Eskil	Eynar	Favor	Flannan	Fritzi
Esmay	Ezra	Fawna	Fleta	Frodine
Esme	Faakhir	Faxan	Fletcher	Froma
Esmond	Fabrin	Fealty	Fleurette	Fromel
Espen	Fabron	Fedde	Flora	Froyim
Essence	Fachan	Fede	Florence	Fuchsia
Este	Fagan	Feechi	Flower	Fuji
Estee	Faheem	Feibush	Foigl	Fuller
Estelle	Faiga	Feige	Fola	Fulton
Estes	Faina	Feivel	Folke	Fysal
Esther	Fairfax	Felda	Fonda	Gabai
Estlin	Faiza	Felice	Forster	Gabel
Estus	Faizon	Felix	Fortune	Gabi
Ethan	Fakhr	Felton	Foster	Gabor
Ethban	Falcon	Femke	Franchot	Gada
Ethel	Faldo	Fenton	Francine	Gadil
Ethna	Faline	Ferenc	Francis	Gadmann
Etka	Falkner	Fergus	François	Gaea
Etna	Fallon	Fermin	Frankie	Gainer
Etta	Fanchet	Ferna	Franklin	Gairdner
Etzal	Fancy	Fernand	Franzel	Gaius
Eudo	Fanny	Fernas	Fraser	Galan
Eugene	Farah	Ferrand	Frauke	Galton
Eula	Farand	Festus	Freda	Galuelle
Eunan	Fareed	Fhoki	Freddie	Galvan
Eunice	Fargo	Fia	Fredneish	Gamal
Eustace	Farhat	Fidel	Fredrick	Gamba
Eva	Farkas	Fielding	Freedom	Gamel
Evan	Farley	Fifi	Freeman	Ganges
Evers	Farnall	Fiji	Freena	Gannon
Evette	Farnham	Filbert	Freidel	Garbick
Evi	Farnley	Fillmore	Fremont	Gardal
Evlyn	Farold	Filma	Freta	Gardner
Evonne	Farrah	Fina	Frewen	Gareth
Evreml	Farrell	Finbar	Freya	Garett
Evren	Farris	Finlay	Freydis	Garfield

Gari	Georgette	Gillan	Goldwin	Gunnel
Garlan	Georgia	Gillead	Golin	Gunter
Garland	Georgy	Gilliette	Gomar	Guri
Garmond	Geraint	Gilmer	Gonsalve	Guryon
Garner	Gerald	Gilmore	Goodman	Gustaf
Garnet	Gerard	Gilroy	Goodness	Guthrie
Garnock	Gerben	Gilson	Goodrich	Gutki
Garonne	Gerbold	Gilus	Goral	Guva
Garrick	Gerda	Gimpel	Gordon	Guylaine
Garson	Geri	Gina	Gorje	Gwenda
Garton	Gerius	Ginette	Gorman	Gwyneth
Garvey	Gerlac	Ginger	Goro	Gwynore
Garvin	Gerlind	Gino	Gothar	Gyda
Garwood	Germaine	Giola	Gotthard	Gypsy
Gary	German	Giorsal	Gottlieb	Gytle
Gaspar	Germma	Giosue	Gower	Haadee
Gaston	Gernot	Girvan	Gowon	Haafiz
Gati	Gerold	Gisa	Gracie	Haakon
Gaudenz	Gerrard	Gisbert	Grady	Haalah
Gauthier	Gerrid	Giselle	Graham	Haaris
Gavin	Gerrit	Gitta	Grainne	Habbai
Gavra	Gersham	Gittel	Granger	Habeeb
Gavril	Gertjan	Giusto	Grantland	Hachman
Gaylord	Gertrude	Givon	Granville	Hackett
Gaynor	Gervas	Gladwin	Grayson	Hadad
Gazo	Getzel	Gladys	Greeley	Hadden
Geanna	Geza	Gleason	Gregor	Hadley
Geary	Ghanee	Gleda	Greta	Hadwin
Gebhard	Ghulaam	Glenda	Greyson	Hagai
Geddy	Gibbon	Glenden	Griffith	Hagar
Gefen	Gibe	Glinys	Grimbal	Hagen
Gehrig	Gibor	Glomma	Griswold	Haggar
Geier	Gibson	Glucke	Grover	Hagley
Gemma	Gifford	Glynas	Gudmund	Haidee
Gendel	Gigi	Glynis	Gudrun	Haike
Genie	Gilane	Goddard	Guenna	Hakan
Genna	Gilbert	Godfrey	Guida	Hakeem
Gennie	Gilby	Godric	Guido	Hako
Gentle	Gilchrist	Godwin	Guillaume	Halla
Gentry	Gilda	Goeffrey	Gulai	Haland
Geode	Gildas	Goer	Gunde	Halbert
Geoffrey	Gildor	Golda	Gunhild	Halda
Georgene	Gilford	Golding	Gunnar	Haldan

Haldas	Harlie	Heirnine	Hibbing	Howland
Halden	Harlow	Helbon	Hidde	Hubbard
Haldi	Harmen	Helen	Hidie	Hubert
Haldor	Harmon	Helens	Hilan	Hudel
Halette	Harod	Helga	Hilda	Hudi
Haley	Harold	Helge	Hildar	Hudson
Halfdan	Harper	Helice	Hildreth	Hudya
Halford	Harris	Hella	Hilel	Huette
Hali	Harry	Helle	Hilma	Huey
Hallam	Harsho	Hellfried	Hilton	Hugo
Halle	Hartford	Helma	Hindal	Huila
Halsea	Hartmann	Helmand	Hiram	Hulbard
Halsey	Hartmut	Helmar	Hirza	Hulda
Halstead	Hartwell	Helmut	Hoashis	Humbert
Halston	Harvey	Helsa	Hobert	Humphrey
Halton	Hasheem	Heman	Hodel	Hunter
Halvard	Hashi	Henda	Hoffman	Huntley
Hamal	Hashum	Hendrick	Hogan	Hurley
Hamar	Hasin	Henech	Holbert	Huron
Hamid	Haskel	Henny	Holcomb	Husain
Hamill	Hassan	Henry	Holda	Hutton
Hamish	Hasso	Henson	Holden	Huxford
Hamlet	Hastings	Herbert	Holger	Huxley
Hamlin	Havelock	Herdis	Hollah	Hyatt
Hamon	Haven	Herman	Holland	Hyman
Hamor	Hawthorne	Hernan	Hollis	Iaap
Hampton	Haw-waa	Herra	Holly	Ian
Haneef	Haydon	Herrick	Holman	Ianthe
Hanford	Hayley	Herrod	Holmfrid	Ichal
Hanley	Haymo	Herschel	Homer	Ida
Hannah	Hayward	Hertha	Honda	Ideh
Hansel	Hazel	Hertzel	Honey	Idele
Happy	Heathcliff	Herval	Honor	Iden
Harbin	Heather	Herve	Horace	Idil
Harcourt	Heaven	Hesper	Hortense	Idit
Harden	Heba	Hessel	Horton	Idress
Hardwin	Hector	Hesta	Hosaam	Ierne
Hardy	Hedda	Hester	Hoshi	Iggy
Harel	Hedva	Heston	Hosni	Ignace
Hargrave	Hedwig	Heti	Houghton	Igor
Harim	Hedy	Hetty	Houston	Ihsaan
Harlan	Heidi	Hevel	Howard	I'jaaz
Harley	Heidrun	Heywood	Howell	Ikhlaas

Ikraam	Isleen	Jakeem	Jaya	Jo Anne
Ilda	Isman	Jakob	Jayda	Joappa
Ilene	Ismey	Jalaal	Jayla	Joaquin
Ilka	Isser	Jalen	Jeanette	Joash
Ilsa	Istvan	JaLon	Jebel	JoBeth
Ilya	Ita	Ja'Lyne	Jeffrey	Jobin
Ima	Ithnan	Jamaal	Jehan	Jochbed
Imaad	Iti	Jamece	Jehu	Jochen
Imaam	Itka	Jamie	Jelmer	JoDan
Imre	Itmar	Jamil	Jemine	Jody
Imrich	Itsche	Jamin	Jenci	Joed
Ina	Iva	Jamir	Jeniece	Joep
Inaayat	Ivan	Jamnes	Jenna	Joette
Indus	Ivar	Janal	Jennings	Joewand
Inez	Ivonne	Janelle	Jenny	Johan
Ingalls	Ivy	Janet	Jeno	Johannes
Ingar	Izzie	Janice	Jensen	Johnette
Ingmar	Jaabir	Janine	Jephum	Johnni
Ingo	Jaala	Janis	Jerald	Johnny
Ingolf	Jabbaar	Janna	Jermaine	Johnson
Ingraham	Jabez	Janne	Jerome	Johnston
Ingrid	Jabin	JanMeer	Jerrell	Johnta
Ingvar	Jacek	Jano	Jerri	Johppa
Innes	Jacey	Janusz	Jerry	Jojo
Iqbaal	Jacinth	Japhet	Jervis	Joktan
Ira	Jackson	Jaquaad	Jerzy	Jola
Irene	Jacky	Jaquan	Jesse	Jolie
Irette	Jaclyn	Jared	Jesus	Joline
Irfaan	Jacob	Jari	Jethro	Jollie
Iris	Jacoy	Jarlath	Jevon	Jomo
Irma	Jada	Jaron	Jewel	Jona
Irmgard	Jaddan	Jarreau	Jezreel	Jonah
Irra	Jadeite	Jarren	Jibril	Joplin
Irshaad	Jaden	Jarrett	Jiles	Jordaan
Irvette	Jadon	Jarvis	Jimmy	Jordan
Irving	Jael	Jasmine	Jindrich	Jorgen
Isa	Jaela	Jason	Jinte	Jori
Isaac	Ja'far	Jasper	Jiri	Jorie
Isham	Jagger	Jauhar	Jiro	Joris
Ishmul	Jahdal	Javon	Jivon	Jorren
Isis	Jahod	Javont	Joab	Jorrit
Isla	Jaimie	Jawaad	Joachim	Jorunn
Islam	Jairus	Jawon	Joah	Jory

Jose	Kahlil	Karson	Kelsea	Keyonne
Josee	Kaia	Karsten	Kelsey	Khabeer
Joseph	Kailer	Kashaun	Kelvan	Khaki
Joses	Kaitlyn	Kasheif	Kemi	Khalan
Josette	Kala	Kasia	Kenard	Khalid
Joshi	Kaleb	Kaski	Kenay	Khari
Joshwuan	Kaleem	Kaspar	Kenaz	Khateeb
Josie	Kalen	Kasril	Kenda	Khawlah
Joslyn	Kalie	Kassie	Kendall	Kheino
Josnelle	Kalikst	Kasten	Kenden	Khingan
Jostein	Kalil	Kathe	Kendra	Kiah
Josue	Kalin	Kathleen	Kendrick	Kian
Jotham	Kalli	Kathryn	Kendy	Kiefer
Jovi	Kalvin	Katiann	Kenelm	Kierre
Juba	Kama	Katie	Kenlay	Kiki
Judah	Kamau	Katrine	Kennan	Kila
Judith	Kamba	Katsu	Kenndale	Kilan
Judsen	Kamil	Kauffman	Kenneth	Kilby
Judy	Kamille	Kayla	Kensell	Kileen
Julie	Kamren	Kaylee	Kensey	Kiley
July	Kamron	Kazuo	Kenta	Kilmer
Junaid	Kanaye	Kea	Kentac	Kimbal
Junko	Kandice	Kealy	Kenton	Kimble
Juno	Kanean	Keaton	Kenward	Kimmie
Juraj	Kani	Kedma	Kenway	Kimon
Jurgen	Kanko	Keegan	Kenya	Kincaid
Jusitn	Kansas	Keelan	KenYan	Kindness
Justice	Kanton	Keeley	Kenyon	Kingdon
Justin	Kanya	Keenen	Keon	Kingsley
Justine	Kaoru	Keicha	Kerill	Kingston
Justus	Kapel	Keifer	Kermit	Kingswell
Jutta	Kapil	Keiko	Kerrie	Kinji
Jwahir	Kara	Keiron	Kerrith	Kinnard
Kaare	Kareem	Keirrick	Kerry	Kinnell
Kaatje	Kareen	Keisha	Kershawn	Kino
Kacey	Karel	Kelby	Kerwin	Kinofe
Kachine	Karen	Kelda	Kesey	Kinsey
Kadar	Kari	Kellan	Kesia	Kinsley
Kadeem	Karla	Keller	Keskel	Kipling
Kaden	Karlee	Kelley	Kester	Kira
Kadence	Karmel	Kellie	Keto	Kirby
Kady	Karne	Kelly	Kevin	Kirin
Kaelyn	Karol	Kellyn	Keyla	Kirkley

Kirkwood	Krisol	Laila	Laverne	Levan
Kirstin	Krista	Laius	Lawford	Levi
Kisha	Kristal	Lajos	Lawler	Levin
Kita	Kristen	Laken	Lawley	Lewis
Kitei	Krister	Lala	Lawrence	Lexa
Kitra	Kristian	Lalage	Lawson	Lexine
Kitron	Kristine	Lamar	Lawton	Lia
Kitson	Kristy	Lambert	Layna	Liam
Kitty	Kriten	Lamont	Lazer	Lian
Kiva	Krolik	Lana	Lazine	Liane
Klara	Krystal	Landa	Le Var	Liba
Klemen	Kunle	Lander	Leah	Liban
Kleon	Kurile	Landre	Leanne	Libby
Knowledge	Kurtis	Lanette	Lectra	Libna
Koa	Kusuo	Langford	Leda	Lieber
Kody	Kveta	Langston	Leger	Lieke
Koen	Kwacha	Langworth	Leggitt	Liggett
Koji	Kwaco	Lantha	Legra	Lila
Kolby	Kwasi	Lara	Leila	Lilac
Kolin	Kya	Laraine	Leland	Lilis
Kolton	Kyla	Largent	Lelia	Lilith
Konad	Kyleen	Laron	Lelith	Lilly
Konane	Kyler	LaRoux	Lema	Lilo
Konrad	Kylie	Laroy	Lemuel	Liman
Kontar	Kyna	Larry	Lena	Limbe
Koppel	Kynos	Larson	Lendl	Lincoln
Kora	Kyo	Lasca	Lenka	Linda
Korey	Kyra	LaShawn	Lennon	Lindberg
Korinne	Kyras	LaShay	Leno	Lindell
Kornel	Kyree	Lasse	Lenore	Linden
Korwin	Kyrene	Lassie	Lenox	Lindley
Koryak	Kyron	Lathan	Leo	Lindsay
Kosey	Label	Lathrop	Leon	Line
Kostas	Labib	Lati	Leonard	Linette
Kota	Labor	Latia	LeRon	Liney
Koty	Lacey	Latrice	Lerone	Linford
Kourtney	Lachlan	Latton	Leroy	Lino
Kramer	Lachus	Laura	Leshem	Linor
Krayna	Ladda	Laurel	Lesil	Linsey
Kreindel	LaDrew	Lauren	Lesley	Linton
Krijn	La'eeq	Laurette	Lester	Linus
Krishna	Lagee	Laurie	Leszek	Lipman
Krislyn	Laggett	Lavelle	Letha	Lisa

Lisbeth	Luane	Maddie	Manchu	Marney
Lisette	Luay	Maddock	Mandel	Marnin
Lisha	Luba	Madelle	Mandy	Maro
Liska	Lubbock	Madglaine	Manfred	Ma'roof
Lissa	Lucas	Madra	Mani	Maroon
Lissle	Lucette	Madu	Manish	Marquel
Litha	Lucia	Maelee	Manley	Marques
Litta	Lucierne	Magda	Manning	Marquis
Litton	Lucille	Maggie	Mannis	Marquise
Livei	Lucius	Magic	Mansfield	Marra
Liya	Lucky	Magna	Manshel	Marsden
Llisel	Lucy	Magne	Manton	Marsha
Lockwood	Ludlow	Magnus	Manuel	Marshall
Lodah	Ludly	Maher	Manville	Marshawn
Loden	Ludolf	Mahla	Manya	Marshay
Lodie	Ludwig	Maia	Mara	Marston
Logan	Luelle	Maida	Maranne	Martha
Loire	Luise	Maika	Marcel	Martial
Lois	Lulu	Mailand	Marcelle	Marties
Lola	Luna	Mailyn	Marcia	Martin
Loma	Lundy	Maimon	Marcin	Marvel
Lombard	Lupe	Mairead	Marcus	Marvin
Lona	Lurline	Maise	Marcy	Marwood
London	Luther	Maisel	Mareld	Mary
Loni	Lyan	Maisha	Maren	Maryse
Lonneke	Lydell	Maite	Marette	Mashael
Lonnie	Lydie	Maitland	Marga	Maslin
Lopez	Lyman	Maitlynne	Margie	Mason
Lorant	Lyndon	Major	Margot	Ma'soom
Lorcan	Lynus	Malak	Margrit	Massif
Loren	Lyric	Malan	Marice	Mather
Loring	Lyris	Malca	Marie	Matin
Loris	Maacah	Malchus	Maris	Matisse
Lorna	Maaike	Malcolm	Marit	Matland
Lorraine	Maartje	Mali	Marjon	Mato
Lothar	Mabel	Malik	Markel	Matsu
Lotta	Macie	Malin	Markie	Matthew
Lotus	Macklin	Malinde	Marla	Mattie
Louis	Maclain	Malise	Marlene	Matza
Louise	MacNair	Malva	Marley	Maura
Lourdes	Macon	Malvie	Marlin	Maureen
Lovedeep	Macy	Malwine	Marloes	Mauri
Lowell	Madai	Mamie	Marlow	Maurice

Mavis	Menshel	Miller	Morgan	Myrtle
Maxfield	Merced	Millford	Moria	Naaman
Maxine	Mercer	Millman	Moritz	Naarah
Maxwell	Mercia	Milo	Morley	Naashom
Maybelle	Mercy	Milore	Morna	Naasir
Mayer	Merline	Milos	Morrin	Nabal
Mayfield	Merras	Milton	Morris	Nabor
Maynard	Merrick	Mimba	Morta	Nadab
Mayon	Merrill	Mimi	Morton	Nadav
Mayor	Merritt	Mina	Morven	Nadda
Mayotte	Merry	Minda	Mosa	Nadeem
Mayra	Mertice	Mindy	Moselle	Nadine
Mayson	Mertie	Mine	Moses	Nadire
Mazal	Merton	Minette	Mosi	Naghmah
McGill	Mesen	Minna	Motel	Nagy
McKay	Meshach	Minta	Mouldon	Nahash
McLean	Meta	Mira	Moya	Nahshu
Meagan	Metis	Mirel	Muel	Nahum
Meara	Mette	Mirsab	Muir	Naida
Mechtild	Metzger	Miru	Mukhtaar	Naim
Meda	Meyer	Mischa	Muki	Naimah
Medor	Mia	Misty	Mumtaaz	Najmah
Medwin	Miai	Mita	Muna	Naka
Megan	Micah	Mitchell	Muncie	Naldo
Mehla	Michael	Mitzi	Muneer	Nalon
Mehmet	Michelle	Mma	Mungo	Nalor
Meike	Michener	Moina	Mura	Naman
Meindert	Michi	Moira	Muraad	Namir
Meir	Mickey	Moises	Murdoch	Nancy
Meisha	Mieke	Moline	Murphy	Nando
Melar	Mignon	Molly	Murray	Nandor
Melbourne	Mikayle	Molton	Murtough	Nanette
Melchor	Mikear	Mona	Musa	Nanna
Melda	Miki	Monae	Musette	Nara
Meldon	Miklos	Monday	Muslim	Narda
Melis	Mila	Monet	Muta	Nari
Mella	Milan	Monroe	Mutka	Narjis
Melville	Milda	Monty	Myra	Nashom
Melvin	Mildred	Monya	Myrie	Nasia
Memphis	Milford	Moonstone	Myrka	Nasreen
Menas	Milhous	Morel	Myrlene	Nassor
Mendel	Milla	Moreland	Myrna	Nassos
Mensa	Millard	Morette	Myron	Nata

Natal	Newcomb	Nolan	Ofar	Orman
Nathan	Newland	Noma	Ogden	Orna
Nathene	Newlin	Nona	Oira	Ornas
Naveed	Newman	Noortje	Oisin	Oro
Naylor	Newton	Nora	Oka	Oron
Nayo	Nia	Norbert	Okei	Orrick
Nayton	Niamh	Noreen	Olaf	Orson
Nazar	Nichelle	Norma	Olaug	Orten
Nazheer	Nico	Norman	Olcott	Orterd
Nduka	Nicole	Northrop	Oldrich	Ortfried
Nealah	Nidri	Norton	Oleg	Orton
Necha	Niene	Norval	Olen	Ortrud
Neco	Nigel	Norward	Olette	Orva
Neda	Nike	Norwell	Olga	Orval
Nedra	Nikha	Norwin	Oline	Orville
Neela	Nikki	Norwood	Olive	Orvin
Neeltje	Nikon	Norword	Ollie	Orwell
Neely	Nila	Nosson	Olnay	Orwin
Neema	Nilla	Nova	Olva	Osbert
Neesa	Nina	Nunu	Oma	Osborn
Nelda	Ninette	Nuri	Omar	Oscar
Nella	Nino	Nuru	Omen	Oseye
Nelli	Nipha	Nuteh	Omri	Osgood
Nellwyn	Nipsey	Nyrell	Ona	Oshri
Nelson	Nisha	Nysa	Ondine	Osithe
Neman	Nissa	Nyshae	Ondrej	Oslo
Nemo	Nita	Oakley	Ontine	Osman
Neneh	Niven	Obed	Onyx	Osred
Neom	Nixie	Obel	Opal	Osric
Nepal	Nixon	Obert	Oprah	Ossa
Nerine	Niyra	Obla	Ora	Oswald
Nessa	Nizaam	Octave	Oram	Oswin
Nessan	Noah	Oda	Oran	Otha
Nesta	Noaz	Odab	Orange	Othman
Nestor	Noble	Oddvar	Orchid	Otis
Netra	Nodab	Odeen	Ordway	Otmar
Netta	Noe	Odele	Orel	Otto
Netzel	Noel	Odette	Oren	Ove
Neva	Noelle	Odin	Orford	Ovid
Nevil	Noemi	Odine	Ori	Owen
Nevin	Noga	Odlo	Orla	Oxford
Nevlin	Noha	Odolf	Orlan	Oyvind
Newbold	Nola	Odrick	Orland	Oza

Ozan	Paxon	Phia	Precious	Quita
OZire	Paxton	Phibba	Prentice	Raaghib
Ozmo	Peabo	Phil	Prescott	Raama
Ozzie	Pearline	Philbert	Presley	Raashid
Pablo	Pecos	Philene	Preto	Rabbi
Pacian	Pedro	Philippe	Prima	Rabi
Paco	Pega	Phillip	Primo	Rabul
Padget	Peggy	Phira	Primrose	Rachel
Pageman	Pegma	Phoebe	Prisca	Rachins
Paisley	Pelle	Phoenix	Priya	Racine
Paiton	Pelton	Phonsa	Procter	Racqueab
Paki	Pembroke	Phyllis	Prosper	Radbert
Palla	Penley	Pia	Prudence	Radborne
Pallas	Penny	Pickford	Psyche	Radcliff
Palma	Penrod	Pico	Purvis	Radcliffe
Palmer	Penrose	Pierette	Qaadir	Raden
Palti	Pentha	Pierre	Qamar	Radka
Pankraz	Pentige	Pierrepont	Qawee	Radley
Panos	Peony	Pierson	Quaco	Radnor
Pansy	Pepin	Pilar	Quadai	Radolf
Panya	Pepper	Pincas	Quadrey	Raelyn
Paolo	Percy	Pinya	Quamere	Rafeé
Paris	Perel	Piper	Quami	Rafeeq
Parker	Peril	Pippa	Quanah	Raffin
Parnell	Perkin	Pippin	Quartas	Raghib
Parrish	Perla	Pirney	Quartus	Ragnar
Parry	Pernille	Pity	Quashee	Ragnhild
Parthik	Peron	Pius	Quddos	Rahab
Pascal	Perrin	Plato	Quenby	Rahmaan
Pascale	Perry	Pollard	Quenna	Raina
Pasia	Persis	Pollock	Quentin	Rainer
Passion	Pesha	Pollux	Queri	Rainier
Patience	Peshe	Polly	Quertnel	Raleigh
Patrice	Pesye	Polo	Quesstin	Ralik
Patrick	Peter	Pontus	Questa	Ralis
Patsy	Petra	Poonam	Quigley	Ralston
Patton	Peyton	Poppy	Quillan	Rama
Patty	Pfeiffer	Pora	Quilmes	Ramah
Paula	Pheba	Porsha	Quinby	Rambert
Paulette	Phedra	Porter	Quincy	Ramel
Pauline	Phelan	Portia	Quinlan	Rami
Paulo	Phelgen	Potter	Quinta	Ramla
Pavlof	Phenice	Powell	Quintez	Ramsden

Ramsey	Regal	Richman	Rodney	Ruby
Rana	Regan	Richmond	Rodwell	Rudelle
Ra'naa	Regis	Richshae	Rogan	Rudo
Ranceford	Reidar	Rickard	Roger	Rudolph
Randall	Reidun	Ricki	Roiza	Rudyard
Randolph	Reiko	Riddock	Roland	Ruelle
Randy	Reilly	Rider	Rollin	Rufus
Ranen	Reine	Ridglee	Rolshawn	Rugby
Ranger	Reinhard	Ridhaa	Roma	Ruiz
Rankin	Rema	Riely	Romaine	Rula
Rannveig	Remus	Riemer	Roman	Rumford
Ransell	Remy	Rif'at	Rombert	Rupert
Ransford	Rena	Rifka	Romney	Rurik
Ransley	Renaud	Riga	Romy	Rushford
Ransom	Rene	Rigby	Rona	Ruskeh
Rante	Renferd	Rigmor	Ronald	Ruskin
Raoul	Renny	Rika	Ronan	Ruslan
Rasean	Reno	Rilda	Rondell	Russell
RaSha	Renshaw	Riley	Roni	Russet
RaShaad	Renton	Rimon	Ronnie	Rustice
Rashad	Renwick	Ringo	Ronson	Rusty
Rasheed	Renzo	Rio	Rooney	Rutledge
Rasine	Reshard	Riordan	Roper	Rutley
Rasline	Reuben	Ripley	Roque	Ruvim
Rasmus	Reva	Risa	Rory	Ryan
Rasool	Rexford	Rishab	Roscoe	Ryker
Raul	Reyes	Rishon	Roseanne	Rylan
Raven	Reyna	Rita	Roselle	Rylee
Ravid	Reynard	Rito	Rosemay	Ryman
Rawdan	Reynold	Riva	Rosette	Ryton
Rawlins	Rhawann	Rivan	Rosine	Saadiq
Raybourne	Rhea	River	Roslin	Saarah
Raymond	Rhetta	Riyaadh	Roswell	Saba
Raynard	Rhoda	Roald	Rosy	Sabelle
Rayzel	Rhona	Robbie	Rothwell	Saber
Razi	Rhonda	Robert	Rover	Sabine
Reba	Ria	Robin	Rowan	Sabra
Reddy	Rian	Rocco	Rowell	Sabu
Redford	Riao	Rochelle	Rowley	Sacco
Redman	Ribal	Rockwell	Roxane	Sacha
Redmond	Rica	Rocky	Royal	Sachi
Reeba	Richard	Rodas	Royden	Sa'd
Reeta	Richma	Rodman	Royla	Saddie

Sadey	Sapphire	Serwa	Sharnice	Shimon
Sadir	Sappho	Sessue	Sharon	Shinsei
Sadoc	Sarah	Seta	Sharvay	Shipton
Saeed	Sarette	Seton	Shasta	Shira
Safdar	Sargent	Setta	Shateek	Shirley
Safford	Sarine	Severn	Shatner	Shivon
Sageon	Sarna	Sewall	Shaundel	Shloimeh
Sagiv	Sasha	Seward	Shawna	Shmiel
Saida	Sassille	Sewell	Shawntae	Shoji
Saide	Saulat	Sexton	Shaya	Shota
Sajoir	Saval	Sextus	Shaylynn	Shoze
Saka	Savando	Seymour	Sheba	Shraga
Saki	Savil	Shaafee	Shebsil	Shujaa
Salaam	Sawao	Shadoe	Sheedy	Shyan
Salba	Sawyer	Shadrach	Sheehan	Shyla
Saleem	Saxon	Shahaab	Sheena	Sibley
Salem	Sayah	Shahlaa	Shefer	Sibyl
Sally	Saychelle	Shakeel	Sheffield	Sida
Salmah	Scarlet	Shakur	Sheila	Siddell
Salud	Schuyler	Shalah	Shelah	Siddeq
Salween	Scota	Shalem	Shelby	Siddon
Sama	Scotty	Shalin	Sheldon	Sidney
Samal	Seamus	Shalva	Shelia	Sidon
Sameer	Sebald	Shamel	Shelley	Sidra
Samson	Sedgwick	Shamfa	Shelsie	Sidsel
Samuele	Segel	Shamil	Shepherd	Sidwel
Sana	Seito	Shamir	Shepley	Siegbert
Sanborn	Sekel	Shamma	Shepsil	Siegfried
Sancho	Sela	Shamrose	Sherard	Sieglinde
Sanders	Selby	Shanda	Sherborne	Sigleif
Sandi	Seldon	Shandeigh	Sherine	Sigmund
Sandip	Seled	Shandy	Sherlock	Signe
Sandon	Selene	Shanelle	Sherman	Sigrid
Sandra	Selfridge	Shani	Shermarke	Sigurd
Sanford	Selig	Shanice	Sherrice	Sigwald
Sanfred	Selma	Shanley	Sherrod	Sihon
Sangay	Selwyn	Shannah	Sherry	Silaah
Sanger	Semele	Shannon	Sherwin	Silas
Sanne	Sena	Shanta	Sherwood	Silda
Sanson	Sennett	Shantrelle	Sheryl	Silene
Santo	Senta	Shara	Sheya	Siloam
Saphra	Seon	Shareef	Shiloh	Siloum
Sapir	Sera	Sharif	Shima	Silsby

Silva	Sophie	Stilwell	Sylvie	Tarus
Silver	Sorcha	Stina	Syna	Taryn
Sima	Sorele	Stinson	Synjin	Tasha
Simon	Sorka	Stockard	Syshe	TaSheem
Simone	Sorrell	Stockley	Szeja	Tasneem
Simpson	Soslan	Stockton	Taalib	Tatu
Sinclair	Southwell	Stockwell	Tabber	Tatum
Sinead	Sowa	Stoddard	Taggert	Tauri
Siobhan	Spalding	Stonwin	Tahoe	Tavis
Sion	Spencer	Stormy	Tailor	Tavon
Sippie	Spengler	Strahan	Taima	Tawqeer
Siraaj	Spiro	Stratford	Taiwo	Taybah
Sirel	Spokane	Struthers	Taja	Tayib
Siri	Spyros	Suffield	Tala	Tayla
Sisel	Sroli	Sughraa	Tal'at	Taylor
Sishe	Stacy	Suha	Talbot	Tayon
Sissy	Staffan	Sujith	Talie	Tayor
Sivan	Stafford	Sula	Talis	Taysean
Sive	Stancliff	Sully	Talmadge	Teara
Sixto	Standfield	Sultan	Talyn	Tecla
Sjoerd	Standice	Suma	Tama	Teclo
Skelly	Stanford	Summer	Tameez	Teddman
Skelton	Stanhope	Sumner	Tami	Tegan
Skerrit	Stanley	Sunday	Tamir	Teiko
Skerry	Stanmore	Sunni	Tamkeen	Teillo
Skipper	Stanton	Sunny	Tammy	Teivel
Skylar	Stanway	Sura	Tanel	Telford
Slader	Stanwick	Surele	Tani	Telly
Slaven	Stanwin	Surem	Tanner	Teman
Smedley	Stanwood	Susan	Tansey	Tempest
Snowden	Stashu	Suskov	Tanton	Templa
Snyder	Stathis	Sutcliff	Tanya	Teneah
Sohil	Stavros	Sutton	Taqee	Tengger
Sola	Stedman	Suzu	Tara	Teo
Solange	Steinar	Sverre	Taran	Teri
Solerne	Stella	Sweeney	TaRay	Terje
Solfrid	Stephen	Swithbart	Tari	Terrance
Solon	Sterling	Swoosie	Tarim	Terrell
Solveig	Steven	Sybil	Tariq	Terren
Soma	Stevie	Sybren	Taro	Terrene
Sona	Stewart	Sydelle	Tarrant	Terrill
Sonia	Stilla	Sydney	Tarrsus	Terris
Sonnie	Stillman	Sylvan	Tartan	Terry

Terza	Thoreau	Toni	Trevon	TyZhier
Terzas	Thorley	Tony	Trevor	Tzigane
Tesei	Thorma	Tooru	Trilby	Tzipa
Tesfay	Thorndike	Topaz	Trina	Tzipi
Tesia	Thornley	Topez	Trinette	Uba
Tesla	Thornton	Torbjorn	Trisha	Ubald
Tessa	Thurber	Torborg	Trista	Uda
Tesslyn	Thurgood	Torey	Tristan	Udeh
Tethyan	Thurlow	Torfinn	Trixie	Udel
Teton	Thurman	Torgrim	Troyal	Udele
Tevin	Thursday	Tori	Trudy	Udell
Thaabit	Thurston	Torild	Truesdale	Udo
Thais	Thyra	Torkild	Truman	Udolf
Thambo	Tia	Tormey	Trumble	Uela
Tharwat	Tibor	Torolf	Trygve	Ugo
Thatcher	Tica	Torpin	Tucker	Ula
Thayer	Tierell	Torrance	Tudor	Ulas
Thea	Tiernan	Torray	Tuesday	Ulbrich
Thecie	Ties	Torrens	Tulip	Ulda
Thede	Tikey	Torrlow	Tully	Ule
Thelma	Tilda	Torsten	Tupper	Ulfat
Thema	Tilden	Torunn	Turid	Ulfred
Themis	Tilford	Torvald	Turlough	Ulgar
Thenna	Tillo	Tovah	Turner	Ulick
Theon	Tilton	Towland	Turquois	Ulla
Therese	Tima	Townley	Tutto	Ulland
Theron	Timon	Townsend	Tuxford	Ullock
Thesda	Tina	Towrey	Twimell	Ulmer
Thetes	Tirso	Toyo	Twyford	Ulphi
Thetis	Tirza	Tracay	Tybalt	Ulric
Thetos	Tisbe	Tracy	Tycell	Ultan
Thia	Tita	Trahern	Tychon	Ulva
Thien	Titus	Trana	Tyler	Ulysee
Thierry	Toby	Traugott	Tylow	Uma
Thila	Toda	Travis	Tynan	Umar
Thilde	Toiba	Trechelle	Tyra	Una
Thirze	Toland	Tredway	Tyran	Undine
Thisbe	Tollman	Treindel	Tyriek	Unique
Thistle	Tomer	Trella	Tyrone	Unni
Thomas	Tomiek	Tremayne	Tyshawn	Unwin
Thora	Tomkin	Trenton	Tyson	Updike
Thorald	Tomlin	Trequan	Tyus	Upton
Thorbert	Tomo	Treva	Tzerin	Upwood

Ural	Vaydell	Vita	Wardell	Wheaton
Urbai	Veda	Vitold	Wardley	Wheeler
Urban	Vedette	Vitus	Warfeld	Whistler
Urbi	Vedi	Vivi	Warford	Whitby
Uri	Vega	Vlasta	Warren	Whitelaw
Ursa	Vegard	Vola	Warring	Whitfield
Urso	Velda	Volga	Warton	Whitford
Urta	Velma	Volker	Warwick	Whitlee
Usaid	Velore	Volkhard	Washburn	Whitley
Uta	Velvel	Volkov	Wather	Whitlock
Utah	Velvet	Volney	Watkins	Whitman
Utas	Venice	Vona	Watson	Whitmore
Ute	Venke	Vyatt	Wayland	Whitney
Uwe	Venture	Wadley	Waylon	Wickham
Vachel	Venus	Wadsworth	Wazeer	Wickley
Vacla	Vera	Wagner	Weaver	Widnie
Vaclav	Verald	Wahab	Weber	Wiep
Vadnee	Verda	Waheed	Webley	Wieslav
Vakhtang	Verek	Wainwright	Webster	Wilbur
Vala	Verene	Waka	Wednesday	Wilda
Valborg	Verla	Wakefield	Welborne	Wildon
Valda	Verna	Wakeley	Welby	Wiley
Valdes	Verney	Wakeman	Welcome	Wilford
Vallis	Vernon	Walburg	Weldon	Wilfred
Valma	Vero	Walcott	Welford	Wilfrede
Vanda	Verrall	Walda	Welton	Willard
Vander	Veste	Walden	Wendell	Willette
Vandyke	Vevine	Waldron	Wendy	William
Vani	Vicky	Walford	Wenston	Willie
Vanna	Victor	Walker	Wentforth	Willis
Van Ness	Vida	Wallace	Wentworth	Willow
Vanthe	Vidal	Waller	Wenzel	Willtrude
Van Wyck	Vigdis	Wallis	Wera	Wilma
Varda	Viggo	Wallmond	Werdah	Wilmar
Varden	Vignette	Walston	Werner	Wilmot
Vareck	Vigor	Walter	Wescott	Wilson
Varna	Villette	Walton	Wesla	Wilton
Vasco	Vina	Waltraut	Wesley	Wilva
Vashti	Vincent	Walworth	Westbrook	Winchell
Vasso	Vinne	Walwyn	Weston	Windsor
Vasta	Vinson	Wanda	Weylin	Winfield
Vasti	Virgil	Wandell	Wharton	Winfred
Vasya	Vision	Warda	Wheatley	Wingate

Winnie	Xipto	Yudel	Zarrah	Zjateek
Winslow	Xochil	Yudis	Zavad	Zlata
Winston	Xylon	Yui	Zayna	Zoara
Winter	Yaameen	Yuji	Zbigniew	Zoba
Winthrop	Yachna	Yukon	Zbik	Zoe
Winton	Yadon	Yuma	Zdenek	Zoha
Winward	Yagil	Yurik	Zdenka	Zoila
Wira	Yaira	Yursa	Zea	Zoilo
Wisdom	Yakar	Yuta	Zeeman	Zoisite
Wiske	Yama	Yvette	Zeenat	Zokaa
Witold	Yancy	Yvonne	Zeidel	Zoltan
Witter	Yanee	Zaahid	Zela	Zona
Witton	Yangtze	Zaahir	Zelda	Zora
Wolcott	Yanis	Zadok	Zelig	Zoser
Wolfgang	Yankel	Zafar	Zemel	Zosi
Wolfram	Yardley	Zafeer	Zena	Zufar
Woodley	Yarkon	Zagros	Zenas	Zuhrah
Woodman	Yarom	Zaheer	Zeno	Zulay
Woodrow	Yasir	Zahraa	Zenon	Zundel
Woodruff	Yasmine	Zahtwon	Zenzi	Zusa
Woodward	Yasu	Zahur	Zephan	Zussman
Woolcott	Yasuo	ZaiMel	Zera	Zwena
Woolsey	Yazeed	Zaida	Zerah	
Wordsworth	Yedda	Zaire	Zere	
Worton	Yemin	Zajac	Zerem	
Wouter	Yemyo	Zaji	Zero	
Wyanda	Yeoman	Zakaa	Zeta	
Wyatt	Yero	Zakai	Zetan	
Wyborn	Yesel	Zakoc	Zeva	
Wycliff	Yesher	Zalkin	Zevon	
Wylie	Yeta	Zalman	Zeynep	
Wyman	Yigal	Zamir	Ziegier	
Wymer	Yitzhak	Zander	Ziggy	
Wyndham	Yngvar	Zandra	Zillah	
Wynee	Yogi	ZaNique	Zima	
Wystan	Yoko	Zanna	Zimra	
Xanthe	Yona	Zanvil	Zintars	
Xanthus	Yoosef	ZaQuon	Zintis	
Xaver	Yoran	Zara	Zion	
Xena	Yoshe	Zared	Zisel	
Xenos	Yossel	Zarek	Zissa	
Xerxes	Yotti	Zari	Zita	
Xianne	Yseult	Zarna	Ziyaad	

3 Syllables

Aabidah	Adalard	Agatha	Aleda	Almira
Aaminah	Adalbert	Agave	Aledis	Alodie
Aamirah	Adaline	Agnella	Aleeca	Aloha
Aanisah	Adama	Ahava	Aleesa	Alona
Aarionne	Adamek	Ahlexa	Aleighsha	Alondra
Aasimah	Adamsen	Ahola	Aleldra	Alonso
Aasiyah	Adanma	Ahuva	Alemet	Alonza
Aatiqah	Adara	Aillsa	Alena	Alonzo
Aba'ye	Adaucus	Airlia	Aleron	Alora
Ababno	Addison	Airliah	Alesia	Alpena
Abaddon	Adedewe	Aislara	Aleta	Alpheus
Abahu	Adela	Akaka	Aleutian	Alphonsa
Abana	Adelaide	Akevy	Alexa	Alphonsine
Abasi	Adelbert	Akeyla	Alexei	Alphonso
Abbottson	Adelfo	Akia	Alexis	Althea
Abdullah	Adelheid	Akili	Alfalfa	Altinure
Abebi	Adelmo	Akira	Alfonsine	Alufa
Abeeku	Adelpho	Akiva	Alfreda	Alula
Abellard	Adena	Akshara	Alfredo	Alura
Abeo	Adewale	Akuako	Algernon	Alvado
Aberdeen	Adira	Akwasi	Alia	Alvaro
Aberlin	Adiva	Akwate	Aliceson	Alvina
Abidla	Adiya	Alage	Alicia	Alvita
Abiezer	Adlare	Alana	Alicja	Alyda
Abigail	Adolphus	Alani	Alida	Alyssa
Abijah	Adonis	Alanson	Alidis	Alzado
Abioye	Adora	Alara	Alima	Alzena
Abira	Adoree	Alaric	Alina	Amabel
Abiri	Adorna	Alarice	Alipi	Amada
Abosi	Adria	Alasia	Alisa	Amadis
Abraham	Adrian	Alaska	Alisen	Amadour
Abramo	Adriel	Alastair	Alisia	Amaila
Abrasha	Adrienne	Alayla	Alita	Amaline
Absalom	Aenea	Albany	Aliyah	Amamda
Acantha	Aeneas	Alberta	Allare	Amana
Achille	Afafa	Alberto	Allegra	Amanda
Acima	Afeefah	Albina	Allena	Amani
Acisclo	Africa	Albion	Alleras	Amanique
Ackerley	Afryea	Aldarcie	Allison	Amara
Adaego	Agala	Aldarcy	Allista	Amargo
Adaha	Agape	Aldercy	Allveta	Amaris
Adaia	Agata	Aldora	Almagor	Amary
Adalai	Agate	Alea	Almeta	Amasa

Amata	Anita	Aribert	Athena	Balthasar
Amaty	Ankoma	Aribold	Atherton	Baptista
Amazon	Annabell	Arica	Atida	Barabas
Amazu	Annaliese	Ariel	Atira	Barbara
Amberlynn	Annegret	Ario	Atlanta	Barnaby
Ambria	Annemarie	Arissa	Atronna	Barrington
Ambrosia	Annerose	Arita	Attalie	Bashaarat
Ambrosine	Annibale	Arkady	Atthia	Bathilda
Ambrosius	Annika	Arlena	Attila	Bathsheba
Amedee	Annisia	Arleta	Attracta	Beata
Ameenah	Annorah	Armando	Atwater	Beatrice
Amena	Anntonette	Armani	Atzhiry	Beauregard
Amery	Anona	Armelda	Auberta	Behira
Amethyst	Anselma	Armesha	Augusta	Belia
Amias	Anselme	Armida	Augustine	Belinda
Amichai	Antanae	Armilla	Augustus	Belino
Amina	Antero	Armina	Aurea	Bellamy
Aminta	Anthea	Armona	Aurelie	Belshazzar
Amira	Anthony	Armoni	Aurita	Beluchi
Amitan	Antipas	Arnalda	Aurora	Belvia
Amity	Antoinette	Arnina	Austria	Beneba
Ammaarah	Antonin	Arnoldo	Avena	Benedict
Amoni	Antoya	Arnona	Avenall	Benigna
Amora	Anysia	Arola	Avera	Benigno
Amorette	Anyssa	Aroldo	Averil	Benilda
Amparo	Apollo	Arria	Avery	Benita
Amrita	Appoline	Arrigo	Aviaz	Benito
Anatol	Aquila	Artema	Avigail	Benjamin
Anceline	Aquinnah	Artina	Avinoam	Benoni
Andea	Arabelle	Arturo	Aviva	Beora
Anderson	Aracin	Aruba	Avrumel	Beresford
Andorra	Araldo	Arundel	Ayana	Berkeley
Andrea	Ararat	Arvidas	Ayesha	Berlinda
Andreas	Arbogast	Aselma	Aylandra	Bermudo
Andrere	Archibald	Ashanti	Azeezah	Bernadette
Andromede	Ardara	Ashia	Aziza	Bernadine
Aneesah	Ardella	Asifa	Azriel	Bernardo
Angela	Arela	Aspia	Azura	Bernia
Angelo	Arelus	Asriel	Babita	Bernica
Angelou	Aretha	Assunta	Bahati	Bernita
Angola	Argenta	Astilbe	Balbina	Bertilla
Anibal	Aria	Atalie	Baldemar	Bertoldo
Anika	Arian	Atanas	Balogun	Bertrando

Berura	Cadena	Carnation	Chavakuk	Clematis
Bethany	Calandra	Carolanne	Chavivi	Clemente
Bethesda	Calantha	Caroline	Chemarin	Clementine
Bethezel	Calgary	Carollan	Cheritta	Cleodal
Bethia	Calia	Cartier	Cherokee	Cleofas
Bethina	Calida	Casilda	Chevalier	Cliona
Betsabe	Calixto	Casimir	Chevona	Clorinda
Bettina	Callista	Caspian	Chiante	Clotilda
Beverly	Callula	Cassandra	Chiara	Colberdee
Bianca	Calvina	Cassia	Chibale	Colier
Bibienne	Calvino	Cassidy	Chicago	Colima
Binetta	Calypso	Cassius	Chijioke	Colinette
Birgitta	Camaren	Castara	Chikosi	Collier
Bithia	Cambria	Castellan	Chimanga	Columba
Blumele	Cameo	Catherine	Chinasia	Columbus
Boguslaw	Camerero	Catima	Chinenye	Commodore
Bolivar	Cameron	Catriona	Chiquita	Compassion
Boniface	Camilla	Ceara	Chiura	Conchita
Bonita	Camillo	Cecily	Chiyena	Coniah
Bozena	Camron	Ceirra	Chiyoko	Conradine
Bradbury	Candenza	Celandine	Chizoba	Conrado
Brandio	Candida	Celia	Chriselda	Conseja
Brassica	Candido	Celina	Chrissa	Constantine
Braulia	Canute	Celisha	Christabelle	Consuela
Breina	Cardamine	Celosia	Christina	Contrado
Brianna	Caridad	Ceporah	Christopher	Corabelle
Brietta	Carina	Cerelly	Ciandra	Coraline
Brigido	Carino	Cerina	Ciara	Corazon
Brionna	Cariota	Cesare	Cicero	Corcoran
Brittany	Carissa	Chaika	Cinnamon	Cordaro
Broccoli	Carita	Chamaran	Cinzia	Corina
Broderick	Carleas	Chancellor	Ciprian	Corisa
Bronislaw	Carlessa	Chanina	Cirillo	Corlinda
Brunetta	Carleton	Chardonnae	Clarabelle	Cornecia
Brunhilde	Carlianne	Charian	Claresta	Cornela
Buffalo	Carlina	Charilaos	Clareta	Corodon
Bukeda	Carlita	Charissa	Clarinda	Corona
Burgundy	Carlotta	Charity	Clarissa	Corrado
Burnaby	Carlton	Charleston	Clasina	Cosetta
Buruku	Carmelo	Charlotta	Claudia	Cosima
Buttercup	Carmichael	Charlton	Claudio	Cosimo
Bwerani	Carmiel	Chasity	Clavero	Costanza
Cabrina	Carmiela	Chastity	Cleantha	Costanzo

Cotia	Darina	DeNesha	Dontavis	Ehrenfried
Courtesy	Darius	Deniko	Dorcea	Eirena
Crescentia	Darivin	Deondre	Dorian	Ekechi
Cressida	Daroma	Deonsha	Dorina	Elaina
Cresusa	Darona	Derrico	Dorinda	Elana
Crisanto	Dartagnon	Desiah	Dorothy	Elatia
Crispino	Dativa	Desiree	Dosia	Elberta
Cristobal	Davina	Destiny	Druella	Elboa
Cubbenah	Davita	DeVanta	Drusilla	Eldora
Cymbeline	Daymiane	Devashka	Duana	Eldreda
Cynara	DeAjah	Deverell	Duena	Eleanor
Cynthia	De'Andre	Devirtna	Durango	Electra
Cyperus	Deandre	Devona	Dylana	Elena
Cyprian	Deanna	Dhariel	Dymphia	Elesha
Cyprio	Deasa	Diana	Dynasty	Elexys
Cyrano	Debarath	DiAndre	Eberhard	Elfrida
Cyrena	Deborah	Diante	Eberta	Elia
Cyrilla	December	Diantha	Ebony	Elias
Cyrillus	Decima	Diaya	Econah	Elidad
Dachia	DeForest	Dibia	Edana	Eliezer
Daffodil	Degenhard	Didier	Edelbert	Elijah
Dagobert	De'Jana	Diego	Edeline	Eliphaz
Dahlia	Dekari	Diella	Edelmar	Elisa
Daigoro	Delace	Dieuwertje	Edgardo	Elisha
Dakarai	Delaney	Dioma	Edina	Elishka
Dakota	Delanie	Dionna	Edison	Elisif
Dalia	Delano	Dmitri	Edissa	Elita
Dalila	Delanos	Docilla	Edita	Ellata
Damalas	Delante	Dolores	Editha	Ellerey
Damara	Delcia	Domela	Ediva	Ellga
Damarcus	Delfino	Domina	Edmea	Elliot
Damaso	Deliah	Dominic	Edmonda	Ellison
Damien	Delida	Dominique	Edmonton	Ellora
Damita	Delilah	Donahue	Edmundo	Elmina
Danasia	Delora	Donalda	Edora	Elmira
Dania	Delphina	Donaldo	Edrea	Elodie
Danica	Demarcus	Donata	Edwardine	Eloise
Daniella	Demeko	Donato	Edwardo	Elondra
Danilo	Demery	Donavon	Edwina	Elrica
Danuta	Demetrig	Donela	Efrona	Elura
Daquisha	Deminko	Donia	Efua	Elvina
Daria	DeMonte	Donica	Egarton	Elvira
Darienne	Denedra	Donovan	Eglantine	Elviro

292

Elwina	Ernaline	Fadia	Fortuna	Genaida
Emani	Ernestine	Faheemah	Fortuno	Genaro
Emelda	Ernesto	Faraji	Fotina	Genesa
Emeline	Erwina	Fareedah	Francesca	Genesis
Emerald	Erzsebet	Farica	Francisco	Geneva
Emerson	Escriba	Fatima	Frantisek	Genevieve
Emily	Esmero	Faustino	Fredela	Gennady
Emina	Esquilo	Favian	Frederick	Gentilis
Emmerich	Esteban	Fayola	Frederique	Georgina
Emmuela	Estella	Fedora	Fridolin	Georgios
Emmylou	Etana	Felicia	Fronnia	Geraldine
Emogene	Ethaniel	Felimy	Froyimke	Geraldo
Emonie	Ethelind	Felipa	Fuensanta	Gerardo
Emory	Etienne	Felipe	Fujita	Gereron
Enalda	Ettore	Fenella	Fukuda	Gergely
Enchantra	Euclea	Fenimore	Fulvia	Gergory
Encratia	Eudice	Feodor	Furuta	Gerita
Endia	Eudoca	Ferdinand	Gabino	Germana
Endora	Eudora	Feriga	Gabriel	Gervaso
Endoro	Eugenie	Fernanda	Gabrielle	Gevante
Eneas	Eulalie	Festatus	Gaerity	Ghazaalah
Engedi	Eurosia	Fiachra	Galatia	Giachem
Engelbert	Eustacie	Fidelas	Galina	Giana
Ennea	Eustrate	Fidele	Gallagher	Gianni
Enrica	Evadne	Fidelma	Gamali	Gibeon
Enrique	Evander	Filberte	Gamaliel	Gibrian
Eradis	Evante	Filide	Garcia	Gideon
Eraldo	Evelyn	Fillander	Gardia	Gilada
Eranthe	Everard	Fineas	Gardiner	Gilberta
Erasmo	Everest	Finian	Garibald	Gilberto
Erasmus	Everett	Fiona	Garielle	Gilboa
Erastus	Evetta	Fiora	Garlanda	Gilead
Erebus	Evromel	Fitzgerald	Garretson	Giletta
Erela	Ezarra	Fitzpatrick	Garrison	Gileyla
Erica	Ezio	Fitzroya	Garroway	Gillian
Erida	Faadilah	Flavia	Gaspare	Ginebra
Erlia	Faa'izah	Flavian	Gastone	Ginendel
Erlina	Fabia	Florentin	Gatias	Giordano
Erlinda	Fabian	Florida	Gavino	Giorgio
Ermanno	Fabienne	Florina	Gavrilke	Gisleno
Ermelind	Fabria	Foluke	Gazella	Gitana
Ermina	Fachanan	Fornasa	Gedraitis	Giuditta
Ernaldus	Facundo	Forrester	Gemino	Giulio

Giuseppe	Halona	Hideko	Ila	Islean
Giustina	Hamilton	Hideyo	Ilana	Isoke
Giustino	Hamony	Hilary	Ildiko	Isolde
Gloria	Hanako	Hildebrand	Ilia	Isotta
Godiva	Hanani	Hildegarde	Illana	Israel
Goffredo	Haneefah	Hildemar	Ilona	Isserel
Goliath	Hanisi	Hilina	Ilyssa	Istifaa
Gonzago	Hannelore	Hillary	Imani	Ithaman
Gonzales	Hannibal	Hilliard	Imari	Iveta
Grania	Hansuli	Hirata	Imelda	Ivona
Gregory	Haralda	Hiroko	Imena	Ivory
Grimona	Harmony	Hiroshi	Imogene	Ivriya
Griselda	Haroldo	Hisaye	Inaki	Iwata
Grunella	Harriet	Holiness	Inazo	Iwona
Gualtiero	Harrison	Holmaitn	India	Iyana
Guillermo	Harshita	Honesty	Indigo	Iynd'go
Guinevere	Haruki	Honora	Indira	Izebe
Guiseppa	Haseenah	Horiya	Ineke	Jabari
Gunilla	Hasina	Hosea	Ingalill	Jabrial
Gurias	Hawaii	Huberta	Ingeborg	Jacari
Gustava	Hazael	Huberto	Ingegerd	Jacinda
Gustavo	Heiiri	Humairaa	Ingemar	Jacinto
Gwendolyn	Heirrierte	Humberto	Inglebert	Jacoba
Gyorgy	Helbona	Humbleness	Ingrida	Jacobo
Gyozo	Helena	Huntington	Inigo	Jacomine
Gyula	Helicon	Hyacinth	Ioannis	Jacqueline
Haafizah	Heloise	Iantha	Iolanthe	Jadwiga
Haarisah	Henia	Ibraaheem	Iona	Jahnea
Haarithah	Henrika	Ibratum	Ireneusz	Jahnika
Habakkuk	Heraldo	Ichabod	Ireta	Jairia
Habeebah	Herberto	Idaline	Irmela	Jakira
Habika	Heremon	Idola	Isabel	Jamaica
Hachiro	Hermina	Idolia	Isacco	Jamarcus
Hadasa	Hermino	Idona	Isaiah	Ja'-Mari
Hadrian	Hermione	Idowu	Isami	Jamica
Hadriel	Hermosa	Iesha	Isamu	Jamila
Haldana	Hernanda	Iftikhaar	Isao	Jamisha
Haletta	Hernando	Ignatus	Isauro	Jamison
Halfrida	Hespera	Ihtishaam	Ishiko	Jamonte
Halima	Hezeklah	Ijada	Ishmael	Janaya
Hallela	Hibiscus	Ikeia	Ishrnael	Janesa
Halliwell	Hidalgo	Ikenna	Ishtiyaaq	Janiqua
Halloween	Hideaki	Ikuko	Isidore	Janira

Janitza	Jobina	Kahaleel	Kelula	Kristina
Janneke	Jocasta	Kahtia	Kemara	Kristopher
Jaquale	Jocelyn	Kainoah	Kenadi	Ksawery
Jaquita	Jochebed	Kalila	Kenesha	Kumiko
Jarius	Jocosa	Kalina	Kennedy	Kumiwa
Jariya	Joelia	Kameko	Kennetha	Kunibert
Jarmila	Joellen	Kameron	Kennison	Kuroda
Jarnescia	Johanan	Kamila	Kenshiro	Kwabena
Jaromir	Johanna	Kampihe	Kentaro	Kwame
Jaroslav	Johiah	Kamuzu	Kentucky	Kyshana
Jarqueese	Johnico	Kania	Kenyetta	Kyuzo
JarQuisa	Johntria	Kanichi	Keonta	La Reina
Jasira	Jokichi	Karaamat	Kerinci	Laa'iqah
Jasmarie	Jolande	Kareemah	Kerrigan	Labana
Javaris	Jolanta	Karianne	Ketina	Ladislaus
Javier	Joletta	Karissa	Ketura	Ladonna
Javontae	Jonathan	Karita	Kevellin	Laisha
Jawara	Jonati	Karoly	Kevina	Lakayla
Jayare	Jonina	Karrigan	Keziah	Lakeesha
Jealousy	Jonovan	Karynza	Khaalidah	Lakelyn
Jediah	Jordanny	Kashira	Khadijha	Lalita
Jefferson	Josefat	Kasimir	Kianna	Lamberto
Jelana	Josephine	Kasiya	Kiara	LaMesha
Jelinek	Josephus	Kasmira	Kiari	Lancaster
Jemima	Joshana	Kasrileke	Killian	Lancelot
Jenavieve	Joshua	Kassandra	Kimani	Landberto
Jenaya	Josiah	Kassidy	Kimberly	Landrada
Jenilee	Jovanah	Katana	Kineta	Lanfranco
Jennifer	Jovani	Katherine	Kiona	Lania
Jeremy	Jovita	Katina	Kirima	Laoghaire
Jerica	Juanita	Katrina	Kirkpatrick	Laquitta
Jericho	Jucundo	Kayode	Kissiah	Lareeka
Jerilee	Jueta	Kazimierz	Kiyomi	Larentia
Jeritah	Julia	Keaira	Kiyoshi	Larimer
Jerusha	Julian	Keanjaho	Klarissa	Larina
Jessica	Julio	Keanu	Klavdia	Larissa
Jezebel	Julius	Kefira	Klementine	LaShawnda
Jianni	Ju'nesha	Keiandra	Kolyma	LaTasha
Jiichiro	Junius	Keiichi	Konstantin	Latea
Jillmary	Kabria	Keinesha	Korina	Lateefah
Jirina	Kadija	Kelana	Kotaro	Latimer
Joachima	Kadisha	Kelechi	Kristalen	Latona
Joakirna	Kadiya	Kelisa	Kristaney	Latricia

Lauretta	Lilybelle	Lykaon	Maleana	Marino
Lavella	Lilybet	Lysandra	Malesha	Mario
Lavender	Linares	Lyubov	Malia	Marisol
Lavonte	Linetta	Maajidah	Malinda	Marissa
Lazarus	Linnea	Maariyah	Malita	Marita
Lazauskas	Lionel	Mablevi	Malkiya	Marium
Leander	Liora	MacAdam	Mallorie	Marjorie
Leandra	Lisandro	MacDonald	Maloney	Markeisa
Lebechi	Lise-Marie	MacDougal	Malvia	Marlaina
Leeara	Lisimba	MacEgan	Malvina	Marliese
Leilani	Livia	Machiko	Manasseh	Marmaduke
Lemiah	Livingston	Machute	Manchester	Marmara
Lemmuela	Lizabeth	Mackenzie	Mandella	Marmion
Leneta	Llewellyn	MacMurray	Mandelyn	Marolda
Leola	Lodema	Madea	Manisha	Marona
Leoma	Lolita	Madelief	Manuela	Marquala
Leona	Lomasi	Madeline	Maragret	Marquetta
Leonel	Lombardy	Madella	Marala	Marrigje
Leonid	Loredo	Madiah	Maranda	Marsalis
Leonora	Lorelei	Madigan	Marcasia	Martella
Leontine	Lorena	Madison	Marcella	Martina
Leopold	Lorenzo	Madocock	Marcellus	Martinique
Leota	Loretta	Madora	Marcial	Martino
Leotie	Lorimer	Madria	Mareena	Martita
Leslyane	Lorola	Magaidi	Marelda	Maryann
Letitia	Louella	Magena	Marella	MaryLynn
Levanna	Lovilla	Magenta	Margaret	Marysette
Leveda	Luana	Magnilda	Margila	Maryvonne
Leverett	Lubomir	Mahala	Marguerite	Marzena
Leverton	Lucano	Mahatma	Maria	Masaaki
Levina	Lucerna	Mahluli	Mariah	Masada
Levona	Lucinda	Mahmoodah	Mariam	Masaji
Lewanna	Lucio	Majesta	Marianne	Masamba
Liana	Lucretia	Makahla	Mariatt	Masami
Lianda	Ludmila	Makala	Maribel	Massimo
Liatrice	Luella	Makena	Marieileen	Masura
Lidia	Luigi	Makio	Marigold	Matana
Lidio	Lunetta	Makoto	Marika	Mathias
Lieselotte	Lupita	Malachi	Mariko	Matilda
Lilia	Lutero	Malaiah	Marilla	Matina
Liliane	Luvena	Malawa	Marilu	Matrona
Lillemor	Luzero	Malaysia	Marilyn	Matsuda
Lillian	Lydia	Malbina	Marina	Matsuo

Mattea	Messiah	Monserrat	Namono	Ninetta
Matteson	Messina	Montague	Naomi	NKeyvah
Matunde	Miami	Montana	Naoto	Noboru
Mauretta	Miasia	Montero	Napea	Nobuhle
Maurilla	Michaela	Morasha	Narcissus	Nofiya
Maurisha	Michaelsa	Mordecai	Nariko	Nokomis
Mawali	Micheline	Moreno	Nashoma	Nolita
Mawasi	Michiko	Morgana	Nastassja	Nolizwe
Maxantia	Mieczyslaw	Moriah	Natale	Nomikos
Maxia	Mihaly	Morrisa	Natalie	Norberta
Maxima	MiKenna	Morrison	Natari	Norberto
Maximo	Mikenzie	Mortimer	Natasha	Nordica
Mayuko	Mikera	Mosera	Nathania	Norsalus
Mayumi	Mikia	Mubaarak	Nathaniel	Noshavyah
McKayla	Mikoali	Mudiwa	Natia	Notburga
McKenna	Milada	Muhammad	Natori	Novella
McKinley	Milagros	Mulogo	Navea	November
Medarda	Millicent	Muntean	Nazeela	Novia
Medea	Minerva	Muriel	Neala	Nuala
Medina	Minetta	Musetta	Nebraska	Nuncia
Medora	Minoru	Mustafa	Nebula	Nuncio
Meghana	Mirabel	Myeasha	Nediva	Nuriel
Megumi	Miracle	Myliah	Neeoma	Nwaoma
Meingolda	Miranda	Naadirah	Nelia	Nyagwa
Melanie	Miranti	Naafi'ah	Nelleke	Nyasa
Melantha	Mireille	Naajidah	Nereida	Nydia
Melesha	Miriah	Naamana	Netanel	Obadiah
Melina	Miriam	Nabeha	Nevada	Obala
Melinda	Mirian	Nachmanke	Nevara	Obinna
Melissa	Miroslav	Nadaba	Ngoli	Obispo
Melita	Misael	Nadabus	Ngozi	October
Melito	Missoula	Nadia	Niabi	Odera
Melody	Missouri	Naftali	Niagara	Odessa
Melone	Mitchella	Nafula	Niamke	Odilo
Melvina	Mitsuo	Nahama	Nicanor	Odoardo
Menjuiwe	Miyoshi	Nahtanha	Nichola	Odoric
Meraree	Modesto	Nairobi	Nicholas	Ofira
Mercedes	Modesty	Najia	Nicolette	Ogilvie
Mercury	Mohamed	Nakeya	Nicoline	Oglesby
Merdyce	Monaco	Nakisa	Nicoya	Ohara
Meredith	Moneta	Nalani	Nieves	Okpara
Merete	Monica	Naliaka	Niketa	Olean
Merial	Monisha	Nalyssa	Nikita	Oleia

Olenek	Osakwe	Percival	Prunella	Rashida
Olenka	Osamu	Perdita	Publias	Rashidi
Olentá	Osana	Perfecta	Pulchia	Rasia
Oleta	Osarma	Perfecto	Purity	Rathana
Oletta	Osvaldo	Peridot	Pyrena	Rayanna
Olida	Otakar	Perikles	Pyrenees	Raynata
Olinda	Otina	Pernella	Pythia	Rebecca
Oliver	Otniel	Pethuel	Qualisha	Rechaba
Olympus	Ottilie	Petula	Quanisha	Regina
Omari	Ottone	Peverel	Qudsiyyah	Reginald
Omora	Ovida	Phemia	Querdia	Regulo
Onawa	Owena	Philana	Quianna	Rehema
Ondreja	Oyama	Philander	Quintera	Rehoboam
Onega	Ozias	Philantha	Quintessa	Reina
Oneida	Ozora	Philberta	Quintino	Remington
Onia	Palila	Philemon	Quirino	Renaldo
Onida	Pallaton	Philetus	Quirita	Renata
Onofre	Palmira	Philida	Quiteris	Reseda
Ontina	Paloma	Philippa	Raadhiyah	Rexana
Ophelie	Pamela	Phineas	Raashidah	Rhiamon
Orabel	Panama	Phiona	Rabbaanee	Rhiana
Oralie	Pandora	Photina	Rachaba	Rhiannon
Orbelin	Panfilo	Photius	Rachelyn	Rhumani
Ordella	Panphila	Picardus	Radella	Ricarda
Orea	Panthea	Piedad	Radinka	Ricardo
Oregon	Pantias	Pineleh	Radmilla	Ridhiyyah
Oreille	Paradise	Pitana	Radomir	Rihana
Orela	Parnella	Placida	Ra'eesah	Rivera
Orella	Parthena	Placido	Rafaelle	Roanna
Orenda	Partholon	Platinum	Rafee'ah	Roberta
Orenthal	Pascasia	Platona	Rafeeqah	Roberto
Orestes	Paterson	Polonice	Rafferty	Robinson
Oringa	Patricia	Pomeroy	Raheemah	Rochester
Oriole	Pechora	Pomona	Raihaanah	Roderick
Orion	Pedaias	Pomposo	Raimondo	Rodolfo
Orlanda	Pegasus	Pontias	Raissa	Rodriego
Orlando	Pelagla	Portero	Ralayah	Roemello
Orlena	Pelion	Praxedes	Ramiah	Rohana
Orola	Penina	Priscilla	Ramiro	Rolanda
Oroville	Penthea	Pristina	Ramona	Rolando
Orseline	Penuel	Prochora	Ramonda	Romanus
Orsola	Pepita	Prospera	Raphael	Romeo
Ortensia	Peppino	Prospero	Raquana	Romilda

Romola	Sadao	Selena	Sheymonie	Sonio
Romulus	Sadella	Selila	Shiaja	Sophia
Ronalda	Sadira	Selima	Shiana	Sorilda
Ronaldus	Sa'diyah	Semira	Shianhan	Sosthena
Roosevelt	Sadora	Senalda	Shigeo	Sotero
Rosabel	Safiyyah	Senedra	Shohaci	Sotoli
Rosalba	Sahara	Sepia	Shoshana	Speranza
Rosalind	Sainvilus	September	Shotaro	Spiridon
Rosamond	Sakeenah	Septima	Shulamith	Stanbury
Rosanna	Salaamah	Septimus	Shydaisa	Stanislaus
Rosary	Salangi	Seraphim	Sidonie	Stefano
Rosemary	Saleemah	Serena	Sienna	Stephanie
Rosetta	Salina	Sereno	Sierra	Stephenson
Roshanda	Salinger	Sergio	Sigfreda	Suhailah
Rosina	Salome	Serica	Sigfrido	Sullivan
Roswitha	Salvador	Serilda	Sigismund	Sultaanah
Rotislav	Salvia	Servando	Sigita	Sumaali
Rovonte	Samantha	Sethrida	Sigourney	Sumiko
Rowena	Samara	Severen	Silvester	Suria
Rudiger	Samdisha	Sexybeth	Silvia	Sutemi
Ruella	Sameerah	Shabsi	Simeon	Sutherland
Rufano	Samuel	Shafeeqah	Simeone	Svetlana
Rufina	Samuela	Shaiyena	Siorhan	Swanhilda
Rufino	Sanchia	Shakea	Sippora	Sylvia
Ruggero	Sancia	Shakeelah	Sireesha	Symington
Rumaanah	Sanderson	Shakira	Sirena	Sympathy
Ruperto	SanJuana	Shalia	Slawomir	Synneove
Rusticus	Santana	Shalina	Sobenna	Syria
Rutgerus	Santino	Shamaamah	Socorro	Taahirah
Rutherford	Sanura	Shamira	Socrates	Taa'ibah
Rwanda	Sarahann	Shamiya	Sofia	Tabansi
Sa'aadat	Sarahbeth	Shamoodah	Sofio	Tabassum
Saadiqah	Sardonyx	Shanahan	Sofonie	Tabina
Saahirah	Sarina	Shandalee	Sojourner	Tabitha
Saalihah	Sarita	Shaniqua	Solana	Tacio
Sabella	Satoru	Sharaya	Soledad	Tacita
Sabian	Saturday	Shareefah	Solita	Tacoma
Sabina	Savannah	Sharesa	Soloma	Tadaatsu
Sabino	Sawandi	Sharia	Solomon	Tadashi
Sabola	Sebastian	Shawnkayzia	Somerset	Tadeo
Sabrina	Secunda	Shekayl	Somerton	Tagawa
Saburo	Segrada	Sheridan	Somerville	Tahanie
Sachiko	Sekani	Sherika	Sonesu	Tahaw-wur

Takashi	Terina	Tobias	Ulrica	Velika
Takehide	Terrilyn	Tolasa	Ulrico	Velonie
Takeo	Terrishea	Tomaso	Ultima	Venceslao
Takeyla	Territus	Tomila	Ulysses	Venetia
Takora	Tertia	Tonino	Umberto	Ventura
Takuji	Teryri	Topeka	Umeko	Verbena
Talanta	Tesaura	Torkwase	Unitas	Verina
Talashah	Tetsuo	Toshiko	Unity	Verlita
Talia	Tevonna	Tourmaline	Urbana	Verneta
Talitha	Thabana	TraShonda	Urbano	Vernita
Tallulah	Thackeray	Trayvarous	Uria	Verona
Tamara	Thaddea	Trevina	Urian	Vespera
Tamarcus	Thaddeus	Trevino	Urias	Vevila
Tamatra	Thaelassa	Triana	Uriel	Vevina
Tamayo	Thalia	Tricilla	Urien	Vianca
Tamia	Thameenah	Trinetta	Ursula	Vibeke
Tamio	Thanksgiving	Trinia	Usaku	Vicente
Tanabe	Theano	Trinidad	Utica	Vidonie
Tanaka	Thecia	Trinity	Uttasta	Viera
Tanana	Themetri	Trivini	Uzia	Vigilie
Tancredo	Theobald	Tryphena	Uziel	Vincente
Tanisha	Theodore	Tsalani	Uzoma	Vincentia
Tarleton	Theola	Tsutomu	Uzondu	Vinia
Tarsila	Theone	Tullia	Vaclava	Vinita
Tasadduq	Theora	Tullio	Valborga	Viole
T'aunsanae	Theresa	Tullius	Valdemar	Violet
Taurino	Thetisa	Turnina	Valeda	Viridas
Tavanna	Thirzia	Tyesha	Valentin	Virtudes
Tavaris	Thomasine	Tykearon	Valentine	Vistula
Tawanna	Thorberta	Tykesha	Valerie	Vitaly
Tayana	Thorida	Tylonda	Valeska	Viterbo
Tay-yibah	Thormund	Tzaitel	Vancouver	Vitezslav
Tehillah	Thurai-yaa	Ubaldo	Vanessa	Viveka
Temperance	Tiaja	Ubanwa	Vania	Vivienne
Templeton	Tiana	Uchechi	Vanora	Vladimir
Templia	Tiara	Udella	Varian	Vladislav
Tempora	Tibelda	Udenwa	Varina	Vlastibor
Tenika	Tiffany	Uella	Vasallo	Vlastimil
Teniya	Tillio	Uganda	Vasilek	Volante
Tennessee	Timothy	Ulexite	Vassily	Voleta
Tennyson	Tinaret	Ulfrido	Vasyuta	Vovcenko
Tereso	Tineke	Ulima	Vedetta	Vyera
	Tobago	Ulphia	Velacy	Waahidah

Wahkuna
Waldemar
Wanetta
Warburton
Waseme
Washington
Watende
Waverly
Wellington
Wenceslaus
Wendelin
Wetherby
Wetherell
Wetherly
Whittaker
Wichita
Wieteke
Wilesha
Wilfrido
Willamson
Willebald
Willeke
Willoughby
Wilona
Winema
Winifred
Winola
Winona
Wisconsin
Wivina
Wojciech
Worcester
Worthington
Wyoming
Xantipa
Xavier
Xenia
Xenophon
Ximena
Ximenes
Xiomara
Xylia
Xylona

Yadua
Yahaira
Yamato
Yamilet
Yamina
Yanina
Yaritza
Yasema
Yasmuji
Ydia
Yediel
Yehuda
Yelana
Yesifin
Yevgeny
Yevgenya
Yianni
Yisrael
Yobachi
Yojiro
Yolanda
Yomara
Yoshiko
Yoshio
Yosuke
Yukichi
Yukio
Yulia
Yvonnda
Zaahidah
Zaakirah
Zabrina
Zabulon
Zacchaeus
Zachary
Zaelea
Zahara
Zaheerah
Zainabu
Zaitoonah
Zajicka
Zakiya
Zakura

Zamara
Zambesi
Zaphnozy
Zapopan
Zarrita
Zavier
Zebada
Zebedee
Zebulon
Zelia
Zelotes
Zenaido
Zerelda
Zerlina
Zetana
Zevida
Zimmerman
Zinaida
Zinnia
Zipporah
Zobeida
Zoerina
Zofia
Zohara
Zoraida
Zosima
Zosimo
Zotico
Zsuzsanna
Zuberi
Zuleika
Zulema
Zuriel

4 Syllables

Abanobi
Abayomi
Abednego
Abelino
Abercius
Abimbola
Abimelech
Abinadab
Abirio
Abisia
Abrasia
Abrianna
Abundio
Acacia
Acacius
Accalia
Aconcagua
Adalberto
Adalia
Adamina
Adelaido
Adelina
Adeola
Adeoye
Adilmira
Adonaldo
Adonia
Adonijah
Adorabelle
Adoria
Adriana
Adrianus
Afanasy
Agapito
Agapius
Agricola
Agripino
Agueleo
Aharona
Ahaziah
Ahimelech
Aiyetoro
Akeyleeah

Akinori
Alameda
Alarica
Alatea
Alauna
Albertina
Albinia
Alcina
Aldegundo
Alelina
Aleria
Alessio
Aletheia
Alevtina
Alexander
Alexandra
Alexia
Alianna
Alicio
Alireza
Alivia
Allajawaan
Aloisa
Aloisia
Aloysius
Alyssia
Amadea
Amadeo
Amadeus
Amalio
Amancio
Amarachi
Amaramto
Amarillo
Amaryllis
Amatullah
Amber-Marie
Ambernesha
Ambrosio
Amelia
Amelinda
America
Amerigo

Ameritia	Arsenio	Bonifatius	Cleopatra	Dohnnishia
Amilinda	Artemio	Botavia	Cocinero	Dominica
Amoreta	Artemisa	Brandelyn	Colorado	Dominico
Analissa	Artinias	Brasenia	Columbia	Domitilo
Anancia	Asharious	Breonia	Concepcion	Doroteo
Ananias	Aspasia	Brittanylynn	Concordia	Dorothea
Anastasie	Astoria	Cacalia	Consistency	Drahomira
Anatola	Asuncion	Caesaria	Consolata	Dulciana
Anatoly	Atalani	Caitrianne	Constancio	Dumisani
Andreanna	Athalia	Calliope	Constantina	Ebenezer
Andromeda	Atiana	Camassia	Constantino	Eberardo
Andronicus	Atilano	Camelia	Corcovado	Edelmira
Anemone	Atinuwa	Camelina	Cordeelia	Edesio
Anfanio	Attilio	Caractacus	Cordilio	Eduvigis
Angelica	Aubriana	Carmelina	Cordillera	Efrosini
Anibelis	Aurelia	Carmencita	Coriander	Egbertina
Annacotty	Aurelius	Carolina	Corinthian	Egidio
Annamarie	Avaria	Casiano	Cornelia	Ekechukwu
Annapolis	Aviana	Casimiro	Cornelio	Elayasia
Annapurna	Azalea	Castalina	Cornelius	Eldreonna
Anquavia	Azaria	Catalina	Crescencio	Eleazaro
Anshanika	Azariah	Caterina	Crisoforo	Eleonora
Antanisha	Azubuike	Catharina	Cristiana	Eliana
Antonella	Bacilio	Cayetano	Cytherea	Eliathas
Antonetta	Balandria	Cecilia	Damario	Elijahuan
Antonia	Baldassarre	Cecilio	Damiano	Elimelech
Antonina	Baldomero	Ceferino	Daravia	Eliseo
Antonio	Baldovino	Celestina	Davianna	Elisheva
Arabella	Banelia	Celestino	DeAngelo	Elizabeth
Araceli	Bartholomew	Cerelia	Delorita	Elodia
Arainne	Basilia	Cerulean	Delphinia	Elysian
Araminta	Basilio	Cesaria	Demetria	Emanuel
Archibaldo	Bedelia	Chateria	Demetrio	Emelia
Ardelia	Belicia	Chiamaka	Demetrius	Emerencia
Ardenia	Benedicta	Christiana	Denoriel	Emereo
Aretina	Benedicto	Christiano	Dernitna	Emilio
Ariadine	Bergenia	Christodoulous	Devahuti	Emmanuel
Ariana	Bernardena	Cinderella	Devonzia	Engelberta
Ariandrah	Biagio	Cipriano	Dexhiana	Engracia
Ariela	Bidelia	Ciriaco	Deyanira	Enrichetta
Aristides	Bohumila	Clarabella	Diamanta	Ephemia
Arizona	Bolivia	Clementia	Dianthia	Erasatus
Armillia	Bonavento	Clementius	Dionysus	Ereaunna

Eredina	Felicity	Giovanna	Idonia	Josefina
Eremita	Feodosia	Giovanni	Ieronimo	Julianna
Erendira	Ferdinanda	Giroiamo	Ifeanacho	Juvencio
Esmeralda	Ferdnando	Giuliana	Ignacia	Kamania
Esperanza	Fidelia	Giuseppina	Ignatius	Kamaria
Estacada	Fidelio	Gloriana	Iheoma	Kamulira
Estanislao	Filiberto	Godavari	Ilaria	Karolina
Estrellita	Filomeno	Grabriela	Ilario	Katarina
Ethelinda	Fionnula	Graciela	Ildebrando	Kazuhiro
Eudocia	Florencia	Gratiana	Ildefonso	Koleanna
Eufenia	Florencio	Gregorio	Ileana	Kornelia
Eugenia	Forsythia	Grimonia	Imelida	Kvetoslava
Eugenio	Fortunia	Guadalupe	Immanuel	Kyutaro
Eulalia	Fortunio	Guendalina	Imperia	Ladarius
Eulalio	Frederica	Guglielmo	Independence	Lagenia
Euphemia	Frederico	Guillelmina	Indiana	Larianna
Eurydice	Gabriana	Gumersindo	Infiniti	Latavia
Eusebio	Gabriella	Habimama	Innocenzo	Lateshia
Eustachio	Galatea	Halimeda	Ippolito	Latonia
Eustacia	Galiana	Hananiah	Isabella	Laurencia
Eutimia	Ganeshia	Harmonia	Isadora	Lavinia
Evalina	Gardenia	Helbonia	Isidoro	Lazario
Evangeline	Garibaldo	Henrietta	Isleana	Leonardo
Evangelos	Gelasia	Hermelinda	Ismenia	Leopoldine
Evania	Gelasias	Hersilia	Jaazaniah	Leopoldo
Everardo	Geminian	Hesiquio	Jabulani	Levinicha
Everildis	Generosa	Hezekiah	Jacobina	Liberato
Ezaria	Genisia	Hibernia	Jaleshia	Lilliana
Ezeamaka	Genoveva	Higinio	Jamarius	Lotachukwu
Ezekiel	Georgiana	Hilaria	Jameilla	Lotario
Ezenachi	Geraldina	Hilario	Jametrius	Luciana
Ezeoha	Geremia	Himalaya	January	Luciano
Fabiana	Gerolamo	Hiramatsu	Jaqualia	Lucrezia
Fabiano	Giacinta	Horacio	Jaroslava	Macario
Fabiola	Giacomina	Horatia	Jedediah	Madzimoyo
Fabrioni	Giacomo	Hortensia	Je'hoshua	Magdalena
Fabrizio	Gianina	Humility	Jenario	Magdaleno
Favianus	Gianpaolo	Hypatia	Jenesia	Magnificent
Faviola	Gilbertina	Iacopo	Jeramiah	Magnolia
Febronio	Ginikanwa	Ibeamaka	Jeronimo	Mahalia
February	Gioacchino	Icario	Jesenia	Mahogany
Federica	Giolia	Idalia	Johneshia	Malgorzata
Federico	Gionata	Idasia	Jomaralee	Malynia

Marabella	Melchizedek	Oleander	Petronella	Salangia
Maralina	Meletius	Oliana	Petronilo	Salisbury
Maranela	Melisenda	Olivia	Petulia	Salonia
Marcelino	Melquiades	Oliviero	Petunia	Salvatore
Marcellina	Mercurio	Olubayo	Philomena	Samanthia
Marciana	Michalina	Olujuwan	Phylicia	Samaria
Margareta	Migdalia	Olympia	Pioquinto	Samuella
Margarito	Miltiades	Omolara	Placidia	Sanovea
Mariana	Minnesota	Oneshia	Policarpo	Santiago
Mariano	Mississippi	Onesimo	Polygnotos	Saturnino
Mariasa	Mitsuyoshi	Ontario	Ponciano	Saverio
Mariasha	Montgomery	Opalina	Porfirio	Serafiel
Mariela	Musidora	Ophelia	Presencia	Seraphina
Mariena	Nabulungi	Opportina	Primavera	Serapio
Marie-Theres	Nakedria	Oralia	Primitivo	Servacio
Marietta	Nakisisa	Orazio	Procopio	Shamekia
Marigolda	Naoichi	Oriana	Prudencia	Shaquria
Mariorie	Napoleon	Oribella	Pulcheria	Shenandoah
Mariposa	Natalia	Oriella	Quaneria	Shontieria
Marisela	Natalio	Orinoco	Quasimodo	Sidonia
Marsilio	Nathaneal	Osceola	Quiteria	Sidonius
Mary-Alice	Natividad	Othieno	Quontavius	Sieralyn
Maryhelen	Nazario	Othilia	Rafaello	Silvanus
Masajiro	Nazarius	Othineil	Raphaela	Silverio
Masamitsu	Nebedaeus	Ottavia	Rasoliia	Simonetta
Masanao	Nehemiah	Ottavito	Refugio	Slavario
Masayuki	Nemesio	Ovidio	Reginaldo	Sobriety
Massillion	Nicodemus	Ozioma	Remigio	Sophronia
Matsuhira	Nicolina	Pacifica	Ricadonna	Stephania
Matsukawa	Nicomedes	Pamelina	Ricanora	Stephanio
Matsumoto	Nobutaka	Panagiotis	Roderica	Sunserrea
Matsunaka	Noelani	Pancrazio	Rogerio	Sybilia
Matsuoka	Numidia	Pantaleon	Ronnisia	Takahiro
Matsushima	Nwabudike	Parthenia	Rosalia	Talorian
Matsushita	Obelia	Patricio	Rosalio	Tarkisseya
Matsuyama	Obioma	Patrizia	Rosamunda	Tatiana
Mauralia	Obsidian	Pefilia	Rosario	Telesforo
Maurizio	Octavia	Pelagia	Roselinda	Teobaldo
Mawulolo	Octavius	Penelope	Ryoichiro	Teodoro
Maxmilian	Odelia	Peoria	Sabiryhan	Teofilo
Mehitabel	Odelinda	Peregrino	Sadakichi	Teogenes
Melania	Odericus	Periwinkle	Sadonia	Terencio
Melanio	Ofelio	Perpetua	Sagrario	Terentia

5 Syllables

Teresita	Vesuvius	Abejundio	Hermenegildo
Thelonious	Vetaria	Afililio	Hospitality
Themistoklis	Victoria	Alexandria	Ianthiria
Theodora	Vidonia	Alocasia	Ifigenia
Theodoric	Vigilia	Aloisio	Imanuela
Theodoros	Vihelmina	Altagracia	Indalecio
Theodosia	Vinefrida	Analysia	Inocencio
Theophila	Violeta	Anarolio	Macedonio
Theophilos	Virgilia	Anastacio	Mariarosa
Theophrastos	Virgilio	Anastasia	Massimiliano
Thomasina	Virginia	Anastatius	Maximilian
Tiberia	Vitorio	Anatolio	Natasiana
Tiberio	Vivianna	Annamaria	Nebuchadnezzar
Timothea	Viviano	Annunciata	Nepomuceno
Timotheus	Vyacheslav	Apolonio	Obiajulu
Titania	Wendelina	Artemisia	Olegario
Titilayo	Wilhelmina	Athanasius	Oliverio
Tivona	Wivinia	Bartolomeo	Oliviana
Toribio	Xaviera	Belisario	Osediame
Tormoria	Xaykevia	Beniamino	Patroncinio
Toyokazu	Yasutaro	Berengaria	Prisciliano
Tranquilino	Yatavia	Bonifacio	Sebastiana
Traviata	Yehoshua	Caledonia	Sebastiano
Trinotera	Yesenia	California	Tanzenakia
Turquoisia	Yevgenia	Candelario	Teodosio
Tyberrius	Yosemite	Celedonio	Theophania
Uberio	Yoshiaki	DeAngelio	Tokunosuke
Ulielmi	Yoshikatsu	Desiderio	
Umberlina	Yoshinobu	Diamantina	
Urania	Zacharias	Dionisia	
Valencia	Zaragoza	Dionisio	
Valentina	Zebadiah	Donaciano	
Valentino	Zedekiah	Ekaterina	
Valerian	Zenobia	Eleuterio	
Vallonia	Zenobio	Elisabetta	
Valydia	Zephaniah	Emanuela	
Vasilios		Emeterio	
Venancio		Epifanio	
Veneranda		Epitacio	
Venerio		Evangalista	
Veradia		Feliciana	
Veremundo		Gabrielia	
Veronica		Heliodoro	

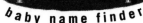

On-Line Baby Name Resources

While we hope this book gives you all the information and inspiration you need to find the perfect name for your baby, we know we might not be the only stop on your baby name quest. We also know there are some great sites on the World Wide Web that add a whole new dimension to a name search. Following are the best of the best: the most useful, the most interesting, and the most fun. Enjoy!

www.parentsoup.com/babynames

All of the names listed in this book came from our interactive Baby Name Finder. What makes it interactive? Say you want a boy's name beginning with *M* from the Bible. Using our fabulous Find-o-Matic, you can find a list of names meeting all your requirements—how about Malachai or Matthew? Or if you're looking for something unusual, try our Finder Potpourri. (You know, Petunia makes a lovely name.) You can also plug in your last name and desired middle name so every search will show you exactly what your child's name will look like on the birth certificate.

www.jellinek.com/baby

If you've tried everything to find a name and just haven't found one that jumps out at you, this is the site for you. Jellinek's Baby Name Chooser picks a boy or girl's name at random—maybe the one you get will be the one you love! The site doesn't show the meanings of the name or any other related information, but it sure is fun. It's also been recognized by the search engines Yahoo! (as a Pick of the Week) and Excite (as a "Must See" site).

307

www.icus.com/names/

This self-described Name Analyzer lets you find out just where your baby's full name stands in popularity. Based on a 1990 census sampling of 1 million households, the Name Analyzer show you the most and least common first names and will give you a specific ranking for all names (first and last) that fall somewhere in between. Another labor of love that provides invaluable insight into your baby's potential name.

www.babynames.com

Created by sisters Jennifer Moss and Mallory Moss Lubofsky, this site has more than 4,200 names listed in an easy-to-use, easy-to-read layout. But the real kicker of this site is its listing of soap opera names. These gals know their soaps!

www.kabalarians.com/html/babyname.htm

This is one heck of a database—50,000 names and growing, including nicknames, medieval names, and names of all nationalities. The Society of Kabalarians is a registered nonprofit organization in Vancouver, British Columbia. It maintains that names have hidden power to shape an individual's "true Inner Potential." You go to the site, look up a name, and get a small personality analysis of individuals with that name. If you don't believe in horoscopes, you are certainly not going to believe in what is said here. But it is interesting and certainly a new take on the query "What's in a name?"

About the Authors

Kate Hanley

Kate is a member of the founding team of Parent Soup. A writer and an editor, she is the original staff writer of Parent Soup. Kate is also the author of *The Parent Soup A-to-Z Guide to Your New Baby*. Physically she lives in New York, but virtually she lives in the Parent Soup message boards, mingling with the members.

Nancy Evans

Nancy is the co-creator of Parent Soup. Before going on-line, she created *Family Life* magazine, was the president and publisher of Doubleday and editor-in-chief of the Book-of-the-Month Club. She lives in New York and is the mother of a nine-year-old named Samantha.